Help Yourself!

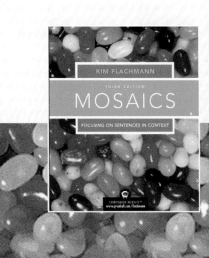

KIM FLACHMANN

THIRD EDITION

MOSAICS

FOCUSING ON SENTENCES IN CONTEXT

COMPANION WEBSITE™
www.prenhall.com/flachmann

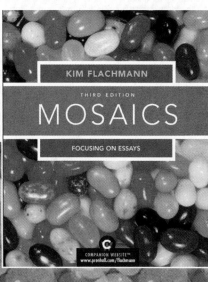

KIM FLACHMANN

THIRD EDITION

MOSAICS

FOCUSING ON ESSAYS

COMPANION WEBSITE™
www.prenhall.com/flachmann

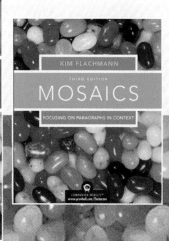

KIM FLACHMANN

THIRD EDITION

MOSAICS

FOCUSING ON PARAGRAPHS IN CONTEXT

COMPANION WEBSITE™
www.prenhall.com/flachmann

As much as you would love to help yourself to the jellybeans on this cover, this new edition of MOSAICS: Focusing on Essays, Third Edition helps your students **help themselves** as they study their own writing. It contains a multitude of exercises and activities that encourage students to apply the techniques and skills of good writing to their own assignments.

With **MOSAICS**, your students start writing when the learning **begins**, not when the learning **ends.**

MOSAICS: Focusing on Essays, Third Edition takes students to a higher level of thinking and performing in all their college courses. The Third Edition demonstrates the interrelationship among thinking, reading, and writing on progressively more difficult levels and helps prepare students for success in college throughout the curriculum.

With MOSAICS, students study *their own writing* to learn to write well. After being introduced to each new concept, students are asked to start writing. Then, they return to their initial writing to learn and practice each skill.

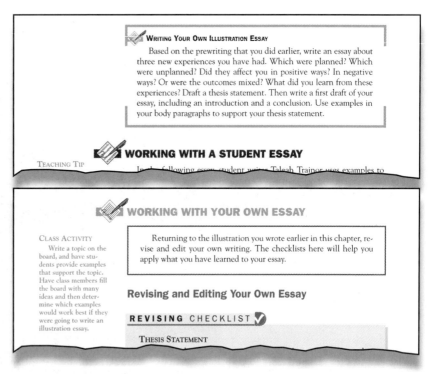

The Third Edition of MOSAICS: Focusing on Essays is easier to use because it's *more accessible.* We have strived to make the Third Edition streamlined, updated, and more accessible for your writing classroom.

Full color design.
This edition has a colorful and open format that invites students into the book!

Streamlined Content.

We now provide the revising and editing checklists on a special insert that students can take with them when they write.

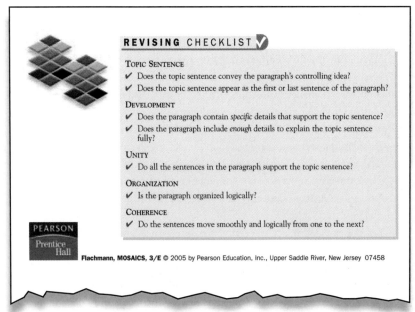

REVISING CHECKLIST ✔

TOPIC SENTENCE
✔ Does the topic sentence convey the paragraph's controlling idea?
✔ Does the topic sentence appear as the first or last sentence of the paragraph?

DEVELOPMENT
✔ Does the paragraph contain *specific* details that support the topic sentence?
✔ Does the paragraph include *enough* details to explain the topic sentence fully?

UNITY
✔ Do all the sentences in the paragraph support the topic sentence?

ORGANIZATION
✔ Is the paragraph organized logically?

COHERENCE
✔ Do the sentences move smoothly and logically from one to the next?

PEARSON
Prentice Hall

Flachmann, MOSAICS, 3/E © 2005 by Pearson Education, Inc., Upper Saddle River, New Jersey 07458

Service Learning Writing Assignments.

Service Learning Writing Assignments are added to the new edition to encourage your students to participate in community service through their writing. As you know, many schools require specific activities or time spent in the community. These writing assignments facilitate the service learning aspect of any course. The essay level text also has a complete chapter on Service Learning (Chapter 22).

PRACTICING ILLUSTRATION

Reading Suggestions

In Chapter 27, you will find two essays that use examples to make their point: "I Just Wanna Be Average" by Mike Rose gives examples from his life to show the importance to him of being average, and "Getting to Know About You and Me" by Chana Schoenberger uses examples to talk about personal biases. You might want to read these selections before writing another illustration essay. As you read, notice how the writers use examples to support and advance their ideas.

Service Learning Project

This assignment is based on a Service Learning project of your choice. If your instructor has already introduced service learning to the class, you will be doing these exercises when they are assigned. At this point, choose a project you would like to pursue, or continue work on a project you have already begun. This assignment in Part II will help you prepare for an essay on this project in Part III. Here is another stage in the preparation for this essay:

For the Service Learning project you have taken on, record a point you want to make and then list as many examples as you can think of from your project that illustrate your point. Use the guidelines you have learned in this chapter to help you create your list. But remember that these are just thoughts that will be developed into an essay in Part III.

SERVICE LEARNING PROJECT
This assignment is another step in the Service Learning Project. If you choose to use this feature of the text, each chapter in Part II has an assignment that asks students to use a different rhetorical mode to reflect on their Service Learning project. These reflections will lead to an essay assignment in Part III (Chapter 22). You can assign as many or as few of these exercises as you want in preparation for this essay. For more information on service learning, see the *Instructor's Resource Manual*, Section I, Part III.

Accuracy Initiative.

In a course where accuracy is crucial to success, we realize textbook errors can be frustrating and might distract students from their ultimate goal—becoming better writers.

We are committed to providing the best and most accurate textbooks for students and instructors alike. In addition to our standard three rounds of copyediting and proofreading, we have asked an independent company, *nSight Publishing Services*, to perform a three-step accuracy check on this text. *nSight* has checked for any typographical errors, completed every exercise to make sure the answers provided were correct, and worked with the author to guarantee every explanation is as clear as possible.

nSight has a stellar reputation for working closely with authors to help make texts as error-free as possible. We are very excited to have this wonderful company on board with us.

Sample page excerpts are reduced from their original size and are accurate as of presstime. © 2005 Pearson Prentice Hall, Upper Saddle River, New Jersey.

Instructor Support

Prentice Hall is committed to helping every instructor, whether a new adjunct or a seasoned professional, by offering the following Instructor Support Package. Ask your Prentice Hall sales representative for more information.

- **Annotated Instructor's Edition (AIE) (0-13-185021-0)**
  The AIE features the answers to all of the exercises and includes marginal annotations to enhance instruction. Written by Kim Flachmann, these annotations are derived from her many years of experience in teaching writing.
  The AIE includes many exciting teaching ideas, including the following:
  —*Teaching Tips* offer practical suggestions for getting the most out of each class session and specific activities to help students master the material.
  —*Class Activities* consist of ideas that promote class interaction.
  —*Answers to Questions* furnish possible responses to the questions in the student text.
  —*Teaching on the Web* provides chapter cross-references and suggestions for helping students learn online.

- **Instructor's Resource Manual (0-13-185022-9)**
  An additional free supplement for instructors, the Instructor's Resource Manual provides over 350 pages of additional teaching strategies, collaborative activities, sample syllabi, chapter summaries, and two quizzes for each chapter.
  Free to adopters.

- **The Prentice Hall Writing Center**
  This online resource is an exciting forum where writing instructors can exchange teaching strategies and ideas as well as contribute their own essays or suggestions for future topics. To find out more, please visit *www.prenhall.com/phwritingcenter.*

- **The Prentice Hall Writing Skills Test Bank (0-13-111628-2)**
  This printed test bank includes hundreds of additional exercises. Covering many of the basic skills of writing, The Prentice Hall Writing Skills Test Bank can be used with any writing text as a source of extra practice or testing. Free to adopters.

- **Instructors 1st Program**
  You are not alone. Incorporating technology or a new book into your classroom is just the first step. Prentice Hall not only provides you with the best tools, but we also stay with you to provide training and support as you develop your course.

Kim Flachmann is coming to YOUR campus!

HOW?

With the
MOSAICS Instructor CD-ROM

Writing effective essays

Instructor CD-ROM Contents:
Introduction:
I. Why I Wrote the Series. II. Students Studying Their Own Writing.

MOSAICS: Focusing on Sentences in Context, Third Edition
I. The Writing Process. II. Writing Effective Sentences. III. Paragraphs: Sentences in Context. IV. From Reading to Writing. Supplements: I. Using the AIE and IRM. II. Student Supplements. III. Instructor Supplements.

MOSAICS: Focusing on Paragraphs in Context, Third Edition
I. The Writing Process. II. Writing Effective Paragraphs. III. Essays: Paragraphs in Context. IV. From Reading to Writing. V. Handbook. Supplements: I. Using the AIE and IRM. II. Student Supplements. III. Instructor Supplements.

MOSAICS: Focusing on Essays, Third Edition
I. The Writing Process. II. Writing Effective Essays. III. Writing a Research Paper. IV. From Reading to Writing. V. Handbook. Supplements: I. Using the AIE and IRM. II. Student Supplements. III. Instructor Supplements.

This invaluable CD-ROM contains video clips of Kim Flachmann explaining the best way to use the MOSAICS series in your classroom. It is designed for both the new and the seasoned instructor and is organized around the specific parts of each text. Plus, it provides concrete teaching strategies from Kim Flachmann's own classroom. The new edition of this CD-ROM also contains electronic versions of the Instructor's Manuals. The CD-ROM is free to adopters and is packaged in the Instructor's Resource Manual.

Student Support
Customize your classroom!

Enrich your classroom beyond the textbook with the following Student Support Packages designed to connect your students to the power of the written word. Ask your Prentice Hall sales representative for more information or for other packaging options.

● **Text-specific Companion Website™ at *www.prenhall.com/flachmann***
The Companion Website™ allows students to gain a richer perspective and a deeper understanding of the concepts and issues discussed in **MOSAICS: Focusing on Essays, Third Edition**. This site is free to all students. Features of the site include the following:
—Online quizzes for each chapter with instant scoring and coaching
—Essay questions that test students' critical thinking skills
—Chapter objectives and web destinations

● **The New American Webster Handy College Dictionary**
Available free to students when packaged with **MOSAICS**, this dictionary has over 1.5 million Signet copies in print and over 115,000 definitions, including current phrases, slang, and scientific terms. It offers more than 1,500 new words, with over 200 not found in any other competing dictionary, and features boxed inserts on etymologies and language. **Use this ISBN to order MOSAICS: Focusing on Essays, Third Edition with FREE Dictionary: 0-13-160362-0**

● **The Prentice Hall ESL Workbook**
Available free to students when packaged with **MOSAICS**, this 138-page workbook is divided into seven major units, providing explanations and exercises in the most challenging grammar topics for non-native speakers. With over 80 exercise sets, this guide provides ample instruction and practice in nouns, articles, verbs, modifiers, pronouns, prepositions, and sentence structure.
Stand Alone ISBN: 0-13-092323-0
Use this ISBN to order MOSAICS: Focusing on Essays, Third Edition with FREE ESL Workbook: 0-13-147264-X

MOSAICS

THIRD EDITION

MOSAICS

FOCUSING ON ESSAYS

KIM FLACHMANN

PEARSON

Prentice
Hall

Upper Saddle River, New Jersey 07458

Library of Congress Cataloging-in-Publication Data

Flachmann, Kim.
    Mosaics, focusing on essays / Kim Flachmann.—3rd ed.
        p. cm.
    Includes index.
        ISBN 0-13-185019-9 (student ed.)—ISBN 0-13-185021-0 (annotated instructor's ed.)
        1. English language—Rhetoric.   2. English language—Grammar—Problems, exercises, etc.
    3. Report writing.   I. Title.

PE1408.F469 2005
808'.042—dc22   2003060750

Editor-in-Chief: *Leah Jewell*
Senior Acquisitions
    Editor: *Craig Campanella*
Assistant Editor: *Karen Schultz*
Editorial Assistant: *Joan Polk*
Developmental Editor-in-Chief: *Rochelle*
    Diogenes
Development Editor: *Marta Tomins*
Media Project Manager: *Christy Schaack*
Marketing Director: *Beth Mejia*
Marketing Manager: *Rachel Falk*
Marketing Assistant: *Adam Laitman*
VP/Director of Production and
    Manufacturing: *Barbara Kittle*
Production Editor: *Maureen Benicasa*
Production Assistant: *Marlene Gassler*
Copyeditor: *Krystyna Budd*
Permissions Coordinator: *Ron Fox*
Text Permission Specialist: *Jane Scelta*
Prepress & Manufacturing
    Manager: *Nick Sklitsis*

Prepress & Manufacturing
    Buyer: *Ben Smith*
Creative Design Director: *Leslie Osher*
Interior & Cover Designer: *Carmen*
    DiBartolomeo, C2K, Inc.
Director, Image Resource
    Center: *Melinda Reo*
Manager, Rights and Permissions: *Zina*
    Arabia
Interior Image Specialist: *Beth Boyd-*
    Brenzel
Image Permission Coordinator: *Charles*
    Morris
Cover Art: *Jellybeans, Omni-Photo*
    Communications, Inc
Composition: *Interactive Composition*
    Corporation
Printer/Binder: *Quebecor World Book Services*
Cover Printer: *Phoenix Color Corporation*

This book was set in 11/13 Goudy.
Credits and acknowledgments borrowed from other sources and reproduced, with permission, in this
textbook appear on appropriate page within text (or on pages 825–827).

Pearson Education LTD., London
Pearson Education Australia PTY, Limited
Pearson Education Singapore, Pte. Ltd
Pearson Education North Asia Ltd
Pearson Education, Canada, Ltd
Pearson Educación de Mexico, S.A. de C.V.
Pearson Education–Japan
Pearson Education Malaysia, Pte. Ltd
Pearson Education, Upper Saddle River, New Jersey

For
Michael

10 9 8 7 6 5 4 3 2 1
ISBN 0-13-185021-0 (Annotated Instructor's Edition)
ISBN 0-13-185019-9 (Student Edition)

BRIEF CONTENTS

CONTENTS

PREFACE

Experience tells us that students have the best chance of succeeding in college if they learn how to respond productively to the varying academic demands made on them throughout the curriculum. One extremely important part of this process is being able to analyze ideas and think critically about issues in many different subject areas. *Mosaics: Focusing on Essays* is the third in a series of three books that teach the basic skills essential to all good academic writing. This series illustrates how the companion skills of reading and writing are parts of a larger, interrelated process that moves back and forth through the tasks of prereading and reading, prewriting and writing, and revising and editing. In other words, the *Mosaics* series shows how these skills are integrated at every stage of the writing process.

THE *MOSAICS* SERIES

This third edition of the *Mosaics* series consists of three books, each with a different emphasis: *Focusing on Sentences in Context, Focusing on Paragraphs in Context,* and *Focusing on Essays.* The first book highlights sentence structure, the second book paragraph development, and the third the composition of essays. Each book introduces the writing process as a unified whole and asks students to begin writing in the very first chapter. Each volume also moves from personal to more academic writing. The books differ in the length and level of their reading selections, the complexity of their writing assignments, the degree of difficulty of their revising and editing strategies, and the length and level of their student writing samples.

This entire three-book series is based on the following fundamental assumptions:

- Students build confidence in their ability to read and write by reading and writing.
- Students learn best from discovery and experimentation rather than from instruction and abstract discussions.
- Students need to discover their personal writing process.
- Students learn both individually and collaboratively.

- Students profit from studying both professional and student writing.
- Students benefit most from assignments that actually integrate thinking, reading, and writing.
- Students learn how to revise by following clear guidelines.
- Students learn grammar and usage rules by editing their own writing.
- Students must be able to transfer their writing skills to all their college courses.
- Students must think critically and analytically to succeed in college.

HOW THIS BOOK WORKS

Mosaics: Focusing on Essays teaches students how to write effective essays. For flexibility and easy reference, this book is divided into five parts:

Part I: The Writing Process
Part II: Writing Effective Essays
Part III: The Essay with Sources
Part IV: From Reading to Writing
Part V: The Handbook

Part I: The Writing Process   All eight chapters in Part I demonstrate the cyclical nature of the writing process. They begin with the logistics of getting ready to write and then move systematically through the interlocking stages of the process by following a student essay from prewriting to revising and editing. Part I ends with a quiz that students can take to identify their "Editing Quotient"—their strengths and weaknesses in grammar and mechanics.

Part II: Writing Effective Essays   Part II, the heart of the instruction in this text, teaches students how to write essays by introducing the rhetorical modes as patterns of development. It moves from personal writing to more academic types of writing: describing, narrating, illustrating, analyzing a process, comparing and contrasting, dividing and classifying, defining, analyzing causes and effects, and arguing. Within each chapter, students write their own essays, read professional essays, study the essays of other students, and finally revise and edit the essay they wrote earlier in the chapter. By following specific guidelines, students learn how to produce a successful essay using each rhetorical mode.

Part III: The Essay with Sources   The next section of this text helps students move from writing effective essays to writing an essay with sources.

It systematically illustrates the details of writing a source paper. Then it explains the paper through student examples. Part III ends with a series of writing assignments and workshops designed to encourage students to write, revise, and edit an essay with sources and then reflect on their own writing process.

Part IV: From Reading to Writing Part IV of this text is a collection of readings arranged by rhetorical mode. Multiple rhetorical strategies are at work in most of these essays, but each is classified according to its primary rhetorical purpose. As a result, you can refer your students to particular essays in this part that demonstrate a rhetorical mode you are studying in Part II. In this way, students can actually see the features of each rhetorical mode at work in different pieces of writing. Each professional essay is preceded by prereading activities that will help your students focus on the topic at hand and then is followed by 10 questions that move students from literal to analytical thinking as they consider the essay's content, purpose, audience, and paragraph structure.

Part V: The Handbook Part V is a complete handbook, including exercises, that covers eight main categories: Sentences, Verbs, Pronouns, Modifiers, Punctuation, Mechanics, Effective Sentences, and Choosing the Right Word. These categories are coordinated with the Editing Checklist that appears periodically throughout this text. Each chapter starts with five self-test questions so that students can determine their strengths and weaknesses in a specific area. The chapters provide at least three types of practice after each grammar concept, moving the students systematically from identifying grammar concepts to writing their own sentences. Each chapter ends with a practical editing workshop that asks students to use the skills they just learned as they work with another student to edit their own writing. Unit Tests—including practice with single sentences and paragraphs—complete each unit.

APPENDIXES

The appendixes will help your students keep track of their progress in the various skills they are learning in this text. References to these appendixes are interspersed throughout the book so that students know when to use them as they study the concepts in each chapter:

Appendix 1: Critical Thinking Log
Appendix 2: Revising and Editing Peer Evaluation Forms
Appendix 3: Revising and Editing Peer Evaluation Forms for an Essay with Sources

Appendix 4: Test Yourself Answers
Appendix 5: Editing Quotient Error Chart
Appendix 6: Error Log
Appendix 7: Spelling Log

OVERALL GOAL

Ultimately, each book in the *Mosaics* series portrays writing as a way of thinking and processing information. One by one, these books encourage students to discover how the "mosaics" of their own writing process work together to form a coherent whole. By demonstrating the interrelationship among thinking, reading, and writing on progressively more difficult levels, these books promise to help prepare your students for success in college throughout the curriculum.

UNIQUE FEATURES

Several unique and exciting features separate this book from other basic writing texts:

- It moves students systematically from personal to academic writing.
- It uses both student writing and professional writing as models.
- It demonstrates all aspects of the writing process through student writing.
- It integrates reading and writing throughout the text.
- It teaches revising and editing through student writing.
- It features culturally diverse reading selections that are of high interest to students.
- It teaches rhetorical modes as patterns of thought.
- It helps students discover their own writing process.
- It includes a complete handbook with exercises.
- It offers worksheets for students to chart their progress in reading and writing.

ACKNOWLEDGMENTS

I want to acknowledge the support, encouragement, and sound advice of several people who have helped me through the development of the *Mosaics* series. First, Prentice Hall has provided guidance and inspiration for this project through the enduring wisdom of Craig Campanella, senior acquisitions editor; the insights and vision of Marta Tomins and Harriett Prentiss, development editors; the diligence and clairvoyance of Maureen Benicasa, production editor; the foresight and prudence of Leah Jewell, editor-in-chief; the boundless creative inspiration of Rachel Falk, senior marketing manager; resourceful oversight of Rochelle Diogenes, editor-in-chief of development; the brilliant leadership of Yolanda de Rooy, President of Humanities and Social Sciences; the hard work and patience of Ron Fox and Jane Scelta, permissions editors; the guidance and fortitude of Krystyna Budd, copyeditor; and the common sense and organization of Joan Polk, administrative assistant for developmental English. Also, this book would not be a reality without the insightful persistence of Phil Miller, publisher for modern languages.

I want to give very special thanks to Cheryl Smith, my constant source of inspiration in her role as consultant and adviser for the duration of this project. She was also the author of the margin annotations and the coordinator of the *Mosaics Instructor's Resource Manuals*. I am also grateful to Rebecca Hewett, Valerie Turner, and Li'i Pearl for their discipline and hard work on the *Instructor's Resource Manuals* for each of the books in the series. And I want to thank Crystal Huddleston, Zandree Stidham, and Anne Elrod for their expertise and assistance.

In addition, I am especially indebted to the following reviewers who have guided me through the development and revision of this book: Lisa Berman, Miami-Dade Community College; Patrick Haas, Glendale Community College; Jeanne Campanelli, American River College; Dianne Gregory, Cape Cod Community College; Clara Wilson-Cook, Southern University at New Orleans; Thomas Beery, Lima Technical College; Jean Petrolle, Columbia College; David Cratty, Cuyahoga Community College; Allison Travis, Butte State College; Suellen Meyer, Meramec Community College; Jill Lahnstein, Cape Fear Community College; Stanley Coberly, West Virginia State University at Parkersville; Jamie Moore, Scottsdale Community College; Nancy Hellner, Mesa Community College; Ruth Hatcher, Washtenaw Community College; Thurmond Whatley, Aiken Technical College; W. David Hall, Columbus State Community College; Marilyn Coffee, Fort Hays State University; Teriann Gaston, University of Texas at Arlington; Peggy Karsten, Ridgewater College; Nancy Hayward, Indiana University of Pennsylvania; Carol Ann Britt, San Antonio College; Maria C. Villar-Smith, Miami-Dade Community College; Jami L. Huntsinger, University of New Mexico at Valencia Campus; P. Berniece Longmore, Essex County College; Lee Herrick, Fresno City College; Elaine Chakonas, North Eastern Illinois University; Roy Warner, Montana State University.

I also want to express my gratitude to my students, from whom I have learned so much about the writing process, about teaching, and about life itself, and to Cheryl Smith's students, who tested various sections of the books and gave me good ideas for revising them over the past three years. Thanks finally to the students who contributed paragraphs and essays to this series: Josh Ellis, Jolene Christie, Mary Minor, Michael Tiede, and numerous others.

Finally, I owe a tremendous personal debt to the people who have lived with this project for the last two years; they are my closest companions and my best advisers: Michael, Christopher, and Laura Flachmann. To Michael, I owe additional thanks for the valuable support and feedback he has given me through the entire process of creating and revising this series.

Kim Flachmann

PART

I

THE WRITING PROCESS

Writing, like life itself, is a voyage of discovery.

—HENRY MILLER

In Part I, you will be working with the entire writing process. The goal of this part is to help you develop self-confidence as a writer. It will give you the tools you need to construct your personal writing process. Then, as you move through these eight chapters, you will discover how to adjust the writing process to suit your own needs and preferences. As you become more aware of the choices you have to make, you will also develop a better understanding of your strengths and weaknesses as a writer. With practice, your personalized writing process will soon be a routine part of your academic life and will help you confirm your place in the community of writers.

1

WRITING IN COLLEGE

Words help us solve problems, discover new ideas, feel better, make people laugh, and understand the world around us. Writing is simply one way of using words. It lets us connect with our immediate environment. Eric Zorn, a reporter for the *Chicago Tribune*, tries to explain more precisely the power of writing in our everyday lives:

> We write to enlarge and preserve that which we know, that which we have felt. We write because organizing our jumbled impressions into sentences is sometimes the only way to figure out what we think. We write because words—inadequate as they always are—are the best and most lasting way to connect with ourselves and with others.

WHY LEARN HOW TO WRITE WELL?

The better you write, the more completely you can connect with your environment and the more control you have over your daily routine. Writing well lets you communicate exactly what you mean and actually helps you get what you want out of life. So writing well can give you power—in a variety of ways.

Writing as Discovery

Often you will not really know the points you want to make until you start writing. When you write, a very interesting process takes place: the physical act of writing helps your mind sort through lots of ideas and helps you decide exactly what you want to say. Sometimes new ideas will come out of something you have written. Or you might understand an idea better once you start writing about it.

The simple act of writing leads to understanding. Also, the more you write, the more ideas you generate. This is why your instructor might suggest that you write if you are stuck on a topic or don't know what to say next. Writing helps you discover and express the good ideas that are already in your mind.

TEACHING WRITING IN COLLEGE

Ask your students to bring in a visual representation of their writing process. It can be anything—cut-up magazines, something with props, a drawing—that conveys how they go through their writing process. Be careful not to give students too many ideas so you don't limit the scope of their imaginations. For this exercise, the more vague you are, the more creative students get.

Writing as Critical Thinking

Writing can also help you think critically. Critical thinking is the highest form of mental activity that human beings engage in, and it is a major source of success in college and in life.

Thinking critically involves grappling with the ideas, issues, and problems that surround you in your immediate environment and in the larger world. It means constantly questioning and analyzing different aspects of life. Since critical thinking is complex, it requires a great deal of concentration and practice. Once you have a sense of how your mind works at this level, you will be able to think critically whenever you want.

With some guidance, learning how to write according to different rhetorical modes or strategies (such as describing, narrating, or dividing and classifying) can give you the mental workout you need to think critically in much the same way that physical exercise warms you up for various sports. As you move through the chapters in Part II, you will be asked to isolate each rhetorical mode—just as you isolate your abs, thighs, and biceps in a weight-lifting workout. Each rhetorical mode offers a slightly different way of seeing the world, processing information, and solving problems. So each rhetorical mode is really a different way of thinking and making sense of the world.

Writing as Necessity

Most important of all, writing is necessary for surviving both in college and on the job. You will have to write more in today's electronic age than any previous generation has. Some of your writing will be reports or projects that extend over a long period of time. Other writing tasks will have to be completed immediately, such as responses to e-mail messages. Whatever the terms, writing will be a significant part of your life throughout college and beyond.

The better your writing skills, the better grades you will make in college and the further you will get in a career. Everything you learn about writing in this text applies to writing in all your courses. These strategies will also be helpful on the job, especially when you have to write that difficult report or when you are asked to summarize your accomplishments so far. The same writing guidelines apply to all writing tasks.

◆ **P r a c t i c e 1**   Answer the following questions.

1. Why should you learn to write?

Writing helps us solve problems, discover new ideas, feel better, make

people laugh, and understand the world around us.

TEACHING ON THE WEB

Discussion Topic: Divide students into groups of three or four. Ask the members of each group to think about the recursive steps they go through when researching with a search engine (for example, how many variations do they try in a search?). Have them compare the process of searching for information on the Web to the writing process. How are the two cyclical activities similar? How are they different? Have each group explain its answer.

TEACHING ON THE WEB

Mosaics Web Site: To learn more about the writing process, students can go to www.prenhall.com/ mosaics.

INSTRUCTOR'S RESOURCE MANUAL

For additional material about teaching writing in college, for journal entries, and for various tests, see the *Instructor's Resource Manual,* Section II, Part I.

2. Why should you learn to write well?

   Writing well lets us communicate exactly what we mean and actually helps

   us get what we want out of life.

3. In what ways is writing a process of discovery?

   Writing helps our minds sort through ideas and decide what we want to

   say. New ideas can come from writing, and we may understand ideas

   better once we start writing about them.

4. How can writing help you think critically?

   Learning how to write according to different rhetorical modes can give us

   the mental workout we need to think critically just as physical exercise

   warms us up for various sports.

5. Why is writing necessary in today's world?

   Writing is necessary for surviving both in college and on the job. We will have

   to write more in today's electronic age than any previous generation has.

THINKING OF YOURSELF AS A WRITER

Using words on paper or on the computer screen makes a person a writer. Whether you write a note on the refrigerator, e-mail a friend, write a paper for economics class, or draft a report for your boss, you are part of a community of writers. In fact, you *are* a writer.

Any piece of writing more formal than a note on the refrigerator, however, is usually the result of a sequence of activities that may seem on the surface to have nothing directly to do with the act of writing itself. This sequence of activities is called the **writing process,** and learning to use this process is what this book is all about.

Even though each writer is different, some general principles apply to everyone—students and professional writers alike. Before you actually begin to write, a wise move is to get your surroundings ready. That involves setting aside a time and place to write, gathering supplies, and establishing a routine.

1. ***Set aside a special time to write, and plan to do nothing else during that time.*** The bird's cage can wait to be cleaned until tomorrow, the furniture doesn't have to be dusted today, the garage can be hosed down some other time, and the dirt on your kitchen floor won't turn to concrete overnight. When you first get a writing assignment, a little procrastination can be good. Procrastinating lets your mind plan your approach to the writing task. The trick is to know when to quit procrastinating and get down to work.

2. ***Find a comfortable place with few distractions.*** Joyce Carol Oates, a famous contemporary writer, claims that writing is a very private act that requires lots of patience, time, and space. First, you need to set up a place to write that suits your specific needs as a writer. It should be a place where you are not distracted or interrupted. Some people work best in a straight-backed chair sitting at a table or desk, while others get their best ideas sitting cross-legged in bed. The exact place doesn't matter, as long as you can write there.

   Even if you are fortunate enough to have a private study area, you may find that you still want to make some adjustments. You may decide to unplug your phone during your writing time. Or you may discover that an all-night R&B radio station helps you shut out all kinds of noises but doesn't distract you the way talk shows and rock stations do. One student may do her best writing after soaking in a hot tub; another might play jazz when he is getting down to work; and still another may have a Pepsi on one side of his table and a Snicker's bar on the other as he writes. Whatever your choices, you need to set up a comfortable working environment.

3. ***Gather your supplies before you begin to write.*** Don't risk losing your great ideas by not being able to find a pen and paper or a formatted disk. Some writers use a yellow tablet and a mechanical pencil to get started on a writing task; others go straight to their computers. One of the main advantages of working on a computer is that once you type your ideas in to it, changing them or moving them around is easy. As a result, you are more likely to make revisions when you work on a computer, and you will therefore turn in a better paper. Whatever equipment you choose, make sure it is ready at the time you have set aside to write.

4. ***Establish a personal writing ritual.*** As a member of the community of writers, acknowledging your own writing habits and rituals is a major

part of discovering your writing process. These rituals begin the minute you are given a writing assignment. What activities help you get ready to write? Some people exercise, others catch up on e-mail, and still others clean their rooms before they write. Most people do these activities without even realizing why. But they are preparing their minds for writing. So in the course of confirming yourself as a writer, take a moment now to record some of your own preferences and rituals connected with your writing.

P r a c t i c e 2   Explain the rituals you instinctively follow as you prepare to write. How do you prepare your mind for writing? Where do you write? At what time of day do you produce your best work? Do you like noise? Quiet? What other details describe your writing environment? What equipment do you use to write? *Answers will vary.*

KEEPING A JOURNAL

The word **journal** refers to a daily log of your writing. It is a place where you can record ideas, snatches of conversation, dreams, descriptions of people, pictures of places, and thoughts about objects—whatever catches your attention.

If you use a notebook for your journal, choose one that you really like. You might even keep your journal on your computer. However, unless you have a hand–held computer, you won't have your electronic journal with you all the time. The choice is yours (unless your instructor has specific requirements). Just remember that a journal should be a notebook you enjoy writing in and carrying with you.

As you move from college to the professional world, you will find a personal journal a particularly valuable tool because—in the case of writing as in many other activities—the more you write, the more you will improve your writing. In addition, your journal can become an excellent bank of thoughts and topics for you. If used thoughtfully, it can become an incredible resource—a place to both generate and retrieve your ideas. Writing in your journal can help you discover your thoughts and feelings about specific issues as well as let you think through important choices you have to make. So writing can help you solve problems and work your way through various college projects.

A good way to establish the habit of journal writing is to use your journal for answering the questions that accompany the instruction in Parts II and III of this text, the readings in Part IV, and the writing exercises in the handbook (Part V). You can also use your journal to jot down ideas and plans for essays as they occur to you. In addition, you might want to complete your prewriting activities in your journal. Keeping track of a journal is much easier than finding notes on assorted scraps of paper.

Keeping a section of your journal private is also a good idea. Sometimes, when you think on paper or let your imagination run free, you don't want to share the results with anyone. Yet those notes can be very important in finding a subject to write about or in developing a topic.

The content of your journal entries depends to a great extent on your instructor's directions. But some basic advice applies to all entries, whether on paper or on a computer.

1. Date your entries, and note the time; you may find it useful to see when your best ideas occur.
2. Record anything that comes to your mind, and follow your thoughts wherever they take you (unless your instructor gives you different directions).
3. Glue or tape anything into your journal that stimulates your thinking or writing—cartoons, magazine ads, poems, pictures, advice columns; add URLs for useful Web sites.
4. Think of your journal as someone to talk to—a friend who will keep your cherished ideas safe and sound and won't talk back to or argue with you.

Practice 3 Begin your own journal.

1. Buy a notebook that you like, and write in it.
2. Make at least two journal entries on your computer.
3. Which type of journal do you prefer—notebook or disk? Write an entry explaining your preference. *Answers will vary.*

WRITING WITH A COMPUTER

Many people—in school and at work—find that they write most efficiently directly on a computer. This strategy saves them time and energy and helps them meet deadlines. First of all, writing directly on a computer lets you change words and sentences as you go along. It also saves you time since you don't have to write out a draft by hand and then input it later. When you complete a first draft on a computer, you can move your ideas around without having to rewrite the whole paper. Finally, you can correct your grammar and spelling errors right on the final draft.

To compose on your computer, follow some simple rules so you don't lose your work or make word processing more complex than it is. Here are five essential guidelines for writing on a computer:

1. Give your document a name before you start writing.

2. Save your work often (or set the computer to save at short intervals). This will help you avoid losing your writing in a power failure or other accident.

3. Save your work in two different places—on your hard drive and on a disk. Then if one becomes damaged, you always have the other.

4. Name and number each draft so that you can go back to earlier drafts if you want. For example, you might name and number an assignment this way: Description Essay D1, Description Essay D2, and so forth (D = draft).

5. Print out your work frequently so that you can refer to printed copies as well as electronic copies.

◆ **Practice 4**   Answer the following questions.

1. What are the advantages of writing directly on a computer?

   Writing directly on a computer lets you change words and sentences as

   you go along. It also saves you time because you don't have to write out a

   draft by hand and then type it up later. When you complete a first draft on

   a computer, you can move your ideas around without having to rewrite

   your whole paper. Finally, you can correct your grammar and spelling errors

   right on the final draft.

2. What five guidelines should you remember if you write on a computer?

   1. Give your document a name before you start writing.

   2. Save your work often.

   3. Save your work in two different places—on the hard drive and on a disk.

   4. Name and number each of your drafts so you can go back to earlier
   *   drafts if you want.*

   5. Print out your work frequently so you can refer to printed as well as
   *   electronic copies.*

THE WRITING PROCESS

The writing process begins the minute you get a writing assignment. It involves all the activities you do, from choosing a topic to turning in a final draft, including trips to the library, phone calls, and late-night snacks. The main parts of the process are outlined here.

Prewriting

Prewriting refers to activities that help you explore a general subject, generate ideas about it, select a specific topic, establish a purpose, and learn as much as possible about your readers. Chapter 2 will teach you different strategies for accomplishing these goals before you actually begin to write a draft of your essay. Your mission at this stage is to stimulate your thinking before and during the act of writing. Whenever you generate new material throughout the writing process, you are prewriting.

Writing

You can start writing after you have some ideas to work with. Writing includes developing some of your ideas further, organizing your thoughts with your purpose in mind, and writing a first draft. To begin writing, you should go back to your notes, journal entries, and other prewriting activities and then mold these ideas into a logical, coherent essay. As you write, you should concentrate on what you are saying and how your ideas fit together. Don't let grammar and spelling distract you from your task at this point. You can correct your grammar and mechanical errors later.

Revising

Most people do not want to take the time to revise their writing. But revising always pays off, because it will make your writing stronger and better. Revising involves rethinking your content and organization so that your words say exactly what you mean. (Editing, the last step, focuses on your grammar, punctuation, mechanics, and spelling.) Your main goal in revising is to make sure that the purpose of your essay is clear to your audience and that your main ideas are supported with adequate details and examples. In addition, you should check that your paper is organized logically.

Editing

Editing is the final stage of the writing process. After you revise, read your writing slowly and carefully to find errors in grammar, punctuation, mechanics, and spelling. Such errors can distract your reader from the message you are trying to convey or can even cause communication to break down altogether. Editing gives you the chance to clean up your draft so that your writing is clear, precise, and effective.

Once you start writing, these "stages" do not necessarily occur in any specific order. You may change a word (revise) in the very first sentence that you write, then think of another detail that you want to add to your opening sentence (prewrite), and next cross out and rewrite a misspelled word (edit)—all in the first two minutes of writing. Although you may never approach any two writing projects in the same way, the chapters in Part I will help you establish a framework for your personal writing process and start to feel comfortable as a writer working within that framework.

◆ *P r a c t i c e 5*   Answer the following questions.

1. When does the writing process start for a writing assignment?

   The writing process begins the minute you get a writing assignment.

   _____

2. Explain "prewriting" in your own words.

   Prewriting helps you explore a general subject, generate ideas about it,

   select a specific topic, establish a purpose, and learn as much as possible

   about your readers.

3. Describe your writing environment.

   Answers will vary.

   _____

4. What does "writing" consist of?

   Writing includes developing some of your ideas further, organizing your

   thoughts with your purpose in mind, and writing a first draft.

5. What is the difference between "revising" and "editing"?

Revising involves rethinking your content and organization so that your

words say exactly what you mean. Editing, the last step, focuses on your

grammar, punctuation, mechanics, and spelling.

VISUALIZING THE WRITING PROCESS

Even though we talk about the stages of writing, writing is actually a cyclical process, which means that at any point you may loop in and out of other stages. As you work with the writing process in this textbook, the following graphic might help you understand how various stages of the process can overlap.

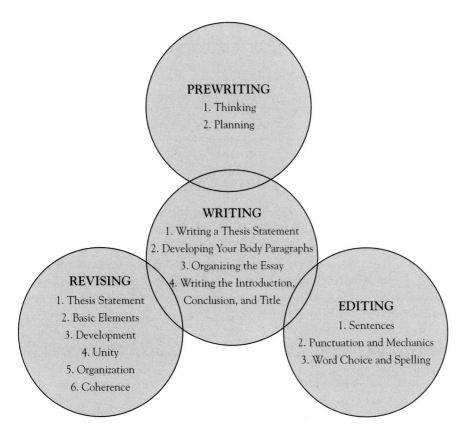

PREWRITING
1. Thinking
2. Planning

WRITING
1. Writing a Thesis Statement
2. Developing Your Body Paragraphs
3. Organizing the Essay
4. Writing the Introduction, Conclusion, and Title

REVISING
1. Thesis Statement
2. Basic Elements
3. Development
4. Unity
5. Organization
6. Coherence

EDITING
1. Sentences
2. Punctuation and Mechanics
3. Word Choice and Spelling

◆ ***P r a c t i c e 6***   Answer the following questions.

1. List the two elements of prewriting.

   Thinking, planning

   _____

2. List the four elements of writing.

   Writing the thesis statement; developing your body paragraphs; organiz-

   ing the essay; writing the introduction, conclusion, and title

3. List the six elements of revising.

   Thesis statement, basic elements, development, unity, organization,

   coherence

4. List the three elements of editing.

   Sentences, punctuation and mechanics, word choice and spelling

   _____

WRITING IN TANDEM WITH A STUDENT

In the rest of Part I, you will be writing in tandem with (along with) another student, Beth Olson, who has already completed the assignments you will be doing. In other words, this student writer will be demonstrating what you have to do for each essay. This approach will make the requirements for each writing task easy to follow, but you might find that you want to borrow Beth's ideas. When this happens, concentrate on discovering your own original ideas as you do each assignment.

◆ ***P r a c t i c e 7***   Answer the following questions.

1. What does writing in tandem mean in this text?

   It means writing along with another student who has already completed

   the assignments.

2. How can this approach help you?

   This approach will make the requirements for each writing task easy to

   follow.

3. What problem can it cause?

   You might find that you want to borrow the student's ideas.

4. How can you best deal with this problem?

   Force yourself to discover the original ideas in your mind as you do each

   assignment.

WRITING ASSIGNMENT

This first writing assignment is much like the writing tasks you will be asked to do throughout this book. You'll be working on this assignment yourself over the next seven chapters as you apply what you are learning about the writing process. At the same time, we will follow the work of student Beth Olson so you can see how she approaches and completes the same assignment. By the end of Chapter 8, you will have a feel for the entire writing process, which is essential to strengthening your writing and your identity as a writer.

Write Your Own Essay

We all learn about life in a variety of ways. These lessons help us become who we are. What have you learned over the years? How did you learn these lessons? What experiences have made you the person you are today? Based on a combination of your observations, your reading, and your personal experience, write an essay explaining how you learn best.

CHAPTER **2**

PREWRITING

Activities that take place before you actually start writing your paper fall into the general category of **prewriting.** This is a time when you should be generating as many new ideas on a topic as you can, using the right side of your brain over the left. This is the part of your brain that thinks up new ideas and sees relationships among old ideas. More specifically, prewriting consists of activities that help you do the following tasks:

- Explore a subject
- Generate ideas about the subject
- Settle on a specific topic
- Establish a purpose
- Analyze your audience

Let's begin by looking at activities that many writers use to stimulate their minds as they approach a writing task. You will get a chance to try each one. Record your responses to the following exercises and questions in your journal or on a separate piece of paper so that you can refer to them throughout the course.

THINKING

Thinking is always the place to start any writing project. Thinking means exploring your topic and letting your mind run freely over the ideas you generate. We'll explore six activities that students often use to stimulate their best thoughts: reading, freewriting, brainstorming, clustering, questioning, and discussing. You will see how Beth Olson uses each strategy before you have a chance to try out the strategy yourself.

Reading

Sometimes a good way to start your writing process is to surf the Net or read an article on your topic. Taking notes on your reading will give you material to work with as you begin to write. In fact, you may find yourself wandering off into your own thoughts on the subject, which you should also get down in writing.

Beth's Reading   Beth read the following paragraph from an essay titled "Survive the Savage Sea" by Dougal Robertson. It stimulated her thoughts about learning in general because she believes that the most important part of learning is taking risks. She jotted several notes to herself in the margins as she read.

TEACHING ON THE WEB
Discussion Topic: Divide students into groups of three or four, and have them talk about how the Internet can help them generate ideas during the prewriting stage. What are the advantages of using the Web for prewriting in this manner? In what ways is the Internet a disadvantage?

TEACHING ON THE WEB
Mosaics Web Site: To learn more about prewriting, students can go to www.prenhall.com/mosaics.

INSTRUCTOR'S RESOURCE MANUAL
For additional material about teaching prewriting, for journal entries, and for various tests, see the *Instructor's Resource Manual,* Section II, Part I.

That Sunday morning stands out clearly in my memory, however, as one of the nice days. I had put the kettle on the hot plate of the solid fuel cooker and while waiting for it to boil switched on the radio to listen to news, which contained a commentary on the Round the World yacht race. I had carried the mugs of tea upstairs on a tray, calling out to Anne, our sixteen-year-old daughter, to come through to our room where nine-year-old twins Neil and Sandy rocked with laughter as they lay in bed with their mother watching our son Douglas perform one of

My family would never have a Sunday like this.

his special slapstick comedy acts. As Douglas rolled his eyes and cavorted around the bedroom in stiff-legged imitation of a disabled robot, Neil's face reddened as he laughed all the breath from his lungs, and even the more serious-minded Sandy chuckled in ecstasy as he watched his fifteen-year-old brother's antics.

Neil and Sandy had become silent while Anne and Douglas questioned and Lyn talked of our sailing adventures in Hong Kong before we had started farming, but suddenly Neil shouted, "Daddy's a sailor. Why can't we go round the world?" Lyn burst out laughing, and "What a lovely idea!" she exclaimed. "Let's buy a boat and go round the world." I realized that Neil, who thought Manchester was one

I wish my dad were a sailor.

Sounds like a great learning experience!

of the four brown corners of the earth, had no conception of the meaning of his remark, and that his mother was entering into the spirit of the game, but suddenly, to me, it was no game. Why not? I looked at Anne and Douglas, both handsome children but the horizons of their minds stunted by the limitations of

I can't believe they sold every- thing.

their environment. In two years they would both have reached school leaving age and neither had shown any leaning toward academic aptitude, and the twins, already backward compared with their contemporaries in town, were unlikely to blossom into sudden educational prodigies. In two years' time they would finish their primary schooling and then. . . . Why not indeed?

I can't imagine spending so much time with my family.

Two years later, after selling our entire holdings in stock and land, we had acquired enough money to embark on the initial stage of our planned circum- navigation of the world.

Later, Beth made this entry in her journal.

> The more I think about Robertson's essay, the more I think about how much I could learn from a trip like this. How great it would be to pick up and leave for a while! I could get some perspective on the world. I can't imagine not having any responsibilities except for those on a boat. My head might actually be clear. I would like to travel around the States for about a year or so, but in an RV or something. I've only been to Texas, Illinois, and New York, but I'd love to see the rest of the country. I can't imagine leaving my family or school, though. I think it would be a waste of time for me right now to just leave. I guess I can plan for that after I retire. That is, if I can get through school.

Your Reading   Read "I Just Wanna Be Average," an essay by Mike Rose (p. 421) on learning, and take notes in the margins as you read. Then, in your journal, write down any thoughts this essay stimulates.

Freewriting

The strategy of freewriting involves writing about anything that comes to your mind. You should write without stopping for five to ten minutes be- cause the act of writing alone will make you think of other ideas. Do not worry about grammar, punctuation, mechanics, or spelling. If you get stuck, repeat an idea or start rhyming words. Just keep writing.

Beth's Freewriting   Beth had trouble freewriting, but she got going and then repeated some words to keep herself writing.

> My English teacher wants us to freewrite about whatever comes to our minds, but I can't think of anything to say. It's hard for me to just start writing. I still can't think of anything to say. And it's hard for me to just write. I don't even know what to write about. Everyone in here is writing furiously in their notebooks; I wonder what they're writing about. How many are writing about their girlfriends? their families? their dreams? I wonder what their dreams are. No one could ever guess that one of my dreams is to someday be my own boss in a company that will make enough money for my family to live comfortably. I suppose that's everyone's dream, really, but I don't think many people would think I had enough guts to go out on my own. But I will someday, and it's going to be a great life.

Focused freewriting is the same procedure focused on a specific topic—either one your instructor gives you or one you choose. Apply your guidelines for freewriting to a specific topic. Just write freely about a designated topic so that you find words for your thoughts and impressions.

Beth's Focused Freewriting   Beth produced the following focused freewriting in her journal. She is trying to get her mind ready to write her essay about learning.

> People can learn about life from just about everything they do. It seems that every action can result in some sort of lesson. It's like all those fairy tales that have morals at the end of the story. If we keep our eyes open, everything we do can have a moral at the end. We can learn about how to study when we join a study group. We can decide how to treat our boyfriends or girlfriends when we watch our friends. And we can even learn from what's on the tube. I also like asking questions and talking to people about problems I'm having. I often get answers that way. Everywhere we look there's something to learn.

Your Freewriting   Try a focused freewriting assignment to prepare for the essay you are going to write by writing in your journal about ways that you learn.

Brainstorming

Like freewriting, brainstorming is based on free association. When you are brainstorming, you let one thought naturally lead to another, generally in the form of a list. You can brainstorm by yourself, with a friend, or with a group. Regardless of the method, list whatever comes into your mind on a topic—ideas, thoughts, examples, facts. As with freewriting, don't worry about grammar, punctuation, mechanics, or spelling.

Beth's Brainstorming   Here is Beth's brainstorming on learning about life:

- everyone learns about life through everyday lessons
- from my parents
- from my brothers and sisters
- from friends
- by watching our friends make mistakes
- by listening to others
- by listening to the radio
- by making my own mistakes
- by asking questions
- by listening to music
- by taking risks
- by succeeding and failing
- by reading books or newspapers
- by studying or going to school
- by observing

Your Brainstorming   Brainstorm in your journal about how you think you learn.

Clustering

Clustering, like brainstorming, is based on free association, but it also shows how your thoughts are related. To cluster, take a sheet of blank paper, write a key word or phrase in the center of the page, and draw a circle around it. Next, write down and circle any related ideas that come to mind. As you add ideas, draw lines to the thoughts they came from. After two or three minutes, you'll have a map of your ideas that can guide you toward a good essay.

Beth's Cluster   Here is Beth's cluster on learning about life:

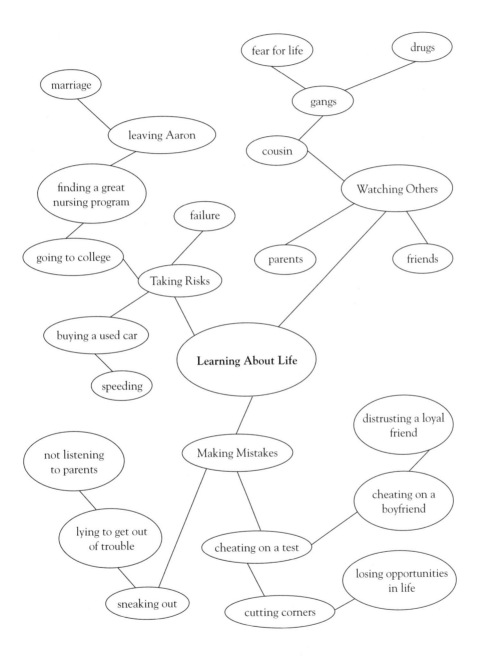

Your Cluster   Write "Learning About Life" in the middle of a piece of paper, circle it, and create a cluster of your own associations with this concept.

Questioning

Journalists use the questions known as the "five *W*s and one *H*"—*Who? What? When? Where? Why?* and *How?*—to check that they've covered all the important information in a news story. Other writers use these questions to generate ideas on a writing topic. Ask yourself each question as it relates to a particular topic. Then answer the questions one by one.

Beth's Questions   Here is how Beth used questioning to generate ideas on her topic, learning about life:

Who?	everyone I know learns about life
What?	learning about life
When?	all day, every day
Where?	depends on what's being learned
Why?	to better themselves in life, for fun, for a variety of reasons
How?	by paying attention and taking action I guess we can even learn without realizing it.

Your Questions   In your journal, answer these six questions about learning in preparation for your essay: Who? What? When? Where? Why? How?

Discussing

Discussing involves talking your ideas out with friends, relatives, class-mates, tutors, or anyone who will listen. Often someone else will have a completely new perspective on your topic that will help you come up with even more ideas. Be sure to record your notes from these conversations so that you don't lose the ideas.

Beth's Discussion   Here are Beth's notes from a conversation she had with her running partner about how we learn about life.

> When I spoke with my friend Alison, I realized that we all learn about life in just about everything we do. I guess it really depends on how much we want to pay attention. Alison talked about the risks I took when I decided to leave my hometown and study nursing at my current college. She also reminded me how much I learned from my cousin when she was involved in gangs. And we even reminisced about some of the bad choices I made and what they taught me. We talked about all the

ways we learn in life, but realized we learn by watching what other people do, by taking risks throughout our lives, and by actually making mistakes. We figured these were the best ways to learn about life—for us.

Your Discussion   Discuss learning about life with someone, and record notes from your conversation in your journal.

Practice 1A   Now that you have been introduced to several prewriting strategies, which is your favorite? Why do you like it best?
Answers will vary.

Practice 1B   Using two prewriting strategies on one assignment is often a good idea. What is your second favorite prewriting strategy? Why do you like this strategy? *Answers will vary.*

PLANNING

In this course, you'll be writing essays. Although essays may differ a great deal in design, organization, and content, they share certain identifying features that distinguish them from other types of writing. At the simplest level, how an essay looks on the page tells its audience "Here's an essay!" An essay usually has a title that names its broad subject. Many longer, more complex essays also have subtitles. When writers move from one topic to another, they indicate this shift by indenting a new paragraph. Most essays have a thesis that is either stated or implied in the introduction, several body paragraphs explaining or supporting that thesis, and a conclusion.

In content, essays are nonfiction, as opposed to short stories, poetry, or drama; that is, they deal with real-life subjects rather than made-up ones. Most essays concentrate on one specific subject and focus on a single purpose. For an essay to be successful, most writers choose methods of development that both suit their purpose and appeal to the audience they hope to inform or persuade. A successful essay gets the reaction from the readers that its author hopes for—whether this response is to appreciate a special scene, identify with someone's grief, or leap into action.

If you haven't already discovered it, you will learn in this book that writing an essay takes planning. If you make some decisions about your topic, audience, and purpose before you actually write, the job of writing will be much smoother and less stressful.

- **What is your subject (person, event, object, idea, etc.)?** An essay focuses on a single subject, along with related thoughts and details. In approaching an essay assignment, then, deciding what you are going to write about is very important. Sometimes your topic is given to you, as when your sociology instructor assigns a paper on abused children. But other times, you choose your own subject. In such cases, choosing a subject that interests you is best. You will have more to say, and you will enjoy writing much more if you know something about your topic.

- *What is your purpose?* Your purpose is your reason for writing an essay. Your purpose could be to explore your feelings on a topic (*to do personal writing*), to tell a friend about something funny that happened to you (*to entertain*), to explain something or share information (*to inform*), or to convince others of your position on a controversial issue (*to persuade*). Whatever your purpose, deciding on it in advance makes writing the rest of your essay easier.

- *Who is your audience?* Your audience consists of the people for whom your message is intended. The more you know about your audience, the more likely you are to accomplish your purpose. The audience for your writing in college is usually your instructor, who represents what is called a "general audience"—people with an average amount of knowledge on most subjects. A general audience is a good group to aim for in all your writing unless you are given other directions.

Practice 2   Identify the subject, purpose, and audience of each of the following paragraphs.

1. Schools have been dealing with the issue of bilingual education for many years. The big debate is whether or not students should be allowed to study in their native language in order to learn English. Many people believe that students should be forced to learn in English, even if they don't know the language. Other people believe that this method of teaching will cause students not to learn, but they know bilingual education programs aren't teaching the students. Obviously, a compromise must be reached in order to help the students.

   Subject: *Bilingual education*

   Purpose: *To inform or persuade*

   Audience: *People who teach or people who need or have children who need these programs*

2. The world of computers has reached a point where people can conduct all of their business transactions from the comfort of their

homes. Internet companies have made it possible for people to shop and do all of their business online. While most people using these services enjoy the convenience of being able to have a business meeting in their bathrobes, the idea of never having to leave the house worries other computer users. People will be able to do everything from home and won't have to interact with other people face to face. Eventually, the art of human interaction will be lost.

Subject: *Effects of using computers in the home*

Purpose: *To inform*

Audience: *General*

3. Playing sports came naturally to me and also taught me a valuable lesson. I began playing soccer and T-ball when I was five years old and continued playing all different types of sports through high school. I had times when I would get tired of constantly having to be at practice for one sport or another. Having a social life became very difficult because I was always busy with sports or trying to stay caught up in my classes. However, through the years of playing sports, I realized I had learned something that none of the teachers in my classes could ever teach me. I had learned how to deal with people. Competing against people taught me how to play with a team and how to keep calm when something wasn't going my way.

Subject: *Using sports to learn about how to deal with people*

Purpose: *Personal writing or to inform*

Audience: *General*

4. Reading a good book can be a fine substitute for a vacation. Every once in a while, people get the feeling that they need to get away from their normal routine and take a trip. Unfortunately, dropping everything and leaving town is not always possible. In this case, reading a book about somewhere far away can make people believe that they have really left their normal surroundings. People can become so involved in a book that they are completely oblivious to the world around them. Sometimes reading a book is just what people need to get away.

Subject: *Reading as a form of vacationing*

Purpose: *To inform*

Audience: *General*

5. Last summer, my family and I went on a two-day rafting trip. The morning our trip began, we loaded all of the camping gear and food into the gear trailer and were on our way. The first day the rapids were Class 2 and 3, which meant that they were moderate rapids and perfect for beginners. Everyone had fun playing in the rapids, swimming, and jumping off of the rocks on the side of the river. That night in camp, the entire group was tired from such a full day on the river, so everyone was ready to go to bed early. The rapids the second day were Class 4 because they had large holes and waves and were considered intermediate. I have to admit that the second day was more exciting than the first day. At the end of the trip, everyone was ready to get a good night's sleep but eager to come back and do it all again.

Subject: *A rafting trip*

Purpose: *Personal writing or to entertain*

Audience: *General*

Beth's Plans   Beth made the following decisions before beginning to write on learning about life:

Subject: learning about life

Purpose: informative—to really talk about the different ways of learning

Audience: general—anyone from the general population

Your Plans   Identify the subject, purpose, and audience of the essay you will write on learning about life.

Subject: _____

Purpose: _____

Audience: _____

WRITING A THESIS STATEMENT

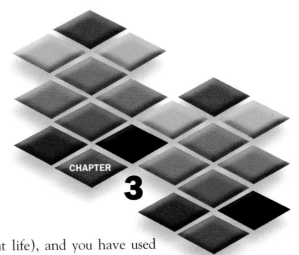

By now, you have a subject (learning about life), and you have used several prewriting techniques with this subject, which means you have generated a number of thoughts that you can use in your essay. You have also decided on a purpose and an audience. In this chapter, you will learn how to write a thesis statement, which you will develop into an essay in the next three chapters. Again, you will be writing alongside Beth Olson as she works through her writing process.

Writing assignments in college are most often broad subjects. To compose a good essay, you need to narrow a broad subject to an idea that you can discuss in a limited number of pages. Your thesis statement is what puts limits on your essay. A **thesis statement** is the controlling idea of an essay. It is the main point that all other sentences relate to. Like a high-powered telescope, your thesis statement zooms in on the specific topic that you will discuss in the body of your essay. The decisions you made in Chapter 2 about subject, purpose, and audience lead you to your thesis statement.

A thesis statement is usually in the first paragraph of an essay. It works best as the last sentence of the opening paragraph. Ending the introduction with the thesis statement lets the writer use the beginning of the paragraph to capture the reader's interest or give background information.

A thesis statement has two parts—a topic and an opinion you hold on that topic.

Subject	Limited Subject	+	Opinion	=	Thesis Statement
Sports	Playing a team sport		has lots of benefits		Playing a team sport teaches a person self-discipline, cooperation, and leadership.

TEACHING WRITING A THESIS
Provide students with thesis statements for many different topics. Make sure you include statements that are too broad ("Sports on TV is an American pastime"), too narrow ("My favorite football player will always be Trent Dilfer"), vague ("Monday Night Football is great"), very specific ("Monday Night Football may be a sports program, but it teaches people about teamwork and sports ethics"), and boring ("My paper will be about Monday Night Football"). Have students discuss the value of each statement and explain why they would or would not use the statement as a thesis statement. This discussion will help students learn how to concentrate their thoughts into one sentence.

Subject	Limited Subject	+	Opinion	=	Thesis Statement
Anger	Road rage		is very dangerous		Road rage is dangerous because it puts the driver, the victim, and the surrounding cars at risk.
Writing	College writing		is similar to writing in the business world		College writing is similar to writing in the business world in three important ways: Both types of writing must be logical, well-developed, and clear.

Practice 1   Fill in the blanks.

1. A thesis statement is _the controlling idea of an essay. It is the main_

   _point that all other sentences relate to_____.

2. A thesis statement has two parts, a _topic_____

   and an _opinion you hold on that topic_____.

3. Where should you put your thesis? _It works best as the last sentence of_

   _the opening paragraph_____.

Practice 2   Limit the following subjects that aren't already limited.
Then add an opinion to all subjects, and make them into thesis statements.
Answers will vary.

Subject	Limited Subject	+	Opinion	=	Thesis Statement
1. Friendship	_____		_____		_____
2. Work	Managers		_____		_____
3. Winning	_____		_____		_____
4. Love	Dating		_____		_____
5. Winter	_____		_____		_____

When you write a thesis statement, keep the following guidelines in mind:

INSTRUCTOR'S
RESOURCE MANUAL

For additional material about teaching the thesis, for journal entries, and for various tests, see the *Instructor's Resource Manual*, Section II, Part I.

1. ***Your subject should not be too broad or too narrow.*** A subject or topic that is too broad would need a book to develop it. One that is too narrow leaves you nothing to say. A manageable subject is one that you can write about in roughly three body paragraphs. You may find it necessary to limit your subject several times before you arrive at one that will work.

Subject:	Television
Too broad:	Prime-time TV
Still too broad:	New TV shows of the 2004 season
Good:	*The Bachelor*
Too narrow:	My favorite competitor

2. ***State your opinion clearly.*** When you give your opinion on the topic, choose your words carefully. Be direct and take a stand. Opinions such as "is interesting," "are not good," "is a problem," or "can teach us a lot" are vague and boring. In fact, if you are specific enough about the opinion you hold, you will be very close to a thesis statement.

Vague Opinion:	*The Bachelor* is fun to watch.
Specific Opinion:	*The Bachelor* teaches us about choosing a mate.

3. ***Do not simply announce your topic.*** Make an interesting statement about your topic.

Announcement:	My paper is going to be about *The Bachelor*.
	The Bachelor is the topic of this essay.
Statement:	*The Bachelor* is a TV show that teaches us how to choose a mate.

4. ***Try your thesis statement (TS) as a question.*** This does not mean that you should actually express your thesis statement as a question in your essay. Rather, you should try thinking of your thesis statement as a question that you will answer in the rest of your essay. You might want to write out your "TS Question" and keep it in front of you as you draft your paper. It will help you keep your focus.

Thesis Statement: The television program *The Bachelor*
teaches us how to choose a mate.

TS Question: How does *The Bachelor* teach us about
choosing a mate?

◆ **P r a c t i c e   3**   Which of the following are good thesis statements?
Mark B for too broad, N for too narrow, MO for missing opinion, and C for
complete. Test each thesis statement by turning it into a question.

___B___ 1. Schools have good education programs.

___MO___ 2. In America today, we face the problem of keeping our air clean.

___C___ 3. Vehicles powered by natural gas will cut down on the pollution
expelled by automobiles.

___B___ 4. When using a computer, the user should know many things.

___MO___ 5. Human cloning is being studied to determine the scientific and
moral consequences of the process.

___C___ 6. Children in America are becoming desensitized to violence
because of TV.

___N___ 7. Many people do not eat meat because they cannot stand the
thought of eating something that was once alive.

___N___ 8. A lot of people avoid math because they have difficulty with
analytical problem solving.

___MO___ 9. Our campus drama department will be performing *Noises Off*
this spring.

___MO___ 10. Since the early 1980s, people have been on various health-craze
diets and exercise programs.

◆ **P r a c t i c e   4**   Complete the following thesis statements. *Answers
will vary.*

1. Marriage today _____.

2. _____ is my favorite class because _____.

3. Sleeping ————————————————————————————.

4. TV award shows ——————————————————————————.

5. ————————————————— is a role model for college students today.

Beth's Thesis Statement Beth writes a thesis statement by stating her opinion about her subject.

Limited Subject   **Opinion**
I know that I learn   from many things in life.

Your Thesis Statement Write a thesis statement here that can serve as the controlling idea for your essay.

Limited Subject   **Opinion**

————————————————   ————————————————————————

Thesis Statement

——————————————————————————————————————

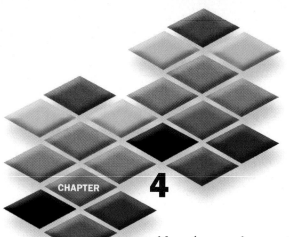

CHAPTER **4**

DEVELOPING BODY PARAGRAPHS

Now that you have written a thesis statement that comes at the end of your introduction, you are ready to write the body paragraphs of your essay. The body paragraphs explain and support the thesis statement.

SUPPORT FOR YOUR THESIS STATEMENT

What ideas will support the statement you make in your thesis? This is the question you need to answer at this point. The supporting ideas are what make up the body of your essay. Each body paragraph covers one major idea of your thesis. The body paragraphs consist of a topic sentence and concrete details that support that topic sentence.

◆ **P r a c t i c e   1 A**   For each of the following lists, cross out any ideas that do not support the thesis statement.

1. Thesis: Children are desensitized to violence by television, video games, and comic books.

> Children don't react to the violent acts they see on TV.
>
> Children do not care when the heroes beat up the villains in comic books.
>
> ~~Many video games cost too much.~~
>
> ~~Children often want to be just like the sports figures they watch on TV.~~
>
> Most children learn very early in life to shoot figures in video games.

2. Thesis: Political campaigns often bring out the worst in candidates.

> ~~Most people are either Republican or Democrat.~~
>
> Candidates try to find secrets from their opponents' pasts.

Candidates use the media to help ruin other candidates' reputations. ~~Presidential campaigns occur every four years.~~

Some candidates even resort to name-calling and twisting their opponents' words.

3. Thesis: To qualify for the FBI, applicants must meet certain requirements.

People interested in joining the FBI must have a college degree.

FBI applicants must be in great physical shape and have excellent eyesight.

~~The events on 9/11 have created a great interest in the CIA.~~

~~FBI agents work within the United States, while CIA agents work outside the United States.~~

FBI applicants must be willing to go through rigorous training and to move anywhere in the United States.

4. Thesis: Starting your own business takes a lot of planning and work.

Prospective business owners must create a business plan in order to borrow money from a bank.

~~Owning your own business is rewarding.~~

People should research the current trends in the market for the type of business they plan to open.

~~Sometimes business owners can get their families to work for free.~~

People should determine how much money they will spend and how much money they will make so they can project possible earnings.

5. Thesis: To maintain a long-distance relationship, both people must be willing to sacrifice.

~~Couples often separate when they go to different universities.~~

Both parties must be sensitive to the other's needs—even at a distance.

People have to communicate often with each other, even if it's hard to find the time.

Both people must put extra effort into the relationship to make it work.

~~My parents had a long-distance relationship.~~

TEACHING ON THE WEB

Discussion Topic: Divide students into groups of three or four, and have them discuss how the Internet has changed the way they view writing. How much writing do they do in a single day on the Internet? How much writing did they do prior to the Internet? How have writing and the Internet changed their lives?

TEACHING ON THE WEB

Mosaics Web Site: To learn more about body paragraphs, students can go to www.prenhall.com/ mosaics.

INSTRUCTOR'S RESOURCE MANUAL

For additional material about teaching body paragraphs, for journal entries, and for various tests, see the *Instructor's Resource Manual,* Section II, Part I.

◆ *P r a c t i c e   1 B*   For each of the following thesis statements, list three supporting ideas. *Answers will vary.*

1. People should always look for three qualities when searching for a job.

   _____

   _____

   _____

2. Moving away from home for the first time can be hard.

   _____

   _____

   _____

3. Animals can help people live longer.

   _____

   _____

   _____

4. Vacations can often be more strenuous than restful.

   _____

   _____

   _____

5. Studying the right way can make a difference in a test grade.

   _____

   _____

   _____

Essays can be different lengths and often have a varying number of ideas that support their thesis statements. The thesis statement generally determines the length of an essay and the amount of support necessary to make a point. Some statements require very little proof and might need only one body paragraph; others require much more support and might need four or more body paragraphs for a complete explanation. An essay that falls somewhere in the middle has an introduction, three body paragraphs, and a conclusion.

Beth's Supporting Ideas   Beth decided on three supporting ideas for her essay, which call for three body paragraphs.

Thesis Statement: I know that I learn from many things in life.
  Supporting Idea 1:   Taking risks
  Supporting Idea 2:   Watching others
  Supporting Idea 3:   Making mistakes

Your Supporting Ideas   Now list the support you might use for your thesis statement.

Your Thesis Statement: _____

  Supporting Idea 1: _____

  Supporting Idea 2: _____

  Supporting Idea 3: _____

OUTLINING

At this stage of the writing process, many people benefit from putting their main ideas in the form of a rough, or working, outline. A rough outline can help you plan your essay and let you see the relationship of your ideas to one another. In this way, you can easily identify ideas that don't support your thesis and locate places where you need more information. A rough outline can evolve and become more detailed as your paper develops.

Beth's Rough Outline   Here is a rough outline of Beth's ideas so far:

Thesis Statement: I know that I learn from many things in life.
  A. I learn from taking risks.
  B. I learn from watching others.
  C. I learn from making mistakes.

Your Rough Outline   Now put your ideas so far in outline form.

Thesis Statement: _____

   A. _____

   B. _____

   C. _____

TOPIC SENTENCES

Writing is made up of several steps that lead you to your first draft. So far, you have been given a subject (learning about life) and worked through a number of prewriting techniques. You also have generated ideas that you can use in your essay and have decided on a purpose and audience. Now you will learn how to write topic sentences for your body paragraphs. Then you will add some specific, concrete details from your prewriting activities and choose a method of organization for each paragraph. At that point, you will be ready to write your essay. This portion of the chapter will help you start your first draft, which you will then revise and edit in Chapters 7 and 8. Again, you will be writing alongside Beth as she works through the writing process with you.

First, you need to state each of your supporting ideas in the form of a topic sentence that will be developed into a body paragraph. The decisions you made in Chapter 2 about subject, purpose, and audience will lead you to your topic sentences. Look back at your prewriting notes and think about which topics will best support your thesis statement. These will be the topics of your body paragraphs. These paragraphs will each include a topic sentence.

The **topic sentence** of a paragraph is its controlling idea. A typical paragraph consists of a topic sentence and details that expand on that topic sentence. A topic sentence performs two important tasks in its paragraph: (1) It supports the essay's thesis statement, and (2) it tells what the paragraph will be about. It functions best as the first or last sentence in its paragraph. Beginning or ending a paragraph with the topic sentence gives direction to the paragraph and provides a kind of road map for the reader.

Like a thesis statement, a topic sentence has two parts—a topic and a statement about that topic. The topic should be limited enough that it can be developed in a paragraph. It should also be focused and not vague or scattered.

Topic	Limited Topic	Statement
Reading	Frequent reading	improves thinking skills.
Lotteries	Winning the lottery	will change a person's life forever.
Children	Having children	is a huge responsibility.
Hate	Hate crimes	are one of life's worst horrors.

P r a c t i c e   2 A   Limit the following topics. Then develop them into statements that could be topic sentences. *Answers will vary.*

Topic	Limited Topic	Statement
1. Mondays	_____	_____
2. Hobbies	_____	_____
3. Theme parks	_____	_____
4. Writing	_____	_____
5. Summer	_____	_____

P r a c t i c e   2 B   Complete the following topic sentences. Make sure they are general enough to be developed into a paragraph but not too broad. *Answers will vary.*

1. Work-related injuries _____.

2. _____ is my favorite television show.

3. Sex education _____.

4. Stray dogs and cats _____.

5. _____ must be looked at on my college campus.

P r a c t i c e   2 C   Write topic sentences for the following paragraphs. *Answers may vary.*

1. *My mom loves to watch mystery shows on TV.* _____

She watches the old ones like *Perry Mason* and can't get enough of the newer ones like *CSI*. But my mom really prefers the not-old and not-new mystery shows like *Matlock* and *Murder She Wrote*. My mom will watch any of these shows for hours. My dad has a joke that she's watching all these TV shows so she can learn how to get rid of him and get away with it. I think she's just gathering information to write a book similar to these shows she loves to watch.

2.   *Learning how to master a new computer program can be difficult.*

First, you must follow the directions to install it onto your computer. Then you must read the directions to learn what you should do first with the program. It's best to read all the directions first, but most of the time people just go straight to the program and try to navigate their way through it. Once you get a handle on how to work the program, it's best just to play around and use the book only when you have questions. Mastering computer programs can be hard, but once you've done it, you can be sure you'll never forget how to use them.

3.   *My sister should have hired a professional consultant to help with her*

wedding plans.

Because she wanted to save money for other parts of her wedding, the consultant was the first expense she cut. Everything went fine until the day of the wedding. My sister didn't get the flowers she ordered, but the ones that were delivered were OK. The cake arrived four hours late, and the reception hall wouldn't let us attach anything to the walls. And just before my sister walked into the church, she discovered that the train on her wedding dress was completely inside out. Luckily, no one but my sister and our family knew of the mishaps, but a consultant would have been worth every penny on the actual day of the wedding.

◆ **P r a c t i c e   3 A**   Supply three topic sentences for each thesis statement. *Answers will vary.*

1. Many people enjoy resting on Sundays.

_____

_____

_____

2. Teachers should encourage all students to learn.

_____

_____

_____

3. Computers will enable people to function more efficiently at work, at home, and at play.

_____

_____

_____

4. Planning is the key to a successful vacation.

_____

_____

_____

5. The abilities to think critically, act quickly, and communicate clearly are essential in the business world.

_____

_____

_____

◆ *Practice* **3B** Fill in the following rough outlines. *Answers will vary.*

1. Subject: College life

Limited Subject: _____

Thesis Statement: _____

Topic Sentence: _____

Topic Sentence: _____

Topic Sentence: _____

2. Subject: Animal rights

Limited Subject: _____

Thesis Statement: _____

Topic Sentence: _____

Topic Sentence: _____

Topic Sentence: _____

3. Subject: Intercollegiate sports

Limited Subject: _____

Thesis Statement: _____

Topic Sentence: _____

Topic Sentence: _____

Topic Sentence: _____

4. Subject: Summer jobs

Limited Subject: _____

Thesis Statement: _____

Topic Sentence: _____

Topic Sentence: _____

Topic Sentence: _____

5. Subject: The Internet

Limited Subject: _____

Thesis Statement: _____

Topic Sentence: _____

Topic Sentence: _____

Topic Sentence: _____

Beth's Topic Sentences   Beth writes three topic sentences that she thinks will support her thesis statement.

> **Thesis Statement:**   I know that I learn from many things in life.
>
> **Topic Sentence:**   I have discovered that I learn a lot by taking risks.
>
> **Topic Sentence:**   I also benefit from watching other people.
>
> **Topic Sentence:**   I believe that I learn from making mistakes.

Your Topic Sentences   Develop each of the ideas you listed on page 33 into a topic sentence that is directly related to your thesis statement. List your thesis first.

> **Thesis Statement:** _____
>
> **Topic Sentence:** _____
>
> **Topic Sentence:** _____
>
> **Topic Sentence:** _____

SPECIFIC DETAILS

Now you are ready to generate the specific details that will make up the bulk of your body paragraphs. Later in this text, you will learn about different methods of developing your ideas, such as describing, comparing and contrasting, and analyzing causes and effects. For now, we are simply going to practice generating concrete supporting details and examples that are directly related to a specific topic. Concrete words refer to anything you can see, hear, touch, smell, or taste, such as *trees, boats, water, friends, fire alarm,* and *bread.* They make writing come alive because they help the reader picture what the writer is talking about.

Practice 4A   Put a check by the details and examples listed that support each topic sentence.

1. Many people are addicted to soap operas.

    ____✔____ viewers get caught up in the story

    ____✔____ people care about the characters

_____ soap operas are often springboards for actors wanting more work

___✔___ people are anxious to see what happens next

_____ mindless but entertaining TV

___✔___ viewers often strongly identify with the characters

_____ CBS has had the number one soap opera for years

2. My parents have reversed the stereotypical roles in their marriage.

___✔___ my dad decorates the house

_____ my mom and dad both work

_____ my sister wants to be just like our mom

___✔___ my mom mows and takes care of the lawn

___✔___ my dad cleans the inside of the house

_____ I hope to marry someone like my mom

3. The members of every generation think they'll understand their kids' music—until they actually hear it.

___✔___ parents don't appreciate today's rock music

___✔___ parents who listened to rock-and-roll don't understand heavy metal

___✔___ parents become wary of musicians like Kid Rock and Marilyn Manson

___✔___ no parents understand new wave or punk music

_____ Dick Clark has helped all kinds of music get established

_____ parents have a hard time letting their kids listen to rap music

_____ Elvis helped put rock-and-roll on the map

4. Students change their majors often throughout their academic careers.

_____ general education courses make students learn about a variety of subjects

___✓___ in college, students discover new interests in subjects they have never been exposed to

_____ professors bring new subjects to life for many students

_____ math is difficult for many students

___✓___ other students often influence a student's decision about a major

___✓___ the reality of the job market creates changes in majors

___✓___ academic performance sometimes makes students look for alternative interests

5. The best way to lose weight is through a good diet and exercise.

___✓___ snacking all day long can cause a person to eat more than usual

_____ people who exercise a lot need enough sleep

___✓___ skipping meals is counterproductive for people on diets

___✓___ people should exercise at least three times per week

___✓___ running is great exercise

___✓___ people should eat three sensible meals per day

_____ ESPN has many exercise shows

◆ ***Practice 4B***   For each of the following topic sentences, list five details or examples to develop them. *Answers will vary.*

1. Everywhere I go, I seem to see someone that I know.

_____

_____

_____

_____

_____

2. When I was in high school, I enjoyed many different extracurricular activities.

_____

_____

_____

_____

_____

3. People are beginning to use their personal computers for many different types of business transactions.

_____

_____

_____

_____

_____

4. Friends and family are very important parts of life.

_____

_____

_____

_____

_____

5. People must be careful when they are swimming.

_____

_____

_____

_____

_____

Beth's Development   To come up with concrete details and examples that would support her topic sentence, Beth uses the brainstorming and focused freewriting techniques she learned in Chapter 2. This is what she wrote:

I have discovered that I learn a lot by taking risks.

- buying a used car
- quitting my new job
- leaving Aaron to come to this school
- driving way too fast
- trying new foods
- changing majors
- procrastinating in school

I also benefit from watching other people.

- moving in with roommates I don't know
- watching my friends make mistakes with their boyfriends
- looking at my parents make rules
- seeing my cousin ruin her life
- watching my brother mess up
- observing people around me get involved with drugs
- learning about other people's mistakes from my friends

I believe that I learn from making mistakes.

- cheating on the test
- believing the rumor about my best friend
- lying to my parents
- not believing my sister
- waiting too long to write a paper
- watching TV instead of studying

Here is Beth's new freewriting:

> I know I learn a lot by taking risks, watching other people, and making mistakes. I'm sure I learn in other ways too, but these are the ways that seem to give me the most information about life in general.
>
> Taking risks really helps everyone learn in life, but I think this is especially true for me. I mean, right now I'm sitting here in this class thinking about Aaron and how we want to get married some day. But I left my hometown and Aaron to come here for the nursing program. So far everything is great, but I knew it was a risk coming here. But how could I learn if I didn't?
>
> I also learn by watching other people. My parents are great role models, but it's hard to really learn because they are so much older. I mean, they *tell* me not to join a gang, but they're my parents. I learned more about gangs from my cousin than from my parents. Watching my cousin go through her experiences was way better than just listening to my parents. I definitely learn by watching others.
>
> And I definitely learn by making mistakes. And boy do I have tons of those. Most of my mistakes are pretty small, but I still learn from them. I think I learned the most from Mr. Turner, though, when he caught me cheating on his test. He talked to me, and that really helped. In fact, I think it's because of him that I started paying attention in class and decided to pursue nursing at this school.
>
> I will always learn about life from these sources. I guess I will always learn about life as long as I keep my eyes open, but these ways seem the most important to me right now.

Your Development   Choose at least one of the prewriting strategies that you learned in Chapter 2, and use it to generate more specific details and examples for each of your topic sentences.

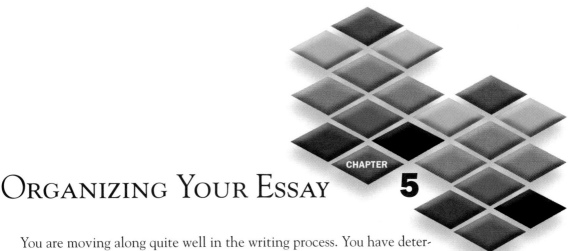

ORGANIZING YOUR ESSAY

You are moving along quite well in the writing process. You have determined your subject, purpose, and audience, and you have written your thesis statement. You have also written topic sentences for your body paragraphs and thought of details, examples, and facts to develop those topic sentences. You are now ready to organize your ideas. What should come first? What next?

To organize the ideas in your essay, you need to consider the purpose of your essay and the way each body paragraph serves that purpose. Then you should arrange your body paragraphs in a logical manner to achieve that purpose. If your essay's main purpose is informative—to describe the layout of a building, for example—you would probably arrange the details spatially. That is, you might begin with the entrance and move to the other parts of the building as if you were strolling through it. If, however, you want to persuade a reader to buy one type of car over another, you might arrange the essay so that it moves from one extreme to another—for example, from the least important feature of the car to the most important. Once you decide on the order of your paragraphs, you need to organize the details in each paragraph.

Most paragraphs and essays are organized in one of five ways:

1. From general to particular
2. From particular to general
3. Chronologically (by time)
4. Spatially (by physical order)
5. From one extreme to another

Let's look at these methods of organization one by one.

GENERAL TO PARTICULAR

The most common method of organizing an essay or paragraph is from general to particular. This method begins with a general topic and becomes more specific as it progresses. A paragraph organized from general to

TEACHING
ORGANIZING THE
ESSAY
Bring to class newspaper articles that you have cut into sections. Divide your students into groups of three or four, and give each group two or three cut-up articles (be sure not to mix up the articles). Have each group try to organize the articles in a logical way. Have students organize at least one of the articles in more than one way. Have each group present one article that can be organized in a couple of different ways and justify the organization in each case.

particular might look like this:

Topic Sentence
    Detail
    Detail
    Detail
    Detail

Here is an example of a paragraph organized from general to particular:

   When I began attending college, I was very nervous because I was afraid I would not do very well in my classes. My first year, I took general education classes that reviewed a lot of the material I learned in high school. There was a lot of studying involved in these classes, but I was able to pass all of them. Soon I decided that my major would be business, so I began taking classes that dealt with business. All of the business classes were harder than the classes I had taken in general education. Just when I thought I would not pass a class, I would do well on a test, which would raise my confidence level again. I worked very hard in every class I took and was able to pass every one. Tomorrow I am graduating with my bachelor's degree in business.

This paragraph moves from the general idea of going to college to the specific notion of taking classes, graduating, and receiving a degree. Notice that it includes such transitions as *when, but, soon,* and *which*. They show the relationship among the writer's thoughts.

   The skeleton of a general-to-particular essay looks like this, although the number of paragraphs and details will vary:

Introduction
    Topic sentence stating the most general point
        Detail
        Detail
        Detail
    Topic sentence stating a more specific supporting point
        Detail
        Detail
        Detail
    Topic sentence stating the most specific supporting point
        Detail

Detail
Detail
Conclusion

An example of an essay organized from general to particular is "A Family Dilemma: To Scout or Not to Scout" on page 474. The essay begins by introducing the nephew of the author and the Supreme Court's ruling that the Boy Scouts can legally fire gay men from their organization. The author then explains how these two general topics are affecting his present life, moving to topics that become more and more specific as the essay progresses. You might want to read this selection to see how this method of organization works in a full essay.

◆ **Practice 1A** Turn to the essay "El Hoyo" on page 400, and find two paragraphs organized from general to specific. *Paragraphs 2, 3, or 4.*

◆ **Practice 1B** Write a topic sentence for the following group of sentences. Then organize the sentences into a paragraph using general-to-particular order. Add words, phrases, or sentences as necessary to smooth out the paragraph.

Topic Sentence: *Nowadays sports figures are constantly on television.*

3 During these events, not only do you get to watch the athletes play their games, but you get to see former athletes announcing the action play-by-play.

1 Anytime you turn on the TV, there are at least 14 sporting events happening at one time.

2 You can see anything from basketball to golf to racing to fishing.

5 Let's face it; the likelihood of seeing a sports figure on TV is great.

4 And just when you think you've seen enough of the players, you are flooded with commercials that have athletes selling various products.

PARTICULAR TO GENERAL

When you reverse the first method of organization, you arrange your material from particular to general. In this case, more specific ideas start the essay or paragraph and lead up to a general statement. This type of organization is particularly effective if you suspect that your reader might not agree with the final point you are going to make. With this method, you can lead your reader to your opinion slowly and carefully.

A paragraph organized from particular to general looks like this:

Detail

Detail

Detail

Detail

Topic Sentence

Here is a paragraph of particular-to-general organization.

> The water is so crystal-clear that I can see every pebble settled on the bottom. A small sandy beach reaches the water's edge and makes a perfect spot to spend the afternoon. Across the water I can see the mountainside covered in the greenest trees imaginable. A log cabin also sits among the trees halfway up the mountain, so peaceful and secluded. The puffy white clouds make the sky appear to be a brighter blue, and the birds seem to enjoy floating on the soft breeze. I could sit all day next to the lake in the valley and just stare at my surroundings.

This paragraph starts with specific details about the area around the lake and ends with a topic sentence. Such transitions as *and, across the water*, and *also* move readers through the paragraph.

This is how a particular-to-general essay looks, though the number of details will vary:

Introduction

  Topic sentence stating the most specific point

    Detail

    Detail

    Detail

  Topic sentence stating a less specific point

    Detail

    Detail

    Detail

  Topic sentence stating the most general point

    Detail

    Detail

    Detail

Conclusion

The essay titled "Healing Myself with the Power of Work" on page 470 is a good example of organization from particular to general. It moves from examples out of the writer's life to his thesis at the end—that work is his therapy. If you read this selection, you will see firsthand how this method of organization works in a complete essay.

Practice 2A Turn to the essay "What Are Friends For?" on page 462, and find two paragraphs that demonstrate particular-to-general organization. *Paragraphs 6 and 12.*

Practice 2B Write a topic sentence for the following group of sentences. Then organize the sentences into a paragraph using particular-to-general order. Add words, phrases, or sentences as necessary to smooth out the paragraph.

Topic Sentence: *Pepperoni pizza is my very favorite food.* _____

6 My mom hopes I'll order something more grown-up, but I never will.

4 My family knew I loved pizza and always let me order one once a week.

1 I have always loved pepperoni, even on sandwiches and in soups.

3 I used to love pizza night when I lived at home.

2 I believe that pizza is the best food ever created.

5 Now when I go home, we just go to an Italian restaurant where I can order pizza.

CHRONOLOGICAL ORDER

When you organize ideas chronologically, you are organizing them according to the passage of time—in other words, in the order in which they occurred. Most of the time, when you tell a story or explain how to do something, you use chronological order: First this happened, and then that. Or first you do this, next you do that, and so on.

A paragraph organized chronologically looks like this:

Topic Sentence
   First
   Then
   Next
   Finally

Here is an example of a paragraph organized chronologically:

> Preparing to go snowboarding for the first time can be a lot of fun. First of all, you must get into full gear when you arrive at the mountain. Then you ride a ski lift to the top of the mountain. Once at the top, it is time to buckle your boots into the bindings on the board. The bindings must be tight, but not so tight that they are uncomfortable. Next, you are ready to begin your descent. On the way down the mountain, pay attention to how the board moves when pressure is applied to the toes and heels of the feet. Finally, you need to learn which way to lean in order to turn right and left so you can fly down the mountain. Once you have mastered the basics, you will have fun perfecting your new hobby.

This paragraph is chronological because it explains snowboarding according to a time sequence and uses transitions such as *first of all, then, next,* and *finally.*

Here is what an essay organized chronologically looks like:

Introduction
    What happened first
        Detail
        Detail
        Detail
    What happened next
        Detail
        Detail
        Detail
    What happened after that
        Detail
        Detail
        Detail
Conclusion

A good example of this method of organization is the essay titled "Black Music in Our Hands" on page 456. It begins with the author explaining the three types of music she sang in the early 1960s. She then explains according to a time sequence all the circumstances that caused her to look at music differently. Reading through it will help you understand this method of organization.

Practice   3A   Turn to the essay "Writer's Retreat" on page 414, and find two paragraphs that are organized chronologically. *Most paragraphs in this essay are arranged chronologically.*

Practice   3B   Write a topic sentence for the following group of sentences. Then organize the sentences into a paragraph using chronological order. Add words, phrases, or sentences as necessary to smooth out the paragraph.

Topic Sentence: _*Making a peanut butter and jelly sandwich is easy.*_____

7   Spread the jelly on top of the peanut butter.

3   Unscrew the lid from a jar of peanut butter and from a jar of jelly.

6   Using the knife again, remove a small amount of jelly from the jar.

2   Place two slices of bread on a plate.

4   Using the knife, remove a small amount of peanut butter from the jar.

8   Place the second slice of bread on top of the slice with the peanut butter and jelly on it.

1   First, remove a butter knife from the drawer.

5   Spread the peanut butter on one slice of bread with the knife.

SPATIAL ORDER

Another method of arranging details is by their relationship to each other in space. You might describe the layout of your campus from its front entrance to its back exit or the arrangement of a beautiful garden from one end to the other. Explaining a home page from top to bottom and a screened-in porch from inside to outside are also examples of spatial order. Beginning at one point and moving detail by detail around a specific area is the simplest way of organizing by space.

A paragraph organized spatially might look like this:

Topic Sentence
   Here
   There
   Next
   Across
   Beyond

Here is an example of a paragraph organized spatially:

It was the first football game of the season and her first football game ever as a cheerleader. Standing in front of the huge crowd made the butterflies in her stomach begin to flutter again. In the front row sat a group of her friends cheering her on. Two rows behind them sat her psychology professor. Next to her professor sat a few of her new sorority sisters. As the cheerleader looked across the aisle, she noticed a group of rowdy students screaming and cheering for their team. Beyond the crowd, the tall announcer's booth where all of the press people and the athletic director sat seemed to glare down at her. Any minute the music would begin to blare from that very booth, and she would begin her first half-time dance routine.

This paragraph is arranged spatially because it moves physically around the football stadium, using such words as *in front of, behind, next to,* and *beyond* as transitions.

Here is what an essay organized spatially looks like:

Introduction
  Here
    Detail
    Detail
    Detail
  There
    Detail
    Detail
    Detail
  Next
    Detail
    Detail
    Detail
  Across
    Detail
    Detail
    Detail
  Beyond
    Detail

Detail

Detail

Conclusion

An example of this method of organization is the essay titled "Dwellings" on page 404. It moves in spatial order around the vicinity of the author's home. Reading through it will help you understand this method of organization.

◆ *P r a c t i c e   4 A*   Turn to the essay "Sanctuary of School" on page 411, and find two paragraphs that use spatial organization. *Paragraphs 8 and 12*

◆ *P r a c t i c e   4 B*   Write a topic sentence for the following group of sentences. Then write a paragraph putting the sentences in spatial order. Add words, phrases, or sentences as necessary to smooth out the paragraph.

Topic Sentence: *There are many things to see at the front of the hotel.*

4   The hotel's check-in desk is located on the left side of the lobby.

5   Two little boys are sitting quietly on the couches next to the check-in desk, waiting for their parents to finish checking in.

7   In the center of the lobby are four massive couches arranged in a conversational setting.

6   Directly across from the check-in desk is the activities counter where people can plan their days.

2   Inside the front door, the guests' attention is immediately drawn to the ceiling.

3   Painted as a sky, the ceiling gives guests the feeling that they have never left the outdoors.

1   Framing the front door are two huge dolphins, each perched in the center of a water fountain.

ONE EXTREME TO ANOTHER

Sometimes the best way to organize a paragraph is from one extreme to another: from most expensive to least expensive, from most humorous to least humorous, from most frustrating to least frustrating, and so on. (Of course, you can also move from least to most.) Use whatever extremes make sense for your topic. You might explain how to choose a pet by elaborating on the most important qualities of an animal and then considering the least important. For example, an apartment dweller's most important consideration would be the size of the pet and its need for exercise. Least important would be watchdog qualities. To accomplish another purpose, you might reverse this order and begin with the least important quality; this method is good in persuasive writing because you end with your most important idea.

This method of organization has one distinct advantage over the other four approaches: It is the most flexible. When no other method of organization works, you can always arrange details from one extreme to another.

Here is an outline of a paragraph organized from one extreme to another:

Topic Sentence
  Most
  Next most
  Somewhat
  Least

Here is an example of a paragraph that moves from one extreme to another:

> Ever since I was old enough to join Little League teams, I have played a variety of sports. I would have to say that my favorite sport has always been football. Absolutely nothing can top the feeling of running for a touchdown and passing the defensive safety. My next favorite sport would have to be baseball. I used to love to pitch to catchers when we would work as though we were one athlete. My next favorite sport is basketball. As a teenager, I played guard in basketball, but eventually I got bored with the position. My least favorite sport is soccer. No matter how much I trained and ran before soccer season, I always got exhausted during the games—all we did was run up and down the field. Now that I'm in college, I'm grateful for the intramural teams that let me keep playing the sports that I love.

This paragraph moves from most to least preferred sports and is marked by such words as *favorite*, *next favorite*, and *least favorite*.

Here is what an essay organized according to extremes looks like:

Introduction
  Most
    Detail
    Detail
    Detail
  Next most
    Detail

                Detail
                Detail
          Somewhat
                Detail
                Detail
                Detail
          Least
                Detail
                Detail
                Detail
    Conclusion

"What Are Friends For?" on page 462 is a good example of this method of organization. It begins with a discussion of "relative friends" and moves to an explanation of "new friends." The author organizes her essay from least meaningful to most meaningful friends. Reading through it will help you understand this strategy.

P r a c t i c e   5 A   Turn to the essay "Happiness Is Catching" on page 477, and find two paragraphs that are organized from one extreme to another. *Paragraphs 10 and 11*

P r a c t i c e   5 B   Write a topic sentence for the following group of sentences. Then write a paragraph arranging the sentences from one extreme to another. Add words, phrases, and sentences as necessary to smooth out the paragraph. Also, label your system of classification (from most to least or from least to most). *Answers will vary.*

Topic Sentence: _New employees who must collect money have a difficult time._

1   First, they have a hard time asking people for money.

3   Consequently, they allow debtors extra time to pay the bill.

6   But after a few months, the new employee has heard all the sob stories and is immune to their power.

4   That just makes it harder to get the money.

2   This may be because they believe the sob stories they hear, which probably aren't true.

5   Unfortunately, once the date has been extended, we all have to agree to it.

System of Classification: _Chronological_

◈ *P r a c t i c e   6 A*   List the best method of development for paragraphs on the following topics.

1. How to make homemade salsa. *Chronological*
2. I think I am going to rearrange my dorm room to create more space. *Spatial*
3. What I will have for dinner tonight. *General to particular*
4. Today, people question the ethics of capital punishment. *General to particular*
5. I lift weights for an hour and run five miles every day. *Particular to general*

◈ *P r a c t i c e   6 B*   Write a topic sentence that introduces the following details in a paragraph. Then arrange the details in logical order, and write a paragraph. *Answers will vary.*

Topic Sentence: *Although sometimes difficult, exercise is an essential part of life.*

exercising three times a week

the advantages of aerobic exercise

exercising with a friend

the difficulty of starting an exercise routine

Beth's Organization   Beth decided to organize her essay from one extreme to another—from the most important ways of learning for her to the least important. She first wants to introduce the idea of taking risks, which she believes is very important. Next she will discuss watching others and finally learning from mistakes because she thinks she learns a lot from her own mistakes. She thinks this order might work, so she lists as many concrete details as she can under each main idea.

Here is Beth's working outline at this point:

Thesis Statement: I know that I learn from many things in life.

   Taking Risks (*most important*):   taking risks and learning from them

     Specific Details: finding a good nursing program
                  leaving my boyfriend back home
                  going to college

  Watching Others (*less important*):   learning from watching others

     Specific Details: watching my cousin in gangs
                  living in fear
                  not in a gang because of her

Making Mistakes (*least important*):   making mistakes and learning from those mistakes

Specific Details: cheating on test
talking with Mr. Turner
learning to pay more attention in school
for a better future

Concluding Thoughts: people can learn from everything they do

Specific Details: taking risks
watching others
making mistakes

Does the method of organization that Beth has chosen suit her topic? Would any other method of organization work as well?

Your Organization   What method of organization will work best for your ideas about learning? Why do you think this method will be best?

WRITING
THE INTRODUCTION,
CONCLUSION, AND TITLE

By now, you have written your thesis statement and topic sentences for your body paragraphs. You've thought of supporting details, facts, examples, and the most effective way of organizing your thoughts. At the end of this chapter, you will write a complete first draft of your essay. First, though, let's look at three important parts of your essay: the introduction, the conclusion, and the title.

You might have written some of these parts already. Some people write their introduction with their thesis; others write the introduction last. Some have an idea of how they want to conclude from the time they begin their papers; others write the conclusion last. Some struggle with a title; others write their titles as they generate their drafts. The order in which you write these three parts of an essay depends on your own personal writing process. All that matters is that your papers have a title, an introduction, several body paragraphs, and a conclusion that work together.

INTRODUCTION

The introduction to your essay—your first paragraph—should both introduce your subject and stimulate your audience's interest. The introduction of an essay captures the readers' interest, gives necessary background information, and presents your thesis statement. This paragraph essentially tells readers what the essay is going to cover without going into detail or discussing specifics.

Writers generally use the introduction to lead up to their thesis statement. As a result, the sentences at the beginning of the introductory paragraph need to grab your readers' attention. Some effective ways of capturing your audience's interest and giving necessary background information are to (1) furnish a vivid description, (2) tell a brief story, (3) give a revealing fact, statistic, or definition, (4) make an interesting comparison, (5) present a dramatic example, and (6) use an exciting quotation.

TEACHING WRITING THE INTRODUCTION, CONCLUSION, AND TITLE

Divide students into six groups. Provide each group with an extremely dull, short introduction on a topic familiar to them (perhaps a current TV show or an issue in the news). Then assign each group a different strategy for revising the introduction: (1) furnish vivid descriptions, (2) tell a brief story, (3) give a revealing fact, statistic, or definition, (4) make an interesting comparison, (5) present a dramatic example, and (6) use an exciting quotation. Have the members of each group rewrite the introduction using their assigned technique and read their revisions to the class. Have the students vote for the introduction that is the most interesting.

Also be sure that your introduction gives your readers any information that they may need to follow your train of thought. One way to check that your readers have all the necessary background is to apply the five Ws and one H: *Who, What, When, Where, Why,* and *How.* Any of this information that is important to your readers' understanding of your thesis statement should go in the introduction. You might also ask a friend to read your first draft and tell you if any background information is missing.

Beth's Introduction and Thesis   Beth wrote a first draft of her introduction just to get started. She knew she would have to work with it later, but at least she was able to get some of her ideas down on paper.

> Everyone learns in different ways. Some people learn by watching, some by reading, and others by themselves. The way people learn is a part of who they are. Knowing how we learn can help us understand ourselves better. I know that I learn from many things in life.

Your Introduction   Use the guidelines suggested here to capture your readers' interest and, if necessary, give them background information. Write two different introductions for your essay. End each with your thesis statement.

CONCLUSION

The concluding paragraph is the final paragraph of an essay. It completes your essay, giving readers a sense of closure. That is, readers feel that all the loose ends are wrapped up and the point of the essay is clear. As with introductions, there are many good techniques for writing a conclusion. You might (1) summarize the main ideas, (2) highlight the most important issue, (3) ask a question that gets readers to think about something in particular, (4) predict the future, (5) offer a solution to a problem, or (6) call readers to action. In some cases, you might want to use several of these strategies.

You should avoid two common problems in writing a conclusion. First, do not begin your conclusion with the words "in conclusion," "in summary," or "as you can see." Your conclusion should *show*—not *tell*—that you are at the end of your essay. Second, do not introduce a new idea. The main ideas of your essay should be in your body paragraphs. The conclusion is where you *finish* your essay, leaving your readers with a sense of closure or completeness.

Repeat the same exercise with a very dull conclusion. Have groups (1) summarize main ideas, (2) highlight the most important issue, (3) ask a question that gets the reader to think about something in particular, (4) predict the future, (5) offer a solution to a problem, and (6) call the reader to action.

Finally, provide some very dull titles, and have each group try to come up with catchier versions. You might bring tabloid headlines to help demonstrate how titles can entice people to read an article or essay.

TEACHING ON THE WEB
Discussion Topic: How do Internet advertisers use catchy titles or short introductions to lure customers to their Web sites? What would happen if Web sites were dull and uninviting? Would people still read the information? How important are attention-getters to the Web?

TEACHING ON THE WEB
Mosaics Web Site: To learn more about the introduction, conclusion, and title, students can go to www.prenhall.com/mosaics.

INSTRUCTOR'S
RESOURCE MANUAL
For additional material
about teaching the in-
troduction, conclusion,
and title; for journal
entries; and for
various tests, see the
*Instructor's Resource
Manual*, Section II,
Part I.

Beth's Conclusion   Here is a rough outline of what Beth wants to include in her conclusion. These are the notes that she came up with at this point.

People can learn about life from just about anything.

—made me the person I am

—watching other people

—taking some risks myself

—making mistakes

Your Conclusion   Sketch an outline or write a draft of a possible conclusion for your essay.

TITLE

A title is a phrase, usually no more than a few words. A title gives a hint about the subject, purpose, or focus of what is to follow. For example, the main title chosen for this book, *Mosaics*, reflects a particular view of the writing process—as many bright pieces logically connected to complete a picture. In other words, that title expresses in capsule form this textbook's purpose, which is to guide writers through the process of fitting the separate pieces of their ideas into a single meaningful whole to make an essay. The title of this chapter, however, is a straightforward naming of its contents: "Writing the Introduction, Conclusion, and Title."

Besides suggesting an essay's purpose, a good title catches an audience's attention or "hooks" readers so that they want to read more. Look at some of the essay titles in the readings in Part IV. For example, "Happiness Is Catching: Why Emotions Are Contagious" attracts the readers' attention because they will probably want to find out exactly how happiness is catching. "What Are Friends For?" is a title that will naturally draw in most readers. And "I Just Wanna Be Average" is intriguing because the title is not a typical goal for most people. Do not underline or use quotation marks around your essay titles. Do not put a period at the end of your titles, and be sure to capitalize them correctly. The first word and last word in a title are always capitalized. Capitalize all other words except articles (*a, an, the*) and short prepositions (such as *in, by, on,* or *from;* see page 514 for a more complete list of prepositions).

Beth's Title   Beth has several possible titles for her essay. She doesn't really know which one to use.

Learning About Life

The Way We Learn

Everyone Can Learn

Your Title   Write three titles for your essay: (1) one that gives a hint of your subject, (2) one that gives a hint of your purpose, and (3) one that gives a hint of your focus. Make each title as catchy as you can.

Beth's First Draft   In Chapters 1 through 5, and again in this chapter, you have watched Beth thinking about, planning, developing, and organizing her essay. It is time now to get a complete first draft down on paper. Here is Beth's first draft, including a few grammar errors that we will deal with later in this unit.

The Way We Learn

Everyone learns in different ways. Some people learn by watching, some by reading, and others by themselves. The way people learn is a part of who they are. Knowing how we learn can help us understand ourselves better. I know that I learn from many things in life.   1

I have discovered that I learn a lot by taking risks. Being at this college was a risk. I have a boyfriend back home, we want to get married some day. We are hoping for a spring wedding with all of our friends and family. I left my boyfriend to come here. Coming here was a risk to our relationship. But if I am ever going to make it, I have to be willing to take risks.   2

I also benefit from watching other people. When my cousin became heavily involved with gangs, I watched my cousin live in constant fear. By watching my cousin, I made a conscious decision to be nothing like my cousin. By watching and understanding my cousin's life. I learned to live mine better.   3

I believe that I learn from making mistakes. When I was in high school, I didn't study for a major science   4

test. So I cheated. My sister cheated once. I was so
scared to do it. The teacher caught me. The teacher took
the time to talk to me about the mistake I was making.
This mistake made me reevaluate my education. I could
have laughed off the cheating experience. I decided to
slow down and learn from the experience.

5   People can learn about life from almost anything
they do. They just have to be willing to do so. When I
take risks, I think about what I will learn. I definitely
try to learn as much as I can from watching others.
When I make mistakes, I figure out why I made each
mistake and how to avoid it a second time.

Your First Draft   Now write a complete first draft of your essay on how you
learn.

REVISING

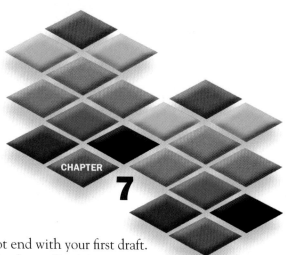

No matter how hard you wish, writing does not end with your first draft. The fun of revising and editing still lies ahead of you. **Revising** means "seeing again," and that is exactly what you should try to do when you revise to improve your writing—see it again from as many different angles as possible.

More specifically, revising your writing means changing it so that it says exactly what you mean in the most effective way. Revision involves both *content* (what you are trying to say) and *form* (how you deliver your message). Having a friend or tutor read your paper before you revise it is a good idea so that you can see if you are communicating clearly.

Revising content means working with your words until they express your ideas as accurately and completely as possible. Revising form consists of working with the organization of your writing. When you revise, you should look closely at the six basic categories listed in the following checklist.

REVISING CHECKLIST ✔

THESIS STATEMENT
✔ Does the thesis statement contain the essay's controlling idea and an opinion about that idea?

✔ Does the thesis appear as the last sentence of the introduction?

BASIC ELEMENTS
✔ Does the title draw in the readers?

✔ Does the introduction capture the readers' attention and build up to the thesis statement effectively?

✔ Does each body paragraph deal with a single topic?

✔ Does the conclusion bring the essay to a close in an interesting way?

TEACHING REVISING
Divide students into groups of three or four, and have them exchange papers. Have the first student read his or her paper aloud while the other students listen for and take notes on suggested revisions. When the reader finishes, have each listener explain his or her suggestions; make sure the reader does not talk or try to clarify any points during this interchange. After all suggestions have been relayed, have the next writer read his or her paper, and so on. Allow only 10 minutes per paper.

TEACHING ON THE WEB
Discussion Topic: Divide students into groups of three or four, and have them discuss how the Internet can be a tool for revision.

What types of Web sites will help students get revising feedback for their papers? How else can the Internet help?

TEACHING ON THE WEB
Mosaics Web Site: To learn more about revising, students can go to www.prenhall.com/ mosaics.

INSTRUCTOR'S RESOURCE MANUAL
For additional material about teaching revising, for journal entries, and for various tests, see the *Instructor's Resource Manual,* Section II, Part I.

DEVELOPMENT
✔ Do the body paragraphs adequately support the thesis statement?
✔ Does each body paragraph have a focused topic sentence?
✔ Does each body paragraph contain specific details that support the topic sentence?
✔ Does each body paragraph include enough details to explain the topic sentence fully?

UNITY
✔ Do the essay's topic sentences relate directly to the thesis statement?
✔ Do the details in each body paragraph support its topic sentence?

ORGANIZATION
✔ Is the essay organized logically?
✔ Is each body paragraph organized logically?

COHERENCE
✔ Are transitions used effectively so that paragraphs move smoothly and logically from one to the next?
✔ Do the sentences move smoothly and logically from one to the next?

Let's look at these revision strategies one by one.

Thesis Statement

✔ Does the thesis statement contain the essay's controlling idea and an opinion about that idea?
✔ Does the thesis appear as the last sentence of the introduction?

As you learned in Chapter 3, every successful essay has a thesis statement that states the essay's controlling idea. This sentence gives direction to the rest of the essay. It consists of a limited subject and the writer's position on that subject. Although a thesis statement can appear anywhere in an essay, it is usually the last sentence of the introduction.

Here are two examples:

Limited Subject	+ Opinion	= Thesis Statement
1. Children today	grow up too fast	Children today grow up too fast.
2. Children today	grow up too fast	Children today grow up too fast because of television, advertising, and working parents.

As in the second example, the thesis statement should introduce all the topics in its essay. The first example includes the limited subject and the writer's position on that subject but also needs to introduce its topics.

Practice 1A   Review the guidelines for developing a thesis statement in Chapter 3. Then write a thesis statement for each group of topic sentences listed here.

1. Thesis Statement: *Friends are wonderful people with whom you can share activities, good news, and bad times.*

   Everyone needs a friend who likes to do the same things.

   Everyone needs someone to share the good news with.

   Equally important, everyone needs a good listener during bad times.

2. Thesis Statement: *Seeing a movie in a theater is much better than watching one at home.*

   Watching a movie on the big screen of a theater makes the story and characters bigger and more interesting than life.

   The sound system in a movie theater makes me feel that I'm right there in the action.

   The concession stand has all sorts of candy and goodies, and I don't have to clean up my own mess afterward.

3. Thesis Statement: *There are many ways to become upset while driving.*

   Being behind slow drivers can cause people to experience road rage.

Likewise, tailgating can cause people to get angry.

People who weave in and out of traffic at extreme speeds make many drivers furious.

4. Thesis Statement: *No matter what, everything about a first date is awkward.*

Asking someone out on a first date can take a lot of courage.

Suggesting places to go or things to do is harder than it sounds.

It seems that there's always one very embarrassing moment on a first date that would never happen on a later date.

5. Thesis Statement: *Skydiving is scary but a lot of fun.*

Signing up for a skydiving class is exciting, and all your friends think you're really cool.

Boarding the plane for your first jump is a strong dose of reality, but not quite like getting up the nerve to actually jump.

Free-falling and landing safely provide a rush that skydivers never forget.

Practice 1B Write thesis statements for the following introductions.

1. *I have great difficulty getting out of bed, which affects my plans for the morning.*

No matter how much I tell myself I am going to get up in the morning and go, I cannot seem to do it. Every night before I go to bed, I lay out my sweats and shoes and set my alarm. In the morning when the alarm rings, I push the snooze button and promise myself that I will get up in 10 minutes. This routine goes on for the next hour until I have to get up in order to make it to work on time. Once again, I have failed to get up and go to the gym, and I have deprived myself of one more hour of sleep.

2. *People need to consider many things when buying a new house.*

The most important detail is to determine the number of rooms in the house. A family must consider the needs of the people living in the house and their plans for the near future. Of course, don't forget the backyard. Does the family need a fenced yard for animals or an area for the kids to play? And the family must pay attention to how well the house has been kept up. All of these items are very important details when looking for a new home.

3. *A couple in my neighborhood follows the same routine every day.*

Every morning, at precisely 8:00, the couple eats breakfast at the corner café. Afterward, they go to the market for fresh fruit or vegetables and run errands. If they have no shopping to do, the couple goes home and does housework or yard work. Every afternoon at 1:00, they sit down to lunch and watch a little television. In the late afternoon, they go for a walk around the lake for a bit of exercise before preparing their dinner. After dinner, they watch the news and play a hand of cards. Soon the sun dips behind the mountain, and the couple retires for the night.

Beth's Revision   When Beth looks back at her thesis statement, she realizes it does not completely introduce what she talks about in her essay. Her thesis tells readers only that she learns about life from different things, not that she has three important ways that she learns about life.

Thesis Statement: I know that I learn from many things in life.

She decides to expand her thesis statement so that it more accurately introduces the topics that will follow in her essay:

Revised Thesis Statement: I know that I learn ~~from many things in life~~ best from taking risks, watching others, and making mistakes.

She feels that this thesis statement introduces the notion of learning and the different ways that she has learned.

Your Revision   With these guidelines in mind, revise your thesis statement.

Your Revised Thesis Statement: _____

Basic Elements

✔ Does the title draw in the readers?
✔ Does the introduction capture the readers' attention and build up to the thesis statement effectively?
✔ Does each body paragraph deal with a single topic?
✔ Does the conclusion bring the essay to a close in an interesting way?

These revision items ask you to check that all the basic elements of the essay are present and are doing the jobs they are supposed to do. If all the essay's parts are in place, you can spend more time polishing what you have to say.

Now that you have written a complete draft of your essay, this is the time to review these basic elements. What changes do you want to make in your title? In your introduction? In your conclusion? Is your thesis statement at the end of your introduction? Do you need to split any body paragraphs?

Practice 2A Write an alternative title for "Between Worlds" (page 451). *Answers will vary.*

Practice 2B Write an alternative introduction for "Don't Be Cruel" (page 431). *Answers will vary.*

Practice 2C Write an additional body paragraph for "Sanctuary of School" (page 411). *Answers will vary.*

Practice 2D Write an alternative conclusion for "Writer's Retreat" (page 414). *Answers will vary.*

Beth's Revision   Beth sets out to answer each of these questions one by one. Here are her responses.

✔ Does the title draw in the readers?

No. It's kind of boring.

✔ Does the introduction capture the readers' attention and build up to the thesis statement effectively?

Not really—it's too short; I could use one of the ideas introduced in Chapter 6 to make it more interesting.

✔ Does each body paragraph deal with a single topic?

Yes. So I don't have to break any of them into two or more paragraphs.

✔ Does the conclusion bring the essay to a close in an interesting way?

Sort of. I guess I should look at it again and try to apply some of the material in Chapter 6 to my conclusion.

You saw Beth's first draft at the end of Chapter 6. Here is the second draft of her introduction, conclusion, and title with her changes highlighted.

Introduction

Everyone learns in different ways. Some people learn by watching, **while others learn by doing.** Some learn by reading, **while others learn by listening** ~~and others by themselves.~~ **Some learn best when they work independently, while others do better in groups.** The way people learn is a **major** part of who they are. Knowing how we learn can help us understand ourselves better. I know that I learn best from taking risks, watching others, and making mistakes.

Conclusion

People can learn about life from almost anything they do. They just have to be willing to do so. When I take risks, I think about what I will learn. I definitely try to learn as much as I can from watching others, **which I believe, in the case of my cousin, has already saved my life.** When I make mistakes, I figure out why I made each mistake and how to avoid it a second time. **These three ways of learning are all part of who I am today. I know I'm not finished learning yet. In fact, I don't know if I ever will be.**

Title

~~The Way We Learn~~

The Learning Curve

Your Revision   Apply these questions one by one to your essay.

- ☐ Does the title draw in the readers?
- ☐ Does the introduction capture the readers' attention and build up to the thesis statement effectively?
- ☐ Does each body paragraph deal with a single topic?
- ☐ Does the conclusion bring the essay to a close in an interesting way?

Development

- ✔ Do the body paragraphs adequately support the thesis statement?
- ✔ Does each body paragraph have a focused topic sentence?

> ✔ Does each body paragraph contain specific details that support the topic sentence?
>
> ✔ Does each body paragraph include enough details to explain the topic sentence fully?

When you develop an essay, you build the body paragraphs. Body paragraphs provide supporting evidence for the thesis statement. They are made up of a clearly focused topic sentence and details that support the topic sentence. Supporting details should be as specific as possible, and you need to provide enough details to support the point you are making in each paragraph.

Specific Details

An important part of developing a good essay is being able to recognize ideas that are more general (for example, *entertainment* and *exercise*) and more specific (the opening scene in *The Green Mile*). Two other essential terms to know in choosing details are *abstract* and *concrete*. As you learned in Chapter 3, concrete words refer to items you can see, hear, touch, smell, or taste—as opposed to abstract words, which refer to ideas and concepts, such as *entertainment, frustration,* and *peacefulness*. Look at the following examples, and notice how each line becomes more detailed.

entertainment (general, abstract)

  movies

    suspense films

      Stephen King films

        The Green Mile

          opening scene in *The Green Mile* (specific, concrete)

exercise (general, abstract)

  sports

    team sports

      football

        college football

          college football championship

            Rose Bowl

              2004 Rose Bowl in Pasadena (specific, concrete)

Don't confuse levels of detail with examples. Compare the previous ladder with this one:

sports
    team sports
        football
            college football
                UCLA Bruins
                Wisconsin Wolverines
                University of Texas Longhorns
                Florida State Gators

In this ladder, the four college teams are at the same level of detail. One is not more specific than another. So these last four items are just a list of examples.

As a rule, your thesis statement should be the most general statement in your essay. Your topic sentences are more specific than your thesis, and the details in your body paragraphs are the most specific items in the essay. So an outline of these elements looks like this:

Thesis statement (general)
    Topic sentence
        Detail (specific and concrete)
        Detail (specific and concrete)
        Detail (specific and concrete)

Making your essay more specific involves adding as well as rewriting words, phrases, and whole sentences. Here is one of Beth's body paragraphs with more specific details in bold type in her revision.

First Draft

I have discovered that I learn a lot by taking risks. Being at this college was a risk. I have a boyfriend back home, we want to get married some day. We are hoping for a spring wedding with all of our friends and family. I left my boyfriend to come here. Coming here was a risk to our relationship. But if I am ever going to make it, I have to be willing to take risks.

Revised with Specific Details

I have discovered that I learn a lot by taking risks. **If I didn't take risks, I think I'd never mature.** Being at this college was a risk. I have a boyfriend back home, we want to get married some day. We are hoping for a spring wedding with all of our friends and family. I left my boyfriend to come here. Coming here was a risk to our relationship. **Taking this risk taught me to be responsible and trust my boyfriend back home.** But if I am ever going to ~~make it~~ **reach my potential,** I have to be willing to take risks.

Practice 3A   Underline the most specific word or phrase in each group.

1. books, library, shelves, page 42, stairs *page 42*

2. computer, technology, software, power button, online help *power button*

3. backyard, swimming pool, Coppertone lotion, pool party *Coppertone lotion*

4. drinks, thirst, soda, Dr. Pepper, root beer in a frosty mug *root beer in a frosty mug*

5. pink candles on a birthday cake, dessert dinner, sweets, chocolate candy *pink candles on a birthday cake*

Practice 3B   Fill in each blank with a new level of concrete detail as indicated by the indentions. *Answers will vary.*

1. _____

   state lottery

   _____

   _____

2. _____

   brother

   _____

   _____

3. boat

_____

_____

_____

4. _____

_____

_____

blue shirt with stripes

5. _____

_____

Thursday's newspaper

_____

Enough Details

Not only should your details be specific and concrete, but you should furnish enough details to support your topic sentence. No matter how good one detail is, it is not adequate to develop a topic sentence. Without enough details, facts, or reasons, a paragraph can be too short and weak to support a thesis statement. So Beth needs to add more details to her paragraph.

Here is Beth's body paragraph on learning with more details.

Revised with More Details

I have discovered that I learn a lot by taking risks. If I didn't take risks, I think I'd never mature. Being at this college was a risk. I have a boyfriend back home, we want to get married some day. We are hoping for a spring wedding with all of our friends and family. **But I knew that this school's nursing program was better than the one in my hometown.** I left my boyfriend to come here. Coming here was a risk to our relationship. **Not coming here would have been a risk to my career.** Taking this risk taught me to be responsible and trust

my boyfriend back home. **I know that I will take many
risks like this throughout my life and that not all of them
will work out.** But if I am ever going to reach my
potential, I have to be willing to take risks.

◆ *Practice 4 A*   List three details that could support each of the following topic sentences. *Answers will vary.*

1. My favorite pastime is swimming.

_____

_____

_____

2. Eating a balanced diet is an important part of feeling good.

_____

_____

_____

3. A simple gift is often the best.

_____

_____

_____

4. Working for people you like is easy.

_____

_____

_____

5. Spending time outside can change a person's mood.

_____

_____

_____

Practice 4B   Develop the following topic sentences with enough specific details. *Answers will vary.*

1. Before taking a test, take a moment to relax.
2. Always discuss major decisions with someone you trust.
3. When interviewing for a job, dress appropriately.
4. My roommate is a real neat freak.
5. When reading a book, think about what you are reading.

Beth's Revision   Beth's essay needs *more* details and *more specific* details to help it communicate its message. She accomplishes this by adding more details about learning throughout her essay. The details she added to her first draft are highlighted below.

The Learning Curve

Everyone learns in different ways. Some people learn   1
by watching, while others learn by doing. Some learn by
reading, while others learn by listening. Some learn
best when they work independently, while others do
better in groups. The way people learn is a major part
of who they are. Knowing how we learn can help
us understand ourselves better. I know that I learn
best from taking risks, watching others, and making
mistakes.

I have discovered that I learn a lot by taking risks.   2
If I didn't take risks, I think I'd never mature. Being at
this college was a risk. I have a boyfriend back home,
we want to get married some day. We are hoping for a
spring wedding with all of our friends and family. But
I knew that this school's nursing program was better
than the one in my hometown. I left my boyfriend to
come here. Coming here was a risk to our relationship.
Not coming here would have been a risk to my career.
Taking this risk taught me to be responsible and trust
my boyfriend back home. I know that I will take many
risks like this throughout my life and that not all of
them will work out. But if I am ever going to reach my
potential, I have to be willing to take risks.

I also benefit from watching other people. When my   3
cousin became heavily involved with gangs **and drugs,**
I watched my cousin live in constant fear. **She was**

worried that she would end up in jail, overdose on drugs, or become a "plaything" for other gang members. **She worked hard to overcome that lifestyle. She talked a lot to me about those experiences.** By watching my cousin **go through these horrible experiences,** I made a conscious decision ~~to be nothing like my cousin~~ **never to make the bad choices that my cousin made. I had plenty of opportunities to do so. Turning away from this life was difficult, but I did it.** By watching and understanding my cousin's life. I learned to live mine better.

4   I believe that I learn from making mistakes. When I was **a sophomore** in high school, I didn't study for a major science test. **I knew the test was important, but I decided to go to a party with my friends. I really needed the grade,** ~~S~~so I cheated. My sister cheated once. I was so scared to do it. **I cut my notes into small strips of paper that I put in my desk, but** ~~T~~the teacher caught me. **Thank goodness the teacher was a nice person.** The teacher took the time to talk to me about the mistake I was making, **not only cheating for a grade, but cheating myself out of the knowledge that I could have.** This mistake made me reevaluate my education. **This mistake led me into nursing by making me reevaluate what subjects I really enjoyed.** I could have laughed off the cheating experience **and the teacher.** I decided to slow down and learn from the experience.

5   People can learn about life from almost anything they do. They just have to be willing to do so. When I take risks, I think about what I will learn. I definitely try to learn as much as I can from watching others, which I believe, in the case of my cousin, has already saved my life. When I make mistakes, I figure out why I made each mistake and how to avoid it a second time. These three ways of learning are all part of who I am today. I know I'm not finished learning yet. In fact, I don't know if I ever will be.

Your Revision   Add more relevant details to your essay, making your explanations and descriptions as specific as possible. Also make sure all of your body paragraphs have focused topic sentences that support your thesis statement.

Unity

> ✔ Do the essay's topic sentences relate directly to the thesis statement?
> ✔ Do the details in each body paragraph support its topic sentence?

An essay is unified when its topic sentences are all related to the thesis statement and when each body paragraph discusses only one idea. Irrelevant paragraphs in essays are those that don't support their essay's thesis statement. They should be deleted or revised to fit into the essay's plan.

A paragraph's main idea is introduced in its topic sentence. All other sentences in a paragraph should expand on this idea and relate to it in some way. Information that is not about the topic sentence is irrelevant and does not belong in the paragraph.

 P r a c t i c e   5 A   Cross out the topic sentences that don't support each thesis statement.

1. Thesis: Holidays are fun times in my family.

   My favorite holiday is Thanksgiving.

   July 4th always scares my dogs.

   Chanukah is a time of great celebration in my house.

   ~~My boyfriend doesn't understand my family.~~

2. Thesis: I love working with children.

   Children's games still make me laugh.

   ~~I hate foods that are good for me.~~

   ~~I want a job that pays well.~~

   I have always liked babysitting.

   I have applied to work at the Children's Center on our campus.

3. Thesis: Exercise is essential for good health.

   Exercise keeps our hearts in good shape.

   ~~Exercise is fun.~~

   ~~Exercise is difficult when you are on a tight schedule.~~

   Exercise is necessary for weight control.

   Exercise is good for us emotionally.

4. Thesis: I have learned over the years how to control my anger.

    One way is to count to 10 before I do anything.

    ~~I get angry easily.~~

    Another solution is to take a deep breath before I act.

    The solution I use most often is to take a walk.

5. Thesis: I really like to cook, but I never have the time.

    I am most creative at breakfast.

    The dish I like to make the most is fritatta.

    My class schedule keeps me busy right through dinner.

    ~~My philosophy class is my toughest class.~~

    ~~I don't like spicy foods.~~

P r a c t i c e   5 B   Cross out the three irrelevant sentences in the following paragraph.

I have a very bad habit of waiting until the night before an exam to begin studying, so it is very important for me to have a well-planned and productive cramming session. ~~One time during my junior year of high school, I failed a test.~~ I begin by putting on comfortable clothes so that when I begin to squirm and twist to try and get comfortable, I am able to move around. Next, I get a large glass of milk and several cookies to snack on. ~~Peanut butter cookies have always been my favorite.~~ Once I have my snack, I spread all my books and study materials out on the living room floor. ~~I have a hardwood floor.~~ Finally, I am ready to begin studying for the next few hours.

P r a c t i c e   5 C   Cross out the three irrelevant sentences in the following paragraph.

Most people wonder what it would be like to win the lottery and be able to spend money as they please. ~~The odds are that even the people who buy a lottery ticket every day will never win the lottery.~~ Winning the lottery would change most people's lives drastically. Many people say that they would begin by paying all their debts. ~~There are people in the world who buy so many items on credit that they are constantly trying to get out of debt.~~ Other people say that they would buy a new house or a new car to spoil themselves a little bit. Some people simply say that they would invest the money and use it when they retire so that they can live comfortably. ~~Many elderly people are unable to continue the lifestyles they are accustomed to after retirement.~~

Beth's Revision   When Beth reads her paper for unity, she sees that three sentences are off topic. So she deletes them.

In Paragraph 2:   ~~We are hoping for a spring wedding with all of our friends and family.~~

In Paragraph 3:   ~~My sister cheated once. I was so scared to do it.~~

Your Revision   Read your essay carefully, and cross out any irrelevant sentences or paragraphs.

Organization

> ✔ Is the essay organized logically?
>
> ✔ Is each body paragraph organized logically?

In Chapter 3, you learned five ways to organize your paragraphs and essays:

1. From general to particular
2. From particular to general
3. Chronologically (by time)
4. Spatially (by physical arrangement)
5. From one extreme to another

The organization that you choose for your essay depends chiefly on your topic and overall purpose. What are you trying to accomplish? In what order should you present your evidence? Is point A the most important? Maybe it should be the last paragraph so you can build up to it.

After you put your paragraphs in order, you are ready to look at the organization of each individual paragraph. It's very likely that your essay will be organized one way (say, from least important to most important) and each of your body paragraphs will have its own method of organization. As you revise, you should check to see that your essay is organized as effectively as possible for what you are trying to accomplish and that your body paragraphs are each arranged logically as well.

Practice 6A Reorganize the following topics so that they are in a logical order. Then label your method of organization. *The order of the items will vary.*

1. east at the mall to the stop light

   west at the grocery store to the flower shop

   north at the flower shop until you get to Anita's

   south at the stop light until you hit the grocery store

   Method of Organization: *Spatial*

2. sitcoms

   dramas

   documentaries

   musicals

   awards shows

   Method of Organization: *From one extreme to another*

3. community servants

   police badges

   police officers

   police office staff

   police uniforms

   Method of Organization: *Either particular to general or general to particular*

Practice 6B Reorganize the following sentences so that they are in a logical order. Then identify your method of organization.

4 Next, I decide what I will have for dinner and begin to cook.

3 Then I change into comfortable clothes.

8 Before I completely wind down, I lay out my clothes for the next day and set my alarm clock.

7 This is always a good time to look at the mail or return phone calls.

5 While I am cooking, I listen to music or turn on the evening news.

2 First, I begin to relax by taking a shower.

1 When I return home in the evenings, I always follow the same routine.

6 After I eat, I do the dishes and sit down in the living room.

9 Finally I watch television or read a book until I fall asleep.

Method of Organization: _Chronological_

Practice 6C   Reorganize the following sentences so that they are in a logical order. Then identify your method of organization.

4 Sweatshirts belong next to long-sleeved shirts, so they come next.

2 When I walk in the closet door, all of my T-shirts are hanging directly to my left in the closet.

9 My shoes follow the same pattern on the floor as the clothes on hangers.

3 Next to the T-shirts are my long-sleeved shirts.

8 Starting the summer clothes are the tank-tops, followed by summer dresses.

1 Everything in my closet must be in order, or I will never be able to find anything.

5 All of my sweaters can be found stacked neatly on the shelf just above my long-sleeved sweatshirts.

6 Jackets, of course, go along with sweatshirts, so they are hanging next to the sweatshirts.

10 I have winter shoes immediately as I walk in the door, with sandals for summer toward the back of the closet.

7 After the jackets come the summer clothes.

Method of Organization: _Spatial_

Beth's Revision   In Chapter 3, Beth decided that the best way to organize her essay was from one extreme to another (from most to least important). But now she needs to make sure that this is the most effective order for her ideas and that every paragraph is in the right place.

This is the order of the main ideas in her first draft:

Most important: Taking risks
Next most important: Watching others
Least important: Making mistakes

After thinking about this order, Beth realizes that she learns more from making mistakes than from watching others. So she decides to reverse these two topics. She also remembers that she has to revise her thesis statement and her conclusion to reflect this new order.

Revised Thesis Statement:	I know that I learn best from taking risks, making mistakes, and watching others.
Revised Conclusion:	People can learn about life from almost anything they do. They just have to be willing to do so. When I take risks, I think about what I will learn. **When I make mistakes, I figure out why I made each mistake and how to avoid it a second time. I definitely try to learn as much as I can from watching others, which I believe, in the case of my cousin, has already saved my life.** These three ways of learning are all a part of who I am today. I know I'm not finished learning yet. In fact, I don't know if I ever will be.

Also in Chapter 3, Beth organized her three body paragraphs from general to particular. At this point, she checks to see if this is the most effective order for these ideas. She thinks that this order is a good choice for her body paragraphs.

Your Revision   Double-check the method of organization you chose in Chapter 3 for your essay. Do you still think this is the most effective order for what you are trying to say? Then check each body paragraph to see that the details are arranged logically.

Coherence

> ✔ Are transitions used effectively so that paragraphs move smoothly and logically from one to the next?
> ✔ Do the sentences move smoothly and logically from one to the next?

A well-written paragraph is coherent—that is, its parts cohere or stick together. It is smooth, not choppy, and readers move logically from one thought to the next, seeing a clear relationship among the ideas. Here are four different strategies that writers use to help their readers follow their train of thought from one paragraph to the next and within paragraphs: *transitions*, *repeated words*, *synonyms*, and *pronouns*.

Transitions

Transitional words and phrases provide bridges or links between paragraphs and ideas. They show your readers how your paragraphs or thoughts are related or when you are moving to a new point. Good use of transitions makes your writing smooth rather than choppy.

Choppy: I could have laughed off the cheating experience and the teacher. I decided to slow down and learn from the experience.

Smooth: I could have laughed off the cheating experience and the teacher. **However,** I decided to slow down and learn from the experience.

Transitions have very specific meanings, so you should take care to make logical choices that help you communicate your exact thoughts.

Confusing: I could have laughed off the cheating experience and the teacher. **In addition,** I decided to slow down and learn from the experience.

Here is a list of some common transitional words and phrases that will make your writing more coherent. They are classified by meaning.

Some Common Transitions

Addition:	*again, and, and then, also, besides, finally, first, further, furthermore, in addition, last, likewise, moreover, next, nor, second, third, too*
Comparison:	*in like manner, likewise, similarly*
Contrast:	*after all, and yet, at the same time, but, however, in contrast, nevertheless, on the contrary, on the other hand, otherwise, still, yet*
Emphasis:	*actually, after all, essentially, in any event, indeed, in fact, of course, to tell the truth*

Example:	for example, for instance, in this case
Place:	adjacent to, beyond, here, near, nearby, opposite, there
Purpose:	for this purpose, to this end, with this objective
Result:	accordingly, as a result, consequently, hence, so, then, therefore, thus
Summary:	as I have said, in brief, in other words, in short, in sum, on the whole, that is, to conclude, to sum up, to summarize
Time:	after a few days, afterward, at length, (at) other times, immediately, in the meantime, later, meanwhile, now, sometimes, soon, still, then

See pages 516–517 in the Handbook (Part V) for more information on transitions.

Sometimes longer phrases provide transitions between paragraphs or main ideas. See if you can find the long transition that Beth adds to the beginning of one of the paragraphs that she moved (pages 89–90). This phrase helps her readers shift gears to a new topic and makes her essay easier to follow.

Practice 7A   Fill in the blanks in the following paragraph with logical transitions. *Answers may vary.*

Today, an unlimited amount of information is available through the Internet. *However*, some of this information may not be suitable for younger audiences. Many concerned parents asked for a way to block Internet sites that they did not want their children to view. *Therefore*, a system was developed by which a parent uses a password to choose which Internet sites the household computer will and won't access. *Now*, children who do not know the password cannot access the blocked Internet sites. *Finally*, parents have control over the technology in their homes and feel their children are safe when they use the Internet.

◈ *P r a c t i c e **7 B***   Rewrite the following paragraph, adding at least three transitions to make it more coherent. *Answers will vary.*

> In high school, I thought I had everything figured out. I never considered what I would do after graduation. I never made any plans. When I graduated, I was completely lost. I went to see a guidance counselor at the local college. I decided to go to college. I am in college and have made many plans for the future.

Repeated Words

Repeating key words is another way of binding the ideas of an essay together and guiding readers through the details. A key word is usually a main idea in an essay. You should also know that too much repetition becomes boring.

Effective Repetition: Coming here was a **risk** to our relationship. Not coming here would have been a **risk** to my career.

◈ *P r a c t i c e **8 A***   Underline five effective repeated words in the following paragraph.

> All my life, I have gone to my grandmother's house near a lake out in farm country during the summer. This year, I'm taking my best friend from college with me. What I like most about summers at the lake is that the weather is so warm that I can <u>swim</u> all day long. I <u>swim</u> near the bridge and see the small fish <u>swimming</u> around the columns. Sometimes I even <u>swim</u> over to the docks where all of the people are loading and unloading their boats. I used to try to <u>swim</u> faster and faster to beat my own record. Now I just go to relax, forget about school, and think about the future.

◈ *P r a c t i c e **8 B***   Underline at least five effective repeated words in the following paragraph.

> For many people, reading the daily <u>newspaper</u> is their main source of information about the world. The front page usually gives the national <u>news</u> or an international political event that affects the United States. Major world events, such as an earthquake, always make front-page <u>news</u>. On the second page of the first section is the op-ed (opposite editorial) page, where editors and readers give their opinions on current <u>news</u>. The editorial and op-ed pages are among the few places in the <u>newspaper</u> where the writing is not objective, along with book and movie reviews and columnists such as Molly

Ivins or Dear Abby. Most <u>newspapers</u> have separate sections for sports, business, entertainment, classified ads, and comics. All in all, a half hour spent with the <u>newspaper</u> over morning coffee keeps a person up-to-date on world affairs and local people, places, and events.

Synonyms

Synonyms are another way to link your ideas and help you avoid ineffective repetition. Synonyms are words that have identical or similar meanings—*movie/film, feeling/emotion, fantastic/unbelievable*. They add variety and interest to your writing. A thesaurus, or book of synonyms, can help you choose synonyms for specific words. Be aware, however, that all the words in a thesaurus listing are not interchangeable. *Retreat,* for example, is listed as a synonym for *escape,* but the two words suggest two very different ways of leaving a place. In the following example from Beth's essay, Beth uses *incidents* in place of one of her references to *experiences.*

Boring Repetition:	She talked a lot to me about those **experiences.** By watching my cousin go through these horrible **experiences,** I made a conscious decision never to make the bad choices that my cousin made.
Synonym:	She talked a lot to me about those **experiences.** By watching my cousin go through these horrible ~~**experiences**~~ **incidents,** I made a conscious decision never to make the bad choices that my cousin made.

◆ *P r a c t i c e   9 A*   Underline four different synonyms for *friend* in the following paragraph.

My younger brother and his friends were always starting clubs when I was young. The clubhouse and the club name were very important. The <u>pals</u> usually decided on a name first. I think my favorite name that they had was "The Three <u>Amigos</u>," even though it was not very original. Every once in a while, an <u>acquaintance</u> of the boys would be allowed to join the club, and the name would have to be changed. Since the boys always thought that they were such sophisticated <u>companions</u>, they had a sign on the door that read "Associates Only—No Girls Allowed." The boys are all grown now, but I still smile every time I think about all of the meetings of "The Three <u>Amigos</u>" that I sat outside of and listened to.

Practice 9B Replace two uses of the word *actor* with two different synonyms in the following paragraph. *Answers will vary.*

> Being an actor seems like a glamorous career choice, but becoming famous is not easy. Many actors start out waiting on tables in restaurants, hoping to be discovered by agents dining there. Other actors go from bit part to bit part in movies and never really earn enough for a living. In the unlikely event that an actor makes it big, he or she suddenly loses all privacy. Still, there are advantages to fame, and most actors adjust quite well to the lifestyle.

Pronouns

Finally, you can link your sentences with *pronouns*. Pronouns not only help you avoid needless repetition, but they also keep your writing moving at a fairly fast pace. Personal pronouns (*I, you, he, she, it, we, they*) and indefinite pronouns (*any, some, other, one*) are the ones most commonly used as replacements.

Beth can use a pronoun to get rid of her repetition of the words *my cousin*.

> **Repetition:** When my cousin became heavily involved with gangs and drugs, I watched my cousin live in constant fear.
>
> **Revision:** When my cousin became heavily involved with gangs and drugs, I watched ~~my cousin~~ her live in constant fear.

For more information on pronouns, see pages 508–509 in the Handbook (Part V).

Practice 10A Underline 10 personal and indefinite pronouns in the following paragraph.

> The people down the street have a very large family, which means that there is always <u>something</u> going on in <u>their</u> house. Sometimes when <u>I</u> am at <u>their</u> house, <u>I</u> cannot keep up with <u>everything</u> that is happening. For example, when Sandy answers the phone, <u>she</u> yells that <u>it's</u> for Ryan. Of course, Ryan has to know who it is, and the yelling continues back and forth until Ryan decides to finally pick up the phone. Sometimes when the family members are really busy, <u>they</u> all make dinner individually. <u>Everyone</u> is in the kitchen at one time

trying to find <u>something</u> to eat while trying not to step on <u>one</u> <u>ano-</u><u>ther</u>. <u>I</u>'m not sure <u>I</u> could live at the Mitchells' house, but <u>I</u> definitely like visiting.

Practice 10B   Add five pronouns where appropriate in the following paragraph.

A few days ago, Brian, Carol, Katie, and I went out to dinner. ~~Brian, Carol, Katie, and I~~ *We* went to a new Italian restaurant on First Street. As soon as ~~Brian, Carol, Katie, and I~~ *we* walked in the door, ~~Brian, Carol, Katie, and I~~ *we* could smell the garlic, basil, and oregano in the rich tomato sauces of pizza, lasagna, and, of course, spaghetti and meatballs. ~~Brian, Carol, Katie, and I~~ *We* couldn't stand it, so ~~Brian, Carol, Katie, and I~~ *we* ordered immediately. The food was even better than it smelled. Before the dinner was over, Brian, Carol, Katie, and I set a date to return.

Beth's Revision   When Beth checks her essay for coherence, she thinks her writing could be smoother if she used some of these techniques. So she makes the following revisions that help bind her sentences together and show the specific relationships between her ideas.

Here is Beth's essay with transitions, repeated words, synonyms, and pronouns highlighted.

The Learning Curve

Everyone learns in different ways. Some people learn by watching, while others learn by doing. Some learn by reading, and others learn by listening. Some learn best when they work independently, but others do better in groups. *Transition* **In fact, t**~~T~~he way people learn is a major part of *Transition* who they are. **So** knowing how we learn can help us understand ourselves better. I know that I learn best from taking risks, making mistakes, and watching others.

Transition   **First,** I have discovered that I learn a lot by taking risks. If I didn't take risks, I think I'd never mature. Being at this college was a risk. I have a boyfriend back home, we want to get married some day. But I knew that this school's nursing program was better than the one in my hometown~~,~~ **so** I left my boyfriend to come here. Coming here was a risk to our relationship.   *Transition*

Transition   **However, n~~N~~**ot coming here would have been a risk to my career. Taking this risk taught me to be responsible and trust my boyfriend back home. I know that I will take many risks like this throughout my life and that not all of them will work out. But if I am ever going to reach my potential, I have to be willing to take risks.

Transition   **Also,** I believe that I learn from making mistakes.
Transition   **For example, w~~W~~**hen I was a sophomore in high school, I didn't study for a major science test. I knew the test was important, but I decided to go to a party with my friends. I really needed the grade, so I cheated. I cut my notes into small strips of paper that I put in my desk, but the teacher caught me. Thank goodness ~~the teacher~~
Pronoun   **he** was a nice person. ~~The teacher~~ **He** took the time to   *Pronoun*
talk to me about the mistake I was making, not only
Repetition   **cheating** for a grade, but **cheating** myself out of the   *Repetition*
knowledge that I could have. This mistake made me
reevaluate my education. ~~This mistake~~ **It** led me into   *Pronoun*
nursing by making me ~~reevaluate~~ **realize** what subjects   *Synonym*
I really enjoyed. I could have laughed off the cheating experience and the teacher. However, I decided to slow down and learn from the experience.

Transition   **In addition to learning from my own actions,** I also benefit from watching other people. **For instance,**   *Transition*
w~~W~~hen my cousin became heavily involved with gangs and drugs, I watched her live in constant fear. She was worried that she would end up in jail, overdose on drugs, or become a "plaything" for other gang members. She worked hard to overcome that lifestyle. She talked a lot to me about those experiences. By watching my cousin go through these horrible incidents, I made a conscious decision never to make the bad choices that
Pronoun   ~~my cousin~~ **she** made. I had plenty of opportunities to do

so. Turning away from this life was difficult, but I did it.
By watching and understanding my cousin's life. I
learned to live mine better.

Transition   **Essentially, pP**eople can learn about life from almost
anything they do. They just have to be willing to do so.

Transition   **Now, wW**hen I take risks, I think about what I will learn.
When I make mistakes, I figure out why I made each
mistake and how to avoid it a second time. **Also,** I   *Transition*
definitely try to learn as much as I can from watching
others, which I believe, in the case of my cousin, has
already saved my life. These three ways of learning are
all part of who I am today. I know I'm not finished
learning yet. In fact, I don't know if I ever will be.

Transitions   In addition to *however*, Beth added 12 more transitions to
her essay. What are they?

In fact, So, First, so, However, Also, For example, In addition to learning from

my own actions, For instance, Essentially, Now, Also

List the meaning of five of these transitions:

1. Transition: _____   Meaning: _____

2. Transition: _____   Meaning: _____

3. Transition: _____   Meaning: _____

4. Transition: _____   Meaning: _____

5. Transition: _____   Meaning: _____

Repeated Words   When Beth checked her essay for repeated key words,
she saw that she referred directly to *cheating* twice in the same sentence. She
decided this was an effective repetition and chose to keep it in her essay.

Effective Repetition: He took the time to talk to me about the
mistake I was making, not only **cheating**
for a grade, but **cheating** myself out of the
knowledge that I could have.

Synonyms   When Beth looked at her essay again, she found another
opportunity to use a synonym to link her ideas more clearly. Besides the

addition of *incidents* for *experiences*, what other synonym does Beth use in her revision?

_____ *realize* _____ for _____ *reevaluate* _____

Pronouns   Finally, in addition to substituting *her* for *my cousin*, Beth found four more places to use pronouns to bind key parts of her essay together. Where are these places in her essay?

_____ *he* _____ for _____ *the teacher* _____

_____ *He* _____ for _____ *The teacher* _____

_____ *It* _____ for _____ *This mistake* _____

_____ *she* _____ for _____ *my cousin* _____

Your Revision   Now it's time to make your essay more coherent.

Transitions   Check the transitions in your essay. Do you use enough transitions so that your essay moves smoothly and logically from one paragraph to the next and from one sentence to the next? Do you use your transitions logically?

Repeated Words   Look at your essay to see when you might want to repeat a key word. Then revise your essay accordingly.

Synonyms   Now look for places in your essay where you might add synonyms to link your sentences. Use a thesaurus (in book or electronic form) if you need help.

Pronouns   Now check your essay for opportunities to use pronouns. Add appropriate pronouns.

Beth's Revised Essay   After revising her thesis statement, her development of ideas, and the unity, organization, and coherence of her writing, Beth produced the following revised essay. All of her revisions are highlighted.

~~**The Way We Learn**~~

The Learning Curve

Everyone learns in different ways. Some people learn 1
by watching, **while others learn by doing.** Some **learn** by
reading, ~~while~~ and others learn by listening ~~and others~~

~~by themselves.~~ Some learn best when they work independently, ~~while~~ but others do better in groups. In fact, t~~T~~he way people learn is a **major** part of who they are. Knowing how we learn can help us understand ourselves better. I know that I learn ~~from many things in life~~ best from taking risks, making mistakes, and watching others.

2   First, I have discovered that I learn a lot by taking risks. **If I didn't take risks, I think I'd never mature.** Being at this college was a risk. I have a boyfriend back home, we want to get married some day. ~~We are hoping for a spring wedding with all of our friends and family.~~ But I knew that this school's nursing program was better than the one in my hometown~~,~~ so I left my boyfriend to come here. Coming here was a risk to our relationship. However, n~~N~~ot coming here would have been a risk to my career. Taking this risk taught me to be responsible and trust my boyfriend back home. I know that I will take many risks like this throughout my life and that not all of them will work out. But if I am ever going to ~~make it~~ reach my potential, I have to be willing to take risks.

3   Also, I believe that I learn from making mistakes. **For example, w**~~W~~hen I was **a sophomore** in high school, I didn't study for a major science test. **I knew the test was important, but I decided to go to a party with my friends. I really needed the grade,** S~~s~~o I cheated. ~~My sister cheated once. I was so scared to do it.~~ I cut my notes into small strips of paper that I put in my desk, but T~~t~~he teacher caught me. **Thank goodness** ~~the teacher~~ he was a nice person. ~~The teacher~~ He took the time to talk to me about the mistake I was making, **not only cheating for a grade, but cheating myself out of the knowledge that I could have.** This mistake made me reevaluate my education. ~~This mistake~~ It led me into nursing by making me ~~reevaluate~~ realize what subjects I really enjoyed. I could have laughed off the cheating experience **and the teacher. However,** I decided to slow down and learn from the experience.

4   **In addition to learning from my own actions,** I also benefit from watching other people. **For instance, w**~~W~~hen my cousin became heavily involved with gangs

and drugs, I watched ~~my cousin~~ her live in constant fear.
~~My cousin~~ She was worried that she would end up in
jail, overdose on drugs, or become a "plaything" for
other gang members. She worked hard to overcome that
lifestyle. She talked a lot to me about those experiences.
By watching my cousin **go through these horrible
experiences** ~~experiences~~ incidents, I made a conscious decision ~~to be
nothing like my cousin~~ never to make the bad choices
that ~~my cousin~~ she made. I had plenty of opportunities
to do so. Turning away from this life was difficult, but I
did it. By watching and understanding my cousin's life. I
learned to live mine better.

    Essentially, p People can learn about life from almost   5
anything they do. They just have to be willing to do so.
Now, w~~W~~hen I take risks, I think about what I will learn.
When I make mistakes, I figure out why I made each
mistake and how to avoid it a second time. Also, I
definitely try to learn as much as I can from watching
others, which I believe, in the case of my cousin, has
already saved my life. These three ways of learning are
all part of who I am today. I know I'm not finished
learning yet. In fact, I don't know if I ever will be.

Your Revised Essay   Now that you have applied all the revision strategies
to your own writing, rewrite your revised essay.

EDITING

After you have revised your writing, you are ready to edit it. Editing involves finding and correcting errors in grammar, punctuation, mechanics, and spelling. Correct writing is as important to communicating as well-chosen words. Nothing distracts readers from what you are saying more than editing errors.

As the checklist here shows, we have divided the editing strategies into three categories: sentences, punctuation and mechanics, and word choice and spelling. This checklist doesn't cover all the grammar and usage problems you may find in your writing, but it focuses on the main errors college students make.

EDITING CHECKLIST ✔

SENTENCES
✔ Does each sentence have a main subject and verb?
✔ Do all subjects and verbs agree?
✔ Do all pronouns agree with their nouns?
✔ Are modifiers as close as possible to the words they modify?

PUNCTUATION AND MECHANICS
✔ Are sentences punctuated correctly?
✔ Are words capitalized properly?

WORD CHOICE AND SPELLING
✔ Are words used correctly?
✔ Are words spelled correctly?

YOUR EQ (EDITING QUOTIENT)

A good way to approach editing is by finding your EQ (Editing Quotient). Knowing your EQ will help you look for specific errors in your writing and make your editing more efficient.

◆ *P r a c t i c e 1* **EQ Test** In each of the following paragraphs, underline the errors you find, and label them a, b, c, and so on. Then list them on the lines below the paragraph. The number of lines corresponds to the number of errors in each paragraph. *Answers are in Practice 2.*

The possible errors are listed here:

apostrophe	end punctuation	pronoun agreement
capitalization	fragment	spelling
comma	fused sentence	subject-verb agreement
comma splice	modifier error	verb form
confused word	pronoun	

1. Many people seem to have a telephone permanently attached to one ear people have several phone lines going into their homes. And cell phones hanging off of their belts. People are talking on their cell phones in restaurants, in cars, and even in public bathrooms. When they go home, they go online to check e-mail. While the second line is ringing off the hook. Why would someone want to be available every second of the day? This rushed society will eventually have to slow down, people can't live at this pace for long.

   a. _____

   b. _____

   c. _____

   d. _____

2. Recently, a major computer software company was accused of being a monopoly. That is, it seemed to be trying to control the whole software industry. The company, reality software, sells many different types of software at reasonable prices. Which results in the company selling more products than its competitors. Reality Software also signed contracts with Computer Manufacturers that allow the manufacturers to install Reality programs on computers before they are

sold. The courts, which guard against monopolies, say this is unfair to consumers, buyers should be able to choose their software. It is also unfair to other software companies. Because they are not given a fair chance to sell their products.

    (a.) _____

    (b.) _____

    (c.) _____

    (d.) _____

    (e.) _____

3. Public speaking is a valuable tool no matter what career path a person take. At some point in every career, if a person is going to advance, they will have to speak to a group. In fact, the higher up the career ladder a person climb, the more public speaking will be required. It is good preparation, therefore, to take a public speaking course in college, a public speaking course not only teaches the skills involved in making a presentation but also builds a person's confidence.

    (a.) _____

    (b.) _____

    (c.) _____

    (d.) _____

4. Anyone who thinks a surprise birthday party takes a lot of time and work should try planning a wedding. Until a person plans his or her own wedding, they can't fully understand all the details that must be considered. Too my way of thinking, long engagements aren't to find out how compatible the couple is. There to allow enough time to find a place to hold the reception. On the date you want. Plus a good caterer and music. Even the smallest detail must be considered, such as whether guests should throw rice birdseed or confetti at the happy couple after the ceremony.

    (a.) _____

    (b.) _____

    (c.) _____

d. _____

e. _____

f. _____

g. _____

5. A famous author once said that his messy handwriting, almost kept him from becoming a writer. Struggling to be legible, the pages were impossible to read. No matter how hard he tried, his handwriting would become rushed and scribbled. He would write wonderful novels that only he could read, for his twenty-third birthday, his wife bought him a typewriter. He then began to write books. That people all over the world have read. If he were alive today, he could write on a computer.

a. _____

b. _____

c. _____

d. _____

6. Everyone has heard the term "best freind." What is a best friend? Some people beleive that their oldest friend is they're best friend. Yet a best friend can be someone from college or even someone who is family. Such as a brother or sister. No matter who qualifies as a best friend, two facts is true: A best freind is someone special and trustworthy. People may wonder how they could get along without their best friend? Most people couldn't.

a. _____

b. _____

c. _____

d. _____

e. _____

f. _____

g. _____

7. If I had my way, I would require every college student to take a course in geography. It is embarassing how little the average American knows about his own country, to say nothing of other countries. For instance, do you know the capital of virginia? Could you name all the Great Lakes? On which continent is greece? If you can answer these questions you are one of very few people. People think geography is boring but it isn't. Its fascinating to learn about the world we live in.

(a.) _____

(b.) _____

(c.) _____

(d.) _____

(e.) _____

(f.) _____

(g.) _____

8. I believe that fast-food restaurants should change there names to "fast food sometimes, but at least faster than a sit-down restaurant." When I go through the drive-up window at a fast-food restaraunt, it is because I am in a hurry and want to get something to eat quickly, however, sometimes it would be quicker for me to go home and cook a three-course meal. I do not understand what could take so long. I pull up to the intercom, order my food, procede to the window, and wait. If fast food always lived up to its name I would be able to get food fast.

(a.) _____

(b.) _____

(c.) _____

(d.) _____

(e.) _____

9. Doing the family laundry used to be a chore for me but now I am a pro. First, I sort the clothes according to colors or whites. Before I learned this basic rule, my poor brother had to wear pink underwear from time to time. Next, I put the clothes in the washing machine, and add detergent. If I'm doing whites I also add bleach. I close the

lid, turn the dial to hot wash and cold rinse, and push the "start" button. I allow the washing machine to do it's work while I read a magazine. When it's time to put the clothes in the dryer, I pay attention to the drying instructions on the tags. Once I neglected this step, and my favorite pants shrinked. When the dryer has done its work, I remove the clothes immediately so they do not become rinkled.

(a.) _____

(b.) _____

(c.) _____

(d.) _____

(e.) _____

(f.) _____

10. It's fun to watch a person with their animals. For instance, the lady down the street takes her dog for a walk every morning. The dog is a tiny rat terrier, it is really cute. The lady puts a little leash on the dog. To keep him from running away. Even though the dogs legs are short, he can run real fast. The dog seems so happy during his walks. He jumps and yips. The lady and her dog are a good pair they enjoy walking with each other and keeping each other company.

(a.) _____

(b.) _____

(c.) _____

(d.) _____

(e.) _____

(f.) _____

P r a c t i c e 2 EQ Answers Score your answers in Practice 1 using the following answer key.

1. (a)Many people seem to have a telephone permanently attached to their ear people have several phone lines going into their homes. (b)And cell phones hanging off of their belts. People are talking on

their cell phones in restaurants, in cars, and even in public bathrooms. When they go home, they go online to check e-mail. ©<u>While
the second line is ringing off the hook.</u> Why would someone want to
be available every second of the day? [ⓓ]<u>This rushed society will eventually have to slow down, people can't live at this pace for long.</u>

_ⓐ   fused sentence or end punctuation
_____

_ⓑ   fragment
_____

_ⓒ   fragment
_____

_ⓓ   comma splice or end punctuation
_____

2. Recently, a major computer software company was accused of being a
monopoly. That is, it seemed to be trying to control the whole software industry. The company, [ⓐ]<u>reality software</u>, sells many different
types of software at reasonable prices. [ⓑ]<u>Which results in the company
selling more products than its competitors.</u> Reality Software also
signed contracts with©<u>Computer Manufacturers</u> that allow the manufacturers to install Reality programs on computers before they are
sold. [ⓓ]<u>The courts, which guard against monopolies, say this is unfair
to consumers, buyers should be able to choose their software.</u> It is also
unfair to other software companies. ©<u>Because they are not given a
fair chance to sell their products.</u>

_ⓐ   capitalization
_____

_ⓑ   fragment
_____

_ⓒ   capitalization
_____

_ⓓ   comma splice or end punctuation
_____

_ⓔ   fragment
_____

3. Public speaking is a valuable tool no matter what career path a[ⓐ]<u>person
take</u>. At some point in every career, if a person is going to
advance,[ⓑ]<u>they</u> will have to speak to a group. In fact, the higher up the
career ladder a ©<u>person climb</u>, the more public speaking will be required. [ⓓ]<u>It is good preparation, therefore, to take a public speaking
course in college, a public speaking course not only teaches the skills involved in making a presentation but also builds a person's confidence.</u>

_ⓐ   subject-verb agreement
_____

_ⓑ   pronoun agreement
_____

(c.)   *subject-verb agreement* _____

(d.)   *comma splice or end punctuation* _____

4. Anyone who thinks a surprise birthday party takes a lot of time and work should try planning a wedding. Until a person plans his or her own wedding, ⓐ<u>they</u> can't fully understand all the details that must be considered. ⓑ<u>Too</u> my way of thinking, long engagements aren't to find out how compatible the couple is. ⓒ<u>There</u> to allow enough time to find a place to hold the reception. ⓓ<u>On the date you want.</u> ⓔ<u>Plus a good caterer and music.</u> Even the smallest detail must be considered, such as whether guests should throw rice ⓕ<u>birdseed</u> ⓖ<u>or</u> confetti at the happy couple after the ceremony.

(a.)   *pronoun agreement* _____

(b.)   *confused word* _____

(c.)   *confused word* _____

(d.)   *fragment* _____

(e.)   *fragment* _____

(f.)   *comma* _____

(g.)   *comma* _____

5. A famous author once said that his messy handwriting, ⓐ<u>almost</u> kept him from becoming a writer. ⓑ<u>Struggling to be legible</u>, the pages were impossible to read. No matter how hard he tried, his handwriting would become rushed and scribbled. ⓒ<u>He would write wonderful novels that only he could read, for his twenty-third birthday his wife bought him a typewriter.</u> He then began to write books. ⓓ<u>That people all over the world have read.</u> If he were alive today, he could write on a computer.

(a.)   *comma* _____

(b.)   *modifier error* _____

(c.)   *comma splice or end punctuation* _____

(d.)   *fragment* _____

6. Everyone has heard the term "best ⓐ<u>freind</u>." What is a best friend? Some people ⓑ<u>beleive</u> that their oldest friend is ⓒ<u>they're</u> best friend.

Yet a best friend can be someone from college or even someone who is family. [ⓓ]<u>Such as a brother or sister.</u> No matter who qualifies as a best friend, two[ⓒ]<u>facts is</u> true: A best[ⓕ]<u>freind</u> is someone special and trustworthy. People may wonder how they could get along without their best friend?[ⓖ]Most people couldn't.

(a.) _spelling_____

(b.) _spelling_____

(c.) _confused word_____

(d.) _fragment_____

(e.) _subject-verb agreement_____

(f.) _spelling_____

(g.) _end punctuation_____

7. If I had my way, I would require every college student to take a course in geography. It is [ⓐ]<u>embarassing</u> how little the average American knows about[ⓑ]<u>his</u> own country, to say nothing of other countries. For instance, do you know the capital of[ⓒ]<u>virginia</u>? Can you name all the Great Lakes? On which continent is[ⓓ]<u>greece</u>? If you can answer these questions[ⓔ]<u>you</u> are one of very few people. People think geography is boring[ⓕ]<u>but</u> it isn't.[ⓖ]<u>Its</u> fascinating to learn about the world we live in.

(a.) _spelling_____

(b.) _pronoun_____

(c.) _capitalization_____

(d.) _capitalization_____

(e.) _comma_____

(f.) _comma_____

(g.) _confused word or apostrophe_____

8. I believe that fast-food restaurants should change[ⓐ]<u>there</u> names to "fast food sometimes, but at least faster than a sit-down restaurant."[ⓑ]<u>When I go through the drive-up window at a fast-food[ⓒ]restaraunt, it is because I am in a hurry and want to get something to eat quickly,</u>

<u>however, sometimes it would be quicker for me to go home and cook a three-course meal</u>. I do not understand what could take so long. I pull up to the intercom, order my food, [ⓓ]<u>procede</u> to the window, and wait. If fast food always lived up to its name [ⓔ]I would be able to get food fast.

ⓐ ___confused word_____

ⓑ ___comma splice or end punctuation_____

ⓒ ___spelling_____

ⓓ ___spelling_____

ⓔ ___comma_____

9. Doing the family laundry used to be a chore for me [ⓐ]but now I am a pro. First, I sort the clothes according to colors or whites. Before I learned this basic rule, my poor brother had to wear pink underwear from time to time. Next, I put the clothes in the washing machine, [ⓑ]and add detergent. If I'm doing whites [ⓒ]I also add bleach. I close the lid, turn the dial to hot wash and cold rinse, and push the "start" button. I allow the washing machine to do [ⓓ]<u>it's</u> work while I read a magazine. When it's time to put the clothes in the dryer, I pay attention to the drying instructions on the tags. Once I neglected this step, and my favorite pants [ⓔ]<u>shrinked</u>. When the dryer has done its work, I remove the clothes immediately so they do not become [ⓕ]<u>rinkled</u>.

ⓐ ___comma_____

ⓑ ___comma_____

ⓒ ___comma_____

ⓓ ___confused word_____

ⓔ ___verb form_____

ⓕ ___spelling_____

10. It's fun to watch a person with [ⓐ]<u>their</u> animals. For instance, the lady down the street takes her dog for a walk every morning. [ⓑ]<u>The dog is a tiny rat terrier, it is really cute</u>. The lady puts a little leash on the dog. [ⓒ]<u>To keep him from running away</u>. Even though the [ⓓ]<u>dogs</u> legs are short, he can run [ⓔ]<u>real</u> fast. The dog seems so happy during his

walks. He jumps and yips.[Ⓕ]<u>The lady and her dog are a good pair they</u>
<u>enjoy walking with each other and keeping each other company.</u>

(a.)   *pronoun agreement* _____

(b.)   *comma splice or end punctuation* _____

(c.)   *fragment* _____

(d.)   *apostrophe* _____

(e.)   *modifier error* _____

(f.)   *fused sentence or end punctuation* _____

◆ *P r a c t i c e   3*   **Finding Your EQ**   Turn to Appendix 5, and chart the
errors you didn't identify in Practice 1. Then place your errors on the second
EQ chart, and see what pattern they form. *Answers will vary.*

HOW TO EDIT

Editing is a two-part job: First, you must locate the errors. Then you must
know how to correct them.

Finding Your Errors

A major part of editing is proofreading. Proofreading is reading to catch
grammar, punctuation, mechanics, and spelling errors. If you do not proofread carefully, you will not catch your errors and make the final changes that
will improve your writing.

There are some specific techniques for finding errors. One good method
is to read your essay backward, sentence by sentence, starting with the last
sentence. Taking sentences out of context lets you concentrate on individual sentences and not get caught up in reading for meaning.

Many students like to keep error logs like the one for grammar, punctuation, and mechanics in Appendix 6 and the one for spelling in Appendix 7. By the second or third paper you write, the logs will show you the
types of errors you make most frequently. Then you can proofread your
paper for one type of error at a time. For example, if you often write run-on
sentences, you should read your paper once just to catch run-ons. Then read
it again to find a second type of error, and so on. The error logs can help you
reduce the number of errors in your writing. By recording the correction for
each error you find, you will eventually learn the corrections.

You can also use the grammar-check or spell-check features on your computer. The grammar check will point out possible grammar errors and suggest ways to reword sentences, but it is not foolproof. You need to decide if you want to accept or reject the grammar suggestions the computer makes. The spell-check is also not completely reliable because it misses errors. So you should use it cautiously.

Asking a tutor or a friend to read your writing is also a good idea. A fresh pair of eyes may see errors you have missed. When others read your writing, they might want to use the editing symbols on the inside back cover to highlight your errors for you. You can then use the page references on the chart to guide you to the part of this textbook that explains how to correct those errors.

Correcting Your Errors

Whenever you find errors, you need to correct them. To guide you through this phase of the writing process, Part V of this text provides a complete handbook of grammar and usage. The cross-references in the EQ Score Yourself section direct you to pages in this handbook. You may also want to refer to the list on the inside back cover if your instructor uses editing symbols when reading your essays.

As you proofread, record your errors in the Error Log in Appendix 6 and the Spelling Log in Appendix 7. If you do this regularly as you write, these logs will eventually help you control the most common errors in your writing.

Finally, use the Editing Checklist at the beginning of this chapter. Apply each question in the checklist to your essay. If you are not sure whether you have made an error or not, look up the problem in Part V. Work with your writing until you can answer yes to every question on the checklist.

◆ *P r a c t i c e 4*   **Using the Handbook**   Using the Handbook in Part V, list the page references for the 15 different types of errors you worked with in Practice 1. This will help you learn to use the Handbook as a reference guide.

apostrophe   page _____

capitalization   page _____

comma   page _____

comma splice   page _____

confused word   page _____

dangling modifier   page _____

end punctuation	page _____
fragment	page _____
fused sentence	page _____
modifier error	page _____
pronoun	page _____
pronoun agreement	page _____
spelling	page _____
subject-verb agreement	page _____
verb form	page _____

P r a c t i c e   5 **Using the Error Log and Spelling Log** Turn to Appendixes 6 and 7, and start an Error Log and a Spelling Log of your own with the errors you didn't identify in Practice 1. For each error, write out the mistake and the rule from the Handbook. Then make the correction. See Appendix 6 for an example. *Answers will vary.*

P r a c t i c e   6 **Using the Editing Checklist** Using the Editing Checklist at the beginning of this chapter, edit two of the paragraphs from Practice 1. Rewrite the entire paragraphs, and correct all errors. *Answers will vary.*

Beth's Editing   When Beth proofreads her paper for grammar, punctuation, mechanics, and spelling, she finds two errors that she looks up in Part V and corrects. The first error is a comma splice:

Comma Splice: I have a boyfriend back home, we want to get married some day.

Beth realizes that this sentence has too many subjects and verbs without any linking words or end punctuation between them. She looks up "comma splice" on page 000 of Part V and corrects the error by putting a coordinating conjunction (*and*) between the two clauses.

Correction: I have a boyfriend back home, **and** we want to get married some day.

Beth also finds a sentence that doesn't sound complete—it's not a sentence but a fragment:

Fragment: By watching and understanding my cousin's life.

When she looks up the problem in Part V (page 000), she learns that a fragment is easily corrected by connecting it to another sentence.

Correction: By watching and understanding my cousin's life~~.~~, I learned to live mine better.

Beth's Edited Draft   Both of these errors are corrected here in Beth's edited draft.

The Learning Curve

Everyone learns in different ways. Some people learn by watching, while others learn by doing. Some learn by reading, and others learn by listening. Some learn best when they work independently, but others do better in groups. In fact, the way people learn is a major part of who they are. Knowing how we learn can help us understand ourselves better. I know that I learn best from taking risks, making mistakes, and watching others.   1

First, I have discovered that I learn a lot by taking risks. If I didn't take risks, I think I'd never mature. Being at this college was a risk. **I have a boyfriend back home, and we want to get married some day.** But I knew that this school's nursing program was better than the one in my hometown, so I left my boyfriend to come here. Coming here was a risk to our relationship. However, not coming here would have been a risk to my career. Taking this risk taught me to be responsible and trust my boyfriend back home. I know that I will take many risks like this throughout my life and that not all of them will work out. But if I am ever going to reach my potential, I have to be willing to take risks.   2

Also, I believe that I learn from making mistakes. For example, when I was a sophomore in high school, I didn't study for a major science test. I knew the test was important, but I decided to go to a party with my friends. I really needed the grade, so I cheated. I cut my notes into small strips of paper that I put in my desk, but the teacher caught me. Thank goodness he was a nice person. He took the time to talk to me about the mistake I was making, not only cheating for a grade, but cheating   3 myself out of the knowledge that I could have. This mistake made me reevaluate my education. It led me into nursing by making me realize what subjects I really enjoyed. I could have laughed off the cheating experience and the teacher. However, I decided to slow down and learn from the experience.

4   In addition to learning from my own actions, I also benefit from watching other people. For instance, when my cousin became heavily involved with gangs and drugs, I watched her live in constant fear. She was worried that she would end up in jail, overdose on drugs, or become a "plaything" for other gang members. She worked hard to overcome that lifestyle. She talked a lot to me about those experiences. By watching my cousin go through these horrible incidents, I made a conscious decision never to make the bad choices that she made. I had plenty of opportunities to do so. Turning away from this life was difficult, but I did it. **By watching and understanding my cousin's life, I learned to live mine better.**

5   Essentially, people can learn about life from almost anything they do. They just have to be willing to do so. Now, when I take risks, I think about what I will learn. When I make mistakes, I figure out why I made each mistake and how to avoid it a second time. Also, I definitely try to learn as much as I can from watching others, which I believe, in the case of my cousin, has already saved my life. These three ways of learning are all a part of what I am today. I know I'm not finished learning yet. In fact, I don't know if I ever will be.

Your Editing   Proofread your paragraph carefully to find errors, using at least two of the methods described in this chapter. Record your grammar, punctuation, and mechanics errors in the Error Log (Appendix 6) and your spelling errors in the Spelling Log (Appendix 7).

Your Edited Draft   Now write out a corrected draft of your essay.

Review of the Writing Process

Clues for Review

- **The writing process** is a series of tasks that involve prewriting, writing, revising, and editing. At any time, one activity may loop in and out of another.

- **Prewriting** consists of thinking about and planning your essay.
  Thinking: Reading, freewriting, brainstorming, clustering, questioning, discussing
  Planning: Deciding on a subject, purpose, and audience

- **Writing** includes writing a thesis statement, developing your ideas, organizing your essay, and writing a first draft.
  Writing a thesis statement: Stating a limited subject and an opinion about that subject
  Developing: Explaining your ideas and adding specific details, examples, facts, and reasons
  Organizing: Arranging ideas from general to particular, particular to general, chronologically, spatially, or from one extreme to another
  Drafting: Writing a first draft, then revising to write a second draft, a third draft, and so on, until you have written your final draft

- **Revising** means "seeing again" and improving all aspects of an essay's organization and development.
  Thesis statement
  Basic elements
  Development
  Unity
  Organization
  Coherence

- **Editing** involves proofreading and correcting your grammar, punctuation, mechanics, and spelling errors.

◆ **Review P r a c t i c e 1**

1. What are the four main parts of the writing process?

   Prewriting, writing, revising, and editing

2. What is your favorite prewriting activity? Why is it your favorite?

   Answers will vary.

3. What personal rituals do you go through when you write?

   Answers will vary.

4. Where do you usually do your academic writing? Do you write your first draft on a computer? What time of day do you do your best writing?

   Answers will vary.

5. What is a thesis statement?

   The controlling idea of an essay

6. What is the difference between topic sentences and details?

   Topic sentences relate directly to the thesis statement of an essay.

   Details support their topic sentences.

7. What are the five main methods of organization?

   General to particular, particular to general, chronological, spatial, and from

   one extreme to another

8. Do you usually ask a tutor or friend to look at your draft before you revise it?

   Answers will vary.

9. What is the difference between revising and editing?

    Revising deals with development and organization; editing deals with

    grammar, punctuation, mechanics, and spelling.

10. Draw a picture or graphic version of your own writing process. What happens first, second, third, and so on from the time you get a writing assignment? Don't use any words in your picture.

    Answers will vary.

Review Practice 2 Write a thesis statement for five of the following topics. Then develop one thesis statement into a first draft of an essay. *Answers will vary.*

1. My best friend
2. Politics
3. My best adventure
4. Animals
5. In the middle of the night
6. My family
7. My future career
8. The best car
9. Parents should never
10. Sports

Review Practice 3 Revise the essay you wrote for Review Practice 2, using the checklist on page 63–64. *Answers will vary.*

Review Practice 4 Edit the essay you wrote for Review Practice 2, using the checklist on page 94. *Answers will vary.*

II

WRITING EFFECTIVE ESSAYS

We do not write in order to be understood; we write
in order to understand.

—CECIL DAY LEWIS

In Part I of *Mosaics,* you learned about the different stages of the writing process—prewriting, writing, revising, and editing—and the form of an essay. You know that essays typically have an introduction with a thesis statement, several body paragraphs, and a conclusion. Part II of *Mosaics* focuses on ways to develop and organize an essay's body paragraphs. You will learn strategies for thinking on paper that will help you discover your best thoughts on a particular topic. Then you will find out your options for organizing those ideas.

The nine basic writing strategies—also called rhetorical modes—are introduced in this part. Each chapter begins with an explanation of a strategy and then gives specific guidelines for using that strategy with examples from a model essay. Then the chapter helps you apply the chapter guidelines to two writing samples: (1) a real student essay and (2) your own essay. Students can usually see patterns in other students' writing more easily than they can in their own. As a result, you are asked to look at another student's writing first. In both cases, however, you can see systematically how to improve your writing with detailed instruction on a writing strategy, on revising, and on editing.

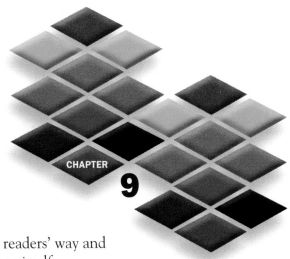

DESCRIBING

When you show, you get out of the readers' way and
let them come right at the experience itself.

—DONALD MURRAY

Description is an essential part of your life every day. Your friends might
want to know what kind of car you just bought; your parents may ask what
your new friend is like; your supervisor might need a description of the
project you just finished. You constantly need to describe people, places,
objects, and activities for different audiences if you want to communicate
clearly and effectively.

In addition, you frequently use description when writing. Actually, description is a major part of our writing in our personal lives, in college, and
at work:

> You describe your new leather jacket in an e-mail message to a
> friend.
>
> You describe the damage to your car in an insurance report.
>
> A student describes a cell and its parts on a biology exam.
>
> A nurse describes the appearance of a wound in a patient report.
>
> A landscape contractor describes a design for a rock garden.

Description creates a picture in words to help a reader visualize something a writer has seen, heard, or done. It helps the reader understand or share
a sensory experience through "showing" rather than "telling." Description is
one of our primary forms of self-expression.

At times, description is used as an end in itself. That is, you write a description for the sole purpose of telling what something looks, sounds, feels,
tastes, or smells like. For instance, you might use pure description to tell a
friend about your new apartment. More often, though, description is used to
help accomplish another purpose—to explain a problem, to analyze the

TEACHING
DESCRIPTION

Divide students into
five groups, and assign
each group one sense—
seeing, hearing,
touching, smelling,
or tasting.

Provide each group
with a word that is not
usually associated with
its sense. For example,
have students describe
the smell of a desk,
the taste of rain, the
sight of "irritation,"
the sound of autumn,
or the feel of sour
(opposite of sweet).
Make sure the groups
don't know each other's
words. Have each
group describe its word
using only sensory
details assigned to its
group. For example,
the group that is
describing the smell of
a closet can use only
words associated with
smell—not sight.

Have one person
from each group

describe the group's word to the other groups to see if the other groups can guess the word. This exercise will compel students to see the power of description by focusing on only one sense in an unusual way.

causes and effects of an event, or to persuade your readers to change their thinking or take some specific action.

WRITING A DESCRIPTION ESSAY

Writing about the dust storms of the 1930s, Margaret Bourke-White describes their various trails of destruction. In what ways has nature played a role in your life? What is this role? Is it a positive or negative one?

DUST CHANGES AMERICA
by Margaret Bourke-White

1   Vitamin K they call it—the dust which sifts under the door sills, and stings in the eyes, and seasons every spoonful of food. The dust storms have distinct personalities, rising in formation like rolling clouds, creeping up silently like formless fog, approaching violently like a tornado. Where has it come from? It provides topics of endless speculation. Red, it is the topsoil from Oklahoma; brown, it is the fertile earth of western Kansas; the good grazing land of Texas and New Mexico sweeps by as a murky yellow haze. Or, tracing it locally, "My uncle will be along pretty soon," they say; "I just saw his farm go by."

2   The town dwellers stack their linen in trunks, stuff wet cloths along the window sills, estimate the tons of sand in the darkened air above them, paste cloth masks on their faces with adhesive tape, and try to joke about Vitamin K. But on the farms and ranches there is an attitude of despair.

3   By coincidence I was in the same parts of the country where last year I photographed the drought. As short a time as eight months ago there was an attitude of false optimism. "Things will get better," the farmers would say. "We're not as hard hit as other states. The government will help out. This can't go on." But this year there is an atmosphere of utter hopelessness—nothing to do: no use digging out your chicken coops and pigpens after the last "duster" because the next one will be coming along soon; no use trying to keep the house clean; no use fighting off that foreclosure any longer; no use even hoping to give your cattle anything to chew on when their food crops have literally blown out of the ground.

4   It was my job to avoid dust storms, since I was commissioned by an airplane company to take photographs of its course from the air, but frequently the dust storms caught up with us, and as we were grounded anyway, I started to photograph them. Thus I saw five dust-storm states from the air and from the ground.

In the last several years, there have been droughts and sand storms 5 and dusters, but they have been localized, and always one state could borrow from another. But this year the scourge assumes tremendous proportions. Dust storms are bringing distress and death to 300,000 square miles; they are blowing over all of Kansas, all of Nebraska and Wyoming, strips of the Dakotas, about half of Colorado, sections of Iowa and Missouri, the greater part of Oklahoma, and the northern panhandle of Texas, extending into the eastern parts of New Mexico.

Last year, I saw farmers harvesting the Russian thistle. Never before 6 had they thought of feeding thistles to cattle. But this prickly fodder became precious for food. This year even the Russian thistles are dying out and the still humbler soap weed becomes as vital to the farmer as the fields of golden grain he tended in the past. Last year's thistle-fed cattle dwindled to skin and bone. This year's herds on their diet of soap weed develop roughened hides, ugly growths around the mouth, and lusterless eyes.

Years of the farmers' and ranchers' lives have gone into the building up 7 of their herds. Their herds were like their families to them. When AAA [American Agricultural Association] officials spotted cows and steers for shooting during the cattle-killing days of last summer, the farmers felt as though their own children were facing the bullets. Kansas, a Republican state, has no love for the AAA. This year, winds whistled over land made barren by the drought and the crop-conservation program. When Wallace [Henry Agard Wallace, Secretary of Agriculture under Franklin D. Roosevelt] removed the ban on the planting of spring wheat, he was greeted by cheers. But the wheat has been blown completely out of the ground. Nothing is left but soap weed, or the expensive cotton-seed cake, and after that—bankruptcy.

The storm comes in a terrifying way. Yellow clouds roll. The wind blows 8 such a gale that it is all my helper can do to hold my camera to the ground. The sand whips into my lens. I repeatedly wipe it away trying to snatch an exposure before it becomes completely coated again. The light becomes yellower, the wind colder. Soon there is no photographic light, and we hurry for shelter to the nearest farmhouse.

Three men and a woman are seated around a dust-caked lamp, on their 9 faces grotesque masks of wet cloth. The children have been put to bed with towels tucked over their heads. My host greets us: "It takes grit to live in this country." They are telling stories: A bachelor harnessed the sandblast which ripped through the keyhole by holding his pots and pans in it until they were spick and span. A pilot flying over Amarillo got caught in a sand storm. His motor clogged; he took to his parachute. It took him six hours to shovel his way back to earth. And when a man from the next county was struck by a drop of water, he fainted, and it took two buckets of sand to revive him.

10   The migrations of the farmer have begun. In many of the worst-hit counties, 80 percent of the families are on relief. In the open farm country, one crop failure follows another. After perhaps three successive crop failures, the farmer can't stand it any longer. He moves in with relatives and hopes for a job in Arizona or Illinois or some neighboring state where he knows he is not needed. Perhaps he gets a job as a cotton picker, and off he goes with his family, to be turned adrift again after a brief working period.

11   We passed them on the road, all their household goods piled on wagons, one lucky family on a truck—lucky, because they had been able to keep their truck when the mortgage was foreclosed. All they owned in the world was packed on it; the children sat on a pile of bureaus topped with mattresses, and the sides of the truck were strapped up with bed springs. The entire family looked like a Ku Klux Klan meeting, their faces done up in masks to protect them from the whirling sand.

12   Near Hays, Kansas, a little boy started home from school and never arrived there. The neighbors looked for him till ten at night, and all next day a band of two hundred people searched. At twilight they found him, only a quarter of a mile from home, his body nearly covered with silt. He had strangled to death. The man who got lost in his own ten-acre truck garden and wandered around choking and sniffling for eight hours before he found his house considered himself lucky to escape with his life. The police and sheriffs are kept constantly busy with calls from anxious parents whose children are lost, and the toll is mounting of people who become marooned and die in the storms.

13   But the real tragedy is the plight of the cattle. In a rising sand storm, cattle quickly become blinded. They run around in circles until they fall and breathe so much dust that they die. Autopsies show their lungs caked with dust and mud. Farmers dread the birth of calves during a storm. The newborn animals will die within twenty-four hours.

14   And this same dust that coats the lungs and threatens death to cattle and men alike, that ruins the stock of the storekeeper lying unsold on his shelves, that creeps into the gear shifts of automobiles, that sifts through the refrigerator into the butter, that makes housekeeping, and gradually life itself, unbearable, this swirling drifting dust is changing the agricultural map of the United States. It piles ever higher on the floors and beds of a steadily increasing number of deserted farmhouses. A half-buried plowshare, a wheat binder ruffled over with sand, the skeleton of a horse near a dirt-filled water hole are stark evidence of the meager life, the wasted savings, the years of toil that the farmer is leaving behind him.

PREPARING TO WRITE YOUR OWN DESCRIPTION

What are some memorable experiences you have had with nature (for example, a snowstorm, a sunny day, a drought, a tornado, a thunderstorm)? Why do you remember these experiences? Do any of them form a single impression when you think about them? Use one or more of the prewriting techniques that you learned in Chapter 2 to generate your thoughts about these memories.

How To Write a Description Essay

Describing is a very natural process that is based on good observing. But some people describe things more vividly than others. When they describe an experience, you feel as though you were there too. We can all improve our skill at describing by following a few simple guidelines:

1. *Decide on a dominant impression—the feeling or mood you want to communicate.* How do you want your readers to feel after reading your description? Good about the characters in the scene? Angry at the situation? Satisfied with the outcome? Choosing a dominant impression gives your description focus and unity. You can't possibly write down everything you observe about a person, place, incident, or object. The result would be a long, confusing—and probably boring—list. But if you first decide on a dominant impression for your description, you can then choose the details that will best convey that impression.

   The dominant impression Bourke-White conveys is a feeling of frustration and despair at the thought of the destruction that nature can bring. This dominant impression gives her essay focus and helps her choose the details that will best communicate this feeling.

2. *Decide how much of your description should be objective (factual) and how much should be subjective (personal reactions).* An objective description is like a dictionary definition—accurate and without emotion. Scientific and technical writing are objective. If, for example, you are describing a piece of equipment used in a chemistry experiment or the packaging needed to ship a computer, you would be objective. Subjective description, in contrast, tries to produce a specific emotional response in the reader. It focuses on feelings rather than facts and tries to activate as many senses as possible. An advertisement describing a Caribbean cruise might be very subjective, as might a restaurant or movie review. Most descriptive writing has a combination of objective

INSTRUCTOR'S RESOURCE MANUAL For additional material about teaching description; for journal entries; and for multiple-choice, short-answer, and paragraph tests, see the *Instructor's Resource Manual*, Section II, Part II.

and subjective elements. The degree to which you emphasize one over the other depends on your purpose and your audience.

Bourke-White's essay demonstrates a good balance of objective and subjective writing. She presents the facts about the dust storms and the ways the midwesterners deal with the dust—putting linen in trunks, stuffing wet cloths in window sills, using masks on their faces, and so on. Then she mixes these facts with subjective stories about families who are suffering, children who never make it home from school, and cattle who are like family to their owners. This combination of objective and subjective elements makes the essay realistic and powerful at the same time.

3. ***Draw on your five senses to write a good description.*** Although observing is at the heart of good description, limiting yourself to what you see is a mistake. Good description relies on all five senses: seeing, hearing, touching, smelling, and tasting. If you use all your senses to relay your description, your readers will be able to see, hear, touch, smell, and taste what you are describing as if they were there with you participating in the same experience.

Look again at Bourke-White's description. She draws on sight throughout the essay but especially in paragraph 8 when she describes her attempts at taking pictures. She refers to our sense of touch when she talks about the dust stinging the eyes (paragraph 1) and the cloth masks on people's faces (paragraph 2). She relies on taste when she mentions the dust seasoning the food (paragraph 1) and the cattle eating thistles (paragraph 6). Her description of the wind whistling over the barren land (paragraph 7) appeals to our sense of hearing. Her entire essay is vivid because of all the specific sensory details she furnishes.

4. ***When you describe, try to show rather than tell your readers what you want them to know.*** Your ultimate goal in writing a descriptive essay is to give your readers an experience as close to yours as possible. Therefore, do not simply tell your readers what you saw or experienced; show them. Use your writing skills to re-create the event so that your readers can see, hear, feel, smell, taste, and understand as if they were there. For example, you can tell someone you bought a "terrific new car." But if you say you bought a "beautiful, new blue Mustang with a gray interior, custom wheels, and an awesome stereo," you're *showing* your readers why you are so excited about your purchase.

If Bourke-White had simply stated her dominant impression (that dust storms bring frustration and despair to the Midwest) with no examples or details to support her statement, she would only be *telling* her readers how she felt. Instead, she *shows* them. Her sensory details demonstrate her main point.

5. *Organize your description so that your readers can easily follow it.*
Most descriptions are organized from general to particular (from main
idea to details), from particular to general (from details to main idea),
or spatially (from top to bottom or left to right). Because the organization of your essay often depends on your point of view, you should
choose a specific perspective from which to write your description. If
your description jumps around your house, referring to a picture on the
wall in your bedroom, then to the refrigerator in the kitchen, and next
to the quilt on your bed, your readers are likely to become confused and
disoriented. They will not be able to follow you. If, however, you move
from room to room in a logical way, your audience will be able to stay
with you. In fact, your vision will become their vision.

Bourke-White organizes her essay from one extreme to another—in
this case, from least to most tragic. She starts by describing the incon-
veniences of the dust storms on a personal level—the dirty houses, the
piles of dust in the fields, the health problems. Then she moves on to
the more serious issues of death on 300,000 square miles of land. The
essay ends with references to farms collapsing financially, children
dying from the dust, and whole families being displaced. The author
leaves us at the end of her essay with a sense of loss and hopelessness
that reflects the feelings of the farmers in the Midwest during a
drought.

 WRITING YOUR OWN DESCRIPTION ESSAY

What direct encounters have you had with nature? What are some of
the details of these encounters? Was your general impression good or
bad? Write an essay describing one of these encounters. Describe
your experience through the senses, following the guidelines for writing a description essay. Remember to show rather than tell your readers about your memory. Begin by reviewing your prewriting notes.
Then choose your dominant impression, and put it into a thesis
statement.

 # WORKING WITH A STUDENT ESSAY

TEACHING TIPS
The following eight
teaching tips are based
on Howard Gardner's
multiple intelligences:

In an essay about a fond memory, a student named Abby Reed remi-
nisces about her grandfather. As you read this draft, ask yourself what dominant impression Abby is trying to communicate to her readers.

Verbal/Linguistic
Have students write a
short but extremely
detailed account of the
last vacation they took.
How many sensory
words can they use to
describe one aspect of
the trip?

Musical/Rhythmic
Have students listen
to a pastoral piece
of music, such as
Mendelssohn's *Song
Without Words* or
Vivaldi's *Spring* from
Four Seasons. Then
have them list the
sights, sounds, smells,
tastes, and textures that
the music conjures up.

**Logical/
Mathematical**
Have students list in
chronological order all
the sensory details they
experience from the
moment they arrive
home for the day to the
moment they go to
sleep.

Visual/Spatial
Have students draw a
scene that includes all
five senses; it might
be a busy city street
corner, a country fair,
or some other location.
Which senses are pre-
dominant in the scene?

Bodily/Kinesthetic
Suggest that students
bicycle for a few miles,
run through a park,

Grandma's House

1   My grandma lives in the country, near a large, blue lake and a small, green forest. I look forward to visiting her house. I think of my grandpa when I'm there.

2   Whenever I walk into my grandma's house, I always go directly to my grandpa's favorite room—the den. I am immediately reminded of my grandpa in this room. My grandma has a soft, brown sofa and a brown leather loveseat in this small, dark room, but all I see is the old, worn chair that was my grandpa's. The chair was re-covered in an itchy tweed fabric. I used to pretend to be asleep in his chair so my grandpa would gently lift me from the coarse fabric and place me on his lap. I would lie there even though I wasn't sleeping and enjoy the warmth of his body. I remember the times I sat on his sturdy lap in that chair while he read One Fish, Two Fish, Red Fish, Blue Fish or The Cat in the Hat in his deep voice.

3   Now when I sit in his chair, I look on the mantle and see an old Air Force picture of my grandpa and three of his Air Force buddies. They are all dressed in informal flight clothes and are standing in front of a World War II airplane. Next to this picture is a single portrait of my grandpa when he was 70. This picture represents the way I still see him in my mind. His gray hair is thin, his face has light brown sun spots on it that show his years of working outdoors. His gentle, light blue eyes sparkle in a way that usually meant he was up to something mischievous. But most of all. I love looking at his smile. The right side of his mouth always turned slightly downward, but it is a smile that I would give anything to see in person just one more time.

4   I also love to play with the pipe stand that sits on the table next to my grandpa's chair. I like the worn feeling of the pipe. It once was rough with ridges but is now smooth from use. When I quietly pick up his pipe and smell the sweet tobacco that was once housed in its shell, I think of all the times I knew my grandpa were near me because of this same aroma.

5   I have wonderful memories of my grandpa. When I go to my grandma's house, I can sit in my grandpa's old chair in my grandpa's favorite room and reminisce about all the times I felt safe when my grandpa was near. I will always treasure this one tiny room, with its smells from the past and its picture of my grandpa smiling.

Discovering How the Essay Works

1. This essay creates a certain mood. What is the dominant impression that Abby creates?

   She feels happy and content when she thinks of her grandfather.

2. Is this description primarily subjective or objective? Explain your answer.

   It is subjective because most of the details she mentions are not

   facts but personal memories of her grandfather.

3. In this particular essay, the student writer describes her subjects mainly through the sense of sight, with a few references to hearing, touching, and smelling. Find at least one example of each of these senses in this essay. *Answers will vary. Here are some possibilities.*

   Seeing: *blue lake; an old Air Force picture; light brown sun spots*

   Hearing: *he read; deep voice; quietly pick up his pipe*

   Touching: *soft, brown sofa; itchy tweed fabric; sturdy lap; coarse fabric*

   Smelling: *sweet tobacco; this same aroma; smells from the past*

4. Abby works hard in this essay to *show* rather than *tell* us what she sees in the house. List three details that go beyond telling to *show* us what she observes?

   Answers will vary.

5. How does Abby organize her essay? List the topics of each of her body paragraphs, and then identify her method of organization.

   going to the den

   sitting in her grandpa's chair

   touching the pipe

   Method of organization: *Spatial*

play tennis, or do some other activity to see if they experience a heightened awareness of sensory details when they are active versus inactive. What senses do they experience differently?

Intrapersonal

Ask students to close themselves in their rooms and think about the most peaceful place they would like to visit. What sensory details do they think they would find most satisfying about this special place? What sensory details would make them think of this place when they are not there?

Interpersonal

Put students in groups of five to discuss a childhood vacation they took. What sensory details do they remember from the experience? Can they still see, hear, feel, smell, or taste any of the trip?

Naturalist

Suggest that students walk on a beach, kayak in a lake, roller-blade down a walkway, or otherwise move through nature and watch for vivid sensory details. What sounds are loudest? What sights are brightest? What smells are strongest? What tastes or textures are most obvious?

Revising and Editing the Student Essay

This essay is Abby's first draft, which now needs to be revised and edited. First, apply the Revising Checklist on this page to the content of Abby's draft. When you are satisfied that her ideas are fully developed and well organized, use the Editing Checklist on page 128 to correct her grammar and mechanics errors. Answer the questions after each checklist. Then write your suggested changes directly on Abby's draft.

REVISING CHECKLIST

THESIS STATEMENT

✔ Does the thesis statement contain the essay's controlling idea and an opinion about that idea?

✔ Does the thesis appear as the last sentence of the introduction?

BASIC ELEMENTS

✔ Does the title draw in the readers?

✔ Does the introduction capture the readers' attention and build up to the thesis statement effectively?

✔ Does each body paragraph deal with a single topic?

✔ Does the conclusion bring the essay to a close in an interesting way?

DEVELOPMENT

✔ Do the body paragraphs adequately support the thesis statement?

✔ Does each body paragraph have a focused topic sentence?

✔ Does each body paragraph contain *specific* details that support the topic sentence?

✔ Does each body paragraph include *enough* details to explain the topic sentence fully?

UNITY

✔ Do the essay's topic sentences relate directly to the thesis statement?

✔ Do the details in each body paragraph support its topic sentence?

ORGANIZATION

✔ Is the essay organized logically?

✔ Is each body paragraph organized logically?

> COHERENCE
> ✔ Are transitions used effectively so that paragraphs move smoothly and logically from one to the next?
> ✔ Do the sentences move smoothly and logically from one to the next?

Thesis Statement

1. Put brackets around the last sentence in Abby's introduction. Does it contain her dominant impression?

   No

2. Rewrite Abby's thesis statement if necessary so that it states her dominant impression as clearly as possible.

   Here is one possibility: I love my grandma's house because I can go to

   my grandpa's favorite room and remember him in detail.

Basic Elements

1. Give Abby's essay an alternate title.

   Answers will vary.

2. Rewrite Abby's introduction so that it captures the readers' attention and builds up to the thesis statement at the end of the paragraph.

   Answers will vary.

3. Does each of Abby's body paragraphs deal with only one topic?

   Yes

4. Rewrite Abby's conclusion using at least one suggestion from Part I.

Answers will vary.

_____

_____

_____

_____

Development

1. Write out Abby's thesis statement (revised, if necessary), and list her three topic sentences below it. *Thesis may vary.*

   Thesis statement: *I love my grandma's house because I can go to my grandpa's favorite room and remember him in detail.*

   Topic 1: *Whenever I walk into my grandma's house, I always go directly to my grandpa's favorite room—the den.*

   Topic 2: *Now when I sit in his chair, I look on the mantle and see an old Air Force picture of my grandpa and three of his Air Force buddies.*

   Topic 3: *I also love to play with the pipe stand that sits on the table next to my grandpa's chair.*

2. Do Abby's topics adequately support her thesis statement?

   Yes

3. Does each body paragraph have a focused topic sentence?

   Yes

4. Does the essay draw on all five senses?

   There is no tasting in the essay.

5. Add at least one detail to Abby's essay that refers to a new sense. Label the detail you are adding. *Answers will vary.*

   Sense: _____   Detail: _____

6. In what way does Abby's essay *show* rather than *tell* her readers about her memories of her grandfather?

   She uses many sensory details to make an image of her grandfather

   for readers. They can almost see and feel him.

Unity

1. Read each of Abby's topic sentences with her thesis statement (revised, if necessary) in mind. Do they go together?

   Answers will vary.

2. Revise them if necessary so they are directly related.
3. Drop or rewrite any of the sentences in her body paragraphs that are not directly related to their topic sentences. *All sentences are directly related to their topic sentences.*

Organization

1. Read Abby's essay again to see if all the paragraphs are arranged logically.
2. Move any paragraphs that are out of order. *All paragraphs are arranged logically.*
3. Look closely at Abby's body paragraphs to see if all her sentences are arranged logically within paragraphs.
4. Move any sentences that are out of order. *All sentences are in order.*

Coherence

1. Circle five transitions Abby uses. *Answers will vary.*
2. Explain how two of these make Abby's essay easier to read.

   Answers will vary.

   _____

For a list of transitions, see pages 83–84.

   Now rewrite Abby's essay with your revisions.

EDITING STRATEGIES
This chapter focuses on the following editing problems:
Fragments
Run-together sentences
Subject-verb agreement

EDITING CHECKLIST ✔

SENTENCES

✔ Does each sentence have a main subject and verb?

✔ Do all subjects and verbs agree?

✔ Do all pronouns agree with their nouns?

✔ Are modifiers as close as possible to the words they modify?

PUNCTUATION AND MECHANICS

✔ Are sentences punctuated correctly?

✔ Are words capitalized properly?

WORD CHOICE AND SPELLING

✔ Are words used correctly?

✔ Are words spelled correctly?

Sentences

Subjects and Verbs

For help with subjects and verbs, see Chapter 34.

1. Underline the subjects once and verbs twice in paragraphs 3 and 4 of your revision of Abby's essay. Remember that sentences can have more than one subject-verb set.

2. Does each of the sentences have at least one subject and verb that can stand alone?

   No

For help with fragments, see Chapter 35.

3. Did you find and correct Abby's fragment? If not, find and correct it now. *Paragraph 3, sentence 7*

For help with run-togethers, see Chapter 36.

4. Did you find and correct Abby's run-together sentence? If not, find and correct it now. *Paragraph 3, sentence 5*

Subject-Verb Agreement

For help with subject-verb agreement, see Chapter 39.

1. Read aloud the subjects and verbs you underlined in your revision of Abby's essay.

2. Did you find and correct the subject and verb that do not agree?

   Paragraph 4, sentence 4

Pronoun Agreement

1. Find any pronouns in your revision of Abby's essay that do not agree with their nouns. *All pronouns agree with their nouns.*
2. Correct any pronouns that do not agree with their nouns.

For help with pronoun agreement, see Chapter 43.

Modifiers

1. Find any modifiers in your revision of Abby's essay that are not as close as possible to the words they modify. *There are no modifier errors.*
2. Rewrite sentences if necessary so that modifiers are as close as possible to the words they modify.

For help with modifier errors, see Chapter 46.

Punctuation and Mechanics

Punctuation

1. Read your revision of Abby's essay for any errors in punctuation.
2. Find the fragment and the run-together sentence you revised, and make sure they are punctuated correctly.

For help with punctuation, see Chapters 47–51.

Mechanics

1. Read your revision of Abby's essay for any errors in capitalization. *There are no capitalization errors.*
2. Be sure to check Abby's capitalization in the fragment and run-together sentence you revised.

For help with capitalization, see Chapter 52.

Word Choice and Spelling

Word Choice

1. Find any words used incorrectly in your revision of Abby's essay. *All words are used correctly.*
2. Correct any errors you find.

For help with confused words, see Chapter 58.

Spelling

1. Use spell-check and a dictionary to check the spelling in your revision of Abby's essay.
2. Correct any misspelled words. *All words are spelled correctly.*

For help with spelling, see Chapter 59.

Now rewrite Abby's essay again with your editing corrections.

WORKING WITH YOUR OWN ESSAY

Returning to the description you wrote earlier in this chapter, revise and edit your own writing. The checklists here will help you apply what you have learned to your essay.

Revising and Editing Your Own Essay

CLASS ACTIVITY

Put a sentence on the board that *tells* readers information, and have the students, as a class, offer suggestions to change it to *show* readers that information. For example, change "The boat went down the river" to "The red and white paddleboat gently glided down the murky Guadalupe River."

REVISING CHECKLIST ✔

THESIS STATEMENT

☐ Does the thesis statement contain the essay's controlling idea and an opinion about that idea?

☐ Does the thesis appear as the last sentence of the introduction?

BASIC ELEMENTS

☐ Does the title draw in the readers?

☐ Does the introduction capture the readers' attention and build up to the thesis statement effectively?

☐ Does each body paragraph deal with a single topic?

☐ Does the conclusion bring the essay to a close in an interesting way?

DEVELOPMENT

☐ Do the body paragraphs adequately support the thesis statement?

☐ Does each body paragraph have a focused topic sentence?

☐ Does each body paragraph contain *specific* details that support the topic sentence?

☐ Does each body paragraph include *enough* details to explain the topic sentence fully?

UNITY

☐ Do the essay's topic sentences relate directly to the thesis statement?

☐ Do the details in each body paragraph support its topic sentence?

ORGANIZATION

☐ Is the essay organized logically?

☐ Is each body paragraph organized logically?

> COHERENCE
> ☐ Are transitions used effectively so that paragraphs move smoothly and logically from one to the next?
> ☐ Do the sentences move smoothly and logically from one to the next?

Thesis Statement

1. What dominant impression are you trying to communicate in your essay?

   _____

2. Put brackets around the last sentence in your introduction. Does it contain your dominant impression?

   _____

3. Rewrite your thesis statement if necessary so that it states your dominant impression as clearly as possible.

Basic Elements

1. Give your essay a title if it doesn't have one.

   _____

2. Does your introduction capture your readers' attention and build up to your thesis statement at the end of the paragraph?

   _____

3. Does each of your body paragraphs deal with only one topic?

   _____

4. Does your conclusion follow some of the suggestions offered in Part I?

   _____

Development

1. Write out your thesis statement (revised, if necessary), and list your topic sentences below it.

   Thesis statement: _____

       Topic 1: _____

       Topic 2: _____

       Topic 3: _____

2. Do your topics adequately support your thesis statement?

   _____

3. Does each body paragraph have a focused topic sentence?

   _____

4. Does your essay draw on all five senses?

   _____

5. Record three details from your essay that draw on three different senses. Label each example with the sense it refers to.

Detail	**Sense**
_____	_____
_____	_____
_____	_____

6. Add at least one new detail to your essay.

7. Does your essay *show* rather than *tell* readers what they need to know? Give three examples.

   _____

   _____

   _____

Unity

1. Read each of your topic sentences with your thesis statement in mind. Do they go together?

   _____

2. Revise them if necessary so they are directly related.
3. Drop or rewrite any of the sentences in your body paragraphs that are not directly related to their topic sentences.

Organization

1. Read your essay again to see if all the paragraphs are arranged logically.
2. Refer to your answers to the development questions. Then identify your method of organization.

   _____

3. Is the order you chose for your paragraphs the most effective approach to your topic?

   _____

4. Move any paragraphs that are out of order.
5. Look closely at your body paragraphs to see if all the sentences are arranged logically within paragraphs.
6. Move any sentences that are out of order.

Coherence

1. Circle five transitions you use.
2. Explain how two of these make your essay easier to read.

   For a list of transitions, see pages 83–84.

   _____

   _____

   Now rewrite your essay with your revisions.

EDITING CHECKLIST ✔

SENTENCES

☐ Does each sentence have a main subject and verb?

☐ Do all subjects and verbs agree?

☐ Do all pronouns agree with their nouns?

☐ Are modifiers as close as possible to the words they modify?

PUNCTUATION AND MECHANICS

☐ Are sentences punctuated correctly?

☐ Are words capitalized properly?

WORD CHOICE AND SPELLING

☐ Are words used correctly?

☐ Are words spelled correctly?

Sentences

Subjects and Verbs

For help with subjects and verbs, see Chapter 34.

1. Underline the subjects once and verbs twice in a paragraph of your revised essay. Remember that sentences can have more than one subject-verb set.

2. Does each of your sentences have at least one subject and verb that can stand alone?

For help with fragments, see Chapter 35.

3. Correct any fragments you have written.

For help with run-togethers, see Chapter 36.

4. Correct any run-together sentences you have written.

Subject-Verb Agreement

For help with subject-verb agreement, see Chapter 39.

1. Read aloud the subjects and verbs you underlined in your revised essay.

2. Correct any subjects and verbs that do not agree.

Pronoun Agreement

For help with pronoun agreement, see Chapter 43.

1. Find any pronouns in your revised essay that do not agree with their nouns.

2. Correct any pronouns that do not agree with their nouns.

Modifiers

1. Find any modifiers in your revised essay that are not as close as possible to the words they modify.
2. Rewrite sentences if necessary so that your modifiers are as close as possible to the words they modify.

For help with modifier errors, see Chapter 46.

Punctuation and Mechanics
Punctuation

1. Read your revised essay for any errors in punctuation.
2. Make sure any fragments and run-together sentences you revised are punctuated correctly.

For help with punctuation, see Chapters 47–51.

Mechanics

1. Read your revised essay for any errors in capitalization.
2. Be sure to check your capitalization in any fragments or run-together sentences you revised.

For help with capitalization, see Chapter 52.

Word Choice and Spelling
Word Choice

1. Find any words used incorrectly in your revised essay.
2. Correct any errors you find.

For help with confused words, see Chapter 58.

Spelling

1. Use spell-check and a dictionary to check your spelling.
2. Correct any misspelled words.

Now rewrite your essay again with your editing corrections.

PRACTICING DESCRIPTION
Reading Suggestions

In Chapter 25, you will find two essays that demonstrate good descriptive writing: "El Hoyo" by Mario Suarez describes a small town near Tucson and its citizens, and "Dwellings" by Linda Hogan focuses on the habitats of different animals. You might want to read these selections before writing another description essay. As you read, notice how the writers pull you into each experience through sensory details.

SERVICE LEARNING PROJECT
This assignment is another step in the Service Learning project. If you choose to use this feature of the text, each chapter

Service Learning Project

This assignment is based on a Service Learning project of your choice. If your instructor has already introduced service learning to the class, you will be doing these exercises when they are assigned. At this point, choose a project you would like to pursue, or continue work on a project you have already begun. This assignment in Part II will help you prepare for an essay on this project in Part III. Here is another stage in the preparation for this essay:

For the Service Learning project you have taken on, describe the people, places, or objects involved in your project. Use the guidelines you have learned in this chapter to help you write your description. But remember that these are just thoughts that will be developed into an essay in Part III.

Writing Workshop

Guidelines for Writing a Description Essay

1. Decide on a dominant impression—the feeling or mood you want to communicate.
2. Decide how much of your description should be objective (factual) and how much should be subjective (personal reactions).
3. Draw on your five senses to write a good description.
4. When you describe, try to *show* rather than *tell* your readers what you want them to know.
5. Organize your description so that your readers can easily follow it.

1. Place yourself in the scene on previous page, and describe it in as much detail as possible. Imagine that you can see, hear, touch, smell, and taste everything in this picture. What are your sensations? How do you feel? Before you begin to write, decide on the dominant impression you want to convey. Then choose your details carefully.

2. Describe for your classmates a class environment that is ideal for you. What kind of classroom atmosphere makes you thrive? What should the people in your class understand about you as a student? What kind of instructor brings out the best in you? Why?

3. A national travel magazine is asking for honest descriptions (positive or negative) of places people have visited. They are offering $100 to the writers of the essays chosen for publication. You may decide to write about a place with a marvelous beach or about an absolutely awful hotel. In either case, remember to begin with the dominant impression you want to create.

4. Create your own description assignment (with the help of your instructor), and write a response to it.

Revising Workshop

Small Group Activity (5–10 minutes per writer)   Working in groups of three or four, each person should read his or her description essay to the other members of the group. Those listening should record their reactions on a copy of the Peer Evaluation Form in Appendix 2A. After your group goes through this process, give your evaluation forms to the appropriate writers so that each writer has two or three peer comment sheets for revising.

Paired Activity (5 minutes per writer)   Using the completed Peer Evaluation Forms, work in pairs to decide what you should revise in your essay. If time allows, rewrite some of your sentences, and have your partner look at them.

Individual Activity   Rewrite your paper, using the revising feedback you received from other students.

Editing Workshop

Paired Activity (5–10 minutes per writer)   Swap papers with a classmate, and use the editing portion of your Peer Evaluation Form to identify as many grammar, punctuation, mechanics, and spelling errors as you can. If time allows, correct some of your errors, and have your partner look at them. Record your grammar, punctuation, and mechanics errors in the Error Log (Appendix 6) and your spelling errors in the Spelling Log (Appendix 7).

TEACHING ON THE WEB
Discussion Topic: The Internet has become indispensable in today's society. Put students in groups of three or four, and have them discuss whether or not they think people are growing out of touch with their senses because they spend so much time on the Internet instead of experiencing life firsthand. Have one person from each group report the group's conclusions to the class.

TEACHING ON THE WEB
Links: Have students link to world-renowned museums and view famous pieces of art. How do some of these masterpieces convey the five senses?
Possible sites:
Tate Britain, London, www.tate.org.uk/britain
Guggenheim Museum, Venice, www.guggenheim-venice.it
Smithsonian American Art Museum, Washington, D.C., www.nmaa.si.edu

TEACHING ON THE WEB
Research: Have students search various Web sites to find one that incorporates all five senses. How difficult was it to

find this site? How
are all the senses
represented?

TEACHING ON
THE WEB
Mosaics Web Site:
To learn more
about description,
students can go to
www.prenhall.com/
mosaics.

Individual Activity   Rewrite your paper again, using the editing feedback you received from other students.

Reflecting on Your Writing

When you have completed your own essay, answer these six questions.

1. What was most difficult about this assignment?
2. What was easiest?
3. What did you learn about description by completing this assignment?
4. What do you think are the strengths of your description? Place a wavy line by the parts of your essay that you feel are very good.
5. What are the weaknesses, if any, of your paper? Place an X by the parts of your essay you would like help with. Write any questions you have in the margin.
6. What did you learn from this assignment about your own writing process—about preparing to write, about writing the first draft, about revising, and about editing?

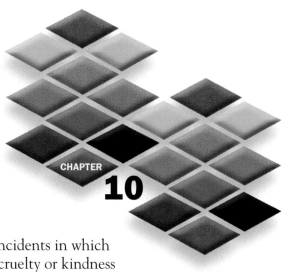

NARRATING

I try to remember times in my life, incidents in which
there was the dominating theme of cruelty or kindness
or generosity or envy or happiness or glee. Then I
select one.

—MAYA ANGELOU

Because we are constantly telling other people about various events in
our lives, we all know how to use narration. Think of how many times a day
you tell someone about an event that happened to you: your accident on the
way to school; the conversation you had at the bus stop yesterday; your
strange experience at the restaurant last night. Narrating is an essential part
of all of our lives. In fact, stories can teach us how to live our lives.

Narration also plays an important role in our writing. Think about how
many times we tell a story when we write—in our personal lives, in classes,
and at work:

You tell a friend in an e-mail about how you met the person you're
now dating.

On a history exam, a student summarizes the chain of events that
led to the United States' entry into World War II.

A student summarizes a short story in an English class.

An emergency medical technician gives an account of her 911 calls
for the day.

A supervisor writes a report explaining an employee's accident on
the job.

Narration, or storytelling, is an interesting way of getting someone's attention by sharing thoughts or experiences. Like description, narration is
sometimes used as an end in itself (for example, when you tell a friend a joke

TEACHING
NARRATION
Write an introduction
that could lead to an
unusual story line
(such as "Ballerina
leaves company to join
Navy SEALS"). At the
beginning of class, read
the introduction aloud
to all your students.
Give the introduction
to a student, and have
him or her add a line or
two to begin an essay.
Then have the student
pass the paper to the
next student.
   The next student
should read only the
lines written by the
student before him or
her and then add a line
or two to the essay.
Students should not
read the entire essay,
just the last lines that
were written. This
should continue until

every student has contributed to the essay.

After class, type the essay out and add natural paragraph breaks and a conclusion, if necessary. Hand out copies of the essay to the class next time you meet.

Using the essay as a guide, use whatever disorganized connections or lucky coincidences that were written to discuss how to write an effective narrative essay.

or the plot of a movie). But very often it's used in conjunction with explaining or persuading. You might start a term paper analyzing drug abuse, for example, with a brief story of one addict's life, or a lawyer might seek a not-guilty verdict by telling the jury about the hardships his or her client suffered as a child. Basically, people use storytelling to help focus their readers' or listeners' attention.

WRITING A NARRATION ESSAY

Jane Maher, who teaches college in New York City, wrote the following autobiographical essay to help her come to terms with the loss of her father. Can you think of an event that taught you something important about life? What was the event? What did you learn?

GIRL
by Jane Maher

1   I don't remember exactly when I began to be offended when my father called me, or other girls or women, "girl." I guess he always did it; at least I don't remember him ever not doing it. He'd often use it as a term of affection: "How's my girl today?" But just as often, he'd use it carelessly or callously, the way some men use the expression "sweetie." "Listen girl," my father would say, "I make the rules around here."

2   Women, girls, were perceived by my father as less than men: less important, less intelligent, less capable, less in need of education or direction. In fact, for a long period of my life, I was so indoctrinated by my father's views, and by society's confirmation of those views, that I agreed with him.

3   But as I grew older, the term "girl" began to hurt me and make me angry. As my father became aware of my strong and growing aversion to the word, he'd use it even more often. "What's the matter," he'd ask. "You don't like it anymore when your old man calls you girl? You're my daughter; I'll call you whatever I want." Or he'd ask my mother, pretending I wasn't in the room, "What kind of daughter did you raise that she wants to become a man? Is she ashamed to be a girl?" The word took on stronger and stronger connotations for me as I began to realize how permanently, and adversely, my father's attitudes had affected my life. I had been sent to an all-girls commercial high school. "Listen, girl," my father declared,

"as long as you know typing and stenography, you'll never starve." College was not mentioned very much in our house. I was one of three daughters. If one of us had a date, my father would tell my mother to remind us "what can happen to a girl if she's not careful." When I got married, I heard my father joking with my uncle: "One down, two to go." We were objects to be dispensed with, burdens of no conceivable use to him.

This does not mean that he did not love us or care for us; for my entire childhood, he worked two jobs so that he could afford to send us away to the country every summer. But it was the terms upon which he loved and cared for us which were so distressing to me. Nor did I always get angry when he used the term. When my first daughter was born, he arrived at the hospital carrying a silver dollar he had saved in his collection for many years as a gift for her. "Now I've got four of you girls instead of three," he said, knowing that I knew at this special time he was only teasing and did not intend to hurt me.

I saw less and less of my father after I moved to Connecticut in 1980. He and my mother kept their house in Brooklyn but spent most of the winter months in Florida. Sometimes when I called on the phone, I could tell how happy he was to hear my voice. "Hey, girl, is that husband of yours taking as good care of you as I did?" But other times, over Thanksgiving dinner or while opening Christmas presents, he'd use the term as he had when I was young. "Girl, get me a little more coffee will you?" Or when I enrolled my daughter in an expensive private school: "Why spend money you don't have to, girl? She's just going to get married the way you did." I'd keep my countenance at those times; I had grown wise to my father—I wouldn't give him the satisfaction of showing my anger. That's not to say he didn't keep trying: "So now you like it when your old man calls you girl, huh? You're finally getting wise to the fact that men aren't so bad to have around when you need something."

And I suspected that secretly he was proud of me. Soon after I got married, I returned to college, part-time, in the evening, and graduated magna cum laude. By then, both of my daughters were in school, so I earned my master's degree from Columbia University, again part-time. It was my father who picked up my daughters from the school bus stop on the day I took my comprehensive exam. When I began to teach part time at a local community college, my father asked my mother, again pretending I wasn't in the room, "if there was a girl around here who thought her father was going to start calling her Professor."

My father had always had a heart condition, exacerbated by twenty-two years as a New York City fireman, two packs of cigarettes a day, and my mother's delicious Italian cooking. When he suddenly became seriously

4

5

6

7

ill, my mother got him home from Florida and into a hospital in Brooklyn in less than 24 hours. But it still wasn't soon enough. My father died before they could perform a triple bypass, and before I got to say goodbye to him.

8   I had left Connecticut at nine in the morning, intending to wait out the surgery with my mother and to be with my father when he awoke. Instead, when I arrived at the hospital, one of my sisters and my mother were in a small, curtained-off section of the intensive care unit being told by a busy, preoccupied young resident that my father had experienced very little discomfort before he died. It sounded too pat, too familiar, too convenient to me. I was overcome with the fear that my father had been alone that entire morning, that no one in that overcrowded municipal hospital had even known that he was dead until they arrived to prepare him for surgery.

9   They left us alone to say goodbye to him, but I was so concerned over my mother's anguish that I didn't take the time I should have to kiss him or even to touch his forehead. A nurse came in and suggested, gently, that it was time to leave. She was right, of course; another moment and my mother would have collapsed.

10   I thanked the nurse and asked her, nonchalantly, if she knew exactly when my father had died, secretly convinced that she didn't have an answer, that he had been alone all morning. "I didn't see him this morning," she replied, "but I'll get the nurse who did."

11   A young, pretty nurse appeared several minutes later. "My shift is over," she said, "but I was waiting around to see the family."

12   "Was he in pain?" my mother asked.

13   "No, not at all. He even teased me a bit. I remember his exact words. "Go take care of the patients who need you, girl," he said. "I'm perfectly fine."

14   I wasn't exactly fine, but I have never felt more comforted in my life than when I heard that word.

✎ Preparing to Write Your Own Narration Essay

We have all learned important lessons from various events in our lives. Over time, we find that some lessons are more worthwhile than others. What events in your life have taught you important lessons? Use one or more of the prewriting techniques you learned in Chapter 2 to gather your thoughts on these events. What lessons did you learn?

How to Write a Narration Essay

Narrating involves telling a story about an experience—one of yours or someone else's. When you write a narrative essay, you focus on a particular event and make a specific point about it. You should provide enough detail so that readers can understand as completely as possible what your experience was like. Here are some guidelines to help you make your narrative interesting.

1. ***Make sure your essay has a point.*** The most important feature of a narrative essay is that it makes a point. Simply recording your story step by step is a boring exercise for both writer and reader. Writing an account of your walk to class in the morning might not be particularly interesting. But the walk becomes interesting when something important or significant happens on the way. An event is significant if it helps both writer and reader understand something about themselves, about other people, or about the world we live in. If you can complete one of the following sentences, you will produce a focused narrative:

> This essay shows that . . .
> This essay teaches us that . . .

In Jane Maher's essay, the narrator focuses on the pain she felt, growing up, when her father referred to her as a "girl." She thought the term was degrading until she understood, after he died, that it was really a term of endearment. Maher is able to communicate the process of growing up through her experience with this one word. Her essay teaches us that the relationship between words and emotions is complex.

2. ***Use the five Ws and one H to construct your story.*** The five Ws and one H are the six questions—*Who? What? When? Where? Why?* and *How?*—that journalists use to make sure they cover all the basic information when they write a news story. These questions can help you come up with details and ideas for a well-developed narrative essay. You should make sure that your essay answers each of these questions in detail.

When you look at Maher's narrative again, you can see that she covered the answers to all these questions:

> *Who* was involved? Maher, her father, her mother, and the nurses
> *What* was the central problem? Maher was offended by her father's use of the word "girl."
> *When* did this story take place? As Maher was growing up

INSTRUCTOR'S RESOURCE MANUAL For additional material about teaching narration; for journal entries; and for multiple-choice, short-answer, and paragraph tests, see the *Instructor's Resource Manual*, Section II, Part II.

Where were they? At home

Why was Maher offended? Because she thought the word "girl" was degrading to her as a person and to other females

How did the author learn from this event? She finally understood that her father's use of "girl" wasn't as offensive as she thought it was.

Since Maher covers all these basic details, the reader can appreciate her full story and understand its significance.

3. ***Develop your narrative with vivid details.*** Your readers will be able to imagine the events in your narrative essay if you provide them with specific details. In fact, the more specific your details, the more vivid your essay will become. These details should develop the ideas you generated with the six journalistic questions. At the same time, you should omit any irrelevant details that don't support your thesis statement.

   Look again at Maher's essay. In this narrative, the author provides many vivid details about the narrator: She is a girl whose father thinks girls are less important than boys; he calls her "girl"; this term starts to bother the narrator as she is growing up; she gets married and moves to Connecticut; she has two daughters; she gets her master's degree at Columbia University and starts teaching at a local community college; and her father dies of a heart attack. The amount of detail in Maher's essay helps us participate in her narrative.

4. ***Build excitement in your narrative with careful pacing.*** To be most effective, narration should prolong the exciting parts of a story and shorten the routine facts that simply move the reader from one episode to another. If you were robbed on your way to work, for example, a good narrative describing the incident would concentrate on the traumatic event itself rather than on such boring details as what you had for breakfast or what clothes you were wearing. One writer might say, "I was robbed this morning." A better writer would draw out the exciting parts: "As I was walking to work around 7:30 this morning, a huge, angry-looking man ran up to me, thrust a gun into my stomach, and demanded my money, my new wristwatch, my credit cards, and my pants—leaving me broke and embarrassed." The details themselves tell the story.

   Maher reveals the details in her story through some of her father's quotations that bothered her: "Listen girl, I make the rules around here"; "Listen girl, as long as you know typing and stenography, you'll never starve." She feels frustrated and belittled by her father, even as an adult: "Hey, girl, is that husband of yours taking as good care of you as I did?" Finally, she works through the hurtfulness when her father dies. At this point, Maher draws out the search for the nurse who could tell her if her father died alone. The pacing of her story holds our interest throughout the essay.

5. ***Organize your narration so that your readers can easily follow it.*** Most narrative essays follow a series of actions through time, so they are organized chronologically, or according to a time sequence. Once you choose the details you will use, you should arrange them so that your story has a clear beginning, middle, and end. If you add clear, logical transitions, such as "then," "next," "at this point," and "suddenly," you will guide your readers smoothly through your essay from one event to the next.

   Jane Maher organizes her narrative chronologically. It moves through time from her childhood to going to high school to getting married and having a baby as her father raises her, retires, and grows old. In other words, the two main characters—Maher and her father—move through normal life events. Because it follows a logical time sequence and does not jump around, Maher's narrative is easy to follow. She guides her readers through her essay with such transitions as "in fact," "as I grew older," "when," "sometimes," and "soon."

 WRITING YOUR OWN NARRATION ESSAY

Choose one of the events from your prewriting notes that taught you an important lesson in life, and write a narration essay explaining this incident and the lesson you learned. Follow the guidelines in this chapter to develop your essay.

 WORKING WITH A STUDENT ESSAY

In an essay about a dramatic incident, student writer Tommy Poulos tells a story that taught him an important lesson in life. Here is his first draft. As you read this paragraph, try to figure out what Tommy's main point is.

TEACHING TIPS
The following eight teaching tips are based on Howard Gardner's multiple intelligences:

"My Brother"

My family and I lead a fairly quiet life. My parents go to work, and my   1
brother and I go to school. We never make headlines with sports events

or science fairs. We essentially live a normal American life out of the spotlight. It was quite a shock, then, when a lot of attention was focused on our family.

2   My brother, Wayne, was driving on a highway that is nicknamed "The Death Loop." It got its name because it's a two-lane highway that loops around the city, and many people have died because of drivers who take too many chances and cause head-on collisions. One afternoon, Wayne saw a woman's car wrecked into a guardrail with her passenger side of the car completely smashed in. The driver's side was mangled, and my brother could tell the woman inside was in trouble. Wayne didn't think twice about running up to help them. She was badly injured, but my brother knew not to move her!

3   The woman had not been wearing her seat belt. Her car was too old to have an airbag. She had obviously hit her head because she had blood gushing from a gaping wound in her forehead. She was conscious, so my brother sat with her, trying to keep her calm and awake. He kept asking her questions like if she had any children? Two other cars stopped, and my brother remembers telling one man to call 911. Wayne stayed with the woman until the paramedics arrived.

4   Wayne left the scene after giving a statement to the police. Later, he heard from the local newspapers and news stations that his heroic actions had saved the woman. In these stories, the woman's husband said he believed his wife was still alive because she had a guardian angel keeping her awake. Even the paramedics said Wayne probably kept her alive. By keeping her awake. In public, Wayne acts very humble, but in private, he is loving the attention.

5   Now my brother is the local hero. Our house used to be quiet, but since Wayne's act of heroism, it's become Grand Central Station. Everyone wants to talk to Wayne. I'm happy for him. But most of all, I'm glad Wayne realizes the importance of seat belts. He used to be macho and say seat belts were too uncomfortable to wear. Now he won't leave the driveway until everyone has buckled their seat belts. Perhaps the woman will save Wayne's life as well.

Discovering How the Essay Works

1.   All the details in Tommy's essay lead to one main point. What is that point?

His brother became a hero and learned an important lesson.

2. Tommy covers all the journalistic questions in his essay. Record at least one detail he uses for each question: *Answers may vary.*

Who? *Wayne*

What? *Wayne saved a woman's life.*

When? *One afternoon*

Where? *"The Death Loop"*

Why? *She was injured.*

How? *By staying with her and keeping her awake*

3. In your opinion, which two details of Tommy's are most vivid? What makes them so vivid?

Answers will vary.

4. How does Tommy pace his essay to build excitement?

He spreads out important details. For example, the driver wasn't wearing a seat belt, and the woman might have died if she didn't stay awake. Then, right at the end, Tommy tells us that his brother didn't wear a seat belt until this incident.

5. How does Tommy organize his essay? List the topic of each of his body paragraphs; then identify his method of organization.

Paragraph 2: *Wayne found an injured motorist.*

Paragraph 3: *Wayne helped the badly injured woman.*

Paragraph 4: *Wayne was considered a hero by the media.*

Method of organization: *Chronological*

Intrapersonal

Have students evaluate the latest episode they saw of their favorite TV show. Did it follow the guidelines of narration? What aspects of the story did they find most enjoyable? Why?

Interpersonal

Have students choose their favorite hero from a popular movie. Have them act out a scene from the movie to see if other students can guess who the hero might be.

Naturalist

Have students go outdoors to a park, lake, ocean, or mountain. Have them imagine what could have happened on this spot 100 years ago. What story did they envision while reflecting on this place?

REVISING AND
EDITING OPTIONS
Consider varying your
approach to revising
and editing. You could
teach these skills in a
class discussion, in
small groups, or in
pairs.

Revising and Editing the Student Essay

This essay is Tommy's first draft, which now needs to be revised and edited. First, apply the Revising Checklist below to the content of Tommy's draft. When you are satisfied that his ideas are fully developed and well organized, use the Editing Checklist on page 151 to correct his grammar and mechanics errors. Answer the questions after each checklist. Then write your suggested changes directly on Tommy's draft.

REVISING
STRATEGIES
This chapter focuses on
the following revising
elements:
 Thesis statement
 Basic elements
 Development

REVISING CHECKLIST

THESIS STATEMENT
✔ Does the thesis statement contain the essay's controlling idea and an opinion about that idea?
✔ Does the thesis appear as the last sentence of the introduction?

BASIC ELEMENTS
✔ Does the title draw in the readers?
✔ Does the introduction capture the readers' attention and build up to the thesis statement effectively?
✔ Does each body paragraph deal with a single topic?
✔ Does the conclusion bring the essay to a close in an interesting way?

DEVELOPMENT
✔ Do the body paragraphs adequately support the thesis statement?
✔ Does each body paragraph have a focused topic sentence?
✔ Does each body paragraph contain *specific* details that support the topic sentence?
✔ Does each body paragraph include *enough* details to explain the topic sentence fully?

UNITY
✔ Do the essay's topic sentences relate directly to the thesis statement?
✔ Do the details in each body paragraph support its topic sentence?

ORGANIZATION
✔ Is the essay organized logically?
✔ Is each body paragraph organized logically?

> **COHERENCE**
> ✔ Are transitions used effectively so that paragraphs move smoothly and logically from one to the next?
> ✔ Do the sentences move smoothly and logically from one to the next?

Thesis Statement

1. Put brackets around the last sentence in Tommy's introduction. Does it contain his main point? Does it express his opinion about that point?

   No

2. Rewrite Tommy's thesis statement if necessary so that it states his main point and an opinion about that main point.

   Here is one possibility: It was quite a shock, then, when my brother

   suddenly became the town hero and a lot of attention was focused

   on our family.

Basic Elements

1. Give Tommy's essay an alternate title. Also drop the quotation marks, since original titles should not be in quotation marks.

   Answers will vary.

2. Rewrite Tommy's introduction so that it captures the readers' attention and builds up to the thesis statement at the end of the paragraph.

   Answers will vary.

3. Does each of Tommy's body paragraphs deal with only one topic?

   Yes

4. Rewrite Tommy's conclusion using at least one suggestion from Part I.

   Answers will vary.

   _____

   _____

Development

1. Write out Tommy's thesis statement (revised, if necessary), and list his three topic sentences below it. *Thesis may vary.*

   Thesis statement: *It was quite a shock, then, when my brother suddenly*

   became the town hero and a lot of attention was focused on our family.

   Topic 1: *My brother, Wayne, was driving on a highway that is nick-named "The Death Loop."*

   Topic 2: *The woman had not been wearing her seat belt.*

   Topic 3: *Wayne left the scene after giving a statement to the police.*

2. Do Tommy's topics adequately support his thesis statement?

   Yes

3. Does each body paragraph have a focused topic sentence?

   Yes

4. Add more specific information to two of Tommy's supporting details.
5. Add two new details to Tommy's essay that support his main idea.

Unity

1. Read each of Tommy's topic sentences with his thesis statement (revised, if necessary) in mind. Do they go together?

   Answers will vary.

2. Revise them if necessary so they are directly related.

3. Drop or rewrite any of the sentences in his body paragraphs that are not directly related to their topic sentences. *All sentences are directly related to their topic sentences.*

Organization

1. Read Tommy's essay again to see if all the paragraphs are arranged chronologically.

2. Move any paragraphs that are out of order. *All paragraphs are in order.*

3. Look closely at Tommy's body paragraphs to see if all his sentences are arranged logically within paragraphs.

4. Move any sentences that are out of order. *All sentences are in order.*

Coherence

1. Circle five words or phrases Tommy repeats. *Answers will vary.*

2. Explain how two of these make Tommy's essay easier to read.

_____

_____

Now rewrite Tommy's essay with your revisions.

EDITING CHECKLIST ✔

SENTENCES

✔ Does each sentence have a main subject and verb?

✔ Do all subjects and verbs agree?

✔ Do all pronouns agree with their nouns?

✔ Are modifiers as close as possible to the words they modify?

PUNCTUATION AND MECHANICS

✔ Are sentences punctuated correctly?

✔ Are words capitalized properly?

WORD CHOICE AND SPELLING

✔ Are words used correctly?

✔ Are words spelled correctly?

EDITING STRATEGIES
This chapter focuses on the following editing problems:

Fragments
Pronoun agreement
End punctuation

Sentences

Subjects and Verbs

For help with subjects and verbs, see Chapter 34.

1. Underline the subjects once and verbs twice in paragraph 4 of your revision of Tommy's essay. Remember that sentences can have more than one subject-verb set.

2. Does each of the sentences have at least one subject and verb that can stand alone?

    No

For help with fragments, see Chapter 35.

3. Did you find and correct Tommy's fragment? If not, find and correct it now. *Paragraph 4, sentence 5*

Subject-Verb Agreement

For help with subject-verb agreement, see Chapter 39.

1. Read aloud the subjects and verbs you underlined in your revision of Tommy's essay.

2. Correct any subjects and verbs that do not agree with each other. *All subjects and verbs agree.*

Pronoun Agreement

For help with pronoun agreement, see Chapter 43.

1. Find any pronouns in your revision of Tommy's essay that do not agree with their nouns.

2. Did you find and correct the two pronouns that do not agree with their nouns? If not, find and correct them now. *Paragraph 2, sentence 5; paragraph 5, sentence 7*

Modifiers

For help with modifier errors, see Chapter 46.

1. Find any modifiers in your revision of Tommy's essay that are not as close as possible to the words they modify. *There are no modifier errors.*

2. Rewrite sentences if necessary so that modifiers are as close as possible to the words they modify.

Punctuation and Mechanics

Punctuation

For help with punctuation, see Chapters 47–51.

1. Read your revision of Tommy's essay for any errors in punctuation.

2. Find the fragment you revised, and make sure it is punctuated correctly.

3. Did you find and correct Tommy's two other punctuation errors? *Paragraph 2, sentence 6; paragraph 3, sentence 4*

Mechanics

1. Read your revision of Tommy's essay for any errors in capitalization. *There are no capitalization errors.*
2. Be sure to check Tommy's capitalization in the fragment you revised.

For help with capitalization, see Chapter 52.

Word Choice and Spelling

Word Choice

1. Find any words used incorrectly in your revision of Tommy's essay. *All words are used correctly.*
2. Correct any errors you find.

For help with confused words, see Chapter 58.

Spelling

1. Use spell-check and a dictionary to check the spelling in your revision of Tommy's essay. *All words are spelled correctly.*
2. Correct any misspelled words.

For help with spelling, see Chapter 59.

Now rewrite Tommy's essay again with your editing corrections.

WORKING WITH YOUR OWN ESSAY

Returning to the narration you wrote earlier in this chapter, revise and edit your own writing. The checklists here will help you apply what you have learned to your essay.

Revising and Editing Your Own Essay

REVISING CHECKLIST ✔

THESIS STATEMENT

☐ Does the thesis statement contain the essay's controlling idea and an opinion about that idea?

☐ Does the thesis appear as the last sentence of the introduction?

BASIC ELEMENTS

☐ Does the title draw in the readers?

☐ Does the introduction capture the readers' attention and build up to the thesis statement effectively?

CLASS ACTIVITY
Provide students with an essay that is missing part of the five Ws and one H and has few descriptive details. In groups of three or four, have the students fill in the gaps to make the story more vivid and interesting.

☐ Does each body paragraph deal with a single topic?

☐ Does the conclusion bring the essay to a close in an interesting way?

DEVELOPMENT

☐ Do the body paragraphs adequately support the thesis statement?

☐ Does each body paragraph have a focused topic sentence?

☐ Does each body paragraph contain *specific* details that support the topic sentence?

☐ Does each body paragraph include *enough* details to explain the topic sentence fully?

UNITY

☐ Do the essay's topic sentences relate directly to the thesis statement?

☐ Do the details in each body paragraph support its topic sentence?

ORGANIZATION

☐ Is the essay organized logically?

☐ Is each body paragraph organized logically?

COHERENCE

☐ Are transitions used effectively so that paragraphs move smoothly and logically from one to the next?

☐ Do the sentences move smoothly and logically from one to the next?

Thesis Statement

1. What is the main point of your essay?

2. What is your opinion about the main point?

3. Put brackets around the last sentence in your introduction. Does it contain your main point and your opinion about that point?

4. Rewrite your thesis statement if necessary so that it states your main point and your opinion.

Basic Elements

1. Give your essay a title if it doesn't have one.

    _____

2. Does your introduction capture your readers' attention and build up to your thesis statement at the end of the paragraph?

    _____

3. Does each of your body paragraphs deal with only one topic?

    _____

4. Does your conclusion follow some of the suggestions offered in Part I?

    _____

Development

1. Write out your thesis statement (revised, if necessary), and list your topic sentences below it.

    Thesis statement: _____

    Topic 1: _____

    Topic 2: _____

    Topic 3: _____

2. Do your topics adequately support your thesis statement?

    _____

3. Does each body paragraph have a focused topic sentence?

    _____

4. Record at least one detail you use in response to each journalistic question.

    Who? _____

What? _____

When? _____

Where? _____

Why? _____

How? _____

5. Add at least two new details to your essay that support your main idea.

Unity

1. Read each of your topic sentences with your thesis statement in mind. Do they go together?

   _____

2. Revise them if necessary so they are directly related.
3. Drop or rewrite any of the sentences in your body paragraphs that are not directly related to their topic sentences.

Organization

1. Read your essay again to see if all the paragraphs are arranged logically.
2. Refer to your answers to the development questions. Then identify your method of organization:

   _____

3. Is the order you chose for your paragraphs the most effective approach to your topic?

   _____

4. Move any paragraphs that are out of order.
5. Look closely at your body paragraphs to see if all the sentences are arranged logically within paragraphs.
6. Move any sentences that are out of order.

Coherence

1. Circle five words or phrases you repeat.
2. Explain how two of these make your essay easier to read.

_____

_____

Now rewrite your essay with your revisions.

EDITING CHECKLIST ✔

SENTENCES

☐ Does each sentence have a main subject and verb?

☐ Do all subjects and verbs agree?

☐ Do all pronouns agree with their nouns?

☐ Are modifiers as close as possible to the words they modify?

PUNCTUATION AND MECHANICS

☐ Are sentences punctuated correctly?

☐ Are words capitalized properly?

WORD CHOICE AND SPELLING

☐ Are words used correctly?

☐ Are words spelled correctly?

Sentences

Subjects and Verbs

1. Underline the subjects once and verbs twice in a paragraph of your revised essay. Remember that sentences can have more than one subject-verb set.

2. Does each of your sentences have at least one subject and verb that can stand alone?

_____

3. Correct any fragments you have written.
4. Correct any run-together sentences you have written.

For help with subjects and verbs, see Chapter 34.

For help with fragments, see Chapter 35.

For help with run-togethers, see Chapter 36.

Subject-Verb Agreement

For help with subject-verb agreement, see Chapter 39.

1. Read aloud the subjects and verbs you underlined in your revised essay.
2. Correct any subjects and verbs that do not agree.

Pronoun Agreement

For help with pronoun agreement, see Chapter 43.

1. Find any pronouns in your revised essay that do not agree with their nouns.
2. Correct any pronouns that do not agree with their nouns.

Modifiers

For help with modifier errors, see Chapter 46.

1. Find any modifiers in your revised essay that are not as close as possible to the words they modify.
2. Rewrite sentences if necessary so that your modifiers are as close as possible to the words they modify.

Punctuation and Mechanics
Punctuation

For help with punctuation, see Chapters 47–51.

1. Read your revised essay for any errors in punctuation.
2. Make sure any fragments and run-together sentences you revised are punctuated correctly.

Mechanics

For help with capitalization, see Chapter 52.

1. Read your revised essay for any errors in capitalization.
2. Be sure to check your capitalization in any fragments or run-together sentences you revised.

Word Choice and Spelling
Word Choice

For help with confused words, see Chapter 58.

1. Find any words used incorrectly in your revised essay.
2. Correct any errors you find.

Spelling

For help with spelling, see Chapter 59.

1. Use spell-check and a dictionary to check your spelling.
2. Correct any misspelled words.

Now rewrite your essay again with your editing corrections.

PRACTICING NARRATION

Reading Suggestions

In Chapter 26, you will find two essays that illustrate good narrative writing: "The Sanctuary of School," in which Lynda Barry tells a story about using her school as an escape from her home life, and "Writer's Retreat" by Stan Higgins, which talks about his life as a writer in prison. You might want to read these selections before writing another narration essay. As you read, notice how the writers cover the journalistic questions and use vivid descriptive details to pull you into their narratives, making the main point of the essays all the more meaningful.

Service Learning Project

This assignment is based on a Service Learning project of your choice. If your instructor has already introduced service learning to the class, you will be doing these exercises when they are assigned. At this point, choose a project you would like to pursue, or continue work on a project you have already begun. This assignment in Part II will help you prepare for an essay on this project in Part III. Here is another stage in the preparation for this essay:

For the Service Learning project you have taken on, tell a story about a specific aspect of your community project. Make sure your story has a point. Use the guidelines you have learned in this chapter to help you write your narrative. But remember that these are just thoughts that will be developed into an essay in Part III.

Writing Workshop

Guidelines for Writing a Narration Essay

1. Make sure your essay has a point.
2. Use the five *W*s and one *H* to construct your story.
3. Develop your narrative with vivid details.
4. Build excitement in your narrative with careful pacing.
5. Organize your narration so that your readers can easily follow it.

---

1. Place yourself in the scene pictured on the next page, and write a narrative about what is happening. How did you get here? Why are you here? Where are you going from here? Be sure to decide on a main point before you begin to write.

SERVICE LEARNING PROJECT
This assignment is another step in the Service Learning project. If you choose to use this feature of the text, each chapter in Part II has an assignment that asks students to use a different rhetorical mode to reflect on their Service Learning project. These reflections will lead to an essay assignment in Part III (Chapter 22). You can assign as many or as few of these exercises as you want in preparation for this essay. For more information on service learning, see the *Instructor's Resource Manual*, Section I, Part III.

ADDITIONAL WRITING TOPIC
Have your students turn to Chapter 26 and read Lynda Barry's "Sanctuary of School" or Stan Higgins's "Writer's Retreat." Then ask them to write an essay on one of the topics from "Writing Topics: Narrating" at the end of the chapter.

2. Your old high school has asked you, as a graduate, to submit an essay to the newsletter recalling a job or volunteer experience that you enjoyed. The editors want to inform current high school students about options for volunteer and paid work. Your purpose is to tell your story in enough interesting detail so that you convince the current high school students that the job you had is worth looking into.

3. Your college class is putting together a collection of essays that explain how classmates decided to go to their college. What happened first? When did you decide? What helped you decide? What activities or people influenced your decision the most? Tell your story in vivid detail.

4. Create your own narration assignment (with the help of your instructor), and write a response to it.

Revising Workshop

Small Group Activity (5–10 minutes per writer)   Working in groups of three or four, each person should read his or her narration essay to the other members of the group. Those listening should record their reactions on a copy of the Peer Evaluation Form in Appendix 2B. After your group goes through this process, give your evaluation forms to the appropriate writers so that each writer has two peer comment sheets for revising.

Paired Activity (5 minutes per writer)   Using the completed Peer Evaluation Forms, work in pairs to decide what you should revise in your essay. If time allows, rewrite some of your sentences, and have your partner look at them.

Individual Activity   Rewrite your paper, using the revising feedback you received from other students.

Editing Workshop

Paired Activity (5–10 minutes per writer)   Swap papers with a classmate, and use the editing portion of your Peer Evaluation Form to identify as many grammar, punctuation, mechanics, and spelling errors as you can. If time allows, correct some of your errors, and have your partner look at them. Record your grammar, punctuation, and mechanics errors in the Error Log (Appendix 6) and your spelling errors in the Spelling Log (Appendix 7).

Individual Activity   Rewrite your paper again, using the editing feedback you received from other students.

Reflecting on Your Writing

When you have completed your own essay, answer these six questions.

1. What was most difficult about this assignment?

2. What was easiest?

3. What did you learn about narration by completing this assignment?

4. What do you think are the strengths of your narration? Place a wavy line by the parts of your essay that you feel are very good.

5. What are the weaknesses, if any, of your paper? Place an X by the parts of your essay you would like help with. Write any questions you have in the margin.

6. What did you learn from this assignment about your own writing process—about preparing to write, about writing the first draft, about revising, and about editing?

TEACHING ON THE WEB

Research: Have students search online for Web sites that teach how to write novels or short stories for future publication. What advice do these Web sites give that will help students learn more about narration?

TEACHING ON THE WEB

Mosaics Web Site: To learn more about narration, students can go to www. prenhall.com/mosaics.

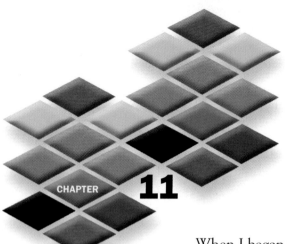

CHAPTER **11**

ILLUSTRATING

When I began to write, I found it was the best way to
make sense out of my life.

—JOHN CHEEVER

TEACHING
ILLUSTRATION
Provide students
with a concept like
"generation gaps," and
ask them to find as
many examples of the
concept in the media as
possible—both where
it is present and where
it is not. They can
look on billboards, in
magazines, in movies,
on TV, and so on.
    Have students make
a list of where they find
examples and where
examples are conspicu-
ously missing. Which
types of media show
the most examples?
Which show the least?
Why do your students
think this is so?

Giving examples to make a point is a natural part of communication. For
example, if you are trying to demonstrate how much time you waste, you
can cite the fact that you talk on the phone about two hours every day. Or
to tell your friends how much fun you are having, you might say, "College is
great because no one tells me what to do or when to go to bed. I am completely on my own." The message is in the examples you choose.

We also use examples every day to make various points in our writing.
Think about the following situations that take place in our personal lives, at
school, and at work.

In a letter to your parents, you tell them how hard you are studying
in college by giving them examples of your weekend study schedule.

A student gives examples of gestures, facial expressions, and posture
in a paper on nonverbal communication for a psychology course.

A student answers a sociology exam question by giving examples
to show how children are integrated into society.

A human resource director of a large company writes a memo on
sexual harassment in the workplace, including examples of inappro-
priate behavior.

The owner of a catering business writes a brochure listing examples
of dinners available in different price ranges.

An example is an **illustration** of the point you want to make. Well-
chosen examples, then, are the building blocks of an illustration essay. You
draw examples from your experience, your observations, and your reading.
They help you show rather than tell what you mean, usually by supplying

concrete details (what you see, hear, touch, smell, or taste) to support abstract ideas (such as faith, hope, understanding, and love), by providing specifics ("I like chocolate") to explain generalizations ("I like sweets"), and by giving definite references ("Turn left at the second stoplight") to clarify vague statements ("Turn left in a few blocks").

Not only do examples help you make your point, but they also add interest to your writing. Would you like to read an essay stating that being a server in a restaurant is a lot harder than it looks? Or would you be more interested in reading an essay describing what it is like having to serve too many tables, carrying heavy trays, taking the wrong order to a table, and dealing with rude customers? The first statement tells, but vivid examples show your readers the point you want to make.

WRITING AN ILLUSTRATION ESSAY

In her essay "Hold the Mayonnaise," Julia Alvarez uses examples to explain the difficulties involved in blending two cultures—American and Latino—in a stepfamily. Have you ever visited a foreign country? What was it like to be in a different culture? Have you ever been part of a group that blended two or more cultures? What did you learn?

HOLD THE MAYONNAISE

by Julia Alvarez

"If I die first and Papi ever gets remarried," Mami used to tease when   1
we were kids, "don't you accept a new woman in my house. Make her life impossible, you hear?" My sisters and I nodded obediently and a filial shudder would go through us. We were Catholics, so, of course, the only kind of remarriage we could imagine had to involve our mother's death.

We were also Dominicans, recently arrived in Jamaica, Queens, in   2
the early '60s, before waves of other Latin Americans began arriving. So, when we imagined whom exactly my father might possibly ever think of remarrying, only American women came to mind. It would be bad enough having a *madrastra*, but a "stepmother. . . ."

All I could think of was that she would make me eat mayonnaise, a food   3
which I identified with the United States and which I detested. Mami understood, of course, that I wasn't used to that kind of food. Even a *madrastra*, accustomed to our rice and beans and *tostones* and *pollo frito*, would understand. But an American stepmother would think it was normal

to put mayonnaise on food, and if she were at all strict and a little mean, which all stepmothers, of course, were, she would make me eat potato salad and such. I had plenty of my own reasons to make a potential stepmother's life impossible. When I nodded obediently with my sisters, I was imagining not just something foreign in our house, but in our refrigerator.

4   So it's strange now, almost 35 years later, to find myself a Latina stepmother of my husband's two tall, strapping, blond, mayonnaise-eating daughters. To be honest, neither of them is a real aficionado of the condiment, but it's a fair thing to add to a bowl of tuna fish or diced potatoes. Their American food, I think of it, and when they head to their mother's or off to school, I push the jar back in the refrigerator behind their chocolate pudding and several open cans of Diet Coke.

5   What I can't push as successfully out of sight are my own immigrant childhood fears of having a *gringa* stepmother with foreign tastes in our house. Except now, I am the foreign stepmother in a *gringa* household. I've wondered what my husband's two daughters think of this stranger in their family. It must be doubly strange for them that I am from another culture.

6   Of course, there are mitigating circumstances—my husband's two daughters were teenagers when we married, older, more mature, able to understand differences. They had also traveled when they were children with their father, an eye doctor, who worked on short-term international projects with various eye foundations. But still, it's one thing to visit a foreign country, another altogether to find it brought home—a real bear plopped down in a Goldilocks house.

7   Sometimes, it's a whole extended family of bears. My warm, loud Latino family came up for the wedding: my *tía* from Santo Domingo; three dramatic, enthusiastic sisters and their families; my papi, with a thick accent I could tell the girls found it hard to understand; and my mami, who had her eye trained on my soon-to-be stepdaughters for any sign that they were about to make my life impossible. "How are they behaving themselves?" she asked me, as if they were 7 and 3, not 19 and 16. "They're wonderful girls," I replied, already feeling protective of them.

8   I looked around for the girls in the meadow in front of the house we were building, where we were holding the outdoor wedding ceremony and party. The oldest hung out with a group of her own friends. The younger one whizzed in briefly for the ceremony, then left again before the congratulations started up. There was not much mixing with me and mine. What was there for them to celebrate on a day so full of confusion and effort?

9   On my side, being the newcomer in someone else's territory is a role I'm used to. I can tap into that struggling English speaker, that skinny, dark-haired, olive-skinned girl in a sixth grade of mostly blond and

blue-eyed giants. Those tall, freckled boys would push me around in the playground. "Go back to where you came from!" *"No comprendo!"* I'd reply, though of course there was no misunderstanding the fierce looks on their faces.

Even now, my first response to a scowl is that old pulling away. (My hus-   10
band calls it "checking out.") I remember times early on in the marriage when the girls would be with us, and I'd get out of school and drive around doing errands, killing time, until my husband, their father, would be leaving work. I am not proud of my fears, but I understand—as the lingo goes—where they come from.

And I understand, more than I'd like to sometimes, my stepdaughters'   11
pain. But with me, they need never fear that I'll usurp a mother's place. No one has ever come up and held their faces and then addressed me, "They look just like you." If anything, strangers to the remarriage are probably playing Mr. Potato Head in their minds, trying to figure out how my foreign features and my husband's fair Nebraskan features got put together into these two tall, blond girls. "My husband's daughters," I kept introducing them.

Once, when one of them visited my class and I introduced her as such,   12
two students asked me why. "I'd be so hurt if my stepmom introduced me that way," the young man said. That night I told my stepdaughter what my students had said. She scowled at me and agreed. "It's so weird how you call me Papa's daughter. Like you don't want to be related to me or something."

"I didn't want to presume," I explained. "So it's O.K. if I call you my   13
stepdaughter?"

"That's what I am," she said. Relieved, I took it for a teensy inch of ac-   14
ceptance. The takings are small in this stepworld, I've discovered—sort of like being a minority. It feels as if all the goodies have gone somewhere else.

Day to day, I guess I follow my papi's advice. When we first came, he   15
would talk to his children about how to make it in our new country. "Just do your work and put in your heart, and they will accept you!" In this age of remaining true to your roots, of keeping your Spanish, of fighting from inside your culture, that assimilationist approach is highly suspect. My Latino students—who don't want to be called Hispanics anymore—would ditch me as faculty adviser if I came up with that play-nice message.

But in a stepfamily where everyone is starting a new life together, it   16
isn't bad advice. Like a potluck supper, an American concept my mami never took to. ("Why invite people to your house and then ask them to bring the food?") You put what you've got together with what everyone else

brought and see what comes out of the pot. The luck part is if everyone brings something you like—no potato salad, no deviled eggs, no little party sandwiches with you know what in them.

  PREPARING TO WRITE YOUR OWN ILLUSTRATION ESSAY

When did you last try something new in your life? Was it difficult? Did you plan this new experience, or did it just happen? Do you like new experiences, or do you prefer keeping your life routine? Use one or more of the prewriting strategies you learned in Chapter 2 to recall several times you tried something new, planned or not. Then think about the positive and negative aspects of trying new experiences. What value do they have in your life? What are the disadvantages of trying new experiences?

INSTRUCTOR'S
RESOURCE MANUAL
For additional material about teaching illustration; for journal entries; and for multiple-choice, short-answer, and paragraph tests, see the *Instructor's Resource Manual,* Section II, Part II.

How to Write an Illustration Essay

In the art world, a good illustrator is someone who makes an image or an idea come alive with the perfect drawing. The same principle applies in writing: Someone who uses illustrations, or examples, effectively makes an essay or other piece of writing come alive. Moreover, in college, most essay exam questions are based on illustration—finding the best examples to support your main point. Here are some guidelines to help you use examples effectively:

1. *State your main point and your opinion about that point in the last sentence of your introduction.* Write a thesis statement that clearly and plainly states the main idea of your essay, and place it at the end of your introduction. This is the controlling idea of your essay and should consist of a limited subject and your opinion about that subject. You will explain this main point through the examples you furnish in the following body paragraphs.

   In the sample essay, Alvarez's introduction is two paragraphs long. She expresses her main point in the last sentence of the second paragraph: "It would be bad enough having a *madrastra,* but a 'stepmother.'" She introduces this idea as the focus of her essay, including her opinion ("bad enough"), and then explains it with examples.

Through her examples, the author is talking about her new family as much as her fears as a child.

2. ***Choose examples that are relevant to your point.*** In an illustration essay, examples serve as the writer's explanation. Well-chosen examples are an essay's building blocks. They help you prove your point and must directly support the point you are trying to make. Examples that are not relevant are distracting, causing readers to lose their train of thought. Your readers will appreciate the point you are making not because you tell them what to think but because you show them with relevant examples what you are trying to say. Keep in mind, too, that the more specific your examples are, the more likely your readers are to agree with your point.

Finding relevant examples is a fairly easy task. The best examples often come from your own experience and observation. You can also draw examples from your reading—books, newspapers, magazines. In addition, as technology advances, more and more information is available online, making the Internet a good place to find examples for an illustration essay.

In Alvarez's essay, all of her examples focus on how difficult the role of stepmother is. Since Alvarez's point has to do with merging two cultures in a stepfamily, her examples refer to either her Dominican experience or her stepdaughters' American experience. Alvarez uses her dislike of mayonnaise to help her illustrate some of the differences people have to deal with when they combine cultures. These focused examples make her essay coherent and unified.

3. ***Choose examples that your readers can identify with.*** To do this, you need to know as much as possible about your audience. Once you know who your readers are, you can tailor your examples to them. In this way, your readers are most likely to follow your line of reasoning. Suppose, for instance, that you want your parents to finance an off-campus apartment for you. You are not likely to make your point by citing examples of European universities that do not provide any student housing because this is not an example that American parents can identify with. You need to furnish examples that address your specific situation.

Alvarez's essay was first published in the *New York Times*, so she chose examples that a diverse group of educated people would relate to. She knew that many of these readers would also be parents, so they would understand the issue of merging families and cultures. In that way, she could keep the attention of her readers for her entire essay and get them to sympathize with her particular point of view.

4. *Use a sufficient number of examples to make your point.* Nobody has a set formula for determining the perfect number of examples, because that depends on the point you are trying to make. Sometimes several short examples will make your point best. Or perhaps three or four fairly detailed examples—each in its own body paragraph—work best. At other times the most effective way to develop an essay is with a single extended example. Usually, however, three or four examples are sufficient. If you are in doubt whether to add another example or more vivid details, you should probably do so. Most students err on the side of using too few examples or not adding enough detail to their examples.

Alvarez opens her essay with a fairly extended example (three paragraphs) to show her dislike of mayonnaise and stepmothers. Later, in paragraph 7, she provides four short examples—all in one sentence—of how her stepdaughters might find her Dominican family difficult to be around. In paragraphs 9 and 11 through 14, Alvarez develops her examples in single paragraphs. She also tries to put herself in her stepdaughters' place. Overall, she gives enough examples from many perspectives so that we understand the complexity and importance of the point she is making. These different types of examples give her essay variety and make it interesting.

5. *Organize your examples to make your point in the clearest, strongest way.* When you have gathered enough relevant examples, you are ready to organize them into an essay. Most illustration essays are organized from general to particular (from a general statement—the thesis—to specific examples that support the general statement) or chronologically (according to a time sequence).

The examples themselves must also be organized within their paragraphs in some logical way—chronologically, spatially, or by extremes. Which example should come first? Second? Last? The simple act of arranging examples can help you and your reader make sense of an experience or idea. Use basic logic to guide you to different patterns.

Alvarez opens her essay with a childhood memory (fearing a stepmother), moves to present time (she's now a stepmother), and then looks back at episodes in her life and her stepdaughters' lives that show how blending two cultures can be difficult. For every point she makes, she provides an example. Overall, her organization is chronological, though someone else might have arranged these examples a different way.

WRITING YOUR OWN ILLUSTRATION ESSAY

Based on the prewriting that you did earlier, write an essay about three new experiences you have had. Which were planned? Which were unplanned? Did they affect you in positive ways? In negative ways? Or were the outcomes mixed? What did you learn from these experiences? Draft a thesis statement. Then write a first draft of your essay, including an introduction and a conclusion. Use examples in your body paragraphs to support your thesis statement.

WORKING WITH A STUDENT ESSAY

In the following essay, student writer Taleah Trainor uses examples to explain her relationship with Murphy's Law. As you read this draft of her essay, try to find Taleah's main point.

Murphy's Law

Murphy's Law: If something can go wrong, it will. I have always been familiar with the concept of this law, but never from actual experience. It was not until the summer before my first year in college that different events taught me about Murphy's Law.

The first event was when my father informed me that on our family trip to Washington D.C. we would be using my car. Since I had made previous plans I was not bubbling with enthusiasm. I had 14 "fun-filled" days in D.C. And to top it all off, on the way home from D.C., my car decided to have a breakdown between two Louisiana towns. Louisiana has a really long stretch of highway that driver's hate. People feel like they're on it forever. Luckily, my father had AAA, our delay was short.

This particular instance had familiarized me with Murphy's Law, and for the remainder of the summer, I began to notice it every time I turned around. At first it was little things like catching the flu just hours before a date. After a while, it turned into bigger hassles, like getting flat tires on the way to job interviews. I prayed my luck would take a turn for the better rather then the worse.

Murphy showed up again on August 29, when I left my hometown to travel to my new school. Having to entrust my 397-mile journey to an old AAA map, I pictured getting sidetracked onto an out-of-the-way farm road leading me to an uncharted town. But I did not get lost until arriving

1

2

3

4

TEACHING TIPS
The following eight teaching tips are based on Howard Gardner's multiple intelligences:

Verbal/Linguistic
Have students create lists of every example they can think of on a topic of their choice (such as teen pregnancy, air pollution, or aerobic exercise). How many can they come up with?

Musical/Rhythmic
Choose a word such as "rejection" or "love," and have students find examples of the term in at least three different pieces of music.

Logical/ Mathematical
Provide students with a list of examples on at least two different topics. Have students

sort the examples into
categories to determine
which specifics go with
which topic. Include
examples that don't fit
either topic.

Visual/Spatial
Provide each student
with an art book, and
assign a topic such as
"peace." Then have
students find examples
from many different
artistic time periods
that portray the topic.

Bodily/Kinesthetic
Divide students into
groups of three, and
send them on a pseudo
scavenger hunt around
your campus to find
examples of items that
relate to athletics. The
students should list the
items and their loca-
tions. The group that
brings back the longest
list wins.

Intrapersonal
Have students reflect
on times when they
realized that they think
best when they are
alone. What examples
can help them show
that this is true?

Interpersonal
Have a small group of
students think of a
current issue affecting
your city or state. How
does the group think
the issue should be
resolved? Have the
students provide as
many examples as

at the infamous "traffic circle" in my new home town. Realizing my highway map was of know use in town, I frantically looked around and happened to catch a glimpse of the "I ♥ Bulldogs" bumper sticker plastered
on the car in front of me. I said to myself, "Now how many cars could have
<u>that</u> sticker?" I convinced myself that I was in luck and that the car in
front of me was headed toward campus. I decided to follow it. After arriving in a gruesome alley, which accurately resembled the pictures I had
seen of a Third World country, I came to the conclusion the car was not
headed toward campus but probably to the local chicken fights. Pulling
in to the nearest Texaco station, directions were given to me. Three service stations later, their I was, at my new dorm on campus. Once again, I
knew that Murphy's Law had decided to play with me.

5   I realized Murphy's Law was becoming a permanent part of my life. If
something in my life could possibly go wrong, Murphy would be there to
make sure of it. I had finally come to the conclusion that Murphy, and I
would be friends for life—unless, of course, something went wrong.

Discovering How the Essay Works

1. What main idea do you think Taleah is trying to communicate in this
   essay?

   Murphy's Law is going to haunt her forever.

   Does her thesis communicate this main idea?

   It could be stronger.

2. How is each of Taleah's examples related to her main point? List
   three examples she furnishes, and explain how they are related to her
   thesis statement. *Answers will vary.*

3. Knowing that this essay was written for her college writing class, do
   you think Taleah's audience could identify with these examples?
   Explain your answer. *Answers will vary.*

possible to help illustrate their views.

Naturalist
Have students recall times they have spent outdoors and determine how they feel about being out in nature. Have them provide numerous examples that illustrate why they feel the way they do.

4. Does Taleah include enough examples to make her point? Explain your answer.

   Yes, except in paragraph 3.

5. How are the examples in Taleah's essay arranged? List some of her examples in the order they appear; then identify her method of organization. *Answers may vary.*

   going to D.C., having to change plans   *flat tires before job interviews*

   car breakdown between two Louisiana towns   *getting lost in new town*

   getting flu before a date   *ending up in a strange alley*

   Method of organization: *chronological*

Revising and Editing the Student Essay

This essay is Taleah's first draft, which now needs to be revised and edited. First, apply the Revising Checklist below to the content of Taleah's draft. When you are satisfied that her ideas are fully developed and well organized, use the Editing Checklist on page 175 to correct her grammar and mechanics errors. Answer the questions after each checklist. Then write your suggested changes directly on Taleah's draft.

REVISING AND EDITING OPTIONS
Consider varying your approach to revising and editing. You could teach these skills in a class discussion, in small groups, or in pairs.

REVISING CHECKLIST ✔

THESIS STATEMENT
✔ Does the thesis statement contain the essay's controlling idea and an opinion about that idea?
✔ Does the thesis appear as the last sentence of the introduction?

BASIC ELEMENTS
✔ Does the title draw in the readers?
✔ Does the introduction capture the readers' attention and build up to the thesis statement effectively?

REVISING STRATEGIES
This chapter focuses on the following revising elements:
Thesis statement
Basic elements
Development
Unity

✔ Does each body paragraph deal with a single topic?

✔ Does the conclusion bring the essay to a close in an interesting way?

DEVELOPMENT

✔ Do the body paragraphs adequately support the thesis statement?

✔ Does each body paragraph have a focused topic sentence?

✔ Does each body paragraph contain *specific* details that support the topic sentence?

✔ Does each body paragraph include *enough* details to explain the topic sentence fully?

UNITY

✔ Do the essay's topic sentences relate directly to the thesis statement?

✔ Do the details in each body paragraph support its topic sentence?

ORGANIZATION

✔ Is the essay organized logically?

✔ Is each body paragraph organized logically?

COHERENCE

✔ Are transitions used effectively so that paragraphs move smoothly and logically from one to the next?

✔ Do the sentences move smoothly and logically from one to the next?

Thesis Statement

1. Put brackets around the last sentence in Taleah's introduction. Does it introduce her main point? Does it include her opinion about that point?

   It could be a little stronger.

2. Rewrite Taleah's thesis statement if necessary so that it states her main point and her opinion about that point.

   Here is one possibility: It wasn't until my first year in college that I

   realized Murphy's Law would constantly disrupt my life.

Basic Elements

1. Give Taleah's essay an alternate title.

    Answers will vary.

2. Rewrite Taleah's introduction so that it captures the readers' attention and builds up to the thesis statement at the end of the paragraph.

    Answers will vary.

3. Does each of Taleah's body paragraphs deal with only one topic?

    Yes

4. Rewrite Taleah's conclusion using at least one suggestion from Part I.

    Answers will vary.

Development

1. Write out Taleah's thesis statement (revised, if necessary), and list her three topic sentences below it. *Thesis may vary.*

    Thesis statement: *It wasn't until my first year in college that I realized that Murphy's Law would constantly disrupt my life.*

    Topic 1: *The first event was when my father informed me that on our family trip to Washington D.C. we would be using my car.*

    Topic 2: *This particular instance had familiarized me with Murphy's Law, and for the remainder of the summer, I began to notice it every time I turned around.*

Topic 3: _Murphy showed up again on August 29, when I left my home town to travel to my new school._

2. Do Taleah's topics adequately support her thesis statement?

   Yes

3. Does each body paragraph have a focused topic sentence?

   Yes

4. Are Taleah's examples specific?

   Answers will vary.

   Add another more specific detail to one of the examples in her essay.

5. Does she offer enough examples to make her point?

   Answers will vary.

   Add at least one new example to strengthen Taleah's essay.

Unity

1. Read each of Taleah's topic sentences with her thesis statement (revised, if necessary) in mind. Do they go together?

   Answers will vary.

2. Revise them if necessary so they are directly related.
3. Drop or rewrite the two sentences in paragraph 2 that are not directly related to their topic sentence. _Sentences 5 and 6_

Organization

1. Read Taleah's essay again to see if all the paragraphs are arranged logically.
2. Move any paragraphs that are out of order. _All paragraphs are in order._
3. Look closely at Taleah's body paragraphs to see if all her sentences are arranged logically within paragraphs.
4. Move any sentences that are out of order. _All sentences are in order._

Coherence

1. Circle five transitions, repetitions, synonyms, or pronouns Taleah uses.
2. Explain how two of these make Taleah's essay easier to read.

    Answers will vary.

For a list of transitions, see pages 83–84.

For a list of pronouns, see pages 508–509.

Now rewrite Taleah's essay with your revisions.

EDITING CHECKLIST ✔

SENTENCES
- ✔ Does each sentence have a main subject and verb?
- ✔ Do all subjects and verbs agree?
- ✔ Do all pronouns agree with their nouns?
- ✔ Are modifiers as close as possible to the words they modify?

PUNCTUATION AND MECHANICS
- ✔ Are sentences punctuated correctly?
- ✔ Are words capitalized properly?

WORD CHOICE AND SPELLING
- ✔ Are words used correctly?
- ✔ Are words spelled correctly?

EDITING STRATEGIES

This chapter focuses on the following editing problems:

   Run-togethers
   Modifier errors
   Commas
   Confused words

Sentences

Subjects and Verbs

1. Underline the subjects once and verbs twice in paragraph 2 of your revision of Taleah's essay. Remember that sentences can have more than one subject-verb set.

For help with subjects and verbs, see Chapter 34.

2. Does each of Taleah's sentences have at least one subject and verb that can stand alone?

    No

For help with run-togethers, see Chapter 36.

3. Did you find and correct Taleah's run-together sentence? If not, find and correct it now. *Paragraph 2, sentence 7*

Subject-Verb Agreement

For help with subject-verb agreement, see Chapter 39.

1. Read aloud the subjects and verbs you underlined in your revision of Taleah's essay.

2. Correct any subjects and verbs that do not agree. *All subjects and verbs agree.*

Pronoun Agreement

For help with pronoun agreement, see Chapter 43.

1. Find any pronouns in your revision of Taleah's essay that do not agree with their nouns. *All pronouns agree with their nouns.*

2. Correct any pronouns that do not agree with their nouns.

Modifiers

For help with modifier errors, see Chapter 46.

1. Find any modifiers in your revision of Taleah's essay that are not as close as possible to the words they modify.

2. Did you find and correct her dangling modifier? If not, find and correct it now. *Paragraph 4, sentence 9*

Punctuation and Mechanics

Punctuation

For help with punctuation, see Chapters 47–51.

1. Read your revision of Taleah's essay for any errors in punctuation.

2. Find the run-together sentence you revised, and make sure it is punctuated correctly.

3. Did you find and correct Taleah's two comma errors? *Paragraph 2, sentence 2; paragraph 5, sentence 3*

Mechanics

For help with capitalization, see Chapter 52.

1. Read your revision of Taleah's essay for any errors in capitalization.

2. Be sure to check Taleah's capitalization in the run-together sentence you revised.

Word Choice and Spelling

Word Choice

For help with confused words, see Chapter 58.

1. Find any words used incorrectly in your revision of Taleah's essay.

2. Did you find and correct the three confused words in Taleah's essay? If not, find and correct them now. *then/than (paragraph 3), know/no (paragraph 4), their/there (paragraph 4)*

Spelling

1. Use spell-check and a dictionary to check the spelling in your revision of Taleah's essay. *All words are spelled correctly.*

For help with spelling, see Chapter 59.

2. Correct any misspelled words.

   Now rewrite Taleah's essay again with your editing corrections.

 WORKING WITH YOUR OWN ESSAY

Returning to the illustration you wrote earlier in this chapter, revise and edit your own writing. The checklists here will help you apply what you have learned to your essay.

Revising and Editing Your Own Essay

REVISING CHECKLIST ✔

THESIS STATEMENT

☐ Does the thesis statement contain the essay's controlling idea and an opinion about that idea?

☐ Does the thesis appear as the last sentence of the introduction?

BASIC ELEMENTS

☐ Does the title draw in the readers?

☐ Does the introduction capture the readers' attention and build up to the thesis statement effectively?

☐ Does each body paragraph deal with a single topic?

☐ Does the conclusion bring the essay to a close in an interesting way?

DEVELOPMENT

☐ Do the body paragraphs adequately support the thesis statement?

☐ Does each body paragraph have a focused topic sentence?

☐ Does each body paragraph contain specific details that support the topic sentence?

☐ Does each body paragraph include enough details to explain the topic sentence fully?

CLASS ACTIVITY
Write a topic on the board, and have students provide examples that support the topic. Have class members fill the board with many ideas and then determine which examples would work best if they were going to write an illustration essay.

UNITY
- ☐ Do the essay's topic sentences relate directly to the thesis statement?
- ☐ Do the details in each body paragraph support its topic sentence?

ORGANIZATION
- ☐ Is the essay organized logically?
- ☐ Is each body paragraph organized logically?

COHERENCE
- ☐ Are transitions used effectively so that paragraphs move smoothly and logically from one to the next?
- ☐ Do the sentences move smoothly and logically from one to the next?

Thesis Statement

1. What is the main point you are trying to convey in your essay?

   _____

   _____

2. What is your opinion about that main point?

   _____

   _____

3. Put brackets around the last sentence in your introduction. Does it convey your main point and your opinion about that point?

   _____

4. Rewrite your thesis statement if necessary so that it states your main point and your opinion.

Basic Elements

1. Give your essay a title if it doesn't have one.

   _____

2. Does your introduction capture your readers' attention and build up to your thesis statement at the end of the paragraph?

   _____

3. Does each of your body paragraphs deal with only one topic?

   _____

4. Does your conclusion follow some of the suggestions offered in Part I?

   _____

Development

1. Write out your thesis statement (revised, if necessary), and list your topic sentences below it.

   Thesis statement: _____

   Topic 1: _____

   Topic 2: _____

   Topic 3: _____

2. Do your topics adequately support your thesis statement?

   _____

3. Does each body paragraph have a focused topic sentence?

   _____

4. Are your examples specific?

   _____

   Add another more specific detail to an example in your essay.

5. Do you give enough examples to make your point?

   _____

   Add at least one new example to your essay.

6. Can your readers identify with your examples?

_____

Unity

1. Read each of your topic sentences with your thesis statement in mind. Do they go together?

_____

2. Revise them if necessary so they are directly related.
3. Drop or rewrite any of the sentences in your body paragraphs that are not directly related to their topic sentences.

Organization

1. Read your essay again to see if all the paragraphs are arranged logically.
2. Refer to your answers to the development questions. Then identify your method of organization:

_____

3. Is the order you chose for your paragraphs the most effective approach to your topic?

_____

4. Move any paragraphs that are out of order.
5. Look closely at your body paragraphs to see if all the sentences are arranged logically within paragraphs.
6. Move any sentences that are out of order.

Coherence

For a list of transitions, see pages 83–84.

For a list of pronouns, see pages 508–509.

1. Circle five transitions, repetitions, synonyms, or pronouns you use.
2. Explain how two of these make your essay easier to read.

_____

_____

Now rewrite your essay with your revisions.

(E)DITING CHECKLIST ✔

SENTENCES

☐ Does each sentence have a main subject and verb?

☐ Do all subjects and verbs agree?

☐ Do all pronouns agree with their nouns?

☐ Are modifiers as close as possible to the words they modify?

PUNCTUATION AND MECHANICS

☐ Are sentences punctuated correctly?

☐ Are words capitalized properly?

WORD CHOICE AND SPELLING

☐ Are words used correctly?

☐ Are words spelled correctly?

Sentences

Subjects and Verbs

1. Underline the subjects once and verbs twice in a paragraph of your revised essay. Remember that sentences can have more than one subject-verb set.

2. Does each of your sentences have at least one subject and verb that can stand alone?

For help with subjects and verbs, see Chapter 34.

3. Correct any fragments you have written.

4. Correct any run-together sentences you have written.

For help with fragments, see Chapter 35.

For help with run-togethers, see Chapter 36.

Subject-Verb Agreement

1. Read aloud the subjects and verbs you underlined in your revised essay.

2. Correct any subjects and verbs that do not agree.

For help with subject-verb agreement, see Chapter 39.

Pronoun Agreement

1. Find any pronouns in your revised essay that do not agree with their nouns.

2. Correct any pronouns that do not agree with their nouns.

For help with pronoun agreement, see Chapter 43.

Modifiers

For help with modifier errors, see Chapter 46.

1. Find any modifiers in your revised essay that are not as close as possible to the words they modify.
2. Rewrite sentences if necessary so that your modifiers are as close as possible to the words they modify.

Punctuation and Mechanics

Punctuation

For help with punctuation, see Chapters 47–51.

1. Read your revised essay for any errors in punctuation.
2. Make sure any fragments and run-together sentences you revised are punctuated correctly.

Mechanics

For help with capitalization, see Chapter 52.

1. Read your revised essay for any errors in capitalization.
2. Be sure to check your capitalization in any fragments or run-together sentences you revised.

Word Choice and Spelling

Word Choice

For help with confused words, see Chapter 58.

1. Find any words used incorrectly in your revised essay.
2. Correct any errors you find.

Spelling

For help with spelling, see Chapter 59.

1. Use spell-check and a dictionary to check your spelling.
2. Correct any misspelled words.

   Now rewrite your essay again with your editing corrections.

PRACTICING ILLUSTRATION

Reading Suggestions

SERVICE LEARNING
PROJECT
This assignment is another step in the Service Learning project. If you choose to use this feature of the text, each chapter in Part II has an assignment that asks students

   In Chapter 27, you will find two essays that use examples to make their point: "I Just Wanna Be Average" by Mike Rose gives examples from his life to show the importance to him of being average, and "Getting to Know About You and Me" by Chana Schoenberger uses examples to talk about personal biases. You might want to read these selections before writing another illustration essay. As you read, notice how the writers use examples to support and advance their ideas.

Service Learning Project

This assignment is based on a Service Learning project of your choice. If your instructor has already introduced service learning to the class, you will be doing these exercises when they are assigned. At this point, choose a project you would like to pursue, or continue work on a project you have already begun. This assignment in Part II will help you prepare for an essay on this project in Part III. Here is another stage in the preparation for this essay:

For the Service Learning project you have taken on, record a point you want to make and then list as many examples as you can think of from your project that illustrate your point. Use the guidelines you have learned in this chapter to help you create your list. But remember that these are just thoughts that will be developed into an essay in Part III.

Writing Workshop

> **Guidelines for Writing an Illustration Essay**
>
> 1. State your main point in the last sentence of your introduction.
> 2. Choose examples that are relevant to your point.
> 3. Choose examples that your readers can identify with.
> 4. Use a sufficient number of examples to make your point.
> 5. Organize your examples to make your point in the clearest, strongest way.

1. Identify some common themes in this collage. Then come up with a thesis statement that explains the message of the collage. Write an essay to support your thesis that is developed with relevant examples

to use a different rhetorical mode to reflect on their Service Learning project. These reflections will lead to an essay assignment in Part III (Chapter 22). You can assign as many or as few of these exercises as you want in preparation for this essay. For more information on service learning, see the *Instructor's Resource Manual*, Section I, Part III.

ADDITIONAL WRITING TOPIC
Have your students turn to Chapter 27 and read Mike Rose's "I Just Wanna Be Average" or Chana Schoenberger's "Getting to Know About You and Me." Then ask them to write an essay on one of the topics from "Writing Topics: Illustrating" at the end of the chapter.

from the picture and from your own experience to support your thesis statement.

2. Share with your classmates your opinion on a national issue, such as capital punishment, abortion, or gun laws. Use examples in your body paragraphs to support your main point.

3. Why do you think Americans are interested in exercise and weight loss? What actions illustrate this attitude? Use examples or illustrations to explain your observations on the current interest in health and weight among Americans.

4. Create your own illustration assignment (with the help of your instructor), and write a response to it.

Revising Workshop

Small Group Activity (5–10 minutes per writer)   Working in groups of three or four, each person should read his or her illustration essay to the other members of the group. Those listening should record their reactions on a copy of the Peer Evaluation Form in Appendix 2C. After your group goes through this process, give your evaluation forms to the appropriate writers so that each writer has two or three peer comment sheets for revising.

Paired Activity (5 minutes per writer)   Using the completed Peer Evaluation Forms, work in pairs to decide what you should revise in your essay. If time allows, rewrite some of your sentences, and have your partner look at them.

Individual Activity   Rewrite your paper, using the revising feedback you received from other students.

Editing Workshop

Paired Activity (5–10 minutes per writer)   Swap papers with a classmate, and use the editing portion of your Peer Evaluation Form to identify as many grammar, punctuation, mechanics, and spelling errors as you can. If time allows, correct some of your errors, and have your partner look at them. Record your grammar, punctuation, and mechanics errors in the Error Log (Appendix 6) and your spelling errors in the Spelling Log (Appendix 7).

Individual Activity   Rewrite your paper again, using the editing feedback you received from other students.

Reflecting on Your Writing

When you have completed your own essay, answer these six questions.

1. What was most difficult about this assignment?

2. What was easiest?

3. What did you learn about illustration by completing this assignment?

4. What do you think are the strengths of your illustration? Place a wavy line by the parts of your essay that you feel are very good.

5. What are the weaknesses, if any, of your paper? Place an X by the parts of your essay you would like help with. Write any questions you have in the margin.

6. What did you learn from this assignment about your own writing process—about preparing to write, about writing the first draft, about revising, and about editing?

either side of the issue. How do these Web sites collectively show students the usefulness of illustration?

TEACHING ON THE WEB

Mosaics Web Site: To learn more about illustration, students can go to www.prenhall.com/mosaics.

12   ANALYZING A PROCESS

I see but one rule: to be clear.

—STENDHAL

TEACHING PROCESS
ANALYSIS

Divide students into
pairs. Using one circle,
one triangle, one
square, and one rectan-
gle, have students draw
an abstract picture.
They should not let
their partners see what
they have drawn.

Once the pictures
are drawn, have one
student explain to the
partner, step by step,
how to draw the pic-
ture the student drew.
Since the partners can't
see the drawings, they
can only use the in-
structions provided by
the speaker. Once they
have drawn their part-
ners' pictures, have the
students reverse roles.

When the students
have all drawn their
partners' pictures, have
them show each other
what they actually
drew. How many
students came close to
drawing the correct
picture? Use this

Process analysis satisfies our natural desire for basic information—how to be more assertive, how to invest in the stock market, how to eat more healthfully, or how to help your child do a better job in school.

Process analysis writing, more than other types of writing, helps you understand the world around you and improve yourself—in your personal life, in college, and in the workplace. Consider the following situations:

People who are coming to visit you from out of town e-mail you for directions to your house.

A student needs to write a paper on how to improve employee morale for a course in business management.

A student needs to explain how to be a good listener for the midterm exam in speech communication.

The owner of an apartment building posts a notice in the laundry room explaining how to operate the new washers and dryers.

The manager of a shoe store has to write a memo reminding employees about the correct procedure for taking returns.

Process analysis is a form of explaining. Process analysis essays fall into one of two main types—giving directions or giving information. The first type, giving directions, tells *how to do something*, such as how to write a research paper or change the oil in your car. The second type, giving information, analyzes *how something works*, such as satellite TV or a bread machine, or *how something happened*, such as how the Soviet Union broke into separate nations. In each case, the explanation starts at the beginning and moves step by step, usually in chronological order, to the end result. Process analysis can be about something mental (how to solve a math problem) or something physical (how to pitch a tent).

WRITING A PROCESS ANALYSIS ESSAY

In "Dare to Change Your Job and Your Life in 7 Steps," Carole Kanchler explains how to take the right risks in order to change jobs and improve your life. In other words, the essay demonstrates the first type of process analysis: how to do something. Kanchler tells you what to do first, then second, and so on until reaching the desired outcome—success in a job you like. Have you ever held a job that you intensely disliked? Were you able to quit? Why or why not? Do you know what career you want to follow? What steps are you taking to prepare for it?

exercise to show the importance of providing accurate directions when writing a process analysis.

DARE TO CHANGE YOUR JOB AND YOUR LIFE IN 7 STEPS

by Carole Kanchler

Small, dark-haired, attractive, and warm, Melissa belies her 44 years. In a sharp gray suit and becoming blouse, she projects a professional yet approachable image. She is now director of training and development for a large retail outlet—and loves it. 1

"I feel good about myself," she says, "and at the end of the day, I have lots of energy left over." Melissa feels content because she believes she is doing something worthwhile. Her new position gives her life meaning and purpose. But getting there wasn't easy. 2

First a flight attendant, then a high school English teacher, then a manager in a retail store, Melissa stumbled about from what was for her one dead-end job to another. How did she finally find a meaningful, fulfilling, well-paid career? And how did she do what so many of us fail to do—dare to change? 3

A career change can take months or even years of soul-searching— 10 months in Melissa's case. You need to know the steps, how to master the troublesome feelings that accompany change, where the possible dangers lie, and how to maximize your gains while minimizing your losses. While creating a life worth living isn't easy, Melissa and millions of others have shown that anything is possible. 4

In interviews and surveys with more than 30,000 people over the past 25 years, I have identified seven steps that are key to a successful career and life shift. 5

1. Become AWARE of Negative Feelings

6   Your body and mind may be sending you messages about your job satisfaction. The messages may be physical—lingering colds, flu or headaches—or verbal—"23 minutes till lunch!" or "One more day till Friday!"

7   Perhaps you've been working for several years in your job, and it appears to be going well. You've had steady promotions, praise from superiors, and admiration from colleagues. Then one day you get a queasy feeling that something is lacking. But what? You run the film of your life in reverse but you can't figure it out. These feelings may persist for months or even years, depending on your ability to tolerate them, but, sooner or later, you have to admit you have a problem.

2. DEFINE the Problem

8   A good written definition of your problem can help to put you on the road toward change.

9   First, ask yourself, "What's making me feel this way? What is it about my situation that is unpleasant? Does this job help me reach my goals?" If not, why?

10   Next, describe any barriers that may be blocking you from making a move—perhaps fear of change; fear of losing a secure income, pension or other benefits; fear that the change will interfere with your relationships; or fear that you'll lose power or status.

11   Fear is the result of conditioning, and because it is learned, it can be unlearned. Reprogram your old attitudes and beliefs with new ones by learning and practicing specific ways to overcome the fears blocking your path toward change. Think of FEAR as an acronym for "False Expectations Appear Real." Don't spend time worrying about what might happen. Focus on the now.

3. Listen to AMBIVALENCE

12   Milton, a rehabilitation counselor, was approached by a prospective partner to start an executive recruitment agency. For weeks before making the move, he went straight to bed immediately after dinner and pulled the sheets up over his head. He tried to make light of this behavior, but he had undertaken many risks before and had never felt this way about them.

13   His underlying fears were prophetic. He later discovered that the hardsell, aggressive style required for executive recruiting was not for him. The difference in basic values between Milton and his partner proved such a handicap that, within five months, the two parted ways.

14   The decision to change can provoke mixed feelings. A certain amount of ambivalence is natural. Inner emotional preparation—weighing losses

as well as gains, fears as well as hopes—is a necessary prerequisite for successful risk taking.

But if the prospect of undertaking a change is so great that your stomach   15
is churning, you can't sleep, you have constant headaches. or you feel you're developing an ulcer, your body, in its wisdom, is telling you to forgo the risk.

4. PREPARE for Risk

The key to avoiding potential potholes is to set tentative career goals be-   16
fore you explore new roads. Goals force you to focus on what you really want. Years from now, as you review your life, what would you regret not having done?

Fantasize about the ultimate goal, your shining star. If you could do any-   17
thing in the world, what would it be? Write all of your ideas or fantasies in a notebook. Include everything you want to do, be, and have. The sky is the limit. Once you know what you want, you'll be more willing to take the risks necessary to achieve it.

Choosing a satisfying career and lifestyle also requires a basic under-   18
standing of yourself. A variety of exercises can help. To identify your strengths, for example, list some of the successes you've had—say, substituting for your son's soccer coach. Next to each success, identify what gave you the positive feelings. Did you contribute to the team's first win of the season?

Also list the skills and abilities you used to bring about that success.   19
Were you well organized and adept at working with parents? Finally, decide how your interests, needs, accomplishments, and other personal strengths add up. What pattern do they form?

Self-exploration is just part of the process. You also need to take a care-   20
ful look at your current situation, as well as the available alternatives. Some popular reference tools, available at your local library, can help. Check out the *Occupational Handbook*, the *Dictionary of Occupational Titles*, and the *Encyclopedia of Careers and Work Issues*. The Internet also offers excellent sites for exploring general occupational fields, job descriptions, and educational opportunities.

5. NARROW Your Options

Successful career management hinges on finding a position that's com-   21
patible with your personal qualities and goals. Do you have the necessary intelligence and skills to do the work? Can you afford the training required for the job? Might your shortcomings—health, vision, size, or strength, for example—pose a problem?

22   To help narrow your options, draw a series of vertical and horizontal lines so that your paper is divided into squares. Across the top of the page, list the most important elements of your ideal job: income, responsibility, public image, creativity, challenge, and so on (one in each square). Down the left side of the page, list each occupational option you're considering.

23   Next, for each alternative, place a −1 in the appropriate box if that job option doesn't satisfy the criterion listed at the top of the page. If the criterion is met, but not as much as you'd like, record a 0. If the criterion is well met, record a +1. Add the points for each job option and place them in a column labeled "total" at the far right. The job with the highest score meets the greatest number of criteria that you have deemed important.

6. Take ACTION

24   Once you've determined your occupational goal, take steps to realize it. You'll need a well-planned campaign to market yourself for the job, establish your own business, or return to school.

25   Stay focused on your goals, and believe you will achieve them. View failures along the way as learning experiences—detours that might offer an unexpected dividend.

7. EVALUATE the Decision

26   When you have worked hard at making a decision, take the time not just to enjoy the outcome, but to evaluate it. Ask yourself:

- Do I feel good about the move?
- What other gains did I derive from the move? What did I lose?
- What factors contributed to the success of my move?
- If I could do it all over again, what would I do differently?
- Who was most helpful in the process? Who let me down?

27   Evaluation is a continuous process. Assess your needs, goals, and job satisfaction periodically to determine if your developing personality fits your position and lifestyle. Don't wait for a crisis to clear your vision.

28   There really is no substitute for risk as a way to grow. Knowing you have honestly faced the painful struggle and accepted the trade-offs, and yet proceeded in spite of them, is extremely gratifying.

29   Melissa learned that the tremendous investment of energy a successful job search demands is exactly what enables people to look back and say, "Win, lose, or draw, I gave it my everything." Being able to say with satisfaction that you risked for a dream may be the biggest prize of all.

To remain fulfilled, however, you'll need to risk again and again until   30
you've created a life in which you feel comfortable being yourself, without
apology or pretense—a life in which you can continue to have choices.

PREPARING TO WRITE YOUR OWN PROCESS ANALYSIS

Think of some advice that you would like to give to a friend or classmate—for example, how to survive your first year of college, how to
find the partner of your dreams, how to buy a used car, or how to find
good day care for your child. Use one or more of the prewriting
strategies you learned in Chapter 2 to generate ideas about advice
you have for others.

How to Write a Process Analysis Essay

INSTRUCTOR'S
RESOURCE MANUAL
For additional material
about teaching process
analysis; for journal
entries; and for
multiple-choice,
short-answer, and
paragraph tests, see
the *Instructor's
Resource Manual*,
Section II, Part II.

Both types of a process analysis call for careful step-by-step thinking, but
especially the first—how to do something. If you leave out even one detail,
you may confuse your reader or even endanger someone's life. If, for example,
you forget to tell a patient who is coming to a doctor's office for some tests
that she shouldn't eat after midnight and she has breakfast, the test results
will not be accurate, and a serious medical condition might go unnoticed.

Good process analysis of the second type—how something works or how
something happened—can help your reader see a product or an event in a
totally new light. Someone looking at a product that is already assembled or
at a completed event has no way of knowing how it got to the final stage
without an explanation. Good process analysis gives the reader a new way of
"seeing" something. The following guidelines will help you write clear and
complete process analysis essays.

1. *State in the thesis statement what the reader should be able to do or
   understand by the end of the essay.* Stating the end result at the beginning, in the thesis statement, gives your readers a road map for what
   follows. The thesis statement in a process essay should also state the
   number of steps or stages in the process. For example, someone giving
   directions might start by saying, "It's easy to get to the library from here
   with just four turns." Even if a process involves many separate steps, you
   should divide the list into a few manageable groups: "Most experts agree
   that there are four stages in overcoming an addiction." Stating the end

result and the number of steps or stages in the thesis statement helps the reader follow your explanation. These statements set up the tasks.

Carole Kanchler's thesis statement, which appears in paragraph 5, at the end of her introduction, tells her readers exactly what they will be able to do by the end of her article: make "a successful career and life shift." She also tells them how many steps are involved—seven. In this way, she gives a very clear road map for reading her essay.

2. ***Know your audience.*** In a process analysis essay, more than in others, the success of your essay depends on how well you know your audience. Knowing your audience helps you decide how much detail to include, how many examples to add, and which terms to define. Also keep in mind that your readers won't be able to ask you questions, so if they can't follow your explanation, they will become confused and frustrated. Whoever your audience is, explaining clearly is essential.

Kanchler's essay was first published in *Psychology Today*, which is read mostly by educated adults. The author's audience seems to be working adults of any age who are unhappy in their jobs. Kanchler addresses them in a very businesslike way; she doesn't talk down. Knowing that being unhappy in a job is very depressing, she strives for an upbeat "you can do it" tone.

3. ***Explain the process clearly in the body of your essay.*** By the end of a how-to essay, the reader should be able to perform the activity. By the end of a how-something-works essay, the reader should understand what is going on behind the scenes, and by the end of a how-something-happened essay, the reader should understand more about a specific event.

In writing the body paragraphs of a process essay, pay special attention to transitions. Use transitions such as *first, next, then, after that,* and *finally* to guide your readers through the process from beginning to end.

Since Kanchler's process has seven parts, she numbers each step. This is a good idea if a process is complicated. If you are writing about a process with only three or four steps, you can use transitions to indicate to your readers where you are in the process.

4. ***Organize your material logically.*** Most process analysis essays are organized chronologically or according to a time sequence. The explanation starts at one point and progresses through time to the final point. If a process is complicated, figure out the most logical organization for the process you are explaining. For instance, playing the guitar

involves pressing the strings with the fingers of one hand and strumming with the other hand. You might therefore explain each part of the process separately and then explain how the hands work together to make music.

Kanchler's essay is organized chronologically. She moves from recognizing the problem to taking action and then to evaluating the action. To help readers follow along smoothly, she numbers the steps and uses transitions such as *first, next,* and *then.*

5. ***End your essay by considering the process as a whole.*** Don't just stop after you have explained the last step of a process. Instead, in the conclusion, look at the process as a whole. There are many ways to do this. You might state why knowing about this process is important: Knowing how to perform CPR (cardiopulmonary resuscitation) can save a life; knowing how your car runs might save you money in repair bills. Or you might review your introduction, summarize the steps of the process, call for action, or end with a fitting quotation. Whatever your method, leave your reader feeling that your essay has reached a natural close.

Kanchler concludes by returning to her introduction. She brings back Melissa, the person from the opening example, to emphasize the rewards of taking risks. She ends her essay by saying that a satisfying life requires taking risks again and again.

 WRITING YOUR OWN PROCESS ANALYSIS ESSAY

Look at the prewriting you did earlier on the topic of giving advice to a friend or classmate. If your directions involve many steps, divide them into three groups. Come up with a thesis statement that states the end result of the process and tells how many steps or stages are involved. Then write the first draft of your essay by following the guidelines for writing a process analysis essay. Make sure you have an introduction and a conclusion.

 WORKING WITH A STUDENT ESSAY

A student writer named Emily Bliss wrote the following essay about procrastination. See if you can follow her steps as you read her first draft.

TEACHING TIPS
The following eight teaching tips are based on Howard Gardner's multiple intelligences:

You Too Can Procrastinate

1   My name is Emily, and I am a procrastinator. But I have discovered over the years that procrastination is not all bad. Especially when I have to write. At my college, the English instructors requires rough drafts. I have somehow mastered the art of procrastinating but still meeting deadlines with my papers. So I have perfected a successful plan for procrastinating that I now want to share with the world.

2   You will know the dreaded day you have to write has arrived when you wake up with a start. This day is different from the rest. You actually have to do something about your paper today. But whatever you do, resist the temptation to sit down and write early in the day by following two more steps. First (step 1), to avoid sitting down to write, you can clean, take a bike ride, do the laundry, rearrange the furniture, dust the light bulbs, and so on. But don't write. Then (step 2), when you finally think you are ready to start writing, call a friend. Talk about anything but your paper for about 15 or 20 minutes. This final delay is what creates the tension that a real procrastinator needs to do his or her best work.

3   Whether you want to or not, you will naturally think about the assignment from the moment you get it. If you have two weeks or two months, you will spend most quiet moments haunted by your paper topic. No matter what you do, your paper topic will be bouncing around in your head giving you headaches, making you worry, wanting attention. But that's OK. Don't give in and write. Ignore it until the day before it is due.

4   At this point, your third step is to prepare your immediate environment for work. You need to get ready for serious business. Sharpen your pencils, and lay them in a row. Get out the white paper if you can't think on yellow, or get out the yellow paper if you can't think on white. Go to the kitchen for snacks. Whether or not you actually drink or eat these item's is irrelevant—as long as they are by your side. You can't be distracted if you don't have them next to you. My stomach growls really loudly when I'm hungry. Some sort of bread usually takes away the hunger pangs. Step 4 is to sit back in your chair and stare at the computer while you think long and hard about your paper. Fifth, brainstorm, list, or cluster your ideas on the colored paper of your choice. Sixth, put all your procrastination strategies aside. Its finally time to write.

5   If you follow these six simple steps, you too can become a master procrastinator. You can perform your very own procrastinating ritual and still get your first draft in on time. If you go through the same ritual every time you write. You can perfect it and get your own system for writing essays down to a science. The trick is just to make sure you start writing before you has to join Procrastinators Anonymous.

Discovering How the Essay Works

1. What should the reader be able to do by the end of this essay?

   Procrastinate and still meet deadlines

2. Who do you think Emily's audience is? Does she meet their needs?

   Her audience is students who might have to write papers. Her advice

   might be helpful to them.

3. Do you understand how to procrastinate and still meet your deadlines? If so, list the six steps of this process.

   Step 1: *Do chores to avoid writing.*

   Step 2: *Call a friend.*

   Step 3: *Prepare your environment for writing.*

   Step 4: *Think about your paper while you stare at your computer.*

   Step 5: *Brainstorm, list, or cluster.*

   Step 6: *Write.*

   If you do not understand, what else do you need to know?

   Answers will vary.

4. Are the details in the essay organized logically? Is this order effective for what the author is trying to say? Why or why not?

   Paragraph 3 is out of order, but the rest of the essay is organized

   chronologically. It is effective because the writer clearly outlines the

   steps of the process.

5. Does the essay conclude by considering the process as a whole? Explain your answer.

   Emily concludes by reminding students that procrastination is really

   prewriting. Her reference to "Procrastinators Anonymous" refers to

   her introduction and brings her essay to a clever end.

Make sure students know that if, for instance, the blindfolded student gives the direction to walk through a doorway without saying to open the door, the other student cannot progress beyond the closed door. When the instructions are complete, have the blindfolded students guess where they are.

Intrapersonal

Have students think of the process they typically go through before they write a paper. Does this ritual ever change? What steps may be different from assignment to assignment?

Interpersonal

Divide students into small groups of three or four. Have them list the steps to a process that all students would most likely know (for example, ordering a pizza or making a sandwich), but have them omit some seemingly insignificant steps. See if the other groups can find the omissions.

Naturalist

Have students explain the steps for an outdoor adventure, such as making a campfire, preparing a fish for cooking, or getting into a canoe. What is the consequence if one step is missing?

REVISING AND
EDITING OPTIONS
Consider varying your
approach to revising
and editing. You could
teach these skills in a
class discussion, in
small groups, or in
pairs.

REVISING
STRATEGIES
This chapter focuses on
the following revising
elements:
Thesis statement
Basic elements
Development
Unity
Organization

Revising and Editing the Student Essay

This essay is Emily's first draft, which now needs to be revised and edited. First, apply the Revising Checklist below to the content of Emily's draft. When you are satisfied that her ideas are fully developed and well organized, use the Editing Checklist on page 199 to correct her grammar and mechanics errors. Answer the questions after each checklist. Then write your suggested changes directly on Emily's draft.

REVISING CHECKLIST ✔

THESIS STATEMENT
- ✔ Does the thesis statement contain the essay's controlling idea?
- ✔ Does the thesis appear as the last sentence of the introduction?

BASIC ELEMENTS
- ✔ Does the title draw in the readers?
- ✔ Does the introduction capture the readers' attention and build up to the thesis statement effectively?
- ✔ Does each body paragraph deal with a single topic?
- ✔ Does the conclusion bring the essay to a close in an interesting way?

DEVELOPMENT
- ✔ Do the body paragraphs adequately support the thesis statement?
- ✔ Does each body paragraph have a focused topic sentence?
- ✔ Does each body paragraph contain *specific* details that support the topic sentence?
- ✔ Does each body paragraph include *enough* details to explain the topic sentence fully?

UNITY
- ✔ Do the essay's topic sentences relate directly to the thesis statement?
- ✔ Do the details in each body paragraph support its topic sentence?

ORGANIZATION
- ✔ Is the essay organized logically?
- ✔ Is each body paragraph organized logically?

COHERENCE
- ✔ Are transitions used effectively so that paragraphs move smoothly and logically from one to the next?
- ✔ Do the sentences move smoothly and logically from one to the next?

Thesis Statement

1. Put brackets around the last sentence in Emily's introduction. Does it state her purpose?

    Yes, but it is incomplete.

2. Rewrite Emily's thesis statement if necessary so that it introduces her process and states her purpose.

    Here is one possibility: So I have perfected a successful plan of six

    easy steps for procrastination that I now want to share with the world.

Basic Elements

1. Give Emily's essay an alternate title.

    Answers will vary.

2. Rewrite Emily's introduction so that it captures the readers' attention and builds up to the thesis statement at the end of the introduction.

    Answers will vary.

3. Does each of Emily's body paragraphs deal with only one topic?

    Yes

4. Rewrite Emily's conclusion using at least one suggestion from Part I.

    Answers will vary.

Development

1. Write out Emily's thesis statement (revised, if necessary), and list her three topic sentences below it. *Thesis may vary.*

Thesis statement: *So I have perfected a successful plan of six easy steps for procrastination that I now want to share with the world.*

Topic 1: *You will know the dreaded day you have to write has arrived when you wake up with a start.*

Topic 2: *Whether you want to or not, you will naturally think about the assignment from the moment you get it.*

Topic 3: *At this point, your third step is to prepare your immediate environment for work.*

2. Do Emily's topics adequately support her thesis statement?

   Yes

3. Do Emily's details in the essay explain the process step by step?

   Yes

4. Where do you need more information?

   She could provide more examples for steps 4, 5, and 6.

5. Add at least two new details to make the steps clearer. *Answers will vary.*

Unity

1. Read each of Emily's topic sentences with her thesis statement (revised, if necessary) in mind. Do they go together?

   Answers will vary.

2. Revise them if necessary so they are directly related.

3. Drop or rewrite the two sentences in paragraph 4 that are not directly related to their topic sentence. *Sentences 8 and 9*

Organization

1. Read Emily's essay again to see if all the paragraphs are arranged logically. Look at your list of steps in response to question 3 after Emily's essay.

2. Reverse the two paragraphs that are out of order. *Reverse paragraphs 2 and 3.*
3. Look closely at Emily's body paragraphs to see if all her sentences are arranged logically within paragraphs.

4. Move any sentences that are out of order. *All sentences are in order.*

Coherence

1. Circle five transitions Emily uses.

2. Explain how two of these make Emily's essay easier to read.

For a list of transitions, see pages 83–84.

Answers will vary.

_____

_____

_____

Now rewrite Emily's essay with your revisions.

EDITING CHECKLIST ✔

SENTENCES
✔ Does each sentence have a main subject and verb?
✔ Do all subjects and verbs agree?
✔ Do all pronouns agree with their nouns?
✔ Are modifiers as close as possible to the words they modify?

PUNCTUATION AND MECHANICS
✔ Are sentences punctuated correctly?
✔ Are words capitalized properly?

WORD CHOICE AND SPELLING
✔ Are words used correctly?
✔ Are words spelled correctly?

EDITING STRATEGIES
This chapter focuses on the following editing problems:
    Fragments
    Subject-verb
      agreement
    Apostrophes
      (contractions)

Sentences

Subjects and Verbs

1. Underline the subjects once and verbs twice in paragraphs 1 and 5 of your revision of Emily's essay. Remember that sentences can have more than one subject-verb set.

For help with subjects and verbs, see Chapter 34.

2. Does each of the sentences have at least one subject and verb that can stand alone?

No

For help with fragments, see Chapter 35.

3. Did you find and correct Emily's two fragments? If not, find and correct them now. *Paragraph 1, sentence 3; paragraph 5, sentence 3*

Subject-Verb Agreement

For help with subject-verb agreement, see Chapter 39.

1. Read aloud the subjects and verbs you underlined in your revision of Emily's essay.

2. Did you find and correct the two subjects and verbs that do not agree? If not, find and correct them now. *Paragraph 1, sentence 4; paragraph 5, sentence 5*

Pronoun Agreement

For help with pronoun agreement, see Chapter 43.

1. Find any pronouns in your revision of Emily's essay that do not agree with their nouns. *All pronouns agree with their nouns.*

2. Correct any pronouns that do not agree with their nouns.

Modifiers

For help with modifier errors, see Chapter 46.

1. Find any modifiers in your revision of Emily's essay that are not as close as possible to the words they modify. *There are no modifier errors.*

2. Rewrite sentences if necessary so that modifiers are as close as possible to the words they modify.

Punctuation and Mechanics

Punctuation

For help with punctuation, see Chapters 47–51.

1. Read your revision of Emily's essay for any errors in punctuation.

2. Find the two fragments you revised, and make sure they are punctuated correctly.

3. Did you find and correct Emily's two apostrophe errors? If not, find and correct them now. *Paragraph 4, sentences 6 and 13*

Mechanics

For help with capitalization, see Chapter 52.

1. Read your revision of Emily's essay for any errors in capitalization.

2. Be sure to check Emily's capitalization in the fragments you revised.

Word Choice and Spelling

Word Choice

1. Find any words used incorrectly in your revision of Emily's essay. *All words are used correctly.*
2. Correct any errors you find.

For help with confused words, see Chapter 58.

Spelling

1. Use spell-check or a dictionary to check the spelling in your revision of Emily's essay. *All words are spelled correctly.*
2. Correct any misspelled words.

Now rewrite Emily's essay again with your editing corrections.

 WORKING WITH YOUR OWN ESSAY

Returning to the process analysis you wrote earlier in this chapter, revise and edit your own writing. The checklists here will help you apply what you have learned to your essay.

Revising and Editing Your Own Essay

REVISING CHECKLIST ✔

THESIS STATEMENT
- ☐ Does the thesis statement contain the essay's controlling idea?
- ☐ Does the thesis appear as the last sentence of the introduction?

BASIC ELEMENTS
- ☐ Does the title draw in the readers?
- ☐ Does the introduction capture the readers' attention and build up to the thesis statement effectively?
- ☐ Does each body paragraph deal with a single topic?
- ☐ Does the conclusion bring the essay to a close in an interesting way?

DEVELOPMENT
- ☐ Do the body paragraphs adequately support the thesis statement?
- ☐ Does each body paragraph have a focused topic sentence?

CLASS ACTIVITY
Put on the board or overhead projector a how-to paragraph that is filled with jargon or technical terms. Ask the class to determine what is wrong with the paragraph. Remind students to consider their audience and to be sure that their words are clear; for example, they should be careful not to tell a new employee to "do a JE to compensate for the credit balance in the AR" if the employee has no accounting experience.

☐ Does each body paragraph contain *specific* details that support the topic sentence?

☐ Does each body paragraph include *enough* details to explain the topic sentence fully?

UNITY

☐ Do the essay's topic sentences relate directly to the thesis statement?

☐ Do the details in each body paragraph support its topic sentence?

ORGANIZATION

☐ Is the essay organized logically?

☐ Is each body paragraph organized logically?

COHERENCE

☐ Are transitions used effectively so that paragraphs move smoothly and logically from one to the next?

☐ Do the sentences move smoothly and logically from one to the next?

Thesis Statement

1. What is your purpose in the essay?

_____

2. Put brackets around the last sentence in your introduction. Does it state your purpose?

_____

3. Revise your thesis statement if necessary so that it states your purpose and introduces your topics.

Basic Elements

1. Give your essay a title if it doesn't have one.

_____

2. Does your introduction capture your readers' attention and build up to your thesis statement at the end of the paragraph?

_____

3. Does each of your paragraphs deal with only one topic?

   _____

4. Does your conclusion follow some of the suggestions offered in Part I?

   _____

Development

1. Write out your thesis statement (revised, if necessary), and list your topic sentences below it.

   Thesis statement: _____

   Topic 1: _____

   Topic 2: _____

   Topic 3: _____

2. Do your topics adequately support your thesis statement?

   _____

3. Does each body paragraph have a focused topic sentence?

   _____

4. Do the details in your essay explain the process step by step?

   _____

5. Where do you need more information?

   _____

6. Add at least two new details to make the steps clearer.

Unity

1. Read each of your topic sentences with your thesis statement in mind. Do they go together?

   _____

2. Revise them if necessary so they are directly related.

3. Drop or rewrite any of the sentences in your body paragraphs that are not directly related to their topic sentences.

Organization

1. List the steps in your essay to make sure your process analysis is in chronological order.

2. Move any steps or paragraphs that are out of order.

3. What word clues help your readers move logically through your essay?

_____

4. Look closely at your body paragraphs to see if all the sentences are arranged logically within paragraphs.

5. Move any sentences that are out of order.

Coherence

For a list of transitions, see pages 83–84.

1. Circle five transitions you use.

2. Explain how two of these make your essay easier to read.

_____

_____

Now rewrite your essay with your revisions.

EDITING CHECKLIST ✔

SENTENCES

☐ Does each sentence have a main subject and verb?

☐ Do all subjects and verbs agree?

☐ Do all pronouns agree with their nouns?

☐ Are modifiers as close as possible to the words they modify?

PUNCTUATION AND MECHANICS

☐ Are sentences punctuated correctly?

☐ Are words capitalized properly?

WORD CHOICE AND SPELLING
- [ ] Are words used correctly?
- [ ] Are words spelled correctly?

Sentences

Subjects and Verbs

1. Underline your subjects once and verbs twice in a paragraph of your revised essay. Remember that sentences can have more than one subject-verb set.

2. Does each of your sentences have at least one subject and verb that can stand alone?

For help with subjects and verbs, see Chapter 34.

3. Correct any fragments you have written.

4. Correct any run-together sentences you have written.

For help with fragments, see Chapter 35.

For help with run-togethers, see Chapter 36.

Subject-Verb Agreement

1. Read aloud the subjects and verbs you underlined in your revised essay.

2. Correct any subjects and verbs that do not agree.

For help with subject-verb agreement, see Chapter 39.

Pronoun Agreement

1. Find any pronouns in your revised essay that do not agree with their nouns.

2. Correct any pronouns that do not agree with their nouns.

For help with pronoun agreement, see Chapter 43.

Modifiers

1. Find any modifiers in your revised essay that are not as close as possible to the words they modify.

2. Rewrite sentences if necessary so that your modifiers are as close as possible to the words they modify.

For help with modifier errors, see Chapter 46.

Punctuation and Mechanics

Punctuation

1. Read your revised essay for any errors in punctuation.

For help with punctuation, see Chapters 47–51.

2. Make sure any fragments and run-together sentences you revised are punctuated correctly.

Mechanics

For help with capitalization, see Chapter 52.

1. Read your revised essay for any errors in capitalization.
2. Be sure to check your capitalization in any fragments or run-together sentences you revised.

Word Choice and Spelling
Word Choice

For help with confused words, see Chapter 58.

1. Find any words used incorrectly in your revised essay.
2. Correct any errors you find.

Spelling

For help with spelling, see Chapter 59.

1. Use spell-check or a dictionary to check your spelling.
2. Correct any misspelled words.

Now rewrite your essay again with your editing corrections.

PRACTICING PROCESS ANALYSIS

Reading Suggestions

In Chapter 28, you will find two essays that illustrate good process analysis writing: "Don't Be Cruel" by Dr. Roger Flax explains how to criticize people without humiliating them, and "Why We Have a Moon" by David Levy explains the role of the moon in relation to the earth. You might want to read these selections before writing another process analysis essay. As you read, notice how the writers explain every step of the process carefully and completely.

Service Learning Project

SERVICE LEARNING PROJECT

This assignment is another step in the Service Learning project. If you choose to use this feature of the text, each chapter in Part II has an assignment that asks students to use a different rhetorical mode to reflect on their Service Learning project. These reflections will lead to an essay assignment in Part III (Chapter 22). You can assign as many or as few of these exercises as you want in preparation for this

This assignment is based on a Service Learning project of your choice. If your instructor has already introduced service learning to the class, you will be doing these exercises when they are assigned. At this point, choose a project you would like to pursue, or continue work on a project you have already begun. This assignment in Part II will help you prepare for an essay on this project in Part III. Here is another stage in the preparation for this essay:

For the Service Learning project you have taken on, explain a process involved in any part of your project (for example, how you got started, how you created your first newsletter, how you developed your first ad). Use the guidelines you have learned in this chapter to help you record this process. But remember that these are just thoughts that will be developed into an essay in Part III.

essay. For more information on service learning, see the *Instructor's Resource Manual*, Section I, Part III.

Writing Workshop

Guidelines for Writing a Process Analysis Essay

1. State in the thesis statement what the reader should be able to do or understand by the end of the essay.
2. Know your audience.
3. Explain the process clearly in the body of your essay.
4. Organize your material logically.
5. End your essay by considering the process as a whole.

ADDITIONAL WRITING TOPIC
Have your students turn to Chapter 28 and read Roger Flax's "Don't Be Cruel" or David Levy's "Why We Have a Moon." Then have them write an essay on one of the topics from "Writing Topics: Analyzing a Process" at the end of the chapter.

1. Place yourself in a scene similar to the one above, and write a process analysis essay explaining something that you find as interesting as this person finds this activity. Be sure to cover all steps or stages of the process you are discussing.
2. Choose an appliance or a piece of equipment that you understand well, and write a process analysis essay explaining how it works. Don't

TEACHING ON THE WEB
Discussion Topic: Divide students into groups of three or four, and have them discuss the many ways in which process analysis

can be found on the Internet. How can process analysis on the Net help them in their daily lives?

TEACHING ON THE WEB

Links: Have students find links to Web sites that sell videos about historical events. What three titles in each category sound most interesting to them?
   Possible sites:
   A&E,
      www.aetv.com
   History Channel,
      www.
      historychannel.
      com
   Discovery Channel,
      www.discovery.
      com

TEACHING ON THE WEB

Research: Have students find Web sites that explain how something happened. Have them determine whether all the steps are given or if any were left out. Then ask them to explain how important each step is to the process analysis they found.

TEACHING ON THE WEB

Mosaics Web Site: To learn more about process analysis, students can go to www.prenhall.com/mosaics.

identify the item in your essay. Then see if the class members can guess what device you are talking about.

3. Research the history of your college or university, and write an essay explaining its background to prospective students. Be sure to give a focus to your study and decide on a purpose before you begin writing.

4. Write your own process analysis assignment (with the help of your instructor), and write a response to it.

Revising Workshop

Small Group Activity (5–10 minutes per writer)   In groups of three or four, each person should read his or her process analysis essay to the other members of the group. Those listening should record their reactions on a copy of the Peer Evaluation Form in Appendix 2D. After your group goes through this process, give your evaluation forms to the appropriate writers so that each writer has two or three peer comment sheets for revising.

Paired Activity (5 minutes per writer)   Using the completed Peer Evaluation Forms, work in pairs to decide what you should revise in your essay. If time allows, rewrite some of your sentences, and have your partner look at them.

Individual Activity   Rewrite your paper, using the revising feedback you received from other students.

Editing Workshop

Paired Activity (5–10 minutes per writer)   Swap papers with a classmate, and use the editing portion of your Peer Evaluation Form to identify as many grammar, punctuation, mechanics, and spelling errors as you can. If time allows, correct some of your errors, and have your partner look at them. Record your grammar, punctuation, and mechanics errors in the Error Log (Appendix 6) and your spelling errors in the Spelling Log (Appendix 7).

Individual Activity   Rewrite your paper again, using the editing feedback you received from other students.

Reflecting on Your Writing

When you have completed your own essay, answer these six questions.

1. What was most difficult about this assignment?

2. What was easiest?

3. What did you learn about process analysis by completing this assignment?

4. What do you think are the strengths of your process analysis? Place a wavy line by the parts of your essay that you feel are very good.

5. What are the weaknesses, if any, of your paper? Place an X by the parts of your essay you would like help with. Write any questions you have in the margin.

6. What did you learn from this assignment about your own writing process—about preparing to write, about writing the first draft, about revising, and about editing?

13

COMPARING AND CONTRASTING

The difference between the right word and the
almost-right word is really a large matter—'tis
the difference between the lightning-bug and
the lightning.

—MARK TWAIN

Comparison and contrast are at the heart of our democratic society. Our competitive natures encourage us to compare our lives to those of others so we can try to better ourselves. Even if we simply attempt to improve on our "personal best," comparison and contrast keep us striving for more. In school, we learn about different writers, different cultures, different musical instruments, and different political platforms by comparing them to one an-other. And every day we make decisions based on comparisons of one sort or another—which clothes we should wear, which person we should date, which apartment we should rent, which job we should take. Comparisons help us establish a frame of reference and figure out where we fit into the larger world around us.

On another level, comparison and contrast are also part of our writing. They play an important role in our personal lives, in our college courses, and in the workplace, as in the following situations:

Someone looking for a new car does comparison shopping on the Internet.

A student doing a report in a nursing course compares and contrasts traditional and alternative approaches to medical care.

A student compares and contrasts two Native American cultures for an exam in anthropology.

An insurance agent prepares a report for a client that compares and contrasts several different insurance policies.

A travel agent compares and contrasts two travel packages for a client.

Comparison and contrast help us understand one subject by putting it next to another. When we *compare*, we look for similarities, and when we *contrast*, we look for differences. Nearly always, however, comparison and contrast are part of the same process. For this reason, we often use the word *compare* to refer to both techniques.

WRITING A COMPARISON/CONTRAST ESSAY

In the essay "Thrills and Chills," Eric Minton compares and contrasts roller coasters and haunted houses to show how amusement parks play on our deepest fears. Do you like being scared? Do you like roller coasters and haunted houses? Are they a means of escape for you?

When students have found as many similarities and differences as possible, have a class discussion about how relatively easy it is to do this exercise because everyone can hear the similarities and differences, even though some took longer to spot than others. Then discuss the correlation to writing: When writing comparison/contrast essays, students should be sure to look for what is obvious and what is not so obvious and then compare and contrast in a logical manner.

THRILLS AND CHILLS
by Eric Minton

In Orlando, Florida, David Clevinger stands in a back corridor of *Terror on Church Street* and listens expectantly as customers make their way through the haunted house's passages. Suddenly screams erupt, sending Clevinger, the attraction's artistic director and operations manager, into gales of glee. "I love that sound," he chortles. So does Dave Focke. Watching shrieking riders hurtle through the drops of *The Beast*, the massive wooden coaster at Paramount's Kings Island near Cincinnati, Ohio, Focke beams with pride. "Guests come off breathless, hearts pounding, scared out of their wits," exults Focke, the park's vice president of construction and maintenance, "and wanting to get in line to go again!"   1

Call them shockmeisters, terror tacticians, spookologists, and boo-ologists. The small band of designers who create the roller coasters and haunted houses that are amusement parks' premier attractions are master manipulators of our deepest fears. They get us to walk through pitch black hallways and step into cutaway coaster cars that dangle our arms and legs. They exploit our most closely held vulnerabilities—and make us like it.   2

For designers, primarily engineers for coasters and theatrical artists for haunted houses, turning fear into fun depends on illusion. No matter how precarious a roller coaster or alarming a haunted house may appear, it must be totally safe. "We always try to make them look and feel more   3 dangerous than they really are," says Michael Boodley, president of Great Coasters International, Inc., of Santa Cruz, California.

4   Though the experience offered by roller coasters and haunted houses diverges dramatically—it's the difference between pushing a wagon over a steep hill versus telling campfire ghost stories—the attractions are constructed of common elements. Both draw on all our senses, both rely on surprise for their shocks and both quote heavily from the movies (Coasters replicate action-adventure perils, à la *Indiana Jones* and *Star Wars*, and haunted houses feature quasi-Frankensteins and *Friday the 13th* Jasons).

5   But the biggest common denominator is that the two feed on the same basic fear: loss of control. Once a coaster takes off, passengers can do nothing but sit, or on some rides stand, and scream. "The closest thing to compare it to is driving with an idiot," observes Boodley. Lynton Harris, director of *Madison Scare Garden*, an annual fright fest in New York City, also uses an auto analogy for haunted houses. "It's a hundred degrees outside, and you'd expect to get in a car and have air conditioning, and all of a sudden the heater gets turned on," he says. "Then the doors lock. Cocky as you are, you realize you're not in charge."

6   With roller coasters, the psychological games start before customers even get into the train. Boodley purposely makes his wooden coasters as diabolical looking as possible. "It's kind of like a black widow spider web," he explains. "It's a very, very pretty thing, but when the black widow gets you . . . " Queueing customers at *Outer Limits: Flights of Fear*, one of 12 coasters at Kings Island, are treated to dim lights, alien noises and a video of a space station in the grip of a mysterious force. "Even after having ridden that ride probably close to a hundred times, I sit there anticipating the start, and my palms still sweat," says *Outer Limits* designer Jim Seay, president of Premier Rides of Millersville, Maryland.

7   Whether the traditional chain-driven wooden or steel clackers or the newer linear induction motor (LIM) rides that harness electromagnetic force to blast off trains, all roller coasters play on two related—and universal—terrors: fear of heights and fear of falling. "The loops and elements, they come and go, but the coaster always has to have the big drop," says Focke of Kings Island.

8   Traditional coasters provide an excruciatingly slow buildup to the plunge. "There's a lot of self-abuse on that chain lift," says Boodley. "Your own mind puts you in a state of paralysis." (Wooden coasters also creak, rumble and clickity-clack naturally as they flex, but riders get a queasy feeling that the structure is about to collapse. "That's probably one of the funniest things we as designers get to appreciate," says Boodley.) LIMs, on

the other hand, rocket you into terror with trains that go from 0 to 60 mph in under four seconds. The big drops are actually shorter on LIMs, but the sense of speed sets hearts pounding.

Most coasters travel below 70 miles an hour, slower than many people 9
drive, but designers heighten the sense of speed and danger with close fly-bys of terrain, buildings, people, even other trains. At Busch Gardens Tampa Bay, *Montu* dives riders into five trenches, one of which emerges through the patio of an ersatz Egyptian temple. "Not knowing exactly where the bottom is or where you come out is important," says Mark Rose, the park's vice president of design and engineering. "If you could see the whole thing, then you could kind of play it out in your mind." Some coasters, like *Outer Limits* and Disney World's *Space Mountain*, intensify the fear and suspense by keeping passengers in the dark for the entire ride.

Upping the vulnerability quotient even further is a recent innovation: in- 10
verted coasters which suspend riders below the track and carve away as much of the train as possible. "There is less fiberglass, less coach around you, so your feet are just hanging out there," notes Rose. During one stretch of track on *Montu*, passengers' soles skim just 24 inches above the ground. Riders also get dangled over a pit of live Nile crocodiles.

A coaster's effects, though, are not all illusory. Passengers pull close to 11
4 positive G's on some plummets. They turn upside down on loops and rotate head over heels through corkscrews. They literally feel the wind in their hair and, on a LIM coaster launch, the air in their eyes. Human bodies don't commonly experience such acrobatic maneuvers, and that in itself is psychologically disorienting. "Anytime you put riders in a situation they're not used to, there's an element of the unknown," declares Boodley. "And for 80% of people, fear is the unknown."

The biggest unknown of all is death, and creators of haunted houses are 12
masters at exploiting our fear of dying, especially in a gruesome manner. To unnerve guests, designers depend on two elements. The first is setting a spooky mood with sights, sounds, smells, and "feels"—"all the things that make you uneasy," says Drew Edward Hunter, co-chairman of the International Association of Haunted Attractions and design director of haunted attractions at Sally Corporation of Jacksonville, Florida. "Then you have the second part, the attack, the out-and-out scare. I don't think you can have one without the other."

For the "creep-out" effect, haunts are always dark; skeletons, skulls, fog, 13
ticking clocks, and screaming ghouls abound. "On my sets, I try to capture a claustrophobic feeling," says *Terror on Church Street's* Clevinger. "I bring my ceilings low, the walls close." To further emphasize the sense of enclosure, he hangs tree branches, Spanish moss, rags, and spider webs.

14   Just the suggestion of something loathsome will give customers the screaming meemies. "Do the sounds of insects, and people scratch their heads all the way through," says John Denley, president and owner of Boneyard Productions of Salem, Massachusetts. Run a soundtrack that whispers of rats, turn on ankle-aimed air hoses, and professional football players tap dance. A strong whiff of formaldehyde, and you have the scent of death, "no matter what country you're in," says Clevinger.

15   The second part of the equation is the scare, which, say spookologists, is really a "startle." "All scares are primarily based on two things," instructs Edward Marks, president of Jets Productions of Chatsworth, California. "One, it's there and does something you don't expect it to do, or two, it's not there and it appears."

16   In *Terror on Church Street*, customers come upon Hannibal Lecter, the cannibal psychiatrist of *Silence of the Lambs*. He yells and lunges against his cell's bars, drawing yelps from viewers. The cries quickly subside into nervous tittering. As guests make their way around the bars, Lecter follows along inside. Then, just when viewers feel safest, Lecter opens the cage door and steps out. "The guys who were taunting him usually scream the loudest," observes Clevinger.

17   In the second type of gag, designers have people or objects suddenly emerge from in front, beside, above, or below patrons. A surefire gag—and the simplest of all—is dropping a spider on a person's head. "We call that a $2 scare," says Harris of *Madison Scare Garden*. "It's the best value-for-money scare we've ever used."

18   Another never-fail gotcha goes by the generic term "UV Dot Man." Guests enter a dark room with ultraviolet dots on the wall (variations would be skeletons or geometric patterns). A black-masked actor wearing a black bodysuit, likewise bearing UV dots, stands against the wall and jumps out. "You are actually looking at him before he leaps out at you," Marks says. "It works every time, and it's so simple." (Another certain scare that designers hate, but feel compelled to use, is the hockey-masked goon waving a whirring chainsaw. Customers complain if a haunted house doesn't have one.)

19   For designers, combining the two types of gags may be the most satisfying scare of all. In his favorite trick, Denley once draped sheets over padding, topped them with masked and wigged heads, and attached the forms to the caging on oscillating fans. He plugged the fans into a power strip but left the cords clearly visible. These "monsters" started moving in unison when people entered the room. After the initial surprise, guests noticed the power strip and began mocking the amateurish setup. Suddenly, the middle white-sheeted monster—actually a man with one of the plugged-in extension cords tied to his leg—leaped out.

"It was hilarious," recalls a chuckling Denley, who is also known as   20
Professor Nightmare. "We had a woman hyperventilate. We had people
wet themselves. They thought they knew the gag—and, bam! we hit them
with something totally different." Guests losing control of their bladders is
considered a badge of honor among haunt producers. "We call it yellow
control," Clevinger says. Getting an entire group to cower on the ground is
another measure of success.

While the live actors who sometimes assume roles in haunted produc-   21
tion are forbidden to touch patrons, they are encouraged to invade their
personal space. "Everybody's got this wonderful circle around them," says
Denley, who likes to have actors suddenly appear as close to a person as
possible, then disappear. "We want to leave you thinking, 'What was that?'"

Designers also like to pick their victims. "We call it 'slicing the group,'"   22
says Marks at Jets Productions. "We actually can single out a person from
20 people. A guy and girl clinging together—I can slice them apart with
the right scare." A trained actor watches their body language, whether
they tighten up, stare him down, or avert their eyes.

Male customers are a favorite target. "We try to take the guys who are   23
hecklers and make examples of them," observes Denley. "If you nail them,
the rest of the group will follow." Men also pose a special challenge. "Guys
are harder to read than women," Denley explains. "They don't do body language as much. Women are more animated, more intent on being scared.
Guys play it cool." Designers usually get them with strikes from above or
below, but they're careful. Men sometimes lash out with their fists.

"The scariest things come from your mind," sums up Edward Hunter.   24
"With the right setup, the right imagination, the right story, your mind creates things we couldn't possibly show you." "No matter how good the
makeup or the costume, nothing is more effective than your imagination,"
echoes Denley. One proof: guests at *Terror on Church Street* scream loud
and long when, at a particular point, they catch a glimpse of lurking monsters. The fiends: themselves, reflected in strategically placed mirrors.

 PREPARING TO WRITE YOUR OWN COMPARISON/CONTRAST ESSAY

Think of several ways you escape or relieve stress. What do you like
about these methods of relaxation? Use one or more of the prewriting strategies you learned in Chapter 2 to generate ideas about these
forms of relaxation. Why do they work for you?

INSTRUCTOR'S
RESOURCE MANUAL
For additional material
about teaching compar-
ison and contrast;
for journal entries;
and for multiple-choice,
short-answer, and
paragraph tests, see the
*Instructor's Resource
Manual*, Section II,
Part II.

How to Write a Comparison/Contrast Essay

To write a comparison/contrast essay, you should consider two items that have something in common, such as cats and dogs (both are family pets) or cars and motorcycles (both are means of transportation). A discussion of cats and motorcycles, for example, would not be very interesting or useful because the two do not have common features. This is the basic rule underlying the following guidelines for writing a good comparison/contrast essay.

1. ***Decide what point you want to make with your comparison, and state it in your thesis statement.*** A comparison/contrast essay is usually written for one of two purposes: to examine the subjects separately or to show the superiority of one over the other. This purpose should be made clear in your thesis statement.

   In the sample essay, Minton's main idea is that the experience of roller coasters and of haunted houses plays in a similar manner on people's deepest fears. Minton makes the purpose of his essay clear in his thesis statement at the end of paragraph 2: "They exploit our most closely held vulnerabilities—and make us like it." This thesis promises to examine its subjects separately. If, however, this essay was going to show the superiority of one of its subjects over the other, its thesis statement might read something like this: "Although roller coasters and haunted houses both draw on our deepest fears, roller coasters are far more popular." In either case, readers would be interested in reading further to find out why they are attracted to roller coasters and haunted houses.

2. ***Choose items to compare and contrast that will make your point most effectively.*** Usually, the subjects you plan to compare and contrast have many similarities and differences. Your task, then, is to look over the ideas you generated in prewriting and choose the best points for making your comparison clearly and strongly.

   In his essay, Minton compares his subjects—roller coasters and haunted houses—on four points:

   Point 1: They draw on all five senses.
   Point 2: They rely on surprise.
   Point 3: They refer to movies.
   Point 4: They feed on loss of control.

3. ***Use as many specific details and examples as possible to expand your comparison.*** The most common way of developing a comparison/

contrast essay is to use description and example. Generate as many details and examples as you can for each of your subjects. Try to think of both obvious and not-so-obvious points of comparison.

In "Thrills and Chills," Minton relies heavily on description and examples. First, he describes both of these attractions with equal attention to detail throughout the essay. You can look at almost any body paragraph (paragraphs 6 to 23) in Minton's essay and find an example with vivid description. When he finally gets down to the common elements that make both of these subjects appeal to people who like to be scared, Minton makes his details more and more specific. Here is an example of his varying level of detail:

> haunted houses
> > fear of death
> > > spooky mood
> > > low ceilings
> > > close walls
> > > sound of insects
> > > smell of formaldehyde
> > the attack
> > > unexpected action
> > > jumping from cage
> > > unexpected appearance
> > > spider
> > > "UV Dot Man"

These specific examples draw the readers into the essay.

4. ***Develop your comparison in a balanced way.*** Having selected the points on which you will compare your two subjects, you are ready to develop the comparison in your body paragraphs. You should make sure, however, that your treatment of each subject is balanced. That means, first, you cover the same topics for each subject. In other words, you should give equal coverage to both subjects, no matter what your conclusion is. In addition, you should spend the same amount of time on each point. If you describe one of your subjects in detail, you should also describe the other. In like manner, you should provide a similar number of examples for both subjects. In this way, your readers will feel that you have been fair to both subjects and that you are not presenting a biased discussion that favors one subject over the other.

Minton covers all four of his points for both of his subjects and spends approximately the same amount of time developing both subjects. In discussing the ways that roller coasters make us feel out of control, for example, he names specific roller coasters and describes the way they build fear and suspense. Then he names specific haunted house attractions and describes how they "creep out" and scare people.

5. *Organize your essay subject by subject or point by point—or combine the two approaches.* When you are ready to write, you have three choices for organizing a comparison-and-contrast essay: (1) subject by subject (AAA, BBB), (2) point by point (AB, AB, AB), or (3) a combination of the two.

In the subject arrangement, you say everything you have to say about the first subject, A, before you move on to talk about the second subject, B. In a point-by-point arrangement, both subjects are compared on point 1; then both are compared on point 2; and so on through all the points.

To choose which method of organization would be most effective, just use your common sense. If the subjects themselves are the most interesting part of your essay, use the subject pattern. But if you want single characteristics to stand out, use the point-by-point pattern.

Minton's essay is organized point by point. He spends most of his time on point 4 for both subjects. Here is what Minton's organization looks like:

Point 1: They draw on all five senses.
   A. Roller coasters
   B. Haunted houses

Point 2: They rely on surprise.
   A. Roller coasters
   B. Haunted houses

Point 3: They refer to movies.
   A. Roller coasters
   B. Haunted houses

Point 4: They feed on loss of control.
   A. Roller coasters
     i. Fear of heights
     ii. Fear of falling
   B. Haunted houses
     i. Spooky mood
     ii. The scare

WRITING YOUR OWN COMPARISON/CONTRAST ESSAY

Write an essay comparing and contrasting two methods of escape, based on the ideas you generated in your prewriting activities. How are they alike? How are they different? Decide what point you want to make before you start writing. Then spend some time choosing and organizing your topics and deciding on your method of organization (subject by subject, point by point, or a combination of the two). Form a clear thesis statement, and follow the guidelines for writing a comparison/contrast essay.

WORKING WITH A STUDENT ESSAY

Let's look at a student's management of a comparison/contrast essay. This next essay, called "The Truth About Cats and Dogs," was written by a student named Maria Castillo. See if you can identify her main point as you read this draft of her essay.

The Truth About Cats and Dogs

The majority of people in the world will say that dogs are man's best friends and that cats were put on this earth to aggravate dogs. Some people are closet cat lovers, meaning he or she is afraid to tell family and friends that they actually like cats. Others will proudly state, "I hate cats, except for yours." People who resist cats do so because they believe they are; aloof, self-centered, and dull. People prefer dogs because they are friendly, protective, and playful. However, cats exhibit these same qualities and deserve the same respect as dogs.

Dogs have always been considered to be friendly, but cats can also fit this description. Dogs stay by their owners' sides and live to make their masters happy. They are the first to greet their family at the front door, they want nothing more than to be praised by their owners. Yet cats are much the same way. They, too, will be at the front door when their family gets home and are always excited to see them. They usually sit near their owners just to be by their sides. And despite what some people believe, a cat does come when they're called. Birds do not sit with their owners unless they are trained. Cats are very friendly to their owners.

As much as dogs love to play, so do cats. Most dogs love to play with chew toys, searching for the hidden-squeaker treasure. They often

1

2

3

parade around with their "kill" until their masters notice their triumph. Some owners will awaken to find that their dogs have strewn all their toys all over the house. Dogs love the toys they know are theirs. However, so do cats. Cats will make a toy out of anything that will slide across a tile floor, whether it's a hair clip, a milk jug ring, a toy mouse, or a spool of thread. They can amuse themselves for hours. If the toy-of-the-day gets trapped under the refrigerator, cats will whine and wait for their owner to get the toy. Cats just love to play.

4   Even though dogs are great defenders, cats have been known to protect the family as well. Dogs bark or growl whenever they want to alert their owners to possible danger. They stand at the door and wait for their owners to check for danger. If they see their owner being at-tacked, they will attack the enemy. Most people think cats would just stand by and watch, but this simply isn't true. Cats also alert their owners of danger by growling or standing to stiff attention. They, too, stand near the door waiting for their owner to react. Cats have been known to bite people who harm their loved ones. Cats can be excellent watch animals.

5   Dogs and cats are a lot alike. People say cats are very different from dogs, but this is not the case. The truth is, most people love to hate cats. It's now an old American pastime. But it's time for all cat lovers to unite and prove that it can be a cat-eat-cat world too.

Discovering How the Essay Works

1. What is Maria's main point in this essay?

   That cats are great animals, just like dogs

2. What exactly is Maria comparing or contrasting in this essay? List her points under the subjects below.

Dogs   Cats

Dogs are friendly.   *Cats are just as friendly.*

                                                        Cats love to play with anything
Dogs love to play with toys.   *that will move.*

Dogs signal danger by barking   *Cats signal danger by growling*
and growling.   *or stiffening.*

3. Does Maria use as many specific details and examples as possible? List three of her specific references.

   Answers will vary.

4. Does Maria develop her comparison in a balanced way? Explain your answer.

   Yes. Maria compares the same three points for both dogs and cats,

   and she provides many examples of both subjects for each topic.

5. How does Maria organize her essay: subject by subject, point by point, or a combination of the two?

   The essay is organized point by point.

Revising and Editing the Student Essay

This essay is Maria's first draft, which now needs to be revised and edited. First, apply the Revising Checklist below to the content of Maria's draft. When you are satisfied that her ideas are fully developed and well organized, use the Editing Checklist on page 225 to correct her grammatical and mechanical errors. Answer the questions after each checklist. Then write your suggested changes directly on Maria's draft.

REVISING CHECKLIST ✔

THESIS STATEMENT
- ✔ Does the thesis statement contain the essay's controlling idea?
- ✔ Does the thesis appear as the last sentence of the introduction?

BASIC ELEMENTS
- ✔ Does the title draw in the readers?
- ✔ Does the introduction capture the readers' attention and build up to the thesis statement effectively?

Interpersonal
Have students watch the movie version of a book they have read. Have them compare and contrast the two to determine which one they prefer.

Naturalist
Have students think of their two favorite outdoor sports. If they had to choose one over the other, which one would they choose and why?

REVISING AND EDITING OPTIONS
Consider varying your approach to revising and editing. You could teach these skills in a class discussion, in small groups, or in pairs.

REVISING STRATEGIES
This chapter focuses on the following revising elements:

Thesis statement
Basic elements
Development
Unity
Organization
Coherence

✔ Does each body paragraph deal with a single topic?

✔ Does the conclusion bring the essay to a close in an interesting way?

DEVELOPMENT

✔ Do the body paragraphs adequately support the thesis statement?

✔ Does each body paragraph have a focused topic sentence?

✔ Does each body paragraph contain *specific* details that support the topic sentence?

✔ Does each body paragraph include *enough* details to explain the topic sentence fully?

UNITY

✔ Do the essay's topic sentences relate directly to the thesis statement?

✔ Do the details in each body paragraph support its topic sentence?

ORGANIZATION

✔ Is the essay organized logically?

✔ Is each body paragraph organized logically?

COHERENCE

✔ Are transitions used effectively so that paragraphs move smoothly and logically from one to the next?

✔ Do the sentences move smoothly and logically from one to the next?

Thesis Statement

1. Put brackets around the last sentence in Maria's introduction. Does it contain her main point?

   No

2. Rewrite Maria's thesis statement if necessary so that it states her main point and introduces her topics.

   Here is one possibility: People prefer dogs because they are friendly,

   protective, and playful; however, cats exhibit these same qualities and

   deserve the same respect as dogs.

Basic Elements

1. Give Maria's essay an alternate title.

   Answers will vary.
   _____

2. Rewrite Maria's introduction so that it captures readers' attention and builds up to the thesis statement at the end of the paragraph.

   Answers will vary.
   _____

   _____

   _____

3. Does each of Maria's body paragraphs deal with only one topic?

   Yes
   _____

4. Rewrite Maria's conclusion using at least one suggestion from Part I.

   Answers will vary.
   _____

   _____

   _____

Development

1. Write out Maria's thesis statement (revised, if necessary), and list her three topic sentences below it. *Thesis may vary.*

   Thesis statement: *People prefer dogs because they are friendly, pro-*

   tective, and playful; however, cats exhibit these same qualities and

   deserve the same respect as dogs.

   Topic 1: *Dogs have always been considered to be friendly, but*

   cats can also fit this description.

   Topic 2: *As much as dogs love to play, so do cats.*

Topic 3: *Even though dogs are great defenders, cats have been known to protect the family as well.*

2. Do Maria's topic sentences adequately support her thesis statement?

   Yes

3. Does each body paragraph have a focused topic sentence?

   Yes

4. Do Maria's details adequately characterize both cats and dogs?

   Yes

5. Where do you need more information?

   Answers will vary.

6. Make two of Maria's details more specific. *Answers will vary.*

7. Add at least two new details to make her comparison clearer. *Answers will vary.*

Unity

1. Read each of Maria's topic sentences with her thesis statement (revised, if necessary) in mind. Do they go together?

   Answers will vary.

2. Revise them if necessary so they are directly related.

3. Drop or rewrite the sentence in paragraph 2 that is not directly related to its topic sentence. *Sentence 8*

Organization

1. Read Maria's essay again to see if all the paragraphs are arranged logically.

2. Reverse the two paragraphs that are out of order. *Reverse paragraphs 3 and 4 to match thesis.*

3. Look closely at Maria's body paragraphs to see if all her sentences are arranged logically within paragraphs.

4. Move any sentences that are out of order. *All sentences are in order.*

Coherence

1. Add two transitions to Maria's essay. *Answers will vary.*

2. Circle five synonyms that Maria uses. *Answers will vary.*

3. Explain how two of these make Maria's essay easier to read.

For the list of transitions, see pages 83–84.

   Answers will vary.

   _____

   _____

Now rewrite Maria's essay with your revisions.

EDITING CHECKLIST ✔

SENTENCES
✔ Does each sentence have a main subject and verb?
✔ Do all subjects and verbs agree?
✔ Do all pronouns agree with their nouns?
✔ Are modifiers as close as possible to the words they modify?

PUNCTUATION AND MECHANICS
✔ Are sentences punctuated correctly?
✔ Are words capitalized properly?

WORD CHOICE AND SPELLING
✔ Are words used correctly?
✔ Are words spelled correctly?

EDITING STRATEGIES
This chapter focuses on the following editing problems:
  Run-togethers
  Pronoun agreement
  Semicolons

Sentences

Subjects and Verbs

1. Underline Maria's subjects once and verbs twice in paragraph 2 of your revision of Maria's essay. Remember that sentences can have more than one subject-verb set.

2. Does each of Maria's sentences have at least one subject and verb that can stand alone?

For help with subjects and verbs, see Chapter 34.

   Yes _____

For help with run-togethers, see Chapter 36.

3. Did you find and correct Maria's run-together sentence? If not, find and correct it now. *Paragraph 2, sentence 3*

Subject-Verb Agreement

For help with subject-verb agreement, see Chapter 39.

1. Read aloud the subjects and verbs you underlined in your revision of Maria's essay.
2. Correct any subjects and verbs that do not agree. *All subjects and verbs agree.*

Pronoun Agreement

For help with pronoun agreement, see Chapter 43.

1. Find any pronouns in your revision of Maria's essay that do not agree with their nouns.
2. Did you find and correct the two pronouns that do not agree with their nouns? *Paragraph 1, sentence 2; paragraph 2, sentence 7*

Modifiers

For help with modifier errors, see Chapter 46.

1. Find any modifiers in your revision of Maria's essay that are not as close as possible to the words they modify. *There are no modifier errors.*
2. Rewrite sentences if necessary so modifiers are as close as possible to the words they modify.

Punctuation and Mechanics
Punctuation

For help with punctuation, see Chapters 47–51.

1. Read your revision of Maria's essay for any errors in punctuation.
2. Find the run-together sentence you revised, and make sure it is punctuated correctly.
3. Did you find and correct Maria's semicolon error? If not, find and correct it now. *Paragraph 1, sentence 4*

Mechanics

For help with capitalization, see Chapter 52.

1. Read your revision of Maria's essay for any errors in capitalization.
2. Be sure to check Maria's capitalization in the run-together sentence you revised.

Word Choice and Spelling
Word Choice

For help with confused words, see Chapter 58.

1. Find any words used incorrectly in your revision of Maria's essay. *All words are used correctly.*
2. Correct any errors you find.

Spelling

1. Use spell-check and a dictionary to check the spelling in your revision of Maria's essay. *All words are spelled correctly.*

2. Correct any misspelled words.

   Now rewrite Maria's essay again with your editing corrections.

For help with spelling, see Chapter 59.

WORKING WITH YOUR OWN ESSAY

Returning to the comparison/contrast you wrote earlier in this chapter, revise and edit your own writing. The checklists here will help you apply what you have learned to your essay.

Revising and Editing Your Own Essay

REVISING CHECKLIST ✔

THESIS STATEMENT
- [ ] Does the thesis statement contain the essay's controlling idea?
- [ ] Does the thesis appear as the last sentence of the introduction?

BASIC ELEMENTS
- [ ] Does the title draw in the readers?
- [ ] Does the introduction capture the readers' attention and build up to the thesis statement effectively?
- [ ] Does each body paragraph deal with a single topic?
- [ ] Does the conclusion bring the essay to a close in an interesting way?

DEVELOPMENT
- [ ] Do the body paragraphs adequately support the thesis statement?
- [ ] Does each body paragraph have a focused topic sentence?
- [ ] Does each body paragraph contain *specific* details that support the topic sentence?
- [ ] Does each body paragraph include *enough* details to explain the topic sentence fully?

UNITY
- [ ] Do the essay's topic sentences relate directly to the thesis statement?
- [ ] Do the details in each body paragraph support its topic sentence?

CLASS ACTIVITY
Ask students to think of every instance they compared or contrasted in the past week. Write their examples on the board, trying to fill all available space. Prompt them when necessary. After the board is relatively full, point out that they compare and contrast instinctively, so transferring this process into writing will not be difficult.

ORGANIZATION

☐ Is the essay organized logically?

☐ Is each body paragraph organized logically?

COHERENCE

☐ Are transitions used effectively so that paragraphs move smoothly and logically from one to the next?

☐ Do the sentences move smoothly and logically from one to the next?

Thesis Statement

1. What main point are you trying to make in your essay?

   _____

2. Put brackets around the last sentence in your introduction. Does it contain your main point?

   _____

3. Rewrite your thesis statement if necessary so that it states your main point and introduces your topics.

Basic Elements

1. Give your essay a title if it doesn't have one.

   _____

2. Does your introduction capture your readers' attention and build up to your thesis statement at the end of the paragraph?

   _____

3. Does each of your body paragraphs deal with only one topic?

   _____

4. Does your conclusion follow some of the suggestions offered in Part I?

   _____

Development

1. Write out your thesis statement (revised, if necessary), and list your topic sentences below it.

    Thesis statement: _____

    Topic 1: _____

    Topic 2: _____

    Topic 3: _____

2. Do your topics adequately support your thesis statement?

    _____

3. Does each body paragraph have a focused topic sentence?

    _____

4. Do you cover the same characteristics of both topics?

    _____

5. Where do your readers need more information?

    _____

6. Make two of your details more specific.
7. Add at least two new details to make your comparison clearer.

Unity

1. Read each of your topic sentences with your thesis statement in mind. Do they go together?

    _____

2. Revise them if necessary so they are directly related.
3. Drop or rewrite any of the sentences in your body paragraphs that are not directly related to their topic sentences.

Organization

1. Read your essay again to see if all the paragraphs are arranged logically.

2. How is your essay organized: subject by subject, point by point, or a combination of the two?

   _____

3. Is the order you chose for your paragraphs the most effective approach to your subject?

   _____

4. Move any paragraphs that are out of order.

5. Look closely at your body paragraphs to see if all the sentences are arranged logically within paragraphs.

6. Move any sentences that are out of order.

Coherence

For a list of transitions, see pages 83–84.

1. Add two transitions to your essay.

2. Circle five synonyms you use.

3. Explain how two of these make your essay easier to read.

   _____

   _____

Now rewrite your essay with your revisions.

EDITING CHECKLIST ✔

SENTENCES

- ☐ Does each sentence have a main subject and verb?
- ☐ Do all subjects and verbs agree?
- ☐ Do all pronouns agree with their nouns?
- ☐ Are modifiers as close as possible to the words they modify?

PUNCTUATION AND MECHANICS
- ☐ Are sentences punctuated correctly?
- ☐ Are words capitalized properly?

WORD CHOICE AND SPELLING
- ☐ Are words used correctly?
- ☐ Are words spelled correctly?

Sentences

Subjects and Verbs

1. Underline the subjects once and verbs twice in a paragraph of your revised essay. Remember that sentences can have more than one subject-verb set.
2. Does each of your sentences have at least one subject and verb that can stand alone?

For help with subjects and verbs, see Chapter 34.

3. Correct any fragments you have written.
4. Correct any run-together sentences you have written.

For help with fragments, see Chapter 35.

For help with run-togethers, see Chapter 36.

Subject-verb Agreement

1. Read aloud the subjects and verbs you underlined in your revised essay.
2. Correct any subjects and verbs that do not agree.

For help with subject-verb agreement, see Chapter 39.

Pronoun Agreement

1. Find any pronouns in your revised essay that do not agree with their nouns.
2. Correct any pronouns that do not agree with their nouns.

For help with pronoun agreement, see Chapter 43.

Modifiers

1. Find any modifiers in your revised essay that are not as close as possible to the words they modify.
2. Rewrite sentences if necessary so that your modifiers are as close as possible to the words they modify.

For help with modifier errors, see Chapter 46.

Punctuation and Mechanics

Punctuation

For help with punctuation, see Chapters 47–51.

1. Read your revised essay for any errors in punctuation.
2. Make sure any fragments and run-together sentences you revised are punctuated correctly.

Mechanics

For help with capitalization, see Chapter 52.

1. Read your revised essay for any errors in capitalization.
2. Be sure to check your capitalization in any fragments or run-together sentences you revised.

Word Choice and Spelling

Word Choice

For help with confused words, see Chapter 58.

1. Find any words used incorrectly in your revised essay.
2. Correct any errors you find.

Spelling

For help with spelling, see Chapter 59.

1. Use spell-check and a dictionary to check your spelling.
2. Correct any misspelled words.

Now rewrite your essay again with your editing corrections.

PRACTICING COMPARISON/CONTRAST

Reading Suggestions

In Chapter 29, you will find two essays that illustrate good comparison/contrast writing: "The American Family" by Stephanie Coontz compares the institution of the family over the years, and "Between Worlds" by Tony Cohan compares and contrasts a writer's life in two separate locations. You might want to read these selections before writing another comparison/contrast essay. As you read, notice how the writers make their points through well-thought-out, detailed comparisons and contrasts.

Service Learning Project

SERVICE LEARNING PROJECT

This assignment is another step in the Service Learning project. If you choose to use this feature of the text, each chapter in Part II has an assignment that asks students to use a different rhetorical mode to reflect on their Service Learning project. These reflections will lead to an essay assignment in Part III (Chapter 22). You can assign as many or as few of these

This assignment is based on a Service Learning project of your choice. If your instructor has already introduced service learning to the class, you will be doing these exercises when they are assigned. At this point, choose a project you would like to pursue, or continue work on a project you have already begun. This assignment in Part II will help you prepare for an essay on this project in Part III. Here is another stage in the preparation for this essay:

For the Service Learning project you have taken on, compare and contrast two aspects of your project. This might be two different stages, two tasks, or two separate products. Use the guidelines you have learned in this chapter to help you record your comparison/contrast insights. But remember that these are just thoughts that will be developed into an essay in Part III.

Writing Workshop

> **Guidelines for Writing a Comparison/Contrast Essay**
>
> 1. Decide what point you want to make with your comparison, and state it in your thesis statement.
> 2. Choose items to compare and contrast that will make your point most effectively.
> 3. Use as many specific details and examples as possible to expand your comparison.
> 4. Develop your comparison in a balanced way.
> 5. Organize your essay subject by subject or point by point—or combine the two approaches.

exercises as you want in preparation for this essay. For more information on service learning, see the *Instructor's Resource Manual,* Section I, Part III.

ADDITIONAL WRITING TOPIC

Have your students turn to Chapter 29 and read Stephanie Coontz's "American Family" or Tony Cohan's "Between Worlds." Then have them write an essay on one of the topics from "Writing Topics: Comparing and Contrasting" at the end of the chapter.

TEACHING ON
THE WEB
Discussion Topic:
Divide students into
groups of three or four.
Ask them to compare
and contrast a single
search engine (like
Google.com) with one
that surveys multiple
search engines (like
dogpile.com). In what
circumstances is one
better than the other?
What are the advan-
tages of both?

TEACHING ON
THE WEB
Links: Provide students
with a topic, and have
them link to three Web
sites that deal with that
topic. How are these
sites similar in their
treatment of the topic?
How are they different?
    Possible sites for the
topic "education":
    U.S. Department
        of Education,
        www.ed.gov
    *Chronicle of Higher
        Education,*
        http://chronicle.
        merit.com
    American Council
        on Education,
        www.acenet.edu

TEACHING ON
THE WEB
Research: Have
students find Web sites
that sell the same types
of products. How are
these sites similar?
How are they different?
Which product would
students buy based on
the Web sites? How did

1. Compare and contrast the two buildings on the previous page. What details in both buildings are different? What are the same? What is the overall message you get from these two buildings? Look at both the obvious and the not-so-obvious.

2. Choose a job being advertised in your local newspaper's classified section, and write a cover letter to the employer comparing yourself to your probable competition. What are your best qualifications compared to others who might be applying for this job? What are your weaknesses in comparison to them? Why would you be the best candidate for the job?

3. Discuss the similarities and differences between two cities that you know well. How are they the same? How are they different? What do you think accounts for these similarities and differences? When you write your essay, consider whether a subject-by-subject or a point-by-point organization would be more effective.

4. Create your own comparison/contrast assignment (with the help of your instructor), and write a response to it.

Revising Workshop

Small Group Activity (5–10 minutes per writer)   Working in groups of three or four, each person should read his or her comparison/contrast essay to the other members of the group. Those listening should record their reactions on a copy of the Peer Evaluation Form in Appendix 2E. After your group goes through this process, give your evaluation forms to the appropriate writers so that each writer has two or three peer comment sheets for revising.

Paired Activity (5 minutes per writer)   Using the completed Peer Evaluation Forms, work in pairs to decide what you should revise in your essay. If time allows, rewrite some of your sentences, and have your partner look at them.

Individual Activity   Rewrite your paper, using the revising feedback you received from other students.

Editing Workshop

Paired Activity (5–10 minutes per writer)   Swap papers with a classmate, and use the editing portion of your Peer Evaluation Form to identify as many grammar, punctuation, mechanics, and spelling errors as you can. If time allows, correct some of your errors, and have your partner look at them.

Record your grammar, punctuation, and mechanics errors in the Error Log (Appendix 6) and your spelling errors in the Spelling Log (Appendix 7).

Individual Activity   Rewrite your paper again, using the editing feedback you received from other students.

Reflecting on Your Writing

When you have completed your own essay, answer these six questions.
1. What was most difficult about this assignment?
2. What was easiest?
3. What did you learn about using comparing and contrasting by completing this assignment?
4. What do you think are the strengths of your comparison/contrast essay? Place a wavy line by the parts of your essay that you feel are very good.
5. What are the weaknesses, if any, of your paper? Place an X by the parts of your essay you would like help with. Write any questions you have in the margin.
6. What did you learn from this assignment about your own writing process—about preparing to write, about writing the first draft, about revising, and about editing?

comparison and contrast help them come to this decision?

TEACHING ON THE WEB
Mosaics Web Site: To learn more about comparison and contrast, students can go to www.prenhall.com/mosaics.

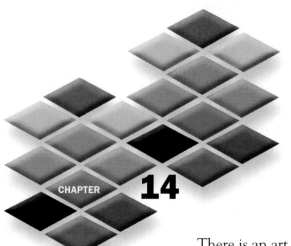

DIVIDING AND CLASSIFYING

There is an art of reading, as well as an art of thinking and an art of writing.

—ISAAC D'ISRAELI

Division and classification ensure that we have a certain amount of order in our lives. In fact, we constantly use these two processes to navigate through our days. Thanks to classification, you know where to find the milk in the grocery store and the chapter on World War II in your history textbook. Also, when you choose a major and a career, you use division and classification to make your choice. Division and classification are such a natural part of everyday life that we often don't even know we are using them.

In addition, we regularly use division and classification when we write. Actually, division and classification are a vital part of our written communication every day—in our personal lives, in college courses, and in the workplace:

You divide your expenses into categories to create a budget.

A student explains three types of bacteria on a biology exam.

A student writes a report on types of hazardous materials for a science course.

A personal banker prepares a flyer about the types of savings accounts that are available.

The manager of a music store suggests to the home office a new system for arranging CDs.

Like comparison and contrast, division and classification are really two parts of the same process. **Division** is sorting—dividing something into its basic parts, such as a home into rooms. Division moves from a single, large category (home) to many smaller subcategories (kitchen, bath, living room, and so forth). **Classification,** grouping items together, moves in the opposite direction, from many subgroups to a single, large category. For example, all the pieces of furniture in a home can be classified as living room furniture or bedroom furniture. Division and classification help us organize information so that we can make sense of our complex world. Dividing large categories into smaller ones (division) and grouping many items into larger categories (classification) both help us put a lot of information into useful groups.

also shows how these strategies work together.

WRITING A DIVISION/CLASSIFICATION ESSAY

Here is a sample division/classification essay by Fran Lebowitz called "The Sound of Music: Enough Already." It classifies the types of music Lebowitz dislikes the most. What are some of your dislikes? Are these also your biggest pet peeves? Why do you dislike these things or behaviors?

THE SOUND OF MUSIC: ENOUGH ALREADY
by Fran Lebowitz

First off, I want to say that as far as I am concerned, in instances where I have not personally and deliberately sought it out, the only difference between music and Muzak is the spelling. Pablo Casals practicing across the hall with the door open—being trapped in an elevator, the ceiling of which is broadcasting "Parsley, Sage, Rosemary, and Thyme"—it's all the same to me. Harsh words? Perhaps. But then again these are not gentle times we live in. And they are being made no more gentle by this incessant melody that was once real life.   1

There was a time when music knew its place. No longer. Possibly this is not music's fault. It may be that music fell in with a bad crowd and lost its sense of common decency. I am willing to consider this. I am willing even to try and help. I would like to do my bit to set music straight in order that it might shape up and leave the mainstream of society. The first thing that music must understand is that there are two kinds of music—good music and bad music. Good music is music that I want to hear. Bad music is music that I don't want to hear.   2

So that music might more clearly see the error of its ways, I offer the following. If you are music and you recognize yourself on this list, you are bad music.   3

1. Music in Other People's Clock Radios

4   There are times when I find myself spending the night in the home of another. Frequently the other is in a more reasonable line of work than I and must arise at a specific hour. Ofttimes the other, unbeknownst to me, manipulates an appliance in such a way that I am awakened by Stevie Wonder. On such occasions I announce that, if I wished to be awakened by Stevie Wonder, I would sleep with Stevie Wonder. I do not, however, wish to be awakened by Stevie Wonder and that is why God invented alarm clocks. Sometimes the other realizes that I am right. Sometimes the other does not. And that is why God invented many others.

2. Music Residing in the Hold Buttons of Other People's Business Telephones

5   I do not under any circumstances enjoy hold buttons. But I am a woman of reason. I can accept reality. I can face the facts. What I cannot face is the music. Just as there are two kinds of music—good and bad—so there are two kinds of hold buttons—good and bad. Good hold buttons are hold buttons that hold one silently. Bad hold buttons are hold buttons that hold one musically. When I hold, I want to hold silently. That is the way it was meant to be, for that is what God was talking about when he said, "Forever hold your peace." He would have added, "and quiet," but he thought you were smarter.

3. Music in the Streets

6   The past few years have seen a steady increase in the number of people playing music in the streets. The past few years have also seen a steady increase in the number of malignant diseases. Are these two facts related? One wonders. But even if they are not—and, as I have pointed out, one cannot be sure—music in the streets has definitely taken its toll. For it is at the very least disorienting. When one is walking down Fifth Avenue, one does not expect to hear a string quartet playing a Strauss waltz. What one expects to hear while walking down Fifth Avenue is traffic. When one does indeed hear a string quartet playing a Strauss waltz while one is walking down Fifth Avenue, one is apt to become confused and imagine that one is not walking down Fifth Avenue at all but rather that one has somehow wound up in Old Vienna. Should one imagine that one is in Old Vienna, one is likely to become upset when one realizes that in Old Vienna there is no sale at Charles Jourdan. And that is why when I walk down Fifth Avenue I want to hear traffic.

4. Music in the Movies

7   I'm not talking about musicals. Musicals are movies that warn you by saying, "Lots of music here. Take it or leave it." I'm talking about regular

movies that extend no such courtesy but allow unsuspecting people to come to see them and then assault them with a barrage of unasked-for tunes. There are two major offenders in this category: black movies and movies set in the fifties. Both types of movies are afflicted with the same misconception. They don't know that movies are supposed to be movies. They think that movies are supposed to be records with pictures. They have failed to understand that if God had wanted records to have pictures, he would not have invented television.

5. Music in Public Places Such as Restaurants, Supermarkets, Hotel Lobbies, Airports, Etc.

When I am in any of the above-mentioned places, I am not there to hear   8
music. I am there for whatever reason is appropriate to the respective place. I am no more interested in hearing "Mack the Knife" while waiting for the shuttle to Boston than someone sitting ringside at the Sands Hotel is interested in being forced to choose between sixteen varieties of cottage cheese. If God had meant for everything to happen at once, he would not have invented desk calendars.

Epilogue

Some people talk to themselves. Some people sing to themselves. Is one   9
group better than the other? Did not God create all people equal? Yes, God created all people equal. Only to some he gave the ability to make up their own words.

 PREPARING TO WRITE YOUR OWN DIVISION/CLASSIFICATION ESSAY

Everyone has pet peeves. What are yours? How did you develop these pet peeves? Do your pet peeves form any particular patterns? Use one or more of the prewriting strategies that you learned in Chapter 2 to explore this topic.

How to Write a Division/Classification Essay

To write a division/classification essay, keep in mind that the same items can be divided and classified in many different ways. Your friends probably don't all organize their closets the way you do, and no two kitchens are

INSTRUCTOR'S
RESOURCE MANUAL
For additional material about teaching division and classification; for

journal entries; and for multiple-choice, short-answer, and paragraph tests, see the *Instructor's Resource Manual,* Section II, Part II.

organized exactly alike. The United States can be divided many different ways—into 50 states, four regions (Northeast, Midwest, South, and Pacific), and six time zones (Eastern, Central, Mountain, Pacific, Alaska, and Hawaii). Similarly, in writing you can divide and classify a topic in different ways. Whatever your method of dividing or classifying, use the following guidelines to help you write an effective division/classification essay.

1. *Decide on your purpose for writing, and make it part of your thesis statement.* Dividing and classifying in themselves are not particularly interesting. But they are very useful techniques if you are trying to make a specific point. That point, or purpose, should be in your thesis statement. Look at these two examples:

   A. There are three types of dangerous drivers on the road today.
   B. Being aware of three types of dangerous drivers on the road today could save your life.

Both thesis statements name a category—dangerous drivers—but only thesis statement B gives the reader a good reason to keep reading: Knowing the three types could save your life.

In our sample essay, Lebowitz uses division and classification to make fun of the types of music she dislikes. She divides all music into good music and bad music. Then she breaks bad music into five categories. She captures the humor of her essay in her thesis at the end of paragraph 3: "If you are music and you recognize yourself on this list, you are bad music."

2. *Divide your topic into categories that don't overlap.* Since most subjects can be classified in different ways, your next task in writing a division/classification essay is to decide on what basis you will divide your subject into categories. First, gather information to come up with a list of all the possible topics. Second, decide on what basis you will put these topics into categories. Next, make sure some of your topics don't fall into two categories. Your categories should be separate enough that your topics fall into one category only. Also, don't add a category at the last minute to accommodate a topic. Keep adjusting your categories until they work with your thesis.

In the sample essay, the author uses a combination of division and classification to make her point. First, she divides all music into good and bad. Then she classifies bad music into five categories: (1) music in other people's clock radios, (2) music in the hold buttons of other people's business telephones, (3) music in the streets, (4) music in the movies, and (5) music in public places such as restaurants, supermarkets, hotel lobbies, and airports. She might have tried to classify bad music in other ways, such as public and private; indoor, outdoor, and a combination of the two; or personal, business-related, and involving other people. But none of these options would be effective. The first two groupings are too general to supply the detailed information that Lebowitz's categories give us. The third set of categories would force the author to classify many topics, like music in the movies and music in public places, in two categories, which would be confusing. Lebowitz's more specific categories are all about the same size and are very effective in sending her humorous message.

3. ***Clearly explain each category.*** With division, you are trying to show what differences break the items into separate groups or types. With classification, you let the similarities in the items help you set up categories that make sense. In either case, you need to explain each category fully and provide enough details to help your readers see your subject in a new way. To do this, use vivid description and carefully chosen examples. Comparison and contrast (Chapter 13) is also a useful technique because when you classify items, you are looking at how they are alike (comparison) and how they are different (contrast).

    Lebowitz uses comparison and contrast to place her ideas into categories. Then she describes each category and provides detailed examples, such as Stevie Wonder, a Strauss waltz, and "Mack the Knife," to fill out her descriptions. As a result, she explains each of her categories fully and clearly.

4. ***Organize your categories logically.*** Your method of organization should make sense and be easy for readers to follow. Most often, this means organizing from one extreme to another. For example, you might organize your types from most obvious to least obvious. Or you might move from least important to most important, from least humorous to most humorous, from largest to smallest—or the other way around. In every case, though, try to end with the category that is most memorable.

    Fran Lebowitz's essay is arranged from one extreme to another—from personal to public. The categories move from clock radios to business phones to music in the streets to music in movies to music in public places. Each category gets farther from the personal realm, which helps Lebowitz prove that bad music is everywhere.

5. *Use transitions to move your readers through your essay.* Transitions will help your readers move from one category to another and follow your train of thought. They will also keep your essay from sounding choppy or boring.

Since Lebowitz gives her categories headings, she doesn't need to use transitions to move from one category to another. But she does use transitions within her paragraphs. Here are some effective transitions from Lebowitz's essay: "first off" (paragraph 1), "there was a time when" (paragraph 2), "frequently" (paragraph 4), "on such occasions" (paragraph 4), "but" (paragraph 5), and "when" (paragraphs 6 and 8). These words and phrases serve as traffic signals that guide Lebowitz's readers through her essay.

 WRITING YOUR OWN DIVISION/CLASSIFICATION ESSAY

Write an essay explaining your various pet peeves. How did these pet peeves start? Why do you have them? Begin by reviewing your prewriting notes. Next, divide your subject into distinct categories, and write a clear thesis statement. Then develop your essay with specific examples that explain each category.

 WORKING WITH A STUDENT ESSAY

TEACHING TIPS
The following eight teaching tips are based on Howard Gardner's list of multiple intelligences:

Verbal/Linguistic
Provide students with four very limited categories, and ask them to determine how many classifications the categories can fall into. For example, show students how "small, eight-week-old golden retriever puppy" might fall into the

Sergio Mendola, a student writer, uses division and classification in an essay about neighbors. Called "Won't You Be My Neighbor?" it divides and classifies neighbors into specific categories to prove a point. See if you can identify his main point as you read this draft of his essay.

WON'T YOU BE MY NEIGHBOR?

1   Neighborhoods can be strange places. Every one is different, but they are all made up of the same ingredient—neighbors. In today's world, though, most people don't know there neighbors. It's not like the '50s. When people knew what their neighbors were doing. But in every neighborhood today, you can find at least one Mystery Neighbor, one Perfect Cleaver Family, and one Good Neighbor Family.

The first type of neighbor everyone has is the Perfect Cleaver Family. This family has the perfect parents and the perfect children. They are the June and Ward Cleavers of today. They have 2.5 perfect children. Although these children get in their share of minor trouble, the children never repeat the same mistake after the parents express their disappointment. And then, to avoid future disappointments, the children always keep their parents' values in mind before making decisions. Eddie Haskell left a lot to be desired. I don't know what his values are. The Cleaver-type children later become heart surgeons or police chiefs in order to help the world around them. These neighbors are the role models for everyone else.

Then there is the Mystery Neighbor. The Mystery Neighbor remains aloof, and the only way the other neighbors know someone lives at the Mystery House is because the newspaper disappears sometime during the day and the lawn somehow gets mowed every week. Every once in a while, a car will sit in the driveway, but no one knows for sure if the car belongs to the people who own the house. Neighborhood children make up stories about the Mystery Neighbor, which are based on nothing and compete with the best urban legends. The Mystery Neighbor is usually a workaholic or a traveling salesperson, but this doesn't stop the neighbors from wondering.

The best type of neighbor in any neighborhood is the Good Neighbor Family. Made up of very reliable people. This family is always reaching out to other neighbors. Whenever something goes wrong, someone from the Good Neighbor Family is the first person at the doorstep to lend a helping hand. These neighbors will water the plants and feed the animals for people on vacation who always want to help others. They create the kinds of friendships that continue even when one family moves away. Sometimes the parents might try to "fix up" their boy and girl children so that the families relationship can be legally cemented for life. The Good Neighbor Family is one that everyone hopes to encounter at least once in a lifetime.

This mixture of neighbors makes up a very good neighborhood. It creates a neighborhood that functions smoothly and thoughtfully. And even though people don't no their neighbors like they used to 50 years ago, they will probably find at least three different types of neighbors if they look hard enough: the Perfect Cleaver Family, the Mystery Neighbor, and the Good Neighbor Family. It would be sad to be missing any one of them.

2 classifications "family," "children," "friend," "playmate," "responsibility," and so on.

Musical/Rhythmic

Have students divide "popular music" into categories and subcategories. How can these categories help someone understand the music of today?

Logical/Mathematic

Provide students with an abundance of related words that can be divided into three levels. Then have students diagram the main classification and the divisions that can stem from this category. For example, use *"fun"* as one level; *sports, leisure,* and *vacation* as a second level; and *soccer, softball, racquetball, reading, watching TV, sunbathing, family trips, spring break,* and *weekend getaways* as a third level.

Visual/Spatial

Bring several books to class. Have students divide the books into logical categories. How many categories can students generate? How many books fit into more than one category?

Discovering How the Essay Works

1. This essay doesn't simply classify neighbors for their own sake. It has a broader message. What is Sergio's general purpose in this essay?

   To explain that every neighborhood has the same three basic types of

   neighbors that make a neighborhood interesting.

2. Does Sergio divide his subject into categories that don't overlap?

   He makes sure that he has three distinct categories, and he develops

   each one separately.

3. Does Sergio clearly explain each of his categories? Explain your answer.

   Sergio clearly explains each category by providing examples that illus-

   trate the different types of neighbors.

4. How does Sergio organize his categories? Is this the most logical order for this purpose? Explain your answer.

   He moves from least to most desirable neighbor. It is effective and

   logical, although the body paragraphs are out of order.

5. What transitions does Sergio use to move his essay along smoothly?

   The first type

   Then

   The best type of neighbor

Revising and Editing the Student Essay

   This essay is Sergio's first draft, which now needs to be revised and edited. First, apply the Revising Checklist on the next page to the content of Sergio's draft. When you are satisfied that his ideas are fully developed and well organized, use the Editing Checklist on page 248 to correct his grammar and mechanics errors. Answer the questions after each checklist. Then write your suggested changes directly on Sergio's draft.

and editing. You could teach these skills in a class discussion, in small groups, or in pairs.

REVISING CHECKLIST ✔

THESIS STATEMENT

✔ Does the thesis statement contain the essay's controlling idea?

✔ Does the thesis appear as the last sentence of the introduction?

BASIC ELEMENTS

✔ Does the title draw in the readers?

✔ Does the introduction capture the readers' attention and build up to the thesis statement effectively?

✔ Does each body paragraph deal with a single topic?

✔ Does the conclusion bring the essay to a close in an interesting way?

DEVELOPMENT

✔ Do the body paragraphs adequately support the thesis statement?

✔ Does each body paragraph have a focused topic sentence?

✔ Does each body paragraph contain *specific* details that support the topic sentence?

✔ Does each body paragraph include *enough* details to explain the topic sentence fully?

UNITY

✔ Do the essay's topic sentences relate directly to the thesis statement?

✔ Do the details in each body paragraph support its topic sentence?

ORGANIZATION

✔ Is the essay organized logically?

✔ Is each body paragraph organized logically?

COHERENCE

✔ Are transitions used effectively so that paragraphs move smoothly and logically from one to the next?

✔ Do the sentences move smoothly and logically from one to the next?

REVISING STRATEGIES
This chapter focuses on the following revising elements:
Basic elements
Development
Unity
Organization
Coherence

Thesis Statement

1. Put brackets around the last sentence in Sergio's introduction. Does it introduce his purpose?

    Yes

2. Rewrite Sergio's thesis statement if necessary so that it states his purpose and introduces his topics.

    His thesis states his purpose and introduces his topics.

Basic Elements

1. Give Sergio's essay an alternate title.

    Answers will vary.

2. Rewrite Sergio's introduction so that it captures the readers' attention and builds up to the thesis statement at the end of the paragraph.

    Answers will vary.

3. Does each of Sergio's body paragraphs deal with only one topic?

    Yes

4. Rewrite Sergio's conclusion using at least one suggestion from Part I.

    Answers will vary.

Development

1. Write out Sergio's thesis statement (revised, if necessary), and list his three topic sentences below it.

Thesis statement: _But in every neighborhood today, you can find at least one Mystery Neighbor, one Perfect Cleaver Family, and one Good Neighbor Family._

Topic 1: _The first type of neighbor everyone has is the Perfect Cleaver Family._

Topic 2: _Then there is the Mystery Neighbor._

Topic 3: _The best type of neighbor in any neighborhood is the Good Neighbor Family._

2. Do Sergio's topics adequately support his thesis statement?

   Yes

3. Does each body paragraph have a focused topic sentence?

   Yes

4. Do Sergio's details adequately explain his categories?

   Yes, but he could use more detail.

5. Where do you need more information?

   Answers will vary.

6. Make two of Sergio's details more specific. _Answers will vary._

7. Add two new details to make his essay clearer. _Answers will vary._

Unity

1. Read each of Sergio's topic sentences with his thesis statement (revised, if necessary) in mind. Do they go together?

   Yes

2. Revise them if necessary so they are directly related.

3. Drop or rewrite the two sentences in paragraph 2 that are not directly related to their topic sentences. *Sentences 7 and 8*

Organization

1. Read Sergio's essay again to see if all the paragraphs are arranged logically.

2. Reverse the two paragraphs that are out of order. *Reverse paragraphs 2 and 3.*

3. Look closely at Sergio's body paragraphs to see if all his sentences are arranged logically within paragraphs.

4. Move any sentences that are out of order. *All sentences are in order.*

Coherence

For a list of transitions, see pages 83–84.

For a list of pronouns, see pages 508–509.

1. Add two transitions to Sergio's essay.

2. Circle five transitions, repetitions, synonyms, or pronouns Sergio uses.

3. Explain how two of these make Sergio's essay easier to read.

_____

_____

Now rewrite Sergio's essay with your revisions.

EDITING STRATEGIES

This chapter focuses on the following editing problems:

Fragments
Modifier errors
Apostrophes
 (possession)
Confused words

EDITING CHECKLIST ✔

SENTENCES

✔ Does each sentence have a main subject and verb?

✔ Do all subjects and verbs agree?

✔ Do all pronouns agree with their nouns?

✔ Are modifiers as close as possible to the words they modify?

PUNCTUATION AND MECHANICS

✔ Are sentences punctuated correctly?

✔ Are words capitalized properly?

WORD CHOICE AND SPELLING

✔ Are words used correctly?

✔ Are words spelled correctly?

Sentences

Subjects and Verbs

1. Underline the subjects once and verbs twice in paragraphs 1 and 4 of your revision of Sergio's essay. Remember that sentences can have more than one subject-verb set.

For help with subjects and verbs, see Chapter 34.

2. Does each of the sentences have at least one subject and verb that can stand alone?

   No

3. Did you find and correct Sergio's two fragments? If not, find and correct them now. *Paragraph 1, sentence 5; paragraph 4, sentence 2*

For help with fragments, see Chapter 35.

Subject-Verb Agreement

1. Read aloud the subjects and verbs you underlined in your revision of Sergio's essay.

2. Correct any subjects and verbs that do not agree. *All subjects and verbs agree.*

For help with subject-verb agreement, see Chapter 39.

Pronoun Agreement

1. Find any pronouns in your revision of Sergio's essay that do not agree with their nouns. *All pronouns agree with their nouns.*

2. Correct any pronouns that do not agree with their nouns.

For help with pronoun agreement, see Chapter 43.

Modifiers

1. Find any modifiers in your revision of Sergio's essay that are not as close as possible to the words they modify.

2. Did you find and correct Sergio's modifier error? If not, find and correct it now. *Paragraph 4, sentence 5*

For help with modifier errors, see Chapter 46.

Punctuation and Mechanics

Punctuation

1. Read your revision of Sergio's essay for any errors in punctuation.

2. Find the two fragments you revised, and make sure they are punctuated correctly.

For help with punctuation, see Chapters 47–51.

3. Did you find and correct the missing apostrophe in Sergio's essay? *Paragraph 4, sentence 7*

Mechanics

1. Read your revision of Sergio's essay for any errors in capitalization.

2. Be sure to check Sergio's capitalization in the fragments you revised.

For help with capitalization, see Chapter 52.

Word Choice and Spelling

Word Choice

For help with confused words, see Chapter 58.

1. Find any words used incorrectly in your revision of Sergio's essay. *there/their (paragraph 1, sentence 3); too/to (paragraph 4, sentence 4); know/no (paragraph 5, sentence 3)*

2. Did you find and correct his three confused words? If not, find and correct them now.

Spelling

For help with spelling, see Chapter 59.

1. Use spell-check and a dictionary to check the spelling in your revision of Sergio's essay. *All words are spelled correctly.*

2. Correct any misspelled words.

Now rewrite Sergio's essay again with your editing corrections.

 WORKING WITH YOUR OWN ESSAY

Returning to the division/classification essay you wrote earlier in this chapter, revise and edit your own writing. The checklists here will help you apply what you have learned to your essay.

Revising and Editing Your Own Essay

REVISING CHECKLIST ✔

CLASS ACTIVITY

Take some of the categories that students created for the "Write Your Own Division/Classification Essay" at the beginning of this chapter, and show how the categories were divided from the classification "pet peeves" and how, when reversed, the divisions create the same main classification.

THESIS STATEMENT

☐ Does the thesis statement contain the essay's controlling idea?

☐ Does the thesis appear as the last sentence of the introduction?

BASIC ELEMENTS

☐ Does the title draw in the readers?

☐ Does the introduction capture the readers' attention and build up to the thesis statement effectively?

☐ Does each body paragraph deal with a single topic?

☐ Does the conclusion bring the essay to a close in an interesting way?

DEVELOPMENT
- ☐ Do the body paragraphs adequately support the thesis statement?
- ☐ Does each body paragraph have a focused topic sentence?
- ☐ Does each body paragraph contain *specific* details that support the topic sentence?
- ☐ Does each body paragraph include *enough* details to explain the topic sentence fully?

UNITY
- ☐ Do the essay's topic sentences relate directly to the thesis statement?
- ☐ Do the details in each body paragraph support its topic sentence?

ORGANIZATION
- ☐ Is the essay organized logically?
- ☐ Is each body paragraph organized logically?

COHERENCE
- ☐ Are transitions used effectively so that paragraphs move smoothly and logically from one to the next?
- ☐ Do the sentences move smoothly and logically from one to the next?

Thesis Statement

1. What is the purpose or general message you want to send to your readers?

   _____

2. Put brackets around the last sentence in your introduction. Does it explain your purpose?

   _____

3. Rewrite your thesis statement if necessary so that it states your purpose and introduces your topics.

Basic Elements

1. Give your essay a title if it doesn't have one.

   _____

2. Does your introduction capture your readers' attention and build up to your thesis statement at the end of the paragraph?

   _____

3. Does each of your body paragraphs deal with only one topic?

   _____

4. Does your conclusion follow some of the suggestions offered in Part I?

   _____

Development

1. Write out your thesis statement (revised, if necessary), and list your topic sentences below it.

   Thesis statement: _____

   Topic 1: _____

   Topic 2: _____

   Topic 3: _____

2. Do your topics adequately support your thesis statement?

   _____

3. Does each body paragraph have a focused topic sentence?

   _____

4. Do your details adequately explain your categories?

   _____

5. Where do you need more information?

   _____

6. Make two of your details more specific.
7. Add at least two new details to make your essay clearer.

Unity

1. Read each of your topic sentences with your thesis statement in mind. Do they go together?

   _____

2. Revise them if necessary so they are directly related.
3. Drop or rewrite any of the sentences in your body paragraphs that are not directly related to their topic sentences.

Organization

1. Read your essay again to see if all the paragraphs are arranged logically.
2. Refer to your answers to the development questions. Then identify your method of organization.

   _____

3. Is the order you chose for your paragraphs the most effective approach to your topic?

   _____

4. Move any paragraphs that are out of order.
5. Look closely at your body paragraphs to see if all the sentences are arranged logically within paragraphs.
6. Move any sentences that are out of order.

Coherence

1. Add two transitions to your essay.
2. Circle five transitions, repetitions, synonyms, or pronouns you use.
3. Explain how two of them make your paragraphs easier to read.

   _____

   _____

For a list of transitions, see pages 83–84.

For a list of pronouns, see pages 508–509.

Now rewrite your essay with your revisions.

EDITING CHECKLIST ✔

SENTENCES

☐ Does each sentence have a main subject and verb?

☐ Do all subjects and verbs agree?

☐ Do all pronouns agree with their nouns?

☐ Are modifiers as close as possible to the words they modify?

PUNCTUATION AND MECHANICS

☐ Are sentences punctuated correctly?

☐ Are words capitalized properly?

WORD CHOICE AND SPELLING

☐ Are words used correctly?

☐ Are words spelled correctly?

Sentences

Subjects and Verbs

For help with subjects and verbs, see Chapter 34.

1. Underline the subjects once and verbs twice in a paragraph of your revised essay. Remember that sentences can have more than one subject-verb set.

2. Does each of your sentences have at least one subject and verb that can stand alone?

For help with fragments, see Chapter 35.

For help with run-togethers, see Chapter 36.

3. Correct any fragments you have written.

4. Correct any run-together sentences you have written.

Subject-Verb Agreement

For help with subject-verb agreement, see Chapter 39.

1. Read aloud the subjects and verbs you underlined in your revised essay.

2. Correct any subjects and verbs that do not agree.

Pronoun Agreement

For help with pronoun agreement, see Chapter 43.

1. Find any pronouns in your revised essay that do not agree with their nouns.

2. Correct any pronouns that do not agree with their nouns.

Modifiers

1. Find any modifiers in your revised essay that are not as close as possible to the words they modify.
2. Rewrite sentences if necessary so your modifiers are as close as possible to the words they modify.

For help with modifier errors, see Chapter 46.

Punctuation and Mechanics

Punctuation

1. Read your revised essay for any errors in punctuation.
2. Make sure any fragments and run-together sentences you revised are punctuated correctly.

For help with punctuation, see Chapters 47–51.

Mechanics

1. Read your revised essay for any errors in capitalization.
2. Be sure to check your capitalization in any fragments or run-together sentences you revised.

For help with capitalization, see Chapter 52.

Word Choice and Spelling

Word Choice

1. Find any words used incorrectly in your revised essay.
2. Correct any errors you find.

For help with confused words, see Chapter 58.

Spelling

1. Use spell-check and a dictionary to check your spelling.
2. Correct any misspelled words.

Now rewrite your essay again with your editing corrections.

For help with spelling, see Chapter 59.

PRACTICING DIVISION AND CLASSIFICATION

Reading Suggestions

In Chapter 30, you will find two essays that illustrate good division and classification writing: "Black Music in Our Hands" by Bernice Reagon categorizes different kinds of music she has encountered, while "What Are Friends For?" by Marion Winik discusses different types of friends. You might want to read these selections before writing another division and

SERVICE LEARNING PROJECT
This assignment is another step in the Service Learning project. If you choose to use this feature of the text, each chapter in

Part II has an assignment that asks students to use a different rhetorical mode to reflect on their Service Learning project. These reflections will lead to an essay assignment in Part III (Chapter 22). You can assign as many or as few of these exercises as you want in preparation for this essay. For more information on service learning, see the *Instructor's Resource Manual*, Section I, Part III.

classification essay. As you read, notice how the authors' categories support the points they are making.

Service Learning Project

This assignment is based on a Service Learning project of your choice. If your instructor has already introduced service learning to the class, you will be doing these exercises when they are assigned. At this point, choose a project you would like to pursue, or continue work on a project you have already begun. This assignment in Part II will help you prepare for an essay on this project in Part III. Here is another stage in the preparation for this essay:

For the Service Learning project you have taken on, divide and/or classify the basic chores connected with your project. Use the guidelines you have learned in this chapter to help you write your division/classification notes. But remember that these are just thoughts that will be developed into an essay in Part III.

ADDITIONAL
WRITING TOPIC
Have your students turn to Chapter 30 and read Marion Winik's "What Are Friends For?" or Bernice Reagon's "Black Music in Our Hands." Then have them write an essay on one of the topics from "Writing Topics: Dividing and Classifying" at the end of the chapter.

Writing Workshop

Guidelines for Writing a Division/Classification Essay

1. Decide on your purpose for writing, and make it part of your thesis statement.
2. Divide your topic into categories that don't overlap.
3. Clearly explain each category.
4. Organize your categories logically.
5. Use transitions to move your readers through your essay.

---

1. Looking at the picture on the previous page, think of the types of activities college students do in their spare time. Classify these activities into a few categories, and explain their advantages and disadvantages.

2. What are some rituals that you follow in your own life? Do these rituals serve a purpose in your life? Use division and classification to explain three rituals that you follow.

3. We all dream about trips we'd like to take. Sometimes we get to take one of these trips. Others have to remain dreams. What are your ideal trips? Discuss the types of trips you would like to take. What categories do they fall into? Why do you dream about these types of travel?

4. Create your own division/classification assignment (with the help of your instructor), and write a response to it.

Revising Workshop

Small Group Activity (5–10 minutes per writer)   Working in groups of three or four, each person should read his or her division/classification essay to the other members of the group. Those listening should record their reactions on a copy of the Peer Evaluation Form in Appendix 2F. After your group goes through this process, give your evaluation forms to the appropriate writers so that each writer has two or three peer comment sheets for revising.

Paired Activity (5 minutes per writer)   Using the completed Peer Evaluation Forms, work in pairs to decide what you should revise in your essay. If time allows, rewrite some of your sentences, and have your partner look at them.

Individual Activity   Rewrite your paper, using the revising feedback you received from other students.

Editing Workshop

Paired Activity (5–10 minutes per writer)   Swap papers with a classmate, and use the editing portion of your Peer Evaluation Form to identify as many grammar, punctuation, mechanics, and spelling errors as you can. If time allows, correct some of your errors, and have your partner look at them. Record your grammar, punctuation, and mechanics errors in the Error Log (Appendix 6) and your spelling errors in the Spelling Log (Appendix 7).

Individual Activity   Rewrite your paper again, using the editing feedback you received from other students.

TEACHING ON THE WEB
Discussion Topic: Bring in printouts from a Web site that shows the various links people go through as they navigate around the site. Divide students into groups of three or four, and have them discuss how the Web site divides the links by categories. What are these categories? Have students discuss the different ways that the Web site uses division and classification.

TEACHING ON THE WEB
Links: Provide students with a topic, and have them link to Web sites that will divide the topic into categories. What are the different divisions that Web sites make? Which Web site is easiest to follow?
  Possible sites for the topic "movies":
  DreamWorks SKG Fansite, www.dreamworks.com
  Walt Disney Pictures, www.disney.com/DisneyPictures
  Paramount Pictures, www.paramount.com

TEACHING ON THE WEB
Research: Have students go to educational or government Web sites to determine

how these sites use division and classification. Then have students do the same with a commercial Web site. Do these Web sites use division and classification differently? If so, in what ways? How do division and classification help sell the products on a commercial site?

TEACHING ON THE WEB

Mosaics Web Site: To learn more about division and classification, students can go to www.prenhall.com/mosaics.

Reflecting on Your Writing

When you have completed your own essay, answer these six questions.

1. What was most difficult about this assignment?

2. What was easiest?

3. What did you learn about dividing and classifying by completing this assignment?

4. What do you think are the strengths of your division/classification essay? Place a wavy line by the parts of your essay that you feel are very good.

5. What are the weaknesses, if any, of your paper? Place an X by the parts of your essay you would like help with. Write any questions you have in the margin.

6. What did you learn from this assignment about your own writing process—about preparing to write, about writing the first draft, about revising, and about editing?

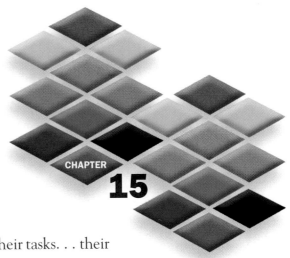

DEFINING

CHAPTER 15

Writers, most of all, need to define their tasks. . . their themes, their objectives.

—HENRY SEIDAL CANBY

All communication depends on our understanding of a common set of definitions. If we did not work from a set of shared definitions, we would not be able to carry on coherent conversations, write clear letters, or understand any form of media.

It's no surprise, then, that we regularly use definitions in writing as well—in our personal lives, in college courses, and in the workplace:

You e-mail a friend to tell him or her about the equipment at the fitness center you just joined.

A student has to define melody, harmony, and rhythm on a music appreciation quiz.

A student begins a report for a criminal justice course with a definition of criminal law and civil law.

A financial planner prepares a summary sheet defining the basic financial terms a client should know.

The manager of a sporting goods shop writes a classified ad for an opening on the staff.

Definition is the process of explaining what a word, an object, or an idea is. A good definition focuses on what is special about a word or an idea and what sets it apart from similar words or concepts. Definitions help us understand basic concrete terms (*cell phone, large fries, midterm exams*), discuss events in our lives (*baseball game, graduation, dentist appointment*), and grasp complex ideas (*friendship, courage, success*). Definitions are the building blocks that help us make certain both writer and reader (or speaker and listener) are working from the same basic understanding of terms and ideas.

TEACHING DEFINITION
Divide students into groups of four or five, and give each group five abstract words that the other groups don't see (for example, *abandonment, freedom, ethnicity, boredom,* and *hope*). Have the groups define each of their words using three sentences: one using synonyms, one using negation, and one using categories. Make sure students do not use the actual word in the definition.

After each group has defined its words, have a spokesperson for each group read the definitions. As soon as another group knows the word being defined, its members should shout out the answer. Limit guessing time to three minutes. The group that guesses the most definitions correctly wins.

259

Definitions vary greatly. They can be as short as one word (a "hog" is a motorcycle) or as long as an essay or even a book. Words or ideas that require such extended definitions are usually abstract, complex, and controversial. Think, for example, how difficult it might be to define an abstract idea like *equality* compared to concrete words such as *dog* or *cat*.

WRITING A DEFINITION ESSAY

In the following essay, Lars Eighner writes an extended definition of the fine art of "Dumpster diving" or living out of Dumpsters, the big containers designed to be raised and emptied into a garbage truck. Have you ever witnessed someone Dumpster diving? Have you yourself ever found something in the trash that you took home? How would you feel if you lost your home and with it your sense of security?

DUMPSTER DIVING
by Lars Eighner

1   I began Dumpster diving about a year before I became homeless. I prefer the term *scavenging*. I have heard people, evidently meaning to be polite, use the word *foraging*, but I prefer to reserve that word for gathering nuts and berries and such, which I also do, according to the season and opportunity.

2   I like the frankness of the word *scavenging*. I live from the refuse of others. I am a scavenger. I think it a sound and honorable niche, although if I could I would naturally prefer to live the comfortable consumer life, perhaps—and only perhaps—as a slightly less wasteful consumer owing to what I have learned as a scavenger.

3   Except for jeans, all my clothes come from Dumpsters. Boom boxes, candles, bedding, toilet paper, medicine, books, a typewriter, a virgin male love doll, coins sometimes amounting to many dollars—all came from Dumpsters. And, yes, I eat from Dumpsters, too.

4   There is a predictable series of stages that a person goes through in learning to scavenge. At first the new scavenger is filled with disgust and self-loathing. He is ashamed of being seen.

5   This stage passes with experience. The scavenger finds a pair of running shoes that fit and look and smell brand-new. He finds a pocket calculator in perfect working order. He finds pristine ice cream, still frozen, more

than he can eat or keep. He begins to understand: People do throw away perfectly good stuff, a lot of perfectly good stuff.

At this stage he may become lost and never recover. All the Dumpster 6 divers I have known come to the point of trying to acquire everything they touch. Why not take it, they reason; it is all free. This is, of course, hopeless, and most divers come to realize that they must restrict themselves to items of relatively immediate utility.

The finding of objects is becoming something of an urban art. Even re- 7 spectable, employed people will sometimes find something tempting sticking out of a Dumpster or standing beside one. Quite a number of people, not all of them of the bohemian type, are willing to brag that they found this or that piece in the trash.

But eating from Dumpsters is the thing that separates the dilettanti from 8 the professionals. Eating safely involves three principles: using the senses and common sense to evaluate the condition of the found materials; knowing the Dumpsters of a given area and checking them regularly; and seeking always to answer the question Why was this discarded?

Yet perfectly good food can be found in Dumpsters. Canned goods, for 9 example, turn up fairly often in the Dumpsters I frequent. I also have few qualms about dry foods such as crackers, cookies, cereal, chips, and pasta if they are free of visible contaminants and still dry and crisp. Raw fruits and vegetables with intact skins seem perfectly safe to me, excluding, of course, the obviously rotten. Many are discarded for minor imperfections that can be pared away.

A typical discard is a half jar of peanut butter—though non-organic 10 peanut butter does not require refrigeration and is unlikely to spoil in any reasonable time. One of my favorite finds is yogurt—often discarded, still sealed, when the expiration date has passed—because it will keep for several days, even in warm weather.

No matter how careful I am I still get dysentery at least once a month, of- 11 tener in warm weather. I do not want to paint too romantic a picture. Dumpster diving has serious drawbacks as a way of life.

I find from the experience of scavenging two rather deep lessons. The 12 first is to take what I can use and let the rest go. I have come to think that there is no value in the abstract. A thing I cannot use or make useful, perhaps by trading, has no value, however fine or rare it may be.

The second lesson is the transience of material being. I do not suppose that 13 ideas are immortal, but certainly they are longer-lived than material objects.

The things I find in Dumpsters, the love letters and rag dolls of so many 14 lives, remind me of this lesson. Now I hardly pick up a thing without envisioning the time I will cast it away. This, I think, is a healthy state of mind.

Almost everything I have now has already been cast out at least once, proving that what I own is valueless to someone.

15   I find that my desire to grab for the gaudy bauble has been largely sated. I think this is an attitude I share with the very wealthy—we both know there is plenty more where whatever we have came from. Between us are the rat-race millions who have confounded their selves with the objects they grasp and who nightly scavenge the cable channels for they know not what.

16   I am sorry for them.

 PREPARING TO WRITE YOUR OWN DEFINITION ESSAY

What do you think of when you hear the word *security?* What associations do you make with this word? What examples does it bring to mind? Use one or more of the prewriting strategies you learned in Chapter 2 to generate ideas for writing an extended definition of *security.*

INSTRUCTOR'S
RESOURCE MANUAL
For additional material about teaching definition; for journal entries; and for multiple-choice, short-answer, and paragraph tests, see the *Instructor's Resource Manual,* Section II, Part II.

How to Write a Definition Essay

Clear definitions give writer and reader a mutual starting point on the road to successful communication. Sometimes a short summary and an example are all the definition that's needed. But in the case of abstract and complex words or ideas, a writer may use several approaches to a definition. Use the following guidelines to help you write an extended definition essay.

1. ***Choose your word or idea carefully, and give a working definition of it in your thesis statement.*** First, you need to choose a word or idea that can be defined and explained from several angles, or you will end up with a short, lifeless essay. At the same time, you need to give your readers a working definition right at the start. Put that brief, basic definition in your thesis statement so that readers have a mental hook on which to hang the definitions and explanations in the rest of your essay. Also include the purpose of your essay in your thesis statement.

    At the start of his essay, Eighner defines *Dumpster diving* as "scavenging," explaining "I live from the refuse of others." This simple, direct definition—given at the beginning—guides readers through the rest of the essay.

2. ***Decide how you want to define your term: by synonym, by negation, or by category.*** These are the three common ways to develop a definition.

   When you define by using a *synonym*, you furnish readers with a similar word or a short explanation with synonyms. Eighner uses a synonym right at the beginning of his essay. "Dumpster diving" is an informal term that is used by city people to refer to taking garbage out of trash bins. Apartment houses and office buildings often use Dumpsters to hold garbage until it is taken to the dump. Because *Dumpster* is not a term that everyone knows and because the meaning of the expression "Dumpster diving" is not immediately obvious, Eighner provides the synonym "scavenging," which most people understand.

   When you define a word by *negation*, you say what the term is not. That is, you define a term by contrasting it with something else. Eighner uses definition by negation twice in his essay. First, he states that "scavenging" is not "foraging," meaning that it is not gathering nuts and berries. He also says that life as a scavenger is not a comfortable consumer life. The rest of his essay explains his life as a scavenger.

   Defining a term by *category* is a more formal type of definition, as in a dictionary. Defining by category has two parts: the class or general category that the word belongs to and the way the word is different from other words in that group. For example, *heart* might be defined as "the organ that pumps blood through the body." The general category is *organ*, and it is different from other organs (brain, lungs, stomach, liver, and so on) because it pumps blood. Eighner doesn't use this type of definition directly. He does, however, suggest that scavenging falls into the category of *lifestyle* in paragraph 2 when he compares his life as a scavenger to the life of a consumer.

3. ***Develop your definition with examples.*** Nearly every definition can be improved by adding examples. Well-chosen examples show your definition in action. Definitions can be *objective*—strictly factual, as in a dictionary definition—or *subjective*—combined with personal opinions. A definition essay is usually more subjective than objective because you are providing your personal opinions about a word or concept. You are explaining to your readers your own meaning, which is what makes your essay interesting. If your readers wanted an objective definition, they could go to a dictionary.

   Eighner uses examples throughout his essay to expand on his definition. Paragraph 3 consists entirely of examples of things he has found in Dumpsters. Later he gives examples of the kinds of food he finds, including canned goods, cookies and crackers, raw fruits and vegetables, peanut butter, and yogurt. These examples help Eighner strike a balance in his definition between objective (factual) and subjective (personal) references. From these and Eighner's other examples, we get a very clear idea of how a person could live by Dumpster diving.

4. ***Use other rhetorical strategies, such as description, comparison, or process analysis, to support your definition.*** When you write a definition essay, you want to look at your word or idea in many different ways. The other techniques you have learned for developing body paragraphs can help you expand your definition even further. Perhaps a description, a short narrative, or a comparison will make your definition come alive.

In addition to examples, Eighner uses process analysis, classification, and cause and effect to expand his definition. He uses process analysis to explain the four stages that new Dumpster divers go through—how something happens. His three rules for eating safely are also process analysis—how to do something. He draws on classification to name the types of foods he finds and then gives examples of each category. At the end of his essay, he uses cause and effect when he explains that Dumpster diving (the cause) has taught him two lessons (the effects): that only items you can use are valuable and that material objects don't last.

5. ***Organize your essay in a logical way.*** Because a definition essay can be developed through several strategies and techniques, there is no set pattern of organization. So you need to figure out the most logical way to explain your word or idea. You might move from particular to general or from general to particular. Or you might arrange your ideas from one extreme to the other, such as from most important to least important, least dramatic to most dramatic, or most familiar to least familiar. In some cases, you might organize your definition chronologically or spatially. Or you might organize part of your essay one way and the rest another way. What's important is that you move in some logical way from one point to another so that your readers can follow your train of thought.

Eighner organizes his essay chronologically. He says he started Dumpster diving about a year before he became homeless. Now he is homeless and lives by Dumpster diving. He defines the term in two ways (synonym and negation) and gives examples of what he finds. Then he switches to a general-to-particular organization in paragraphs 7 to 11, explaining how someone learns to dive in general and then to actually dive for food in particular. The last five paragraphs conclude the essay.

> **WRITING YOUR OWN DEFINITION ESSAY**
>
> If you have a roof over your head, food to eat, and money in your pocket, you have a sense of security. Write an essay defining "security." Begin by reviewing your prewriting notes. Then decide how you are going to approach your subject. Next, write your essay, starting with a clear thesis statement.

 # WORKING WITH A STUDENT ESSAY

In the following essay, titled "True Friends," a student named Francine Feinstein defines friendship. See if you can identify her main point as you read this draft of her essay.

True Friends

Many people throw the term "friend" around loosely. They think they have friends at work, friends at school, and friends from the Internet. But is all these people really friends? The word "friend" seems to be used today to refer to anyone from long-term to short-term relationships. However, a true friend is someone who will always be there in times of need, who will always be the best company, and who will always listen and give advice.

Without any questions asked, a good friend will always be there in times of need. No matter how bad a problem is, a true friend will be the person who sits up nights and take days off work just to sit with a friend. If someone is in trouble with a difficult paper a friend will help brainstorm to figure out the problem. If someone is sick, a friend will be the first one at the door with chicken soup and will baby-sit the kids until the sick person feel better. I hate the feeling of being sick. If someone is stranded across town with a broken-down car, a friend will drop everything to make a rescue and drive the person wherever he or she needs to go. Not everyone has a friend like this a true friend will always be the first one there, no matter what.

Most of all, a true friend is also someone who will listen and give reliable advice. Some people will listen to problems and then give the advice that they think will work best for them, but that advice isn't necessarily best for their friend. Other people will listen but then interject personal stories that relate to the problem but don't solve it. But a true friend listens to a problem and gives suggestions to help a friend figure

TEACHING TIPS
The following eight teaching tips are based on Howard Gardner's list of multiple intelligences:

Verbal/Linguistic
1 Provide students with a list of words and a list of definitions, and have them try to match the words with their definitions. Don't let students use a dictionary until after they have guessed.

Musical/Rhythmic
2 Have students listen to a song in a language they don't speak. Based solely on the music, what do they think the song is about?

Logical/ Mathematical
Provide students with a list of words that sound like they would have one definition but actually have another (such as *noisome*, which sounds like it should have something to do with noise but actually means "foul-smelling" or "unwholesome").

out the best solution for himself or herself. In other words, a true friend knows how to <u>listen</u> and help a person solve problems.

4   In addition, a friend is someone who is always great company, because friends have so much in common with each other. Imagine working out together, grabbing a sandwich, and then spending the evening just talking—about life, about good times, about bad times, about classes at school. Right now my classes are really hard. At the end of the day, friends might rent their favorite DVD and make some fresh popcorn. Sometimes they even seem to be on the same biological clock, getting tired and waking up at the same time. Friends can always be themselves around each other.

5   The word "friend" may be misused in the English language, but at least we can agree on what true friends are. True friends are hard to find. But once you find them, they will always be there, listen to you and be the best people to spend time with. No wonder true friends are so rare!

Discovering How the Essay Works

1. What is this essay defining?

   The meaning of a true friend

2. Does this author define mainly by synonym, by negation, or by category in her essay? Explain your answer.

   She relies mainly on category. She starts with a broad definition of

   "friend" and then talks about how a true friend differs from other friends.

3. List three specific examples that Francine uses to develop her definition.

   Answers will vary.

   Are her examples more objective or subjective?

   Subjective

4. What other techniques does Francine use to develop her definition?

   Paragraph 2 uses examples, paragraph 3 uses comparison and

   contrast, and paragraph 4 uses narration.

5. How does Francine organize the examples in her essay?

   From least to most important

Explain your answer.

   She begins by discussing how friends will always be there in times of

   need, moves to how friends always give great advice, and finishes with

   how friends are fun to be with. But paragraph 3 is out of place.

Revising and Editing the Student Essay

This essay is Francine's first draft, which now needs to be revised and edited. First, apply the Revising Checklist below to the content of Francine's draft. When you are satisfied that her ideas are fully developed and well organized, use the Editing Checklist on page 271 to correct her grammar and mechanics errors. Answer the questions after each checklist. Then write your suggested changes directly on Francine's draft.

REVISING CHECKLIST ✔

THESIS STATEMENT
✔ Does the thesis statement contain the essay's controlling idea?
✔ Does the thesis appear as the last sentence of the introduction?

BASIC ELEMENTS
✔ Does the title draw in the readers?
✔ Does the introduction capture the readers' attention and build up to the thesis statement effectively?
✔ Does each body paragraph deal with a single topic?
✔ Does the conclusion bring the essay to a close in an interesting way?

DEVELOPMENT
✔ Do the body paragraphs adequately support the thesis statement?
✔ Does each body paragraph have a focused topic sentence?
✔ Does each body paragraph contain *specific* details that support the topic sentence?
✔ Does each body paragraph include *enough* details to explain the topic sentence fully?

Naturalist
Have students recall one of their favorite outdoor activities and provide a definition of it that would make other students want to try it. Which part of the students' definition most entices others to try the activity?

REVISING AND EDITING OPTIONS
Consider varying your approach to revising and editing. You could teach these skills in a class discussion, in small groups, or in pairs.

REVISING STRATEGIES
This chapter focuses on the following revising elements:
   Development
   Unity
   Organization
   Coherence

UNITY
✔ Do the essay's topic sentences relate directly to the thesis statement?
✔ Do the details in each body paragraph support its topic sentence?

ORGANIZATION
✔ Is the essay organized logically?
✔ Is each body paragraph organized logically?

COHERENCE
✔ Are transitions used effectively so that paragraphs move smoothly and logically from one to the next?
✔ Do the sentences move smoothly and logically from one to the next?

Thesis Statement

1. Put brackets around the last sentence in Francine's introduction. Does it state her purpose?

   Yes

2. Rewrite Francine's thesis statement if necessary so that it states her purpose and introduces her topics.

   Her thesis states her purpose and introduces her topics.

Basic Elements

1. Give the writer's essay an alternate title.

   Answers will vary.

2. Rewrite Francine's introduction so that it captures the readers' attention and builds up to the thesis statement at the end of the paragraph.

   Answers will vary.

3. Does each of Francine's body paragraphs deal with only one topic?

   Yes

4. Rewrite Francine's conclusion using at least one suggestion from Part I.

   Answers will vary.

Development

1. Write out Francine's thesis statement (revised, if necessary), and list her three topic sentences below it.

   Thesis statement: However, a true friend is someone who will always be there in times of need, who will always be the best company, and who will always listen and give advice.

   Topic 1: Without any questions asked, a good friend will always be there in times of need.

   Topic 2: Most of all, a true friend is also someone who will listen and give reliable advice.

   Topic 3: In addition, a friend is someone who is always great company, because friends have so much in common with each other.

2. Do Francine's topic sentences adequately support her thesis statement?

   Yes

3. Does each body paragraph have a focused topic sentence?

   Yes

4. Do the examples in the essay help define "friend"?

They do, but many more could be added.

5. Where do you need more information?

Answers will vary.

6. Make two of Francine's details more specific. *Answers will vary.*

7. Add at least two new details to make her essay clearer. *Answers will vary.*

Unity

1. Read each of Francine's topic sentences with her thesis statement in mind. Do they go together?

Answers will vary.

2. Revise them if necessary so they are directly related.

3. Drop or rewrite the sentences in paragraph 2 and in paragraph 4 that are not directly related to their topic sentence. *Paragraph 2, sentence 5; paragraph 4, sentence 3*

Organization

1. Read Francine's essay again to see if all the paragraphs are arranged logically.

2. Reverse the two paragraphs that are out of order. *Reverse paragraphs 3 and 4.*

3. Look closely at Francine's body paragraphs to see if all her sentences are arranged logically within paragraphs.

4. Move any sentences that are out of order. *All sentences are in order.*

Coherence

For a list of transitions, see pages 83–84.

1. Add two transitions to Francine's essay. *Answers will vary.*

2. Circle five transitions Francine uses.

3. Explain how two of these make Francine's essay easier to read.

Answers will vary.

Now rewrite Francine's essay with your revisions.

EDITING CHECKLIST ✔

SENTENCES

✔ Does each sentence have a main subject and verb?

✔ Do all subjects and verbs agree?

✔ Do all pronouns agree with their nouns?

✔ Are modifiers as close as possible to the words they modify?

PUNCTUATION AND MECHANICS

✔ Are sentences punctuated correctly?

✔ Are words capitalized properly?

WORD CHOICE AND SPELLING

✔ Are words used correctly?

✔ Are words spelled correctly?

EDITING STRATEGIES
This chapter focuses on
the following editing
problems:
  Run-togethers
  Subject-verb
    agreement
  Commas

Sentences

Subjects and Verbs

1. Underline the subjects once and verbs twice in paragraphs 1 and 2 of your revision of Francine's essay. Remember that sentences can have more than one subject-verb set.

For help with subjects and verbs, see Chapter 34.

2. Does each of the sentences have at least one subject and verb that can stand alone?

   Yes

3. Did you find and correct Francine's run-together sentence? If not, find and correct it now. *Paragraph 2, sentence 7*

For help with run-togethers, see Chapter 36.

Subject-Verb Agreement

1. Read aloud the subjects and verbs you underlined in your revision of Francine's essay.

For help with subject-verb agreement, see Chapter 39.

2. Did you find and correct the three subjects and verbs that do not agree? *Paragraph 1, sentence 3; paragraph 2, sentence 2; paragraph 2, sentence 4*

Pronoun Agreement

1. Find any pronouns in your revision of Francine's essay that do not agree with their nouns. *All pronouns agree with their nouns.*

For help with pronoun agreement, see Chapter 43.

2. Correct any pronouns that do not agree with their nouns.

Modifiers

For help with modifier errors, see Chapter 46.

1. Find any modifiers in your revision of Francine's essay that are not as close as possible to the words they modify.

2. Rewrite sentences if necessary so that modifiers are as close as possible to the words they modify. *There are no modifier errors.*

Punctuation and Mechanics

Punctuation

For help with punctuation, see Chapters 47–51.

1. Read your revision of Francine's essay for any errors in punctuation.

2. Find the run-together sentence you revised, and make sure it is punctuated correctly.

3. Did you find and correct the two comma errors in Francine's essay? *Paragraph 2, sentence 3; paragraph 5, sentence 3*

Mechanics

For help with capitalization, see Chapter 52.

1. Read your revision of Francine's essay for any errors in capitalization.

2. Be sure to check Francine's capitalization in the run-together sentence you revised.

Word Choice and Spelling

Word Choice

For help with confused words, see Chapter 58.

1. Find any words used incorrectly in your revision of Francine's essay. *All words are used correctly.*

2. Correct any errors you find.

Spelling

For help with spelling, see Chapter 59.

1. Use spell-check and a dictionary to check the spelling in your revision of Francine's essay. *All words are spelled correctly.*

2. Correct any misspelled words.

Now rewrite Francine's essay again with your editing corrections.

 WORKING WITH YOUR OWN ESSAY

Returning to the definition essay you wrote earlier in this chapter, revise and edit your own writing. The checklists here will help you apply what you have learned to your essay.

Revising and Editing Your Own Essay

REVISING CHECKLIST ✅

THESIS STATEMENT
- ☐ Does the thesis statement contain the essay's controlling idea?
- ☐ Does the thesis appear as the last sentence of the introduction?

BASIC ELEMENTS
- ☐ Does the title draw in the readers?
- ☐ Does the introduction capture the readers' attention and build up to the thesis statement effectively?
- ☐ Does each body paragraph deal with a single topic?
- ☐ Does the conclusion bring the essay to a close in an interesting way?

DEVELOPMENT
- ☐ Do the body paragraphs adequately support the thesis statement?
- ☐ Does each body paragraph have a focused topic sentence?
- ☐ Does each body paragraph contain *specific* details that support the topic sentence?
- ☐ Does each body paragraph include *enough* details to explain the topic sentence fully?

UNITY
- ☐ Do the essay's topic sentences relate directly to the thesis statement?
- ☐ Do the details in each body paragraph support its topic sentence?

ORGANIZATION
- ☐ Is the essay organized logically?
- ☐ Is each body paragraph organized logically?

COHERENCE
- ☐ Are transitions used effectively so that paragraphs move smoothly and logically from one to the next?
- ☐ Do the sentences move smoothly and logically from one to the next?

CLASS ACTIVITY
Put a few words on the board (such as "vacation," "Ford Ranger," "friendship," and "peace"), and have the class provide definitions for each by using all three defining strategies: synonym, negation, and category. Which one do they think is most effective?

Thesis Statement

1. What are you defining?

_____

2. What is the purpose of your definition essay?

_____

3. Put brackets around the last sentence in your introduction. Does it state your purpose?

_____

4. Rewrite your thesis statement if necessary so that it states your purpose and introduces your topics.

Basic Elements

1. Give your essay a title if it doesn't have one.

_____

2. Does your introduction capture your readers' attention and build up to your thesis statement at the end of the paragraph?

_____

3. Does each of your body paragraphs deal with only one topic?

_____

4. Does your conclusion follow some of the suggestions offered in Part I?

_____

Development

1. Write out your thesis statement (revised, if necessary), and list your topic sentences below it.

Thesis statement: _____

Topic 1: _____

Topic 2: _____

Topic 3: _____

2. Do your topics adequately support your thesis statement?

   _____

3. Does each body paragraph have a focused topic sentence?

   _____

4. Do the examples in the essay help develop your definition?

   _____

5. Where do you need more information?

   _____

6. Make two of your details more specific.
7. Add at least two new details to make your definition clearer.

Unity
1. Read each of your topic sentences with your thesis statement in mind. Do they go together?

   _____

2. Revise them if necessary so they are directly related.
3. Drop or rewrite any of the sentences in your body paragraphs that are not directly related to their topic sentences.

Organization
1. Read your essay again to see if all the paragraphs are arranged logically.
2. Refer to your answers to the development questions. Then identify your method of organization:

   _____

3. Is the order you chose for your paragraphs the most effective approach to your topic?

   _____

4. Move any paragraphs that are out of order.

5. Look closely at your body paragraphs to see if all the sentences are arranged logically within paragraphs.

6. Move any sentences that are out of order.

Coherence

For a list of transitions, see pages 83–84.

1. Add two transitions to your essay.

2. Circle five transitions you use.

3. Explain how two of them make your essay easier to read.

_____

_____

Now rewrite your essay with your revisions.

EDITING CHECKLIST ✔

SENTENCES

☐ Does each sentence have a main subject and verb?

☐ Do all subjects and verbs agree?

☐ Do all pronouns agree with their nouns?

☐ Are modifiers as close as possible to the words they modify?

PUNCTUATION AND MECHANICS

☐ Are sentences punctuated correctly?

☐ Are words capitalized properly?

WORD CHOICE AND SPELLING

☐ Are words used correctly?

☐ Are words spelled correctly?

Sentences

Subjects and Verbs

For help with subjects and verbs, see Chapter 34.

1. Underline the subjects once and verbs twice in a paragraph of your revised essay. Remember that sentences can have more than one subject-verb set.

2. Does each of your sentences have at least one subject and verb that can stand alone?

_____

3. Correct any fragments you have written.

For help with fragments, see Chapter 35.

4. Correct any run-together sentences you have written.

For help with run-togethers, see Chapter 36.

Subject-Verb Agreement

1. Read aloud the subjects and verbs you underlined in your revised essay.

For help with subject-verb agreement, see Chapter 39.

2. Correct any subjects and verbs that do not agree.

Pronoun Agreement

1. Find any pronouns in your revised essay that do not agree with their nouns.

For help with pronoun agreement, see Chapter 43.

2. Correct any pronouns that do not agree with their nouns.

Modifiers

1. Find any modifiers in your revised essay that are not as close as possible to the words they modify.

For help with modifier errors, see Chapter 46.

2. Rewrite sentences if necessary so that your modifiers are as close as possible to the words they modify.

Punctuation and Mechanics

Punctuation

1. Read your revised essay for any errors in punctuation.

For help with punctuation, see Chapters 47–51.

2. Make sure any fragments and run-together sentences you revised are punctuated correctly.

Mechanics

1. Read your revised essay for any errors in capitalization.

For help with capitalization, see Chapter 52.

2. Be sure to check your capitalization in any fragments or run-ons you revised.

Word Choice and Spelling

Word Choice

1. Find any words used incorrectly in your revised essay.

For help with confused words, see Chapter 58.

2. Correct any errors you find.

Spelling

For help with spelling, see Chapter 59.

1. Use spell-check and a dictionary to check your spelling.
2. Correct any misspelled words.

Now rewrite your essay again with your editing corrections.

PRACTICING DEFINITION

Reading Suggestions

In Chapter 31, you will find two good definition essays: "Ways of Ai" by Wang Ping defines love from the point of view of her Chinese heritage, and "Healing Myself with the Power of Work" by Michael Norlen reveals through definition how work helps the author overcome depression. You might want to read these selections before writing another definition essay. As you read, notice how the writers make their points through well-chosen examples and details.

Service Learning Project

SERVICE LEARNING PROJECT
This assignment is another step in the Service Learning project. If you choose to use this feature of the text, each chapter in Part II has an assignment that asks students to use a different rhetorical mode to reflect on their Service Learning project. These reflections will lead to an essay assignment in Part III (Chapter 22). You can assign as many or as few of these exercises as you want in preparation for this essay. For more information on service learning, see the *Instructor's Resource Manual*, Section I, Part III.

This assignment is based on a Service Learning project of your choice. If your instructor has already introduced service learning to the class, you will be doing these exercises when they are assigned. At this point, choose a project you would like to pursue, or continue work on a project you have already begun. This assignment in Part II will help you prepare for an essay on this project in Part III. Here is another stage in the preparation for this essay:

For the Service Learning project you have taken on, define your project in as much detail as possible. Use the guidelines you have learned in this chapter to help you write your definition from many different angles. But remember that these are just thoughts that will be developed into an essay in Part III.

Writing Workshop

ADDITIONAL WRITING TOPIC
Have your students turn to Chapter 31 and read Wang Ping's "Ways to Ai" or Michael Norlen's "Healing Myself with the Power of Work." Then have them write an essay on one of the

---

Guidelines for Writing a Definition Essay

1. Choose your word or idea carefully, and give a working definition of it in your thesis statement.
2. Decide how you want to define your term: by synonym, by negation, or by category.
3. Develop your definition with examples.

topics from "Writing Topics: Defining" at the end of the chapter.

4. Use other rhetorical strategies, such as description, comparison, or process analysis, to support your definition.
5. Organize your essay in a logical way.

1. What does education mean to you? Define "education" as portrayed in this picture.
2. The concept of "family" has undergone a number of changes over the past few years. How would you define this term in our current society?
3. Define one of the following abstract terms: *fear, love, inferiority, wonder, pride, self-control, discipline, anger, freedom, violence, assertiveness, courtesy, kindness.*
4. Create your own definition assignment (with the help of your instructor), and write a response to it.

Revising Workshop

Small Group Activity (5–10 minutes per writer) Working in groups of three or four, each person should read his or her definition essay to the other members of the group. The listeners should record their reactions on a copy of the Peer Evaluation Form in Appendix 2G. After your group goes through this process, give your evaluation forms to the appropriate writers so that each writer has two or three peer comment sheets for revising.

Paired Activity (5 minutes per writer) Using the completed Peer Evaluation Forms, work in pairs to decide what you should revise in your essay. If time allows, rewrite some of your sentences, and have your partner look at them.

TEACHING ON THE WEB
Discussion Topic: Have students as a class discuss how definition is used on the Internet. In what ways can students find uses of definition other than simply defining words? What else is defined on the Internet?

TEACHING ON THE WEB
Links: Provide students with a complex term, and have them link to Web sites that define the term. How does each of the sites use definition? Which site defines the term most clearly?
   Possible sites for the topic "pathology":
   World Wide Web Pathology Case Review,

Individual Activity   Rewrite your paper, using the revising feedback you received from other students.

Editing Workshop

Paired Activity (5–10 minutes per writer)   Swap papers with a classmate, and use the editing portion of your Peer Evaluation Form to identify as many grammar, punctuation, mechanics, and spelling errors as you can. If time allows, correct some of your errors, and have your partner look at them. Record your grammar, punctuation, and mechanics errors in the Error Log (Appendix 6) and your spelling errors in the Spelling Log (Appendix 7).

Individual Activity   Rewrite your paper again, using the editing feedback you received from other students.

Reflecting on Your Writing

When you have completed your own essay, answer these six questions.

1. What was most difficult about this assignment?
2. What was easiest?
3. What did you learn about using definition by completing this assignment?
4. What do you think are the strengths of your definition essay? Place a wavy line by the parts of your essay that you feel are very good.
5. What are the weaknesses, if any, of your paper? Place an X by the parts of your essay you would like help with. Write any questions you have in the margin.
6. What did you learn from this assignment about your own writing process—about preparing to write, about writing the first draft, about revising, and about editing?

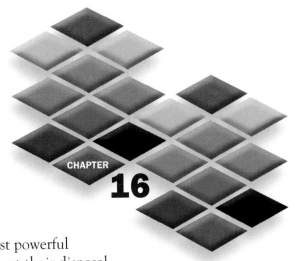

ANALYZING CAUSES AND EFFECTS

CHAPTER 16

The act of writing is one of the most powerful
problem-solving tools humans have at their disposal.

—TOBY FULWILER

We are born with a natural curiosity. Wanting to know why things happen is one of our earliest, most basic instincts: Daddy, why is the sky blue? Closely related to this desire to understand *why* is our interest in *what* will happen as a result of some particular action: If I stay outside much longer, will I get a bad sunburn? But thinking about causes and effects is not only part of human nature but also an advanced mental process and the basis for most decisions we make. When faced with a decision, we naturally consider it from different perspectives. If we choose option A, what will happen? What if we choose B—or C? In other words, we look at the possible results—the effects—of the choices and then make up our minds.

Analyzing causes and effects is also an essential part of our writing lives. We use cause-and-effect writing in our personal lives, in college, and in the marketplace:

A volunteer for a mayor's campaign designs a poster telling how a vote for this candidate will benefit the city.

A student discusses the causes of schizophrenia in a paper for a psychology course.

A student explains the effects of the Civil Rights Act of 1964 on a history exam.

A sales representative writes a report to her manager explaining why she didn't meet her sales projections.

The owner of a florist shop writes a letter of complaint to one of the suppliers about the negative effect of late deliveries on sales.

TEACHING CAUSE
AND EFFECT
Show the first part of a
movie, just enough for
students to understand
what the movie is about
and what effects will
occur based on the
causes they saw. Be
sure to show them a
film that has a shocking
and unexpected ending,
based on the portion of
the movie students saw
(for example, *Along
Came a Spider* with
Morgan Freeman and
Monica Potter). Ask
them what they think
will happen in the
movie and what causes
and effects will occur.
   Then show students
enough of the end of
the film that they can
see the twist and
understand the plot.
How close were the
students' predictions?
Knowing now what
happens in the end of

the movie, what causes and effects do the students think happened in between the portions of the movie they saw?

Analyzing causes and effects requires the ability to look for connections between two or more items or events and to analyze the reasons for those connections. As the name implies, this writing strategy is composed of two parts: cause and effect. To understand **causes,** we look in the past for reasons why something happened. To discover **effects,** we look to the future for possible results of an action. In other words, we break a situation into parts so we can look at the relationships between these parts and then reach conclusions that are logical and useful.

WRITING A CAUSE/EFFECT ESSAY

In "Why Do Schools Flunk Biology?" Lynnell Hancock makes the point that education in the United States is stuck in the nineteenth century. She deals with both the causes and the effects of students' ability to learn. What do you think of our educational system on the high school level? What do you think of your local high schools?

WHY DO SCHOOLS FLUNK BIOLOGY?
by Lynnell Hancock

1   Biology is a staple at most American high schools. Yet when it comes to the biology of the students themselves—how their brains develop and retain knowledge—school officials would rather not pay attention to the lessons. Can first graders handle French? What time should school start? Should music be cut? Biologists have some important evidence to offer. Not only are they ignored, but their findings are often turned upside down.

2   Force of habit rules the hallways and classrooms. Neither brain science nor education research has been able to free the majority of America's schools from their 19th-century roots. If more administrators were tuned in to brain research, scientists argue, not only would schedules change, but subjects such as foreign language and geometry would be offered to much younger children. Music and gym would be daily requirements. Lectures, worksheets, and rote memorization would be replaced by hands-on materials, drama, and project work. And teachers would pay greater attention to children's emotional connections to subjects. "We do more education research than anyone else in the world," says Frank Vellutino, a professor of educational psychology at State University of New York at Albany, "and we ignore more as well."

Plato once said that music "is a more potent instrument than any other   3
for education." Now scientists know why. Music, they believe, trains the
brain for higher forms of thinking. Researchers at the University of
California, Irvine, studied the power of music by observing two groups of
preschoolers. One group took piano lessons and sang daily in chorus. The
other did not. After eight months the musical 3-year-olds were expert puz-
zlemasters, scoring 80 percent higher than their playmates did in spatial
intelligence—the ability to visualize the world accurately.

This skill later translates into complex math and engineering skills.   4
"Early music training can enhance a child's ability to reason," says Irvine
physicist Gordon Shaw. Yet music education is often the first "frill" to be cut
when school budgets shrink. Schools on average have only one music
teacher for every 500 children, according to the National Commission on
Music Education.

Then there's gym—another expendable hour by most school standards.   5
Only 36 percent of school children today are required to participate in daily
physical education. Yet researchers now know that exercise is good not only
for the heart. It also juices up the brain, feeding it nutrients in the form of
glucose and increasing nerve connections—all of which make it easier for
kids of all ages to learn. Neuroscientist William Greenough confirmed this
by watching rats at his University of Illinois at Urbana-Champaign lab. One
group did nothing. A second exercised on an automatic treadmill. A third
was set loose in a Barnum & Bailey obstacle course requiring the rats to perform acrobatic feats. These "supersmart" rats grew "an enormous amount
of gray matter" compared with their sedentary partners, says Greenough.
Of course, children don't ordinarily run such gantlets; still, Greenough
believes, the results are significant. Numerous studies, he says, show that
children who exercise regularly do better in school.

The implication for schools goes beyond simple exercise. Children also   6
need to be more physically active in the classroom, not sitting quietly in
their seats memorizing subtraction tables. Knowledge is retained longer if
children connect not only aurally but emotionally and physically to the material, says University of Oregon education professor Robert Sylwester in *A
Celebration of Neurons*.

Good teachers know that lecturing on the American Revolution is far   7
less effective than acting out a battle. Angles and dimensions are better
understood if children chuck their work sheets and build a complex model
to scale. The smell of the glue enters memory through one sensory system,
the touch of the wood blocks another, the sight of the finished model still
another. The brain then creates a multidimensional mental model of the

experience—one easier to retrieve. "Explaining a smell," says Sylwester, "is not as good as actually smelling it."

8   Scientists argue that children are capable of far more at younger ages than schools generally realize. People obviously continue learning their whole lives, but the optimum "windows of opportunity for learning" last until about the age of 10 or 12, says Harry Chugani of Wayne State University's Children's Hospital of Michigan. Chugani determined this by measuring the brain's consumption of its chief energy source, glucose. (The more glucose it uses, the more active the brain.) Children's brains, he observes, gobble up glucose at twice the adult rate from the age of 4 to puberty. So young brains are as primed as they'll ever be to process new information. Complex subjects such as trigonometry or foreign language shouldn't wait for puberty to be introduced. In fact, Chugani says, it's far easier for an elementary-school child to hear and process a second language—and even speak it without an accent. Yet most U.S. districts wait until junior high to introduce Spanish or French—after the "windows" are closed.

9   Reform could begin at the beginning. Many sleep researchers now believe that most teens' biological clocks are set later than those of their fellow humans. But high school starts at 7:30 a.m., usually to accommodate bus schedules. The result can be wasted class time for whole groups of kids. Making matters worse, many kids have trouble readjusting their natural sleep rhythm. Dr. Richard Allen of Johns Hopkins University found that teens went to sleep at the same time whether they had to be at school by 7:30 a.m. or 9:30 a.m. The later-to-rise teens not only get more sleep, he says; they also get better grades. The obvious solution would be to start school later when kids hit puberty. But at school, there's what's obvious, and then there's tradition.

10   Why is this body of research rarely used in most American classrooms? Not many administrators or school-board members know it exists, says Linda Darling-Hammond, professor of education at Columbia University's Teachers College. In most states, neither teachers nor administrators are required to know much about how children learn in order to be certified. What's worse, she says, decisions to cut music or gym are often made by noneducators, whose concerns are more often monetary than educational. "Our school system was invented in the late 1800s, and little has changed," she says. "Can you imagine if the medical profession ran this way?"

PREPARING TO WRITE YOUR OWN CAUSE/EFFECT ESSAY

What can be improved in our educational system on the high school level? What do you want to change? What would be the possible results of these changes? What do you want to keep the same? Use one or more of the prewriting techniques that you learned in Chapter 2 to generate ideas on this subject.

How to Write a Cause/Effect Essay

When you write a cause/effect essay, your purpose is to give your readers some insight into the causes and effects of an event or a situation. Cause/ effect writing is based on your ability to analyze. Good cause/effect essays follow a few simple guidelines.

1. *Write a thesis statement that tells what you are analyzing.* Cause/ effect thinking requires that you look for connections between two or more situations. That is, you want to discover what caused an incident or what its results might be. Then you can focus on the causes (what made something else happen) or the effects (the results), or some combination of the two.

   In her essay, Hancock puts her thesis statement at the end of her first paragraph: "Not only are they [the biology lessons] ignored, but their findings are often turned upside down." She goes on to say that if school administrators paid attention to research (the cause), we would see many changes (the effects), which she names. The rest of the essay examines each effect in detail.

2. *Choose facts, details, and reasons to support your thesis statement.* Cause/effect essays are usually written to prove a specific point. As a result, your body paragraphs should consist mainly of facts, details, and reasons—not opinions. Your reader should be able to check what you are saying, and any opinions that you include should be based on clear evidence.

   Since Hancock sets out to prove that American education ignores research, she must name specific research studies that help her prove her point. She breaks her subject into five areas: music, gym, teaching methods, curriculum (subjects studied), and school hours. She then cites evidence in each area. For example, in the area of music, she describes

INSTRUCTOR'S RESOURCE MANUAL

For additional material about teaching cause and effect; for journal entries; and for multiple-choice, short-answer, and paragraph tests, see the *Instructor's Resource Manual*, Section II, Part II.

research at the University of California, Irvine; for gym, she discusses rat studies from the University of Illinois; for curriculum, she describes research done at Wayne State University's Children's Hospital.

Hancock also quotes many experts, such as Frank Vellutino, a professor of educational psychology at State University of New York at Albany (paragraph 2), and gives statistics from the National Commission on Music Education (paragraph 4). A reader could check every one of Hancock's research studies, quotations, statistics, and observations (such as when most high schools begin classes in the morning). By providing facts and reasons rather than opinions in her body paragraphs, Hancock proves her point—that American education is not paying attention to current research about learning.

3. ***Do not mistake coincidence for cause or effect.*** If you get up every morning at 5:30, just before the sun rises, you cannot conclude that the sun rises *because* you get up. The relationship between these two events is coincidence. Confusing coincidence with cause and effect is faulty reasoning—reasoning that is not logical. To avoid this kind of faulty reasoning, you can look deeper into the issues connected with your subject. The more you search for real causes and effects, the less likely you will be thrown off by coincidence.

    Hancock does not seem to mistake coincidence for cause or effect in any part of her essay. If, however, she had said that ignoring research on how teens learn has resulted in fewer students studying foreign languages today compared to 40 years ago, her reasoning would be faulty. She has no evidence to prove that the research about how students learn and the decline in students taking foreign languages in high school are related. It's only a coincidence that the research has been ignored and that fewer students study foreign languages today.

4. ***Search for the real causes and effects connected with your subject.*** Just as you wouldn't stop reading halfway through a good murder mystery, you shouldn't stop too early in your analysis of causes and effects. Keep digging. The first reasons or results that you uncover are often not the real reasons or results. Suppose that a character in a mystery dies by slipping in the shower. You should try to find out what caused the fall. A good detective who keeps digging might find that someone administered a drug overdose, which caused her to fall in the shower. In other words, you are looking for the most basic cause or effect.

    Hancock shows us through the large amount of evidence she presents that she has searched hard to discover the real causes and effects of education's lagging behind the times. She names two causes—administrators ignore research and noneducators make decisions about education—and gives the effects of ignoring research in five areas of education.

5. ***Organize your essay so that your readers can easily follow your analysis.*** Though it may be difficult to think through the causes and effects of a situation, organizing this type of essay is usually straightforward. Your thesis statement tells what you are going to analyze. Then your body paragraphs discuss the main causes or main effects in the order they occurred, from one extreme to another, from general to particular, or from particular to general. You might, for example, use chronological order to show how one effect led to another and then to a third. Or you might move from the most important cause or effect to the least important. Your goal in a cause/effect essay is to get your readers to agree with you and see a certain issue or situation the way you do. To accomplish this purpose, your readers need to be able to follow what you are saying.

Hancock discusses five effects of ignoring research on how students learn, moving from particular to general. First, she deals with the two subjects that school boards cut for budget reasons, music and gym. From these specific classes she moves to more general concerns—teaching methods and curriculum. Finally, she discusses high school hours, the most general topic of all. In other words, she organizes her essay from specific to general, moving from specific classes to the general logistics of the school day.

 WRITING YOUR OWN CAUSE/EFFECT ESSAY

Write an essay analyzing one of the changes you think is necessary in our high school educational system. What caused the current problem as you see it? Why is this change necessary? What will be the results of this change? Review your prewriting notes first. Then draft a thesis statement and write your analysis, following the guidelines for writing a cause/effect essay.

 # WORKING WITH A STUDENT ESSAY

Jefferson Wright, the student writer of the following essay, titled "The Budget Crisis," explores the problems of budget cuts at his college. Can you find the points in this draft of his essay when he deals with causes? When does he focus on effects?

The Budget Crisis

1   The local college has a budget crisis. Now, when a staff person quits their job or retires, no one is hired to replace that person. This wouldn't be of great concern to most students, except now the lack of money is starting to affect the campus grounds. The college no longer has the money to replace some of the maintenance and facilities crew, which means the campus grounds, classrooms, and offices are no longer well maintained.

2   A campus that used to be beautiful has turned into a wasteland because of the neglect in keeping up its grounds. The small maintenance crew simply cannot handle the workload necessary to maintain the campus. The flower beds in front of the buildings have not been weeded, so now it has more weeds than flowers. Trash that is thrown around the campus has not been picked up. Around every doorway are cigarette butts ground into the concrete. People shouldn't smoke anyway. It's not a great habit. There are old newspapers and candy wrappers caught on grass that has not been mowed in over two weeks, making the grounds look like the aftermath of a concert. Trash cans are overflowing with garbage and have colonies of flies circling them. The outside of the campus just looks unkempt and uncared for.

3   However, the campus grounds are not all that is ugly. The classroom buildings are also neglected. Everything inside is as messy as outside. The floors that used to shine are now covered with a sticky gray film. There are spills on the floors by all the soft drink machines. The bulletin boards are never cleaned off, so people just put new flyers over three or four layers of old flyers. On warm days, a strange smell overwhelms the classrooms, which the students have named "the biohazard." Restrooms are in desperate need of attention. And would probably fail any government check. The campus is really disgusting.

4   But the students aren't the only people suffering; the teachers are feeling the effects also. Their offices have ants crawling from various cracks in the walls. The dust in their offices is two inches thick. Spiders have woven cobwebs high in the windows and corners of the offices. Making both teachers and students wonder exactly where the insects hide during the day. Many light bulbs are broken near the offices, and the fluorescent bulbs flicker as if it is dancing to an unheard rhythm. The offices are as bad as the rest of the campus.

5   The condition of the campus can hardly be blamed on the maintenance crew. They are constantly working and trying to keep up with the workload. The problem lies in the fact that by the time they finish one job, two or more weeks pass by before they can get back to that job. There just

isn't enough money to hire the necessary personnel to cover the demands of the job. The college should put money into hiring more maintenance personnel before students transfer to other colleges because of the condition of this one. Why can't the college just spend the necessary money to make the campus beautiful again.

Discovering How the Essay Works

1. What is Jefferson analyzing in this essay?

   He is examining how the budget crisis is affecting his college campus.

2. Do Jefferson's facts, details, and reasons support his thesis statement? Explain your answer.

   They are all directly related to his thesis statement.

3. Does Jefferson confuse any coincidences with causes and effects? Explain your answer.

   He does not confuse coincidences with causes and effects.

4. Do you feel that Jefferson gets to the real problems connected with his college's budget crisis? Explain your answer.

   Yes, because he shows how the budget crisis affects the hiring of

   personnel, which affects the campus grounds, classrooms, and offices.

5. How does Jefferson organize the topics in his essay?

   From farthest to closest

Revising and Editing the Student Essay

   This essay is Jefferson's first draft, which now needs to be revised and edited. First, apply the Revising Checklist below to the content of Jefferson's draft. When you are satisfied that his ideas are fully developed and well organized, use the Editing Checklist on page 293 to correct his grammar and mechanics errors. Answer the questions after each checklist. Then write your suggested changes directly on Jefferson's draft.

Intrapersonal
Have students think about times when they tried to study or work but were distracted. What were the causes of the distraction? What effects did these causes produce? How would students make sure these distractions don't occur again?

Interpersonal
Have a group of students go to a fitness center and look closely at some of the machines. Then have students try to figure out what (causes) makes the machines work (effects).

Naturalist
Have students film a video or take pictures that show the influence of nature on humans. Then have them explain the causes and effects of nature on humans from their collection of pictures.

REVISING AND EDITING OPTIONS
Consider varying your approach to revising and editing. You could teach these skills in a class discussion, in small groups, or in pairs.

it will cause them to fall on the next move"). If they miscalculate, have them state the reasons the marbles fell.

REVISING STRATEGIES
This chapter focuses on the following revising elements:
Unity
Organization
Coherence

REVISING CHECKLIST ✔

THESIS STATEMENT
✔ Does the thesis statement contain the essay's controlling idea?
✔ Does the thesis appear as the last sentence of the introduction?

BASIC ELEMENTS
✔ Does the title draw in the readers?
✔ Does the introduction capture the readers' attention and build up to the thesis statement effectively?
✔ Does each body paragraph deal with a single topic?
✔ Does the conclusion bring the essay to a close in an interesting way?

DEVELOPMENT
✔ Do the body paragraphs adequately support the thesis statement?
✔ Does each body paragraph have a focused topic sentence?
✔ Does each body paragraph contain *specific* details that support the topic sentence?
✔ Does each body paragraph include *enough* details to explain the topic sentence fully?

UNITY
✔ Do the essay's topic sentences relate directly to the thesis statement?
✔ Do the details in each body paragraph support its topic sentence?

ORGANIZATION
✔ Is the essay organized logically?
✔ Is each body paragraph organized logically?

COHERENCE
✔ Are transitions used effectively so that paragraphs move smoothly and logically from one to the next?
✔ Do the sentences move smoothly and logically from one to the next?

Thesis Statement

1. Put brackets around the last sentence in Jefferson's introduction. What does it say he is analyzing?

   The effect of the budget crisis on the campus grounds, classrooms,

   and offices

2. Rewrite Jefferson's thesis statement if necessary so that it states his purpose and introduces all his topics.

_____

Basic Elements

1. Give Jefferson's essay an alternate title.

   Answers will vary.
   _____

2. Rewrite Jefferson's introduction so that it captures the readers' attention and builds up to the thesis statement at the end of the paragraph.

   Answers will vary.
   _____

   _____

   _____

3. Does each of Jefferson's body paragraphs deal with only one topic?

   Yes
   _____

4. Rewrite Jefferson's conclusion using at least one suggestion from Part I.

   Answers will vary.
   _____

   _____

   _____

Development

1. Write out Jefferson's thesis statement (revised, if necessary), and list his topic sentences below it.

   Thesis statement: *The college no longer has the money to replace*

   some of the maintenance and facilities crew, which means the cam-

   pus grounds, classrooms, and offices are no longer well maintained.

   Topic 1: *A campus that used to be beautiful has turned into a*

   wasteland because of the neglect in keeping up its grounds.

Topic 2: _However, the campus grounds are not all that is ugly._

_____

Topic 3: _But the students aren't the only people suffering; the_

teachers are feeling the effects also.

2. Do the topics adequately develop the essay's thesis statement?

   Yes

3. Does each body paragraph have a focused topic sentence?

   Yes

4. Does Jefferson get to the *real* causes and effects in his essay?

   He does examine the real causes and effects.

5. Where do you need more information?

   Answers will vary.

6. Make two of Jefferson's details more specific.
7. Add at least two new details to make his essay clearer.

Unity

1. Read each of Jefferson's topic sentences with his thesis statement. Do they go together?

   Answers will vary.

2. Revise them if necessary so they are directly related.
3. Drop or rewrite the two sentences in paragraph 2 that are not directly related to their topic sentence. _Sentences 6 and 7_

Organization

1. Read Jefferson's essay again to see if all the paragraphs are arranged logically.
2. Move any paragraphs that are out of order. _All paragraphs are arranged logically._

3. Do you think his method of organization is the most effective one for his purpose? Explain your answer.

   It is the most effective because it moves the crisis from outside to

   the office space that affects people personally.

4. Look closely at Jefferson's body paragraphs to see if all his sentences are arranged logically within paragraphs.

5. Move the sentence in paragraph 2 that is out of order. *Move sentence 9 after sentence 4.*

Coherence

1. Add two transitions to Jefferson's essay.

2. Circle five pronouns Jefferson uses.

3. Explain how two of these make Jefferson's essay easier to read.

For a list of transitions, see pages 83–84.

For a list of pronouns, see pages 508–509.

   Answers will vary.

Now rewrite Jefferson's essay with your revisions.

EDITING CHECKLIST ✔

EDITING STRATEGIES
This chapter focuses on the following editing problems:
   Fragments
   Pronoun agreement
   End punctuation

SENTENCES

✔ Does each sentence have a main subject and verb?

✔ Do all subjects and verbs agree?

✔ Do all pronouns agree with their nouns?

✔ Are modifiers as close as possible to the words they modify?

PUNCTUATION AND MECHANICS

✔ Are sentences punctuated correctly?

✔ Are words capitalized properly?

WORD CHOICE AND SPELLING

✔ Are words used correctly?

✔ Are words spelled correctly?

Sentences

Subjects and Verbs

For help with subjects and verbs, see Chapter 34.

1. Underline the subjects once and verbs twice in paragraphs 3 and 4 of your revision of Jefferson's essay. Remember that sentences can have more than one subject-verb set.

2. Does each of the sentences have at least one subject and verb that can stand alone?

No

For help with fragments, see Chapter 35.

3. Did you find and correct Jefferson's two fragments? If not, find and correct them now. *Paragraph 3, sentence 9; paragraph 4, sentence 5*

Subject-Verb Agreement

For help with subject-verb agreement, see Chapter 39.

1. Read aloud the subjects and verbs you underlined in your revision of Jefferson's essay.

2. Correct any subjects and verbs that do not agree. *All subjects and verbs agree.*

Pronoun Agreement

For help with pronoun agreement, see Chapter 43.

1. Find any pronouns in your revision of Jefferson's essay that do not agree with their nouns.

2. Did you find and correct the three pronoun agreement errors in Jefferson's essay? If not, find and correct them now. *Paragraph 1, sentence 2; paragraph 2, sentence 3; paragraph 4, sentence 6*

Modifiers

For help with modifier errors, see Chapter 46.

1. Find any modifiers in your revision of Jefferson's essay that are not as close as possible to the words they modify. *There are no modifier errors.*

2. Rewrite sentences if necessary so that modifiers are as close as possible to the words they modify.

Punctuation and Mechanics

Punctuation

For help with punctuation, see Chapters 47–51.

1. Read your revision of Jefferson's essay for any errors in punctuation.

2. Find the two fragments you revised, and make sure they are punctuated correctly.

3. Did you find and correct Jefferson's two errors in end punctuation? If not, find and correct them now. *Paragraph 3, sentence 10; paragraph 5, sentence 6*

Mechanics

1. Read your revision of Jefferson's essay for any errors in capitalization.
2. Be sure to check Jefferson's capitalization in the fragments you revised.

For help with capitalization, see Chapter 52.

Word Choice and Spelling

Word Choice

1. Find any words used incorrectly in your revision of Jefferson's essay.
   All words are used correctly.
2. Correct any errors you find.

For help with confused words, see Chapter 58.

Spelling

1. Use spell-check and a dictionary to check the spelling in your revision of Jefferson's essay. *All words are spelled correctly.*

2. Correct any misspelled words.

Now rewrite Jefferson's essay again with your editing corrections.

For help with spelling, see Chapter 59.

 WORKING WITH YOUR OWN ESSAY

Returning to the cause/effect essay you wrote earlier in this chapter, revise and edit your own writing. The checklists here will help you apply what you have learned to your essay.

Revising and Editing Your Own Essay

REVISING CHECKLIST ✔

THESIS STATEMENT
- ☐ Does the thesis statement contain the essay's controlling idea?
- ☐ Does the thesis appear as the last sentence of the introduction?

BASIC ELEMENTS
- ☐ Does the title draw in the readers?
- ☐ Does the introduction capture the readers' attention and build up to the thesis statement effectively?
- ☐ Does each body paragraph deal with a single topic?
- ☐ Does the conclusion bring the essay to a close in an interesting way?

CLASS ACTIVITY
Find a published cause/effect essay that also incorporates many of the other modes. Have the students identify the instances of the other modes, and then ask them how they think these other modes help establish the cause and effect relationships in the essay as a whole.

DEVELOPMENT

☐ Do the body paragraphs adequately support the thesis statement?

☐ Does each body paragraph have a focused topic sentence?

☐ Does each body paragraph contain *specific* details that support the topic sentence?

☐ Does each body paragraph include *enough* details to explain the topic sentence fully?

UNITY

☐ Do the essay's topic sentences relate directly to the thesis statement?

☐ Do the details in each body paragraph support its topic sentence?

ORGANIZATION

☐ Is the essay organized logically?

☐ Is each body paragraph organized logically?

COHERENCE

☐ Are transitions used effectively so that paragraphs move smoothly and logically from one to the next?

☐ Do the sentences move smoothly and logically from one to the next?

Thesis Statement

1. What are you analyzing?

_____

2. Put brackets around the last sentence in your introduction. What do you say you are analyzing in this sentence?

_____

3. Rewrite your thesis statement if necessary so that it states your purpose and introduces your topics.

Basic Elements

1. Give your essay a title if it doesn't have one.

_____

2. Does your introduction capture your readers' attention and build up to your thesis statement at the end of the paragraph?

   _____

3. Does each of your body paragraphs deal with only one topic?

   _____

4. Does your conclusion follow some of the suggestions offered in Part I?

   _____

Development

1. Write out your thesis statement (revised, if necessary), and list your topic sentences below it.

   Thesis statement: _____

       Topic 1: _____

       Topic 2: _____

       Topic 3: _____

2. Do your topics adequately support your thesis statement?

   _____

3. Does each body paragraph have a focused topic sentence?

   _____

4. Do you get to the *real* causes and effects in your essay?

   _____

5. Where do you need more information?

   _____

6. Make two of your details more specific.
7. Add at least two new details to make your cause/effect clearer.

Unity

1. Read each of your topic sentences with your thesis statement in mind. Do they go together?

_____

2. Revise them if necessary so they are directly related.
3. Drop or rewrite any of the sentences in your body paragraphs that are not directly related to their topic sentences.

Organization

1. Read your essay again to see if all the paragraphs are arranged logically.
2. Refer to your answers to the development questions. Then identify your method of organization:

_____

3. Move any paragraphs that are out of order.
4. Look closely at your body paragraphs to see if all the sentences are arranged logically within paragraphs.
5. Move any sentences that are out of order.

Coherence

For a list of transitions, see pages 83–84.

For a list of pronouns, see pages 508–509.

1. Add two transitions to your essay.
2. Circle five pronouns you use.
3. Explain how two of these make your essay easier to read.

_____

_____

Now rewrite your essay with your revisions.

EDITING CHECKLIST ✔

SENTENCES
☐ Does each sentence have a main subject and verb?
☐ Do all subjects and verbs agree?

☐ Do all pronouns agree with their nouns?

☐ Are modifiers as close as possible to the words they modify?

PUNCTUATION AND MECHANICS

☐ Are sentences punctuated correctly?

☐ Are words capitalized properly?

WORD CHOICE AND SPELLING

☐ Are words used correctly?

☐ Are words spelled correctly?

Sentences

Subjects and Verbs

1. Underline the subjects once and verbs twice in a paragraph of your revised essay. Remember that sentences can have more than one subject-verb set.

   For help with subjects and verbs, see Chapter 34.

2. Does each of your sentences have at least one subject and verb that can stand alone?

   _____

   For help with fragments, see Chapter 35.

3. Correct any fragments you have written.

4. Correct any run-together sentences you have written.

   For help with run-togethers, see Chapter 36.

Subject-Verb Agreement

1. Read aloud the subjects and verbs you underlined in your revised essay.

2. Correct any subjects and verbs that do not agree.

   For help with subject-verb agreement, see Chapter 39.

Pronoun Agreement

1. Find any pronouns in your revised essay that do not agree with their nouns.

2. Correct any pronouns that do not agree with their nouns.

   For help with pronoun agreement, see Chapter 43.

Modifiers

1. Find any modifiers in your revised essay that are not as close as possible to the words they modify.

   For help with modifier errors, see Chapter 46.

2. Rewrite sentences if necessary so that your modifiers are as close as possible to the words they modify.

Punctuation and Mechanics

Punctuation

For help with punctuation, see Chapters 47–51.

1. Read your revised essay for any errors in punctuation.
2. Make sure any fragments and run-together sentences you revised are punctuated correctly.

Mechanics

For help with capitalization, see Chapter 52.

1. Read your revised essay for any errors in capitalization.
2. Be sure to check your capitalization in any fragments or run-together sentences you revised.

Word Choice and Spelling

Word Choice

For help with confused words, see Chapter 58.

1. Find any words used incorrectly in your revised essay.
2. Correct any errors you find.

Spelling

For help with spelling, see Chapter 59.

1. Use spell-check and a dictionary to check your spelling.
2. Correct any misspelled words.

Now rewrite your essay again with your editing corrections.

PRACTICING CAUSE/EFFECT

Reading Suggestions

SERVICE LEARNING
PROJECT
This assignment is
another step in the
Service Learning
project. If you choose
to use this feature of
the text, each chapter
in Part II has an assign-
ment that asks students
to use a different
rhetorical mode to
reflect on their Service
Learning project. These
reflections will lead to
an essay assignment in
Part III (Chapter 22).
You can assign as many

In Chapter 32, you will find two essays that follow the guidelines you have studied in this chapter. "A Family Dilemma: To Scout or Not to Scout?" by Michael Alvear discusses the dilemma that the ruling about gay scout leaders puts on one family, and "Happiness Is Catching: Why Emotions Are Contagious" by Stacey Colino analyzes the role of moods in our daily lives. You might want to read these selections before writing another cause/effect essay. As you read, notice how the writers make their points through well-thought-out, detailed reasoning.

Service Learning Project

This assignment is based on a Service Learning project of your choice. If your instructor has already introduced service learning to the class, you will be doing these exercises when they are assigned. At this point, choose a project you would like to pursue, or continue work on a project you have already begun. This assignment in Part II will help you prepare for an essay on this project in Part III. Here is another stage in the preparation for this essay:

For the Service Learning project you have taken on, discuss some causes and effects of various chores you have completed. Use the guidelines you have learned in this chapter to help you write your discussion. But remember that these are just thoughts that will be developed into an essay in Part III.

or as few of these exercises as you want in preparation for this essay. For more information on service learning, see the *Instructor's Resource Manual,* Section I, Part III.

Writing Workshop

Guidelines for Writing a Cause/Effect Essay

1. Write a thesis statement that tells what you are analyzing.
2. Choose facts, details, and reasons to support your thesis statement.
3. Do not mistake coincidence for cause or effect.
4. Search for the real causes and effects connected with your subject.
5. Organize your essay so that your readers can easily follow your analysis.

ADDITIONAL WRITING TOPIC
Have your students turn to Chapter 32 and read Michael Alvear's "Family Dilemma: To Scout or Not to Scout" or Stacey Colino's "Happiness Is Catching." Then have them write an essay on one of the topics from "Writing Topics: Analyzing Causes and Effects" at the end of the chapter.

1. Explain how the scene above got started. What caused this reaction? Why did it happen? What were the results of the actions pictured here? Write an essay focusing on either the causes or the effects of this scene.

2. We all deal with change differently, but it is generally difficult to accept change in our lives. Think of a significant change in your life,

TEACHING ON THE WEB
Discussion Topic: Divide students into groups of three or four, and have them discuss the effects of the

Internet on college
life today. In what
other ways does the
Internet affect a stu-
dent's life? Which
effects are negative,
and which are positive?

TEACHING ON
THE WEB
Links: Think of a
recent disaster in the
United States, and have
students link to news
Web sites to see how
the news agencies
reported the story.
How does each use
cause and effect
differently to recount
what happened?
    Possible sites:
    CNN,
        www.cnn.com
    Newsweek,
        www.newsweek.
        com
    *The New York
    Times,*
        www.nytimes.com

TEACHING ON
THE WEB
Research: Have stu-
dents find a Web site
that explains a recent
scientific discovery.
What is the discovery,
and how will it affect
the world? What causes
made this discovery
possible?

TEACHING ON
THE WEB
Mosaics Web Site: To
learn more about cause
and effect, students can
go to www.prenhall.
com/mosaics.

and write about its causes and effects. What was the incident? What were the circumstances connected with the incident?

3. Write an essay that analyzes a current social problem—homelessness, drugs, environmental concerns—including the reasons for its existence.

4. Create your own cause/effect assignment (with the help of your instructor), and write a response to it.

Revising Workshop

Small Group Activity (5–10 minutes per writer)   Working in groups of three or four, each person should read his or her cause/effect essay to the other members of the group. Those listening should record their reactions on a copy of the Peer Evaluation Form in Appendix 2H. After your group goes through this process, give your evaluation forms to the appropriate writers so that each writer has two or three peer comment sheets for revising.

Paired Activity (5 minutes per writer)   Using the completed Peer Evaluation Forms, work in pairs to decide what you should revise in your essay. If time allows, rewrite some of your sentences, and have your partner look at them.

Individual Activity   Rewrite your paper, using the revising feedback you received from other students.

Editing Workshop

Paired Activity (5–10 minutes per writer)   Swap papers with a classmate, and use the editing portion of your Peer Evaluation Form to identify as many grammar, punctuation, mechanics, and spelling errors as you can. If time allows, correct some of your errors, and have your partner look at them. Record your grammar, punctuation, and mechanics errors in the Error Log (Appendix 6) and your spelling errors in the Spelling Log (Appendix 7).

Individual Activity   Rewrite your paper again, using the editing feedback you received from other students.

Reflecting on Your Writing

When you have completed your own essay, answer these six questions.

1. What was most difficult about this assignment?

2. What was easiest?

3. What did you learn about using cause and effect by completing this assignment?

4. What do you think are the strengths of your cause/effect essay? Place a wavy line by the parts of your essay that you feel are very good.

5. What are the weaknesses, if any, of your paper? Place an X by the parts of your essay you would like help with. Write any questions you have in the margin.

6. What did you learn from this assignment about your own writing process—about preparing to write, about writing the first draft, about revising, and about editing?

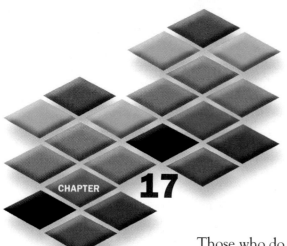

17

ARGUING

Those who do not know their opponent's arguments
do not completely understand their own.

—DAVID BENDER

Argument may be our most important form of communication because
it helps us get what we want in life. The main reason people argue is to persuade someone of something. When you want to get a certain job, sell your
car, or borrow some money, you need to present your request clearly and
convincingly. On the flip side, others try to persuade you to do things all the
time: Politicians make speeches trying to persuade you to vote for them;
your friends try to persuade you to go to a movie when you know you should
study for an exam; TV commercials, magazine ads, and billboards everywhere try to persuade you to buy this cereal or that car.

As you might suspect, your ability to argue in writing is also important in
life. In fact, writing arguments is fundamental to your success on a personal
level, in college courses, and in the workplace:

The chairperson for your college reunion sends a letter with clear
reasons why everyone should attend this year.

A student writes an essay in a freshman composition course arguing
for or against the death penalty.

A student writes a paper in a sociology course arguing that laws
against hate crimes need to be stronger.

A sales representative writes a letter arguing that customers should
order supplies from him rather than from his competitor.

A restaurant owner writes an advertisement to persuade people to
eat at her restaurant.

The purpose of **arguing** is to persuade someone to take a certain action
or to think or feel a specific way. You can use either logical arguments (based

on facts and reasoning) or emotional arguments (based on vivid description and details) to achieve your purpose.

Some of the most important laws affecting people's lives in the United States are the result of arguments made to the Supreme Court. Lawyers argue such issues as gun control, abortion, immigrants' rights, and drunk driving. If, for instance, lawmakers are trying to get stricter jail sentences for drunk driving, they might rely heavily on facts and statistics (logical evidence). But then they might add an emotional element by describing the mangled bike, the bloodstained clothes, and the grief in the faces of the parents of a 12-year-old girl killed by a drunk driver as she rode her bike home from school. Such an appeal to feelings would create a much stronger argument than statistics alone.

The better you become at arguing—in both thinking and writing—the more you will get what you want out of life (and out of college). Arguing effectively means getting the pay raises you hope for, the refund you deserve, and the grades you've worked hard for. Argumentation is a powerful tool.

WRITING AN ARGUMENT ESSAY

The following argument, "Racial Profiling Is Unjust" by Bob Herbert, tries to persuade its readers that law-enforcement agents should not take action based on race alone. It uses a combination of logic and emotion to achieve its purpose. Have you ever been stopped by the police because of your appearance? If you have, what was your reaction? If you haven't, what do you think your reaction would be?

years. How has the intended audience changed? What elements from the old advertisements would not work on consumers today?

RACIAL PROFILING IS UNJUST

by Bob Herbert

An anti-loitering law that allowed the Chicago police to arrest more than 42,000 people from 1992 to 1995 was declared unconstitutional in June of 1999 by the Supreme Court.   1

[Supreme Court justice] Antonin Scalia howled in dissent, which should tell you something. The law was an abomination, just like the practice in New York of stopping and frisking black and Hispanic people by the tens of thousands for no good reason and just like the practice of pulling over and harassing perfectly innocent black and Hispanic motorists on streets and highways in many parts of the country.   2

The Faces of Ethnic Profiling

3   Ethnic profiling by law-enforcement authorities in the United States comes in many forms, and all of them are disgusting.

4   In the summer of 1998, sadistic members of the State Police in Oklahoma spent more than two hours humiliating Rossano Gerald, a 37-year-old Army sergeant, and his 12-year-old son, Greg.

5   Sergeant Gerald was pulled over and interrogated. He was ordered out of his car and handcuffed. The troopers asked if he had any guns. They asked permission to search the car and when he refused they searched it anyway. They separated Greg from his father and locked him in a police vehicle. They interrogated him. They brought drug-sniffing dogs to the scene. They dismantled parts of the car. When they finally tired of the madness, they told Sergeant Gerald he was free to go. No arrest was made. Greg, of course, was petrified. When the ordeal ended he wept uncontrollably.

6   Why did this happen? Greg and Sergeant Gerald were guilty of America's original sin. They were born black.

Profiling Targets the Innocent

7   In New York, profiling was not only perpetuated but elevated to astonishing new heights during the regime of [New York City mayor] Rudolph Giuliani. Here, the targets are mostly pedestrians, not motorists. Young black and Hispanic males (and in some cases females) are stopped, frisked, and harassed in breathtaking numbers.

8   By the Police Department's own count, more than 45,000 people were stopped and frisked by members of the Street Crimes Unit in 1997 and 1998. But the total number of arrests made by the unit over those two years was less than 10,000. And it is widely believed that the number of people stopped during that period was far higher than the 45,000 reported by the cops. The true number likely was in the hundreds of thousands.

9   Ira Glasser, executive director of the American Civil Liberties Union [ACLU], noted that two things characterize the New York City stops: "Virtually everybody is innocent, and virtually everybody is not white."

10   Mayor Giuliani, like most public officials, will not acknowledge that his police officers are targeting people by race. "The stops are driven by the descriptions of the person who committed the crime," Mr. Giuliani said.

11   Spare me. The vast majority of these stops are in no way connected to the commission of a specific crime, and the mayor knows it. They are arbitrary and unconscionable intrusions on the rights of New Yorkers who are supposed to be protected, not humiliated, by the police.

Profiling Is Extensive

Most Americans have no idea of the extent of the race-based profiling 12
that is carried out by law-enforcement officials and the demoralizing effect
it has on its victims. The ACLU, in a report called "Driving While Black:
Racial Profiling on Our Nation's Highways," said: "No [people] of color [are]
safe from this treatment anywhere, regardless of their obedience to the law,
their age, the type of car they drive, or their station in life."

The Chicago law that resulted in more than 42,000 arrests over three 13
years was aimed at curbing gang activity. It was clearly unconstitutional. It
made it a crime for anyone in the presence of suspected gang members to
"remain in any one place with no apparent purpose" after being told by the
police to move on.

Why should one's purpose for being in a public place have to be ap- 14
parent? As a reporter for *The New York Times*, I might be in the presence of
a suspected gang member. What business is that of the police? And how
could that possibly be a legitimate basis for an arrest?

The suit challenging the law was brought by the Chicago office of the 15
ACLU. A spokesman for the group noted that the "vast majority" of the people arrested under the law were African-American or Hispanic. What a
surprise.

 PREPARING TO WRITE YOUR OWN ARGUMENT ESSAY

Choose a controversial issue on your campus or in the news that
is important to you, and use one or more of the prewriting techniques
that you learned in Chapter 2 to generate ideas on the issue. Consult
your campus or local newspaper for ideas if you want. What is the
exact issue? Why is it important? Why do people care about it? How
do you think the issue should be resolved?

How to Write an Argument Essay

When you write an argument essay, choose a subject that matters to you.
If you have strong feelings, you will find it much easier to gather evidence
and convince your readers of your point of view. Keep in mind, however,
that your readers might feel just as strongly about the opposite side of the
issue. The following guidelines will help you write a good argument essay.

INSTRUCTOR'S
RESOURCE MANUAL
For additional material
about teaching argu-
ment or persuasion;
for journal entries;
and for multiple-choice,
short-answer, and

paragraph tests, see the *Instructor's Resource Manual,* Section II, Part II.

1. ***State your opinion on your topic in your thesis statement.*** To write a thesis statement for an argument essay, you must take a stand for or against an action or an idea. In other words, your thesis statement should be debatable—a statement that can be argued or challenged and will not be met with agreement by everyone who reads it. Your thesis statement should introduce your subject and state your opinion about that subject.

   Bob Herbert's thesis is in his third paragraph: "Ethnic profiling by law-enforcement authorities in the United States comes in many forms, and all of them are disgusting." This is a debatable thesis. Some other statements on the topic of ethnic profiling would not be good thesis statements.

Not debatable:	Ethnic profiling by law-enforcement authorities in the United States often involves African Americans and Hispanics.
Not debatable:	Some law-enforcement agencies have strict rules regarding ethnic profiling.

   Herbert sets up his essay with some facts about anti-loitering laws and a reference to the practice in New York of stopping and frisking blacks and Hispanics. This background information leads up to his thesis statement.

2. ***Find out as much as you can about your audience before you write.*** Knowing your readers' background and feelings on your topic will help you choose the best supporting evidence and examples. Suppose that you want to convince people in two different age groups to quit smoking. You might tell the group of teenagers that cigarettes make their breath rancid, their teeth yellow, and their clothes smell bad. But with a group of adults, you might discuss the horrifying statistics on lung and heart disease associated with long-term smoking.

   Herbert's essay was first published in *The New York Times,* which addresses a fairly educated audience. The original readers probably thought a lot like he does on this issue. So he chooses his support as if he is talking to people who agree with him.

3. ***Choose evidence that supports your thesis statement.*** Evidence is probably the most important factor in writing an argument essay. Without solid evidence, your essay is nothing more than opinion; with it, your essay can be powerful and persuasive. If you supply convincing evidence, your readers will not only understand your position but perhaps agree with it.

Evidence can consist of facts, statistics, statements from authorities, and examples or personal stories. Examples and personal stories can be based on your own observations, experiences, and reading, but your opinions are not evidence. You can also develop your ideas with the writing strategies you've learned in Chapters 9 through 16. Comparison/contrast, definition, and cause/effect can be particularly useful in building an argument. Use any combination of evidence and writing strategies that will help you support your thesis statement.

In his essay, Herbert uses several different types of evidence. Here are some examples:

Facts
> An anti-loitering law was declared unconstitutional in June 1999 (paragraph 1)
> Sergeant Rossano Gerald was stopped by the Oklahoma police in the summer of 1998 (paragraph 4)

Statistics
> Chicago police arrested over 42,000 people from 1992 to 1995 for loitering (paragraph 1)
> In New York, more than 45,000 people were stopped and frisked by the Street Crimes Unit in 1997 and 1998 (paragraph 8)
> Only 10,000 arrests were made in New York in 1997 and 1998 (paragraph 8)

Statements from Authorities
> Quotation by Ira Glasser, ACLU director (paragraph 9)
> Quotation by Mayor Giuliani (paragraph 10)
> ACLU report (paragraph 12)

Examples and Personal Stories
> Story about Sergeant Gerald and his son (paragraphs 4–6)

4. ***Anticipate opposing points of view.*** In addition to stating and supporting your position, anticipating and responding to opposing views is important. Presenting only your side of the argument leaves half the story untold—the opposition's half. If you admit that there are opposing arguments and answer them, you will move your reader more in your direction.

   In paragraph 10, Herbert acknowledges a statement made by Mayor Giuliani as his opposition. Giuliani flatly denies the claims against his police force. "The stops are driven by the descriptions of the person who committed the crime." Acknowledging this statement raises Herbert's credibility and then lets him counter Giuliani's claim, which he does in the next paragraph.

5. ***Find some common ground.*** Pointing out common ground between you and your opponent is also an effective strategy. Common ground refers to points of agreement between two opposing positions. For example, one person might be in favor of gun control and another strongly opposed. But they might find common ground—agreement—in the need to keep guns out of teenagers' hands. Locating some common ground is possible in almost every situation. When you state in your essay that you agree with your opponent on certain points, your reader sees you as a fair person.

Herbert assumes that most of his readers know that ethnic profiling by law-enforcement agencies is going on around the country. His job, then, is to prove the extent and unfairness of it.

6. ***Maintain a reasonable tone.*** Just as you probably wouldn't win an argument by shouting or making nasty or sarcastic comments, don't expect your readers to respond well to such tactics. Keep the "voice" of your essay calm and sensible. Your readers will be much more open to what you have to say if they think you are a reasonable person.

Herbert maintains a reasonable tone throughout his essay. Even when he quotes some unbelievable statistics, as in paragraphs 1 and 8 or uses an occasional harsh word ("abomination" in paragraph 2 or "disgusting" in paragraph 3), he keeps his voice under control and therefore earns the respect of his readers.

7. ***Organize your essay so that it presents your position as effectively as possible.*** By the end of your essay, you want your audience to agree with you. So you want to organize your essay in such a way that your readers can easily follow it. The number of your paragraphs may vary, depending on the nature of your assignment, but the following outline shows the order in which the features of an argument essay are most effective:

> **Outline**
> Introduction
>> Background information
>> Introduction of subject
>> Statement of your opinion
> Body Paragraphs
>> Common ground
>> Lots of evidence (logical and emotional)

          Opposing point of view
          Response to opposing point of view
     Conclusion
          Restatement of your position
          Call for action or agreement

The arrangement of your evidence in an argument essay depends to a great extent on your readers' opinions. Most arguments will be organized from general to particular, from particular to general, or from one extreme to another. When you know that your readers already agree with you, arranging your details from general to particular or from most to least important is usually most effective. With this order, you are building on your readers' agreement and loyalty as you explain your thinking on the subject.

If you suspect that your audience does not agree with you, reverse the organization of your evidence and arrange it from particular to general or from least to most important. In this way, you can take your readers step by step through your reasoning in an attempt to get them to agree with you.

Bob Herbert's essay follows the general outline just presented. Here is a skeleton outline of his essay.

Introduction
     Background statistics and facts about anti-loitering laws and stopping and frisking

Body Paragraphs
     The Faces of Ethnic Profiling

Subject introduced:	racial profiling
Statement of opinion:	racial profiling is disgusting
Evidence—example:	Sergeant Gerald's story

     Profiling Targets the Innocent

Evidence—fact:	blacks and Hispanics stopped in New York
Evidence—statistics:	more than 45,000 people stopped, less than 10,000 arrested
Evidence—statements from authorities:	Ira Glasser, ACLU director
Opposing point of view:	Mayor Giuliani
Response to opposition:	Herbert's opinion

Conclusion: Profiling Is Extensive

Restatement of problem:	extent of race-based profiling
Evidence—statements from authorities:	quotation from ACLU report
Evidence—statistics:	over 42,000 arrests in Chicago in three years
Herbert's opinion	
Evidence—fact:	ACLU lawsuit
Herbert's final comment	

 WRITING YOUR OWN ARGUMENT ESSAY

Write an essay that presents your opinion on the controversial issue you considered in your prewriting. Begin with a debatable thesis statement. Then follow the guidelines for writing an argument essay. As you write your essay, be sure you support your opinions with reasons. If a newspaper article inspired this assignment, attach it to your paper before you turn it in.

WORKING WITH A STUDENT ESSAY

TEACHING TIPS
The following eight teaching tips are based on Howard Gardner's list of multiple intelligences:

Verbal/Linguistic
Have students prepare a list of words and phrases that can help their communication in an argument essay. How can choosing the right word strengthen or weaken an argument? What are some words and phrases that can weaken arguments?

Melinda Jackson, the student writer of the following essay, titled "A Call for Policies on Drinking," argues that drinking on college campuses is a serious problem. See if you can identify her main point and supporting evidence as you read this draft of her essay.

A Call for Policies on Drinking

1   College and drinking, drinking and college—most students believe the two go hand in hand. If asked, they would say that drinking in college is just a part of life, and it is not a major concern. However, when we examine drinking in college more closely, we see it is a serious problem that people on all levels are not facing. Drinking on college campuses is a bigger problem than parents and administrators realize, and something needs to be done about it—now.

2 No one would ever realistically believe that college students will never drink. In fact, most students, parents, and administrators are in favor of students taking a break and having fun. Studying during every available minute, parents and administrators realize the strain students

are under. And they know that students will probably drink. What they don't understand is the trap students can fall into.

Jerry, a college student, explained how he got involved with alcohol and how it soon took over his life. Jerry went to a different fraternity party every weekend night, where his main goal was to get as drunk as possible. What he didn't know was that he was confrontational when he drank and that people didn't want to be around him. He didn't know his limit, so he often exceeded it. He usually passed out on someone's couch after drinking. In the morning he would wake up and find the next party. Jerry is just one of many students on every U.S. college campus.

Whereas most people think drinking occurs just during parties, it actually occurs for many students on a daily basis. Students like Jerry begin by drinking on weekends then they all too easily start drinking every day. They begin to need alcohol in order to feel normal. Once they fall into this pattern, several other serious problems can occur. Not only are they missing classes and falling behind in their coarses, but they are also endangering their lives. Drinking becomes the most important aspect in their lives. But it's not just the drinker who's life is effected. Drinkers disrupt their roommates, who are either distracted from their studying or awakened from their sleep. When the roommate complains about being disturbed. The drinker gets angry. And so the pattern repeats itself again and again.

According to our dean of students, students who drink often take risks that endanger their lives and the lives of others. The most obvious risk involves a drinker who gets behind the wheel of a car. Drinkers also tend to get into more fights, because they mistakenly believe they are invincible. In this case, they risk harming the people they fight with and themselves, because they are in no condition to defend themselves. Everyone on the road is a potential victim of the drinker. Drinkers are also likely to have unprotected sex. This could lead to unwanted pregnancies, sexually transmitted diseases, or even AIDS. With the widespread drinking that occurs on college campuses, these consequences are very likely to occur to a student who drinks.

Drinking is a major problem on college campuses, but like every other controversial issue, some people say it has been given too much publicity by overzealous worriers. They believe that the college knows light drinking occurs and that the administration has control of the students who drink. They believe that kids will be kids, students will drink no matter what. These people say that letting students have fun is what's important. But to adopt this attitude is possibly placing someone's life in danger. If even one person is in danger from a drunken student. Then the college must take action.

Musical/Rhythmic

Have students create a rap song that tries to persuade people that either rap music has value in our society or rap music should be banned from the airwaves. At what audience should this song be aimed?

Logical/Mathematical

Provide students with a short argumentative speech. Have students identify key arguments and explain why they are organized as they are. Have them change the order of the argumentative points and explain why the new order either strengthens or weakens the argument.

Visual/Spatial

Provide students with a short argumentative essay, and have them make a rough outline of the essay. Does knowing the blueprint of the argument make the essay more or less persuasive?

Bodily/Kinesthetic

Have students, without using words, try to persuade a friend on campus to do something for them, such as carry their books or cross the street. Then ask students to explain how difficult it was to persuade people with only their facial expressions and actions.

7   Drinking in college is definitely going to happen, but there are measures that can be taken to prevent serious harm to students who do decide to drink. Campuses could have alcohol awareness programs and give students easy access to condoms. Campuses could set up a response team that would pick up any student who was incapable of driving. They could require all sororities and fraternities to confiscate keys before anyone is given a drink to ensure that a person who has been drinking won't drive. They can offer literature on organizations that can help students who become addicted to alcohol. Its time for students, parents, and administrators to see the problem before them and take steps to fix it before it's too late.

Discovering How the Essay Works

1A. What is Melinda's thesis statement?

Drinking on college campuses is a bigger problem than parents and administrators realize, and something needs to be done about it—now.

1B. Does it state her opinion clearly? Explain your answer.

It lets the reader know she thinks drinking on college campuses is a bigger problem than parents and administrators realize.

1C. Is it debatable? (Does it have more than one side?)

Yes, people can certainly argue that drinking is not a problem on college campuses.

2. Who do you think Melinda is addressing in this essay? How did you come to this conclusion?

She is addressing parents, administrators, and students. She states her audience.

3. What evidence does the author use to support her thesis statement? Find an example of each type of evidence in her essay.

Facts: *Students are drinking in college.*

Statistics: *No statistics provided.*

Statements from authorities: ___*Statement from the dean of students*___

Examples and personal stories: ___*Jerry's story is one example.*___

4. Does Melinda anticipate an opposing point of view? Explain your answer.

   In paragraph 6, Melinda acknowledges her opponents.

5. Did Melinda find some common ground with her readers? Explain your answer.

   In paragraph 2, she says her readers know that most students drink

   at some time during their college years.

6. Does Melinda maintain a reasonable tone? Explain your answer.

   Yes. Beyond this, answers will vary.

7. How does Melinda organize the topics in her essay: general to particular, particular to general, or from one extreme to another?

   From general to particular

Revising and Editing the Student Essay

This essay is Melinda's first draft, which now needs to be revised and edited. First, apply the Revising Checklist below to the content of Melinda's draft. When you are satisfied that her ideas are fully developed and well organized, use the Editing Checklist on page 320 to correct her grammar and mechanics errors. Answer the questions after each checklist. Then write your suggested changes directly on Melinda's draft.

REVISING AND EDITING OPTIONS
Consider varying your approach to revising and editing. You could teach these skills in a class discussion, in small groups, or in pairs.

REVISING STRATEGIES
This chapter focuses on the following revising elements:
Organization
Coherence

REVISING CHECKLIST ✔

THESIS STATEMENT
✔ Does the thesis statement contain the essay's controlling idea?
✔ Does the thesis appear as the last sentence of the introduction?

BASIC ELEMENTS
✔ Does the title draw in the readers?
✔ Does the introduction capture the readers' attention and build up to the thesis statement effectively?

✔ Does each body paragraph deal with a single topic?

✔ Does the conclusion bring the essay to a close in an interesting way?

DEVELOPMENT

✔ Do the body paragraphs adequately support the thesis statement?

✔ Does each body paragraph have a focused topic sentence?

✔ Does each body paragraph contain *specific* details that support the topic sentence?

✔ Does each body paragraph include *enough* details to explain the topic sentence fully?

UNITY

✔ Do the essay's topic sentences relate directly to the thesis statement?

✔ Do the details in each body paragraph support its topic sentence?

ORGANIZATION

✔ Is the essay organized logically?

✔ Is each body paragraph organized logically?

COHERENCE

✔ Are transitions used effectively so that paragraphs move smoothly and logically from one to the next?

✔ Do the sentences move smoothly and logically from one to the next?

Thesis Statement

1. Put brackets around the last sentence in Melinda's introduction. Does it contain her opinion?

   Yes

   _____

   Is it debatable?

   Yes

   _____

2. Rewrite Melinda's thesis statement if necessary so that it states her opinion and is debatable.

   _____

   _____

Basic Elements

1. Give Melinda's essay an alternate title.

   Answers will vary.

2. Rewrite Melinda's introduction so that it captures the readers' attention and builds up to the thesis statement at the end of the paragraph.

   Answers will vary.

3. Does each of Melinda's body paragraphs deal with only one topic?

   Yes

4. Rewrite Melinda's conclusion using at least one suggestion from Part I.

   Answers will vary.

Development

1. Write out Melinda's thesis statement (revised, if necessary), and list her topic sentences below it.

   Thesis statement: *Drinking on college campuses is a bigger problem than parents and administrators realize, and something needs to be done about it—now.*

   Topic 1: *No one would ever realistically believe that college students will never drink.*

   Topic 2: *Jerry, a college student, explained how he got involved with alcohol and how it soon took over his life.*

Topic 3: *Whereas most people think drinking occurs just during parties, it actually occurs for many students on a daily basis.*

Topic 4: *According to our dean of students, students who drink often take risks that endanger their lives and the lives of others.*

Topic 5: *Drinking is a major problem on college campuses, but like every other controversial issue, some people say it has been given too much publicity by overzealous worriers.*

2. Do Melinda's topics adequately support her thesis statement?

Yes

3. Does each body paragraph have a focused topic sentence?

Yes

4. Does her evidence support her topic sentences?

Yes

5. What type of evidence does Melinda provide in each body paragraph?

Paragraph 2: *Facts*

Paragraph 3: *Example*

Paragraph 4: *Fact, examples*

Paragraph 5: *Facts, statement from authority, examples*

Paragraph 6: *Facts*

What type of evidence does she use the most? *Facts*

6. Is this a good choice for what she is trying to argue?

Yes, because she is showing the scope of the problem.

7. Where do you need more information?

Answers will vary.

Unity

1. Read each of Melinda's topic sentences with her thesis statement in mind. Do they go together?

   Yes

2. Revise them if necessary so they are directly related.
3. Drop or rewrite any sentences in her body paragraphs that are not directly related to their topic sentences. *All sentences are directly related to their topic sentences.*

Organization

1. Outline Melinda's essay to see if all her ideas are arranged logically.

   _____

   _____

   _____

   _____

   _____

   _____

   _____

   _____

2. Do you think her method of organization is the most effective one for her purpose? Explain your answer.

   It is logical because it moves from general to particular, from the

   problem to the solution.

3. Move any paragraphs that are out of order. *All paragraphs are in order.*
4. Look closely at Melinda's body paragraphs to see if all her sentences are arranged logically within paragraphs.
5. Move any sentences that are out of order. *In paragraph 5, put sentence 5 before sentence 3.*

Coherence

For a list of transitions, see pages 83–84.

For a list of pronouns, see pages 508–509.

1. Add two transitions to Melinda's essay.

2. Circle five transitions, repetitions, synonyms, or pronouns Melinda uses.

3. Explain how two of these make Melinda's essay easier to read.

   Answers will vary.

   _____

   _____

   _____

Now rewrite Melinda's essay with your revisions.

EDITING STRATEGIES
This chapter focuses on the following editing problems:

Fragments
Run-togethers
Modifier errors
Confused words

EDITING CHECKLIST ✔

SENTENCES

✔ Does each sentence have a main subject and verb?

✔ Do all subjects and verbs agree?

✔ Do all pronouns agree with their nouns?

✔ Are modifiers as close as possible to the words they modify?

PUNCTUATION AND MECHANICS

✔ Are sentences punctuated correctly?

✔ Are words capitalized properly?

WORD CHOICE AND SPELLING

✔ Are words used correctly?

✔ Are words spelled correctly?

Sentences

Subjects and Verbs

For help with subjects and verbs, see Chapter 34.

1. Underline the subjects once and verbs twice in paragraphs 4 and 6 of your revision of Melinda's essay. Remember that sentences can have more than one subject-verb set.

2. Does each of Melinda's sentences have at least one subject and verb that can stand alone?

   No

3. Did you find and correct Melinda's two fragments and two run-together sentences? If not, find and correct them now. *Fragments: paragraph 4, sentence 9; paragraph 6, sentence 6. Run-ons: paragraph 4, sentence 2; paragraph 6, sentence 3*

   For help with fragments and run-togethers, see Chapters 35 and 36.

Subject-Verb Agreement

1. Read aloud the subjects and verbs you underlined in your revision of Melinda's essay.

2. Correct any subjects and verbs that do not agree. *All subjects and verbs agree.*

   For help with subject-verb agreement, see Chapter 39.

Pronoun Agreement

1. Find any pronouns in your revision of Melinda's essay that do not agree with their nouns. *All pronouns agree with their nouns.*

2. Correct any pronouns that do not agree with their nouns.

   For help with pronoun agreement, see Chapter 43.

Modifiers

1. Find any modifiers in your revision of Melinda's essay that are not as close as possible to the words they modify.

2. Did you find and correct Melinda's two modifier errors? If not, find and correct them now. *Paragraph 2, sentence 3; paragraph 3, sentence 5*

   For help with modifier errors, see Chapter 46.

Punctuation and Mechanics

Punctuation

1. Read your revision of Melinda's essay for any errors in punctuation.

2. Find the two fragments and two run-together sentences you revised, and make sure they are punctuated correctly.

   For help with punctuation, see Chapters 47–51.

Mechanics

1. Read your revision of Melinda's essay for any errors in capitalization.

2. Be sure to check Melinda's capitalization in the fragments and run-ons you revised.

   For help with capitalization, see Chapter 52.

Word Choice and Spelling

Word Choice

For help with confused words, see Chapter 58.

1. Find any words used incorrectly in your revision of Melinda's essay.
2. Did you find and correct the four words Melinda uses incorrectly? If not, find and correct them now. *coarses/courses (paragraph 4, sentence 5); who's/whose (paragraph 4, sentence 7); effected/affected (paragraph 4, sentence 7); Its/It's (paragraph 7, sentence 6)*

Spelling

For help with spelling, see Chapter 59.

1. Use spell-check and a dictionary to check the spelling in your revision of Melinda's essay. *All words are spelled correctly.*
2. Correct any misspelled words.

Now rewrite Melinda's essay again with your editing corrections.

 WORKING WITH YOUR OWN ESSAY

Returning to the argument essay you wrote earlier in this chapter, revise and edit your own writing. The checklists here will help you apply what you have learned to your essay.

Revising and Editing Your Own Essay

CLASS ACTIVITY
Write some argument statements on the board that begin with "I believe," "I think," and "In my opinion." Demonstrate to students how these types of personal statements can weaken rather than strengthen arguments.

REVISING CHECKLIST ✔

THESIS STATEMENT

☐ Does the thesis statement contain the essay's controlling idea?

☐ Does the thesis appear as the last sentence of the introduction?

BASIC ELEMENTS

☐ Does the title draw in the readers?

☐ Does the introduction capture the readers' attention and build up to the thesis statement effectively?

☐ Does each body paragraph deal with a single topic?

☐ Does the conclusion bring the essay to a close in an interesting way?

DEVELOPMENT

☐ Do the body paragraphs adequately support the thesis statement?

☐ Does each body paragraph have a focused topic sentence?

☐ Does each body paragraph contain *specific* details that support the topic sentence?

☐ Does each body paragraph include *enough* details to explain the topic sentence fully?

UNITY

☐ Do the essay's topic sentences relate directly to the thesis statement?

☐ Do the details in each body paragraph support its topic sentence?

ORGANIZATION

☐ Is the essay organized logically?

☐ Is each body paragraph organized logically?

COHERENCE

☐ Are transitions used effectively so that paragraphs move smoothly and logically from one to the next?

☐ Do the sentences move smoothly and logically from one to the next?

Thesis Statement

1. What is the subject of your essay?

   _____

2. Put brackets around the last sentence in your introduction. Does it contain your opinion?

   _____

   Is it debatable?

   _____

3. Rewrite your thesis statement if necessary so that it states your opinion and is debatable.

Basic Elements

1. Give your essay a title if it doesn't have one.

   _____

2. Does your introduction capture your readers' attention and build up to your thesis statement at the end of the paragraph?

   _____

3. Does each of your body paragraphs deal with only one topic?

   _____

4. Does your conclusion follow some of the suggestions offered in Part I?

   _____

Development

1. Write out your thesis statement (revised, if necessary), and list your topic sentences below it.

   Thesis statement: _____

   Topic 1: _____

   Topic 2: _____

   Topic 3: _____

   Topic 4: _____

   Topic 5: _____

2. Do your topics adequately support your thesis statement?

   _____

3. Does each body paragraph have a focused topic sentence?

   _____

4. Does your evidence support your topic sentences? List and label at least one type of evidence you use for each of your topics.

   Topic 1: Evidence: _____

   Type: _____

   Topic 2: Evidence: _____

   Type: _____

Topic 3: Evidence: _____

    Type: _____

Topic 4: Evidence: _____

    Type: _____

Topic 5: Evidence: _____

    Type: _____

What type of evidence do you use the most?

_____

Is this a good choice for what you are trying to argue?

_____

5. Where do you need more information?

_____

Unity

1. Read each of your topic sentences with your thesis statement in mind. Do they go together?

_____

2. Revise them if necessary so they are directly related.
3. Drop or rewrite any of the sentences in your body paragraphs that are not directly related to their topic sentences.

Organization

1. Outline your essay to see if all the paragraphs are arranged logically.
2. Do you think your method of organization is the most effective one for your purpose? Explain your answer.

_____

_____

3. Move any paragraphs that are out of order.

4. Look closely at your body paragraphs to see if all the sentences are arranged logically within paragraphs.

5. Move any sentences or ideas that are out of order.

Coherence

For a list of transitions, see pages 83–84.

For a list of pronouns, see pages 508–509.

1. Add two transitions to your essay.

2. Circle five transitions, repetitions, synonyms, or pronouns you use.

3. Explain how two of these make your essay easier to read.

_____

_____

Now rewrite your essay with your revisions.

EDITING CHECKLIST ✔

SENTENCES

☐ Does each sentence have a main subject and verb?

☐ Do all subjects and verbs agree?

☐ Do all pronouns agree with their nouns?

☐ Are modifiers as close as possible to the words they modify?

PUNCTUATION AND MECHANICS

☐ Are sentences punctuated correctly?

☐ Are words capitalized properly?

WORD CHOICE AND SPELLING

☐ Are words used correctly?

☐ Are words spelled correctly?

Sentences

Subjects and Verbs

For help with subjects and verbs, see Chapter 34.

1. Underline the subjects once and verbs twice in a paragraph of your revised essay. Remember that sentences can have more than one subject-verb set.

2. Does each of your sentences have at least one subject and verb that can stand alone?

_____

For help with fragments, see Chapter 35.

3. Correct any fragments you have written.
4. Correct any run-together sentences you have written.

For help with run-togethers, see Chapter 36.

Subject-Verb Agreement

1. Read aloud the subjects and verbs you underlined in your revised essay.
2. Correct any subjects and verbs that do not agree.

For help with subject-verb agreement, see Chapter 39.

Pronoun Agreement

1. Find any pronouns in your revised essay that do not agree with their nouns.
2. Correct any pronouns that do not agree with their nouns.

For help with pronoun agreement, see Chapter 43.

Modifiers

1. Find any modifiers in your revised essay that are not as close as possible to the words they modify.
2. Rewrite sentences if necessary so that your modifiers are as close as possible to the words they modify.

For help with modifier errors, see Chapter 46.

Punctuation and Mechanics

Punctuation

1. Read your revised essay for any errors in punctuation.
2. Make sure any fragments and run-together sentences you revised are punctuated correctly.

For help with punctuation, see Chapters 47–51.

Mechanics

1. Read your revised essay for any errors in capitalization.
2. Be sure to check your capitalization in any fragments or run-together sentences you revised.

For help with capitalization, see Chapter 52.

Word Choice and Spelling

Word Choice

1. Find any words used incorrectly in your revised essay.
2. Correct any errors you find.

For help with confused words, see Chapter 58.

Spelling

For help with spelling, see Chapter 59.

1. Use spell-check and a dictionary to check your spelling.
2. Correct any misspelled words.

Now rewrite your essay again with your editing corrections.

PRACTICING ARGUMENT

Reading Suggestions

In Chapter 33, you will find three examples of good argument essays: "We are Training Our Kids to Kill" by Dave Grossman, which tries to persuade readers that our children are conditioned to kill from the violence they are exposed to through TV, movies, and video games, and two essays on loitering and gang violence—"Anti-Loitering Laws Can Reduce Gang Violence" by Richard Willard and "Anti-Loitering Laws Are Ineffective and Biased" by David Cole. You might want to read these selections before writing another argument essay. As you read, notice how the writers make their points through well-thought-out, detailed reasoning.

SERVICE LEARNING
PROJECT
This assignment is another step in the Service Learning project. If you choose to use this feature of the text, each chapter in Part II has an assignment that asks students to use a different rhetorical mode to reflect on their Service Learning project. These reflections will lead to an essay assignment in Part III (Chapter 22). You can assign as many or as few of these exercises as you want in preparation for this essay. For more information on service learning, see the *Instructor's Resource Manual*, Section I, Part III.

Service Learning Project

This assignment is based on a Service Learning project of your choice. If your instructor has already introduced service learning to the class, you will be doing these exercises when they are assigned. At this point, choose a project you would like to pursue, or continue work on a project you have already begun. This assignment in Part II will help you prepare for an essay on this project in Part III. Here is another stage in the preparation for this essay:

For the Service Learning project you have taken on, record your opinions on a controversial issue related to your project. Use the guidelines you have learned in this chapter to help you write down your ideas. But remember that these are just thoughts that will be developed into an essay in Part III.

ADDITIONAL
WRITING TOPIC
Have your students turn to Chapter 33 and read Dave Grossman's, "We Are Training Our Kids to Kill," Richard Willard's "Anti-Loitering Laws Can Reduce Gang Violence," or David

Writing Workshop

Guidelines for Writing an Argument Essay

1. State your opinion on your topic in your thesis statement.
2. Find out as much as you can about your audience before you write.
3. Choose evidence that supports your thesis statement.
4. Anticipate opposing points of view.

5. Find some common ground.

6. Maintain a reasonable tone.

7. Organize your essay so that it presents your position as effectively as possible.

Cole's "Anti-Loitering Laws Are Ineffective and Biased." Then have them write an essay on one of the topics from "Writing Topics: Arguing" at the end of the chapter.

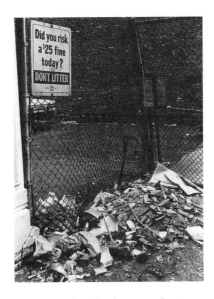

1. Explain what the photographer had in mind in creating this pictorial statement about littering. How does it appeal to its viewers? Write an essay explaining what the ad communicates.

2. Argue for or against a controversial political issue. Take a firm stand, and develop an essay supporting your position. You might want to look at the headlines in the newspaper to get some ideas for this assignment.

3. Write a letter to a potential employer for the job of your dreams, arguing that you are the best candidate for the job. Try to convince the employer not only that you are the perfect person for the job but also that you can take the position into new directions. Follow the format for a well-developed argument essay.

4. Create your own argument essay assignment (with the help of your instructor), and write a response to it.

Revising Workshop

Small Group Activity (5–10 minutes per writer) Working in groups of three or four, each person should read his or her argument essay to the other

TEACHING ON THE WEB
Discussion Topic: Divide students into groups of three or four, and ask them to discuss the different ways the Internet uses argument. When is the use of argument appropriate on the Internet? When is it not appropriate?

TEACHING ON THE WEB
Links: Have students link to Web sites that argue a controversial issue. How do the Web sites try to persuade people to believe a certain way? Are the sites biased in any way?

Possible sites for the issue "Should food be genetically altered?":

Center for Food Safety polls page, www.centerforfoodsafety.org/facts&issues/polls.html

Genetic Engineering News, www.genengnews.com

International Forum for Genetic Engineering, www.anth.org/ifgene/index.htm

TEACHING ON THE WEB

Research: Have students find a Web site that tries to persuade people to do something. Have them examine the argument the Web site uses to determine if the argument is sound. Ask students to explain their answers.

TEACHING ON THE WEB

Mosaics Web Site: To learn more about argument and persuasion, students can go to www.prenhall.com/mosaics.

members of the group. Those listening should record their reactions on a copy of the Peer Evaluation Form in Appendix 2I. After your group goes through this process, give your evaluation forms to the appropriate writers so that each writer has two or three peer comment sheets for revising.

Paired Activity (5 minutes per writer)   Using the completed Peer Evaluation Forms, work in pairs to decide what you should revise in your essay. If time allows, rewrite some of your sentences, and have your partner look at them.

Individual Activity   Rewrite your paper, using the revising feedback you received from other students.

Editing Workshop

Paired Activity (5–10 minutes per writer)   Swap papers with a classmate, and use the editing portion of your Peer Evaluation Form to identify as many grammar, punctuation, mechanics, and spelling errors as you can. If time allows, correct some of your errors, and have your partner look at them. Record your grammar, punctuation, and mechanics errors in the Error Log (Appendix 6) and your spelling errors in the Spelling Log (Appendix 7).

Individual Activity   Rewrite your paper again, using the editing feedback you received from other students.

Reflecting on Your Writing

When you have completed your own essay, answer these six questions.

1. What was most difficult about this assignment?
2. What was easiest?
3. What did you learn about arguing by completing this assignment?
4. What do you think are the strengths of your argument? Place a wavy line by the parts of your essay that you feel are very good.
5. What are the weaknesses, if any, of your paper? Place an X by the parts of your essay you would like help with. Write any questions you have in the margin.
6. What did you learn from this assignment about your own writing process—about preparing to write, about writing the first draft, about revising, and about editing?

III

THE ESSAY WITH SOURCES

In order to understand complex issues and situations and events,
we need to analyze them from multiple perspectives; every position
or every viewpoint ought to have reasons to support it; and the quality
of the conclusion is dependent on the quality of the reasoning that
went before it.

—JOHN CHAFFEE

Part III discusses the college essay with sources from assignment to final draft. It explains not only what this type of essay is but also how to write one, step by step. It provides you with a student model of an essay with sources and then guides you through the process of writing one on a topic of your own.

RECOGNIZING AN ESSAY WITH SOURCES

TEACHING AN ESSAY
WITH SOURCES
Have students bring in
an essay with sources
or a research paper
they have written in
another class (or use
the student essay in
Chapter 23), and have
them annotate the
essay. Where do they
use facts, statistics, and
other supporting mate-
rial or evidence? Is the
evidence effective, and
does it help the writers
make their point? What
transitions do they use?
How can students learn
to write more effective
essays with sources by
analyzing old ones?

The content of an essay with sources is based mainly on facts, statistics, and the opinions of others. The main difference between an essay with sources and other essays is that writers use information from outside reading material when writing an essay with sources. In other words, writers consult books, periodicals, and the Internet to find facts, statistics, and other material or evidence to support their main point.

Just as you develop the body of most essays with common knowledge or personal experience, you develop this type of essay with trustworthy evidence from outside sources. To begin choosing appropriate sources, you must have a good sense of your thesis statement. Then you must set out to find information in various sources that will back up your thesis statement.

In an essay with sources, the title gives the reader a clue to the subject of the essay. The introduction gives some background for understanding the topic and states the purpose of the paper in a thesis statement. Body paragraphs provide evidence to back up the thesis statement. And the conclusion wraps up the essay by restating the thesis statement and bringing the paper to a close.

The following essay by Mary Minor, a student, is a good example of an essay with sources. She solidly proves her thesis statement using books and articles from many different sources as evidence in her supporting paragraphs. As you read the first paragraph of this draft of her essay, notice her thesis statement. Then, in each supporting paragraph that follows the introductory paragraph, be aware of how the author develops her essay and supports her thesis statement with material from outside sources.

Children as Robots

Catchy title

1   When children are infants, there are certain "norms"
they are measured by to see if they are progressing
through developmental stages at the rate of other infants
their age. The "norms" are never clear-cut and leave
room for individual differences. When a child hits the age
of two or enters day care, "norms" become all-important.

More than in any other time in history, the 1990s brought about a change in "norms" that left parents confused. The "terrible twos" and "trying threes" no longer seem to be the best descriptions of toddlerhood. Today children who are "too" terrible at the age of two or "too" trying at the age of three are diagnosed with either "Attention Deficit Disorder (ADD) or its more severe variation, Attention Deficit Hyperactivity Disorder (ADHD). Both neurological conditions seem to be the childhood plague of the '90s" (Higdon 84). Children are often misdiagnosed with ADD or ADHD and suffer unnecessarily when medicated for a disorder they may not have.

Because medical professionals cannot agree on "whether this is one disease with subcategories or two entirely different diseases" (Brink 80), the terms ADD and ADHD are often used interchangeably. Both terms, however, refer to "a short attention span" (Schmitt), with or without hyperactivity. The Diagnostic and Statistical Manual of Mental Disorders (DSM-IV) (American Psychiatric Association, 1994) defines ADHD as a "persistent pattern of inattention and/or hyperactivity-impulsivity that is more frequent and severe than typically observed in individuals at a comparable level of development" (Kendall 839). What's more, the disease ADD has become "one of the most commonly diagnosed" childhood diseases in the United States today (LeFever, Dawnson, and Morrow 1359), afflicting "approximately 4 to 7 percent" of American children (Durall 38). The National Institute of Mental Health (NIMH) claims that "differences do not a disorder make. The differences could simply be part of human variation.... We don't know if perhaps we shouldn't treat ADD as the far end of normal behavior, just like height, weight, or muscle mass" (Koch 918). Given the fact that children are identified as having this disease based on what a person may consider "normal" behavior, it is unfortunate for the children being diagnosed that nobody can agree on what "normal" means. So specialists need to be careful when recommending treatments for what could be everyday behavior.

Many children today who do not fit the "norm" of adult expectations may be diagnosed with ADD.

Margin annotations (left):
In-text citation (MLA)
Statistic

Margin annotations (center):
Interesting comparison
Direct quotation
Thesis statement
2
Quotation used to define problem
3

Author
and book
introduced
before
quotation

Only page
number
needed
since
author
already
introduced

Transition
sentence
to new
topic

Labeling a child's behavior based on a set of "norms" is ludicrous since these qualities cannot accurately be measured, let alone defined. According to Thomas Armstrong, author of <u>The Myth of the ADD Child,</u> "Once the influential American Psychiatric Association (APA) declared ADD a disorder in 1980, the DSM defined it more and more broadly. . . . Increasing numbers of children are caught in the ever-widening definition net and are then labeled ADD" (914). But even though we have a definition for this disorder, nobody really knows for sure what the disorder is. According to psychologist Stephen P. Hinshaw, "There's clearly not a single cause of all cases of well-diagnosed ADHD" (qtd. in Bower 343). Other professionals agree that accurate diagnosis "remains elusive and controversial" (Koch 907). If our leading professionals in the field don't know what a "well-diagnosed" case is, how can we be sure that they even know what any case of ADHD is?

Transition
from
definition
to further
problems

Question
used as
transition

4   Because there are no reliable tests for ADD, nobody is really able to tell if a child actually has the disorder. "Given the explosion in ADHD diagnoses . . . , the disorder is surprisingly ill defined. . . . There is no blood test, no PET scan, no physical exam that can determine who has it and who does not" (Gibbs 90). Professionals in the field argue over what the disease is, what causes it, how it should be treated, or whether it is a disease at all (Bower 343). Yet numerous children are diagnosed with this disease and are medicated because of it.

Transition
sentence
to next
paragraph
about
Ritalin

5   There are as many speculations about the causes of ADD and ADHD as there are experts. Unfortunately, the ones lost in the confusion are the children, and this is due to one fact: Ritalin, the most widely used method of treatment for this disorder, works so well that additional medical tests are not done. According to Dr. Sydney Walker, neither doctors nor insurance companies want to take the time or spend the money to track down the "real" cause of the problem. Instead, they mask the symptoms with Ritalin (Barkley and Walker 921). While Ritalin seems to work for many children, nobody knows why or how it works, not to mention what the long-term effects of the drug might be (Gibbs 89). We have no

Citation
after
paraphrase

absolute information about ADD, only a set of symptoms, which include excessive talking, fidgeting, and similar behaviors. In other words, parents face the decision of whether or not to put their child on strong drugs when nobody has yet proved that a disorder exists.

Unfortunately, teachers are often the first to be   6 involved in diagnosing a child, and "sometimes the school systems insist on a brain-disorder label" (Brink 81). One parent describes his experience and feelings about the matter in a U.S. News and World Report article:

Block indention for long quotations

> First it was the teacher. Then the school counselor. Then the heavies in the school, the principal, start to show up. You go to meetings, and everybody thinks your child has a problem. . . . Doctors and therapists each had a different diagnosis—ADHD, anxiety disorder, obsessive-compulsive disorder, depression—and each diagnosis called for a different drug. . . . Social conformity and mental health are becoming the same terms. . . . The person with a different perspective is seen as a candidate for medication. (Brink 81)

Parents are often pressured into placing their children on drugs with the hope that their children will achieve "academic and social success" (Brink 76). However, this pressure may be unwarranted. "There is no solid evidence that stimulant medicine [such as Ritalin] has any impact on scholastic achievement. . . . Teachers and parents tend to approve of the drug because it makes unruly kids more manageable and more social" (Sheppard 46). So what may be disruptive to teachers or other students may simply be normal behavior for some children.

Some children are so hard to control that mind-   7 altering drugs such as Ritalin appear to be a blessing; but drugs, if used at all, should be used only for a short period of time—until the "real" cause of the problem behavior is found. Pediatrician Lawrence Diller states his opinion on the subject well when he says, "I just don't believe a pill is the moral equivalent of good parenting and good schooling. . . . I prescribe it because . . . my job is to relieve suffering, and Ritalin, in the short term, will ease suffering" (qtd. in Brink 81). One must wonder, however, whose suffering this doctor is relieving; is it the teachers' and parents' or the

Credible opinion used to support argument

children's? Diller's good intentions demonstrate why children should not be medicated for an ill-defined disease.

8   Despite major controversy in the medical field, however, there has been no proof that drugs are being overprescribed for American children. Some experts even feel that children may be undertreated (Koch 912). No studies have been found that would prove one claim over the other, which again means that each child is treated according to the most popular opinion. As a result, "Students who were younger than their classmates were <u>21</u> times more likely to be medicated" for ADD or ADHD (920). With a statistic like this, it's astonishing that experts disagree on this subject.

Opposite argument addressed

Opposite argument refuted with quotation

9   Even if drugs can be beneficial in some instances, long-term usage is potentially dangerous because these drugs are presently "classified as 'having a high potential for abuse with severe liability for physical and/or psychic dependence'" (Morrow, Morrow, and Haislip 1121). Also, "a very small percentage of children treated at high doses have hallucinogenic responses" (Gibbs 90). To give a prescription for drugs to a child without comprehensive medical testing is, as Walker states, "inexcusable" (Barkley and Walker 921). Doctors need to agree that children are overmedicated for a disease that may not exist and find more acceptable ways to curb "disruptive behavior." Many children exhibit the symptoms of ADHD due to family problems or other environmental factors. Diet may also play a major role in this scenario. The removal of certain foods, especially those containing "allergenic food additives and dyes" (Koch 916), may very well eliminate the symptoms. When doctors quote the Hippocratic Oath, they say these words: "I will apply dietetic measures for the benefit of the sick according to my ability and judgment; I will keep them from harm and injustice" ("Hippocratic Oath"). Sworn to dietetically treat their patients, doctors should remember this oath before prescribing drugs for a disease that nobody can prove exists.

Facts used to show other possible reasons for hyperactivity in children

10   Perhaps these "diseases" are nothing more than a belief system in an ever-increasing "conformist" society.

Conclusion

Every effort should be made to find the cause of the "real" medical problems underlying ADD and ADHD before we even think about giving our children drugs. A doctor who doesn't order medical tests for a child with symptoms of ADD is negligent, to say the least, and the failure of a doctor to discuss alternatives to drug therapy with parents when diagnosing ADHD is more than "inexcusable"; it's unforgivable. More parents would seek alternative treatments if they knew that their child was diagnosed on the basis of nothing more than a list of symptoms that cannot be defined or measured. After all, most parents do not want their child placed on long-term stimulant drugs. It's time to say good-bye to "conformist" American classrooms and diagnoses. People don't fit "norms"; they have personalities.

Reference to thesis statement

Call to action

Concluding statement

Works Cited

Alphabetical order

American Psychiatric Association. The Diagnostic and

   Statistical Manual of Mental Disorders. 4th ed.

   Washington: APA, 1994.

Book

Double spaced with no extra spaces between entries

Armstrong, Thomas. The Myth of the ADD Child: 50 Ways to

   Improve Your Child's Behavior and Attention Span Without

   Drugs, Labels, or Coercion. New York: Dutton, 1995.

Barkley, Russell, and Sydney Walker III. "At Issue: Are

   Attention Deficit Disorder (ADD) and Attention Deficit

   Hyperactivity Disorder (ADHD) Legitimate Medical

   Diagnoses?" CQ Researcher 9 (1999): 921.

All lines after the first indented

Bower, Bruce. "Kid's Attention Disorder Attracts Concern."

   Science News 154 (1998): 343.

Brink, Susan. "Doing Ritalin Right." U.S. News and World

   Report 23 Nov. 1998: 76–81.

Durall, John. "Toward an Understanding of ADHD: A

   Developmental Delay in Self-Control." Camping

   Magazine Jan. 1999: 38–41.

General-circulation magazine

Gibbs, Nancy. "The Age of Ritalin." <u>Time</u> 30 Nov. 1998: 86–96.

Higdon, Hal. "Getting Their Attention." <u>Runner's World</u> July
1999: 84–87.

Encyclopedia   "Hippocratic Oath." <u>World Book Encyclopedia</u>. Vol. 9.
1999 ed.

Kendall, Judy. "Outlasting Disruption: The Process of   *Journal*
Reinvestment in Families with ADHD Children."   *article*
<u>Qualitative Health Research</u> 8 (1998): 839–857.

Koch, Kathy. "Rethinking Ritalin." <u>CQ Researcher</u> 9 (1999):
907–914+.

LeFever, Gretchen B., Keila V. Dawson, and Ardythe L.
Morrow. "The Extent of Drug Therapy for Attention
Deficit–Hyperactivity Disorder Among Children in Public
Schools." <u>American Journal of Public Health</u> 89 (1999):
1359–1364.

Morrow, Robert C., Ardythe L. Morrow, and Gene Haislip.
"Methylphenidate in the United States, 1990–1995."
<u>American Journal of Public Health</u> 88 (1998): 1121.

Schmitt, B. D. "Attention Deficit Disorder (Short Attention
Span)." <u>Clinical Reference Systems</u> 1 July 1999. 17 Feb.
Online   2000 <http://www.epnet.com/ehost/login.html>.
source
Sheppard, Robert. "Growing Up Hyperactive." <u>Maclean's</u>
7 Sept. 1998: 45–46.

Before continuing, choose one of the following topics for your own work
in the rest of Part III:

Police brutality	Censorship	Cloning
Alzheimer's disease	Government spending	Date rape
Herbal medicine	Steroids	Child abuse
Assisted suicide	Pollution	Alcohol and crime
Nursing homes	Drug treatment programs	Bilingual education

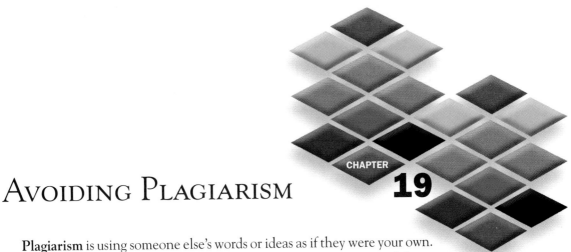

Avoiding Plagiarism

CHAPTER **19**

Plagiarism is using someone else's words or ideas as if they were your own. It is a serious offense in college and in life after college because it is dishonest. When you work with outside sources, you must give credit to them. In other words, if you quote, paraphrase, or summarize from another source, you must provide your reader with information about that source, such as the author's name, the title of the essay, and the identity of the publisher. If you use other people's words without giving them credit, you are plagiarizing.

When you don't cite your sources properly, your readers will think certain words and ideas are yours when they actually came from someone else. When you steal material in this way in college, you can get dismissed from school. When you commit the same offense in the professional world, you can end up in court. So make sure you understand what plagiarism is as you move through this chapter.

TEACHING AVOIDING PLAGIARISM
Have students submit an old essay to www.turnitin.com, an online service that checks student papers for instances of plagiarism. This site can help students identify plagiarism in their own writing when they write research papers. For fun, you might have students submit a highly plagiarized paper just to see how thorough the site really is.

COMMON KNOWLEDGE

If you are referring to information such as historical events, dates of presidents' terms, and known facts, like the effects of ultraviolet rays or smoking, you do not have to cite a source. This material is called *common knowledge* because it can be found in a number of different sources. You can use this information freely because you are not dealing with anyone's original words or ideas.

ORIGINAL IDEAS

If, however, you want to use someone's words or ideas, you must give that person credit by recording where you found this information. This process is called *citing* or *documenting* your sources, and it involves noting in your paper where you found the idea. Since essays based on sources are developed around sources that support your position, citations are an essential ingredient in any source paper.

As you can see in Mary Minor's paper in Chapter 18, every source is ac-knowledged at least twice in her paper: (1) in the paper right after a quota-tion or idea and then (2) at the end of the paper in a list of sources used in the paper. At the note-taking stage, you simply have to make sure that you have all the information on your sources that you need to acknowledge them in proper form in your paper. Having to track down missing details when you prepare your lists of works cited is frustrating and time consuming.

Practice 1 Identify the following information as either common knowledge (CK) or original (O).

1. __O__ In a typical day, for human beings to drink the equivalent of what the glassy-winged sharpshooter insect drinks, humans would have to drink 4,000 gallons of liquid, half the amount in a standard swim-ming pool.

2. __CK__ William Shakespeare was born and died on the same day, April 23, 52 years apart.

3. __CK__ Abraham Lincoln was shot in Ford's Theater by John Wilkes Booth.

4. __CK__ A human being cannot survive beyond three days without water.

5. __O__ The Paleozoic era produced the first shellfish and corals in the Cambrian period, the first fishes in the Ordovician period, and the first land plants in the Silurian period.

6. __CK__ Tom Hanks has won two Oscars, one for his role in *Philadelphia* and one for the title role in *Forrest Gump*.

7. __O__ Aerobic respiration consists of oxygen plus organic matter that produces carbon dioxide, water, and energy.

8. __CK__ The success of *Survivor* caused many other reality shows to be produced.

9. __O__ The longest palindromic word in the English language is *saippuakivikauppias*.

10. __CK__ AIDS is a disease that can be caught through unprotected sex.

USING AND SYNTHESIZING SOURCES

When writers use more than one source in an essay, they are *synthesizing* their sources. In other words, they are taking pieces of information from various sources and weaving them into an argument to form their own essay. If you've written any type of paper using outside sources, including a research paper, you were synthesizing material.

Once you have figured out your topics, you'll most likely start writing. You'll have done some prewriting to help you choose what method of organization to use. You may realize later that you'll have to change your organization around, but you can worry about that in revising.

Once you have written the introduction, ending with a thesis statement, you will probably begin working with your sources. This doesn't mean that you shouldn't use any sources in your introduction, but you'll want to save the majority of them for the body of your paper. As you write the paper, you want to make sure that you develop your argument and use sources as evidence for your claims. You should *not* write your paper around your sources. If you do this, you may end up with a disjointed argument, and your readers will not be able to determine what you really think about the issue. So when you write with sources, be sure to use them to back up your own argument and not the other way around.

Look at one of Mary Minor's paragraphs from her first draft:

> Many children today who do not fit the "norm" of adult expectations may be diagnosed with ADD. Labeling a child's behavior based on a set of "norms" is ludicrous since these qualities cannot accurately be measured, let alone defined. According to Thomas Armstrong, author of The Myth of the ADD Child, "Once the influential American Psychiatric Association (APA) declared ADD a disorder in 1980, the DSM defined it more and more broadly. . . . Increasing numbers of children are caught in the ever-widening definition net and are then labeled ADD" (914). According to psychologist Stephen P. Hinshaw, "There's clearly not a single cause of all cases of well-diagnosed ADHD" (qtd. in Bower 343). Other professionals agree that accurate diagnosis "remains elusive and controversial" (Koch 907).

As Mary was revising this paragraph, she realized she was forcing the reader to make connections between her sources and her argument because she was not providing explanations that made those connections. So she revised her paragraph connecting her sources to her own ideas and making her argument clearer.

> (1) Many children today who do not fit the "norm" of adult expectations may be diagnosed with ADD. (2) Labeling a child's behavior based on a set of "norms" is ludicrous since these qualities cannot accurately be measured, let alone defined. (3) According to Thomas Armstrong, author of <u>The Myth of the ADD Child</u>, "Once the influential American Psychiatric Association (APA) declared ADD a disorder in 1980, the DSM defined it more and more broadly. . . . (4) Increasing numbers of children are caught in the ever-widening definition net and are then labeled ADD" (914). (5) But even though we have a definition for this disorder, nobody really knows for sure what the disorder is. (6) According to psychologist Stephen P. Hinshaw, "There's clearly not a single cause of all cases of well-diagnosed ADHD" (qtd. in Bower 343). (7) Other professionals agree that accurate diagnosis "remains elusive and controversial" (Koch 907). (8) If our leading professionals in the field don't know what a "well-diagnosed" case is, how can we be sure that they even know what any case of ADHD is?

By adding the fifth sentence, "But even though we have a definition for this disorder, nobody really knows for sure what the disorder is," Mary explains the significance of the previous quotation and tells her readers what she wants them to be thinking about after they read it. Similarly, the last sentence in Mary's paragraph also clarifies the quotation before it. "If our leading professionals in the field don't know what a 'well-diagnosed' case is, how can we be sure that they even know what any case of ADHD is?" This sentence, which also acts as the paragraph's concluding sentence, shows readers that the professionals are arguing among themselves about the disease, so we should be careful about any diagnosis of it. Notice, also, how this last sentence provides a transition into Mary's discussion about the scarcity of reliable tests for ADHD.

To better understand how Mary's paragraph works, look at the following breakdown of her paragraph:

(1) Topic sentence
(2) **Explanation of topic sentence**

(3-4) Quotation from Source A, Thomas Armstrong
(with Source A Works Cited information at end)

(5) Statement explaining the significance of Source A

(6) Quotation from Source B, Stephen P. Hinshaw
(with Source B Works Cited information at end)

(7) Paraphrase and quotation from Source C, Kathy Koch
(with Source C Works Cited information at end)

**(8) Concluding sentence showing relevance of Sources B and C
and providing a transition into the next paragraph**

This skeleton outline of Mary's paragraph should help you see how her paragraph works as one unit that supports her main argument. If you get stuck writing your own paragraphs, referring back to this outline might help you see where you need to add information.

Before you get to this stage, however, you must think about what information you want to use from your sources and how you might present that information. The most difficult task when writing an essay with sources is deciding what to quote directly, what to paraphrase, and what to summarize. Once you have a tentative thesis statement, you can start working with your outside sources.

DIRECT QUOTATION, PARAPHRASE, AND SUMMARY

Now that you know how to incorporate your sources, you need to decide whether you will directly quote, paraphrase, or summarize them. This section explains these three options to you. We will begin with an original source and show how to take and acknowledge material from the original in different ways.

The following paragraph is from "A Family Dilemma: To Scout or Not to Scout" by Michael Alvear. It was published in *Newsweek* magazine on November 6, 2000, on pages 12–13. The quoted passage is from page 12.

Original Source

> When my sister first called to tell me she was
> thinking of putting Ricky in the Cub Scouts (a program
> run by Boy Scouts of America), I could hear the torment
> in her voice. Ricky is a bright, athletic boy who suffers
> from a shyness so paralyzing he doesn't have any

friends. The other day my sister asked who he had
played with at recess. "Nobody," he mumbled, looking at
the floor. "I just scratched the mosquito bites on my leg
till it was time to go back to class."

Direct Quotation

If you use a direct quotation from another source, you must put the exact
material you want to use in quotation marks:

Michael Alvear, in his essay "A Family Dilemma: To Scout or Not to
Scout," states, "Ricky is a bright, athletic boy who suffers from a shyness so paralyzing he doesn't have any friends" (12).

Direct Quotation with Some Words Omitted

If you want to leave something out of the quotation, use three dots (with
spaces before and after each dot). Omitting words is known as *ellipsis*.

Michael Alvear, in his essay "A Family Dilemma: To Scout or Not to
Scout," states, "Ricky is a bright, athletic boy who . . . doesn't have
any friends" (12).

Paraphrase

When you paraphrase, you are restating the main ideas of a quotation in
your own words. *Paraphrase* literally means "similar phrasing," so it is usually about the same length as the original. Paraphrasing is one of the most
difficult skills to master in college, but one trick you can use is to read the
material, put it aside, and write a sentence or two about what you think it
said. Then compare what you wrote with the original to make sure they are
relatively the same. If you look at the source while you are trying to paraphrase it, you might inadvertently take a word or phrase from the original.

Then, even though this information is in your own words, you still need
to let your readers know where you found it. A paraphrase of our original
source might look like this:

Michael Alvear, in his essay "A Family Dilemma: To Scout or Not to
Scout," states that he could hear his sister's worry when he talked to
her. She was thinking of putting her very shy son in the Cub Scouts.
Even though his nephew, Ricky, was both athletic and intelligent, his
shyness prevented him from making any friends (12).

Summary

When you summarize, you state the author's main idea in your own words. A summary is much briefer than the original or a paraphrase. As with a paraphrase, you need to cite in your paper where you found the information. Here is a summary of the original source:

> Michael Alvear, in his essay "A Family Dilemma: To Scout or Not to Scout," says his nephew, Ricky, was too shy to have any friends, so Alvear's sister was thinking of signing Ricky up for the Cub Scouts (12).

TAKING NOTES ON SOURCES

As you consider using your sources as direct quotations, paraphrases, and summaries, you will need to keep careful track of them. For your Works Cited page (Modern Language Association documentation style), References page (American Psychological Association documentation style), or Bibliography page (*Chicago Manual of Style*), you will need to provide your reader with several items of information for each source you use. The best time to start keeping track of this information is when you are taking notes.

When you take notes, notecards are an excellent tool because you can move them around as your paper takes shape. Put only one idea on a notecard. Taking notes this way will save you a lot of time in the future because you won't be scrambling around looking for the information on the source you just quoted. Taking notes electronically is another option. Whatever your choice, if you cannot find the original source for some information that you used in your paper and therefore cannot tell your reader where you found the quotation, then you cannot use the material.

As you read your sources, you should consider whether you might want to directly quote, paraphrase, or summarize the material. A general rule to follow is that you never want to use more than 10 percent of directly quoted information, which means 90 percent of the outside information you use in your essay should be paraphrased or summarized. The best way to determine whether you should use direct quotations or not is by asking yourself a question, "Is this the best possible way to relay this information?" If the answer is yes, then you should use a direct quotation. In most cases, however, you should try to put your sources in your own words. Only occasionally should you use the author's exact words in your paper. So when you are reading and taking notes on your sources, you should keep this in mind.

To avoid plagiarism when taking notes and when writing your paper, write down all the information you need to cite a source both in your paper and on the Works Cited page. For a book, you need the following information:

- Book title
- Author or authors
- City where published
- Publisher
- Year of publication

For an article, you must include the following:

- Article title
- Author or authors
- Title of the magazine or journal
- Date of issue (for a magazine)
- Year and volume number (for a journal)
- Pages on which the article appeared

If you put all this information on one card, you can use just the author's last name on all other cards from that source. If an author has more than one book or article, add the source's date to the card. For both books and articles, you should also always record the page where you found the information. That way you can find it again or cite it in your paper. The format in which this information should be presented may depend on the field of study. A good handbook will help you with the formats of the various documentation styles; these include Modern Language Association (MLA) style for the humanities, American Psychological Association (APA) style for the social sciences, and *Chicago Manual of Style* (CMS) style for mathematics and science. Make sure you understand which documentation style your instructor wants you to use because they are all slightly different from each other.

In this book, we are using the Modern Language Association style of citation. The Alvear essay in the MLA format would look like this:

Alvear, Michael. "A Family Dilemma: To Scout or Not to Scout." Newsweek 6 Nov. 2000: 12–13.

Practice 2   Quote from, paraphrase, and summarize the following original sources. Document the source correctly in each case by looking up the MLA documentation style in a handbook.

1. The following paragraph is from "We are Training Our Kids to Kill" by Dave Grossman. It was originally published in the *Saturday Evening Post* in July/August 1999 on pages 64–66, 68, 70, 72. The quoted paragraph appeared on page 65.

> This virus of violence is occurring worldwide. The explanation for it has to be some new factor that is occurring in all of these countries. There are many factors involved, and none should be discounted: for example, the prevalence of guns in our society. But violence is rising in many nations with Draconian gun laws. And though we should never downplay child abuse, poverty, or racism, there is only one new variable present in each of these countries that bears the exact same fruit: media violence presented as entertainment for children.

Quotation: _Answers will vary but must include the in-text citation Grossman 65._

Paraphrase: _Answers will vary but must include the in-text citation Grossman 65._

Summary: _Answers will vary but must include the in-text citation Grossman 65._

Works Cited Citation: _Grossman, Dave. "We Are Training Our Kids to Kill," Saturday Evening Post July/Aug. 1999: 64–66+._

2. The following paragraph is from "Writer's Retreat" by Stan Higgins. It was originally published in *The Writer* in November 1991, volume 104, issue 11, on pages 21–23. The quoted paragraph appeared on page 21.

During the day I wash dishes, clean tables, and mop floors. They call it Vocational Training. And today, as every day at three p.m., I return to my cozy, bathroom-size suite and drag out my tiny portable. We've all night, just the two of us, my blue typewriter that has been my steady cell-mate for six years, through seven facilities across two states, and I. Today's goal is three pages. I blow dust from the cover and clean the keys. The Muse calls. *Tack-tack. Tack. Tack-tack-tack.* My typewriter sings its staccato song as I search for a fertile word or idea, some harmonious junction of thought and paper. Locked in solitary combat with my machine, nothing exists outside my cell, or so I pretend. I type a line. My door opens. Two blue-uniformed guards stand there grinning. "Guess what?" one says. "Your number came up."

Quotation: *Answers will vary but must include the in-text citation*

Higgins 21.

_____

Paraphrase: *Answers will vary but must include the in-text citation*

Higgins 21.

_____

Summary: *Answers will vary but must include the in-text citation*

Higgins 21.

_____

Works Cited Citation: *Higgins, Stan. "Writer's Retreat." The Writer*

104.11 (1991): 21–23.

3. The following paragraph is from "Don't Be Cruel" by Dr. Roger Flax. It was originally published in *TWA Ambassador* in March 1992, on pages 49–51. The quoted paragraph appeared on page 49.

Picture this scenario: Seymour Axshun (we'll call him), a terrific manager who has been a loyal employee for several years, messes up on an assignment. He misses a deadline on a proposal, and that three-day delay costs the company $9,100. Seymour's boss, Sy Kottick, has a near coronary over the incident, lashes out at Seymour, and criticizes him mercilessly. In front of four of Seymour's co-workers, Kottick shouts, "Axshun, how many times do I have to tell you to be more efficient with your planning? You blew it, and your mistake will cost us almost $10,000. I don't know what it takes to drill into your head that you must meet deadlines. It's disgusting, and I'm fed up. If you treated the money as if it were your own, you wouldn't be so careless."

Quotation: _Answers will vary but must include the in-text citation_

Flax 49.

_____

Paraphrase: _Answers will vary but must include the in-text citation_

Flax 49.

_____

Summary: _Answers will vary but must include the in-text citation_

Flax 49.

_____

Works Cited Citation: _Flax, Roger. "Don't Be Cruel." TWA Ambassador_

Mar. 1992: 49–51.

4. The following paragraph is from "Healing Myself with the Power of Work" by Michael Norlen. It was originally published in *Newsweek*, on October 25, 1999, on page 12.

It all changed 12 months ago. For the second time in six years, I abandoned my solo law practice. I stopped returning phone calls, forgot to pay bills, and ignored court dates. I began to sleep 16 hours a day. By July of last year I stopped coming into the office, leaving it to fill up with unopened mail and indignant phone messages. By August I was behind on my office rent, and by October my landlord asked me to leave. I ate, but nothing tasted good. I slept, but woke up tired. I felt like a stranger around my wife and two daughters. Thought of suicide shadowed me. And in the midst of all this, I knew. *It* had returned.

Quotation: *Answers will vary but must include the in-text citation*

Norlen 12.

Paraphrase: *Answers will vary but must include the in-text citation*

Norlen 12.

Summary: *Answers will vary but must include the in-text citation*

Norlen 12.

Works Cited Citation: *Norlen, Michael. "Healing Myself with the Power*

of Work." Newsweek 25 Oct. 1999: 12.

5. The following paragraph is from the essay "What Are Friends For?" by Marion Winik. It was originally published on pages 85–89 in a book titled *Telling: Confessions, Concessions, and Other Flashes of Light*, which was published by Villard Books in New York City in 1994. The quoted paragraph appeared on page 89.

At the other end of the spectrum are Hero Friends. These people are better than the rest of us; that's all there is to it. Their career is something you wanted to be when you grew up—painter, forest ranger, tireless doer of good. They have beautiful homes filled with special handmade things presented to them by villagers in the remote areas they have visited in their extensive travels. Yet they are modest. They never gossip. They are always helping others, especially those who have suffered a death in the family or an illness. You would think people like this would just make you sick, but somehow they don't.

Quotation: _Answers will vary but must include the in-text citation_

Winik 89.

_____

Paraphrase: _Answers will vary but must include the in-text citation_

Winik 89.

_____

Summary: _Answers will vary but must include the in-text citation_

Winik 89.

_____

Works Cited Citation: _Winik, Marion. "What Are Friends For?" Telling:_

Confessions, Concessions, and Other Flashes of Light. New York: Villard,

_1994: 85–89._

20

FINDING SOURCES

No matter what you are studying in college, you should know how to find outside sources using the library through a computer. You can access an enormous amount of information that will help you generate paper topics, teach you new information, challenge your thinking, support your opinions, and make you smile. In today's electronic world, learning how to use the resources available through the library's services is a basic survival skill.

CREDIBILITY OF SOURCES

When you are looking for information to use in your essays, you must be careful about what you choose. Your sources must be relevant, reliable, and recent. This "three *Rs*" approach to finding sources will help you locate convincing evidence to support your argument.

Since anyone can put material on the Internet, you need to make sure you are not using biased or unreliable information in your academic papers. To use Web sites intelligently, follow these four guidelines.

1. ***Check the end of a Web URL address.*** It will be either .com, .edu, .gov, or .org. The last three are generally reputable sources, but you must be very careful of .com sources because this stands for "communication," and anyone can purchase a .com site. For example, www.whitehouse.com is not a site for the President's home, as you might suspect. On the other hand, .edu stands for "education," .gov for "government," and .org for "organization." But any site has the potential for bias, and you should consider the material carefully.

2. ***Pay attention to the argument a site makes.*** Who is the author and what is his or her purpose for entering information on the site? If you log onto a Martin Luther King Jr. site and are inundated with racial slurs, chances are you've found a site that was created by a faction of the Ku Klux Klan. If the argument does not fit the site or if the author has an obvious agenda, avoid the site altogether.

TEACHING FINDING SOURCES

Invite a librarian to your class or plan a visit to the library to discuss the best ways for finding sources in the library. Ask the librarian to outline the design of your library and answer any questions the students may have. If time allows, have the librarian give your students a tour of your campus library.

3. *Make sure the site is providing fact and not opinion.* For academic purposes, facts and evidence are generally more useful than opinions. If you are looking for a site that deals with gun control, you'll want to avoid the site that tells you story after story about innocent children dying or praises American liberty, but fails to give you any specific information. Instead, you'll want to find a site that gives you examples that can be verified and supported with statistics.

4. *Does the site provide information about the other side of the argument?* If a site provides you with details only about its own viewpoint, you should wonder why it is omitting information. If you find a site on prayer in school and see opinions only about why prayer should not be allowed in schools, you should be curious about why they don't present the other side's argument. Will facts about the other side make you change your mind? The best sites provide both sides of an argument so the source can, in turn, show why one side is more valid than the other. If you find a Web site that does not offer balanced information, consider it biased, and avoid the site.

These four guidelines will help you determine whether or not you should use information you find on the Web. But if you want to be certain the information you are using will be acceptable for your instructor, you should stick with academic sources. These sources are different from other sources because they have been "refereed" or "reviewed." This means the authors of the essays send them to the publication and the editors of the publication send the essays anonymously to readers for review. If the readers accept the pieces for publication, they consider the essays to be well-researched and worth reading. If you can, you should use only these sources. The best place to find them is also online, as you will see in the following section.

CONSULTING ONLINE DATABASES, FULL-TEXT INDEXES, AND ELECTRONIC JOURNAL COLLECTIONS

The best places to begin searching for outside sources are online databases, full-text indexes, and electronic journal collections. You should have access to these services from home through your library's home page or from a computer in your library. We will discuss each one separately. You may need a reference librarian to help you find these for the first time.

Online Databases

Online databases can direct you to an incredible number of books and journals on a wide range of subjects. The following are some online indexes found in SilverPlatter's WebSPIRS database, which is an information retrieval system that contains indexes on many different subjects and is used by many libraries.

Index	Primary Use
Biological and Agriculture Index	Science
ERIC	Education
GeoRef	Geology
MLA	Literature, language, and linguistics
Philosopher's Index	Philosophy
Sociological Abstracts	Sociology

Full-Text Indexes

The following indexes take you directly to complete journal articles online. In other words, you can print the journal articles you find right from your computer.

Index	Primary Use
ABI Inform	News and business
Dow Jones	News and business
EBSCOhost*	Many subject areas
Expanded Academic ASAP*	General information in several disciplines
HRAF	Ethnographies
Lexis-Nexis	News, business, and law
WilsonWeb*	Popular magazines and newspapers, social science, humanities, business, general science, and education journals

*Not all articles will be available in full-text.

Electronic Journal Collections

Electronic journal collections are similar to online databases in that you can print complete journal articles directly from your computer. The following collections might help you find information about the topic you have chosen.

Collection	Primary Use
Academic Press's IDEAL	Articles published by academic publishers
American Chemical Society's Web Editions	American Chemical Society's 26 scientific journals
American Mathematical Journals	American Mathematical Society's proceedings and transactions
JSTOR	Back issues of core journals in the humanities, social sciences, and sciences
Project Muse	Humanities, social sciences, and math

Once you access an online database, index, or collection, you can easily find articles and books on your topic. You can do online searches by author, title, or subject; since you will most likely be looking for articles on a topic, you will use the subject function most often. When you are searching for a title by subject, you should be aware of *Boolean connectors or operators*, which are shortcuts to help you narrow the search field.

Using Boolean Connectors or Operators

The Boolean connectors or operators for requesting a search are *AND*, *OR*, and *NOT*. By using these words, you can limit the search and find information directly related to your topic. If you type "AND" between your key words (for example, *TV AND violence*), you are asking the computer to combine the key words for the search. If you put "OR" between the key words (*TV OR video games*), you are separating the words and asking the computer to find articles and books with either one of them. If you add "NOT" (*TV NOT video games*), you limit the search by excluding certain terms from the search.

Accessing Sources

Once you type your topic into the search function of a database, index, or journal collection, the computer will display the number of articles and books it has found in a "results list." Following are some examples of articles found on the topic of *television AND violence* in an online database, a full-text index, and an electronic journal collection.

From an Online Database

Record 40 of 313 in *Sociological Abstracts* [in WebSPIRS] 1986-2001/06
TI: The National Television Violence Studies
AU: Chaffee, -Steven
IN: Stanford U, CA 94305

SO: Journal of Communications; 1997, 47, 4, autumn, 170-173.

DT: aja Abstract-of-Journal-Article

AB: A review essay on books by four university research teams—U California (Santa Barbara), U North Carolina (Chapel Hill), U Texas (Austin), & U Wisconsin (Madison)—(1) National **Television Violence** Study, Vol. 1 (Thousand Oaks, CA: Sage, 1997); & National **Television Violence** Study, Vol. 1. & Vol. 2 (Thousand Oaks, CA: Sage, 1997 & 1998, respectively). These works report on recent university studies of TV **violence** in diverse sectors of the US. The Executive Summary provides an overview of the project & policy recommendations & is appropriate for parents & teachers. The two main volumes present the coding system for **violence,** the effects of ratings & antiviolence advertising, & content analysis based on earlier literature. It is concluded that this team effort offers much useful information for the study of TV **violence,** & presents the studies in such a way that they can be easily replicated. 3 References. M. Cella

DEM: ***Television** (D859500); *Mass-Media-**Violence** (D497700); *Communication-Research (D151900); *Programming-Broadcast (D668400)

AN: 9904482

From a Full-Text Index

Entry 17 of 99 (from the Social Science Index in WilsonWeb)

Formichelli, L. *Programming behavior* [restricting violent **television** programming during hours when children may be watching] *Psychology Today* v. 34 no. 1 (January/February 2001) p. 10

From an Electronic Journal Collection

2. Warning: The Surgeon General Has Determined That TV Violence Is Moderately Dangerous to Your Child's Mental Health

Leo Bogart

Public Opinion Quarterly, Vol. 36, No. 4. (Winter, 1972–1973), pp. 491–521.

[Citation/Abstract] [View Article] [Page of First Match] [Print] [Download]

Notice that these examples contain all of the information you need for citing those works in the text and at the end of your paper. So make sure you keep lists like this when you print them so that you can cite your sources correctly.

◆ **P r a c t i c e   1**   For each of the following topics, find a book from an online database, an article from a full-text journal, and an article from an electronic journal source. Record the title and the database, index, or source where you found it.

Example: Topic: Violence and TV

Database: Sociological Abstracts—in WebSPIRS

Title: *The National Television Violence Studies*

Index: Social Science Index in WilsonWeb

Title: *Programming Behavior*

Electronic Journal: JSTOR

Title: Warning: *The Surgeon General Has Determined That TV Violence Is Moderately Dangerous to Your Child's Mental Health*

1. Topic: Drug testing in college sports

    Database: _Answers will vary._

    Title: _Answers will vary._

    Index: _Answers will vary._

    Title: _Answers will vary._

    Electronic Journal: _Answers will vary._

    Title: _Answers will vary._

2. Topic: Affirmative action and the workforce

    Database: _Answers will vary._

    Title: _Answers will vary._

    Index: _Answers will vary._

    Title: _Answers will vary._

    Electronic Journal: _Answers will vary._

    Title: _Answers will vary._

3. Topic: Prison pampering

Database: *Answers will vary.*

Title: *Answers will vary.*

Index: *Answers will vary.*

Title: *Answers will vary.*

Electronic Journal: *Answers will vary.*

Title: *Answers will vary.*

4. Topic: Women in combat

Database: *Answers will vary.*

Title: *Answers will vary.*

Index: *Answers will vary.*

Title: *Answers will vary.*

Electronic Journal: *Answers will vary.*

Title: *Answers will vary.*

5. Topic: Using animals for testing

Database: *Answers will vary.*

Title: *Answers will vary.*

Index: *Answers will vary.*

Title: *Answers will vary.*

Electronic Journal: *Answers will vary.*

Title: *Answers will vary.*

SEARCHING FOR WEB SITES

To find a Web site related to your topic, you should go to the Internet through whichever browser you have (Netscape Communicator or Navigator, Microsoft Internet Explorer, etc.). Your browser probably has a search engine of its own, which will let you search the Internet. Or you might want to use a search engine that automatically refers you to sites related to your topic: Both www.dogpile.com and www.google.com are examples of search engines that can save you a lot of time. For example, www.google.com searches nearly 1.5 million Web sites in mere seconds and is an excellent source for research.

Once you access a search engine, type in your topic as if you were searching a database. Most search engines will then begin helping you narrow your search and will provide a list of other possible topics. Here are some examples for the topic of Violence and Television.

Topic	Other Possible Topics
Violence and television	TV violence
	On TV violence
	Television violence
	TV violence children
	Violence on television
	Causes of TV violence
	Media violence

When the search is complete, your search engine will list the different Web sites in the order it thinks they will be most helpful to you. It will also briefly describe each Web site. After the description, you will most often find the Web site address. The following are the first three "hits" or Web sites from www.dogpile.com for the topic *violence and television*.

1. National Coalition on TV Violence

   Learn about the effects of TV violence and facts about the V-Chip, and get ideas to help kids avoid violent entertainment.

   www.nctvv.org

2. American Psych. Association—Violence on Television

   Association investigates the effect of television violence on children and discusses ways parents can intervene to minimize its impact.

   www.apa.org

3. APA HelpCenter: Warning Signs of Teen Violence

   The American Psychological Association and MTV team up to get important information to the nation's youth about warning signs of violent behavior, including violence in schools. The Warning Signs site provides a violence prevention guide and resource.

helping.apa.org

Practice 2 For each of the following topics, find a different Web page through a different search engine, and list the Web page title, the explanation, and the Web address.

Example: Topic: Violence and television

Search engine: GoTo.com through dogpile.com

Web page title: Center for Educational Priorities: Two Studies

Explanation: Read brief overview of the 1996 National Violence Study and the 1995 UCLA Television Violence Monitoring Report

Web address: www.cep.org

1. Topic: Bilingual education in California

Search engine: _Answers will vary._

Web page title: _Answers will vary._

Explanation: _Answers will vary._

_____

Web address: _Answers will vary._

2. Topic: Benefits of the U.S. space program

Search engine: _Answers will vary._

Web page title: _Answers will vary._

Explanation: _Answers will vary._

_____

Web address: _Answers will vary._

3. Topic: Legalizing marijuana

Search engine: _Answers will vary._

Web page title: _Answers will vary._

Explanation: _Answers will vary._

Web address: _Answers will vary._

4. Topic: Homeopathic medicine

Search engine: _Answers will vary._

Web page title: _Answers will vary._

Explanation: _Answers will vary._

Web address: _Answers will vary._

5. Topic: Women's soccer

Search engine: _Answers will vary._

Web page title: _Answers will vary._

Explanation: _Answers will vary._

Web address: _Answers will vary._

USING THE LIBRARY

Once you have compiled a list of books and journals from databases and indexes or from Web sites, you should use your library to check out books or copy journal articles that were not available online. First, you need to access your library's online catalog to see if your library has the book. (If your library does not have computers, use the traditional card catalog.) Ask a librarian how to access your particular catalog through your school. You might also ask if this information is available online. You can search for authors and subjects through your library's catalog in much the same way that you would search online databases or program search engines. But since you have already done the preliminary research, all you have to do is search for the books and journals you need. Find the "title" section of the catalog, and type in the title of the book or journal you need in this section. For help finding books and journals in your college library, ask a librarian.

If you are searching for a chapter or an essay contained in a book, be sure to type in the main book title. For example, if you searched for "I Just Wanna Be Average" (by Mike Rose), your library computer will tell you that the library does not carry it. You must type in the title of the book it came from, *Lives on the Boundary,* to find the essay. Once you have located the titles of your books or journals in the library's catalog, you should write down the call numbers so you can find the sources in your library. Then it's just a matter of finding the book itself in the stacks of your library.

Practice 3 Find five books from your research, and using the "title" portion of your library's catalog, locate the call numbers.

Example: **Title:** *Youth Culture: Identity in a Postmodern World*
Call number: HV 1431 Y684 1998

1. Title: *Answers will vary.*

   Call number: *Answers will vary.*

2. Title: *Answers will vary.*

   Call number: *Answers will vary.*

3. Title: *Answers will vary.*

   Call number: *Answers will vary.*

4. Title: *Answers will vary.*

   Call number: *Answers will vary.*

5. Title: *Answers will vary.*

   Call number: *Answers will vary.*

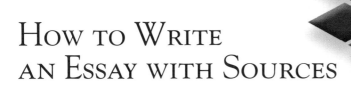

How to Write
an Essay with Sources

21

An essay with sources is really just an essay with supporting material that comes from outside sources. This type of writing assignment has all the elements of a typical essay. The following chart compares a standard essay and an essay with sources.

Standard Essay		Essay with Sources
Introduction with thesis statement	←——→	Introduction with thesis statement
Body paragraphs with facts and personal experience to support thesis statement	←——→	Body paragraphs with documented evidence to support thesis statement
Concluding paragraph	←——→	Concluding paragraph

Keep this outline in mind as you read how to construct a good essay with sources. Laying out some clear guidelines is the best place to start.

1. ***Choose a subject.*** You might be choosing a subject from infinite possibilities or working with an assigned topic. Doing some general reading online or in the library is often necessary to get you started. As you consider various topics, you must ask one very important question before you begin planning your essay: Will you be able to find enough information to back up your thesis statement? To make sure you are able to find enough material to use as good evidence in the body paragraphs of your essay, you must do a good job of choosing a subject, narrowing that subject, and then writing a working thesis statement. You will prove this thesis statement with the information you find when you search for sources on your topic. If you were writing an essay with sources on pursuing a degree in college, for example, your initial prewriting for the thesis statement might look

Teaching How to Write an Essay with Sources

Divide students into 11 groups, and have each group present or teach one of the 11 guidelines for this chapter. Have them come up with examples (if possible) or visual aids to help the other groups understand their guideline.

like this:

General Subject:	College and university degrees
More Specific:	Bachelor's degree
More Specific:	Bachelor's degree in English

This limited subject would be perfect for an essay with sources. You could search for books, catalogs, and periodicals on what it takes to earn a bachelor's degree in English from various colleges and universities. While you are looking, you could be thinking about how to narrow your subject even further.

Mary Minor (in Chapter 18) might have started with a general topic like "childhood disorders," limited it to "childhood behavioral disorders," and finally settled on "ADD and ADHD as childhood behavioral disorders."

 P r a c t i c e 1   Choose a topic from the list on page 338. Why did you choose this topic?

 P r a c t i c e 2   Limit this topic so that you can write a paper about five pages long.

2. *Write a good, clear thesis statement about your subject.* Just as a thesis statement is the controlling idea of an essay, a thesis statement also provides the controlling idea for your argument in an essay with sources. This statement will guide the writing of your entire paper. Your assignments throughout college will usually be broad topics. To compose a good essay with sources, you need to narrow a broad topic to an idea that you can prove within a limited number of pages. A working thesis statement will provide the direction for your essay, and the evidence you collect in your research is what proves the thesis statement.

A good way to start your first draft is to read some general sources on your topic. This reading will help you discover the range of your subject and will guide you toward a thesis. Before you start writing the first draft of your paper, make sure you write a sentence that clearly states your topic and your position on that topic. This is your working thesis statement and will be the controlling idea for your entire paper. Your thesis statement may change several times before your essay is finished, but making this statement and taking a position is a necessary first step. It will help you move from the broad subject of your assignment to your own perspective on the topic. This will also help you focus your essay and save you time in your search for good resources to back up your thesis statement.

Just as in a standard essay, the thesis statement in your essay with sources is a contract between you and your readers. The thesis statement tells your readers what the main idea of your essay will be and sets guidelines for the paragraphs in the body of your essay. If you don't deliver what your thesis statement promises, your readers will be disappointed. The thesis statement is usually the last sentence in the introduction. It outlines your purpose and position on the essay's general topic and gives the reader an idea of the type of resources that you will use to develop your essay.

Mary Minor's controlling idea or thesis statement appears at the end of her first paragraph:

> **Children are often misdiagnosed with ADD or ADHD and suffer unnecessarily when medicated for a disorder they may not have.**

Her entire essay is about children who are too readily diagnosed with ADD or ADHD simply because they do not fall into society's "norm" for children's behavior. The paragraphs following this thesis statement supply evidence that proves that her claim is true.

Practice 3 List your thoughts and opinions on the topic you chose in Practice 1.

Practice 4 Put your topic and your position on that topic into a working thesis statement.

3. **Find sources that are relevant, reliable, and recent to support your thesis statement.** The thesis statement of an essay with sources is really only the beginning. To convince your readers that what you say in your essay is worth reading, you must support your thesis statement with evidence. The evidence of an essay with sources lies in the sources that you use to back up your thesis statement. The sources must be relevant, reliable, and recent. This "three *Rs*" approach to supporting evidence in an essay with sources will help you write a solid essay with convincing evidence.

Mary Minor's thesis statement suggests that young children are being too readily diagnosed with ADD and ADHD. To convince her readers that her thesis is correct, she uses a book, scientific journals, an encyclopedia, online journal articles, and general-circulation magazines as sources of evidence. Here is a breakdown of how she used her sources.

- **Book:** *The Myth of the ADD Child*

  This source provides well-researched information from an expert's point of view. Mary uses this source early in her paper to help define the scope of her study.

- **Scientific journals:** *CQ Researcher, Science News, Qualitative Health Research, American Journal of Public Health*

  These sources supply the reader with specific evidence put forth by experts in the field of ADD and ADHD research and diagnosis. Mary uses this information to prove that her thesis statement is true.

- **Encyclopedia:** *World Book Encyclopedia*

  Mary uses this source to provide the reader with an understandable definition of the Hippocratic Oath. This definition plays an important role in Mary's stance on her topic.

- **Online journal articles:** *Clinical Reference Systems*

  The article from this source was printed from WilsonWeb. The information in this article defines hyperactivity in children for the general reader.

- **General-circulation magazines:** *U.S. News and World Report, Camping Magazine, Time, Runner's World, Maclean's*

  These sources supply information readily available at a newsstand, yet highly informative and applicable to Mary's topic. Information from articles in these magazines speaks to the average citizen. Even though these magazines are not scientific journals, the evidence in them is extremely useful because it was intended to make specialized information understandable to the general reader.

Mary Minor uses sources in her essay that do a thorough job of supporting her thesis statement. Information from articles in these books, journals, and magazines speaks to the average citizen. Even though they are not highly technical scientific sources, the evidence in them is relevant, reliable, and recent, which are also guidelines you should use when looking for your sources.

Practice 5 Review Chapter 20 to make sure that you understand the options available to you for finding sources to use in your essay.

Practice 6 Find five sources that give you information about the limited topic that you chose. Make sure they are relevant, reliable, and recent.

4. ***Take notes to avoid plagiarism.*** Now is the time to read your sources and take careful notes—putting the ideas in your own words or putting the

writer's words in quotation marks if you record the exact words. You should also note the page numbers of all information you take down. If you don't take notes carefully, you will never be able to trace information that you want to use in your paper to its original source. Also, trying to put some-one's ideas into your own words is a very good skill that will help you as you write.

Taking notes on notecards allows you to move your cards around and put ideas into different paragraphs. When you rearrange cards, you can work with them until you think the order will support what you are trying to prove. This notecard method actually saves time in the long run.

Mary Minor had to read and take notes on all the sources she found. She first made a set of bibliography cards with a notecard for every source she found. For the books, she put book title, author, city where published, pub-lisher, and year of publication on each card; for the articles, she recorded article title, author, title of the magazine or journal, date of issue or volume and issue numbers, and page numbers of the article on each card. Then she began to read her sources. She wrote only one idea or quotation on a note-card, and she remembered to record on each notecard the author's name and the page number on which she found the information. She also made sure, as she took notes, to restate information in her own words or else put the author's exact words in quotation marks.

◆ *P r a c t i c e 7*   Review Chapter 19 to make sure you understand what plagiarism is and how to avoid it.

◆ *P r a c t i c e 8*   Read and take notes on your sources using notecards. Make sure each of your cards has a source and page number on it.

5. *Make a working outline of your paper.* To do this, you just need to start re-arranging the notecards you have made. Start by putting all your notecards into small stacks of related ideas. Which ideas will work well together? Which should you put in the introduction? Which do you want to save for your conclusion? When you get all your notecards in stacks, label each group of cards according to its topic. These labels will then become the topics of your paper. You are now ready to start your working outline.

A good way to begin a working outline is to write your tentative thesis statement at the top of a page and then list the topics you have developed under that thesis. These topics should be arranged in some logical order that will help you prove your main point and is easy to follow. Each topic should also directly support your thesis statement. Leave room in your outline to add subtopics and details throughout the paper. This outline then becomes a guide for your writing. It will change and grow with every paragraph that you add to your paper.

Mary started developing her paper by putting related notecards into stacks. Next, she labeled her stacks of notecards and started organizing these topics in different ways until they started making sense to her. Her list of topics, with her thesis statement at the top, became the bulk of her working outline. She eventually turned these topics into topic sentences for her body paragraphs. The stack of cards for each topic became the content of her body paragraphs.

◆ *P r a c t i c e 9*   Divide your notecards into topics that logically support your thesis statement. Then label each stack of cards.

◆ *P r a c t i c e 10*   Start a working outline of your paper by listing your thesis statement and your supporting topics.

6. ***Construct an introduction that leads up to your thesis statement.*** The introduction to an essay with sources is your chance to make a great first impression. Just like a firm handshake and a warm smile in a job interview, an essay's introduction should capture your readers' interest, set the tone for your essay, and state your specific purpose. Introductions often have a funnel effect. They typically begin with general information and then narrow the focus to your position on a particular issue. Regardless of your method, your introduction should "hook" your readers by grabbing their attention and letting them know what you are going to try to prove in your essay.

To lead up to the thesis statement, your introductory paragraph must stimulate your readers' interest. Some effective ways of capturing your audience's attention and giving necessary background information are (1) to use a quotation; (2) to tell a story that relates to your topic; (3) to provide a revealing fact, statistic, or definition; (4) to offer an interesting comparison; or (5) to ask an intriguing question. Be sure your introduction gives readers all the information they may need to follow your train of thought through the rest of your paper.

Mary's introduction starts out with a hypothetical situation that parents face as their children may or may not develop "normally." The paragraph then discusses parents' confusion with their children's behavior and introduces ADD and ADHD. The last sentence of the first paragraph contains Mary's thesis statement and ends the introduction.

Practice 11   Make a rough outline of your ideas for a possible introduction to your essay with sources.

Practice 12   Write a rough draft of your introduction, ending with your thesis statement.

7. *Develop as many supporting paragraphs or body paragraphs as you think are necessary to explain your thesis statement.* Following the introductory paragraph, an essay with sources includes several body paragraphs that support and explain the essay's thesis statement. Each body paragraph covers a topic that is directly related to the thesis statement.

Supporting paragraphs, or body paragraphs, usually include a topic sentence, which is a general statement of the paragraph's contents, and examples or details that support the topic sentence. (See Chapters 4 and 5 for methods to use when you develop and organize paragraphs.)

To write your supporting paragraphs, you should first organize your notecards within each of your stacks. Next, add these details to your working outline. Then write your supporting paragraphs by following your working outline and your notecards. Make adjustments in your outline as you write so that you can keep track of your ideas and make sure you are developing them in a logical order. The body of the paper and your outline should change and develop together with each sentence that you write.

After you write your body paragraphs, you should look at your thesis statement again to make sure it introduces what you say in the rest of your paper. Your thesis statement should refer to all of your topics, even if only indirectly, in the order you discuss them. It should also prepare your readers for the conclusions you are going to come to.

Mary's paper contains eight body paragraphs, each making a separate point that is directly related to her thesis:

Paragraph	Point
2	ADD and ADHD are defined as "a short attention span" and are the most commonly diagnosed childhood diseases.
3	Diagnosing children who do not fit a "norm" is ludicrous, especially since there is no accurate definition or diagnosis of ADD or ADHD.
4	No physical exam can determine if a child has ADD or ADHD.

5   There are as many theories about the causes of ADD as there are experts, so we are only treating the symptoms of these disorders.

6   Teachers, parents, and students get caught up in the diagnosis.

7   Drugs should only be a short-term answer to the hyper-active child.

8   No proof is available that says we overprescribe drugs for American children.

9   Long-term use of drugs for ADD and ADHD is poten-tially dangerous.

Like the foundation of a solid building, these paragraphs provide support for the position Mary takes in her thesis statement. The stronger the support-ing paragraphs are, the stronger the paper will be.

In addition to strong topic sentences, you should also use concluding sentences in your body paragraphs to help reinforce your thesis statement or build a transition to the next paragraph. Concluding sentences wrap up a paragraph just like a conclusion wraps up an essay, and using concluding sentences lets you remind your readers what you are arguing and where you are in your reasoning.

Practice 13   Organize the notecards within each of your stacks so that they make sense. Add these details to your working outline.

Practice 14   Write a rough draft of your body paragraphs. Remem-ber that you will be revising and editing this draft a little later, so just con-centrate on getting your ideas written up in an organized way. Revise your thesis statement, if necessary, to introduce all your body paragraphs.

8. *Make sure you use your sources as evidence for your argument.* Although your argument will evolve as you read your sources, you should decide on a general position on your topic before you begin to take notes. Don't write your essay around your sources, because your essay may become very disjointed and difficult to follow if you do. You should find appropriate sources to help you de-velop your argument. The best way to do this is to tell your reader the signifi-cance of the direct quotations, paraphrases, or summaries that you use. Look, for example, at one of the paragraphs in Mary's paper:

> Despite major controversy in the medical field, however, there has been no proof that drugs are being overprescribed for American children. Some experts

even feel that children may be undertreated (Koch 912).
No studies have been found that would prove one claim
over the other, which again means that each child is
treated according to the most popular opinion. As a
result, "Students who were younger than their
classmates were <u>21</u> times more likely to be medicated"
for ADD or ADHD (920). With a statistic like this, it's
astonishing that experts disagree on this subject.

Notice how Mary does not stop with her source's remarks. Instead, she includes a point about the significance of what each source says. She reminds her readers that she is arguing against drugging young children unnecessarily.

If you simply provide a series of quotations and let them argue for you, you are not demonstrating your understanding of the quotations or showing how they fit into your argument. Make sure to use the quotations as support for your argument and not let them stand for the argument itself.

Practice 15   Consider the different ways your sources will support your argument. Organize them in a way that best helps you prove your main point.

Practice 16   Write your body paragraphs using your sources as evidence in your argument. Be careful not to choose sources haphazardly to include in your body paragraphs. You need to have a reason for using each of your sources.

9. **Write a concluding paragraph.** The concluding paragraph is the final paragraph of an essay. In its most basic form, it should summarize the main points of the essay and remind readers of the thesis statement.

The best conclusions expand on these two basic requirements and bring the essay to a close with one of these creative strategies: (1) Ask a question that provokes thought on the part of the reader, (2) predict the future, (3) offer a solution to a problem, or (4) call the reader to action. Each of these options sends a specific message and creates a slightly different effect at the end of the paper. The most important responsibility of the last paragraph is to bring the essay to an effective close. It is the last information that readers see before they form their own opinions or take action.

Mary's conclusion offers a solution to the problem raised in the second sentence of the paragraph:

Every effort should be made to find the cause of the
"real" medical problems underlying ADD and ADHD
before we even think about giving our children drugs.

Toward the end of her conclusion, she calls the reader to action:

> It's time to say good-bye to "conformist" American classrooms and diagnoses.

She ends by reflecting on her thesis in one last, short line:

> People don't fit "norms"; they have personalities.

Her concluding paragraph refocuses the reader's attention on the problem, offers a solution to the problem, and then calls the reader to action.

◆ *P r a c t i c e* **1 7**   Make a rough outline of your ideas for a possible conclusion to your essay with sources. Choose a strategy that you want to use to bring your paper to a close.

◆ *P r a c t i c e* **1 8**   Write a rough draft of your conclusion, reminding your readers of your thesis statement.

10. ***Think of a catchy title.*** Your title is what readers see first in any essay. A title is a phrase, usually no more than a few words, placed at the beginning of your essay that suggests or sums up the subject, purpose, or focus of the essay. Some titles are very imaginative, drawing on different sources for their meaning. Others are straightforward, like the title of this chapter—"How to Write an Essay with Sources." These are just two of the many different approaches you can take to creating a title.

Besides suggesting an essay's purpose, a good title catches an audience's attention. For instance, Mary Minor's title, "Children as Robots," will catch most readers' attention because referring to children as "robots" is intriguing, and readers will want to find out just how and why this might occur. That's exactly what a title should do—make your readers want to read your paper.

◆ *P r a c t i c e* **1 9**   Jot down some catchy titles for your paper.

◆ *P r a c t i c e* **2 0**   Choose a title for your paper.

11. ***Check your sources and documentation format throughout your paper and at the end.*** Finding and using good, solid sources for evidence in an essay with sources is important, and equally important is the acknowledgment of those sources. If you use a source and do not cite it correctly or forget to cite it altogether, you are guilty of plagiarism, which can lead to a failing grade on the paper. So you need to learn when to cite a

source (see Chapter 19), what documentation style to use (MLA, APA, or other appropriate format), and how to cite sources. You should check with your instructor to find out which format you should use in a particular course.

Citations are of two types: (a) The *in-text citation* indicates the source of a quotation or idea right after it appears in the essay; (b) then, at the end, a list of all the sources cited in the paper must appear on the *Works Cited* or *Reference* page. Many textbooks demonstrate the various forms of documentation, so you should look up the format that your instructor wants you to use. Then keep this text handy when you write papers with sources.

Mary uses the MLA format on her paper, which she wrote for an English class. Usually, English instructors ask their students to use the MLA format. Mary includes a variety of sources in her paper, which we can use to illustrate the two types of citations. Listed here are some sample entries at the end of Mary's paper, with the corresponding in-text citations in parentheses.

Book—name of author, title of book, city of publication, publisher, date of publication

> **Works Cited:**   Armstrong, Thomas. <u>The Myth of the ADD Child: 50 Ways to Improve Your Child's Behavior and Attention Span Without Drugs, Labels, or Coercion.</u> New York: Dutton, 1995.
>
> **In-Text Citation:**   (914)

Note: Notice how Mary introduced Armstrong before providing readers with this page number so she doesn't have to repeat the author's name in the citation.

Journal—name of author, title of article, name of journal, volume number, year, page number

> **Works Cited:**   Bower, Bruce. "Kid's Attention Disorder Attracts Concern." <u>Science News</u> 154 (1998): 343.
>
> **In-Text Citation:**   (Bower 343)

Encyclopedia—name of author, title of article, name of encyclopedia, volume number, year

> **Works Cited:**   "Hippocratic Oath." <u>World Book Encyclopedia.</u> Vol. 9. 1999 ed.
>
> **In-Text Citation:**   ("Hippocratic Oath")

Note: If an article is unsigned, begin with the title of the article.

Online Database—name of author, title of article, name of database, date of publication, date you accessed the material, URL in angle brackets

> **Works Cited:** Schmitt, B. D. "Attention Deficit Disorder (Short Attention Span)." <u>Clinical Reference Systems.</u> 1 July 1999. 17 Feb. 2000 <http://www.epnet.com/ehost/login.html>.
>
> **In-Text Citation:** (Schmitt)

Note: If some information required in the citation is missing, include whatever is available.

General-Circulation Magazine—name of author, title of article, name of magazine, date of publication, page numbers

> **Works Cited:** Sheppard, Robert. "Growing Up Hyperactive." <u>Maclean's</u> 7 Sept. 1998: 45–46.
>
> **In-Text Citation:** (Sheppard 45)

Note: If an article is unsigned, begin with the title of the article.

These examples from Mary's essay are just a few of the various types of sources that you will probably use in your essays with sources. Every source is cited in a slightly different way, depending on the type of source and the documentation style. Not even the best writers know the correct format for every source they use. So when you have chosen your sources and determined that they are relevant, reliable, and recent (the three *R*s), your last step is to consult an appropriate, current manual or Web site to make sure you cite each source correctly.

◆ ***Practice 21*** Make sure that the material from every source in your essay has an in-text citation. Then create a Works Cited, Reference, or Bibliography page, following an approved documentation format.

◆ ***Practice 22*** Check the format of your in-text citations and your list of works cited by consulting a current handbook.

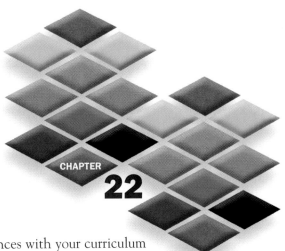

SERVICE LEARNING

Service learning combines real-world experiences with your curriculum in a particular course. It allows you to volunteer for an organization, learn about the organization, understand the population the organization serves, and write about your participation. Service learning works within the traditional curriculum to help you blend life inside and outside college into a meaningful experience. With service learning, you can try out various career paths before making a more permanent decision. It is a way of gaining some experience in a field without really having to commit to it for the long term. Finally, it enables you to gain valuable work experience that can go on a resumé, thus giving you an edge over your peers in the job market.

We all write better when we know what we are talking about. Service learning gives you the opportunity to learn firsthand about a particular experience and then write about it. This chapter will be especially useful if you have been completing the service-learning assignments in Part II.

THINKING ABOUT YOUR SERVICE LEARNING PROJECT

Most students feel slightly overwhelmed when they learn that they will be participating in a Service Learning project in one of their college classes. But the only difficult part of service learning is deciding what organization or project you would like to be involved with.

The first step toward participating in a Service Learning project is to find an organization or project that appeals to you. What are your interests? Are you an athlete? If so, perhaps you could volunteer at the local YMCA, YWCA, or boys' or girls' clubs. If you like crafts or nature, maybe you could volunteer for a local Boy Scout or Girl Scout troop. If you plan on working in the legal field, you could help a local lawyer provide free aid to homeless shelters or women's shelters. Or if you plan on working in the medical field, you could volunteer at a hospital. The possibilities are endless. You just need

TEACHING SERVICE
LEARNING
Invite former students
and/or representatives
from various organiza-
tions to speak to your
class about their
service-learning experi-
ences. What do the
students think went
well with their experi-
ences? What do the
students wish they
knew before beginning
their projects? What do
the representatives
from the organizations
say about the contribu-
tions of the students?
What were some of the
problems they both
had?
    If this is the first
time you have used
service learning, ask
your college's service-
learning office to intro-
duce service learning to
your class or invite
various community
representatives to
discuss possible contri-
butions your students
could make to their
organizations. Your
students will have an

to think of an organization or group that you would like to work with for the term (or for life!).

Below are some service-learning ideas that you may enjoy or that might stimulate another idea for you.

- working as a tutor in an elementary, a middle, or a high school
- studying a problem in a school (any level) and recommending a solution
- reading regularly to elementary school children or to older people in nursing homes
- studying and writing reports on traffic congestion for government agencies
- working for a community or campus organization
- working with adult learners at a community literacy center
- working with parents in schools where English is not spoken at home
- helping a business write and/or edit its daily documents
- assisting a local TV station with its news copy
- working in a homeless shelter
- working for a company that benefits the community
- helping a radio station with special promotions

These are just a few ideas to get you thinking about service learning.

Once you decide on a project and volunteer for a term, most often your instructor will require you to create a written project for or about your organization. For example, if you work with a community or campus organization, you might write a newsletter, create a brochure or special ad, develop a computer program, or design promotional material. As you do your volunteer work, you should find out what written materials your organization needs and then try to supply them. Some instructors may also require a written essay explaining your service-learning experiences. Make sure you understand what written work your instructor wants you to do.

INITIATING YOUR SERVICE LEARNING PROJECT

To begin your Service Learning project, you need to follow six easy steps. If you take them one by one, you will move smoothly into your community project.

1. Because service learning has become so popular on college campuses, your particular campus might have a service learning office. Usually these

offices are associated with campus outreach, community centers, or career centers. Often, you will find that your campus has already established a relationship with different service-learning participants, and all you have to do is choose an office or project that interests you.

entries, and for various tests, see the *Instructor's Resource Manual,* Section II, Part III.

If you do not have a service-learning office on your campus, you need to make the original contacts yourself. This will be similar to searching for a job, but you will often be more kindly received since service-learning work is volunteer and you are not asking for pay.

◆ *P r a c t i c e 1*   Interview people at community organizations where you are thinking of volunteering. If you don't have a service-learning office on your campus, find out if the organization of your choice would be willing to take on a volunteer worker.

◆ *P r a c t i c e 2*   After consulting with your instructor, choose an organization, office, or job for your Service Learning project.

2. When you first make contact with your group or organization, you'll want to explain a little about what you are doing. You need to assure them that you want to volunteer for at least a term and that you would like to complete a writing project tailored to their needs. Tell them you are simply there to volunteer and to produce some sort of written document that can help their organization.

◆ *P r a c t i c e 3*   Prepare a brief description of service learning and a summary of your qualifications to take to the place you have chosen for your Service Learning project.

3. For a Service Learning project, you must make sure to volunteer on a regular basis. If you don't, you will not understand the actual mechanics of your organization, group, or project as well as you should. You should spend at least one hour per week at your service-learning place, yet the more hours you put in, the more benefits you'll receive. You might want to volunteer more hours at the beginning of the term so you can learn about the organization and then settle down to a set schedule. Also, keep your focus on producing a written project that will be useful to the organization. What can you do for this group that will actually help them?

◆ *P r a c t i c e 4*   Put a tentative schedule in writing to take to your organization on your first day.

4. Since you will be volunteering and observing for an entire term, you should keep a journal of all your experiences. By keeping a journal, you can note your daily experiences, your emotions, details about the people you work with, notes on other people you encounter, and so on. You should jot down as much as possible of what you see, hear, and experience because you never know what may be useful at the end of the term.

Since rhetorical modes are effective ways of organizing information, you might want to use your journal to consider various questions that will help you understand your Service Learning project in relation to other essays you will be writing. So you might want to consider the following questions.

Description:	What sights, noises, touches, smells, and tastes do you notice?
Narration:	What stories can you tell about your volunteer experience?
Example:	What examples explain the work that you do? What examples can help you explain the impact you are making on others?
Analyzing a Process:	What are the various steps you go through in a typical day at your organization? What might happen if you forget a step?
Comparing and Contrasting:	How are the various jobs you do similar and different from each other, and why might these differences be important? How are the people you encounter similar and different from each other? How do these similarities and differences help you understand the organization you have volunteered for?
Dividing and Classifying:	What are the different levels of management in your organization? How do these different levels contribute to the overall effectiveness of your organization? Where do you fit into the general scheme of the organization? How does your job help you understand the mission of the organization?
Defining:	Define your organization for someone who knows nothing about it. What is its purpose? Its mission?

Analyzing Causes and Effects:	What are the causes and effects of the work your organization does? What would happen if your organization closed tomorrow? What would happen to the people it serves?
Arguing:	Do you agree with your organization's mission? Explain your reasoning.

◆ ***Practice 5*** Get a journal and record your first journal entry. Then continue to make entries in it every day.

5. You should also try to talk to as many people as you can who work for your service-learning organization. These people work in this environment every day and probably have some very interesting insights into this type of work. You might also ask your service-learning "employer" for permission to interview some of the people you are serving. Talking to others is an excellent way to learn about a work environment.

◆ ***Practice 6*** Talk to as many people at your organization as possible, and record your observations in your journal.

6. As you are working throughout the term, you might also try to do several different types of jobs for your service-learning organization. For example, if you volunteer in a homeless shelter, you might ask to work in a kitchen, in an office, or with a learning activity. Likewise, if you are working in a hospital, you might ask how many different jobs your supervisor will let you do. You may be limited because of your lack of training, but if you can work in several different areas, you will get different perspectives on your volunteer work. These multiple perspectives can be invaluable when you are trying to create your final Service Learning project.

◆ ***Practice 7*** Ask for a new job within your service-learning organization, and record your impressions in your journal.

If you follow these six steps, your service-learning experience should be rewarding and enriching. You should gather enough information to write your final project and/or any other writing project your instructor assigns. Remember this: You will get out of your Service Learning project what you put into it. You can make a difference in the world, and this project gives you the potential to make a significant impact on a specific group of people. Have fun, and let the experience teach you some important lessons about life.

Practice 8 Reread any writing you did in Part II in response to the service-learning assignments. Then reflect on your service-learning experience so far. What have you learned from the experience at this point? What else do you want to learn? Is your service-learning organization a possible career choice for you? Has it helped you make some decisions about your career direction?

Practice 9 Make a list of some possible written projects that will benefit your organization. Record ideas that have been suggested as well as others that you think of on your own.

REVISING AND EDITING AN ESSAY WITH SOURCES

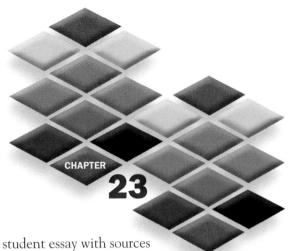

CHAPTER 23

In this chapter, you will revise and edit a new student essay with sources and then revise and edit your own source essay. The checklists for this process are provided here, and the chapter will guide you through this process step by step.

REVISING CHECKLIST ✔

THESIS STATEMENT

✔ Does the thesis statement contain the essay's controlling idea and an opinion about that idea?

✔ Does the thesis appear as the last sentence of the introduction?

BASIC ELEMENTS

✔ Does the title draw in the readers?

✔ Does the introduction capture the readers' attention and build up to the thesis statement effectively?

✔ Does each body paragraph deal with a single topic?

✔ Does the conclusion bring the essay to a close in an interesting way?

DEVELOPMENT

✔ Do the body paragraphs adequately support the thesis statement?

✔ Does each body paragraph have a focused topic sentence?

✔ Does each body paragraph contain *specific* details that support the topic sentence?

✔ Does each body paragraph include *enough* details to explain the topic sentence fully?

✔ Are the sources relevant, reliable, and recent?

✔ Are references given for original sources to avoid plagiarism?

✔ Is the documentation format correct—in the paper and at the end?

TEACHING HOW TO REVISE AND EDIT AN ESSAY WITH SOURCES
Divide students into groups of three or four. Using the guidelines from Chapter 21, have students evaluate Rick Schroeder's essay. Does it follow every guideline? What places in the paper need work? Once students have evaluated the paper based on the guidelines, have them apply the revising and editing checklists to the paper while they keep their evaluations close at hand.

UNITY

✔ Do the essay's topic sentences relate directly to the thesis statement?

✔ Do the details in each body paragraph support its topic sentence?

ORGANIZATION

✔ Is the essay organized logically?

✔ Is each body paragraph organized logically?

COHERENCE

✔ Are transitions used effectively so that paragraphs move smoothly and logically from one to the next?

✔ Do the sentences move smoothly and logically from one to the next?

EDITING CHECKLIST ✔

SENTENCES

✔ Does each sentence have a main subject and verb?

✔ Do all subjects and verbs agree?

✔ Do all pronouns agree with their nouns?

✔ Are modifiers as close as possible to the words they modify?

PUNCTUATION AND MECHANICS

✔ Are sentences punctuated correctly?

✔ Are words capitalized properly?

WORD CHOICE AND SPELLING

✔ Are words used correctly?

✔ Are words spelled correctly?

REVISING AND EDITING A STUDENT ESSAY WITH SOURCES

Here is the first draft of an essay written by Rick Schroeder, a student. It demonstrates the guidelines for writing a successful essay with sources that you have learned in Chapters 18 through 21.

Space Bucks

Every year an enormous amount of money is poured into NASA for space exploration. Does this research justify the expense? Many people would gratefully sacrifice the money just to prove that Americans can compete in the space arena. An overwhelming force drives us into the unknown realms of our universe in the same way that Christopher Columbus was adventurously driven to search for what was once called the New World. On the other hand, many tax-payers believe that more justification is needed for the large amount of money put into NASA research. But what these "non-supporters" tend to overlook is NASA's chance "to lead the exploration and development of the space frontier, advancing science, technology, enterprise, and building institutions and systems that make accessible vast new resources" (United States). NASA is a worthwhile organization that many people benefit from.

Most significantly, technology research that results from space exploration greatly benefit the field of medicine. The International Space Station (ISS), which was built by 16 different nations, is one of the biggest and most costly projects that NASA has constructed and is essential for research in space technology. Scientists aboard the ISS have the opportunity to test various theories and conduct experiments in several different fields of science using the microgravity on this station in space (NASA *Space Station*). Some of the most important research that will be done onboard the ISS involves searching for cures for both osteoporosis and cancer (Von Brook, Siegel, and Foster 67). Also, according to Von Brook, Siegel, and Foster, the authors of <u>Space Exploration: The Dream and the Reality</u>, some additional examples of "space-pioneer medical technology include a cardiac pacemaker that can be automatically recharged without surgery, a human tissue simulator that relieves chronic pain, anti-contamination hospital garments, x-rays that can penetrate bone and produce pictures of body tissues and organs," and several other advances in autism, diabetes, heart disease, and premature birth (69). These are just a few of the contributions from space exploration that help improve the quality of life for humanity on a day-to-day basis. Without NASA's research, scientists would never have discovered these contributions. Therefore, we must continue to fund NASA and all its programs.

The vast number of effective medicines, treatments, and machines used to test for and treat illnesses would be enough to warrant the space exploration funds if they were the only benefits to society from the NASA research. But another benefit of NASA's research is their ability to monitor the environment to ensure continued life on Earth. Since the ISS is a permanent structure that will observe the earth for the next 30 years, scientists will be able to monitor the earth and distinguish changes that have been made over time to its environment (Von Brook, Siegel, and Foster 67). These studies could lead to more breakthroughs and solutions for many environmental problems. For example, the balance between farming and water conservation will soon be made vastly more efficient due to advancements made by NASA using satellite imaging to determine watering priorities for irrigated farm lands (Rumsfeld 11). This information will help both the farmers and the general population—especially in a state like California where water rights are a volatile issue.

4   Not only can the space exploration program help solve environmental problems, but it can also identify those problems. In fact, the space program gave us "our first real perspective on global warming, ozone layer depletion, deforestation, and other environmental scourges" (Von Brook, Siegel, and Foster 69). Yet not all environmental benefits are plans for the future. Von Brook, Siegel, and Foster state,

> we have already achieved very promising results with indoor air pollution and wastewater treatment using NASA technology. Today, NASA researchers are contributing steadily to our knowledge of landfill leachate treatment, hazardous waste disposal, tropical rainforest, and ground water pollution. (69)

5   Recently, astronauts aboard the space station spent ten days creating a topographic map of all locations on the world within 60 degrees of the equator. A topographic map of uniform scale circling the entire globe has never before been created, and NASA accomplished this feat in 10 days. This model of the Earth can now be used to monitor changes on the Earth's surface, providing a very useful tool humanity can use for many reasons, including fighting forest fires (Jet Propulsion Laboratory). The environment must be preserved, and since this task is made easier with the benefits of space exploration, we must continue to fund research for NASA.

6   Science, however, is not the only aspect of life that NASA affects, for it also greatly influences the economy. According to Von Brook, Siegel, and Foster, "Space exploration . . . is the best investment for our future because it sharpens the skills and harnesses the talents of all Americans involved" (70). Sharpening the talents of Americans is important, yet the real question at hand is the economics of space exploration. A single

space shuttle costs, for example, from $10,000–$20,000 per kilogram (Alpert 93). This is definitely a substantial amount of money to pay for a single launch. In 1975, NASA sponsored a study to design a space station it was never funded. A group of scientists created a plan for a circular station that would provide room for 10,000 colonists. The station would have cost $500 billion. However, the station would have paid for itself within 30 years because of enormous solar-power satellites that would be installed. A solar-energy-collection satellite would receive eight times as much energy as a collector on earth. The satellite would also produce five billion watts of electricity. Which is approximately five times that of an average power plant (Alpert 93-94). The economic benefits of this power are enormous considering the energy crises that tend to afflict parts of the United States.

Given the proper chance, much of space exploration could pay for itself. Von Brook, Siegel, and Foster claim that "the Apollo mission yielded a 7-to-1 return of every dollar invested" (70). This does not suggest enormous waste. As Rumsfeld speculates, "An international space industry has developed, with revenues exceeding $80 billion in 2000. Industry forecasts project revenues will more than triple in the next decade" (11). Not only could a space project pay for itself, but the ISS will provide "50,000 jobs directly associated with spin-off technology," which "means greater national pride and fewer Americans that will require public support for basic needs like food and housing."

One major problem of NASA's budget, however, is the cuts it will cause for other programs. Unfortunately, NASA shares a budget with the Environmental Protection Agency (EPA), the Department of Housing and Urban Development (HUD), and the Veterans Administration (Von Brook, Siegel, and Foster 66). This means that budget cuts are mandatory for the other agencies if any one program requires more capital. Von Brook, Siegel, and Foster explain, "This puts some of the nation's most futuristic plans competing directly against some of America's most pressing social needs" (66). Nevertheless, Americans and humanity must look passed the present problems and see into the future for solutions. Social needs have plagued society for centuries. We have tried to throw money at these problems in the past, which has been ineffective, so new solutions must be sought. The answers can be found by looking beyond the problems that humanity faces today and into the future of space exploration.

NASA is an important and vital force in American society. As long as our desire to explore space continues to exist, advances and discoveries will follow. The benefits come not only in the form of space exploration, but also in medical, environmental, and economic advances that are necessary to the survival and progress of humanity. But NASA cannot continue to provide these major discoveries with a diminishing budget. In fact, NASA's 2002 budget allocation was less than the money it received in 1994 (NASA *FY 2003 Budget*). This budget desicion will affect all of American society for hundreds of years to come. An agency with the potential of NASA that has proven its usefulness time and time again should not be inadequately funded. It needs a generous budget that will let it continue to improve the quality of life for all Americans.

Works Cited

Alpert, Mark. "Making Money in Space." The Future of Space Exploration. 1 Jan. 1999: 92-95.

Jet Propulsion Laboratory. "Earth Has a New Look." NASA News. Jet Propulsion Laboratory, California Institute of Technology, Pasadena, California. News Release: 2003-116. August 22, 2003.

National Aeronautical and Space Agency (NASA). Chart: FY 2003 Budget vs. History and Background Material NASA FY 2003 Budget Briefing. 5 Sept. 2003 <http://www1.nasa.gov/audience/formediafeatures/MP_Budget_Previous.html>.

Space Station Benefits. 4 Oct. 2003 <http://spaceflight.nasa.gov/station/benefits/index.html>.

Rumsfeld, Donald H. (chairman). Report of the Commission to Assess United States National Security Space Management and Organization. Pursuant to Public Law 106-65. January 11, 2001. 28 Sept. 2003 <www.defenselink.mil/pubs/space20010111.html>.

United States. The Report of the National Commission on Space. Pioneering the Space Frontier. Toronto: Bantam Books, 1986.

Von Brook, Patricia, Mark A. Siegel, and Carol D. Foster. Space Exploration: The Dream and the Reality. Eds. Patricia Von Brook, Mark A. Siegel, and Carol D. Foster. Wylie, Texas: Information Plus, 1990.

Rick's first draft now needs to be revised and edited. First, apply the Revising Checklist (printed at the beginning of this chapter) to the content of Rick's draft. When you are satisfied that his ideas are fully developed and well organized, use the Editing Checklist on page 382 to correct his grammatical and mechanical errors. The questions below will guide you through this process. Then rewrite the essay with your suggested changes.

Revising

Thesis Statement

1. What is the main idea in Rick's essay with sources?

   NASA's space exploration budget is justified and should be funded.

2. Put brackets around Rick's thesis statement. Does it introduce his main point?

   No

3. Rewrite it to introduce all the topics in his essay.

   Here is one possibility: NASA's space exploration budget is justified;

   therefore, every effort should be made to fund NASA's programs.

Basic Elements

1. Give Rick's essay an alternate title.

   Answers will vary.

2. Rewrite Rick's introduction so that it captures the readers' attention in a different way and builds up to the thesis statement at the end of the paragraph.

   Answers will vary.

3. Does each of Rick's body paragraphs deal with only one topic?

   Yes

4. Rewrite Rick's conclusion with a twist of your own.

   Answers will vary.

TEACHING HOW TO REVISE AND EDIT THEIR OWN ESSAYS WITH SOURCES

Have students send an essay they wrote in your class to an online writing lab (OWL) for revising and editing feedback. Have students include a printout of the OWL's comments when they turn in their final draft of the essay, and have them reflect on the online tutorials by answering the following questions:

What was your most important learning experience from the OWL?

What was your least important learning experience from the OWL?

How can an OWL be beneficial with other papers you may be writing for other classes?

For a complete list of OWLs, go to iwca.syr.edu/iwca/iwcaowls.html. One of the best is owl.english.purdue.edu.

For further help with editing, consult the following sites:

www.prenhall.com/mosaics
www.prenhall.com/troyka

For additional material about teaching students to revise and edit their essays with sources, for journal entries, and for various tests, see the *Instructor's Resource Manual*, Section II, Part III.

TEACHING ON THE WEB

Research: Have students find different ways the Internet can help them revise and edit their writing. Are certain Web sites more helpful than others? How are the sites different?

TEACHING ON THE WEB

Mosaics Web Site: To learn more about revising and editing their own essay with sources, students can go to www.prenhall. com/mosaics.

_____

_____

Development

1. Do Rick's topic sentences support his thesis statement? Write out your revision of Rick's thesis statement, and list his six topic sentences.

   Thesis: *NASA's space exploration budget is justified; therefore,*

   every effort should be made to fund NASA's programs.

   Topics: *Most significantly, technology research that results from*

   space exploration greatly benefit the field of medicine.

   The vast number of effective medicines, treatments, and machines

   used to test for and treat illnesses would be enough to warrant the

   space exploration funds if they were the only benefits to society

   from the NASA research.

   Not only can the space exploration program help solve environ-

   mental problems, but it can also identify those problems.

   Science, however, is not the only aspect of life that NASA affects,

   for it also greatly influences the economy.

   Given the proper chance, much of space exploration could pay for itself.

   One major problem of NASA's budget, however, is the cuts it will

   cause for other programs.

2. Does your revised thesis statement accurately introduce Rick's topic sentences?

   Answers will vary.

   _____

3. Are Rick's examples specific?

   Yes
   _____

   Add an even more specific detail to one of his paragraphs.

4. Does he offer enough examples or details in each paragraph?

   Yes
   _____

5. Are Rick's sources relevant, reliable, and recent?

   Yes
   _____

   For help, see Chapter 20.

6. Does he give references for all original sources in his paper?

   No
   _____

   For help, see Chapter 19.

   Find the one sentence in paragraph 6 that is plagiarized and needs the reference "(Von Brook, Sigel, and Foster 68)."

   Sentence 6
   _____

7. Is the documentation format correct in his paper?

   Yes
   _____

   For help, see Chapter 21.

8. Is the format on his Works Cited page correct?

   Yes
   _____

   For help, see Chapter 21.

Unity

1. Read each of Rick's topic sentences with his thesis statement in mind. Do they go together?

   Yes
   _____

2. Revise any topic sentences that are not directly related to his thesis.
   Topic sentences are all related.

3. Read each of Rick's paragraphs with its topic sentence in mind. Drop or rewrite any sentences that are not directly related to the paragraph's topic sentences. *All sentences are directly related to the paragraph's topic sentences.*

Organization

1. Review your list of Rick's topics in item 1 under "Development," and decide if they are organized logically. *They are logical.*

2. What is his method of organization?

   From one extreme to another (most important to least important)

3. Read Rick's paper again to see if all his sentences are arranged logically.

4. Move any sentences that are out of order. *All sentences are in order.*

Coherence

For a list of transitions, see pages 83–84.

1. Circle five transitions that Rick uses.

2. Explain how three of these transitions make Rick's paper easier to read. *Answers will vary.*

Now rewrite Rick's essay with your revisions.

Editing

Sentences

Subjects and Verbs

For help with subjects and verbs, see Chapter 34.

1. Underline the subjects once and verbs twice in paragraph 5 of Rick's essay. Remember that sentences can have more than one subject-verb set.

2. Does each sentence have at least one subject and verb that can stand alone?

   No

For help with fragments, see Chapter 35.

For help with run-togethers, see Chapter 36.

3. Did you find and correct Rick's fragment in paragraph 6? If not, find and correct it now. *Sentence 12*

4. Did you find and correct Rick's run-together sentence in paragraph 6? If not, find and correct it now. *Sentence 6*

Subject-Verb Agreement

1. Read aloud the subjects and verbs in paragraph 2 of Rick's revised essay.
2. Correct any subjects and verbs that do not agree. *Sentence 1*
3. Now read aloud the subjects and verbs in the rest of his revised essay.
4. Correct any subjects and verbs that do not agree. *The rest of the subjects and verbs agree.*

For help with subject-verb agreement, see Chapter 39.

Pronoun Agreement

1. Find any pronouns in your revision of Rick's essay that do not agree with their nouns. *All pronouns agree with their nouns.*
2. Correct any pronouns that do not agree with their nouns.

For help with pronoun agreement, see Chapter 43.

Modifier Errors

1. Find any modifiers in your revision of Rick's essay that are not as close as possible to the words they modify. *There are no modifier errors.*
2. Rewrite sentences if necessary so that modifiers are as close as possible to the words they modify.

For help with modifier errors, see Chapter 46.

Punctuation and Mechanics

Punctuation

1. Read your revision of Rick's essay for any errors in punctuation.
2. Make sure any fragments and run-together sentences you revised are punctuated correctly. *There are no punctuation errors.*

For help with punctuation, see Chapters 47–51.

Mechanics

1. Read your revisions of Rick's essay for any errors in capitalization.
2. Be sure to check the capitalization in the fragments and run-together sentences you revised. *All capitals are correct.*

For help with capitalization, see Chapter 52.

Word Choice and Spelling

Confused Words

1. Find any words used incorrectly in your revision of Rick's essay.
2. Did you find and correct the confused word? *passed/past (para. 7)*

For help with confused words, see Chapter 58.

Spelling

For help with spelling, see Chapter 59.

1. Use spell-check and a dictionary to check the spelling in your revision of Rick's essay. *dettermine/determine (para 3) and desicion/decision (para. 9)*

2. Did you find and correct his two misspelled words?

Now rewrite Rick's essay again with your editing corrections.

REVISING AND EDITING YOUR OWN ESSAY WITH SOURCES

Now revise and edit the essay that you wrote in Chapter 21. The questions below will help you apply the revising and editing checklists at the beginning of this chapter to your own writing.

Revising

Thesis Statement

1. What is the main idea of your essay with sources?

   _____

2. Put brackets around your thesis statement. Does it introduce your main idea?

   _____

3. How can you change it to introduce all the topics in your paper?

   _____

   _____

Basic Elements

1. Give your essay an alternative title.

   _____

2. Does your introduction capture the readers' attention and build up to the thesis statement at the end of the paragraph?

   _____

3. Does each of your body paragraphs deal with only one topic?

   _____

4. Does your conclusion bring the essay to a close in an interesting way?

   _____

Development

1. Do your topics support your thesis statement? List your revised thesis statement and your topics.

   Thesis: _____

   Topics: _____

   _____

   _____

2. Are your examples specific? Add another more specific detail to at least one of your paragraphs.

3. Do you furnish enough examples or details in each paragraph? Add at least one new example or detail to one of your paragraphs.

4. Check your sources to make sure they are relevant, reliable, and recent. Find new sources if necessary.

   For help, see Chapter 20.

5. Do you give references for all original sources in your paper to avoid plagiarism?

   For help, see Chapter 19.

6. Is the documentation format correct in your paper?

   For help, see Chapter 21.

7. Is the format on your Works Cited page correct?

   For help, see Chapter 21.

Unity

1. Read each of your topic sentences with your thesis statement in mind. Do they go together?

   _____

2. Revise them so that they are directly related.

3. Read each of your paragraphs with its topic sentence in mind.

4. Drop or rewrite any sentences in your body paragraphs not directly related to their topic sentences.

Organization

1. Review the list of your topics in item 1 under "Development," and decide if your topics are organized logically.

2. What is your method of organization?

   _____

3. Do you think your method of organization is the most effective one for your purpose? Explain your answer.

   _____

   _____

4. Read your essay again to see if all your sentences are arranged logically.

5. Move any sentences that are out of order.

Coherence

For a list of transitions, see pages 83–84.

1. Circle five transitions, repetitions, synonyms, or pronouns you use.

2. Explain how two of these make your essay easier to read.

   _____

   _____

   Now rewrite your essay with your revisions.

Editing

Sentences

Subjects and Verbs

For help with subjects and verbs, see Chapter 34.

1. In a paragraph of your choice, underline your subjects once and verbs twice. Remember that sentences can have more than one subject-verb set.

2. Does each sentence have at least one subject and verb that can stand alone?

   _____

For help with fragments, see Chapter 35.

For help with run-togethers, see Chapter 36.

3. Correct any fragments you have written.

4. Correct any run-together sentences you have written.

Subject-Verb Agreement

1. Read aloud the subjects and verbs you underlined in your revised essay.
2. Correct any subjects and verbs that do not agree.

For help with subject-verb agreement, see Chapter 39.

Pronoun Agreement

1. Find any pronouns in your revised essay that do not agree with their nouns.
2. Correct any pronouns that do not agree with their nouns.

For help with pronoun agreement, see Chapter 43.

Modifier Errors

1. Find any modifiers in your revised essay that are not as close as possible to the words they modify.
2. Rewrite sentences if necessary so that your modifiers are as close as possible to the words they modify.

For help with modifier errors, see Chapter 46.

Punctuation and Mechanics

Punctuation

1. Read your revised essay for any errors in punctuation.
2. Make sure any fragments and run-together sentences you revised are punctuated correctly.

For help with punctuation, see Chapters 47–51.

Mechanics

1. Read your revised essay for any errors in capitalization.
2. Be sure to check your capitalization if you revised any fragments or run-together sentences.

For help with capitalization, see Chapter 52.

Word Choice and Spelling

Confused Words

1. Find any words used incorrectly in your revised essay.
2. Correct any errors you find.

For help with confused words, see Chapter 58.

Spelling

1. Use spell-check and a dictionary to check your spelling.
2. Correct any misspelled words.

For help with spelling, see Chapter 59.

Now rewrite your essay again with your editing corrections.

WRITING WORKSHOP

Guidelines for Writing an Essay with Sources

1. Choose a subject.
2. Do some general reading, and write a good, clear thesis statement about your subject.
3. Find sources that are relevant, reliable, and recent to support your thesis statement.
4. Take notes to avoid plagiarism.
5. Make a working outline of your paper.
6. Construct an introduction that leads up to your thesis statement.
7. Develop as many supporting paragraphs or body paragraphs as you think are necessary to explain your thesis statement.
8. Make sure you use your sources as evidence for your argument.
9. Write a concluding paragraph.
10. Think of a catchy title.
11. Check your sources and documentation format throughout your paper and at the end.

---

1. Research the changes in the antidrug ads over the past five years. How have they changed? Are they more or less effective now? Write an essay explaining these changes.

2. Research a controversial political issue of your choice. Then take a firm stand on the issue, and develop an essay supporting your position. You might want to look at headlines in the newspaper to get some ideas for this assignment.

3. Research a special trip that you want to take. Get all the information you need. Then write a letter to a close friend, inviting him or her to join you.

4. Create your own assignment (with the help of your instructor), and write a response to it.

SERVICE LEARNING PROJECT

1. For the Service Learning project you have taken on, prepare a written document that will help the organization: a newsletter, a report, an ad, a brochure, a manual, a documentary, and so on. Use the guidelines you have learned in this chapter to help you.

2. Write a paper describing your service-learning experience and commenting on its significance to you. Refer to your notes in your journal if you recorded comments on your daily experiences with service learning. Use the guidelines you have learned in this chapter to help you.

Revising Workshop

Small Group Activity (10 minutes per writer)   In groups of three or four, each person should read his or her essay with sources to the other members of the group. The listeners should record their reactions on a copy of the Peer Evaluation Form in Appendix 3A. After your group goes through this process, give your evaluation forms to the appropriate writers so that each writer has two or three peer comment sheets for revising.

Paired Activity (5 minutes per writer)   Using the completed Peer Evaluation Forms, work in pairs to decide what you should revise in your essay. If time allows, rewrite some of your sentences, and have your partner check them.

Individual Activity   Rewrite your paper, using the revising feedback you received from other students.

Logical/ Mathematical

Research a special activity that you want to participate in. Get all the facts, including costs, time, and supplies needed. Then write a letter to your parents or guardians asking them to pay for or support this activity in some way. Try to convince them to see the event from your perspective.

Visual/Spatial

Draw a picture of an issue you would like to research. Then list the types of sources you would consult. Write an essay explaining your research plan.

Bodily/Kinesthetic

Produce a short scene from a play, TV show, or movie. Use costumes, create a small set, and choose music and lighting. If possible, videotape the performance. How hard was it to put the production together? Write an essay about the process you went through to produce this show.

Intrapersonal

Go to a children's play in your city, and watch children discover different aspects of the theater. Write an essay describing your observations.

Editing Workshop

Paired Activity (10 minutes per writer)   Swap papers with a classmate, and use the editing portion of your Peer Evaluation Forms to identify as many grammar, punctuation, mechanics, and spelling errors as you can. Mark the errors on the student paper with the correction symbols on the inside back cover. If time allows, correct some of your errors, and have your partner check them.

Individual Activity   Rewrite your paper again, using the editing feedback you received from other students. Record your grammar errors in the Error Log (Appendix 6) and your spelling errors in the Spelling Log (Appendix 7).

Reflecting on Your Writing

When you have completed your own essay, answer these six questions:

1. What was most difficult about this assignment?

2. What was easiest?

3. What did you learn about essays with sources by completing this assignment?

4. What do you think are the strengths of your essay with sources? Place a wavy line in the margin by the parts of your essay that you feel are very good.

5. What are the weaknesses, if any, of your paper? Place an X in the margin by the parts of your essay you would like help with. Write any questions you have in the margin.

6. What did you learn from this assignment about your own writing process—about preparing to write, about writing the first draft, about revising, and about editing?

IV

FROM READING TO WRITING

To read without reflecting is like eating without digesting.

—EDMUND BURKE

Part IV is a collection of essays that demonstrate the rhetorical modes you are studying in this book. Each chapter focuses on a different rhetorical strategy and presents two essays that show the strategy at work with other strategies. After each essay are questions that check your understanding of the selection. By charting your correct and incorrect responses to these questions in Appendix I, you will discover your general level of understanding.

CHAPTER 25

Describing

The following essays describe their subjects through an array of sensory details. The first, "El Hoyo," was written by Mario Suarez. In it, he describes the identity of a city. The second, "Dwellings" by Linda Hogan, discusses how different dwellings suit different people and animals.

Mario Suarez

EL HOYO

SUMMARY
Through sensory details, Suarez describes a small town near Tucson.

READABILITY
(Flesch–Kincaid grade level)
8.9

INSTRUCTOR'S RESOURCE MANUAL
For additional teaching strategies, for journal entries, for vocabulary and reading quizzes, and for more writing assignments, see the *Instructor's Resource Manual*, Section II, Part IV.

Focusing Your Attention

1. Think of a place from your childhood that had special meaning for you as you were growing up. Where was this place? Why was it special?

2. In the essay you are about to read, the writer recounts the many sights, sounds, smells, textures, and tastes that he connects with the place where he grew up. What sights, sounds, smells, textures, and tastes do you remember about the city, town, or farm where you grew up? Can you describe the place you grew up in for someone who has never been there?

Expanding Your Vocabulary

The following words are important to your understanding of this essay:

Tucson: city in southeastern Arizona (paragraph 1)
chicanos: Mexican Americans (paragraph 1)
padre: father, priest (paragraph 1)
paisanos: countrymen (paragraph 1)
bicker: quarrel (paragraph 1)
adobe: sun-dried brick (paragraph 1)
chavalos: small boys (paragraph 1)
inundated: flooded (paragraph 1)

Octavio Perea's Mexican Hour: Spanish radio program (paragraph 2)

"Smoke in the Eyes": song (paragraph 2)

solace: comfort (paragraph 2)

benevolent: kind (paragraph 2)

solicited: asked, begged (paragraph 2)

señora: married woman (paragraph 2)

chicanas: Mexican American females (paragraph 2)

Baja California: peninsula along the western coast of Mexico (paragraph 2)

boleros: music for Spanish dances (paragraph 3)

comadres: gossiping women (paragraph 3)

bloodwell: family ancestry (paragraph 3)

conquistador: a Spanish conqueror (paragraph 3)

capirotada: Mexican bread pudding (paragraph 4)

panocha: corn (paragraph 4)

Sermeños: family name (paragraph 4)

From the center of downtown Tucson the ground slopes gently away to 1
Main Street, drops a few feet, and then rolls to the banks of the Santa Cruz River. Here lies the section of the city known as El Hoyo. Why it is called El Hoyo is not very clear. In no sense is it a hole as its name would imply; it is simply the river's immediate valley. Its inhabitants are chicanos who raise hell on Saturday night and listen to Padre Estanislao on Sunday morning. While the term chicano is the short way of saying Mexicano, it is not restricted to the paisanos who came from old Mexico with the territory or the last famine to work for the railroad, labor, sing, and go on relief. Chicano is the easy way of referring to everybody. Pablo Gutíerrez married the Chinese grocer's daughter and now runs a meat department; his sons are chicanos. So are the sons of Killer Jones who threw a fight in Harlem and fled to El Hoyo to marry Cristina Mendez. And so are all of them. However, it is doubtful that all these spiritual sons of Mexico live in El Hoyo because they love each other—many fight and bicker constantly. It is doubtful they live in El Hoyo because of its scenic beauty—it is everything but beautiful. Its houses are simple affairs of unplastered adobe, wood, and abandoned car parts. Its narrow streets are mostly clearings which have, in time, acquired names. Except for some tall trees which nobody has ever cared to identify, nurse, or destroy, the main things known to grow in the general area are weeds, garbage piles, dark-eyed chavalos, and dogs.

And it is doubtful that the chicanos live in El Hoyo because it is safe—many times the Santa Cruz has risen and inundated the area.

2   In other respects, living in El Hoyo has its advantages. If one is born with a weakness for acquiring bills, El Hoyo is where the collectors are less likely to find you. If one has acquired the habit of listening to Octavio Perea's Mexican Hour in the wee hours of the morning with the radio on at full blast, El Hoyo is where you are less likely to be reported to the authorities. Besides, Perea is very popular and sooner or later to everyone "Smoke in the Eyes" is dedicated between the pinto beans and white flour commercials. If one, for any reason whatever, comes on an extended period of hard times, where, if not in El Hoyo, are the neighbors more willing to offer solace? When Teofila Malacara's house burned to the ground with all her belongings and two children, a benevolent gentleman carried through the gesture that made tolerable her burden. He made a list of five hundred names and solicited from each a dollar. At the end of a month, he turned over to the tearful but grateful señora one hundred dollars in cold cash and then accompanied her on a short vacation. When the new manager of a local store decided that no more chicanas were to work behind the counters, it was the chicanos of El Hoyo who, on taking their individually small but collectively great buying power elsewhere, drove the manager out and the girls returned to their jobs. When the Mexican Army was en route to Baja, California, and the chicanos found out that the enlisted men ate only at infrequent intervals, it was El Hoyo's chicanos who crusaded across town with pots of beans and trays of tortillas to meet the train. When someone gets married, celebrating is not restricted to the immediate friends of the couple. Everybody is invited. Anything calls for a celebration, and a celebration calls for anything. On Memorial Day there are no less than half a dozen good fights at the Riverside Dance Hall. On Mexican Independence Day, more than one flag is sworn allegiance to amid cheers for the queen.

3   And El Hoyo is something more. It is this something more which brought Felipe Sanchez back from the wars after having killed a score of Vietnamese with his body resembling a patchwork quilt to marry Julia Armijo. It brought Joe Zepeda, a gunner, . . . back to compose boleros. He has a metal plate for a skull. Perhaps El Hoyo is proof that those people exist, and perhaps exist best, who have as yet failed to observe the more popular modes of human conduct. Perhaps the humble appearance of El Hoyo justifies the indifferent shrug of those made aware of its existence. Perhaps El Hoyo's simplicity motivates an occasional chicano to move away from its narrow streets, babbling comadres, and shrieking children to deny the bloodwell from which he springs and to claim the blood of a conquistador while his hair is straight and his face beardless. Yet El Hoyo is

ANSWERS TO
QUESTIONS
*Thinking Critically
About Content*
1. According to Suarez, *el hoyo* means "a hole" (para. 1).
2. Answers will vary. Here are some possibilities.
seeing
   "unplastered adobe, wood, and abandoned car parts" (para. 1)
   "body resembling a patchwork quilt" (para. 3)
   "his hair is straight and his face beardless" (para. 3)
hearing
   "many fight and bicker constantly" (para. 1)
   "radio on at full blast" (para. 2)
   "babbling comadres and shrieking children" (para. 3)
touching
   "metal plate for a skull" (para. 3)
   "hard bread" (para. 4)
smelling or tasting
   "pots of beans and trays of tortillas" (para. 2)
   "cooked with peanuts, raisins, onions, cheese, and panocha" (para. 4)

not an outpost of a few families against the world. It fights for no causes except those which soothe its immediate angers. It laughs and cries with the same amount of passion in times of plenty and of want.

Perhaps El Hoyo, its inhabitants, and its essence can best be explained by telling a bit about a dish called capirotada. Its origin is uncertain. But, according to the time and the circumstance, it is made of old, new, or hard bread. It is softened with water and then cooked with peanuts, raisins, onions, cheese, and panocha. It is fired with sherry wine. Then it is served hot, cold, or just "on the weather" as they say in El Hoyo. The Sermeños like it one way, the Garcias another, and the Ortegas still another. While it might differ greatly from one home to another; nevertheless, it is still capirotada. And so it is with El Hoyo's chicanos. While being divided from within and from without, like the capirotada, they remain chicanos.

4

Thinking Critically About Content

1. What does *el hoyo* mean, according to the author?

2. List two details from this essay for each of the five senses: seeing, hearing, touching, smelling, and tasting. How do these details show rather than tell the readers the writer's impressions of El Hoyo?

3. What is the main reason people choose to live in El Hoyo?

Thinking Critically About Purpose and Audience

4. What dominant impression does the writer create in this description? Explain your answer in detail.

5. Do you think readers who have never been to this place can appreciate and enjoy this essay? Why or why not?

6. What details about El Hoyo are most interesting to you? Why do you find them interesting?

Thinking Critically About Essays

7. If an essay is unified, all of its paragraphs are related to one central idea. Based on this explanation, is this essay unified? Explain your answer.

8. How does Suarez organize his ideas and observations in this essay? (Refer to pages 45–57 for information on organization.) Make a rough outline of the essay.

9. Suarez ends his essay with an analogy that compares El Hoyo to a dish called *capirotada*. Is this an effective end for his essay? Why or why not?

10. Describe as fully as possible the inner feelings of the narrator from inside El Hoyo on a typical day.

3. People live in El Hoyo to be in a small community where people care about one another and to "remain chicanos" (para. 4).

Thinking Critically About Purpose and Audience

4. The dominant impression is a sense of community. He creates this by explaining all the ways the people help each other in El Hoyo.

5. Anyone can appreciate this essay because of Suarez's vivid descriptions.

6. Answers will vary.

Thinking Critically About Essays

7. The essay is unified because all the paragraphs describe different aspects of El Hoyo.

8. Suarez organizes his ideas from least to most important.

paragraph 1: background of town
paragraph 2: description of people
paragraph 3: feeling of community
paragraph 4: comparison to *capirotada*

9. The comparison in paragraph 4 is effective because it refers to the discussion of *chicano* in paragraph 1 and shows readers why chicanos like to live in the town.

10. The narrator feels at peace in El Hoyo. Beyond this, answers will vary.

Linda Hogan

DWELLINGS

SUMMARY
Hogan shows readers
habitats of various peo-
ple and animals and
explains why each
dwelling is suitable for
its residents.

READABILITY
(Flesch–Kincaid grade
level)
8.5

INSTRUCTOR'S
RESOURCE MANUAL
For additional teaching
strategies, for journal
entries, for vocabulary
and reading quizzes,
and for more writing
assignments, see the
*Instructor's Resource
Manual,* Section II,
Part IV.

Focusing Your Attention

1. Think about the place you currently live. Does it serve your purposes? In what ways?

2. The essay you are about to read describes different habitats that
   suit different animals and humans. If you could move to a new
   "dwelling," where would you go? Why?

Expanding Your Vocabulary

The following words are important to your understanding of this essay:

eroded: worn down (paragraph 1)

Anasazi: Indian tribe (paragraph 1)

excavations: caves, holes in the earth (paragraph 1)

beetle: jut, project (paragraph 1)

catacombs: tunnels, hollowed-out passageways, burial places
(paragraph 2)

droning: monotonous (paragraph 3)

sanctuary: safe place (paragraph 6)

troglodite: caveman (paragraph 7)

utopia: ideal place (paragraph 7)

felled: cut down (paragraph 8)

spired: rising like a church steeple (paragraph 9)

fledglings: baby birds just learning to fly (paragraph 9)

arid: dry (paragraph 10)

pellets: animal droppings (paragraph 13)

fetal: newborn (paragraph 13)

downy: soft (paragraph 14)

rafter: roof beam (paragraph 14)

Zia Pueblo: an Indian village (paragraph 15)

shards: broken pieces (paragraph 15)

sage: an herb (paragraph 16)

Not far from where I live is a hill that was cut into by the moving water of a creek. Eroded this way, all that's left of it is a broken wall of earth that contains old roots and pebbles woven together and exposed. Seen from a distance, it is only a rise of raw earth. But up close it is something wonderful, a small cliff dwelling that looks almost as intricate and well made as those the Anasazi left behind when they vanished mysteriously centuries ago. This hill is a place that could be the starry skies at night turned inward into the thousand round holes where solitary bees have lived and died. It is a hill of tunneling rooms. At the mouths of some of the excavations, half-circles of clay beetle out like awnings shading a doorway. It is earth that was turned to clay in the mouths of the bees and spit out as they mined deeper into their dwelling places.

This place is where the bees reside at an angle safe from rain. It faces the southern sun. It is a warm and intelligent architecture of memory, learned by whatever memory lives in the blood. Many of the holes still contain gold husks of dead bees, their faces dry and gone, their flat eyes gazing out from death's land toward the other uninhabited half of the hill that is across the creek from the catacombs.

The first time I found the residence of the bees, it was dusty summer. The sun was hot, and land was the dry color of rust. Now and then a car rumbled along the dirt road, and dust rose up behind it before settling back down on older dust. In the silence, the bees made a soft droning hum. They were alive then and working the hill, going out and returning with pollen, in and out through the holes, back and forth between daylight and the cooler, darker regions of the inner earth. They were flying an invisible map through air, a map charted by landmarks, the slant of light, and a circling story they told one another about the direction of food held inside the center of yellow flowers.

Sitting in the hot sun, watching the small bees fly in and out around the hill, hearing the summer birds, the light breeze, I felt right in the world. I belonged there. I thought of my own dwelling places, those real and those imagined. Once I lived in a town called Manitou, which means "Great Spirit," where hot mineral springwater gurgled beneath the streets and rose into open wells. I felt safe there. With the underground movement of water and heat a constant reminder of other life, of what lives beneath us, it seemed to be the center of the world.

A few years after that, I wanted silence. My daydreams were full of places I longed to be, shelters and solitudes. I wanted a room apart from others, a hidden cabin to rest in. I wanted to be in a redwood forest with trees so tall the owls called out in the daytime. I daydreamed of living in a vapor cave a few hours away from here. Underground, warm, and moist, I thought it would be the perfect world for staying out of cold winter, for escaping the noise of living.

6   And how often I've wanted to escape to a wilderness where a human hand has not been in everything. But those were only dreams of peace, of comfort, of a nest inside stone or woods, a sanctuary where a dream or life wouldn't be invaded.

7   Years ago, in the next canyon west of here, there was a man who followed one of those dreams and moved into a cave that could only be reached by climbing down a rope. For years he lived there in comfort, like a troglodite. The inner weather was stable, never too hot, too cold, too wet, or too dry. But then he felt lonely. His utopia needed a woman. He went to town until he found a wife. For a while after the marriage, his wife climbed down the rope along with him, but before long she didn't want the mice scurrying about in the cave or the untidy bats that wanted to hang from the stones of the ceiling. So they built a door. Because of the closed entryway, the temperature changed. They had to put in heat. Then the inner moisture of earth warped the door, so they had to have air-conditioning, and after that the earth wanted to go about life in its own way, and it didn't give in to the people.

8   In other days and places, people paid more attention to the strong-headed will of earth. Once homes were built of wood that had been felled from a single region in a forest. That way, it was thought, the house would hold together more harmoniously, and the family of walls would not fall or lend themselves to the unhappiness or arguments of the inhabitants.

9   An Italian immigrant to Chicago, Aldo Piacenzi, built birdhouses that were dwellings of harmony and peace. They were the incredible spired shapes of cathedrals in Italy. They housed not only the birds, but also his memories, his own past. He painted them the watery blue of his Mediterranean, the wild rose of flowers in a summer field. Inside them was straw and the droppings of lives that laid eggs, fledglings who grew there. What places to inhabit, the bright and sunny birdhouses in dreary alleyways of the city.

10   One beautiful afternoon, cool and moist, with the kind of yellow light that falls on earth in these arid regions, I waited for barn swallows to return from their daily work of food gathering. Inside the tunnel where they live, hundreds of swallows had mixed their saliva with mud and clay, much like the solitary bees, and formed nests that were perfect as a potter's bowl. At five in the evening, they returned all at once, a dark, flying shadow.

Despite their enormous numbers and the crowding together of nests, they didn't pause for even a moment before entering the nests, nor did they crowd one another. Instantly they vanished into the nests. The tunnel went silent. It held no outward signs of life.

But I knew they were there, filled with the fire of living. And what a marriage of elements was in those nests. Not only mud's earth and water, the fire of sun and dry air, but even the elements contained one another. The bodies of prophets and crazy men were broken down in that soil.

I've noticed often how, when a house is abandoned, it begins to sag. Without a tenant, it has no need to go on. If it were a person, we'd say it is depressed or lonely. The roof settles in, the paint cracks, the walls and floorboards warp and slope downward in their own natural ways, telling us that life must stay in everything as the world whirls and tilts and moves through boundless space.

One summer day, cleaning up after long-eared owls where I work at a rehabilitation facility for birds of prey, I was raking the gravel floor of a flight cage. Down on the ground, something looked like it was moving. I bent over to look into the pile of bones and pellets I'd just raked together. There, close to the ground, were two fetal mice. They were new to the planet, pink and hairless. They were so tenderly young. Their faces had swollen blue-veined eyes. They were nestled in a mound of feathers, soft as velvet, each one curled up smaller than an infant's ear, listening to the first sounds of earth. But the ants were biting them. They turned in agony, unable to pull away, not yet having the arms or legs to move, but feeling, twisting away from the pain of the bites. I was horrified to see them bitten out of life that way. I dipped them in water, as if to take away the sting, and let the ants fall in the bucket. Then I held the tiny mice in the palm of my hand. Some of the ants were drowning in the water. I was trading one life for another, exchanging the lives of the ants for those of mice, but I hated their suffering, and hated even more that they had not yet grown to a life, and already they inhabited the miserable world of pain. Death and life feed each other. I know that.

Inside these rooms where birds are healed, there are other lives besides those of mice. There are fine gray globes the wasps have woven together, the white cocoons of spiders in a corner, the downward tunneling anthills. All these dwellings are inside one small walled space, but I think most about the mice. Sometimes the downy nests fall out of the walls where their mothers have placed them out of the way of their enemies. They are so well made and soft, woven mostly from the chest feathers of birds.

white cocoons
of spiders in a
corner, the down-
ward tunneling
anthills"
(para. 14)
hearing
"moving water of a
creek" (para. 1)
"soft droning hum"
(para. 3)
"hearing the
summer birds"
(para. 4)
touching
"faces the southern
sun" (para. 2)
"cooler, darker
regions of the
inner earth"
(para. 3)
"light breeze"
(para. 4)
tasting
"turned to clay in
the mouths of
bees" (para. 1)
"mixed their saliva
with mud and
clay" (para. 10)
"wild grapes would
soon ripen on the
vines" (para. 17)
smelling
No smelling descrip-
tions are in the
essay.
3. Hogan is referring to
her environment that
seems to be perfect as
"the center of the
world." Because
nothing is wrong there,
everything else must
revolve around it.

*Thinking Critically
About Purpose and
Audience*
4. The dominant
impression is that being
able to adapt is
essential in nature.

Sometimes the leg of a small quail holds the nest together like a slender cornerstone with dry, bent claws. The mice have adapted to life in the presence of their enemies, adapted to living in the thin wall between beak and beak, claw and claw. They move their nests often, as if a new rafter or wall will protect them from the inevitable fate of all our returns home to the deeper, wider nests of earth that houses us all.

15   One August at Zia Pueblo during the corn dance, I noticed tourists picking up shards of all the old pottery that had been made and broken there. The residents of Zia know not to take the bowls and pots left behind by the older ones. They know that the fragments of those earlier lives need to be smoothed back to earth, but younger nations, travelers from continents across the world who have come to inhabit this land, have little of their own to grow on. The pieces of earth that were formed into bowls, even on their way home to dust, provide the new people a lifeline to an unknown land, help them remember that they live in the old nest of earth.

16   It was in early February, during the mating season of the great horned owl. It was dusk, and I hiked up the back of a mountain to where I'd heard the owls a year before. I wanted to hear them again, the voices so tender, so deep, like a memory of comfort. I was halfway up the trail when I found a soft, round nest. It had fallen from one of the bare-branched trees. It was a delicate nest, woven together of feathers, sage, and strands of wild grass. Holding it in my hand in the rosy twilight, I noticed that a blue thread was entwined with the other gatherings there. I pulled at the thread a little, and then I recognized it. It was a thread from one of my skirts. It was blue cotton. It was the unmistakable color and shape of a pattern I knew. I liked it, that a thread of my life was in an abandoned nest, one that had held eggs and new life. I took the nest home. At home, I held it to the light and looked more closely. There, to my surprise, nestled into the gray-green sage, was a gnarl of black hair. It was also unmistakable. It was my daughter's hair, cleaned from a brush and picked up out in the sun beneath the maple tree or the pit cherry where the birds eat from the overladen, fertile branches until only the seeds remain on the trees.

17   I didn't know what kind of nest it was or who had lived there. It didn't matter. I thought of the remnants of our lives carried up the hill that way and turned into shelter. That night, resting inside the walls of our home, the world outside weighed so heavily against the thin wood of the house. The sloped roof was the only thing between us and the universe. Everything outside of our wooden boundaries seemed so large. Filled with the night's citizens, it all came alive. The world opened in the thickets of the dark. The

wild grapes would soon ripen on the vines. The burrowing ones were emerging. Horned owls sat in treetops. Mice scurried here and there. Skunks, fox, the slow and holy porcupine, all were passing by this way. The young of the solitary bees were feeding on the pollen in the dark. The whole world was a nest on its humble tilt, in the maze of the universe, holding us.

Thinking Critically About Content

1. How do the dwellings Hogan describes suit their inhabitants? Refer to two specific dwellings to answer this question.

2. Find at least one detail for each of the five senses: seeing, hearing, touching, smelling, and tasting. Does Hogan draw on any one sense more than the others?

3. In paragraph 4, what is Hogan referring to as "the center of the world"? Explain your answer.

Thinking Critically About Purpose and Audience

4. What dominant impression does Hogan create in this essay?

5. Who do you think Hogan's primary audience is?

6. Explain your understanding of this essay's title.

Thinking Critically About Essays

7. Each section of Hogan's essay is about a different dwelling. Is each section unified? Look at the topic sentence of paragraph 7. Do all the sentences in this paragraph relate to its topic sentence? Explain your answer.

8. If a paragraph is coherent, it is considered logical and easy to read. Often, well-chosen transitions help a writer achieve coherence. (Refer to pages 83–84 for a list of transitions.) Underline the words, phrases, and clauses Hogan uses as transitions in paragraph 13. How do these transitions help this paragraph read smoothly? Explain your answer.

9. Look at Hogan's conclusion. Is it effective for this essay? How does the last sentence ("The whole world was a nest on its humble tilt, in the maze of the universe, holding us") tie the whole essay together?

10. Describe in detail what you think the secret to a perfect dwelling is.

---

5. Hogan's primary audience is general readers.
6. The title refers to the different habitats used by the various people and animals described in the essay.

Thinking Critically About Essays
7. The topic sentence of paragraph 7 is "Years ago, in the next canyon west of here, there was a man who followed one of those dreams and moved into a cave that could only be reached by climbing down a rope." The paragraph is unified because all sentences after this refer to his life in the cave.
8. Transitions in paragraph 13 include "One summer day," "Down on the ground," "There," "But," and "Then." The transitions help the paragraph read smoothly by giving the readers indications of shifts in focus or time and showing changes in emphasis.
9. Hogan's conclusion is effective because Hogan is showing how the earth itself is a dwelling for all of its creatures. It ties the essay together because she is referring to the biggest dwelling of all, the one that encompasses all other dwellings.
10. Answers will vary.

Writing Topics: Describing

Before you begin to write, you might want to review the writing process in Part I.

1. In the first descriptive essay, Mario Suarez draws on impressions from all the senses to describe this *barrio*. Think of a place that is very important to you, a place that is a part of your life now or that was a part of your life in the past. Write a description of that place, drawing on as many of the senses as possible—seeing, hearing, touching, smelling, and tasting—so that your reader can experience it the way you did.

2. How well suited to you is the place where you live now? Write a description of the features of your house or apartment that make it most suitable or unsuitable for you.

3. What do you think are the most important features of a good description? Why are they important? What effect do they have on you?

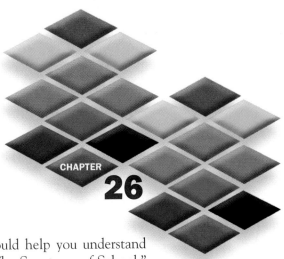

Narrating

The two essays included in this chapter should help you understand more clearly how to write narrative essays. In "The Sanctuary of School," author Lynda Barry recalls an event that occurred during a particularly painful period of her life. In the second essay, "Writer's Retreat" by Stan Higgins, the author tells a story about writing from a prison cell.

Lynda Barry

THE SANCTUARY OF SCHOOL

Focusing Your Attention

1. Can you recall a time in your life when you felt particularly lonely or afraid? Write down as many facts, impressions, and memories as you can recall about that period of your life.

2. In the essay you are about to read, the writer describes a person who had a lasting impact on her. Do you think you have ever had such an important impact on someone that he or she would write an essay about you? Have you had such an impact on more than one person? Who are these people? What would they say about you in their recollections?

Expanding Your Vocabulary

The following words are important to your understanding of this essay:

sanctuary: safe place (title)

nondescript: not distinctive (paragraph 7)

monkey bars: playground equipment (paragraph 8)

breezeway: covered passage between two buildings (paragraph 13)

I was 7 years old the first time I snuck out of the house in the dark. It was winter, and my parents had been fighting all night. They were short on

SUMMARY

Barry explains why her school was a sanctuary in her life and recalls one morning when she particularly needed the safety within its walls.

READABILITY

(Flesch–Kincaid grade level)
8.9

INSTRUCTOR'S RESOURCE MANUAL

For additional teaching strategies, for journal entries, for vocabulary and reading quizzes, and for more writing assignments, see the *Instructor's Resource Manual*, Section II, Part IV.

1

money and long on relatives who kept "temporarily" moving into our house because they had nowhere else to go.

2   My brother and I were used to giving up our bedroom. We slept on the couch, something we actually liked because it put us that much closer to the light of our lives, our television.

3   At night when everyone was asleep, we lay on our pillows watching it with the sound off. We watched Steve Allen's mouth moving. We watched Johnny Carson's mouth moving. We watched movies filled with gangsters shooting machine guns into packed rooms, dying soldiers hurling a last grenade, and beautiful women crying at windows. Then the sign-off finally came, and we tried to sleep.

4   The morning I snuck out, I woke up filled with a panic about needing to get to school. The sun wasn't quite up yet, but my anxiety was so fierce that I just got dressed, walked quietly across the kitchen, and let myself out the back door.

5   It was quiet outside. Stars were still out. Nothing moved, and no one was in the street. It was as if someone had turned the sound off on the world.

6   I walked the alley, breaking thin ice over the puddles with my shoes. I didn't know why I was walking to school in the dark. I didn't think about it. All I knew was the feeling of panic, like the panic that strikes kids when they realize they are lost.

7   That feeling eased the moment I turned the corner and saw the dark outline of my school at the top of the hill. My school was made up of about 15 nondescript portable classrooms set down on a fenced concrete lot in a rundown Seattle neighborhood, but it had the most beautiful view of the Cascade Mountains. You could see them from anywhere on the playfield, and you could see them from the windows of my classroom—Room 2.

8   I walked over to the monkey bars and hooked my arms around the cold metal. I stood for a long time just looking across Rainier Valley. The sky was beginning to whiten, and I could hear a few birds.

9   In a perfect world, my absence at home would not have gone unnoticed. I would have had two parents in a panic to locate me, instead of two parents in a panic to locate an answer to the hard question of survival during a deep financial and emotional crisis.

10   But in an overcrowded and unhappy home, it's incredibly easy for any child to slip away. The high levels of frustration, depression, and anger in my house made my brother and me invisible. We were children with the sound turned off. And for us, as for the steadily increasing number of neglected children in this country, the only place where we could count on being noticed was at school.

11   "Hey there, young lady. Did you forget to go home last night?" It was Mr. Gunderson, our janitor, whom we all loved. He was nice and he was

funny and he was old with white hair, thick glasses, and an unbelievable number of keys. I could hear them jingling as he walked across the playfield. I felt incredibly happy to see him.

He let me push his wheeled garbage can between the different porta- 12 bles as he unlocked each room. He let me turn on the lights and raise the window shades, and I saw my school slowly come to life. I saw Mrs. Holman, our school secretary, walk into the office without her orange lipstick on yet. She waved.

I saw the fifth-grade teacher, Mr. Cunningham, walking under the 13 breezeway eating a hard roll. He waved.

And I saw my teacher, Mrs. Claire LeSane, walking toward us in a red 14 coat and calling my name in a very happy and surprised way, and suddenly my throat got tight and my eyes stung and I ran toward her crying. It was something that surprised both of us.

It's only thinking about it now, 28 years later, that I realize I was crying 15 from relief. I was with my teacher, and in a while I was going to sit at my desk, with my crayons and pencils and books and classmates all around me, and for the next six hours I was going to enjoy a thoroughly secure, warm, and stable world. It was a world I absolutely relied on. Without it, I don't know where I would have gone that morning.

Mrs. LeSane asked me what was wrong, and when I said, "Nothing," 16 she seemingly left it at that. But she asked me if I would carry her purse for her, an honor above all honors, and she asked if I wanted to come into Room 2 early and paint.

She believed in the natural healing power of painting and drawing for 17 troubled children. In the back of her room there was always a drawing table and an easel with plenty of supplies, and sometimes during the day she would come up to you for what seemed like no good reason and quietly ask if you wanted to go to the back table and "make some pictures for Mrs. LeSane." We all had a chance at it—to sit apart from the class for a while to paint, draw, and silently work out impossible problems on 11 × 17 sheets of newsprint.

Drawing came to mean everything to me. At the back table in Room 2, I 18 learned to build myself a life preserver that I could carry into my home. . . .

By the time the bell rang that morning, I had finished my drawing, 19 and Mrs. LeSane pinned it up on the special bulletin board she reserved for drawings from the back table. It was the same picture I always drew—a sun in the corner of a blue sky over a nice house with flowers all around it.

Thinking Critically About Content

1. Notice the way in which the writer describes herself and her brother as "children with the sound turned off" (paragraph 10) and

5. Anyone can appreciate this essay, but readers who have similar home lives will probably understand it best.

6. She probably excludes this information because she doesn't want to put the focus on her parents, and ultimately, their problems don't excuse their behavior.

Thinking Critically About Essays

7. The writer believes that her school is a safe retreat from the rest of the world.

8. Her details are arranged chronologically, which is effective for this essay.

9. The title describes her feelings for the school, which is her sanctuary away from a disturbing home life.

10. If written by Barry's parents, this essay would probably discuss the selfish nature of an ungrateful child. Beyond this, answers will vary.

their environment "as if someone had turned the sound off on the world" (paragraph 5). Is this an effective image? Why? What effect does it have on you? What does it tell you about Lynda Barry's childhood?

2. Why do you think the writer used warm and vivid details to describe the arrival of school employees (paragraphs 11 through 16)? What effect does this description have on you, compared with the description of her home life?

3. Did this essay make you compare your own childhood to Lynda Barry's?

Thinking Critically About Purpose and Audience

4. What do you think Barry's purpose is in writing this narrative essay? Explain your answer.

5. What readers do you think would most understand and appreciate this recollection?

6. In your opinion, why doesn't the writer tell us more about her parents' problems?

Thinking Critically About Essays

7. Describe in a complete sentence the writer's point of view in this essay.

8. How does Barry organize the details in this essay? Is this an effective order?

9. Explain Barry's title for this essay.

10. Explain in detail how this essay would be different if it were written by Lynda Barry's parents.

Stan Higgins

WRITER'S RETREAT

SUMMARY

Higgins, an inmate in prison, ironically talks about his writing getaway, where he attempts to write amid numerous interruptions.

Focusing Your Attention

1. Can you remember a time in your life when you were frustrated trying to meet a goal you set for yourself? Write down as many facts, impressions, and memories as you can about this feeling.

2. In the essay you are about to read, the writer describes a person who is trying to write in prison. What do you think is his motivation?

Have you ever wanted to do something so much you would even do it in prison? Explain your answer.

Expanding Your Vocabulary

The following words are important to your understanding of this essay:

within a pole vault: a few yards away (paragraph 1)

the Muse: inspiration (paragraph 2)

staccato: consisting of short, sharp sounds (paragraph 2)

ransacked: torn apart (paragraph 3)

confiscated: taken away (paragraph 3)

contraband: prohibited items (paragraph 3)

lock down: lock all prisoners in their cells (paragraph 4)

Bugler: brand of tobacco (paragraph 7)

mud: coffee (paragraph 16)

tier: row of prison cells (paragraph 23)

persevere: continue (paragraph 30)

tantamount: equal (paragraph 32)

misdemeanors: minor crimes (paragraph 32)

subsides: decreases (paragraph 34)

nebulous: vague, uncertain (paragraph 34)

girth: size (paragraph 41)

obscenities: offensive comments (paragraph 42)

READABILITY
(Flesch–Kincaid grade level)
9.8

INSTRUCTOR'S RESOURCE MANUAL
For additional teaching strategies, for journal entries, for vocabulary and reading quizzes, and for more writing assignments, see the *Instructor's Resource Manual*, Section II, Part IV.

1   Sandwiched between mountain snow and desert sand, hidden by sandstone walls 150 years old within a pole vault of the Arkansas River, it just doesn't get any better than this writer's retreat I call home. I write from a Colorado prison cell.

2   During the day I wash dishes, clean tables, and mop floors. They call it Vocational Training. And today, as every day at three P.M., I return to my cozy, bathroom-size suite and drag out my tiny portable. We've all night, just the two of us, my blue typewriter that has been my steady cell-mate for six years, through seven facilities across two states, and I. Today's goal is three pages. I blow dust from the cover and clean the keys. The Muse calls. *Tack-tack. Tack. Tack-tack-tack.* My typewriter sings its staccato song as I search for a fertile word or idea, some harmonious junction of thought and paper. Locked in solitary combat with my machine, nothing exists outside my cell, or so I pretend. I type a line. My door opens. Two blue-uniformed guards stand there grinning. "Guess what?" one says. "Your number came up."

3   Somehow I know he doesn't mean the Lottery. One begins searching my cell. The other pats me down as I leave. I return twenty minutes later to find my house ransacked, my bed torn up, papers scattered, pencils and pens strewn about, sox, shorts, and typewriter piled in a heap on the floor. Taped to the shelf above my desk is a slip of yellow paper with a fancily scrawled list of books, magazines, and other confiscated contraband. I can't help but question their appreciation for the written word.

4   I put my house back in order. We lock down, and the guards count us. After ten minutes the Count is cleared. My hands tremble. I can't write, not now. It's time for the ultimate challenge to a prisoner's courage . . . Chow!

5   Buoyed at having survived another meal, I return to my cell and begin anew. *Tack-tack-tack.*

6   "Hey, Bro," a green-uniformed inmate named O'Neil hollers from my doorway. "Think I can get a pinch of tobacco?"

7   This, too, is part of the territory. I pause to hand him a can of Bugler. My attention returns to writing as I study the list of disjointed, unrelated words I have accumulated, but I see out of the corner of my eye that I still have company.

8   "Think I can get a rolling paper?" O'Neil asks as he pops the lid off the can.

9   With a deep breath I fish him a pack of papers from my pocket and hand them over. He fumbles with the paper as I reread my typed words.

10   "Think you could roll it for me, Bro?"

11   "What else, O'Neil?" I say whisking the paper and tobacco from his hands and rolling him a quick, crooked cigarette. He asks for a light as I usher him to the door.

12   *Tack-tack-tack-tack,* I resume. Just more words. I pinch my lips and study the nearly blank sheet of paper. *Write what you know,* memories of books past suggest. What do I know? Steel and concrete, jingling keys, and slamming doors. *Tack-tack-tack. Tack-tack.*

13   "M-m-Mr. Higgins?" another prisoner interrupts. It's a skinny kid in oversize greens, and his voice squeaks. "W-would you maybe have a dictionary I could, you know, sorta read, please?" He hesitates at the door in his stiff, fresh-out-of-the-package uniform that reminds me of pajamas, eyeing my bookshelf from a safe distance until I stand. I pull a *Webster's New Collegiate Dictionary* from my shelf above the desk and sit down again as he thumbs through it. He clears his throat. "Uh, excuse me, how do you spell *the*?"

14   "With two *r*'s instead of one," I tell him, shooing him away with the back of my hand.

15   *Tack-tack. Tack-tack, tack-tack-tack, tack.* Bones of steel, concrete skin, I type, and a soul as slippery as time.

Digger B. struts into my house. "Ya got a cup a mud I can get or what?" 16
He pushes his empty cup in front of me, and as I fill it, he peers over my
shoulder. "So what ya doin'?"

"Trying to write about trying to write." 17

"Man," he says and slurps coffee from his cup. "Whyn't ya write about 18
somethin' interestin', know what I mean? Murder, war, sex, ya know—
interestin'!"

I love encouragement. He wanders out. 19

I stare at my typewriter. I wait a few minutes. Nothing. My fingers creep 20
back into place. *Tack-tack-tack.*

"Got a weed?" asks a gruff voice. It's Thunder. Six-foot-six and almost as 21
wide, 300 pounds of beard and tattoo, he slides sideways into my cell. I
quickly roll him a cigarette and light it.

"Anything else, Mr. Thunder?" 22

"Heared you typing clean down the tier," he grumbles. "What you 23
doing?"

"Typing. Trying to type. Trying to write, I guess." 24

"You ain't writing 'bout me, are you?" He stares at me with eyes like 25
rocks.

"No, sir, Mr. Thunder," I assure him, pointing to my almost blank paper. 26
"Check it out."

He squints at it. "Don't like people writing 'bout me 'hind my back." 27

"I wouldn't do that, Mr. Thunder." 28

"Just so you ain't. 'At's all I care." He turns and sidles out the doorway. 29
Thunder is unpredictable. Thunder hears voices. Thunder caught a guy in
the shower once and stabbed him 53 times with a sharpened Number 2
pencil; he thought the man was talking about him. All in all, I figure it's not
a bad idea to get along with Mr. Thunder.

The sun is setting. I've completed three sentences. My goal of three 30
pages for the day is becoming as gray as my cell. At this rate I'm confident
I can finish an 800-word article by my 2006 discharge date. *Persevere!* I get
up and flip on the light.

Back to my typewriter; back on track. *Tack-tack-tack. Tack-tack, tack-* 31
tackity-tack. I'm into it finally, my head is there, I'm on the verge of something . . . when Thunder stops at my door and pokes his woolly head in.
"You sure you ain't writing things 'bout me?"

In prison, opening a can of tobacco, a bag of potato chips, or brewing a 32
pot of coffee—like trying to type—is tantamount to throwing a side of beef
into shark-infested waters. But these are minor distractions . . . misdemeanors. Prison overcrowding being what it is, Colorado officials have on

several occasions sent inmates to faraway places for temporary storage. Two years ago guards came to my door with a green duffel bag and ordered me to pack up. I surveyed my four-year accumulation of books, magazines, and notes that converted my six-by-ten-foot cell into a private classroom. Each book and magazine, then highlighted for frequent reference, had been a hard-collected treasure. There were works-in-progress scattered on my desk. "Now!" a guard encouraged. "You're going to Washington state. If your stuff don't all fit . . . ," he reassured me with a glint in his eye and a broad sweep of his arm, ". . . you don't need it!" A year later I was returned to sender. Back in Colorado, I set up housekeeping, mailed out another batch of address changes.

33   An aluminum trash can falls to the floor from an upper tier, perhaps with a little help. I try to type. The cell block explodes in cheering and clapping. Pop cans rain from above. I hesitate at the keyboard. It might be boredom; it might be a fight or a stabbing. It might be a riot. Then again, it might be they just discovered what was for breakfast tomorrow.

34   It is dark outside. The noise subsides. I sit for a few minutes blissfully alone, rescuing my thoughts, pondering my last sentence, imagining some nebulous, faraway, fairy tale future where everything is happily-ever-after. I imagine a steak dinner, the meat still sizzling, its pink and brown juice puddling the plate beneath a twice-baked potato and fresh asparagus, steam rising. . . .

35   "You ain't writing 'bout me!?" Thunder startles me. This time I didn't hear or see him fill my doorway.

36   "No, sir," I tell him, cigarette smoke replacing the scent of steak. "Not one word, Mr. Thunder."

37   He scratches his beard and stares. He steps in and looks over my shoulder. When he speaks again, after some moments, his voice is uncharacteristically soft and plaintive. "Not one word?"

38   I shake my head.

39   "Ain't I good enough to be in your stories?"

40   For a minute I think he is about to cry. I tell him I'll write something about him if he likes. He reaches across the desk for the can of Bugler, rolls a cigarette, pats me on the back, and leaves.

41   I sigh into the typewriter keys and look up in time to see a couple of guards making the rounds, parading their girth like badges of authority, jingling keys. "Attention on the Block! Attention on the Block!" blares the loudspeaker. "Five minutes to Count! Lock up now!"

42   Inmates shout obscenities, but they are just pretending. They filter off to their cells. Visions of solitude dance in my head. Alone! Just me and my

ANSWERS TO
QUESTIONS

*Thinking Critically
About Content*

1. Higgins's "writer's
retreat" is a tiny jail
cell that is repeatedly
being invaded by

typewriter! Now I'll get something done. But maybe I am pretending also. Maybe we are all just pretending.

I get up and stretch, close my door, return to my desk, and wait. 43

"Count!" the loudspeaker squawks. "Count!" 44

Doors slam shut. Suddenly it is quiet. I pause to savor the silence. A plas- 45 tic Salvation Army cup rests next to my typewriter, its contents cold, thick, and dark, but it is the best cup I've had all day. For a moment I think I hear crickets, distant, anonymous traffic, dogs barking, the hum of street lights.

Tickticktick . . . complains my clock, its face turned away, hiding time. 46

This is it. I'm either going to write, or I'm not. I remove a three-by-five- 47 inch wire-bound notebook: musings for the day, observations carried with me through the day. Flipped open and set on the desk beside my type-writer, it reminds me that place can also be irrelevant. I turn a page and begin typing. *Tack-tack, tack-tack, tack-tackity-tack. Tack-tack.* What is it like to write from a prison cell? I write. *Tack-tack.*

The glare of a flashlight hits me in the eyes. There is a pounding at my 48 door. A guard is aiming his light in my face. "What're ya doing this time of night?" he asks.

I take a deep breath and count to ten before answering. Writing from 49 prison, I tell myself, just ain't what it used to be. Maybe it never was. I count to twenty.

"Baking a cake," I finally answer. 50

He grins. "Yeah? Is it fun?" 51

"I don't know," I say. "I'll tell you when it's done." 52

Thinking Critically About Content

1. What characterizes this "writer's retreat"?
2. What is Higgins writing about on his typewriter?
3. How does Higgins deal with all the interruptions? In what ways are these incidents part of his writing process?

Thinking Critically About Purpose and Audience

4. Explain your understanding of the writer's main point in this essay.
5. Who do you think Higgins's primary audience is?
6. Why was Higgins frustrated trying to meet his goal of three pages of writing for the day?

Thinking Critically About Essays

7. Describe Higgins's point of view in this essay. Does it change throughout the essay? If so, in what ways?

inmates and authorities.
2. Higgins is explaining how difficult writing from a prison cell is.
3. Higgins tries to keep the amount of time people take away from him to a minimum. The interruptions have become a part of his writing process because he was forced to make them so. Now he uses the interruptions as a form of prewriting; he jots down his "musings for the day" in the hope that they will inspire him (para. 47).

Thinking Critically About Purpose and Audience
4. The main point of the essay is that writing is very important to this author. It's the only freedom he has.
5. Higgins's primary audience is general readers.
6. He was frustrated because he wanted to write three pages, but with the constant interruptions, he was unable to do so.

Thinking Critically About Essays
7. Higgins's point of view is that writing can be therapeutic. Although his point of view doesn't change, he certainly demonstrates how difficult getting to the therapeutic stage can be.
8. Answers will vary.
9. It is an effective ending because it

shows the absurdity
of the disruptions he
faces. It also alludes
to the fact that he is
creating something
that has many
"ingredients."
10. Answers will vary.

8. Higgins uses many details to illustrate his frustration as he tries to write. Which details communicate his frustration most clearly to you?

9. Higgins talks about baking a cake in his conclusion. Is this an effective ending? Why or why not?

10. Tell this same story from Mr. Thunder's perspective.

Writing Topics: Narrating

Before you begin to write, you might want to review the writing process in Part I.

1. In "The Sanctuary of School," Lynda Barry recalls the way her school and her teachers provided a sanctuary, a place where she could escape from the problems of home. Write an essay in which you recall a place, a person, or an event that made you feel safe, secure, and welcome.

2. We all deal with frustration in different ways. Explain the coping strategies you have observed in friends and relatives. Do they work? Are they effective? Write a narrative essay focusing on various coping strategies that you have seen in action.

3. What do you think are the most important features of a good story? Why are they important? What effect do they have on you?

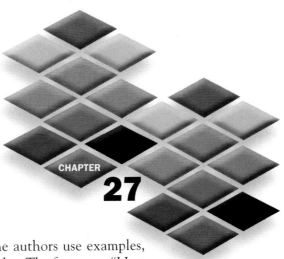

ILLUSTRATING

The two essays in this chapter show how the authors use examples, along with other strategies, to explain their main idea. The first essay, "I Just Wanna Be Average," written by Mike Rose, relates the author's experiences growing up labeled as a slow learner. The second essay, "Getting to Know About You and Me," written by a 16-year-old high school student from Maryland named Chana Schoenberger, was published in *Newsweek* magazine. Chana discusses a problem with prejudice that she recognized while participating in a National Science Foundation program with other high school students.

Mike Rose

I JUST WANNA BE AVERAGE

Focusing Your Attention

1. What do you think about tracking, or separating students by ability level, in high school? What are the advantages and disadvantages of this system of teaching? Did your high school track its students?

2. In the essay you are about to read, the writer claims that students use sophisticated defense mechanisms to get through high school. Have you ever used any defenses in school? How did these defenses make you act?

Expanding Your Vocabulary

The following words are important to your understanding of this essay:

vocational: focused on training for a job (paragraph 1)

Horace's Compromise: a novel by Theodore R. Sizer (paragraph 1)

hypotheses: educated guesses (paragraph 1)

disaffected: rebellious, uncooperative (paragraph 1)

SUMMARY

Rose uses examples to discuss how school systems sometimes drive students toward average goals and beliefs of inferiority.

READABILITY

(Flesch–Kincaid grade level)
10.9

INSTRUCTOR'S
RESOURCE MANUAL
For additional teaching
strategies, for journal
entries, for vocabulary
and reading quizzes,
and for more writing
assignments, see the
*Instructor's Resource
Manual*, Section II,
Part IV.

skeletal: very basic (paragraph 1)

scuttling: moving quickly (paragraph 1)

somnambulant: walking while asleep (paragraph 2)

wherewithal: ability (paragraph 2)

prowess: strength (paragraph 3)

clique: exclusive social group (paragraph 3)

could care less: *slang for* could not care less (paragraph 3)

testament to: proof of (paragraph 3)

dearth: lack (paragraph 3)

much-touted: repeatedly praised (paragraph 4)

salubrious: socially or morally acceptable (paragraph 4)

equivocal: having two or more meanings (paragraph 4)

hit a chuckhole: stumbled (paragraph 4)

Argosy: a science-fiction magazine (paragraph 4)

Field and Stream: a hunting and fishing magazine (paragraph 4)

Daily Worker: a Socialist newspaper (paragraph 4)

The Old Man and the Sea: a novel by Ernest Hemingway (paragraph 4)

rough-hewn: unsophisticated, unpolished (paragraph 4)

apocryphal: a story that is not true but is believed by some people anyway (paragraph 4)

ducktail: a hairstyle in which the hair is swept back at the sides to meet in an upturned point at the back (paragraph 5)

parable of the talents: a story from the New Testament (paragraph 5)

restive: restless, fidgety (paragraph 5)

affect: emotion (paragraph 5)

laryngectomize: surgically remove a person's larynx (paragraph 5)

platitudinous: dull, boring, full of unoriginal thoughts (paragraph 5)

melee: battle (paragraph 5)

dissonant: nonconforming, disagreeing (paragraph 6)

elite: privileged individuals (paragraph 6)

constrained: kept within limits (paragraph 6)

liberate: free (paragraph 6)

gray matter: brain (paragraph 7)

diffuse: scatter (paragraph 7)

cultivate: encourage (paragraph 7)

malady: illness (paragraph 7)

Students will float to the mark you set. I and the others in the vocational 1
classes were bobbing in pretty shallow water. Vocational education was
aimed at increasing the economic opportunities of students who do not do
well in our schools. Some serious programs succeed in doing that, and
through exceptional teachers—like Mr. Gross in *Horace's Compromise*—
students learn to develop hypotheses and troubleshoot, reason through a
problem, and communicate effectively—the true job skills. The vocational
track, however, is most often a place for those who are just not making it, a
dumping ground for the disaffected. There were a few teachers who
worked hard at education; young Brother Slattery, for example, combined
a stern voice with weekly quizzes to try to pass along to us a skeletal outline
of world history. But mostly the teachers had no idea of how to engage the
imaginations of us kids who were scuttling along at the bottom of the pond.

And the teachers would have needed some inventiveness, for none of 2
us was groomed for the classroom. It wasn't just that I didn't know things—
didn't know how to simplify algebraic fractions, couldn't identify different
kinds of clauses, bungled Spanish translations—but that I had developed
various faulty and inadequate ways of doing algebra and making sense of
Spanish. Worse yet, the years of defensive tuning out in elementary school
had given me a way to escape quickly while seeming at least half alert.
During my time in Voc. Ed., I developed further into a mediocre student and
a somnambulant problem solver, and that affected the subjects I did have
the wherewithal to handle: I detested Shakespeare; I got bored with history.
My attention flitted here and there. I fooled around in class and read my
books indifferently—the intellectual equivalent of playing with your food. I
did what I had to do to get by, and I did it with half a mind.

But I did learn things about people and eventually came into my own 3
socially. I liked the guys in Voc. Ed. Growing up where I did, I understood
and admired physical prowess, and there was an abundance of muscle
here. There was Dave Snyder, a sprinter and halfback of true quality.
Dave's ability and his quick wit gave him a natural appeal, and he was
welcome in any clique, though he always kept a little independent. He
enjoyed acting the fool and could care less about studies, but he possessed
a certain maturity and never caused the faculty much trouble. It was a testament to his independence that he included me among his friends—I
eventually went out for track, but I was no jock. Owing to the Latin alpha-
bet and a dearth of *R*'s and *S*'s, Snyder sat behind Rose, and we started
exchanging one-liners and became friends.

There was Ted Richard, a much-touted Little League pitcher. He was 4
chunky and had a baby face and came to Our Lady of Mercy as a seasoned street fighter. Ted was quick to laugh, and he had a loud, jolly laugh,

but when he got angry he'd smile a little smile, the kind that simply raises the corner of the mouth a quarter of an inch. For those who knew, it was an eerie signal. Those who didn't found themselves in big trouble, for Ted was very quick. He loved to carry on what we would come to call philosophical discussions: What is courage? Does God exist? He also loved words, enjoyed picking up big ones like *salubrious* and *equivocal* and using them in our conversations—laughing at himself as the word hit a chuckhole rolling off his tongue. Ted didn't do all that well in school—baseball and parties and testing the courage he'd speculated about took up his time. His textbooks were *Argosy* and *Field and Stream*, whatever newspapers he'd find on the bus stop—from the *Daily Worker* to pornography—conversations with uncles or hobos or businessmen he'd meet in a coffee shop, *The Old Man and the Sea*. With hindsight, I can see that Ted was developing into one of those rough-hewn intellectuals whose sources are a mix of the learned and the apocryphal, whose discussions are both assured and sad.

5   And then there was Ken Harvey. Ken was good-looking in a puffy way and had a full and oily ducktail and was a car enthusiast. . . . One day in religion class, he said the sentence that turned out to be one of the most memorable of the hundreds of thousands I heard in those Voc. Ed. years. We were talking about the parable of the talents, about achievement, working hard, doing the best you can do, blah-blah-blah, when the teacher called on the restive Ken Harvey for an opinion. Ken thought about it, but just for a second, and said (with studied, minimal affect), "I just wanna be average." That woke me up. Average?! Who wants to be average? Then the athletes chimed in with the clichés that make you want to laryngectomize them, and the exchange became a platitudinous melee. At the time, I thought Ken's assertion was stupid, and I wrote him off. But his sentence has stayed with me all these years, and I think I am finally coming to understand it.

6   Ken Harvey was gasping for air. School can be a tremendously disorienting place. No matter how bad the school, you're going to encounter notions that don't fit with the assumptions and beliefs that you grew up with—maybe you'll hear these dissonant notions from teachers, maybe from the other students, and maybe you'll read them. You'll also be thrown in with all kinds of kids from all kinds of backgrounds, and that can be unsettling—this is especially true in places of rich ethnic and linguistic mix, like the L.A. basin. You'll see a handful of students far excel you in courses that sound exotic and that are only in the curriculum of the elite: French, physics, trigonometry. And all this is happening while you're trying to shape an identity, your body is changing, and your emotions are running wild. If you're a working-class kid in the vocational track, the options you'll

ANSWERS TO
QUESTIONS
*Thinking Critically
About Content*
1. Vocational training
was aimed at students
who were deemed
"slow." They were
"placed in a curriculum
that isn't designed to
liberate you but occupy
you, or, if you're lucky,
train you" (para. 6).
2. The examples in
paragraph 2 illustrate
most clearly Rose's aca-
demic life. They point
out his troubles with

have to deal with this will be constrained in certain ways: You're defined by your school as "slow"; you're placed in a curriculum that isn't designed to liberate you but to occupy you, or, if you're lucky, train you, though the training is for work the society does not esteem; other students are picking up the cues from your school and your curriculum and interacting with you in particular ways. If you're a kid like Ted Richard, you turn your back on all this and let your mind roam where it may. But youngsters like Ted are rare. What Ken and so many others do is protect themselves from such suffocating madness by taking on with a vengeance the identity implied in the vocational track. Reject the confusion and frustration by openly defining yourself as the Common Joe. Champion the average. Rely on your own good sense. Fuck this bullshit. Bullshit, of course, is everything you—and the others—fear is beyond you: books, essays, tests, academic scrambling, complexity, scientific reasoning, philosophical inquiry.

The tragedy is that you have to twist the knife in your own gray matter to make this defense work. You'll have to shut down, have to reject intellectual stimuli or diffuse them with sarcasm, have to cultivate stupidity, have to convert boredom from a malady into a way of confronting the world. Keep your vocabulary simple, act stoned when you're not or act more stoned than you are, flaunt ignorance, materialize your dreams. It is a powerful and effective defense—it neutralizes the insult and the frustration of being a vocational kid and, when perfected, it drives teachers up the wall, a delightful secondary effect. But like all strong magic, it exacts a price.

Thinking Critically About Content

1. What was vocational education aimed at in Rose's school? Who is this track for?

2. What examples from this essay illustrate most clearly what Rose's academic life involved?

3. Rose says the Voc. Ed. students "were bobbing in pretty shallow water" and then refers to them "scuttling along at the bottom of the pond" (paragraph 1). In these examples, he is comparing people trying to swim and stay above water to students on a vocational track in high school. This comparison is called a *metaphor*. Find another comparison like this in paragraph 7.

Thinking Critically About Purpose and Audience

4. What do you think Rose's purpose is in this essay? Explain your answer.

5. What type of audience do you think would most understand and appreciate this essay?

8. The topic sentences do support Rose's thesis statement, and the essay is unified. All the paragraphs focus on proving that if teachers don't expect much from their students, they won't get much.

9. Rose's thesis is the first sentence in the essay: "Students will float to the mark you set."

10. Answers will vary.

6. What do you think Ken Harvey meant when he said, "I just wanna be average" (paragraph 5)?

Thinking Critically About Essays

7. Does Rose give you enough examples to understand his learning environment in high school? Explain your answer.

8. Is this essay unified? Does each of the author's topic sentences support the essay's thesis statement? Explain your answer.

9. What is Rose's thesis in this essay? Where is it located?

10. Explain your opinion about tracking students. Is tracking a good idea? Does it help some students? Does it hurt anyone? Can you think of any alternatives to tracking? Respond to these questions in detail.

Chana Schoenberger
GETTING TO KNOW ABOUT YOU AND ME

Focusing Your Attention

1. Think about a problem that you recently solved. How did you go about solving the problem? Did you have to change your lifestyle or behavior in some way, or did you have to convince other people to behave or think differently? Were you happy with the solution, or was it not as satisfying as you expected it to be?

2. In the essay you are about to read, the writer describes an experience she had at a camp where she found herself living with people who did not know very much about her religion. Have you ever been in a situation in which you were misunderstood because of your race, your ethnic background, your religion, your gender, your age, or your appearance? Did this create a problem for you?

Expanding Your Vocabulary

The following words are important to your understanding of this essay:

diversity: variety of ethnic types (paragraph 1)

anti-Semitic: prejudiced against Jewish people (paragraph 7)

benign: harmless (paragraph 8)

EPA: Environmental Protection Agency (paragraph 8)

doctorate: highest academic degree (paragraph 9)

SUMMARY

Schoenberger discusses racism by illustrating an experience she encountered one summer in Wisconsin.

READABILITY

(Flesch–Kincaid grade level)
10.3

INSTRUCTOR'S RESOURCE MANUAL

For additional teaching strategies, for journal entries, for vocabulary and reading quizzes, and for more writing assignments, see the *Instructor's Resource Manual*, Section II, Part IV.

malignantly: with bad intent (paragraph 10)

assimilate: blend into a larger group (paragraph 11)

flawed: incorrect or illogical (paragraph 13)

As a religious holiday approaches, students at my high school who will   1
be celebrating the holiday prepare a presentation on it for an assembly.
The Diversity Committee, which sponsors the assemblies to increase religious awareness, asked me last spring if I would help with the presentation
on Passover, the Jewish holiday that commemorates the Exodus from
Egypt. I was too busy with other things, and I never got around to helping.
I didn't realize then how important those presentations really are, or I definitely would have done something.

This summer I was one of 20 teens who spent five weeks at the University   2
of Wisconsin at Superior studying acid rain with a National Science
Foundation Young Scholars program. With such a small group in such a
small town, we soon became close friends and had a good deal of fun
together. We learned about the science of acid rain, went on field trips, found
the best and cheapest restaurants in Superior, and ate in them frequently to
escape the lousy cafeteria food. We were a happy, bonded group.

Represented among us were eight religions: Jewish, Roman Catholic,   3
Muslim, Hindu, Methodist, Mormon, Jehovah's Witness, and Lutheran. It
was amazing, given the variety of backgrounds, to see the ignorance of
some of the smartest young scholars on the subject of other religions.

On the first day, one girl mentioned that she had nine brothers and   4
sisters. "Oh, are you Mormon?" asked another girl, who I knew was a
Mormon herself. The first girl, shocked, replied, "No, I dress normal!" She
thought Mormon was the same as Mennonite, and the only thing she
knew about either religion was that Mennonites don't, in her opinion,
"dress normal."

My friends, ever curious about Judaism, asked me about everything   5
from our basic theology to food preferences. "How come, if Jesus was a Jew,
Jews aren't Christian?" my Catholic roommate asked me in all seriousness.
Brought up in a small Wisconsin town, she had never met a Jew before, nor
had she met people from most of the other "strange" religions (anything
but Catholic or mainstream Protestant). Many of the other kids were the
same way.

"Do you all still practice animal sacrifices?" a girl from a small town in   6
Minnesota asked me once. I said no, laughed, and pointed out that this was
the 20th century, but she had been absolutely serious. The only Jews she
knew were the ones from the Bible.

7   Nobody was deliberately rude or anti-Semitic, but I got the feeling that I was representing the entire Jewish people through my actions. I realized that many of my friends would go back to their small towns thinking that all Jews liked Dairy Queen Blizzards and grilled cheese sandwiches. After all, that was true of all the Jews they knew (in most cases, me and the only other Jewish young scholar, period).

8   The most awful thing for me, however, was not the benign ignorance of my friends. Our biology professor had taken us on a field trip to the EPA field site where he worked, and he was telling us about the project he was working on. He said that they had to make sure the EPA got its money's worth from the study—he "wouldn't want them to get Jewed."

9   I was astounded. The professor had a doctorate and various other degrees and seemed to be a very intelligent man. He apparently had no idea that he had just made an anti-Semitic remark. The other Jewish girl in the group and I debated whether or not to say something to him about it, and although we agreed we would, neither of us ever did. Personally, it made me feel uncomfortable. For a high-school student to tell a professor who taught her class that he was a bigot seemed out of place to me, even if he was one.

10   What scares me about that experience, in fact about my whole visit to Wisconsin, was that I never met a really vicious anti-Semite or a malignantly prejudiced person. Many of the people I met had been brought up to think that Jews (or Mormons or members of any other religion that's not mainstream Christian) were different and that difference was not good.

11   Difference, in America, is supposed to be good. We are expected—at least, I always thought we were expected—to respect each other's traditions. Respect requires some knowledge about people's backgrounds. Singing Christmas carols as a kid in school did not make me Christian, but it taught me to appreciate beautiful music and someone else's holiday. It's not necessary or desirable for all ethnic groups in America to assimilate into one traditionless mass. Rather, we all need to learn about other cultures so that we can understand one another and not feel threatened by others.

12   In the little multicultural universe that I live in, it's safe not to worry about explaining the story of Passover, because if people don't hear it from me, they'll hear it some other way. Now I realize that's not true everywhere.

13   Ignorance was the problem I faced this summer. By itself, ignorance is not always a problem, but it leads to misunderstandings, prejudice, and hatred. Many of today's problems involve hatred. If there weren't so much ignorance about other people's backgrounds, would people still hate each other as badly as they do now? Maybe so, but at least that hatred would be based on facts and not flawed beliefs.

ANSWERS TO
QUESTIONS
*Thinking Critically
About Content*
1. Schoenberger
wanted to show that
even smart people can
be ignorant about some
issues.
2. The writer felt that
she "was representing
the entire Jewish
people" (para. 7)
because most of the
other students had
not met a Jewish
person. She found their
ignorant remarks a sign
of naiveté and not
deliberate prejudice.
3. She thinks ignorance
is dangerous because
people start basing
judgments on mis-
guided beliefs rather
than facts. She plans to
"get up and tell the
whole school"
(para. 14) about
Judaism in order to
educate people about
her religion.

*Thinking Critically
About Purpose and
Audience*
4. Schoenberger wants
people to become more

I'm now back at school, and I plan to apply for the Diversity Committee. 14 I'm going to get up and tell the whole school about my religion and the tradition I'm proud of. I see now how important it is to celebrate your heritage and to educate others about it. I can no longer take for granted that everyone knows about my religion or that I know about theirs. People who are suspicious when they find out I'm Jewish usually don't know much about Judaism. I would much prefer them to hate or distrust me because of something I've done, instead of them hating me on the basis of prejudice.

Thinking Critically About Content

1. Why do you think the writer stated that the people she attended the program with were "some of the smartest young scholars" (paragraph 3)?

2. What do you think the writer means when she says, "Nobody was deliberately rude or anti-Semitic" (paragraph 7)? Explain your answer.

3. Why does Schoenberger think that ignorance is dangerous? What does she propose to do about people's ignorance regarding her religion?

Thinking Critically About Purpose and Audience

4. What do you think Chana Schoenberger's purpose is in this essay?

5. Do you think this essay should be read by all students? What other groups would benefit from reading this essay? Why?

6. Why do you think the writer chose to send her essay to *Newsweek* magazine rather than to her school newspaper?

Thinking Critically About Essays

7. Why do you think the writer explained people's prejudice and ignorance in reference to other religions as well as toward Judaism?

8. How do you think the biology professor mentioned in the essay would respond to Schoenberger's explanation of prejudice? Explain your answer.

9. How does the writer organize her main points? Is this an effective order? Why or why not?

10. Were your views on religion or on society's ignorance about some religions changed as a result of reading this essay? If so, in what way? Explain your answer in detail.

educated about other religions.
5. All students should read this essay in order to understand that a larger world is out there. Any group can benefit from this essay, however, because it teaches all readers to keep an open mind about the unknown.
6. By sending the essay to *Newsweek*, Schoenberger hopes to reach a larger audience than a school newspaper would.

Thinking Critically About Essays

7. The writer wants people to understand that she is not overreacting to remarks about her own religion; rather, people react strangely to other religions as well. Her examples show that this problem is widespread.
8. The biology professor would probably be mortified if he recognized that Schoenberger was referring to him. The remark was innocent but ignorant, and Schoenberger uses it to make a global statement.
9. The essay is organized chronologically. It is effective because it shows the process Schoenberger went through to educate others.
10. Answers will vary.

Writing Topics: Illustrating

Before you begin to write, you might want to review the writing process in Part I.

1. Contemporary American society rewards students who fit into the educational system and can keep up. But some people just can't keep up with a course for a variety of reasons. Have you ever felt the way Mike Rose says he felt in his essay? What was your reason for not keeping up? Discuss any similarities you see between yourself and Mike Rose.

2. How do you think the generation that is currently in high school handles ethnic and religious differences? Explain how you think these young people will change as they grow up.

3. What do you think writers should consider first when choosing examples in an essay? How should the examples be related to the thesis statement? Why are these criteria important when working with examples?

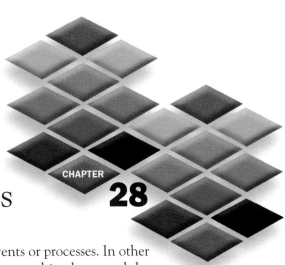

ANALYZING A PROCESS

CHAPTER 28

The essays in this chapter explain different events or processes. In other words, they tell you how to do something or why something happened the way it did. The first essay, "Don't Be Cruel" by Dr. Roger Flax, offers some guidelines for criticizing and motivating at the same time—at work, at home, at school. "Why We Have a Moon," written by David Levy, explains how the moon was formed and what its role is in relation to the earth.

Dr. Roger Flax

DON'T BE CRUEL

Focusing Your Attention

1. Think of a time when you had to explain to someone how to do something. Was it an easy or a difficult task? Did the person understand you? Was the person able to follow your directions?

2. In the process analysis essay you are about to read, the writer tells us how to criticize other people effectively. Have you ever wanted to tell someone about something he or she did wrong without ruining the relationship? What did you do to solve the problem?

Expanding Your Vocabulary

The following words are important to your understanding of this essay:

coronary: heart attack (paragraph 1)

mercilessly: cruelly (paragraph 1)

reprimands: expressions of disapproval (paragraph 4)

manager-subordinate scenarios: boss-employee situations (paragraph 4)

SUMMARY
Flax provides a step-by-step process of reprimanding employees while simultaneously motivating them to perform better.

READABILITY
(Flesch–Kincaid grade level)
10.6

INSTRUCTOR'S
RESOURCE MANUAL
For additional teaching
strategies, for journal
entries, for vocabulary
and reading quizzes,
and for more writing
assignments, see the
*Instructor's Resource
Manual*, Section II,
Part IV.

Project Management Work Teams: groups of individuals who work together in the workforce to improve their management style (paragraph 7)

rapport: sense of trust (paragraph 10)

repercussions: results or effects (paragraph 14)

malice: desire to cause harm or suffering (paragraph 16)

facilitate: guide (paragraph 20)

implementation: the act of putting something into practice (paragraph 21)

misconstrues: misunderstands (paragraph 21)

stroke: flatter, compliment (paragraph 22)

perennial: constant (paragraph 29)

belittle: say negative things about a person (paragraph 31)

1   Picture this scenario: Seymour Axshun (we'll call him), a terrific manager who has been a loyal employee for several years, messes up on an assignment. He misses a deadline on a proposal and that three-day delay costs the company $9,100. Seymour's boss, Sy Kottick, has a near coronary over the incident, lashes out at Seymour, and criticizes him mercilessly. In front of four of Seymour's co-workers, Kottick shouts, "Axshun, how many times do I have to tell you to be more efficient with your planning? You blew it, and your mistake will cost us almost $10,000. I don't know what it takes to drill into your head that you must meet deadlines. It's disgusting, and I'm fed up. If you treated the money as if it were your own, you wouldn't be so careless."

2   "Incidentally, Seymour, on another issue, don't you think you should come to work dressed a bit more professionally? That suit you wore yesterday was a bit outdated, especially since we had our big client, Meyer Fivis, here. And one more thing, while we're at it Seymour . . . "

3   Seymour shrinks from humiliation. He wishes he could push a button and disappear. He looks around him and sees four embarrassed colleagues. His boss storms out of the room and slams the door.

4   This thoughtless, but real-life, managerial scenario happens every minute of every day, in every city of every state. People insensitively and ruthlessly come down on others with reprimands and criticisms that leave permanent scars. And it happens not only in manager-subordinate scenarios, but in parent-child relationships, teacher-student interfaces, sports coach–player affairs, and friendships.

5   It's called *unconstructive, unmotivational criticism* or, in better words, *relationship breaking*.

Put yourself in Seymour Axshun's shoes. Would you ever want to work 6
for that jerk again? And if you did, how dedicated would you really be?
How motivated would you be to make him look good?

The two most critical assets of companies are people and time. Valuable 7
people are hard to replace, and time is irreplaceable. With the evolution of
Project Management Work Teams in companies throughout the world, it's
absolutely imperative that team leaders and managers master the art of
giving constructive, tactful, motivational criticism. After all, if the goal of the
project group is to work as a team to attain a goal, unconstructive criticism
can destroy the group quickly. *Motivation magic,* as I call it, can only enhance the team.

You shouldn't be a robot when giving constructive criticism, but there is 8
a human-relations approach that does work. Here's a several-step process
to follow the next time you have to reprimand another person, but truly
want to motivate that person and enhance the relationship.

1. *Always begin constructive criticism with a positive statement.* Open 9
   with an energizing comment that builds up the person's esteem and
   sincerely expresses your approval and support on a specific item. For
   example, in the Seymour Axshun incident, why not begin with,
   "Seymour, you've done an outstanding job in the Quality Improvement
   Program, and the results are quickly having an impact on our operation. Many people have commented to me about your great work."

2. *Never follow that complimentary opening remark with "but" or* 10
   "however." Those words immediately eliminate the good feeling and
   rapport initiated by the compliment. The person will quickly surmise
   that the opening statement was merely lip service—a manipulative
   tool geared to set up the reprimand or criticism. It's very natural, and
   even habitual, to say "but" or "however" after you open with a positive
   statement, but it will destroy the initial goodwill created and result in
   perceived insincerity.

3. *Use the acronym PEN to plan and verbalize the actual criticism.* 11

   P—Problem. State the problem that exists. Be concise and to the
   point. Remember: Don't begin expressing the problem with
   "but" or "however."

   E—Example. Give an example or two that clearly supports the
   problem or reason for criticism. Get your facts straight, and
   keep them brief. The lengthier the criticism is, the more painful
   it becomes.

   N—Negative Impact. Let the person know what negative effects
   have resulted from the problem or action. It's important to do

some planning before the criticism session. Think through your PEN before giving it. It will come across more concisely, smoothly, and convincingly.

12   4. *Avoid using the word "you" when giving the actual criticism.* This is definitely the most important rule to remember. Discipline yourself to criticize the object or the problem, not the person. Don't let yourself say "you"—it's accusatory, threatening and puts the criticism on a personal, emotional, confrontational level.

13   Example: "Seymour, you've done an outstanding job in the Quality Improvement Program, and the results are quickly having an impact on our operation. There's one situation that could be improved upon, and that is meeting deadlines. On one occasion this month, a deadline was missed by three days, and that has cost our company several thousand dollars. The negative effects not only include a large dollar loss, but a potential loss in credibility for future dealings."

14   Now go back and read the opening example—the confrontational, insensitive way of criticizing. Notice in the second example that the criticizer avoided the word "you" (except for the opening praise) and dealt with the problem, not the person. You need to practice this technique over and over again. Don't just use it at work, but also use it with your spouse, children, friends, relatives—everyone. It goes a long way in relationship building and effective human relations, and it reduces the enormous repercussions that can occur from giving cutthroat criticism.

15   Of course, it's okay to use "you" when you're praising the person or engaging in a subsequent dialogue after the initial criticism has been communicated. However, the word "you" should be avoided when the actual bad news is being stated.

16   If husbands and wives disciplined themselves to avoid the word "you" during potential emotional outbursts, they wouldn't build up years of frustration and marital malice. If coaches stopped publicly criticizing their players and saying "you" every time the players made a mistake, there'd be many more motivated athletes exploiting and reaching their fullest potential.

17   5. *Ask for feedback.* After "PEN-ning" people, find out what their feelings or opinions are on the matter. Let them talk. Let them express their emotions, and don't interrupt. If they're looking to save a little face, go ahead and let them. Lose the battle, but win the war. Open the window of communication, and let the air flow in.

18   6. *Actively listen to their response.* Instead of just gazing at them as they speak, be an active, nonverbal listener. Show facial expressions, nod,

react with sounds, such as "hmmm," "oh, I see," or "really." Show a genuine, caring interest.

When someone has a problem, active listening helps reduce the 19 pain. That's what psychologists do every day. The client reveals painful experiences to the psychologist, and the psychologist uses active listening techniques to show support, concern, and empathy. It's also a technique used by successful sales pros who strive to develop relationships with customers.

7. *Discuss the situation in a low-key manner.* Your two-way communica- 20 tion, although unstructured, should remain focused on the problem. Facilitate the discussion to an agreed-upon action or solution. Clearly state what you want the person to do, if it's not clear, and make sure you obtain a mutual understanding. Don't dominate the communica- tion. If the other person raises his or her voice, keep yours down. That will keep the discussion less emotional and more low-key.

8. *Mutually agree upon an action or next step.* It's always better this 21 way. Forcing a person to do something usually produces substantially less long-term growth and relationship building. Both parties should agree upon an action, set a date for its implementation, and end with a handshake. Try getting the person to verbalize what the action steps will be, thereby ensuring that both people are in sync. You'd be sur- prised how many times the criticized person misconstrues the next action step.

9. *End with a positive.* Now that the hard work is completed (and nobody 22 likes giving criticism), go back and stroke the person a bit. Remind him or her that you greatly appreciate the person's effort and dedication and are very supportive of his or her performance. Make sure that no negative feelings exist, and if they do, probe and uncover them. You want to assure the person that this is a very correctable problem and that, in the big picture, you're a very satisfied manager.

Example: "Seymour, remember, I am extremely pleased with 23 your performance. You are a valuable asset to our department."

A few musts to keep in mind when giving constructive, motivational 24 criticism:

First, *always do it in private.* Nobody is proud of reprimands, so do it 25 when you're alone with the person. It's humiliating when done in public.

Second, *limit the criticism session to one act.* If you bring up things 26 from the past, you're turning the knife and potentially destroying the relationship. You should communicate criticism within a day or two of the

ANSWERS TO QUESTIONS
Thinking Critically About Content
1. "Motivation magic" is a way of offering constructive criticism while motivating employees so that they can all work better as a team.
2. The main steps are as follows:
Always begin constructive criti- cism with a posi- tive statement.
Never follow that complimentary opening remark

with "but" or
"however."
Use the acronym
    PEN to plan and
    verbalize the
    actual criticism.
Avoid using the
    word "you" when
    giving the actual
    criticism.
Ask for feedback.
Actively listen to
    people's responses.
Discuss the situation
    in a low-key
    manner.
Mutually agree on
    an action or a
    next step.
End with a positive.
3. The goal is "to leave
the person feeling
helped, not hurt"
(para. 30).

*Thinking Critically
About Purpose and
Audience*

4. Flax wants to inform
readers how to
reprimand employees
while motivating them
at the same time. He
is probably hoping to
alter some employer
behavior through this
essay.
5. Anyone can benefit
from this essay because
people make mistakes
every day, and not just
in business situations.
Readers can take this
advice and use it in
personal situations.
6. Answers will vary.

*Thinking Critically
About Essays*

7. Flax thinks that
ridiculing others is an
act of small-minded
people and believes

occurrence; otherwise, drop it. Some people bring up events that occurred six months or even six years ago. That's a no-no.

27   Third, *criticize face-to-face, never over the phone.* You never know how the person is reacting. If you're criticizing over the phone, the other person might be dying inside, and you'll never know it. Even if it's timely to do it over the phone, hold it in. Set up an immediate meeting with the person.

28   Finally, *don't dig it in.* Statements such as "you see," "I told you so," or "you don't listen" are worthless. They might make you feel good, but they ruin relationships.

29   A great example of how *not* to criticize can be seen during a sports event—basketball, baseball, or football. How many times does a basketball coach yell at his point guard for missing the play and use the accusatory "you" over and over again? The coach raises his voice in frustration and does it in front of teammates and fans. The player feels abused, his confidence is shaken, and his motivation is drained from within. It's no wonder certain professional coaches go from team to team but continue to lose year after year. They might know the sport, but they know little about human motivation. A little motivational psychology would go a long way for these perennial losers.

30   How do you tie all these points together the next time you must criticize a person? Remember: The goal of motivational criticism should be to leave the person feeling helped, not hurt. So, the next time you're about to criticize a person, think it through before you do. Be tactful, firm, empathetic, and concise.

31   After all, you have to be little to belittle. You hold the key to motivational magic.

Thinking Critically About Content

1. What does Dr. Roger Flax mean by "motivation magic" (paragraph 7)?

2. What are the nine main steps of Flax's method?

3. What does Flax say the main goal of motivational criticism is?

Thinking Critically About Purpose and Audience

4. What do you think Flax's purpose is in this essay?

5. Do you think that only businesspeople can benefit from this essay? Why? Explain your answer.

6. Which piece of Flax's advice do you find most useful for your own life?

Thinking Critically About Essays

7. Describe in a complete sentence Flax's point of view in his last paragraph.

8. How does Flax organize this essay? Write a rough outline to show his method of organization.

9. Choose a paragraph from his essay, and explain how it is developed.

10. Explain in detail whether or not you agree with Flax when he says that using "you" to criticize people makes them feel like they are being attacked.

that everyone has the
potential to criticize
and motivate at the
same time.
8. He organizes his
essay in the order in
which the steps should
occur (chronologi-
cally); see the answer
to question 2.
9. Answers will vary.
10. Answers will vary.

David Levy

WHY WE HAVE A MOON

Focusing Your Attention

1. Astronomy is the study of planets and stars. What interests you about the world of astronomy?

2. In the essay you are about to read, the writer explains his research on how the moon was formed and what its role is in relation to the earth. Have you ever been interested enough in something that you took the time to look into its origins or related facts?

Expanding Your Vocabulary

The following words are important to your understanding of this essay:

orbit: the path of a planet, moon, or satellite (paragraph 3)

gravitational pull: the pull of a planet on an object near its surface (paragraph 3)

supercolossal: extremely large (paragraph 3)

plummeted: fell (paragraph 4)

devastation: severe damage (paragraph 4)

promontory: a piece of land that juts out into the sea (paragraph 7)

mottled: spotted (paragraph 11 and 12)

exhalations: letting air out (paragraph 12)

meteors, comets, asteroids: bodies of rock and air in space (paragraph 13)

SUMMARY

In this essay, Levy
explains the process the
moon went through in
its formation and the
role it plays now.

READABILITY

(Flesch–Kincaid grade
level)
9.3

INSTRUCTOR'S
RESOURCE MANUAL

For additional teaching
strategies, for journal
entries, for vocabulary
and reading quizzes,
and for more writing
assignments, see the
*Instructor's Resource
Manual*, Section II,
Part IV.

imminent: about to happen (paragraph 16)

carbon: a chemical element (paragraph 17)

hydrogen, nitrogen, oxygen: gases in the earth's atmosphere (paragraph 17)

1   I remember the beautiful clear sky the day my granddaughter, then 14 months old, first fell under its spell. She called it the "oon." Soon, I knew, she'd be asking, "How did the Moon get there? Did people really walk on it? Will *I* someday?"—the same questions asked by Moonwatchers of all ages. So, how *did* the Moon get there?

2   About 4.5 billion years ago, the Earth had a bad day. The Sun was shining on our young world, which had no oceans yet and no life, but a surface filled with erupting volcanoes. The sky was awash with stars, though not the ones we see now. But the familiar planets were there—Venus, Jupiter, Saturn, Mars—and another planet the size of Mars but much closer.

3   Had we been alive back then, we would have noticed this other planet looping again and again around the Sun in an odd orbit that brought it very close to Earth, then farther away. On this day, that odd planet, approaching us again, became brighter than ever before, filling the sky and getting bigger by the minute, its gravitational pull now so great that rocks began to stretch and rumble. Then, with unimaginable energy and deafening noise, it sideswiped the Earth, bounced off and, seconds later, tore right back into our planet with a supercolossal force.

4   That Mars-size world broke apart, and huge chunks of Earth's crust flew off into space. Two rings of debris, their particles much larger than those in the fine-grained rings of Saturn, grew and circled the Earth. For many days, pieces of the inner ring plummeted down again, adding to the Earth's devastation. Pieces of the outer ring slowly gathered together around its largest chunks. In just a year, those pieces formed a large new world, a world that we can still see. That world we call the Moon.

5   So goes the prevailing theory, developed in the 1970s. In its earliest days, our Moon was probably no more than 10,000 miles away. The Earth spun around faster then, in a 10-hour day. But over time the Moon slowly veered away from Earth, its gravity forever slowing Earth's rotation. By the time of the dinosaurs, more than 4 billion years after the Moon's formation, a day was about 22 hours long. With our day now at 24 hours, the Moon, still inching away at approximately 3 feet every century, is about 240,000 miles away. But even at this distance, it has a powerful influence on the Earth's waters.

The Moon and the Tides

We have tides on Earth because of the gravitational pull of the Moon (and   6
the Sun, especially when the two are in alignment) across the diameter of
the Earth. If you've ever been to an ocean beach, you have felt the Moon's
whisper as its gravity brings the water in, then out, twice each day. One day
in Nova Scotia, I felt the Moon roar.

At the eastern end of Canada's Bay of Fundy, a flow of water equal to   7
the combined currents of all the rivers on Earth thunders through the Minas
Channel into the Minas Basin twice a day for six hours. To see this mar-
velous sight, I traveled to a remote Nova Scotia promontory called Cape
Split. I arrived as the incoming tidal flow was at its maximum.

A first-quarter Moon hung in the sky as a *million million* gallons of   8
water poured into the Minas Basin. I found it incredible that the Moon, from
a distance of 240,000 miles, was responsible for the tremendous noise in the
channel below. After a few hours, the flow slowed, then stopped. For a half
hour or so, the water was still. Then the huge basin began to empty, flow-
ing *in reverse* like a movie running backward, the noise rising once again.
Such is the power of the Moon's gravity.

The shape of the land makes the tides stronger. In midocean, the daily   9
tidal bulge is about a yard. But at Minas Basin, it's 45 feet—the largest tidal
flow on the planet—owing to the peculiar geography of the Gulf of Maine,
the Bay of Fundy, the Minas Channel and basin. It's like a child playing in
a bathtub, pushing the water to the front, then letting it flow back. A rhythm
builds. If the child lifts up slightly each time, the water sloshes toward one
end. Eventually, the water rides up the side of the tub and spills out. The
child's movement is "in sync" with the natural motion of the water in the
tub. The water's increased momentum, plus the confining shape of the tub,
results in more force on the water—just as the Moon's gravity, aided by the
shape of the land, strengthens the force of the Fundy tides.

The Moon Is a Mirror

When we look at the Moon, we see on its uneven surface a record of   10
billions of years of bashing. The Moon's face is trying to tell us something
about Earth's own past. If the Moon has been hit so often, the Earth, being a
much bigger target, must have been struck even more often.

The first thing you notice about the Moon is its uneven, mottled surface.   11
With binoculars, the unevenness appears more pronounced, with clear
evidence of dark and bright spots. What are they?

To the ancient Greeks, the Moon's "spots" were exhalations from   12
the Earth that rose all the way to the Moon. By the 1500s, it was common to

compare the Moon to green cheese—not because of its mysterious color but because "green cheese" meant round, uncut cheese with a mottled surface. As recently as 1960, most scientists believed craters were the result of volcanic forces beneath the Moon's surface.

13   That was before Gene Shoemaker appeared on the scene. A young geologist, he was studying craters formed by underground nuclear testing near Las Vegas in the late 1950s. He noted that these craters, formed by far greater heat and pressure than a volcano could produce, resembled some of the great natural craters on Earth. Perhaps the latter—as well as the craters on the Moon—had resulted from impacts by meteors, comets or asteroids, whose energy would have been closer to that of an atomic bomb.

14   By 1960, Shoemaker had proved that a 1.2-mile-wide crater near Flagstaff, Ariz., was the result of the crash of an asteroid some 50,000 years ago. By studying detailed photographs of craters on the Moon, plus images taken by the *Ranger* and *Surveyor* spacecraft, Shoemaker established that the Moon's surface was a story of impacts over billions of years.

15   In 1972, the astronaut Harrison Schmidt went to the Moon on *Apollo 17* and confirmed Shoemaker's theory live on television. "Gene defined what the characteristics of the Moon's surface layer would be," Schmidt told me.

16   But the Moon's surface revealed a far more important story—that of the solar system's violent past, when the planets, including Earth, were bombarded by comets and meteors. On March 25, 1993, Shoemaker, his wife, Carol, and I discovered that a collision in the solar system was imminent. And 16 months later, as the world watched, comet Shoemaker-Levy 9 slammed into Jupiter at 37 miles per second—the equivalent of going from New York to Los Angeles *in 70 seconds.*

17   The spectacle of these comets hitting Jupiter was a replay of an ancient scenario in which comets—comprised of carbon, hydrogen, nitrogen, and oxygen—crashed into Earth, starting a slow process that eventually led to the earliest life here.

18   Is the Moon still being bombarded today? On July 10, 1941, Walter Haas, one of the world's most experienced observers, saw a speck of light move across Gassendi, a large lunar crater. Did Haas see a meteorite striking the Moon at enormous speed? Smaller particles did hit the Moon on Nov. 17, 1999, during the Leonid meteor shower.

19   If small objects still hit the Moon, can large ones? In 1178, some monks near Canterbury, England, reported a terrifying experience on a night of a crescent Moon: "Suddenly," the account reads, "the upper horn split in two. From the division, a flaming torch sprang up, spewing out, over a considerable distance, fire, hot coals, and sparks."

ANSWERS TO QUESTIONS
Thinking Critically About Content
1. David Levy's personal stories include his granddaughter's reference to the moon (para. 1), the author's trip to Cape Split (paragraphs 7–9), and his discovery of the forthcoming collision in the solar system in 1993 (para. 16). They make the essay personal and accessible to a general audience.
2. The steps in the moon's formation were (1) a planet hits and bounces off the earth, (2) debris from the earth flies into space, (3) pieces of debris start to circle the earth, and (4) within a year, the moon forms from this debris.
3. The tides are caused by the gravitational pull of the moon.

Thinking Critically About Purpose and Audience
4. The purpose of this essay is to explain in terms anyone can understand how the moon was formed.

Could they have seen a major impact on the Moon? Conceivably, a 20
20-mile crater on the Moon's far side, called Giordano Bruno, was caused
by a large impact. We may never know the answer, but there's a clue.

In the 1970s, the McDonald Observatory in Texas, bouncing laser beams 21
off the Moon, found that it "sways" by a few yards about every three years.
Like a huge bell vibrating after being clanged, the Moon is acting as if it
had been struck by a large object within the last 1000 years. Perhaps, someday, my granddaughter, caught by the Moon's wondrous pull, will walk
there as others once did and find an answer.

Thinking Critically About Content

1. Writers often use personal stories to get the readers' attention or understanding. Where does Levy use stories in this essay? What effect
   do they have?

2. What were the steps in the moon's formation 4.5 billion years ago?

3. According to Levy, what is the relationship between the moon and
   the oceans?

Thinking Critically About Purpose and Audience

4. What do you think the purpose of this essay is?

5. How do you think a general audience would respond to the author's
   description of the moon as a mirror of the earth's past?

6. Levy often relates scientific information to everyday occurrences—
   like comparing the motion of the tides to a child playing in the
   bathtub (paragraph 9). Find one other example of this technique.
   How do you respond to this strategy as a reader?

Thinking Critically About Essays

7. Describe in a complete sentence the writer's point of view.

8. Why do you think Levy introduces current research on the moon in
   the last section of his essay?

9. What are the three main parts of Levy's essay? Why do you think he
   put these topics in this order?

10. If Levy were writing this essay for a publication to be read only by
    scientists, how might it be different? How might it be the same?
    Rewrite the introduction or the conclusion for an audience of
    scientists.

5. Answers will vary.
6. Levy relates scientific information to everyday occurrences in four other instances: comparing spots on the moon to "exhalations" (para. 12); comparing the moon to green cheese (para. 12); comparing the impacts of meteors, comets, and asteroids to the force of an atomic bomb (para. 13); and comparing the vibration of the moon to a huge bell after "being clanged" (para. 21).

Thinking Critically About Essays
7. Answers will vary.
8. He probably introduces current research to show that scientists are still studying the moon today.
9. The three main parts of Levy's essay are (1) how the moon was formed, (2) the moon and the tides, and (3) the moon as a mirror of the past. This order is actually chronological, starting with the formation of the moon and pro-gressing to research on the moon today.
10. For an audience of scientists, the essay would include many more scientific references. Beyond this, answers will vary.

Writing Topics: Analyzing a Process

Before you begin to write, you might want to review the writing process in Part I.

1. In the first essay, Flax talks about motivating people by criticizing without using the word "you." Are you usually aware of your word choice as you talk? How can careful use of words help you get what you want in life? Explain a process that involved getting something you wanted by using words carefully.

2. Think of something in life that you want to study as much as Levy wants to study the moon and stars. Then discuss your plans for achieving your goals in this area of study.

3. Which type of process analysis do you find most interesting—the how-to essays or the background explanations? Explain your answer.

COMPARING AND CONTRASTING

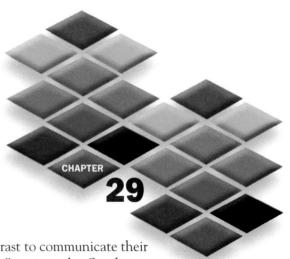

CHAPTER
29

The following essays use comparison and contrast to communicate their main ideas. The first, "The American Family," written by Stephanie Coontz, was originally published in *Life* magazine; it compares the family at the end of the twentieth century with that at the beginning of the century. The second essay, "Between Worlds" by Tony Cohan, compares and contrasts a writer's life in two separate locations.

Stephanie Coontz
THE AMERICAN FAMILY

Focusing Your Attention

1. What do you think are the good qualities of the American family today? What were the good qualities of the family when your parents were children?

2. In the essay you are about to read, the writer compares and contrasts the American family at the turn of the twenty-first century with the family at the turn of the twentieth century. What do you think are some of the differences in family life at these two times? Some of the similarities?

Expanding Your Vocabulary

The following words are important to your understanding of this essay:

litany: list (paragraph 3)

nuclear family: parents and their children, living in the same household (paragraph 5)

nostalgia: a feeling of pleasure and sadness about the past (paragraph 6)

SUMMARY

In this essay, Coontz compares families of today with families 100 years ago, proving that families are better off today.

READABILITY

(Flesch–Kincaid grade level) 10.0

INSTRUCTOR'S RESOURCE MANUAL

For additional teaching strategies, for journal entries, for vocabulary and reading quizzes, and for more writing assignments, see the *Instructor's Resource Manual*, Section II, Part IV.

GI Bill: a series of laws passed after World War II providing low-cost government loans to veterans (paragraph 6)

subsidized: supported by government money (paragraph 6)

coercion: force (paragraph 7)

arbitrary: on a whim, for no clear reason (paragraph 7)

ostracized: excluded, left out (paragraph 7)

Leave It to Beaver: television series of the 1950s featuring the fictional Cleaver family and presenting an idealized picture of family life (paragraph 8)

barbiturate: a drug that calms and relaxes people (paragraph 10)

disparaged: put down, treated unkindly (paragraph 11)

gonorrhea: a sexually transmitted disease (paragraph 12)

syphilis: a sexually transmitted disease (paragraph 12)

Oedipal fantasies: sexual attraction that a child feels for the parent of the opposite sex (paragraph 12)

spousal: of one's husband or wife (paragraph 13)

in flux: changing (paragraph 17)

aberration: a change from the norm (paragraph 19)

breadwinner: person who earns the money on which a family lives (paragraph 19)

impoverished: made poor (paragraph 26)

incapacitated: disabled (paragraph 26)

noncustodial: not having legal authority over one's own child (paragraph 27)

stepfamilies: nuclear families in which one parent is not the original parent of one or more of the children (paragraph 27)

debilitating: causing weakness or loss of strength (paragraph 29)

1   As the century comes to an end, many observers fear for the future of America's families. Our divorce rate is the highest in the world, and the percentage of unmarried women is significantly higher than in 1960. Educated women are having fewer babies, while immigrant children flood the schools, demanding to be taught in their native language. Harvard University reports that only 4 percent of its applicants can write a proper sentence.

2   There's an epidemic of sexually transmitted diseases among men. Many streets in urban neighborhoods are littered with cocaine vials. Youths call

heroin "happy dust." Even in small towns, people have easy access to addictive drugs, and drug abuse by middle-class wives is skyrocketing. Police see 16-year-old killers, 12-year-old prostitutes, and gang members as young as 11. America at the end of the 1990s? No, America at the end of the 1890s.

The litany of complaints may sound familiar, but the truth is that many things were worse at the start of the 20th century than they are today. Then, thousands of children worked full-time in mines, mills, and sweatshops. Most workers labored 10 hours a day, often six days a week, which left them little time or energy for family life. Race riots were more frequent and more deadly than those experienced by recent generations. Women couldn't vote, and their wages were so low that many turned to prostitution.

In 1900 a white child had one chance in three of losing a brother or sister before age 15, and a black child had a fifty-fifty chance of seeing a sibling die. Children's-aid groups reported widespread abuse and neglect by parents. Men who deserted or divorced their wives rarely paid child support. And only 6 percent of the children graduated from high school, compared with 88 percent today.

Why do so many people think American families are facing worse problems now than in the past? Partly it's because we compare the complex and diverse families of the 1990s with the seemingly more standard-issue ones of the 1950s, a unique decade when every long-term trend of the 20th century was temporarily reversed. In the 1950s, for the first time in 100 years, the divorce rate fell while marriage and fertility rates soared, creating a boom in nuclear-family living. The percentage of foreign-born individuals in the country decreased. And the debates over social and cultural issues that had divided Americans for 150 years were silenced, suggesting a national consensus on family values and norms.

Some nostalgia for the 1950s is understandable: Life looked pretty good in comparison with the hardships of the Great Depression and World War II. The GI Bill gave a generation of young fathers a college education and a subsidized mortgage on a new house. For the first time, a majority of men could support a family and buy a home without pooling their earnings with those of other family members. Many Americans built a stable family life on these foundations.

But much nostalgia for the 1950s is a result of selective amnesia—the same process that makes childhood memories of summer vacations grow sunnier with each passing year. The superficial sameness of 1950s family life was achieved through censorship, coercion, and discrimination. People with unconventional beliefs faced governmental investigation and arbitrary firings. African Americans and Mexican Americans were prevented from voting in some states by literacy tests that were not administered to whites. Individuals who didn't follow the rigid gender and sexual rules of the day were ostracized.

8   *Leave It to Beaver* did not reflect the real-life experience of most American families. While many moved into the middle class during the 1950s, poverty remained more widespread than in the worst of our last three recessions. More children went hungry, and poverty rates for the elderly were more than twice as high as today's.

9   Even in the white middle class, not every woman was as serenely happy with her lot as June Cleaver was on TV. Housewives of the 1950s may have been less rushed than today's working mothers, but they were more likely to suffer anxiety and depression. In many states, women couldn't serve on juries or get loans or credit cards in their own names.

10   And not every kid was as wholesome as Beaver Cleaver, whose mischievous antics could be handled by Dad at the dinner table. In 1955 alone, Congress discussed 200 bills aimed at curbing juvenile delinquency. Three years later, *Life* reported that urban teachers were being terrorized by their students. The drugs that were so freely available in 1900 had been outlawed, but many children grew up in families ravaged by alcohol and barbiturate abuse.

11   Rates of unwed childbearing tripled between 1940 and 1958, but most Americans didn't notice because unwed mothers generally left town, gave their babies up for adoption, and returned home as if nothing had happened. Troubled youths were encouraged to drop out of high school. Mentally handicapped children were warehoused in institutions like the Home for Idiotic and Imbecilic Children in Kansas, where a woman whose sister had lived there for most of the 1950s once took me. Wives routinely told pollsters that being disparaged or ignored by their husbands was a normal part of a happier-than-average marriage.

12   Denial extended to other areas of life as well. In the early 1900s, doctors refused to believe that the cases of gonorrhea and syphilis they saw in young girls could have been caused by sexual abuse. Instead, they reasoned, girls could get these diseases from toilet seats, a myth that terrified generations of mothers and daughters. In the 1950s, psychiatrists dismissed incest reports as Oedipal fantasies on the part of children.

13   Spousal rape was legal throughout the period, and wife beating was not taken seriously by authorities. Much of what we now label child abuse was accepted as a normal part of parental discipline. Physicians saw no reason to question parents who claimed that their child's broken bones had been caused by a fall from a tree.

14   There are plenty of stresses in modern family life, but one reason they seem worse is that we no longer sweep them under the rug. Another is that

we have higher expectations of parenting and marriage. That's a good thing. We're right to be concerned about inattentive parents, conflicted marriages, antisocial values, teen violence, and child abuse. But we need to realize that many of our worries reflect how much better we *want* to be, not how much better we *used* to be.

Fathers in intact families are spending more time with their children than at any other point in the past 100 years. Although the number of hours the average woman spends at home with her children has declined since the early 1900s, there has been a decrease in the number of children per family and an increase in individual attention to each child. As a result, mothers today, including working moms, spend almost twice as much time with each child as mothers did in the 1920s. People who raised children in the 1940s and 1950s typically report that their own adult children and grandchildren communicate far better with their kids and spend more time helping with homework than they did—even as they complain that other parents today are doing a worse job than in the past.

Despite the rise in youth violence from the 1960s to the early 1990s, America's children are also safer now than they've ever been. An infant was four times more likely to die in the 1950s than today. A parent then was three times more likely than a modern one to preside at the funeral of a child under the age of 15 and 27 percent more likely to lose an older teen to death.

If we look back over the last millennium, we can see that families have always been diverse and in flux. In each period, families have solved one set of problems only to face a new array of challenges. What works for a family in one economic and cultural setting doesn't work for a family in another. What's helpful at one stage of a family's life may be destructive at the next stage. If there is one lesson to be drawn from the last millennium of family history, it's that families are always having to play catch-up with a changing world.

Take the issue of working mothers. Families in which mothers spend as much time earning a living as they do raising children are nothing new. They were the norm throughout most of the last two millennia. In the 19th century, married women in the United States began a withdrawal from the workforce, but for most families this was made possible only by sending their children out to work instead. When child labor was abolished, married women began reentering the workforce in ever larger numbers.

For a few decades, the decline in child labor was greater than the growth of women's employment. The result was an aberration: the male-breadwinner family. In the 1920s, for the first time, a bare majority of American children grew up in families where the husband provided all the income, the wife stayed home full-time, and they and their siblings went to school instead of work. During the 1950s, almost two thirds of children grew up in such families, an all-time high. Yet that same decade saw an acceleration of workforce participation by wives and mothers that soon made the dual-earner family the norm, a trend not likely to be reversed in the next century.

20   What's new is not that women make half their families' living, but that for the first time they have substantial control over their own income, along with the social freedom to remain single or to leave an unsatisfactory marriage. Also new is the declining proportion of their lives that people devote to rearing children, both because they have fewer kids and because they are living longer. Until about 1940, the typical marriage was broken by the death of one partner within a few years after the last child left home. Today, couples can look forward to spending more than two decades together after the children leave.

21   The growing length of time partners spend with only each other for company has made many individuals less willing to put up with an unhappy marriage, while women's economic independence makes it less essential for them to do so. It is no wonder that divorce has risen steadily since 1900. Disregarding a spurt in 1946, a dip in the 1950s and another peak around 1980, the divorce rate is just where you'd expect to find it, based on the rate of increase from 1900 to 1950. Today, 40 percent of all marriages will end in divorce before a couple's 40th anniversary. Yet despite this high divorce rate, expanded life expectancies mean that more couples are reaching that anniversary than ever before.

22   Families and individuals in contemporary America have more life choices than in the past. That makes it easier for some to consider dangerous or unpopular options. But it also makes success easier for many families that never would have had a chance before—interracial, gay or lesbian, and single-mother families, for example. And it expands horizons for most families.

23   Women's new options are good not just for themselves but for their children. While some people say that women who choose to work are selfish, it turns out that maternal self-sacrifice is not good for children. Kids do better when their mothers are happy with their lives, whether their satisfaction comes from being a full-time homemaker or from having a job.

24   Largely because of women's new roles at work, men are doing more at home. Although most men still do less housework than their wives, the gap has been halved since the 1960s. Today, 49 percent of couples say they share childcare equally, compared with 25 percent in 1985.

Men's greater involvement at home is good for their relationships with   25
their partners and also good for their children. Hands-on fathers make
better parents than men who let their wives do all the nurturing and childcare: They raise sons who are more expressive and daughters who are
more likely to do well in school, especially in math and science.

In 1900, life expectancy was 47 years, and only 4 percent of the popula-   26
tion was 65 or older. Today, life expectancy is 76 years, and by 2025, about
20 percent of Americans will be 65 or older. For the first time, a generation
of adults must plan for the needs of both their parents and their children.
Most Americans are responding with remarkable grace. One in four
households gives the equivalent of a full day a week or more in unpaid
care to an aging relative, and more than half say they expect to do so in the
next 10 years. Older people are less likely to be impoverished or incapacitated by illness than in the past, and they have more opportunity to
develop a relationship with their grandchildren.

Even some of the choices that worry us the most are turning out to be   27
manageable. Divorce rates are likely to remain high, but more noncustodial parents are staying in touch with their children. Child-support receipts
are up. And a lower proportion of kids from divorced families are exhibit-
ing problems than in earlier decades. Stepfamilies are learning to maximize children's access to supportive adults rather than cutting them off
from one side of the family.

Out-of-wedlock births are also high, however, and this will probably   28
continue because the age of first marriage for women has risen to an all-
time high of 25, almost five years above what it was in the 1950s. Women
who marry at an older age are less likely to divorce, but they have more
years when they are at risk—or at choice—for a nonmarital birth.

Nevertheless, births to teenagers have fallen from 50 percent of all non-   29
marital births in the late 1970s to just 30 percent today. A growing proportion of women who have a nonmarital birth are in their twenties and thir-
ties and usually have more economic and educational resources than
unwed mothers of the past. While two involved parents are generally better than one, a mother's personal maturity, along with her educational and
economic status, is a better predictor of how well her child will turn out
than her marital status. We should no longer assume that children raised
by single parents face debilitating disadvantages.

As we begin to understand the range of sizes, shapes, and colors that   30
today's families come in, we find that the differences *within* family types
are more important than the differences *between* them. No particular family form guarantees success, and no particular form is doomed to fail. How

ANSWERS TO
QUESTIONS
Thinking Critically
About Content
1. Answers will vary.
Here are some
possibilities.
    Children are safer
      now.
    Life expectancy is
      higher.
    Men are more active
      in child rearing.
    Women have greater
      individual
      freedom.
    Men help with the
      house.
    People will soon
      take care of
      parents as well
      as children.
2. Answers will vary.
3. Answers will vary,
but families are having
to adapt to women in
the workforce,
women's independence,
longer lives, higher
divorce rates, and male
responsibilities in the
home.

α family functions on the inside is more important than how it looks from the outside.

31   The biggest problem facing most families is not that our families have changed too much but that our institutions have changed too little. America's work policies are 50 years out of date, designed for a time when most moms weren't in the workforce and most dads didn't understand the joys of being involved in childcare. Our school schedules are 150 years out of date, designed for a time when kids needed to be home to help with the milking and haying. And many political leaders feel they have to decide whether to help parents stay home longer with their kids or invest in better childcare, preschool and afterschool programs, when most industrialized nations have long since learned it's possible to do both.

32   So America's social institutions have some bugs to iron out. But for the most part, our families are ready for the new millennium.

Thinking Critically About Content

1. Explain four differences between the American family now and 100 years ago.

2. What difference between family life then and now is most interesting to you? Why?

3. According to Coontz, in what ways are families "always having to play catch-up with a changing world" (paragraph 17)?

Thinking Critically About Purpose and Audience

4. Why do you think Coontz wrote this essay?

5. Who do you think is her main audience?

6. What is Coontz's general opinion about the American family today?

Thinking Critically About Essays

7. What is Coontz's thesis statement? How does she lead up to this thesis?

8. Explain how the topic sentence works in paragraph 5. Does it supply the controlling idea for the entire paragraph?

9. Are the statistics and facts that Coontz cites in this essay effective? Which are most effective in proving her thesis?

10. Do you agree or disagree with her general conclusions about the American family today? Write a detailed response to some of Coontz's observations.

Tony Cohan

BETWEEN WORLDS

Focusing Your Attention

1. Do you ever feel like you live in two or more different worlds? What are they?

2. In the essay you are about to read, the author compares and contrasts the "worlds" of San Miguel de Allende in Mexico and Los Angeles from a writer's point of view. What similarities and differences do you imagine that Cohan discovered?

Expanding Your Vocabulary

The following words are important to your understanding of this essay:

entwine: weave (paragraph 1)

revelatory: revealing (paragraph 1)

mired: buried (paragraph 1)

recession: decline (paragraph 1)

unkempt: messy, untidy (paragraph 4)

la frontera: border (paragraph 5)

calibrations: adjustments (paragraph 6)

referent: point of reference (paragraph 7)

jargon: specialized language (paragraph 7)

deciphering: figuring out (paragraph 7)

corrido: run (paragraph 8)

Proustian: emotional (paragraph 8)

feigned: pretend (paragraph 9)

reticent: uncommunicative, silent (paragraph 9)

xenophobic: afraid of strangers or foreigners (paragraph 9)

primordial: primitive (paragraph 9)

brujos: wizards (paragraph 9)

audibility: hearing (paragraph 10)

near-monastic: almost monk-like (paragraph 13)

muster: create (paragraph 13)

sabor: flavor (paragraph 13)

SUMMARY

In this essay, Cohan compares life in San Miguel de Allende, Mexico, and Los Angeles from a writer's point of view and finds that they are two necessary parts of his life.

READABILITY
(Flesch–Kincaid grade level)
8.2

INSTRUCTOR'S RESOURCE MANUAL

For additional teaching strategies, for journal entries, for vocabulary and reading quizzes, and for more writing assignments, see the *Instructor's Resource Manual*, Section II, Part IV.

ambiente: atmosphere (paragraph 13)

celebratory: festive (paragraph 14)

norteño bands: bands from northern Mexico (paragraph 14)

patina: shine (paragraph 14)

conditional: tentative (paragraph 14)

corrugated: with parallel ridges (paragraph 17)

lumpen detritus: accumulated debris (paragraph 17)

1   Our fourth year in Mexico. We live between worlds these days, frequent flyers. The Mexican cycles of seasons and holidays entwine us deeper in town and country. Friends come and go, fall in love, split up; babies are born. Our life in San Miguel de Allende remains the intimate sum of our days—sensual, revelatory, engaged. Mexico, still mired in post-earthquake recession, muddles through somehow. New friends emerge: Arnaud, a Haitian poet in exile who has awakened me to Caribbean culture; a Chilean painter and his wife; a Mexican professor.

2   Our world widens southward. The sprawling lands below the Rio Grande, a mere blip on CNN or ABC, remain to us norteamericanos, after all these centuries, the New World. Often after a flight from California we remain in Mexico City to explore, see new friends, venture out into other regions—Oaxaca, Guerrero, Yucatán, Chiapas—before returning to San Miguel, the heart's abode.

3   Still we feel unsettled at times, uneasily poised between cultures: losing a foothold in the old country, still on tourist visas in the new one. Masako's art bursts with imagery found here. Slowly Mexico takes root in my work, too: yet the language I hear and speak every day is not the one I write in. Gore Vidal, in an introduction to Paul Bowles's collected short stories, touches on the problem: "Great American writers are supposed not only to live in the greatest country in the world . . . but to write about that greatest of all human themes: the American Experience." A novelist friend I work with in PEN, the international writers group, says only half jokingly, "Careful you don't become a *desaparecido,* a disappeared person, yourself."

4   Sometimes I do fear liking Mexico too much, getting lost in it. One day I saw a scraggly, unkempt gringo on the Mexico City metro around my age with bad teeth and a bad haircut, tangled in another land, beyond return. He reminded me of Russians I'd seen in China, poor and disheveled, hunched atop bundles in train stations—the ones who'd stayed on too long.

5   On plane trips back to California, I gaze down at the Sea of Cortez: tidal blue stripes graduating from pale agate to turquoise to aquamarine. Salty inlets and rust basins, green algal meadows. Violet badlands etched with tiny straight-line roads, barren as Mars. We cross *la frontera,* that invisible,

charged border, and belly down over L.A.'s carpet of light. From the back of a taxi running up the 405, the city spreads away before us, a bobbing, firefly-infested lake.

We stay on friends' couches, house-sit, sublet. We see people necessary   6
to the work we do, thumbing our Rolodexes, trying to make the days count. Observing age's effects upon our parents, we make careful calibrations between desire and duty. Sometimes we talk of buying another place in L.A. just to have an anchor in the home country, but we can't summon the interest. We hurry through our tasks so we can leave all the sooner.

Old friends are busy climbing up, clinging to, falling off career ladders.   7
The conversation is the same one we checked out on six months earlier, different only in detail, with television and movies the referent, not live experience or books. I'm losing the jargon, the codes, the names of things. In conversations I blank on celebrities' names, hip expressions. Car alarms go off like crazy toys. Helicopters throb overhead, spotlighting evil. The nightly news imbues pedestrian acts with hysterical urgency. Few people walk for pleasure. There's little time to talk, and seldom of important things. It's easier to get some tasks done, as long as you don't need another human: I spend hours deciphering new telephone message menus, wading through oceans of calling options, waiting on hold. Arnaud, my Haitian poet friend in San Miguel, refers to revisiting his beloved Haiti as *the exile of return.*

Mexico in memory can be flat, flavorless, a postcard—like trying to   8
remember sex or a good meal. It lives in the senses, not the mind, collapsing all abstractions into the brimming moment. Yet hearing a *corrido* on the radio or Spanish spoken in an L.A. market can unleash a near-overwhelming, Proustian effect, bringing tears. Now I understand better the mariachis' howling laments of memory and loss.

In California we don't talk much about Mexico. We've grown tired of the   9
blank stares, the feigned interest, the allusions to Tijuana and the border towns, the beaches of Cabo or Cancún. Now I know why Mina and Paul used to be so reticent. In glossy, xenophobic, dollar-grubbing late-eighties U.S.A., Mexico is buzzless: a torpid blank somewhere south. Mexico, grail to generations of artists, site of primordial revelation—Mayan temples, *brujos,* muralists, hallucinatory mushrooms—has fallen off the map. This whorled, ornate neighbor civilization, secretly and essentially entwined with ours, is invisible, its people among us silent, nameless wraiths who clip lawns and clear tables.

In a West Hollywood eatery, we sit with friends, poking at endive salad,   10
designer pizza. A plate glass window offers a view of the foothills behind the Strip. A Sade tape teases the threshold of lyric audibility. Noticing the nine-dollar taco on the menu, we glance at each other.

"Yes, but what do you *do* there?" one friend asks.   11

12   How to describe a trip to the Tuesday market? A four-hour dinner with Carlos, Elenita, Arnaud, and Colette in our patio by the Quebrada bridge? Waking up to the bells' sweet clangor? Hurrying along the cobbles in the rain, ducking under archways? How to describe Friday lunches at El Caribe or checking out Thomas More's *Utopia* at the little bilingual library and actually reading it through? It's as if we have a secret life, in a secret place.

13   I used to like L.A.: the cool speed, the indifference to history, the near-monastic life of house, car, house. It freed the mind to run along some ever widening horizon line. Flatness, the absence of affect: not a bad place for a writer. There's no world out there so you invent one. I can't muster that appreciation any longer. I want taste, smell, *sabor, ambiente*. I want the human shape to my days.

14   In another sense, though, Mexico has redeemed L.A. to me. I've discovered a buried city there—a Latino L.A., warm and celebratory, where Spanish traces an invisible heart line deeper than place. In the course of my days, I may encounter a man or woman hailing from Guanajuato or Jalisco or Oaxaca, and matters of truth and fullness of heart may pass between us, and much laughter: riches invisible to most of my other friends. I can trace Los Lobos riffs back to *norteño* bands that come through our part of Mexico: Los Tigres del Norte, Los Bukis. California street names and foods reveal their origins. Suddenly the century-old Anglo patina looks flimsy, conditional.

15   Sometimes I get energy off the displacement, the dislocation, the back-and-forth. Each country seems the antidote to the other's ills. "In Rio, dreaming of New England/In New England, dreaming of Rio," the poet Elizabeth Bishop wrote.

16   Sometimes it feels like the two countries, through me, dream each other.

17   Invariably our L.A. trips end with a visit to the storage bin in Glendale. We introduce the seven-digit code, pass through the security gates, inch down aisles of identical metal containers and cinder-block structures. We remove the lock, raise the corrugated door, and consider the lumpen detritus of our former life.

18   We shut the door, lock it, drive off.

19   Finally, our lists checked off, we head back to Mexico. At journey's end, the Flecha Amarilla bus pulls into the dusty turnaround at the foot of San Miguel. We step out into darkness, as on that first night four years ago. The street dogs, the boys who want a coin to help with the baggage, the waiting taxi driver—those shades that so alarmed us then—appear to us now as town greeters, familiars. Wending up unlit streets once mysterious but intimate now from walking them, we make small talk with the taxi driver. "*Sí*," he says. "*Un poco frío*." A little chilly. At Calle Quebrada we drag our bags down the dark stairwell, brush past a pair of young lovers. We open

the door. The dusky smell of the last mesquite fire we'd built hits us. Our luggage slumps to the stone floor, our hands unclench. We're back.

Thinking Critically About Content

1. What do you think is Cohan's main point in this essay?
2. Why does Cohan call San Miguel "the heart's abode" (paragraph 2)?
3. In what ways is Cohan "poised between cultures" (paragraph 3)

Thinking Critically About Purpose and Audience

4. Why do you think Cohan wrote this essay?
5. Who would be most interested in this essay?
6. How does this essay make you feel about your home town?

Thinking Critically About Essays

7. Name four points of comparison and four points of contrast in this essay.
8. How are most of the paragraphs in this essay organized? Use one paragraph to explain your answer.
9. Is Cohan's title effective? Explain your answer.
10. Write a short fable about a similarity or difference between two cities you know.

especially those who have lived in two different countries or who bring another culture to the place where they now live.
6. Answers will vary.

Thinking Critically About Essays
7. Answers will vary. There are points of comparison in almost every paragraph.
8. Most of the paragraphs discuss both San Miguel and Los Angeles in reference to the topic of the paragraph. If a paragraph deals with only one of these locations in relation to a topic, the next paragraph usually deals with that topic and the other location.
9. Answers will vary.
10. Answers will vary.

Writing Topics: Comparing and Contrasting

Before you begin to write, you might want to review the writing process in Part I.

1. In the first essay, Stephanie Coontz talks about the changes she sees in the past century in the role of the family in American society, but there are also differences between families today. Compare and contrast your family's values with those of another family. What is the same between the two? What is different?
2. Expand the fable you wrote in response to question 10 after Tony Cohan's essay by adding more characters and more points.
3. What process do you have to go through to come up with an interesting comparison or contrast? How is it different from the process you go through for other rhetorical modes?

CHAPTER **30**

DIVIDING AND CLASSIFYING

The essays in this chapter show division and classification at work. The first, "Black Music in Our Hands" written by Bernice Reagon, divides and classifies the role of music in her life. The second essay, "What Are Friends For?" by Marion Winik, divides and classifies various types of friends.

Bernice Reagon

BLACK MUSIC IN OUR HANDS

SUMMARY

In this essay, Reagon explains the different types of music she has encountered that have "helped to shape my present-day use of music" (paragraph 15).

READABILITY
(Flesch–Kincaid grade level)
10.3

INSTRUCTOR'S RESOURCE MANUAL

For additional teaching strategies, for journal entries, for vocabulary and reading quizzes, and for more writing assignments, see the *Instructor's Resource Manual*, Section II, Part IV.

Focusing Your Attention

1. What are some of your main interests in life? Have any of these interests been part of your life for a long time? How have they changed over time?

2. In the essay you are about to read, the writer divides and classifies music from a number of different perspectives. What role does music play in your life? Has it always played this role? How has it changed in your life over the years?

Expanding Your Vocabulary

The following words are important to your understanding of this essay:

Albany State: college in Albany, Georgia (paragraph 1)

contralto soloist: a woman singer with a very low voice (paragraph 1)

arias: songs in an opera (paragraph 1)

lieder: traditional German songs (paragraph 1)

Nathaniel Dett: 1882–1943, American composer and pianist (paragraph 1)

William Dawson: 1899–1990, African American composer (paragraph 1)

unaccompanied: without musical instruments (paragraph 2)

ornate: complex (paragraph 2)

congregational responses: singing by the people in the pews in reply to someone at the front of the church (paragraph 2)

Civil Rights Movement: push for equal rights for African Americans in the 1950s and 1960s (paragraph 5)

integrative: uniting (paragraph 5)

Albany Movement: a movement started in Albany, Georgia, and led by Rev. Martin Luther King Jr. that hoped to gain more freedom for African Americans but ended in racial violence (paragraph 8)

Freedom Singers: African Americans who sang about civic rights during the Civil Rights Movement (paragraph 12)

Georgia Sea Island Singers: international performing artists who sing about African American culture (paragraph 13)

Newport Festival: summer music festival held in Newport, Rhode Island (paragraph 13)

repertoire: collection of songs that an artist is able to perform (paragraph 13)

casings: coverings (paragraph 16)

sit-in: an act of protest in which demonstrators sit down and refuse to leave the premises (paragraph 17)

Wallace: George Wallace, 1919–1998, the segregationist governor of Alabama (paragraph 17)

Freedom Rides: rides taken by civil rights activists to ensure that public facilities had been desegregated (paragraph 17)

ensemble: a group of musicians who perform together (paragraph 17)

Thelonious Monk: 1917–1982, composer and pianist who created a new type of jazz known as bebop (paragraph 18)

Charlie Mingus: 1922–1979, jazz performer on bass and piano, hailed as a composer and a poet (paragraph 18)

SNCC: Student Nonviolent Coordinating Committee, a group of black and white students that promoted peace between races (paragraph 18)

Coltrane: John Coltrane, 1926–1967, jazz saxophonist who also played the flute (paragraph 18)

Charlie Parker: 1920–1955, a bebop jazz artist who played the alto saxophone (paragraph 18)

Coleman Hawkins: 1901–1969, known as the father of the jazz tenor saxophone (paragraph 18)

compost: mixture (paragraph 20)

1   In the early 1960s, I was in college at Albany State. My major interests were music and biology. In music I was a contralto soloist with the choir, studying Italian arias and German lieder. The black music I sang was of three types: (1) Spirituals sung by the college choir. These were arranged by such people as Nathaniel Dett and William Dawson and had major injections of European musical harmony and composition. (2) Rhythm 'n' Blues, music done by and for Blacks in social settings. This included the music of bands at proms, juke boxes, and football game songs. (3) Church music; gospel was a major part of Black church music by the time I was in college. I was a soloist with the gospel choir.

2   Prior to the gospel choir, introduced in my church when I was twelve, was many years' experience with unaccompanied music—Black choral singing, hymns, lined out by strong song leaders with full, powerful, richly ornate congregational responses. These hymns were offset by upbeat, clapping call-and-response songs.

3   I saw people in church sing and pray until they shouted. I knew *that* music as a part of a cultural expression that was powerful enough to take people from their conscious selves to a place where the physical and intellectual being worked in harmony with the spirit. I enjoyed and needed that experience. The music of the church was an integral part of the cultural world into which I was born.

4   Outside of church, I saw music as good, powerful sounds you made or listened to. Rhythm and blues—you danced to; music of the college choir— you clapped after the number was finished.

5   The Civil Rights Movement changed my view of music. It was after my first march. I began to sing a song and in the course of singing changed the song so that it made sense for that particular moment. Although I was not consciously aware of it, this was one of my earliest experiences with how my music was supposed to *function*. This music was to be integrative of and consistent with everything I was doing at that time; it was to be tied to activities that went beyond artistic affairs such as concerts, dances, and church meetings.

6   The next level of awareness came while in jail. I had grown up in a rural area outside the city limits, riding a bus to public school or driving to college. My life had been a pretty consistent, balanced blend of church, school, and proper upbringing. I was aware of a Black educated class that taught me in high school and college, of taxi cabs I never rode in, and of people who used buses I never boarded. I went to school with their children.

In jail with me were all these people. All ages. In my section were   7
women from about thirteen to eighty years old. Ministers' wives and teachers and teachers' wives who had only nodded at me or clapped at a concert or spoken to my mother. A few people from my classes. A large number
of people who rode segregated city buses. One or two women who had
been drinking along the two-block stretch of Little Harlem as the march
went by. Very quickly, clashes arose: around age, who would have authority, what was proper behavior?

The Albany Movement was already a singing movement, and we took   8
the songs to jail. There the songs I had sung because they made me feel
good or because they said what I thought about a specific issue did something. I would start a song, and everybody would join in. After the song, the
differences among us would not be as great. Somehow, making a song required an expression of that which was common to us all. The songs did not
feel like the same songs I had sung in college. This music was like an instrument, like holding a tool in your hand.

I found that although I was younger than many of the women in my sec-   9
tion of the jail, I was asked to take on leadership roles. First as a song leader
and then in most other matters concerning the group, especially in discussions or when speaking with prison officials.

I fell in love with that kind of music. I saw that to define music as some-   10
thing you listen to, something that pleases you, is very different from defining it as an instrument with which you can drive a point. In both instances,
you can have the same song. But using it as an instrument makes it a different kind of music.

The next level of awareness occurred during the first mass meeting   11
after my release from jail. I was asked to lead the song that I had changed
after the first march. When I opened my mouth and began to sing, there
was a force and power within myself I had never heard before. Somehow
this music—music I could use as an instrument to do things with, music that
was mine to shape and change so that it made the statement I needed to
make—released a kind of power and required a level of concentrated energy I did not know I had. I liked the feeling.

For several years, I worked with the Movement eventually doing Civil   12
Rights songs with the Freedom Singers. The Freedom Singers used the
songs, interspersed with narrative, to convey the story of the Civil Rights
Movement's struggles. The songs were more powerful than spoken conversation. They became a major way of making people who were not on the
scene feel the intensity of what was happening in the South. Hopefully, they
would move the people to take a stand, to organize support groups or participate in various projects.

13   The Georgia Sea Island Singers, whom I first heard at the Newport Festival, were a major link. Bessie Jones, coming from within twenty miles of Albany, Georgia, had a repertoire and song-leading style I recognized from the churches I had grown up in. She, along with John Davis, would talk about songs that Black people had sung as slaves and what those songs meant in terms of their struggle to be free. The songs did not sound like the spirituals I had sung in college choirs; they sounded like the songs I had grown up with in church. There I had been told the songs had to do with worship of Jesus Christ.

14   The next few years I spent focusing on three components: (1) The music I had found in the Civil Rights Movement; (2) Songs of the Georgia Sea Island Singers and other traditional groups and the ways in which those songs were linked to the struggles of Black peoples at earlier times; (3) Songs of the church that now sounded like those traditional songs and came close to having, for many people, the same kind of freeing power.

15   There was another experience that helped to shape my present-day use of music. After getting out of jail, the mother of the church my father pastored was at the mass meeting. She prayed, a prayer I had heard hundreds of times. I had focused on its sound, tune, rhythm, chant, whether the moans came at the proper pace and intensity. That morning I heard every word that she said. She did not have to change one word of prayer she had been praying for much of her Christian life for me to know she was addressing the issues we were facing at that moment. More than her personal prayer, it felt like an analysis of the Albany, Georgia, Black community.

16   My collection, study, and creation of Black music has been, to a large extent, about freeing the sounds and the words and the messages from casings in which they have been put, about hearing clearly what the music has to say about Black people and their struggle.

17   When I first began to search, I looked for what was then being called folk music, rather than for other Black forms, such as jazz, rhythm and blues, or gospel. It slowly dawned on me that during the Movement we had used all those forms. When we were relaxing in the office, we made up songs using popular rhythm and blues tunes; songs based in rhythm and blues also came out of jails, especially from the sit-in movement and the march to Selma, Alabama. "Oh Wallace, You Never Can Jail Us All" is an example from Selma. "You Better Leave Segregation Alone" came out of the Nashville Freedom Rides and was based on a bit by Little Willie John, "You Better Leave My Kitten Alone." Gospel choirs became the major musical vehicle in the urban center of Birmingham, with the choir led by

Carlton Reese. There was also a gospel choir in the Chicago work, as well as an instrumental ensemble led by Ben Branch.

Jazz had not been a strong part of my musical life. I began to hear it as I 18 traveled north. Thelonious Monk and Charlie Mingus played on the first SNCC benefit at Carnegie Hall. I heard of and then heard Coltrane. Then I began to pick up the pieces that had been laid by Charlie Parker and Coleman Hawkins and whole lifetimes of music. This music had no words. But, it had power, intensity, and movement under various degrees of pressure; it had vocal texture and color. I could feel that the music knew how it felt to be Black and Angry. Black and Down, Black and Loved, Black and Fighting.

I now believe that Black music exists in every place where Black people 19 run, every corner where they live, every level on which they struggle. We have been here a long while, in many situations. It takes all that we have created to sing our song. I believe that Black musicians/artists have a responsibility to be conscious of their world and to let their consciousness be heard in their songs.

And we need it all—blues, gospel, ballads, children's games, dance, 20 rhythms, jazz, lovesongs, topical songs—doing what it has always done. We need Black music that functions in relation to the people and community who provide the nurturing compost that makes its creation and continuation possible.

Thinking Critically About Content

1. Reagon divides and classifies music into at least three different categories. What are these categories?

2. What are the main differences in these categories?

3. What does Reagon mean when she says, "It takes all that we have created to sing our song" (paragraph 19)?

Thinking Critically About Purpose and Audience

4. What do you think Reagon's purpose is in this essay?

5. What makes this purpose both personal and social?

6. Who do you think is Reagon's main audience?

Thinking Critically About Essays

7. Explain how the topic sentence works in paragraph 5. Does it supply the controlling idea for the entire paragraph?

8. Choose a paragraph from this essay, and explain whether or not it is unified. Be as specific as possible.

Singers, prayer music, and jazz.
3. Reagon is referring to the history of the black people; in order to tell their tales in songs, they must first remember what they have endured.

Thinking Critically About Purpose and Audience
4. Reagon probably wants to educate readers on the evolution of some black music, but she is also informing people of her journey through her appreciation of music.
5. She is describing through narration her journey toward musical discovery (personal) and is showing readers the struggles of blacks and the difficulties they overcame through song (social).
6. Reagon's main audience is general but probably not black people. She is trying to educate those who are unaware of her music.

Thinking Critically About Essays
7. The topic sentence, "The Civil Rights Movement changed my view of music," supplies the controlling idea for paragraph 5 because the following sentences explain this idea.
8. Answers will vary.
9. Reagon uses "in our hands" in her title because she is showing how the music that is available to us (in our

hands) can be used for situations that can help change society.
10. Answers will vary.

9. What do you think "in our hands" means in the title of this essay?

10. What role does music play in your life? Divide and classify its role in your life over the years.

Marion Winik

WHAT ARE FRIENDS FOR?

Focusing Your Attention

1. Who do you rely on to talk out your problems? To confide in? To tell secrets to? How do these people fit into your life? How do you fit into theirs?

2. In the essay you are about to read, the author divides and classifies the types of friends people generally have. What do you think these types are?

Expanding Your Vocabulary

The following words are important to your understanding of this essay:

half-slip: undergarment worn by women (paragraph 1)

innumerable: too many to count (paragraph 2)

Aquarena Springs: a theme park in San Marcos, Texas, that is now a preservation and education center (paragraph 2)

infallible: unfailing (paragraph 6)

indispensable: absolutely necessary (paragraph 8)

wistful: nostalgic (paragraph 10)

ill-conceived: poorly planned (paragraph 10)

inopportune: inconvenient (paragraph 11)

tonic: boost (paragraph 14)

SUMMARY

In this essay, Winik humorously divides "friends" into nine different categories.

READABILITY

(Flesch–Kincaid grade level)
9.8

INSTRUCTOR'S RESOURCE MANUAL

For additional teaching strategies, for journal entries, for vocabulary and reading quizzes, and for more writing assignments, see the *Instructor's Resource Manual*, Section II, Part IV.

1   I was thinking about how everybody can't be everything to each other, but some people can be something to each other, thank God, from the ones whose shoulders you cry on to the ones whose half-slips you borrow to the nameless ones you chat with in the grocery line.

2   Buddies, for example, are the workhorses of the friendship world, the people out there on the front lines, defending you from loneliness and boredom. They call you up, they listen to your complaints, they celebrate your successes and curse your misfortunes, and you do the same for them in return. They hold out through innumerable crises before concluding that the

person you're dating is no good, and even then understand if you ignore their good counsel. They accompany you to a movie with subtitles or to see the diving pig at Aquarena Springs. They feed your cat when you are out of town and pick you up from the airport when you get back. They come over to help you decide what to wear on a date. Even if it is with that creep.

What about family members? Most of them are people you just got stuck with, and though you love them, you may not have very much in common. But there is that rare exception, the Relative Friend. It is your cousin, your brother, maybe even your aunt. The two of you share the same views of the other family members. Meg never should have divorced Martin. He was the best thing that ever happened to her. You can confirm each other's memories of things that happened a long time ago. Don't you remember when Uncle Hank and Daddy had that awful fight in the middle of Thanksgiving dinner? Grandma always hated Grandpa's stamp collection; she probably left the windows open during the hurricane on purpose.   3

While so many family relationships are tinged with guilt and obligation, a relationship with a Relative Friend is relatively worry-free. You don't even have to hide your vices from this delightful person. When you slip out Aunt Joan's back door for a cigarette, she is already there.   4

Then there is that special guy at work. Like all the other people at the job site, at first he's just part of the scenery. But gradually he starts to stand out from the crowd. Your friendship is cemented by jokes about co-workers and thoughtful favors around the office. Did you see Ryan's hair? Want half my bagel? Soon you know the names of his turtles, what he did last Friday night, exactly which model CD player he wants for his birthday. His handwriting is as familiar to you as your own.   5

Though you invite each other to parties, you somehow don't quite fit into each other's outside lives. For this reason, the friendship may not survive a job change. Company gossip, once an infallible source of entertainment, soon awkwardly accentuates the distance between you. But wait. Like School Friends, Work Friends share certain memories which acquire a nostalgic glow after about a decade.   6

A Faraway Friend is someone you grew up with or went to school with or lived in the same town as until one of you moved away. Without a Faraway Friend, you would never get any mail addressed in handwriting. A Faraway Friend calls late at night, invites you to her wedding, always says she is coming to visit but rarely shows up. An actual visit from a Faraway Friend is a cause for celebration and binges of all kinds. Cigarettes, Chips Ahoy, bottles of tequila.   7

Faraway Friends go through phases of intense communication, then may be out of touch for many months. Either way, the connection is always there. A conversation with your Faraway Friend always helps to put your   8 life in perspective: When you feel you've hit a dead end, come to a confusing fork in the road, or gotten lost in some crackerbox subdivision of your life, the advice of the Faraway Friend—who has the big picture, who is so well acquainted with the route that brought you to this place—is indispensable.

9   Another useful function of the Faraway Friend is to help you remember things from a long time ago, like the name of your seventh-grade history teacher, what was in that really good stir-fry, or exactly what happened that night on the boat with the guys from Florida.

10   Ah, the Former Friend. A sad thing. At best a wistful memory, at worst a dangerous enemy who is in possession of many of your deepest secrets. But what was it that drove you apart? A misunderstanding, a betrayed confidence, an unrepaid loan, an ill-conceived flirtation. A poor choice of spouse can do in a friendship just like that. Going into business together can be a serious mistake. Time, money, distance, cult religions: all noted friendship killers. You quit doing drugs, you're not such good friends with your dealer anymore.

11   And lest we forget, there are the Friends You Love to Hate. They call at inopportune times. They say stupid things. They butt in, they boss you around, they embarrass you in public. They invite themselves over. They take advantage. You've done the best you can, but they need professional help. On top of all this, they love you to death and are convinced they're your best friend on the planet.

12   So why do you continue to be involved with these people? Why do you tolerate them? On the contrary, the real question is, What would you do without them? Without Friends You Love to Hate, there would be nothing to talk about with your other friends. Their problems and their irritating stunts provide a reliable source of conversation for everyone they know. What's more, Friends You Love to Hate make you feel good about yourself, since you are obviously in so much better shape than they are. No matter what these people do, you will never get rid of them. As much as they need you, you need them too.

13   At the other end of the spectrum are Hero Friends. These people are better than the rest of us, that's all there is to it. Their career is something you wanted to be when you grew up—painter, forest ranger, tireless doer of good. They have beautiful homes filled with special handmade things presented to them by villagers in the remote areas they have visited in their extensive travels. Yet they are modest. They never gossip. They are always helping others, especially those who have suffered a death in the family or an illness. You would think people like this would just make you sick, but somehow they don't.

14   A New Friend is a tonic unlike any other. Say you meet her at a party. In your bowling league. At a Japanese conversation class, perhaps. Wherever, whenever, there's that spark of recognition. The first time you

ANSWERS TO
QUESTIONS
*Thinking Critically
About Content*
1. Winik introduces
nine categories of
friends: Buddies,
Relative Friends,
Work Friends,
School Friends,
Faraway Friends,
Former Friends,
Friends You Love
to Hate, Hero Friends,
and New Friends.
2. She creates the
categories on the basis
that different kinds of
friends serve different
purposes in people's
lives.
3. New Friends are like
a tonic because they
spark life into both
people. Everything is
new and exciting;

talk, you can't believe how much you have in common. Suddenly, your life story is interesting again, your insights fresh, your opinion valued. Your various shortcomings are as yet completely invisible.

It's almost like falling in love.   15

Thinking Critically About Content

1. How many types of friends does Winik introduce? What are they?
2. On what basis does Winik create these categories?
3. In what ways is a new friend "a tonic" (paragraph 14)?

Thinking Critically About Purpose and Audience

4. Why do you think Winik wrote this essay?
5. Who would be most interested in this essay?
6. How does this essay make you feel about the role of friends in your life?

Thinking Critically About Essays

7. How does Winik organize her essay? Why do you think she puts her categories in this order?
8. How does the author develop each category? Use one paragraph to explain your answer.
9. Explain Winik's title.
10. Write a detailed description of one of your friends. Why is this person a friend of yours?

New Friends are like energy pills.

Thinking Critically About Purpose and Audience
4. Winik wrote this essay to entertain her readers.
5. Anyone would be interested in this essay.
6. Answers will vary.

Thinking Critically About Essays
7. Winik organizes her essay from least to most exciting. In this way, she can hold her readers' attention throughout the essay.
8. She develops her categories by first defining the type of friend and then providing examples. Beyond this, answers will vary.
9. This essay is Winik's answer to the question in her title, "What are friends for?"
10. Answers will vary.

Writing Topics: Dividing and Classifying

Before you begin to write, you might want to review the writing process in Part I.

1. In the first essay, Reagon talks about the changing role of music in her life. Divide and classify one of your interests over the years.
2. Divide and classify your friends into meaningful categories, and write an essay explaining your classification system.
3. What process do you have to go through to come up with an interesting comparison or contrast? How is it different from the process you go through for other rhetorical modes?

CHAPTER **31**

DEFINING

Here are two essays that show how definition works in two completely different contexts: "Ways to *Ai*" by Wang Ping defines "love" from the point of view of her Chinese heritage. The second essay, "Healing Myself with the Power of Work" by Michael Norlen, explains how work has been a form of lifesaving therapy for the author.

Wang Ping

WAYS TO *AI*—爱

SUMMARY
Based on personal experiences from her Chinese heritage, Wang Ping defines "love" in this essay.

READABILITY
(Flesch–Kincaid grade level)
8.2

INSTRUCTOR'S RESOURCE MANUAL
For additional teaching strategies, for journal entries, for vocabulary and reading quizzes, and for more writing assignments, see the *Instructor's Resource Manual*, Section II, Part IV.

Focusing Your Attention

1. How many different kinds of love do you know about? How many have you experienced?

2. The essay you are about to read defines love. What does "love" mean to you? What emotions do you associate with this word?

Expanding Your Vocabulary

The following words are important to your understanding of this essay:

paternal: from the father's side of a family (paragraph 1)

faction: political group (paragraph 3)

filial: involving a son or daughter (paragraphs 4 and 5)

1   "Love? Can love buy you a decent meal with rice and meat? Can it keep you warm in snow? Safe in a storm?" my grandma would answer whenever I asked about her arranged marriage, her long widowed life.

2   "Don't even think about 'talking love' before you turn 25, before you join the Communist Party and have made something of life!" my father warned when I left home at 15.

"There's no such thing as love without a reason, just as there is no such   3
thing as hate without a reason." We chanted Mao's words as we spat and
kicked at the teachers we had once adored, broke windows, burnt books,
beat up Red Guards from a different faction who were once our best
friends.

My grandma's favorite dinner story is about a widow who cut chunks of   4
flesh from her arms and thighs to make broth for her dying mother-in-law.
Such a filial deed moved the gods so much that they let the old woman
revive and live another ten years. As the story proceeded, my mother
would bang her chopsticks and rice bowl louder and louder on the table
and finally stomp out. "Have you heard a better love story than that?" my
grandma would ask, her cheeks sunk deep in a toothless mouth.

"This is for the burnt rice," my mother said as she whipped us with   5
her bamboo stick. "And this is for the bowl you broke, the corner you
didn't sweep, the dirty words that slipped out of your mouth." She aimed at
our thighs, where the meat was the thickest, the pain unforgettable. "A
filial son comes from under a rod. I want you to remember this, with your
flesh. You'll be grateful when you grow up, and you'll pass it on to your
children, and next, and next. And this is the best love a mother can give
you, kiddos."

I've never written a love poem, nor said the word love—*ai*—in Chinese.   6
When pressed by my Chinese boyfriend, I'd say it in English and French
only. (He found it cute in the beginning, but later used it as an excuse to
dump me.) The word sounds like bad luck, too much like a sigh—*ai*. It
makes me feel like an old man bent with heavy loads. We say *teng ai* (pain
love) to our children, *eng ai* (gratitude love), or *ai qing* (love emotion)
between husband and wife, *lian ai* (pity love) to a mistress or a child. Love
is conditioned, heavily.

I trace the word on paper. First is the hand, then the roof of a house. This   7
makes sense. You want to keep a firm hand on your shelter, your safety,
before you can even start talking about love. Is that why my father warned
me over and over again not to "talk love" before I've established myself?
Then comes the part "friend." I open my biggest dictionary, *Ocean of
Words*. 17 years away from China, and I'm losing my mother tongue. It's a
complicated system, each word made with two, three, even six different
components. No, I'm not wrong; the word does end with a friend, a friend
holding up the roof of a house with an assuring hand. So what does it have
to do with love? I look back into the dictionary again. It says "love among
brothers." Ok, brotherly love, love of the same sex before it extends to the
other. Then it says "love = adultery." I squirm in my chair. That explains

why I've been so reluctant to say "I love you" in my mother tongue. The third item: "love = penny-pinch = greed."

8   My palms get clammy with cold sweat. The definitions of love in my Chinese dictionary don't seem friendly, and I can't discard them as rubbish, for they are all backed up by Confucius' writing, history, famous poets and politicians. All of them seem to say: love is a wild animal. Control it or it will tear you apart, drag you into the abyss.

9   "Don't talk love before you turn 25." How the father knows!

10   And the companion words—gratitude, respect, duty, pain, pity, addiction, treasure, and many many others—that go side by side with the taboo word *ai*. Are they meant to tame this beast deep in our hearts? Does it mean we Chinese can't love for the sake of love? And if we do, we must love with all the pain, all the duties, all the consequences? Is this how my grandmas, my ancestors, women of my race find their happiness, though they never met their men before wedding nights, though their husbands may beat them up, sell them to redeem a debt, take in as many concubines as they could afford, whenever they wanted?

11   Does it mean I'm hopeless?

12   "Love?" poofed my mother. "Love is puffed rice. It satisfies you for five minutes. That's all. And men. You can't believe a word they say, they're like commercials. So when you choose a husband, no need to look at his face or crotch, just look into his checking account."

13   "Love is a wild deer in the forest. It won't return no matter how you call it," my twice-divorced sister said on the phone.

14   When pressed to remarry, she replied, "Men are like parking lots. All the good ones are taken, and the rest are handicapped."

15   "It's possible to bear fruit before blossom," my grandma insisted. "Children first, then respect, then love."

16   I suppose, I suppose, I mutter to myself as my index finger goes up and down the dictionary. Security, responsibility, control, all wise and sound. But something is missing. Suddenly my eyes pop wide. At the bottom is the traditional version of the character *ai*: a hand, a roof, a friend, the usual stuff. Then in the middle, between the friend and roof, stands a heart. It was taken out by the government in the 50s to make Chinese words easier to use.

17   "That's it!" I shout out loud. That's what's been missing, the heart—心—*xin*.

18   Dot by dot, I try out the newly found character, adding the heart. Memories rush to me from all sides: first crush, first fight, first betrayal, the whipping, the cursing, my mother and grandmas barking their stories to

my ears, my ancestors, their ways of love, of hatred, cunning and twisted, with its own wisdom and truth. I thought I'd buried them, to make my life easier, more modern, more western, but they've been living with me, all these years, waiting to come out.

爱—the hand comes first, then the roof, then the heart—心. Its three dots 19 spurt and drip like blood over a standing leg. For decades, the heart has been erased from books, papers, magazines. But its pulse has never stopped. It's been pulsing in my grandmas' stories, my sister's waiting for the reunion with her long lost daughter, in the shafts of sunlight, moon rise, fallen leaves, in the whip my mother carefully placed behind the bedroom door.

"Ai," I sigh as I complete the last stroke. The heart looks a bit squashed 20 between the house and people, a bit fragile under the weight of the roof. But it's there, beating with its own rhythm, its own rules of law. Someday, when the heart takes root again, I'll learn how to say the word, in my native tongue, a sound that can also mean a sigh, an obstacle, a sound soaked with pain and joy.

Thinking Critically About Content

1. Restate Wang Ping's definition of "love" in your own words.

2. What was the missing element the author discovered about the Chinese word for love?

3. What does Wang Ping mean when she says, "Love is a wild animal. Control it or it will tear you apart, drag you into the abyss" (paragraph 8)

Thinking Critically About Purpose and Audience

4. What is Wang Ping's purpose in writing this essay?

5. Who do you think is her primary audience?

6. Does Wang Ping capture the essence of love in her essay? Which details communicate this message most effectively?

Thinking Critically About Essays

7. The author uses similes and metaphors (comparisons of two unlike items) to help her explain love. One example is in paragraph 13: "Love is a wild deer in the forest." Explain this comparison, and find one other example of this technique.

8. How does Wang Ping organize her definition? Is this the most effective arrangement for her ideas?

Thinking Critically About Purpose and Audience
4. Wang Ping's main purpose seems to be to reveal a complete definition for the Chinese word for "love."
5. Her primary audience is people who enjoy trivia and/or words.
6. Answers will vary.

Thinking Critically About Essays
7. This first metaphor refers to the unwieldy nature of love. There are four other examples of figurative language (three similes and one metaphor) in this essay:

"Love is like pop-corn. It satisfies you, but only for five minutes" (paragraph 12).
"And men. You can't believe a word they say, because they're like commercials" (paragraph 12).
"Men are like parking lots. All the good ones are taken, and the rest are handicapped" (paragraph 14).
"It's possible to have fruit before the blossom. . . . Children first, then love" (paragraph 15).
8. Wang Ping organizes her essay from personal examples and family stories to dictionary definitions and

characters in the
word *ai* itself.
9. Answers will vary.
10. Answers will vary.

9. Choose three transitions in Wang Ping's essay that you think work well. Explain why they are effective.

10. Write a response to this essay titled "Love in [another language]."

Michael Norlen
HEALING MYSELF WITH THE POWER OF WORK

Focusing Your Attention

1. As a student or as an employee in the job market, what advantages do you get from your work? Are these rewards mostly physical or emotional?

2. The essay you are about to read defines depression. Have you ever been depressed? How did you manage your daily responsibilities? How did you pull yourself out of your depression?

Expanding Your Vocabulary

The following words are important to your understanding of this essay:

Kansas City Star: a daily newspaper published in Missouri (paragraph 1)

perfunctory: indifferent (paragraph 2)

indignant: angry (paragraph 3)

despondency: sadness (paragraph 4)

night-dwellers: people who are active at night (paragraph 6)

Patsy Cline: country singer who died in a plane crash at age 30 in 1963 (paragraph 6)

insidious: slowly destructive (paragraph 8)

neurons: nerve endings (paragraph 8)

synapses: spaces between nerve endings (paragraph 8)

serotonin: a substance that transmits impulses between nerves (paragraph 8)

dopamine: a substance that transmits impulses between nerves (paragraph 8)

manifest: become noticeable (paragraph 8)

dispiriting: depressing (paragraph 8)

regimen: systematic plan, such as a diet (paragraph 9)

antidepressants: medications to fight depression (paragraph 9)

tolerance: resistance, lack of response (paragraph 9)

Jim Beam: a brand of bourbon (paragraph 10)

Coors: a brand of beer (paragraph 10)

introverted: focused on oneself (paragraph 10)

psychotherapy: professional counseling (paragraph 11)

arsenal: collection of weapons (paragraph 12)

satiated: no longer hungry (paragraph 12)

"The paper guy's here!" Every Monday morning a cashier at Eckerd's 1 drugstore greets me with these words. A manager gives her a key, and she fishes $3 and change from the cash drawer and pays me for the copies of the *Kansas City Star* sold the previous week. I pick up the 10 or 12 unsold papers and throw them in my car, next to the returns from the supermarket, the doughnut shop, and the Texaco station.

Quite a difference from a year ago. Then, I would announce myself in 2 response to a judge's perfunctory order: "Counsel, state your appearance." Instead of delivering papers from 1:30 a.m. to 6 a.m., I spent my nights sleeping and my days in an office, a courtroom, or a library.

It all changed 12 months ago. For the second time in six years, I aban- 3 doned my solo law practice. I stopped returning phone calls, forgot to pay bills, and ignored court dates. I began to sleep 16 hours a day. By July of last year, I stopped coming into the office, leaving it to fill up with unopened mail and indignant phone messages. By August I was behind on my office rent, and by October my landlord asked me to leave. I ate, but nothing tasted good. I slept, but woke up tired. I felt like a stranger around my wife and two daughters. Thoughts of suicide shadowed me. And in the midst of all this, I knew. *It* had returned.

Tracy Thompson, the journalist, calls *It* "The Beast." To Winston 4 Churchill, *It* was his "Black Dog." To me, it is both of these: a nameless, faceless thing that infects me with a despondency so bleak I fear that I will never feel joy again. It is depression. Twice now *It* has laid me low.

Trying to throw me a lifeline, a friend offered me a job delivering news- 5 papers. To my great surprise, I found myself almost enjoying the job. Contrasted to the stresses of maintaining a law practice, this mindless work of assembling and bundling papers in a dimly lit warehouse was a welcome distraction. When I left the warehouse to deliver the papers, to vending machines, gas stations, and supermarkets, I began to catch glimpses of small joys.

6   After months of hiding from people and avoiding conversation, little by little I got to know some of the night-dwellers. The clerk at the Phillip's station who plays country music and seems to have an obsession with Patsy Cline. The jogger I always pass at 4 a.m. With friendly greetings and idle conversation, these people, whose names I still don't know, began to draw me out of my darkness.

7   At the end of each night, I look down at my hands, stained with ink from handling 450 newspapers. I stretch and feel a tightness in my shoulders from lifting the 40- or 50-pound bundles into and out of my car. The grime and the pain serve as wake-up calls for my tired body and mind. And every Sunday morning, when my friend hands me a modest check, I begin to feel just a bit more confident.

8   Depression is an insidious disease. On one level, it is about neurons and synapses, seratonin levels, and dopamine readings. On another level, it is memories of trauma stashed in dusty corners of the mind that manifest years later in fear and anxiety. And on yet another level, it is a crippling, dispiriting mind-set that convinces me I am worthless and helpless.

9   For almost five years, I have been on a steady regimen of antidepressants, from Prozac to Serzone. When I build up a tolerance to one drug, my doctor simply switches me to another. Except for some inconvenient side effects, they have been my safety net, stopping my free fall into madness.

10   For most of the same period, I have been in individual or group therapy. I've learned how some of the difficult periods of my life have shaped me and contributed to my depression. The memories of my drunken mother and the Jim Beam and Coors bottles strewn around our rented houses help me understand why I'm so fearful of failure, so introverted and so reluctant to trust others.

11   For all the insight and help I've received from drug therapy and psychotherapy, I still have feelings of worthlessness. Every bout of depression eats away at my self-esteem, and no amount of drugs or talking can restore it. That restoration has to come through a different vehicle. For me, that vehicle is physical work. Every time I look at the calluses on my hands, I realize that this job provides me with a reason to get out of bed.

12   One day soon I'll be ready to leave this job behind, but I'll never again view work as just a paycheck or a daily obligation. It will always be a part of my therapy, my healing. I don't know where my next job will be; in the courtroom, the classroom, or the office. But wherever it is, my work will be a weapon in my arsenal against the attacks I know will come again and again, because the Beast will not be satiated, and the Dog will never be securely leashed.

ANSWERS TO
QUESTIONS
*Thinking Critically
About Content*
1. Answers will vary.
2. He is digging himself
out of his depression by
working as a newspaper
delivery man, and
receiving his small
paycheck each week
is slowly making him
start to feel more
confident and less
depressed.
3. Norlen plans to use
his work as a means to
fight depression; he is
proving to himself that
he can do the job, and
this information will
empower him against
the illness.

*Thinking Critically
About Purpose and
Audience*
4. Norlen wrote this
essay to inform readers
how devastating
depression can be but
also to show that it
can be overcome.

Thinking Critically About Content

1. Restate Norlen's definition of depression in your own words. Does Norlen's definition make sense to you?

2. How does the author say he is digging himself out of his depression?

3. What does Norlen mean when he says, "I'll never again view work as just a paycheck or a daily obligation" (paragraph 12)?

Thinking Critically About Purpose and Audience

4. Why do you think Norlen wrote this essay?

5. Who do you think is his primary audience?

6. Have you ever helped someone who was depressed? What did you do? Explain your answer.

Thinking Critically About Essays

7. Paragraph 7 ends rather than begins with its controlling idea. Explain how Norlen develops this particular paragraph.

8. How is paragraph 3 organized? Why do you think Norlen puts these facts in this particular order?

9. Choose one paragraph, and explain its tone or mood.

10. Write a summary of this essay for your English class.

Writing Topics: Defining

Before you begin to write, you might want to review the writing process in Part I.

1. In the first essay, Wang Ping defines *love*. Write your own definition of another state of mind, such as *joy, fear, loneliness,* or *stress*.

2. Using Norlen's method of development through personal narrative, define *work* for your class.

3. Now that you have studied different approaches to the process of definition, what makes a definition effective or useful for you? Apply what you have studied about definition to your answer.

5. His primary audience is probably people who are suffering from depression or are at risk of doing so, a large part of our population.
6. Answers will vary.

Thinking Critically About Essays

7. Norlen leads up to his controlling idea in paragraph 7 (that he feels more confident now) by providing examples of small accomplishments.
8. Paragraph 3 is organized chronologically. Norlen puts these facts in this order to show readers his imminent downfall.
9. Answers will vary.
10. Answers will vary.

ANALYZING CAUSES AND EFFECTS

In the essays in this chapter, the writers analyze the causes and effects related to their topics. "A Family Dilemma: To Scout or Not to Scout?" by Michael Alvear openly discusses the issue of gay Boy Scout leaders. The second essay, "Happiness Is Catching" by Stacey Colino, discusses the moods in our lives.

Michael Alvear

A FAMILY DILEMMA: TO SCOUT OR NOT TO SCOUT?

SUMMARY

As a gay man, Alvear struggles with the idea that his sister wants her son to join the Boy Scouts, a group that had banned gay Scout leaders.

READABILITY

(Flesch–Kincaid grade level)
10.8

INSTRUCTOR'S RESOURCE MANUAL

For additional teaching strategies, for journal entries, for vocabulary and reading quizzes, and for more writing assignments, see the *Instructor's Resource Manual*, Section II, Part IV.

Focusing Your Attention

1. Think of the last time you had a moral dilemma. What caused the dilemma? How did you handle it?

2. In the essay you are about to read, Michael Alvear looks at the effect on his family of the ruling that the Scouts have a constitutional right to fire gay Scout leaders. What has the greatest impact on your life— your family or your peers? Analyze the effect one of these groups has on your life.

Expanding Your Vocabulary

The following words are important to your understanding of this essay:

backlash: strong negative reaction (paragraph 3)

municipal: owned and operated by the town (paragraph 3)

unsettling: disturbing (paragraph 5)

ethical: moral (paragraph 5)

quandary: dilemma (paragraph 7)

ironically: surprisingly (i.e., opposite of what would have been expected) (paragraph 10)

inconceivable: impossible to imagine (paragraph 11)

My sister constantly tells me how much her 6-year-old son Ricky (not his real name) adores me. So when he came home with a flier about joining a fun and exciting group for kids his age, she had a tough decision to make. Should she let him join a group that doesn't like his beloved uncle Michael?

When the Supreme Court ruled that the Boy Scouts have the constitutional right to fire Scout leaders for being gay, my sister was caught in an agonizing moral dilemma: allowing her son to become a member of America's most family-friendly group meant dishonoring part of her family.

The political backlash since the ruling against the Boy Scouts is clear to anyone who reads the local papers. Many cities, believing the Scouts are engaging in discrimination, have told local Scout troops that they can't use parks, schools, and other municipal sites. Companies and charities have withdrawn hundreds of thousands of dollars in support. But what isn't so easy to see is the division the Supreme Court ruling created in millions of families like mine.

When my sister first called to tell me she was thinking of putting Ricky in the Cub Scouts (a program run by the Boy Scouts of America), I could hear the torment in her voice. Ricky is a bright, athletic boy who suffers from a shyness so paralyzing he doesn't have any friends. The other day my sister asked who he had played with during recess. "Nobody," he mumbled, looking at the floor. "I just scratched the mosquito bites on my leg till it was time to go back to class."

It breaks my sister's heart to see what Ricky's shyness is doing to him. Karate, softball, and soccer leagues helped, but not nearly enough. In another age, my sister wouldn't have thought twice about letting him join the Scouts. But now the decision has taken on an unsettling ethical dimension.

"I don't understand why they're making me take sides in my own family," she said about the Boy Scout policy. "In order to help my son I have to abandon my brother."

My sister was up against some disturbing questions. Should she violate her sense of family loyalty for the social needs of her son? Or keep her values intact and deny her son the possibility of overcoming his shyness? By saying that troops have the right to fire gay leaders, the Boy Scouts created the unimaginable: a moral quandary about joining the most wholesome group in America.

My sister was afraid she'd be doing the same thing many parents did a generation ago when they joined country clubs that didn't allow blacks and Jews. They, too, must have rationalized their membership by saying the clubs' wholesome activities would be good for their kids.

There was one thing my sister and her husband were not conflicted about: me. "No way are we putting Ricky in the Scouts if this is an issue for

ANSWERS TO QUESTIONS *Thinking Critically About Content* 1. Alvear is analyzing how he should handle his sister and the Boy Scouts. 2. The causes of Alvear's dilemma are that (1) the Boy Scouts organization discriminates against gay Scout leaders and (2) his sister's shy son could greatly benefit from the Boy Scouts. The effects of his sister's dilemma are that (1) her son would be in a group that discriminates against her brother, (2) her son might learn negative things that will affect the relationship between her son and her brother, and (3) her brother would know that she made a decision that goes against her brother's lifestyle. 3. Alvear is referring to the fact that his nephew might be told by the Boy Scouts that Alvear's lifestyle is wrong.

Thinking Critically About Purpose and Audience

4. Alvear's purpose is probably to inform readers that decisions like this one by the Boy Scouts to ban gay leaders didn't just affect the organization. It affected families and friends that the organization also touches.
5. Gays would probably find this essay most interesting, but anyone can appreciate the dilemma Alvear is going through.
6. Alvear is trying to evoke emotions of anger against the unfairness of decisions like those of the Boy Scouts. He wants readers to react with sympathy for the position his sister is in.

Thinking Critically About Essays

7. The writer believes he is in a no-win situation, but he believes that most of what the Boy Scouts represents will help his nephew, so he is willing to encourage Ricky's participation.
8. This is an effective beginning because readers first see the relationship that the Boy Scouts may eventually undermine; the beginning brings

you," she said. "Blood is thicker than camping." Still, she wanted to know how I'd feel if my nephew became a Scout.

10   I felt completely torn, but I answered with as much certainty as I could muster. "I am not getting in the way of what's best for a 6-year-old," I told her. Ironically, I found myself trying to persuade her to let Ricky join the Scouts. It's families that teach morality, I argued, not after-school groups. Besides, I added, it's not like the issue will come up during any of the Scouting activities.

11   Or will it? Is it really inconceivable that kids who know why the president of the United States was impeached would ask their Scout leader why gay people aren't allowed in the organization? And what would the scout-master's response be? I was shaken by the possibility of my nephew hearing a trusted grown-up trying to convince him that his uncle Michael is someone to be scared of.

12   One night I had a terrible dream of a Boy Scout official pointing me out to Ricky and saying, "See that guy? The one you love more than any other man except your father? He's not allowed in here."

13   I woke up feeling a kind of enraged helplessness. How could I mean so much to my family and so little to so many outside it? Ultimately, I knew I could live with the indignity of my nephew belonging to a group that discriminates against his uncle; what I couldn't live with was the guilt of denying Ricky a chance to improve his life.

14   How can Ricky's parents know what the right thing to do is in this situation? For starters, they plan to get more information before they make a decision. And so my sister, a mom torn between her devotion to her brother and concern for her son, will go to next month's Scout meeting with her husband.

15   Will they put Ricky in the Scouts? I don't know. But as the date of the meeting approaches, I can't help thinking how unfair it is that my sister will have to pass under that imaginary sign that hangs over every Scout gathering: YOUR SON IS WELCOME, BUT YOUR BROTHER IS NOT.

Thinking Critically About Content

1. What is Alvear analyzing in this essay?

2. What are the causes and effects of the moral dilemma Alvear's sister is struggling with?

3. What is Alvear referring to when he says, "I was shaken by the possibility of my nephew hearing a trusted grown-up trying to convince him that his uncle Michael is someone to be scared of" (paragraph 11)?

Thinking Critically About Purpose and Audience

4. What do you think Michael Alvear's purpose is in this essay?

5. Who do you think would find this essay most interesting? Explain your answer.

6. What emotions do you think Alvear is trying to evoke in his readers as he analyzes his family's moral dilemma?

Thinking Critically About Essays

7. Describe this writer's point of view toward this moral dilemma.

8. The author sets the scene for his essay by explaining his close relationship with his sister's son. Is this an effective beginning? Why or why not?

9. How does Alvear organize his essay? List his main points to answer this question.

10. Analyze your reactions to this situation as Ricky's dad. How would you feel? Why would you feel that way?

Stacey Colino

HAPPINESS IS CATCHING: WHY EMOTIONS ARE CONTAGIOUS

Focusing Your Attention

1. Are you easily influenced by other people's moods? How do you know this?

2. In the essay you are about to read, Stacey Colino explains how we "catch" the feelings of others. Think of someone who generally makes you happy and someone who usually makes you sad. What is the difference between these two people? How do they each approach life? How do they each relate to you?

Expanding Your Vocabulary

The following words are important to your understanding of this essay:

elation: joy, happiness (paragraph 1)

euphoria: extreme happiness (paragraph 1)

inoculate against: become immune to, resist (paragraph 1)

milliseconds: thousandths of a second (paragraph 2)

the problem closer to the readers' personal lives.

9. Alvear organizes his essay from least to most important. He starts by explaining the cause of the dilemma, talks about how Ricky will benefit while Alvear watches Ricky's involvement with an organization that rejects people like Alvear, and moves to the idea that the Boy Scouts will teach Ricky to be frightened of his uncle. The last sentence sums up the essay.

10. Answers will vary.

SUMMARY

Colino explains how people "catch" moods from other people.

READABILITY

(Flesch–Kincaid grade level)

11.4

INSTRUCTOR'S RESOURCE MANUAL

For additional teaching strategies, for journal entries, for vocabulary and reading quizzes, and for more writing assignments, see the *Instructor's Resource Manual,* Section II, Part IV.

synchronize: coordinate (paragraph 2)

extroverts: outgoing people (paragraph 4)

engulfed: completely surrounded, overwhelmed (paragraph 5)

introverts: shy, quiet people (paragraph 5)

susceptible to: easily influenced by (paragraph 8)

mimicry: copying (paragraph 9)

1   Researchers have found that emotions, both good and bad, are nearly as contagious as colds and flus. You can catch elation, euphoria, sadness, and more from friends, family, colleagues, even strangers. And once you understand how to protect yourself, you can inoculate yourself against the bad.

2   Mood "infection" happens in milliseconds, says Elaine Hatfield, Ph.D., a professor of psychology at the University of Hawaii in Honolulu and co-author of *Emotional Contagion* (Cambridge University Press, 1994). And it stems from a primitive instinct: During conversation, we naturally tend to mimic and synchronize our facial expressions, movements, and speech rhythms to match the other person's. "Through this, we come to feel what the person is feeling," explains Dr. Hatfield. In other words, it puts us in touch with their feelings and affects our behavior.

3   Not surprisingly, spouses are especially likely to catch each other's moods, but so are parents, children, and good friends. In fact, a recent study at the University of Texas Medical Branch at Galveston found that depression was highly contagious among college roommates. "The same thing can occur with a spouse or co-worker, where one person is moderately depressed," says study author Thomas E. Joiner Jr., Ph.D., assistant professor of psychiatry and behavioral sciences.

4   Dr. Hatfield's research shows that extroverts and emotionally expressive people tend to transmit their feelings more powerfully. There's also a breed of people who, consciously or not, may want or need you to feel what they feel; they're the ones who live by the adage "misery loves company." They manipulate other people's moods—perhaps without even realizing it—to gain the upper hand or to feel better about themselves. "They express emotion to get a response—perhaps attention or sympathy," says Ross Buck, Ph.D., professor of communication sciences and psychology at the University of Connecticut.

5   On the other hand, some personality types are more likely to be engulfed by others' moods. Introverts are vulnerable because they're easily aroused. So are highly sensitive individuals who react physically to emotionally charged situations—their hearts flutter before giving a speech, for example.

If anyone knows how quickly moods spread, it's Ginny Graves, 33, a 6
San Francisco writer. Last year, when she was pregnant with her first child,
her mood took a nosedive every time she saw a particular friend.

"Basically nothing good was going on in her life—she didn't like her job, 7
and she was obsessed with her weight," recalls Ginny. "I tried to bolster her
up, but whenever I talked to her, I'd feel tense and tired." Afterward, Ginny
was left with a case of the moody blues that lingered a day or so.

Indeed, there's some evidence that women may be particularly suscep- 8
tible to catching moods, perhaps because we're better able to read other
people's emotions and body language, according to psychologist Judith
Hall, Ph.D., professor of psychology at Northeastern University in Boston.

Since women perceive facial expressions so readily that we may be 9
more likely to mimic them—and wind up sharing the feeling. Just how
mimicry leads to catching a mood is not known, notes John T. Cacioppo,
Ph.D., professor of psychology at Ohio State University and coauthor of
Emotional Contagion. One theory holds that when you frown or smile, the
muscular movements in your face alter blood flow to the brain, which in
turn affects mood; another theory maintains that the sensations associated
with specific facial expressions trigger emotional memories—and hence
the feelings—linked with those particular expressions.

With any luck, we catch the happy moods—infectious laughter at a din- 10
ner party or a colleague's enthusiasm for a project, for instance. Some psychologists suspect, however, that negative emotions—especially depression and anxiety—may be the most infectious of all. "For women, stress
and depression are like emotional germs—they jump from one person to
the next," notes Ellen McGrath, Ph.D., a psychologist in Laguna Beach,
California, and author of *When Feeling Bad Is Good* (Bantam, 1994).

Being susceptible to other people's moods does make for a rich emo- 11
tional life. But let's face it: When you catch a happy mood, you don't want to
change it. Downbeat emotions are harder to deal with. And who wants her
life to be ruled by other people's bad moods?

Fortunately, there are ways to protect yourself from unpleasant emo- 12
tions, while letting yourself catch the good ones. For starters, pay attention
to how you feel around different people, suggests Dr. McGrath. Then
label your emotions—noting, for example, whether you feel optimistic
around your best friend or gloomy after seeing your aunt. Then ask yourself if you're feeling what you do because you actually feel that way or
because you've caught a mood from the other person. Just recognizing that
an emotion belongs to someone else, not you, can be enough to short-
circuit its transmission.

Once you know how people affect you, you can be more selective about 13
whom you spend time with. Instead of going on an all-day outing with

ANSWERS TO
QUESTIONS
*Thinking Critically
About Content*
1. Colino is analyzing
how people begin to
feel the way others
feel; they catch the
moods of those around
them. The title pre-
pares readers for this
concept.
2. Answers may vary.
   Causes
   Other people
   Contagious nature
      of moods

Effects
Specific feelings
Specific behaviors
3. We can protect our-
selves from unpleasant
emotions by paying
attention to how we
feel around certain peo-
ple and by recognizing
when we are feeling
low because of someone
else's bad mood.

Thinking Critically
About Purpose and
Audience
4. Colino probably
wrote this essay to
warn readers not to let
other people's moods
affect us.
5. Colino's primary
intended audience is
probably women.
Family Circle is read
primarily by women,
and Colino even men-
tions in her essay that
moods are caught more
easily by women.
6. Answers will vary.

Thinking Critically
About Essays
7. The quotations are
convincing because
they are spoken by
reputable people who
have studied mood
behavior.
8. Colino deals mostly
with causes (paragraphs
1–4, 8–10, 12–14) and
integrates a discussion
of effects at important
points throughout the
essay (paragraphs 5–7
and 11).
9. Answers will vary.
10. Answers will vary.

family members who bring you down, for instance, try spending shorter periods of time with them. Another solution is to give yourself a time-out: It could be as simple as a restroom break during an intense dinner.

14   Putting up emotional barriers is not the answer, though. If the channels are open, both positive and negative influences flow in. Shutting out the bad precludes you from catching joyful moods, too. Instead, it's better to monitor the floodgates—and to come to your own rescue when you feel yourself catching other people's negativity. And if you get swept up in another person's excitement, sit back and enjoy the ride.

Thinking Critically About Content

1. What is Colino analyzing in this essay? How does her title help focus her analysis?

2. Name two causes and two effects of people's moods.

3. How does Colino suggest that you can protect yourself from unpleasant emotions?

Thinking Critically About Purpose and Audience

4. Why do you think Colino wrote this essay?

5. Considering that this essay was originally published in a magazine called *Family Circle*, who do you think Colino's intended audience is? Explain your answer.

6. Are you susceptible to other people's moods? Why or why not?

Thinking Critically About Essays

7. The author of this essay quotes many authorities in the field of psychology. Are these quotations convincing to you? Explain your answer.

8. Which of Colino's paragraphs deal primarily with causes? Which with effects? Do you think this is a good balance? Explain your answer.

9. Find five transitions in Colino's essay that work well, and explain why they are effective.

10. Discuss the emotional climate in the place where you live. Are you able to separate your emotions from those of the people you live with? Are you affected by the emotions of roommates, friends, family? How might you manage emotional swings after reading this essay?

Writing Topics: Analyzing Causes and Effects

Before you begin to write, you might want to review the writing process in Part I.

1. Are you currently dealing with any moral dilemmas? What are they? Does one bother you more than the others? Write an essay analyzing the causes and effects of this particular dilemma.

2. In "Happiness Is Catching," Stacey Colino talks about how contagious moods are. Do you think you might have been responsible for giving a good or bad mood to someone? What were the circumstances? How did someone "catch" your mood? Write an essay analyzing the causes and effects of the situation.

3. How would looking closely at causes and effects help you live a better life? How would the process of discovering causes and effects help you think through your decisions and problems more logically? Explain your answer.

CHAPTER **33**

ARGUING

In all three essays in this chapter, the writers state their evidence clearly and convincingly. In the first essay, "We are Training Our Kids to Kill," Dave Grossman tries to persuade his readers the dangers for children witnessing violence on TV.

The next two essays in this chapter deal with a topic that has been a part of American society for a long time—controlling gang violence. They present two different sides of the issue. The first essay, written by Richard Willard and published in February 1999 in *Supreme Court Debates*, claims that anti-loitering laws can reduce gang violence. The second essay, written by David Cole, argues that anti-loitering laws are not effective. It was first published in February 1999 in The Nation.

Dave Grossman

WE ARE TRAINING OUR KIDS TO KILL

SUMMARY

In this essay, retired colonel Dave Grossman exposes some of the dire consequences of treating violence in various forms of the media as entertainment. Most serious of these is that we are training our children to kill.

READABILITY

(Flesch–Kincaid grade level)
12.0

Focusing Your Attention

1. At what age or in what situation do you think children can handle violence in the media?

2. In the essay you are about to read, the writer discusses the dangers connected with violence on TV for children. What do you think some of these issues are?

Expanding Your Vocabulary

The following words are important to your understanding of this essay:

averted (para. 4): avoided

phenomenally (para. 6): amazingly

Draconian (para. 7): harsh

indiscriminately (para. 8): casually

pervasively (para. 9): universally

anomaly (para. 15): an exception from the normal

desensitized (para. 22): numbed

epidemiological (para. 25): referring to childhood behaviors

variable (para. 25): element being compared

bayonet (para. 28): stab

dismay (para. 32): fear, dread

benign (para. 34): good

INSTRUCTOR'S RESOURCE MANUAL
For additional teaching strategies, for journal entries, for vocabulary and reading quizzes, and for more writing assignments, see the *Instructor's Resource Manual*, Section II, Part IV.

I am from Jonesboro, Arkansas. I travel the world training medical, law enforcement, and U.S. military personnel about the realities of warfare, I try to make those who carry deadly force keenly aware of the magnitude of killing. Too many law enforcement and military personnel act like "cowboys," never stopping to think about who they are and what they are called to do. I hope I am able to give them a reality check.

So here I am, a world traveler and an expert in the field of "killology," when the (then) largest school massacre in American history happens in my hometown of Jonesboro, Arkansas. That was the March 24, 1998, schoolyard shooting deaths of four girls and a teacher. Ten others were injured, and two boys, ages 11 and 13, were jailed, charged with murder.

Virus of Violence

To understand the why behind Littleton, Jonesboro, Springfield, Pearl, and Paducah, and all the other outbreaks of this "virus of violence," we need to first understand the magnitude of the problem. The per capita murder rate doubled in this country between 1957—when the FBI started keeping track of the data—and 1992. A fuller picture of the problem, however, is indicated by the rate at which people are attempting to kill one another—the aggravated assault rate. That rate in America has gone from around 60 per 100,000 in 1957 to over 440 per 100,000 in 2002. As bad as this is, it would be much worse were it not for two major factors.

The first is the increased imprisonment of violent offenders. The prison population in America nearly quintupled between 1975 and 2002. According to criminologist John A. DiIulio, "dozens of credible empirical analyses . . . leave no doubt that the increased use of prisons averted millions of serious crimes." If it were not for our tremendous imprisonment rate (the highest of any industrialized nation), the aggravated assault rate and the murder rate would undoubtedly be even higher.

5   The second factor keeping the murder rate from being even worse is medical technology. According to the U.S. Army Medical Service Corps, a wound that would have killed nine out of ten soldiers in World War II, nine out of ten could have survived in Vietnam. Thus, by a very conservative estimate, if we still had a 1940-level medical technology today, our murder rate would be ten times higher than it is. The murder rate has been held down by the development of sophisticated lifesaving skills and techniques, such as helicopter medevacs, 911 operators, paramedics, CPR, trauma centers, and medicines.

6   Today, both our assault rate and murder rate are at phenomenally high levels. Both are increasing worldwide. In Canada, according to their Center for Justice, per capita assaults increased almost fivefold between 1964 and 2002, attempted murder increased nearly sevenfold, and murders doubled. Similar trends can be seen in other countries in the per capita violent crime rates reported to Interpol between 1977 and 2002. In Australia and New Zealand, the assault rate increased approximately fourfold, and the murder rate nearly doubled in both nations. The assault rate tripled in Sweden and approximately doubled in Belgium, Denmark, England and Wales, France, Hungary, the Netherlands, and Scotland. Meanwhile, all these nations had an associated (but smaller) increase in murder.

7   This virus of violence is occurring worldwide. The explanation for it has to be some new factor that is occurring in all of these countries. There are many factors involved, and none should be discounted: for example, the prevalence of guns in our society. But violence is rising in many nations with Draconian gun laws. And though we should never downplay child abuse, poverty, or racism, there is only one new variable present in each of these countries that bears the exact same fruit: media violence presented as entertainment for children.

Killing Is Unnatural

8   Before retiring from the military, I spent almost a quarter of a century as an army infantry officer and a psychologist, learning and studying how to enable people to kill. Believe me, we are very good at it. But it does not come naturally; you have to be taught to kill. And just as the army is conditioning people to kill, we are indiscriminately doing the same thing to our children, but without the safeguards.

9   After the Jonesboro killings, the head of the American Academy of Pediatrics Task Force on Juvenile Violence came to town and said that children don't naturally kill. It is a learned skill. And they learn it from abuse and violence in the home and, most pervasively, from violence as entertainment in television, the movies, and interactive video games.

Killing requires training because there is a built-in aversion to killing 10
one's own kind. I can best illustrate this fact by drawing on my own military
research into the act of killing.

We all know how hard it is to have a discussion with a frightened or 11
angry human being. Vasoconstriction, the narrowing of the blood vessels,
has literally closed down the forebrain—that great gob of gray matter that
makes one a human being and distinguishes one from a dog. When those
neurons close down, the midbrain takes over and your thought processes
and reflexes are indistinguishable from your dog's. If you've worked with
animals, you have some understanding of what happens to frightened
human beings on the battlefield. The battlefield and violent crime are in
the realm of midbrain responses.

Within the midbrain there is a powerful, God-given resistance to killing 12
your own kind. Every species, with a few exceptions, has a hardwired resistance to killing its own kind in territorial and mating battles. When animals with antlers and horns fight one another, they head-butt in a nonfatal
fashion. But when they fight any other species, they go to the side to gut
and gore. Piranhas will turn their fangs on anything, but they fight one another with flicks of the tail. Rattlesnakes will bite anything, but they wrestle
one another. Almost every species has this hard-wired resistance to killing
its own kind.

When we human beings are overwhelmed with anger and fear, we 13
slam head-on into that midbrain resistance that generally prevents us from
killing. Only sociopaths—who by definition don't have that resistance—
lack this innate violence immune system.

Throughout all human history, when humans have fought each other, 14
there has been a lot of posturing. Adversaries make loud noises and puff
themselves up, trying to daunt the enemy. There is a lot of fleeing and sub-
mission. Ancient battles were nothing more than great shoving matches. It
was not until one side turned and ran that most of the killing happened,
and most of that was stabbing people in the back. All of the ancient military
historians report that the vast majority of killing happened in pursuit when
one side was fleeing.

In more modern times, the average firing rate was incredibly low in 15
Civil War battles. British author Paddy Griffith demonstrates in his book
The Battle Tactics of the Civil War that the killing potential of the average
Civil War regiment was anywhere from five hundred to a thousand men
per minute. The actual killing rate was only one or two men per minute per
regiment. At the Battle of Gettysburg, of the 27,000 muskets picked up from
the dead and dying after the battle, 90 percent were loaded. This is an
anomaly, because it took 90 percent of their time to load muskets and only

5 percent to fire. But even more amazing, of the thousands of loaded muskets, only half had multiple loads in the barrel—one had 23 loads in the barrel.

16   In reality, the average man would load his musket and bring it to his shoulder, but he could not bring himself to kill. He would be brave, he would stand shoulder to shoulder, he would do what he was trained to do; but at the moment of truth, he could not bring himself to pull the trigger. And so he lowered the weapon and loaded it again. Of those who did fire, only a tiny percentage fired to hit. The vast majority fired over the enemy's head.

17   During World War II, U.S. Army Brig. Gen. S. L. A. Marshall had a team of researchers study what soldiers did in battle. For the first time in history, they asked individual soldiers what they did in battle. They discovered that only 15 to 20 percent of the individual riflemen could bring themselves to fire at an exposed enemy soldier.

18   That is the reality of the battlefield. Only a small percentage of soldiers are able and willing to participate. Men are willing to die. They are willing to sacrifice themselves for their nation; but they are not willing to kill. It is a phenomenal insight into human nature; but when the military became aware of that, they systematically went about the process of trying to fix this "problem." From the military perspective, a 15 percent firing rate among riflemen is like a 15 percent literacy rate among librarians. And fix it the military did. By the Korean War, around 55 percent of the soldiers were willing to fire to kill. And by Vietnam, the rate rose to over 90 percent.

19   The method in this madness: desensitization.

20   How the military increases the killing rate of soldiers in combat is instructive because our culture today is doing the same thing to our children. The training methods militaries use are brutalization, classical conditioning, operant conditioning, and role modeling. I will explain each of these in the military context and show how these same factors are contributing to the phenomenal increase of violence in our culture.

21   Brutalization and desensitization are what happens at boot camp. From the moment you step off the bus, you are physically and verbally abused: countless push-ups, endless hours at attention or running with heavy loads, while carefully trained professionals take turns screaming at you. Your head is shaved; you are herded together naked and dressed alike, losing all individuality. This brutalization is designed to break down your existing mores and norms, and force you to accept a new set of values that embraces destruction, violence, and death as a way of life. In the end, you are desensitized to violence and accept it as a normal and essential survival skill in your brutal new world.

Something very similar to this desensitization toward violence is hap-   22
pening to our children through violence in the media—but instead of
18-year-olds, it begins at the age of 18 months when a child is first able to
discern what is happening on television. At that age, a child can watch
something happening on television and mimic that action. But it isn't until
children are six or seven years old that the part of the brain kicks in that lets
them understand where information comes from. Even though young children have some understanding of what it means to pretend, they are de-
velopmentally unable to distinguish clearly between fantasy and reality.

When young children see somebody shot, stabbed, raped, brutalized,   23
degraded, or murdered on TV, to them it is as though it were actually happening. To have a child of three, four, or five watch a "splatter" movie,
learning to relate to a character for the first 90 minutes and then in the last
30 minutes watch helplessly as that new friend is hunted and brutally
murdered, is the moral and psychological equivalent of introducing your
child to a friend, letting her play with that friend, and then butchering that
friend in front of your child's eyes. And this happens to our children hundreds upon hundreds of times.

Sure, they are told, "Hey, it's all for fun. Look, this isn't real; it's just TV."   24
And they nod their little heads and say OK. But they can't tell the difference.
Can you remember a point in your life or in your children's lives when
dreams, reality, and television were all jumbled together? That's what it is
like to be at that level of psychological development. That's what the media
are doing to them.

The *Journal of the American Medical Association* published the defini-   25
tive epidemiological study on the impact of TV violence. The research
demonstrated what happened in numerous nations after television made
its appearance as compared to nations and regions without TV. The two
nations or regions being compared are demographically and ethnically
identical; only one variable is different: the presence of television. In every
nation, region, or city with television, there is an immediate explosion of
violence on the playground, and within 15 years there is a doubling of the
murder rate. Why 15 years? That is how long it takes for the brutalization of
a three-to five-year-old to reach the "prime crime age." That is how long it
takes for you to reap what you have sown when you brutalize and desensi-
tize a three-year-old.

Today the data linking violence in the media to violence in society are   26
superior to those linking cancer and tobacco. Hundreds of sound scientific studies demonstrate the social impact of brutalization by the media.
The *Journal of the American Medical Association* concluded that "the introduction of television in the 1950s caused a subsequent doubling of the

homicide rate, i.e., long-term childhood exposure to television is a causal factor behind approximately one half of the homicides committed in the United States, or approximately 10,000 homicides annually." The article went on to say that "if, hypothetically, television technology had never been developed, there would today be 10,000 fewer homicides each year in the United States, 70,000 fewer rapes, and 700,000 fewer injurious assaults" (June 10, 1992).

Classical Conditioning

27   Classical conditioning is like the famous case of Pavlov's dogs they teach in Psychology 101. The dogs learned to associate the ringing of the bell with food, and once conditioned, the dogs could not hear the bell without salivating.

28   The Japanese were masters at using classical conditioning with their soldiers. Early in World War II, Chinese prisoners were placed in a ditch on their knees with their hands bound behind them. And one by one, a select few Japanese soldiers would go into the ditch and bayonet "their" prisoner to death. This is a horrific way to kill another human being. Up on the bank, countless other young soldiers would cheer them on in their violence. Comparatively few soldiers actually killed in these situations, but by making the others watch and cheer, the Japanese were able to use these kinds of atrocities to classically condition a very large audience to associate pleasure with human death and suffering. Immediately afterwards, the soldiers who had been spectators were treated to sake, to the best meal they had in months, and to so-called comfort girls. The result? They learned to associate committing violent acts with pleasure.

29   The Japanese found these kinds of techniques to be extraordinarily effective at quickly enabling very large numbers of soldiers to commit atrocities in the years to come. Operant conditioning (which we will look at shortly) teaches you to kill, but classical conditioning is a subtle but powerful mechanism that teaches you to like it.

30   This technique is so morally reprehensible that there are very few examples of it in modern U.S. military training, but there are some clear-cut examples of it being done by the media to our children. What is happening to our children is the reverse of the aversion therapy portrayed in the movie *A Clockwork Orange*. In *A Clockwork Orange*, a brutal sociopath, a mass murderer, is strapped to a chair and forced to watch violent movies while he is injected with a drug that nauseates him. So he sits and gags and retches as he watches the movies. After hundreds of repetitions of this, he associates violence with nausea. And it limits his ability to be violent.

We are doing the exact opposite: Our children watch vivid pictures of 31
human suffering and death, and they learn to associate it with their favorite
soft drink and candy bar or their girlfriend's perfume.

After the Jonesboro shootings, one of the high-school teachers told me 32
how her students reacted when she told them about the shootings at the
middle school. "They laughed," she told me with dismay. A similar reaction
happens all the time in movie theaters when there is bloody violence. The
young people laugh and cheer and keep right on eating popcorn and
drinking pop. We have raised a generation of barbarians who have
learned to associate violence with pleasure, like the Romans cheering and
snacking as the Christians were slaughtered in the Colosseum.

The result is a phenomenon that functions much like AIDS, a phenome- 33
non I call AVIDS—Acquired Violence Immune Deficiency Syndrome.
AIDS has never killed anybody. It destroys your immune system, and then
other diseases that shouldn't kill you become fatal. Television violence by
itself does not kill you. It destroys your violence immune system and conditions you to derive pleasure from violence. And once you are at close range
with another human being, and it's time for you to pull that trigger,
Acquired Violence Immune Deficiency Syndrome can destroy your midbrain resistance.

Operant Conditioning

The third method the military uses is operant conditioning, a very pow- 34
erful repetitive procedure of stimulus-response, stimulus-response. A benign example is the use of flight simulators to train pilots. An airline pilot in
training sits in front of a flight simulator for endless hours; when a particular warning light goes on, he is taught to react in a certain way. When
another warning light goes on, a different reaction is required. Stimulus-
response, stimulus-response, stimulus-response. One day the pilot is actually flying a jumbo jet; the plane is going down, and 300 people are
screaming behind him. He is wetting his seat cushion, and he is scared out
of his wits; but he does the right thing. Why? Because he has been conditioned to respond reflexively to this particular crisis.

When people are frightened or angry, they will do what they have been 35
conditioned to do. In fire drills, children learn to file out of the school in
orderly fashion. One day there is a real fire, and they are frightened out of
their wits; but they do exactly what they have been conditioned to do, and
it saves their lives.

The military and law enforcement community have made killing a 36
conditioned response. This has substantially raised the firing rate on the

modern battlefield. Whereas infantry training in World War II used bull's-eye targets, now soldiers learn to fire at realistic, man-shaped silhouettes that pop into their field of view. That is the stimulus. The trainees have only a split second to engage the target. The conditioned response is to shoot the target, and then it drops. Stimulus-response, stimulus-response, stimulus-response—soldiers or police officers experience hundreds of repetitions. Later, when soldiers are on the battlefield or a police officer is walking a beat and somebody pops up with a gun, they will shoot reflexively and shoot to kill. We know that 75 to 80 percent of the shooting on the modern battlefield is the result of this kind of stimulus-response training.

37   Now, if you're a little troubled by that, how much more should we be troubled by the fact that every time a child plays an interactive point-and-shoot video game, he is learning the exact same conditioned reflex and motor skills?

38   I was an expert witness in a murder case in South Carolina offering mitigation for a kid who was facing the death penalty. I tried to explain to the jury that interactive video games had conditioned him to shoot a gun to kill. He had spent hundreds of dollars on video games learning to point and shoot, point and shoot. One day he and his buddy decided it would be fun to rob the local convenience store. They walked in, and he pointed a snub-nosed .38 pistol at the clerk's head. The clerk turned to look at him, and the defendant shot reflexively from about six feet. The bullet hit the clerk right between the eyes—which is a pretty remarkable shot with that weapon at that range—and killed this father of two. Afterward, we asked the boy what happened and why he did it. It clearly was not part of the plan to kill the guy—it was being videotaped from six different directions. He said, "I don't know. It was a mistake. It wasn't supposed to happen."

39   In the military and law-enforcement worlds, the right option is often not to shoot. But you never, ever put your money in that video machine with the intention of not shooting. There is always some stimulus that sets you off. And when he was excited, and his heart rate went up, and vasoconstriction closed his forebrain down, this young man did exactly what he was conditioned to do: he reflexively pulled the trigger, shooting accurately just like all those times he played video games.

40   This process is extraordinarily powerful and frightening. The result is ever more "homemade" sociopaths who kill reflexively. Our children are learning how to kill and learning to like the idea of killing; and then we have the audacity to say, "Oh my goodness, what's wrong?"

41   One of the boys involved in the Jonesboro shootings (and they are just boys) had a fair amount of experience shooting real guns. The other one, to the best of our knowledge, had almost no experience shooting. Between

them, those two boys fired 27 shots from a range of over 100 yards, and they hit 15 people. That's pretty remarkable shooting. We run into these situations often—kids who have never picked up a gun in their lives pick up a real gun and are incredibly accurate. Why? Video games.

Thinking Critically About Content

1. According to Grossman, what is the "virus of violence" (paragraph 3)?

2. What three methods does the military use to train its soldiers to kill?

3. What does Grossman mean when he claims that the media are presenting violence "as entertainment for children"?

Thinking Critically About Purpose and Audience

4. What do you think Grossman's purpose is in this essay?

5. Who do you think would be most interested in this essay?

6. What effect do you think this essay would have on parents?

Thinking Critically About Essays

7. Describe in a complete sentence the writer's argument.

8. Why does Grossman cite statistics to explain the "virus of violence" that concerns him?

9. Explain the title of this essay.

10. This essay discusses the sensitive issues related to children and violence in the media and then ends abruptly. Add a paragraph to the essay making some concrete suggestions for solving the problem the author poses.

ARGUING A POSITION

Focusing Your Attention

1. If you were asked to take a position for or against a topic of great importance to you or to society, what are some of the topics you would consider?

2. In the two essays that you will be reading, one writer claims that if we control loitering, we can control gang activity. The other writer claims loitering is not related to gang activity. Before you read these essays, try to predict some of the arguments each author will make.

Richard Willard

ANTI-LOITERING LAWS CAN REDUCE GANG VIOLENCE

Summary
In this essay, Willard argues that anti-loitering laws are an effective means for reducing gang violence.

Readability
(Flesch–Kincaid grade level)
15.8

Instructor's Resource Manual
For additional teaching strategies, for journal entries, for vocabulary and reading quizzes, and for more writing assignments, see the *Instructor's Resource Manual*, Section II, Part IV.

Expanding Your Vocabulary

The following words are important to your understanding of this essay:

anti-loitering: forbidding people to hang around in a public place without an obvious reason (title)

innovative: clever, original (paragraph 1)

curfew: time by which individuals must be off the public streets (paragraph 1)

statutes: laws (paragraph 1)

court injunctions: orders issued by the courts (paragraph 1)

deterrence: avoidance (paragraph 1)

sanctions: punishments (paragraph 1)

constrained: limited (paragraph 1)

discretion: personal judgment (paragraph 1)

gang-loitering ordinances: laws against gangs hanging around public places without reason (paragraph 2)

implemented: used, enforced (paragraph 2)

pervasiveness: extent (paragraph 2)

engenders: produces, causes (paragraph 3)

panhandling: begging for money (paragraph 5)

vending: the selling of merchandise (paragraph 5)

commons: open public areas such as parks and squares (paragraph 6)

prevalent: widespread (paragraph 7)

skewed: distorted (paragraph 7)

augment: increase (paragraph 10)

condemnation: blame (paragraph 10)

suppression: control (paragraph 11)

abatement: decrease (paragraph 11)

1   Chicago is not alone in seeking to resist the devastating effects of gang violence. Having witnessed the failure of more traditional policing methods, many other threatened localities—from Los Angeles to Washington, D.C.—

have reacted by passing a variety of innovative laws, which range from curfew measures to anti-loitering statutes to court injunctions against specific gang members. All of these measures emphasize prevention and deterrence strategies over increased criminal sanctions. In order to meet the particular challenges of increased gang violence, communities have also strongly supported constrained expansions of police discretion to help communities reassert their own law-abiding norms.

Residents of high-crime communities are much more likely to support   2
gang-loitering ordinances, curfews, and other order-maintenance policies, which they perceive to be appropriately moderate yet effective devices for reducing crime. Communities have implemented these policies in various ways, tailored to their particular needs and depending on the pervasiveness of the problem.

Maintaining Order

Just as community disorder engenders increasing disorder and crime,   3
reinforcement of [existing] community law-abiding norms engenders increasing social order and prevents more serious crime. Modern policing theory has undergone a "quiet revolution" to learn that, in cooperation with community efforts, enforcing community public order norms is one of the most effective means of combating all levels of crime. By focusing on order maintenance and prevention, advocating a more visible presence in policed areas, and basing its legitimacy on the consent of policed populations, police can most effectively prevent the occurrence of more serious crime.

New York City's experience confirms this. Today, that city has much less   4
crime than it did five years ago. From 1993 to 1996, the murder rate dropped by 40 percent, robberies dropped by 30 percent, and burglary dropped by more than 25 percent, more than double the national average.

These drops are not the result of increased police resources, but rather   5
more effectively applied resources. While New York has not increased its law enforcement expenditures substantially more than other cities, since 1993 the city began to focus intensively on "public order" offenses, including vandalism, aggressive panhandling, public drunkenness, unlicensed vending, public urination, and prostitution. This focus on order maintenance is credited for much of the crime reduction.

Anti-loitering ordinances implement community-driven order mainte-   6
nance policing citywide—appropriate to the extreme pervasiveness of Chicago's gang problem—but on a neighborhood scale. Preservation of neighborhood commons is essential to ensuring healthy and vital cities.

Ineffective Strategies

7   Gang loitering works to increase disorder. Order-maintenance policing strikes a reasonable intermediate balance between harsh criminal penalties and inaction. Conventional suppression strategies are ineffective in gang-threatened communities. Where gang activity is prevalent, individuals are more likely to act in an aggressive manner in order to conform to gang norms of behavior. When numerous youths act according to these skewed norms, more are likely to turn to crime: Widespread adoption of aggressive mannerisms sends skewed signals about public attitudes toward gang membership and creates barriers to mainstream law-abiding society, which strongly disfavors aggression.

8   Accordingly, policies that "raise the price" of gang activity can sometimes function at cross-purposes. If juveniles value willingness to break the law, delinquency may be seen as "status-enhancing." As penalties grow more severe, lawbreaking gives increasing status. More severe punishments may also provoke unintended racist accusation, if community minorities view harsher penalties as unfairly applied to their particular groups. Thus, any strategy dependent on harsh penalties may in fact be "at war with itself."

Why Anti-Loitering Laws Work

9   Strategies that instead attack public signals to juveniles' peers about the value of gang criminality are more effective. Gang anti-loitering laws do this, for example, by "authorizing police to disperse known gang members when they congregate in public places" or by "directly prohibiting individuals from displaying gang allegiance through distinctive gestures or clothing." By preventing gangs from flaunting their authority, such laws establish community authority while combating the perception that gangs have high status. As that perception weakens, so does the pressure to join gangs that youths might otherwise perceive.

10   Such strategies also positively influence law-abiding adults. Gang-loitering laws augment law-abiders' confidence so that they can oppose gangs. When public deterrence predominates, individuals are much less likely to perceive that criminality is widespread and much more likely to see private precautions as worthwhile. When the community as a whole is again able to express its condemnation, gang influence quickly wanes.

11   The most successful anti-gang programs combine effective gang suppression programs with targeted community aid efforts: increased social services, job placement, and crisis intervention. Civil gang abatement,

together with other government and community-based efforts, has reduced crime and visibly improved the neighborhood's quality of life.

Chicago has also implemented alternative community aid programs. 12 Since 1992, for example, the Gang Violence Reduction Project has targeted Little Village to serve as a model gang violence reduction program.

The program coordinates increased levels of social services—the 13 carrot—in conjunction with focused suppression strategies—the stick. The result has been a lower level of serious gang violence among the targeted gangs than among comparable gangs in the area. The project also noted improvement in residents' perceptions of gang crime and police effectiveness in dealing with it. Chicago's anti-loitering ordinance is the necessary "stick" of an effective gang violence reduction equation.

David Cole
ANTI-LOITERING LAWS ARE INEFFECTIVE AND BIASED

Expanding Your Vocabulary

The following words are important to your understanding of this essay:

anti-loitering: forbidding people to hang around in a public place without an obvious reason (title)

starkly: boldly (paragraph 1)

ordinance: law (paragraph 1)

due process: the requirement that laws treat all individuals fairly (paragraph 1)

discretion: personal judgment (paragraph 3)

empirical: theoretical (paragraph 4)

aldermen: members of the town council or governing board (paragraph 4)

apartheid regime: political system in which people of different races were separated (paragraph 4)

disparities: differences (paragraph 4)

invalidated: canceled (paragraph 5)

unfettered: free, unlimited (paragraph 6)

mores: moral attitudes (paragraph 6)

SUMMARY

Cole argues that anti-loitering laws are back-firing on the police because (1) they do not deter gang violence and (2) people are losing respect for law agencies.

READABILITY
(Flesch–Kincaid grade level)
13.6

INSTRUCTOR'S RESOURCE MANUAL

For additional teaching strategies, for journal entries, for vocabulary and reading quizzes, and for more writing assignments, see the *Instructor's Resource Manual*, Section II, Part IV.

ANSWERS TO
QUESTIONS
*Thinking Critically
About Content*
1. Willard:
   reasons
   Anti-loitering laws
     can help disperse
     gangs.
   Community
     resources will
     give gang
     members a place
     to go.
   evidence
   New York City's
     crime rate has
     decreased.
   Focusing on minor
     infractions helps
     lower the crime
     rate.
   Community-based
     efforts have
     reduced crime.
   statistics
   From 1993 to 1996,
     the murder rate
     in New York
     dropped by
     40 percent,
     robberies by
     30 percent, and
     burglary by
     25 percent.
Cole:
   reasons
   Anti-loitering laws
     cause mistrust.
   Anti-loitering
     laws focus on
     minorities.
   evidence
   Crime rates have
     dropped every-
     where, not just in
     states with anti-
     loitering laws.
   Communities mis-
     trust the motives

strictures: restraints and limits (paragraph 6)

discriminatory: biased, unfair (paragraph 6)

legitimacy: acceptance as lawful (paragraph 6)

cynicism: doubt, distrust (paragraph 6)

alienation: sense of not belonging (paragraph 6)

Kerner Commission: task force established by President Lyndon Johnson to investigate the causes of race riots (paragraph 7)

street sweeps: stopping and searching everyone on the street as if they are guilty of a crime (paragraph 7)

antithetical: opposing (paragraph 7)

carte blanche: complete freedom (paragraph 7)

impeding: blocking, obstructing (paragraph 7)

1   Do "quality of life" policing and "community" policing, the law enforcement watchwords of the nineties, require the abandonment or dilution of civil rights and civil liberties? On December 9, 1998, the Supreme Court heard arguments in a case that starkly poses that question. At issue is a sweeping Chicago ordinance that makes it a crime for gang members or anyone associated with them merely to stand in public "with no apparent purpose." Chicago calls the offense "gang loitering," but it might more candidly be termed "standing while black." Sixty-six of the more than 45,000 Chicago citizens arrested for this offense in the three years that the law was on the books challenged its constitutionality, and in 1997 the Illinois Supreme Court unanimously ruled that it violated due process.

2   But the Supreme Court agreed to review that decision, and lined up in defense of the ordinance is not only the city of Chicago but also the United States, the attorneys general of thirty-one states, the National District Attorneys Association, the International Association of Chiefs of Police, the U.S. Conference of Mayors, and, perhaps most interesting, a pair of otherwise liberal University of Chicago law professors representing several Chicago neighborhood groups.

Disputing the Arguments for Loitering Laws

3   The ordinance's advocates argue that it played a critical role in making Chicago's high-crime neighborhoods safe and therefore served the interests of the minority poor who live there. They suggest that strict constitutional standards need to be loosened in order to give police the discretion to engage in the day-to-day encounters of "quality of life" or "community"

policing. Most astounding, they argue that criminal laws no longer must be clear in places where minority groups have a voice in the political process and can protect themselves. These arguments resonate with one commonly heard these days, particularly but not exclusively in Mayor Rudolph Giuliani's New York City—namely, that heavy-handed police efforts directed at the inner city benefit minority residents by making their neighborhoods safer places in which to grow up, work, and live.

The arguments fail. First, as an empirical matter it is far from clear that the minority community in Chicago supported the law or that minority communities generally favor "quality of life" policing efforts that send so many of their residents to jail. The majority of Chicago's African-American aldermen voted against the ordinance; one representative, predicting that the law would be targeted at young black men, compared it to South Africa's apartheid regime. And voter turnout rates are so low in the inner city that it is difficult to say whether any elected official speaks for that community. The notion that minorities no longer need the protection of constitutional law simply ignores the racial disparities evident at every stage of the criminal justice system.

It is also not clear that the antigang law actually benefited anyone, much less Chicago's minority communities. Chicago did experience a falling crime rate while the law was in effect, but so did the rest of the nation. And the crime rate continued to fall after the ordinance was invalidated. So it is far from proven that arresting tens of thousands for standing in public had any positive effects.

Law Enforcement Must Build Trust

Most important, giving the police unfettered discretion to sweep the city streets of "undesirable" youth probably undermines safety by incurring distrust among those community members whose trust the police need most. The law's most powerful tool is its legitimacy. The more people believe the law is legitimate, the more likely they are to internalize its mores, obey its strictures, and cooperate with police. When laws are enforced in discriminatory ways, they lose their legitimacy. Cynicism and alienation about the criminal law are nowhere higher than among minorities and the urban poor, and laws like Chicago's only feed the alienation by inviting selective enforcement.

Indeed, law enforcement authorities and experts have long understood the importance of maintaining the community's faith and trust. Thirty years ago, the Kerner Commission reported that such support "will not be present when a substantial segment of the community feels threatened by the

4

5

6

7

of the police and therefore avoid the police.

statistics

45,000 citizens in Chicago were arrested over a three-year period.

2. Willard states that Chicago has attacked loitering on such a scale that gang violence has been reduced. Cole uses Chicago throughout most of his essay to prove that anti-loitering laws cause many arrests but do not deter crime in any way.

3. Answers will vary.

Thinking Critically About Purpose and Audience

4. Willard wants to maintain anti-loitering laws; Cole wants to abolish them.

5. People who are affected by gangs in any way would be most interested in these essays.

6. Answers will vary.

Thinking Critically About Essays

7. Willard believes that anti-loitering laws are effective and are needed to curb violence; Cole believes that anti-loitering laws are unconstitutional and unfairly target minority populations.

8. Willard:
  Introduction
    Background on high-crime communities

Body paragraphs
  Evidence showing
    value of laws
  Statistics proving
    laws are effective
  Opposing viewpoint
  Response to oppos-
    ing viewpoint
  Alternatives to
    loitering
Conclusion
  Anti-loitering laws
    are the solution.

Cole:

Introduction
  Background show-
    ing issue of un-
    constitutionality
Body paragraphs
  Opposing viewpoint
  Response to oppos-
    ing viewpoint:
    facts, examples
  Evidence showing
    laws are
    ineffective
Conclusion
  Anti-loitering laws
    violate civil
    rights.
9. Both writers agree
that loitering is a
problem and that anti-
loitering laws have
cleaned the streets of
many troublesome
youths. However,
Willard believes that
these laws are effective
in curbing violence and
offer gang members a
place to go, whereas
Cole believes that the
laws are targeting
minorities who are not
necessarily gang
members, are infringing
on civil rights, and are
causing distrust for
police officials.
10. Answers will vary.

police and regards the police as an occupying force." The father of "quality of life" policing, George Kelling, has argued that street sweeps are antithetical to its goals precisely because they foster enmity, not community. And Attorney General Janet Reno has written that effective crime control requires "a greater sense of community and trust between law enforcement and the minority community." Yet her Justice Department, the City of Chicago, and the majority of our nation's state attorneys general fail to understand that you don't build trust by unleashing the police on minority communities with carte blanche to arrest anyone standing in public without an apparent purpose. Civil rights and civil liberties, far from impeding law enforcement, are critical to preserving its legitimacy.

Thinking Critically About Content

1. Make a list of the reasons, evidence, and statistics each writer uses to convince the reader of his position.

2. Explain how both writers use the anti-loitering laws in Chicago to argue different positions.

3. Which essay contains the most convincing evidence in your opinion? Why is it so convincing to you?

Thinking Critically About Purpose and Audience

4. What do you think the writers' purposes are in these essays?

5. What type of audience would be most interested in the subject of these two essays? Explain your answer.

6. If you changed your mind as a result of reading one of these essays, what in the essay caused the change?

Thinking Critically About Essays

7. State each writer's point of view in a single sentence.

8. How do both writers organize their essays? Make a rough outline of each essay to demonstrate your answer.

9. Which points do the two writers agree on? Which points do they disagree on? Explain your answer.

10. Write your own argument about the relationship between loitering and gang activity.

Writing Topics: Arguing and Persuading

Before you begin to write, you might want to review the writing process in Part I.

1. In "We Are Training Our Kids to Kill," Grossman tries to convince his readers that various forms of violence in the media teach our kids to kill. Argue for or against government control of violence on TV, in movies, and/or in video games.

2. These pro and con essays deal mainly with loitering as it relates to gang activity. Think of another strategy for fighting gang activity, and attempt to convince a group in authority to try your solution to the problem. Gather as much evidence as you can before you begin to write.

3. How can being able to develop good arguments and persuade people of your point of view help you in life? How might this ability give you the edge over other people on the job market?

THE HANDBOOK

This part of *Mosaics* provides you with a complete handbook for editing your writing. You can use it as a reference tool as you write or as a source of instruction and practice in areas where you need work.

This handbook consists of an Introduction and eight units:

The chapters in each unit start with a self-test to help you identify your strengths and weaknesses in that area. Then the chapter teaches specific sentence skills and provides exercises so you can practice what you have learned. Each chapter also asks you to write your own sentences and then work with another student to edit each other's writing. At the end of each unit, two review tests are provided that ask you to apply to sentences and paragraphs all that you have practiced in the unit.

The Editing Symbols on the inside back cover will give you marks for highlighting errors in your papers. In addition, the Error Log (Appendix 6) and Spelling Log (Appendix 7) will help you tailor the instruction to your own needs and keep track of your progress.

INTRODUCTION: PARTS OF SPEECH, PHRASES, AND CLAUSES

This handbook uses very little terminology. But sometimes talking about the language and the way it works is difficult without a shared understanding of certain basic grammar terms. For that reason, your instructor may ask you to study parts of this introduction to review basic grammar—parts of speech, phrases, and clauses. You might also use this introduction for reference.

This section has three parts:

Parts of Speech
Phrases
Clauses

PARTS OF SPEECH

Test Yourself

In the following paragraph, label the parts of speech listed here:

2 verbs (v)	2 adverbs (adv)
2 nouns (n)	2 prepositions (prep)
2 pronouns (pro)	2 conjunctions (conj)
2 adjectives (adj)	2 interjections (int)

Professional basketball is definitely this nation's best spectator sport. The talented players move around the court so quickly that the audience never has a chance to become bored. Boy, I'll never forget that Saturday night last February when my favorite uncle took me to see the Spurs game against the Trailblazers. It was an important home game for San Antonio, so the arena was packed. The Spurs were behind throughout most of the game, but they pulled

TEACHING PARTS OF SPEECH
Play a game of Memory (Concentration) by creating two identical batches of words on index cards. For instance, have two cards for each of the following words: *walk, house, you, red, never, during, can't,* and *Hey!* Make sure you have many sets of words representing each part of speech. Shuffle the cards, and number the back of each card, starting with 1.

Line your wall with butcher paper, and attach a piece of removable tape to the front of each index card (so that each can be removed and placed back into position many times). Place the index cards, word side down, on the paper in the order of their number. For instance, 1–10 in the first row, 11–20 in the second row, and so on.

Have students form teams of three or four and try to find the matching words. When a team uncovers two words that match, it must identify the part of speech before getting credit for the match. Otherwise, the pair goes back onto the board for another team to uncover and label.

The team that accumulates the most cards wins.

INSTRUCTOR'S RESOURCE MANUAL

For more sample words, for more exercises, and for quizzes, see the *Instructor's Resource Manual*, Section II, Part V.

through and won with a three-pointer in the last few seconds. Wow! I have never seen so many people on their feet, screaming at the top of their lungs.

(Answers are in Appendix 4.)

Every sentence is made up of a variety of words that play different roles. Each word, like each part of a coordinated outfit, serves a distinct function. These functions fall into eight categories:

1. Verbs
2. Nouns
3. Pronouns
4. Adjectives
5. Adverbs
6. Prepositions
7. Conjunctions
8. Interjections

Some words, such as *is*, can function in only one way—in this case, as a verb. Other words, however, can serve as different parts of speech depending on how they are used in a sentence. For example, look at the different ways the word *show* can be used:

Verb:	The artists **show** their work at a gallery.
	(*Show* is a verb here, telling what the artists do.)
Noun:	The **show** will start in 10 minutes.
	(*Show* functions as a noun here, telling what will start in 10 minutes.)
Adjective:	The little boy loves to sing **show** tunes.
	(*Show* is an adjective here, modifying the noun *tunes*.)

Verbs

The **verb** is the most important word in a sentence because every other word depends on it in some way. Verbs tell what's going on in the sentence.

There are three types of verbs: action, linking, and helping. An **action verb** tells what someone or something is doing. A **linking verb** tells what someone or something is, feels, or looks like. Sometimes an action or linking verb has **helping verbs**—words that add information, such as when an action is taking place. A **complete verb** consists of an action or linking verb and all the helping verbs.

Action:	The girl **wandered** too far from the campsite.
Action:	Luca **ran** to the bus stop.
Linking:	He **looks** very tired.
Linking:	It **was** a real surprise to see you.
Helping:	My aunt and uncle **will be** arriving tomorrow.
Helping:	My grandmother **has** been very ill lately.
Complete Verb:	My aunt and uncle **will be arriving** tomorrow.
Complete Verb:	My grandmother **has been** very ill lately.

REVIEWING VERBS

Define each of the following types of verbs, and give an example of each.

Action: Tells what someone or something is doing. Examples will vary.

Linking: Tells what someone or something is, feels, or looks like.

Examples will vary.

Helping: Adds information such as when action is taking place.

Examples will vary.

What is a complete verb? Give an example with your definition.

A complete verb consists of an action or linking verb and all the

helping verbs. Examples will vary.

 P r a c t i c e   1   Identifying In each of the following sentences, underline the complete verbs. Some sentences have more than one verb.

1. I <u>read</u> *Moby Dick* for my literature class.
2. The best place for inexpensive fast food <u>is</u> Taco Bell.
3. You <u>seem</u> tired.

4. I <u>wonder</u> if Chad <u>was going</u> to be attending.

5. The teenager <u>climbed</u> to the top of the mountain before he <u>stopped</u> for lunch.

◆ *P r a c t i c e 2* **Completing** Fill in each blank in the following paragraph with a verb. *Answers will vary.*

This year my sister (1) _____ to get married. She and her fiancé (2) _____ in Dallas, Texas, so I had to buy a plane ticket from Los Angeles. First, I tried the computer and (3) _____ all of the Web sites that people talk about, but I couldn't find any good deals. Finally, I (4) _____ a travel agent and asked her to tell me what my best options were. The best deal she (5) _____ was $280 round-trip, so I charged it to a credit card. I guess my sister is worth it.

◆ *P r a c t i c e 3* **Writing Your Own** Write a sentence of your own for each of the following verbs. *Answers will vary.*

1. was sitting _____

2. handled _____

3. seems _____

4. had been taking _____

5. buy _____

Nouns

People often think of **nouns** as "naming words" because they identify—or name—people (*student, Susan, mom, server*), places (*city, ocean, Thomasville*), or things (*bush, airplane, chair, shirt*). Nouns also name ideas (*liberty, justice*), qualities (*bravery, patience*), emotions (*sadness, happiness*), and actions (*challenge, compromise*). A **common noun** names something general (*singer, hill, water, theater*). A **proper noun** names something specific (*Nicole Kidman, Angel Falls, Coke, McDonald's*).

Hint: To test whether a word is a noun, try putting *a, an,* or *the* in front of it:

    Nouns: a squirrel, an orange, the hope

    NOT Nouns: a funny, an over, the eat

This test does not work with proper nouns:

    NOT   a Natalie, the New York

REVIEWING NOUNS

What is a noun?

A noun names people, places, things, ideas, qualities, emotions, and actions.

What is the difference between a common noun and a proper noun? Give an example of each.

Common noun: *A common noun names something general. Examples*

will vary.

Proper noun: *A proper noun names something specific. Examples*

will vary.

Practice 4 **Identifying** Underline all the nouns in the following sentences.

1. The <u>Golden Gate Bridge</u> is a popular tourist <u>attraction</u> in <u>San Francisco</u>.
2. <u>Collectors</u> will spend much <u>money</u> on limited-edition <u>coins</u>.
3. My <u>son</u> is wearing my favorite <u>shirt</u>.
4. In <u>October</u>, we are planning a <u>trip</u> to <u>Seattle</u>.
5. *<u>Emeril Live</u>* was voted the most popular TV cooking <u>show</u>.

Practice 5 **Completing** Fill in each blank in the following paragraph with a noun that will make each sentence complete. *Answers will vary.*

Last May, I joined a volunteer organization called (1) _____. Within a month, the secretary left, and I was nominated to take his place. I had to put all of the (2) _____ about the organization and its members into my computer and then create a mail merge. With this database, I was able to make labels and (3) _____ very easily. My first assignment was to create a form letter and send it to all of the (4) _____ who promised to send money to the group. I finally saw the (5) _____ of all the grammar lessons I had in my English classes, and I learned that writing good letters is harder than I thought.

P r a c t i c e   6   Writing Your Own Write a sentence of your own for each of the following nouns. *Answers will vary.*

1. pastor _____

2. Sea World _____

3. strength _____

4. audience _____

5. actions _____

Pronouns

Pronouns can do anything nouns can do. In fact, **pronouns** can take the place of nouns. Without pronouns, you would find yourself repeating nouns and producing boring sentences. Compare the following sentences, for example:

George drove **George's** car very fast to **George's** house because **George** had to get home early.

George drove **his** car very fast to **his** house because **he** had to get home early.

There are many different types of pronouns, but you only need to focus on the following four types for now.

Most Common Pronouns

Personal (refer to people or things)

Singular:	First person:	*I, me, my, mine*
	Second person:	*you, your, yours*
	Third person:	*he, she, it, him, her, hers, his, its*

Plural:	First person:	*we, us, our, ours*
	Second person:	*you, your, yours*
	Third person:	*they, them, their, theirs*

Demonstrative (point out someone or something)

| **Singular:** | *this, that* |
| **Plural:** | *these, those* |

Relative (introduce a dependent clause)

who, whom, whose, which, that

Indefinite (refer to someone or something general, not specific)

Singular:	*another, anybody, anyone, anything, each, either, everybody, everyone, everything, little, much, neither, nobody, none, no one, nothing, one, other, somebody, someone, something*
Plural:	*both, few, many, others, several*
Either Singular or Plural:	*all, any, more, most, some*

Hint: When any of these words are used with nouns, they become adjectives instead of pronouns.

| Adjective: | He can have **some candy.** |
| Pronoun: | He can have **some.** |

| Adjective: | The baby wants **that toy.** |
| Pronoun: | The baby wants **that.** |

REVIEWING PRONOUNS

What is a pronoun?

A pronoun is a word that can take the place of a noun.

Define the four most common types of pronouns, and give two examples of each.

Personal: Refer to people or things. Examples will vary.

Demonstrative: *Point out someone or something. Examples will vary.*

Relative: *Introduce a dependent clause. Examples will vary.*

Indefinite: *Refer to someone or something general. Examples will vary.*

P r a c t i c e   7   Identifying Underline all the pronouns in the following sentences. Don't underline words that look like pronouns but are really adjectives.

1. <u>Some</u> of the wedding guests were vegetarians.
2. <u>Those</u> are the biggest shoes <u>I</u> have ever seen.
3. <u>Somebody</u> had better admit to <u>this</u>.
4. After <u>his</u> car was stolen, <u>everything</u> else seemed to go wrong for <u>him</u> too.
5. Does <u>anyone</u> else need <u>anything</u> while <u>I'm</u> up?

P r a c t i c e   8   Completing In the following paragraph, replace the nouns in parentheses with pronouns.

Mike first tried rollerblading when (1) ____*he*____ (Mike) was 19. It was pretty funny to watch (2) ____*him*____ (Mike) buy the shin guards and wrist guards, put (3) ____*them*____ (the shin guards and wrist guards) on, and then roll down the sidewalk out of control. (4) ____*His*____ (Mike's) two best friends, Carl and Luis, wanted to learn also, but when they saw the hard time Mike was having, (5) ____*they*____ (Carl and Luis) were too afraid.

P r a c t i c e   9   Writing Your Own Write a sentence of your own for each of the following pronouns. *Answers will vary.*

1. anyone _____

2. these _____

3. who _____

4. many _____

5. our _____

Adjectives

Adjectives modify—or describe—nouns or pronouns. Adjectives generally make sentences clear and vivid.

Without Adjectives: She brought an umbrella, a towel, and a Walkman to the beach.

With Adjectives: She brought a **bright orange** umbrella, a **striped blue** towel, and a **waterproof** Walkman to the beach.

REVIEWING ADJECTIVES

What is an adjective?

An adjective modifies or describes a noun or pronoun. _____

Give three examples of adjectives.

Examples will vary. _____ _____ _____

P r a c t i c e   1 0   **Identifying** Underline all the adjectives in the following sentences.

1. His long black goatee was formed into two sharp points.
2. The talented musicians gave a two-hour concert for an excited audience.
3. Grisham's best-selling novel, *Runaway Jury*, is about a strange man and his intelligent girlfriend.
4. Getting a good parking place is sometimes impossible.
5. Matthew signed his name using a smooth ballpoint pen.

P r a c t i c e   1 1   **Completing** Fill in each blank in the following paragraph with an adjective. *Answers will vary.*

My girlfriend and I went to a (1) _____ baseball game at the Anaheim Stadium last weekend. The Angels were playing the Texas Rangers, and the Rangers were much more (2) _____. This year, the Rangers have (3) _____ infielders, and their batters are pretty (4) _____ also.

Overall, the teams were unequally matched, and it was (5)
_____ that one of them was going to lose pretty badly.

Practice 12 **Writing Your Own** Write a sentence of your own for each of the following adjectives. *Answers will vary.*

1. gorgeous _____

2. dark _____

3. tempting _____

4. thrifty _____

5. sixth _____

Adverbs

Adverbs modify—or describe—adjectives, verbs, and other adverbs. They do *not* modify nouns. Adverbs also answer the following questions:

How?	thoughtfully, kindly, briefly, quietly
When?	soon, tomorrow, late, now
Where?	inside, somewhere, everywhere, there
How often?	daily, always, annually, rarely
To what extent?	generally, specifically, exactly, very

Hint: Notice that adverbs often end in *-ly*. That might help you recognize them.

REVIEWING ADVERBS

What is an adverb?

An adverb modifies or describes an adjective, a verb, or another adverb.

What are the five questions that adverbs answer?

How?　　*When?*　　*Where?*　　*How often?*　　*To what extent?*

Give one example of an adverb that answers each question.

Examples will vary.

_____　_____　_____　_____

P r a c t i c e 1 3 **Identifying** Underline all the adverbs in the following sentences.

1. He <u>almost</u> passed Stephanie when he was running <u>aimlessly</u> down the hall.
2. That was the <u>very</u> last time George Clooney was on television.
3. It was <u>quite</u> disappointing to lose after <u>nearly</u> six months of training.
4. Are you <u>absolutely</u> sure that you remembered to set the alarm?
5. I try to buy groceries <u>weekly</u> so that we are <u>never</u> missing the basic necessities.

P r a c t i c e 1 4 **Completing** Fill in each blank in the following paragraph with an adverb. *Answers will vary.*

When Shanika (1) _____ lost her job at the grocery store, she felt desperate. She (2) _____ began calling her friends and relatives, asking if they knew of any job openings. (3) _____ for Shanika, her Aunt Betsy owned a hair salon that needed a receptionist. Shanika didn't know anything about beauty parlors, but she (4) _____ agreed to work there because she needed the money. After only three weeks, Shanika became very interested in the salon, and she (5) _____ decided to take classes at a local beauty college and earn a license in cosmetology.

P r a c t i c e 1 5 **Writing Your Own** Write a sentence of your own for each of the following adverbs. *Answers will vary.*

1. sometimes _____

2. hardly _____

3. gently _____

4. too _____

5. tomorrow _____

Prepositions

Prepositions indicate relationship among the ideas in a sentence. Something is *at, in, by, next to, behind, around, near,* or *under* something else. A preposition is always followed by a noun or a pronoun called the **object of the preposition.** Together, they form a **prepositional phrase.**

Preposition	+	Object	=	Prepositional Phrase
near		the beach		near the beach
for		the party		for the party

Here is a list of some common prepositions.

Common Prepositions

about	beside	into	since
above	between	like	through
across	beyond	near	throughout
after	by	next to	to
against	despite	of	toward
among	down	off	under
around	during	on	until
as	except	on top of	up
at	for	out	upon
before	from	out of	up to
behind	in	outside	with
below	in front of	over	within
beneath	inside	past	without

Hint: *To* + a verb (as in *to go, to come, to feel*) is not a prepositional phrase. It is a verb phrase, which we will deal with later in this unit.

REVIEWING PREPOSITIONS

What is a preposition?

A preposition indicates relationships among the ideas in a sentence.

Give two examples of prepositions:

Examples will vary.

_____   _____

What is a prepositional phrase?

A prepositional phrase consists of a preposition and its object.
_____

Give two examples of prepositional phrases:

Examples will vary.

_____   _____

P r a c t i c e   1 6   Identifying Underline all the prepositions in the following sentences.

1. When I stepped off the bus, I looked down the street and saw an old man in a white hat.
2. The cabin is over the big hill, past the creek, and down a winding dirt path.
3. If you go to Maui, stay in Kaanapali at a resort hotel beside the ocean.
4. The paper in my printer is jammed, so the light on the top won't stop blinking.
5. After the party, I found confetti in my hair, on the carpet, behind the sofa, and in all four corners of the room.

P r a c t i c e   1 7   Completing Fill in each blank in the following paragraph with a preposition. *Answers will vary.*

I was so surprised when I saw Carlos walking (1) _____ campus toward me. The last time we talked was eight months ago, when he was still living (2) _____ Kendra. He decided to take some time (3) _____ work to finish his degree, and he was hoping to have it completed (4) _____ the next year. I was very proud (5) _____ him for setting these priorities.

◆ *P r a c t i c e 1 8*   **Writing Your Own** Write a sentence of your own for each of the following prepositions. *Answers will vary.*

1. with _____

2. beside _____

3. on top of _____

4. until _____

5. against _____

Conjunctions

Conjunctions connect groups of words. Without conjunctions, most of our writing would be choppy and boring. The two types of conjunctions are easy to remember because their names state their purpose: *Coordinating conjunctions* link equal ideas, and *subordinating conjunctions* make one idea subordinate to—or dependent on—another.

Coordinating conjunctions connect parts of a sentence that are of equal importance or weight. These parts can be **independent clauses,** a group of words with a subject and verb that can stand alone as a sentence (see pages 522–523). There are only seven coordinating conjunctions:

Coordinating Conjunctions

---

and, but, or, nor, for, so, yet

Coordinating: Johanna **and** Melvin arrived late.

Coordinating: My sister wanted to go shopping **and** I jogging.

Coordinating: The teacher was very demanding, **but** I learned a
                  lot from him.

Subordinating conjunctions join two ideas by making one dependent on the other. The idea introduced by the subordinating conjunction becomes a **dependent clause,** a group of words with a subject and a verb that cannot stand alone as a sentence (see pages 522–523). The other part of the sentence is an independent clause.

Dependent Clause

Subordinating: I won't leave **until** he comes home.

Dependent Clause

Subordinating: **Unless** <u>you study more</u>, you won't be accepted to college.

Common Subordinating Conjunctions

after	because	since	until
although	before	so	when
as	even if	so that	whenever
as if	even though	than	where
as long as	how	that	wherever
as soon as	if	though	whether
as though	in order that	unless	while

REVIEWING CONJUNCTIONS

What is a coordinating conjunction?

A coordinating conjunction connects parts of a sentence that are of

equal importance or weight.

Name the seven coordinating conjunctions.

and   but   for   nor   or   so   yet

What is a subordinating conjunction?

A subordinating conjunction joins two ideas by making one dependent

on the other.

Write a sentence using a subordinating conjunction.

Answers will vary.

P r a c t i c e 1 9 Identifying Underline all the conjunctions in the following sentences.

1. My best personality trait is my sense of humor, <u>but</u> people also say <u>that</u> I'm a good listener.

2. The homecoming game was a lot of fun, <u>yet</u> I didn't see anyone I knew.
3. <u>While</u> the other people were touring the city, Thomas stayed in the hotel room <u>and</u> took a nap.
4. Carmen will be in our study group <u>as long as</u> we meet at her house.
5. Shane volunteered to take us to the airport <u>even though</u> his car seats only four people.

◆ *P r a c t i c e 2 0*   Completing Fill in each blank in the following paragraph with a conjunction. *Answers will vary.*

Babysitting is definitely not an easy job, (1) _____ it is a fast way to make money. One couple I babysit for has two children, and (2) _____ one of them is a perfect angel, the other one is constantly getting into trouble. Michael is the troublemaker, (3) _____ he is 6 years old. (4) _____ I arrive at his house, he runs to his room and begins pulling everything off of his bookshelves. Of course, I clean everything up (5) _____ his parents get home, so they never see how messy the house gets when they leave.

◆ *P r a c t i c e 2 1*   Writing Your Own Write a sentence of your own for each of the following conjunctions. *Answers will vary.*

1. or _____
2. even if _____
3. whether _____
4. yet _____
5. since _____

Interjections

Interjections are words that express strong emotion, surprise, or disappointment. An interjection is usually followed by an exclamation point or a comma.

Interjection: **Whoa!** You're going too fast.

Interjection: **Ouch,** that hurt!

Other common interjections include *aha, alas, great, hallelujah, neat, oh, oops, ouch, well, whoa, yeah,* and *yippee.*

REVIEWING INTERJECTIONS

What is an interjection?

An interjection is a word that expresses strong emotion, surprise, or

disappointment.

Write a sentence using an interjection.

Answers will vary.

Practice 22 **Identifying** Underline all the interjections in the following sentences.

1. <u>My goodness</u>! This wind is going to blow down my fence!
2. I just won the lottery! <u>Hallelujah</u>!
3. <u>Boy</u>, I'm beat. I can't walk another step.
4. We just got a new car! <u>Cool</u>!
5. <u>Good grief</u>! Am I the only one working today?

Practice 23 **Completing** Fill in each blank in the following paragraph with an interjection. *Answers will vary.*

(1) _____, I thought that was the easiest test this professor has ever given. (2) _____! I was really worried about this test. (3) _____, it's over! I spent two weeks solid studying for this test. For the last two nights, I've slept only four hours. (4) _____, am I ever tired. But at least the test is behind me, (5) _____!

◆ *P r a c t i c e 2 4* **Writing Your Own** Write a sentence of your own for each of the following interjections. *Answers will vary.*

1. help _____

2. mercy _____

3. wow _____

4. yippee _____

5. ouch _____

PHRASES

Test Yourself

Underline the phrases in the following sentences.

- Using the computer, I got most of the research done for my report.
- To be totally confident, I checked for spelling and grammar errors twice.
- Susan lives in the gray house at the end of Maple Avenue behind the bank.
- Tess is going to be a professional dancer when she gets older.
- Do you want to join us for dinner this evening?

(Answers are in Appendix 4.)

A **phrase** is a group of words that function together as a unit. Phrases cannot stand alone, however, because they are missing a subject, a verb, or both.

Phrases:	the silver moon, a boneless fish
Phrases:	threw out the trash, navigated the river, floated to the top
Phrases:	after piano lessons, in the crowded boat, by the beach
Phrases:	jumping into the water, to be smart

Notice that all these groups of words are missing a subject, a verb, or both.

REVIEWING PHRASES

What is a phrase?

A phrase is a group of words that function together as a unit but

cannot stand alone.

Give two examples of phrases.

Examples will vary.

◆ *P r a c t i c e   2 5* **Identifying** Underline 8 phrases in the following sentences.

1. Walking to the store, I did see two small boys riding bicycles.
2. My favorite hobbies have to be mountain biking and snow skiing.
3. If you want something for a snack, look in the cabinet above the refrigerator.
4. The grocery store clerk scanned the items and pointed to the total at the bottom of the register tape.
5. I was buying a few antiques at the little store in downtown McKinley.

◆ *P r a c t i c e   2 6* **Completing** Fill in each blank in the following paragraph with a phrase. *Answers will vary.*

Marci, my roommate, drove (1) _____ this weekend because she wanted to visit her relatives there. She also mentioned that there is an outlet mall in the city, where she plans to (2) _____ for some (3) _____. She said the drive is only about two hours, and she listens to the radio (4) _____. I think her relatives are in the food industry, so maybe she'll come home (5) _____.

Give students the cards in random order, and have them try to create five sentences that all make sense. For instance, if they create the sentence *My best friend has enjoyed her new job baking in the morning* and if they get the last three sentences correct, they will be left with *in my father's bakery is causing long days.* Obviously, this does not make sense, so they will have to figure out how to make all the sentences work. The first group to get all five sentences in a logical order wins. Remember that the sentences can be rearranged and still be logical.

The major objective of this exercise is to show students how phrases work as a part of a larger whole—a sentence.

INSTRUCTOR'S RESOURCE MANUAL

For more sample phrases and sentences, for more exercises, and for quizzes, see the *Instructor's Resource Manual,* Section II, Part V.

◆ *P r a c t i c e   2 7*   **Writing Your Own** Write a sentence of your own for each of the following phrases. *Answers will vary.*

1. the brave contestant _____

2. hoping to be chosen _____

3. on the blackboard _____

4. to make a point _____

5. encouraged by the reward money _____

CLAUSES

Test Yourself

Underline the clauses in the following sentences.

* Magdalena will be a great attorney because she argues so well.
* You don't understand the math concept, so I will keep going over it with you.
* If Shane is going to drive, he should have car insurance.
* We finished the big test, and then we all went out for pizza.
* I enjoyed the vacation even though I had one really bad seafood dinner.

(Answers are in Appendix 4.)

Like phrases, **clauses** are groups of words. But unlike phrases, a clause always contains a subject and a verb. There are two types of clauses: *independent* and *dependent*.

An **independent clause** contains a subject and a verb and can stand alone and make sense by itself. Every complete sentence must have at least one independent clause.

Independent Clause: The doctor held the baby very gently.

Now look at the following group of words. It is a clause because it contains a subject and a verb. But it is a **dependent clause** because it is introduced by a word that makes it dependent, *because*.

Dependent Clause: **Because** the doctor held the baby very gently.

This clause cannot stand alone. It must be connected to an independent clause to make sense. Here is one way to complete the dependent clause and form a complete sentence.

      Dependent   Independent

Because the doctor held the baby very gently, the baby stopped crying.

Hint: Subordinating conjunctions (such as *since, although, because, while*) and relative pronouns (*who, whom, whose, which, that*) make clauses dependent. (For more information on subordinating conjunctions, see page 517, and on relative pronouns, see page 509.)

Reviewing Clauses

For a group of words to be a clause, it must have a <u>subject</u>
and a <u>verb</u>.

What is an independent clause?

<u>An independent clause contains a subject and a verb and can stand</u>

<u>alone and make sense by itself.</u>

What is a dependent clause?

<u>A dependent clause contains a subject and a verb but cannot stand alone.</u>

Name the two kinds of words that can begin a dependent clause.

<u>subordinating conjunctions</u>   <u>relative pronouns</u>

Name five subordinating conjunctions.

<u>Answers will vary.</u>   _____   _____   _____

Name the five relative pronouns.

<u>who</u>   <u>whom</u>   <u>whose</u>   <u>which</u>   <u>that</u>

◆ **Practice 28** **Identifying** Each of the following sentences is made up of two clauses. Circle the coordinating or subordinating conjunctions and relative pronouns. Then label each clause either independent (Ind) or dependent (Dep).

Dep   Ind

1. (As soon as) Vanessa arrived, she began telling the others what to do.

Dep   Ind

2. (When) the car approached, the driver turned off the headlights.

Ind   Dep

3. We wanted to know (that) you arrived safely.

Ind   Ind

4. Tomas can turn in his paper late, (but) he will not receive full credit.

Ind   Dep

5. Mr. Johnson was the teacher (who) influenced my life the most.

◆ **P r a c t i c e   2 9   Completing** Add an independent or dependent clause that will complete each sentence and make sense. *Answers will vary.*

Steven, (1) who _____, takes his textbooks to the beach to study. He says that (2) whenever _____, the sound of the ocean relaxes him. Of course, he also enjoys the view. One night he stayed out (3) until _____, and his parents were afraid that something awful had happened to him. I'm sure he just lost track of time, (4) unless _____. He is definitely a "beach bum" (5) because _____.

◆ **P r a c t i c e   3 0   Writing Your Own** Write five independent clauses. Then add at least one dependent clause to each independent clause. *Answers will vary.*

REVIEW

You might want to reread your answers to the questions in all the review boxes before you do the following exercises.

◆ **R e v i e w   P r a c t i c e   1   Identifying** Use the following abbreviations to label the underlined words in these sentences.

v	Verb	adv	Adverb
n	Noun	prep	Preposition

pro	Pronoun	conj	Conjunction
adj	Adjective	int	Interjection
ph	Phrase	cl	Clause

1. <u>Wow</u>, that <u>man</u> looks just like my uncle Bob.
   int n

2. Tiffany <u>is going</u> shopping at the new mall on <u>Harbor Boulevard</u>
   v n
   <u>tomorrow</u>.
   adv

3. Frank is <u>truly</u> my best friend, <u>but</u> sometimes he can't keep a <u>secret</u>.
   adv conj n

4. <u>Whenever Lindsay feels sad</u>, she <u>drives</u> into the mountains and looks
   cl v
   <u>at the stars</u>.
   ph

5. The most popular music <u>artist</u> <u>of</u> the 1960s was <u>definitely</u> Elvis Presley.
   n prep adv

6. <u>Gee</u>, are you sure <u>we</u> had to read the <u>entire</u> novel before class <u>today</u>?
   int pro adj adv

7. Ryan wants <u>to take piano lessons</u>, so he can <u>compose</u> music for the
   ph v
   poetry <u>he</u> has written.
   pro

8. Mikella took her dog to the vet <u>and</u> found out <u>it</u> has a <u>lung</u> infection.
   conj pro adj

9. <u>Though I didn't want to accept the job</u>, I felt pressured <u>by</u> my mother.
   cl prep

10. This morning was <u>dark</u> and cloudy, <u>so</u> I stayed <u>in bed</u> until noon.
    adj conj ph

◆ *Review P r a c t i c e 2* **Completing** Fill in each blank in the following paragraph with an appropriate word, phrase, or clause, as indicated. *Answers will vary.*

The most foolish purchase I ever made was a new (1) _____ (noun) for my computer. When I went to the (2) _____ (adjective) store, the salesman (3) _____ (verb) that I needed this item. I asked him what the part would do (4) _____ (preposition) my computer, and he promised it would make a big difference in the way the computer operated. (5) _____ (interjection), did I believe him! I knew my computer was pretty old, (6) _____ (conjunction) I really didn't want to spend a lot of money on it. Still, I (7) _____ (adverb) bought the part and took (8) _____ (pronoun) home to try it out. After (9) _____ (clause), I turned on the computer, and it began to heat up. Suddenly, smoke began coming (10) _____ (phrase), and I realized the computer had just crashed.

◆ *Review P r a c t i c e 3* **Writing Your Own** Write your own paragraph about your favorite pet. What did you name it? What kind of animal was it? *Answers will vary.*

◆ *Review P r a c t i c e 4* **Editing Your Writing** Exchange paragraphs from Review Practice 3 with a classmate, and do the following: *Answers will vary.*

1. Circle any words that are used incorrectly.
2. Underline any phrases that do not read smoothly.
3. Put an X in the margin where you find a dependent clause that is not connected to an independent clause.

Then return the paragraph to its writer, and use the information in the Introduction to edit your own paragraph. Record your errors on the Error Log in Appendix 6.

SUBJECTS AND VERBS

✔ CHECKLIST for Identifying Subjects and Verbs

> ✔ Does each of your sentences contain a subject?
>
> ✔ Does each of your sentences contain a verb?

Test Yourself

Underline the subjects once and the verbs twice in the following sentences.

- You are my best friend.
- Hang up your clothes.
- They really wanted to be here tonight.
- He made a sandwich and put it in a brown paper bag.
- Susie and Tom went to the dance.

(Answers are in Appendix 4.)

A sentence has a message to communicate, but for that message to be meaningful, the sentence must have a subject and a verb. The subject is the topic of the sentence, what the sentence is about. The verb is the sentence's motor. It moves the message forward to its destination. Without these two parts, the sentence is not complete.

SUBJECTS

To be complete, every sentence must have a subject. The **subject** tells who or what the sentence is about.

TEACHING SUBJECTS AND VERBS

Cut words out of magazines until you have about 20 assorted parts of speech. Place these in an envelope. Create such an envelope for each of your students. Also, bring each student a glue stick and a blank piece of paper.

Have your students create a poem with the words they are given, gluing them in sequence on the paper. When the students have finished, have them underline their subjects once and their verbs twice.

Have the students read their poems aloud. Then have them vote for their favorite poem and perhaps even award prizes.

INSTRUCTOR'S
RESOURCE MANUAL

For more exercises and
for quizzes, see the
*Instructor's Resource
Manual,* Section II,
Part V.

Subject

He   always came home on time.

Action **movies**   appeal to teenagers.

Compound Subjects

When two or more separate words tell what the sentence is about, the sentence has a **compound subject.**

Compound Subject: **Painting** and **sewing** are my hobbies.

Compound Subject: **My brother** and I live with my grandmother.

Hint: Note that *and* is not part of the compound subject.

Unstated Subjects

Sometimes a subject does not actually appear in a sentence but is understood. This occurs in commands and requests. The understood subject is always *you,* meaning either someone specific or anyone in general.

Command: Get up now or you'll be late.

                                         s
Unstated Subject: **(You)** get up now or you'll be late.

Request: Write me an e-mail soon, please.

                                         s
Unstated Subject: **(You)** write me an e-mail soon, please.

Subjects and Prepositional Phrases

The subject of a sentence cannot be part of a prepositional phrase. A **prepositional phrase** is a group of words that begins with a **preposition,** a word like *in, on, under, after,* or *from.* Here are some examples of prepositional phrases:

in the yard	**next to** it	**before** supper
on the plane	**behind** the chair	**instead of** me
under the rug	**around** the circle	**across** the road
after school	**into** the boat	**for** the family
from the White House	**during** the storm	**at** college

(See page 514 for a more complete list of prepositions.)

If you are looking for the subject of a sentence, first cross out all the prepositional phrases. Then figure out what the sentence is about.

~~During the game~~, the coaches and the players had a fight ~~with the other team~~.

The new store ~~around the corner~~ sells designer jeans.

Some ~~of our luggage~~ was lost ~~on the trip~~.

REVIEWING SUBJECTS

What is a subject?

The subject tells who or what the sentence is about.

What is a compound subject?

A compound subject is two or more separate words that tell what the

sentence is about.

What is an unstated subject?

An unstated subject does not appear in the sentence but is understood.

How can you find the subject of a sentence?

First, cross out all the prepositional phrases, and then figure out what

the sentence is about.

◆ **P r a c t i c e   1   Identifying** Cross out the prepositional phrases in each of the following sentences, and then underline the subjects.

1. The <u>golfer</u> stood quietly ~~in front of the ball~~.
2. <u>Marty</u> and <u>Mike</u> gave a presentation ~~at the big convention~~.
3. <u>Two</u> ~~of the graduates~~ had perfect grade point averages.

4. Before I go to the store, I need to balance my checkbook.

5. Get the mayonnaise out of the refrigerator. *"You implied"*

◆ **P r a c t i c e   2   Completing** Fill in each blank in the following sentences with a subject without using a person's name. *Answers will vary.*

1. _____ was voted the best restaurant in this area.

2. Walking to class, _____ thought seriously about changing his major.

3. Sometimes, _____ is a great bargain.

4. _____ and _____ are two very positive personality traits.

5. _____ was late to work again.

◆ **P r a c t i c e   3   Writing Your Own** Write five sentences of your own, and underline the subjects. *Answers will vary.*

Verbs

To be complete, a sentence must have a verb as well as a subject. A **verb** tells what the subject is doing or what is happening.

Verb

He   always **came** home on time.

Action movies   **appeal** to teenagers.

Action Verbs

An **action verb** tells what a subject is doing. Some examples of action verbs are *skip, ski, stare, flip, breathe, remember, restate, sigh, cry, decrease, write,* and *pant.*

    Action Verb: The children **laughed** at the clown.

    Action Verb: The car **crashed** into the tree.

Linking Verbs

A **linking verb** connects the subject to other words in the sentence that say something about it. Linking verbs are also called **state-of-being verbs** because they do not show action. Rather, they say that something "is" a particular way. The most common linking verb is *be* (*am, are, is, was, were*).

Linking Verb: The horses **are** in the stable.

Linking Verb: I **am** unhappy with the results.

Other common linking verbs are *remain, act, look, grow,* and *seem.*

Linking Verb: Darnell **remains** enthusiastic about school.

Linking Verb: I **act** happy even when I'm not.

Linking Verb: The yard **looks** neglected.

Linking Verb: She **grew** fonder of her aunt.

Linking Verb: Lupe **seems** happy with her new house.

Some words, like *smell* and *taste,* can be either action verbs or linking verbs.

Action Verb: I **smell** smoke.

Linking Verb: This house **smells** like flowers.

Action Verb: She **tasted** the soup.

Linking Verb: It **tasted** too salty.

Compound Verbs

Just as a verb can have more than one subject, some subjects can have more than one verb. These are called **compound verbs.**

Compound Verb: She **cooks** and **cleans** every day.

Compound Verb: He **runs** and **swims** twice a week in the summer.

Hint: A sentence can have both a compound subject and a compound verb.

s   s   v   v
Joe and **Mitchell jumped** into the boat and **started** the motor.

Helping Verbs

Often the **main verb** (the action verb or linking verb) in a sentence needs help to convey its meaning. **Helping verbs** add information, such as when an action took place. The **complete verb** consists of a main verb and all its helping verbs.

Complete Verb: The children <u>will</u> **return** tomorrow.

Complete Verb: It <u>might</u> **rain** this weekend.

Complete Verb: We <u>should have</u> **gone** to the concert.

Complete Verb: My uncle <u>has</u> **given** me money for Christmas.

Complete Verb: My sister **will be coming** for my wedding.

Complete Verb: You **should** not **go** home with him.

Hint: Note that *not* isn't part of the helping verb. Similarly, *never, always, only, just,* and *still* are never part of the verb.

Complete Verb: I **have** always **liked** history classes.

The most common helping verbs are

be, am, is, are, was, were
have, has, had
do, did

Other common helping verbs are

may, might
can, could
will, would
should, used to, ought to

REVIEWING VERBS

What is a verb?

A verb tells what the subject is doing or what is happening.

What is the difference between action and linking verbs?

An action verb tells what the subject is doing. A linking verb connects

the subject to other words in the sentence.

Give an example of a compound verb.   Examples will vary

Give an example of a helping verb.   Examples will vary

What is the difference between a subject and a verb?

The subject tells who or what the sentence is about, and the verb tells

what the subject is doing or what is happening.

◆ *P r a c t i c e **4*** **Identifying** Underline the complete verbs in each of the following sentences.

1. The students <u>seemed</u> tired in class Monday morning.
2. One of my professors <u>is</u> a popular public speaker.
3. High school students <u>must read</u> *The Scarlet Letter*.
4. Timothy <u>will go</u> to the championships.
5. <u>Get</u> out of the rain.

◆ *P r a c t i c e **5*** **Completing** Fill in each blank in the following sentences with a verb. Avoid using *is*, *are*, *was*, and *were* except as helping verbs. *Answers will vary.*

1. Chad _____ extreme pain after falling from the ladder and landing on his back.
2. The specialist _____ her client about the different options.
3. Both the parents and the teachers _____ about the need for more meetings.
4. My ill child _____ throughout the night.
5. Red stickers on the price tags _____ the sale items.

◆ *P r a c t i c e **6*** **Writing Your Own** Write five sentences of your own, and underline all the verbs in each. *Answers will vary.*

CHAPTER REVIEW

You might want to reread your answers to the questions in all the review boxes before you do the following exercises.

◆ *Review P r a c t i c e **1*** **Identifying** Underline the subjects once and the verbs twice in each of the following sentences. Cross out the prepositional phrases first.

1. The <u>horses</u> ~~in the corral~~ <u><u>are being trained</u></u> ~~for racing~~.
2. <u>Matilda</u> <u><u>received</u></u> a scholarship ~~for her biology research~~.
3. <u>Salespeople</u> <u><u>can earn</u></u> thousands ~~of dollars in commissions~~ every year.
4. Each month, my <u>office</u> <u><u>pays</u></u> us ~~for overtime~~.
5. The <u>bikes</u> and the <u>helmets</u> <u><u>are</u></u> ~~on sale~~ right now.
6. <u>I</u> <u><u>am going</u></u> ~~to the grocery store for dinner~~.

7. Tonya's <u>computer</u> <u>crashed</u> the other day, and <u>she</u> <u>used</u> mine ~~for her homework~~.

8. <u>Grandma</u> <u>will</u> not <u>join</u> us ~~for dinner~~.

9. <u>Joe</u> and <u>Christine</u> <u>are building</u> a new house.

10. The <u>baby</u> <u>played</u> ~~with the blocks~~ and <u>stacked</u> them ~~on top of each other~~.

◆ **Review Practice 2 Completing** Fill in the missing subjects or verbs in each of the following sentences. *Answers will vary.*

1. Tonight's dinner _____ like leftovers.

2. _____ can't remember where we said we would meet.

3. Taking that midterm _____ my hardest challenge last week.

4. The catcher and the pitcher _____ with the referee.

5. If you want to go with us, you _____ to come along.

6. When Tiffany left this morning, _____ didn't know when she would be back.

7. _____ wear lab coats to set them apart from students.

8. Yesterday I _____ an old box of letters from my friends in high school.

9. (You) _____ your room before we leave.

10. _____ was the best entertainment of the evening.

◆ **Review Practice 3 Writing Your Own** Write a paragraph about a major decision you made within the past three years. How has it affected your life? What did you learn from the process? *Answers will vary.*

◆ **Review Practice 4 Editing Your Writing** Exchange paragraphs from Review Practice 3 with another student, and do the following:
Answers will vary.
1. Underline the subjects once.

2. Underline the verbs twice.

Then return the paragraph to its writer, and edit any sentences in your own paragraph that do not have both a subject and a verb. Record your errors on the Error Log in Appendix 6.

FRAGMENTS

CHAPTER 35

☑ CHECKLIST for Identifying and Correcting Fragments

> ✔ Does each sentence have a subject?
>
> ✔ Does each sentence have a verb?

Test Yourself

Put an X by the sentences that are fragments.

- • _____ I wanted to go to the gym yesterday.
- • _____ Whose tie doesn't match his suit.
- • _____ Giving up his seat for an elderly woman.
- • _____ Paul asked for the most popular menu item.
- • _____ While the captain was away from the cockpit.

(Answers are in Appendix 4.)

One of the most common errors in college writing is the fragment. A fragment is a piece of a sentence that is punctuated as a complete sentence. But it does not express a complete thought. Once you learn how to identify fragments, you can avoid them in your writing.

ABOUT FRAGMENTS

A complete sentence must have both a subject and a verb. If one or both are missing or if the subject and verb are introduced by a dependent word, you have only part of a sentence, a **fragment.** Even if it begins with a capital letter and ends with a period, it cannot stand alone and must be corrected in your writing. The five most common types of fragments are explained in this chapter.

TEACHING
FRAGMENTS
Buy blank flash cards in an educational supply store, and on each card, put words and phrases that can be combined to form sentences: subordinating conjunctions, relative pronouns, phrases, subjects, verbs, and so on.
  Give each student a certain number of flash cards with words on them. Then have the students create sentences out of their words and stand in front of the class in the order of their sentence. For instance, three students might hold up the sentence *the car / was swerving / on the street.* Have another student add *because* to the beginning of the sentence to show how one word can create a fragment.

Have students make other sentences in the same way. Then add and subtract words from these sentences so that students can see the way fragments are both formed and fixed.

INSTRUCTOR'S RESOURCE MANUAL

For suggested words, phrases, and clauses, for more exercises, and for quizzes, see the *Instructor's Resource Manual*, Section II, Part V.

Type 1: Afterthought Fragments

He goes to school during the day. **And works at night.**

Type 2: *-ing* Fragments

Finding no one at the house. Kenny walked back home.

Type 3: *to* Fragments

The school started a tutoring program. **To help improve SAT scores.**

Type 4: Dependent-Clause Fragments

Because I decided to go back to school. My boss fired me.

Type 5: Relative-Clause Fragments

Last summer I visited Rome. **Which is a beautiful city.**

Ways to Correct Fragments

Once you have identified a fragment, you have two options for correcting it. You can connect the fragment to the sentence before or after it or make the fragment into an independent clause.

Correction 1: *Connect the fragment to the sentence before or after it.*

Correction 2: *Make the fragment into an independent clause:*

  (a) either add the missing subject and/or verb, or

  (b) drop the subordinating word before the fragment.

We will discuss these corrections for each type of fragment.

REVIEWING FRAGMENTS

What is a sentence fragment?

A sentence fragment is punctuated like a sentence but is missing a

subject and/or verb or is introduced by a dependent word.

What are the five types of fragments?

afterthought fragment   dependent-clause fragment

-ing fragment   relative-clause fragment

to fragment

What are the two ways to correct a fragment?

1. *Connect it to the sentence before or after it.*

2. *Make it into an independent clause.*

IDENTIFYING AND CORRECTING FRAGMENTS

The rest of this chapter discusses the five types of fragments and the corrections for each type.

Type 1: Afterthought Fragments

Afterthought fragments occur when you add an idea to a sentence but don't punctuate it correctly.

Fragment: He goes to school during the day. **And works at night.**

The phrase *And works at night* is punctuated and capitalized as a complete sentence. Because this group of words lacks a subject, however, it is a fragment.

Correction 1: *Connect the fragment to the sentence before or after it.*

Example: He goes to school during the day **and** works at night.

Correction 2: *Make the fragment into an independent clause.*

Example: He goes to school during the day. **He** works at night.

The first correction connects the fragment to the sentence before it. The second correction makes the fragment an independent clause with its own subject and verb.

REVIEWING AFTERTHOUGHT FRAGMENTS

What is an afterthought fragment?

An idea added to a sentence but not punctuated correctly

Give an example of an afterthought fragment.

Examples will vary.

> **What are the two ways to correct an afterthought fragment?**
>
> 1. *Connect it to the sentence before or after it.*
>
> 2. *Make it into an independent clause by adding the missing subject and/or verb to it.*

◆ **Practice 1A** **Identifying** Underline the afterthought fragments in each of the following sentences.

1. The men on the opposing team were very strong. Everyone was scared to play them. <u>Especially me</u>.
2. Mark peered into the window of his locked car and saw his keys. <u>Stuck in the ignition</u>.
3. I am thinking about buying a really special car next year. <u>For example, a Chevy Tahoe</u>.
4. Carlene turned in her paper on time and knew she would get a good grade. <u>Because she really liked her topic</u>.
5. "Keeping up with the Joneses" is an expression. <u>That my mother uses a lot</u>.

◆ **Practice 1B** **Correcting** Correct the fragments in Practice 1A by rewriting each sentence. *Answers will vary.*

◆ **Practice 2** **Completing** Correct the following afterthought fragments using both correction 1 and correction 2. Rewrite any corrected sentences that you think could be smoother. *Answers will vary.*

1. The child drew in a coloring book. With brand new crayons.
2. I am going to buy some new books to read. For example, the Harry Potter books.
3. Jennifer usually drives very fast. Sometimes running stop signs.
4. My friends are going to the beach. In Santa Barbara for the weekend.
5. He walked over to my desk very slowly. And smiled in a playful way.

◆ **Practice 3** **Writing Your Own** Write five afterthought fragments of your own, and correct them. *Answers will vary.*

Type 2: *-ing* Fragments

Words that end in *-ing* are forms of verbs that cannot be the main verbs in their sentences. For an *-ing* word to function as a verb, it must have a helping verb with it (*be, do,* or *have;* see pages 577–583).

> **Fragment:**   **Finding no one at the house.** Kenny walked back home.

Finding is not a verb in this sentence because it has no helping verb. Also, this group of words is a fragment because it has no subject.

Correction 1:   *Connect the fragment to the sentence before or after it.*

Example: **Finding no one at the house,** Kenny walked home.

Correction 2:   *Make the fragment into an independent clause.*

Example: **He found no one at the house.** Kenny walked home.

Hint: When you connect an *-ing* fragment to a sentence, insert a comma between the two sentence parts. You should insert the comma whether the *-ing* part comes at the beginning or the end of the sentence.

Kenny walked home**,** finding no one at the house.
Finding no one at the house**,** Kenny walked home.

REVIEWING *-ing* FRAGMENTS

How can you tell if an *-ing* word is part of a fragment or is a main verb?

If the -ing verb has a helping verb, it is part of the main verb. Otherwise, it

could be part of a fragment.

Give an example of an *-ing* fragment.

Examples will vary.

What are the two ways to correct an *-ing* fragment?

1. *Connect it to the sentence before or after it.*

2. *Make it into an independent clause by adding the missing subject*

and/or verb to it.

> **What kind of punctuation should you use when you join an -ing fragment to another sentence?**
>
> *Use a comma when joining an -ing fragment to another sentence.*

◆ **P r a c t i c e 4 A**   **Identifying**   Underline the *-ing* fragments in each of the following sentences.

1. <u>Driving to the store.</u> I thought about all of the things I needed to buy.
2. The baseball player dropped the ball. <u>Tripping over his shoelace while running to make the catch.</u>
3. Mr. Holland was the best music teacher I ever had. <u>Treating everyone with respect.</u>
4. I plan to read at least one book each month. <u>Challenging my brother to do the same.</u>
5. <u>Wanting to leave her parents' house.</u> Marissa got married when she was 18 years old.

◆ **P r a c t i c e 4 B**   **Correcting**   Correct the fragments in Practice 4A by rewriting each sentence. *Students will probably connect fragments to independent clauses with commas and change the capitalization after the commas.*

◆ **P r a c t i c e 5**   **Completing**   Correct each of the following *-ing* fragments using both methods. Remember to insert a comma when using correction 1. *Answers will vary.*

1. Making the best grade in the class. Carlos was excited to tell his parents about it.
2. I think I hurt my back. Trying to move the sofa.
3. Looking back at my senior year in high school. I can't believe I dated that guy.
4. Wondering whether he left his car windows down. Shawn saw the rain begin to fall.
5. Jamar was glad he survived the accident. Seeing the damage to his car.

◆ **P r a c t i c e 6**   **Writing Your Own**   Write five *-ing* fragments of your own, and correct them. *Answers will vary.*

Type 3: *to* Fragments

When *to* is added to a verb (*to see*, *to hop*, *to skip*, *to jump*), the combination cannot be a main verb in its sentence. As a result, this group of words is often involved in a fragment.

Fragment: The school started a tutoring program. **To improve SAT scores.**

Because *to* + a verb cannot function as the main verb of its sentence, *to improve SAT scores* is a fragment as it is punctuated here.

Correction 1: *Connect the fragment to the sentence before or after it.*

Example: The school started a tutoring program **to improve SAT scores.**

Correction 2: *Make the fragment into an independent clause.*

Example: The school started a tutoring program. **It wanted to improve SAT scores.**

Hint: A *to* fragment can also occur at the beginning of a sentence. In this case, insert a comma between the two sentence parts when correcting the fragment.

To improve SAT scores, the school started a tutoring program.

REVIEWING *to* FRAGMENTS
....

What does a to fragment consist of?

A to fragment consists of to plus a verb.

Give an example of a to fragment.

Examples will vary.

What are the two ways to correct a to fragment?

1. Connect it to the sentence before or after it.

2. Make it into an independent clause by adding the missing subject

   and/or verb to it.

◆ *P r a c t i c e* **7 A** **Identifying** Underline the *to* fragments in each of the following sentences.

1. <u>To make the crowd more excited.</u> The rodeo clown came out and chased the bull around the arena.
2. <u>To grow perfect roses.</u> You should attend free classes at Home Depot.
3. The baby screamed loudly. <u>To tell his parents he was hungry.</u>
4. We stopped eating fried foods and sweets. <u>To lose weight before summer.</u>
5. <u>To improve their chances at winning the World Series.</u> The Texas Rangers signed Alex Rodriguez.

◆ *P r a c t i c e* **7 B** **Correcting** Correct the fragments in Practice 7A by rewriting each sentence. *Students will probably connect fragments to independent clauses and change the capitalization.*

◆ *P r a c t i c e* **8** **Completing** Correct the following *to* fragments using both correction 1 and correction 2. Try putting the fragment at the beginning of the sentence instead of always at the end. Remember to insert a comma when you add the *to* fragment to the beginning of a sentence. *Answers will vary.*

1. Avoid driving faster than the posted speed limit. To get the best gas mileage.
2. He wanted to buy a new suit. To impress his boss.
3. Suzanne told Warren that she had a boyfriend. To avoid hurting his feelings.
4. The bank is closed on Labor Day. To give the employees time with their families.
5. I put the names and addresses in a mail merge. To make it easier to print labels.

◆ *P r a c t i c e* **9** **Writing Your Own** Write five *to* fragments of your own, and correct them. *Answers will vary.*

Type 4: Dependent-Clause Fragments

A group of words that begins with a **subordinating conjunction** (see the list below) is called a **dependent clause** and cannot stand alone. Even though it has a subject and a verb, it is a fragment because it depends on an independent clause to complete its meaning. An **independent clause** is a group of words with a subject and a verb that can stand alone. (See pages 522–524 for help with clauses.)

Here is a list of some commonly used subordinating conjunctions that create dependent clauses.

Subordinating Conjunctions

after	because	since	until
although	before	so	when
as	even if	so that	whenever
as if	even though	than	where
as long as	how	that	wherever
as soon as	if	though	whether
as though	in order that	unless	while

Fragment: <u>Because</u> I decided to go back to school. My boss fired me.

This sentence has a subject and a verb, but it is introduced by a subordinating conjunction, *because*. As a result, this sentence is a dependent clause and cannot stand alone.

Correction 1:   *Connect the fragment to the sentence before or after it.*

Example: **Because I decided to go back to school,** my boss fired me.

Correction 2:   *Make the fragment into an independent clause.*

Example: ~~Because~~ I decided to go back to school. My boss fired me.

Hint: If the dependent clause comes first, put a comma between the two parts of the sentence. If the dependent clause comes second, the comma is not necessary.

Because I decided to go back to school, my boss fired me.
My boss fired me **because I decided to go back to school.**

REVIEWING DEPENDENT-CLAUSE FRAGMENTS

What is a dependent-clause fragment?

A group of words with a subject and verb that cannot stand alone

What type of conjunction makes a clause dependent?

subordinating conjunction

What is an independent clause?

A group of words with a subject and verb that can stand alone

Give an example of a dependent-clause fragment.

Examples will vary.

What are the two ways to correct a dependent-clause fragment?

1. Connect it to the sentence before or after it.

2. Make it into an independent clause by dropping the subordinating word before it.

◆ **P r a c t i c e 1 0 A** **Identifying** Underline the dependent-clause fragments in each of the following sentences.

1. I love to eat sushi. <u>Although it's sometimes very expensive</u>.
2. It is good to know some trivia. <u>So that you can participate in lots of conversations</u>.
3. <u>After the child finished riding on it</u>. The rocking horse stood in the corner.
4. I will have Thanksgiving dinner at my house again. <u>As long as my parents get along with my in-laws</u>.
5. <u>Before she goes to work in the morning</u>. Margaret takes her children to school.

◆ **P r a c t i c e 1 0 B** **Correcting** Correct the fragments in Practice 10A by rewriting each sentence. *Answers will vary.*

◆ **P r a c t i c e 1 1** **Completing** Correct the following dependent-clause fragments using both correction 1 and correction 2. When you use correction 1, remember to add a comma if the dependent clause comes first. *Answers will vary.*

1. Manny takes his basketball with him. Wherever he goes.
2. While I'm out of town. My mother will take care of my house.
3. The power bill is higher this month. Though we didn't run the air conditioner very often.
4. When she got home from work. Jamie made green beans for dinner.
5. Russ always watches TV for an hour. After he finishes studying.

◆ *P r a c t i c e   1 2* **Writing Your Own** Write five dependent-clause fragments of your own, and correct them. *Answers will vary.*

Type 5: Relative-Clause Fragments

A **relative clause** is a dependent clause that begins with a relative pronoun: *who, whom, whose, which,* or *that.* When a relative clause is punctuated as a sentence, the result is a fragment.

> **Fragment:**   Last summer I visited Rome. **Which is a beautiful city.**

Which is a beautiful city is a clause fragment that begins with the relative pronoun *which.* This word automatically makes the words that follow it a dependent clause, so they cannot stand alone as a sentence.

Correction 1:   *Connect the fragment to the sentence before or after it.*

Example: Last summer I visited Rome, **which is a beautiful city.**

Correction 2:   *Make the fragment into an independent clause.*

Example: Last summer I visited Rome. **It is a beautiful city.**

REVIEWING RELATIVE-CLAUSE FRAGMENTS

How is a relative-clause fragment different from a dependent-clause fragment?

A relative-clause fragment begins with a relative pronoun rather than

a subordinating conjunction.

Give an example of a relative-clause fragment.

Examples will vary.

> **What are the two ways to correct a relative-clause fragment?**
>
> 1. *Connect it to the sentence before or after it.*
>
> 2. *Make it into an independent clause that can stand alone.*

◆ **P r a c t i c e   1 3 A   Identifying** Underline the relative-clause fragments in the following sentences.

1. I made an appointment with the doctor. <u>Whom my cousin recommended.</u>
2. The child ate the pills. <u>That the father left on the bathroom counter.</u>
3. The station got a new captain. <u>Who transferred from another department.</u>
4. At the car wash, I talked to the man. <u>Whose nametag said "Sylvester."</u>
5. Karen got a job at the bakery. <u>Which makes fresh donuts every morning.</u>

◆ **P r a c t i c e   1 3 B   Correcting** Correct the fragments in Practice 13A by rewriting each sentence. *Answers will vary.*

◆ **P r a c t i c e   1 4   Completing** Correct the following relative-clause fragments using both correction 1 and correction 2. *Answers will vary.*

1. Paul studied for the midterm with Charlotte. Who scored the highest on the first exam.
2. My girlfriend works at the bank. That is located on the corner of F Street and Market Avenue.
3. I put more memory in my computer. Which cost me about $70.
4. My boss is the man with the goatee. Whose ties are usually very colorful.
5. Penny shops only at grocery stores. That offer double coupons.

◆ **P r a c t i c e   1 5   Writing Your Own** Write five relative-clause fragments of your own, and correct them. *Answers will vary.*

CHAPTER REVIEW

You might want to reread your answers to the questions in all the review boxes before you do the following exercises.

Review P r a c t i c e   1   Identifying Underline the fragments in the following paragraph.

Buying an old home can be a good experience. If the house is inspected thoroughly before any papers are signed. Thinking we were getting an incredible deal. We rushed into buying a thirty-year-old house in an established neighborhood. The house had lots of personality and big living rooms. To make it perfect for entertaining. Unfortunately, there were several problems with the house that we didn't see right away. For example, plumbing problems. Faulty wiring. Not enough insulation. We put thousands of dollars into repairs. Before we could even invite our friends over for dinner. Even though the house wasn't expensive to buy. It became very expensive for us to maintain. Eventually, we had to sell it. To keep from losing more money. The man who bought it was a contractor. Who could do most of the repairs himself. Which is a big advantage that we didn't have.

Review P r a c t i c e   2   Correcting Correct all the fragments you underlined in Review Practice 1 by rewriting the paragraph. *Answers will vary.*

Review P r a c t i c e   3   Writing Your Own Write a paragraph about your dream vacation. Where would you go? How long would you stay? Who would go with you, or would you go alone? *Answers will vary.*

Review P r a c t i c e   4   Editing Your Writing Exchange paragraphs from Review Practice 3 with another student, and do the following: *Answers will vary.*

1. Put brackets around any fragments that you find.

2. Identify the types of fragments that you find.

Then return the paper to its writer, and use the information in this chapter to correct any fragments in your own paragraph. Record your errors on the Error Log in Appendix 6.

FUSED SENTENCES AND COMMA SPLICES

✔ CHECKLIST for Identifying and Correcting Fused Sentences and Comma Splices

> ✔ Are any sentences run together without punctuation?
> ✔ Are any sentences incorrectly joined with only a comma?

TEACHING FUSED
SENTENCES AND
COMMA SPLICES
One of the major mis-
conceptions about run-
together sentences is
that long sentences are
usually fused sentences
and comma splices.
After all, they run on
and on and on. One
way to dispel this myth
is to write two sen-
tences on the board
(one very short and
one very long) and ask
students to identify the
run-together sentence.
For this to work, make
sure the run-together
is the very short sen-
tence. Here is an
example:
  Which of the fol-
lowing is the run-
together sentence?
  I love chocolate it
    tastes good.

Test Yourself

Mark any incorrect sentences here with a slash between the independent clauses that are not joined properly.

* The rainstorm washed out my garden, I had just planted spring
  bulbs.

* When we cleaned the house, we found the TV remote control it
  was between the sofa cushions.

* People in authority are often criticized and seldom thanked.

* The kids didn't find all of the Easter eggs during the hunt, when
  we finally found them, they were rotten.

* You should ask Aubri to cut your hair she's been cutting mine for
  four years.

(Answers are in Appendix 4.)

When we cram two separate statements into a single sentence without
correct punctuation, we create what are called *fused sentences* and *comma
splices*. These run-together sentences generally distort our message and
cause problems for our readers. In this chapter, you will learn how to identify and avoid these errors in your writing.

IDENTIFYING FUSED SENTENCES AND COMMA SPLICES

Whereas a fragment is a piece of a sentence, **fused sentences** and **comma splices** are made up of two sentences written as one. In both cases, the first sentence runs into the next without the proper punctuation between the two.

Fused Sentence:	The bus stopped we got off.
Comma Splice:	The bus stopped, we got off.

Both of these sentences incorrectly join two independent clauses. The difference between them is one comma.

A **fused sentence** is two sentences "fused" or jammed together without any punctuation. Look at these examples:

Fused Sentence: Rosa's favorite subject is math she always does very well on her math tests.

This example consists of two independent clauses with no punctuation between them:

1. Rosa's favorite subject is math.
2. She always does very well on her math tests.

Fused Sentence: My grandfather likes to cook his own meals he doesn't want anyone to do it for him.

This example also consists of two independent clauses with no punctuation between them:

1. My grandfather likes to cook his own meals.
2. He doesn't want anyone to do it for him.

Like a fused sentence, a **comma splice** incorrectly joins two independent clauses. However, a comma splice puts a comma between the two independent clauses. The only difference between a fused sentence and a comma splice is the comma. Look at the following examples:

Comma Splice: Rosa's favorite subject is math, she always does very well on her math tests.

Comma Splice: My grandfather likes to cook his own meals, he doesn't want anyone to do it for him.

I love chocolate, not only because it tastes good but also because it reminds me of all the fun times that my sister and I had when we were little kids and would buy all different types of candy that we would eat until we got sick.

Students will invariably choose the longer sentence as the run-together sentence because of its length. Showing students that even very short sentences can be run-togethers forces students to look at the grammar of the sentence and not the length.

INSTRUCTOR'S RESOURCE MANUAL

For more sample run-together sentences, for more exercises, and for quizzes, see the *Instructor's Resource Manual,* Section II, Part V.

Both of these sentences consist of two independent clauses. But a comma is not the proper punctuation to separate these two clauses.

REVIEWING FUSED SENTENCES AND COMMA SPLICES

What are the two types of run-together sentences?

fused sentence   *comma splice*

What is the difference between them?

A fused sentence has no punctuation between the run-together

sentences, and a comma splice has a comma between them.

◆ **Practice 1** **Identifying** Put a slash between the independent clauses that are not joined correctly.

1. Paul plays hockey every Thursday/he usually gets home after dark.
2. My mom always tucked me into bed at night,/that's what I remember most about her.
3. Toni borrowed my pencil yesterday/then she lost it.
4. My boyfriend made my favorite cake for my birthday,/I had to eat the whole thing.
5. The child needed a bone marrow transplant,/we raised $10,000 last night for her cause.

◆ **Practice 2** **Identifying** For each incorrect sentence in the following paragraph, put a slash between the independent clauses that are not joined properly.

    The fitness craze is sweeping across America,/it seems like everyone has a gym membership. The best-selling food items have "light," "lite," or "fat free" on the packaging, and people are watching their cholesterol and counting calories. Only the thinnest models are shown in food advertisements/they symbolize good health, responsible eating habits, and overall physical attractiveness. Ironically, thin people are even used in ads for unhealthy food items, like candy and soft drinks,/this sends a very confusing message to the consumer. The stereotypes are not fair/not everyone can have the "perfect" body seen in the ads. Some people are just born with bigger body shapes, and there is nothing wrong or unattractive about that. These people should learn to eat healthy foods,/they should not try to be unnaturally thin.

◆ *P r a c t i c e* **3** **Writing Your Own** Write five fused sentences. Then write the same sentences as comma splices. *Answers will vary.*

CORRECTING FUSED SENTENCES AND COMMA SPLICES

You have four different options for correcting your fused sentences and comma splices.

1. Separate the two sentences with a period, and capitalize the next word.
2. Separate the two sentences with a comma, and add a coordinating conjunction (*and, but, for, nor, or, so,* or *yet*).
3. Change one of the sentences into a dependent clause with a subordinating conjunction (such as *if, because, since, after,* or *when*) or a relative pronoun (*who, whom, whose, which,* or *that*).
4. Separate the two sentences with a semicolon.

Correction 1: Use a Period

Separate the two sentences with a period, and capitalize the next word.

Rosa's favorite subject is math**.** **She** always does very well on her math tests.
My grandfather likes to cook his own meals**.** **He** doesn't want anyone to do it for him.

◆ *P r a c t i c e* **4** **Correcting** Correct all the sentences in Practice 1 using correction 1. *Students should insert a period where the slashes are and capitalize the next word.*

◆ *P r a c t i c e* **5** **Correcting** Correct the paragraph in Practice 2 using correction 1. *Students should insert a period where the slashes are and capitalize the next word.*

◆ *P r a c t i c e 6*   **Writing Your Own** Correct the sentences you wrote in Practice 3 using correction 1. *Answers will vary.*

Correction 2: Use a Coordinating Conjunction

Separate the two sentences with a comma, and add a coordinating conjunction (*and, but, for, nor, or, so,* or *yet*).

> Rosa's favorite subject is math**, so** she always does very well on her math tests.
>
> My grandfather likes to cook his own meals**, and** he doesn't want anyone to do it for him.

◆ *P r a c t i c e 7*   **Correcting** Correct all the sentences in Practice 1 using correction 2. *Students should insert a comma and a coordinating conjunction where the slashes are.*

◆ *P r a c t i c e 8*   **Correcting** Correct the paragraph in Practice 2 using correction 2. *Students should insert a comma and a coordinating conjunction where the slashes are.*

◆ *P r a c t i c e 9*   **Writing Your Own** Correct the sentences you wrote in Practice 3 using correction 2. *Answers will vary.*

Correction 3: Create a Dependent Clause

Change one of the sentences into a dependent clause with a subordinating conjunction (such as *if, because, since, after,* or *when*) or a relative pronoun (*who, whom, whose, which,* or *that*).

> Rosa's favorite subject is math **because** she always does very well on her math tests.
>
> **Since** my grandfather likes to cook his own meals, he doesn't want anyone to do it for him.

For a list of subordinating conjunctions, see page 517.

Hint: If you put the dependent clause at the beginning of the sentence, add a comma between the two sentence parts.

> **Because** she always does very well on her math tests, Rosa's favorite subject is math.

◆ *P r a c t i c e 1 0*   **Correcting** Correct all the sentences in Practice 1 using correction 3. *Students should change one of the sentences in each run-together into a dependent clause with a subordinating conjunction.*

♦ *Practice 11* **Correcting** Correct the paragraph in Practice 2 using correction 3. *Students should change one of the sentences in each run-together into a dependent clause with a subordinating conjunction.*

♦ *Practice 12* **Writing Your Own** Correct the sentences you wrote in Practice 3 using correction 3. *Answers will vary.*

Correction 4: Use a Semicolon

Separate the two sentences with a semicolon.

> Rosa's favorite subject is math; she always does very well on her math tests.
>
> My grandfather likes to cook his own meals; he doesn't want anyone to do it for him.

You can also use a **transition**, a word or an expression that indicates how the two parts of the sentence are related, with a semicolon. A transition often makes the sentence smoother. It is preceded by a semicolon and followed by a comma.

> Rosa's favorite subject is math; **as a result,** she always does very well on her math tests.
>
> My grandfather likes to cook his own meals; **therefore,** he doesn't want anyone to do it for him.

Here are some transitions commonly used with semicolons.

Transitions Used with a Semicolon Before and a Comma After

also	however	furthermore	instead
meanwhile	consequently	for example	similarly
in contrast	therefore	for instance	otherwise
of course	finally	in fact	nevertheless

♦ *Practice 13* **Correcting** Correct all the sentences in Practice 1 using correction 4. *Students should put semicolons where the slashes are.*

♦ *Practice 14* **Correcting** Correct the paragraph in Practice 2 using correction 4. *Students should put semicolons where the slashes are.*

◆ **P r a c t i c e 1 5** **Writing Your Own** Correct the sentences you wrote in Practice 3 using correction 4. *Answers will vary.*

REVIEWING METHODS OF CORRECTING FUSED SENTENCES AND COMMA SPLICES

What are the four ways to correct a fused sentence or comma splice?

1. *Separate the two sentences with a period, and capitalize the next word.*

2. *Separate the two sentences with a comma, and add a coordinating conjunction.*

3. *Change one of the sentences into a dependent clause with a subor- dinating conjunction.*

4. *Separate the two sentences with a semicolon or use a transition.*

Why is correcting fused sentences and comma splices important?

They distort a writer's message and cause readers problems.

CHAPTER REVIEW

You might want to reread your answers to the questions in all the review boxes before you do the following exercises.

◆ **Review P r a c t i c e 1** **Identifying** Label each of the following sentences as fused (F), comma splice (CS), or correct (C).

1. __CS__ My sister woke up late this morning, she made us late for school.

2. __F__ River rafting can be dangerous you need an experienced guide.

3. __CS__ When I dyed my hair black, I didn't know it might turn my scalp black too, it did.

4. __C__ People who compete in triathlons are excellent athletes because the events are very difficult.

5. __F__ Mike made an ice sculpture in his art class it was a penguin with a fish in its mouth.

6. __CS__ Terry needed to mow his lawn, the grass was very high, and the neighbors were complaining.

7. __C__ I drove my car without engine oil, and the repairs were incredibly expensive.

8. __F__ The big earthquake was on the front page of the newspaper many homes and businesses were destroyed.

9. __F__ We had the perfect beach vacation planned, but then it rained the whole time we were so disappointed.

10. __CS__ If you stay out in the sun very long, you should use sunblock, skin cancer is a horrible disease.

◆ *Review   Practice   2* **Completing** Correct the fused sentences and comma splices in Review Practice 1. *Answers will vary.*

◆ *Review   Practice   3* **Writing Your Own** Write a paragraph about your favorite season of the year. Why do you enjoy it? What do you do during this time of year? *Answers will vary.*

◆ *Review   Practice   4* **Editing Through Collaboration** Exchange paragraphs from Review Practice 3 with another student, and do the following:

1. Put brackets around any sentences that have more than one independent clause.
2. Circle the words that connect these clauses.

Then return the paper to its writer, and use the information in this chapter to correct any run-together sentences in your own paragraph. Record your errors on the Error Log in Appendix 6.

UNIT TESTS

Here are some exercises that test your understanding of all the material in this unit: Subjects and Verbs, Fragments, and Run-together Sentences.

Unit Test I

A. Underline the subjects once and the verbs twice in the following sentences. Cross out the prepositional phrases first. Then put the fragments in brackets ([ ]), and put a slash (/) between the run-together sentences.

1. The cars and buses were stuck in traffic for two hours.
2. Spring is my favorite time of year for many reasons. [For example, flowers and trees blooming.] [Lovers holding hands in the park.] [New parents pushing babies in strollers.]
3. I got tickets to Les Misérables in Los Angeles/I have wanted to see that play for years.
4. We're going to watch the Emmy Awards tonight. [Unless the Lakers game is on TV at the same time.]
5. Come with me to the mall. [To pick out a new dress for the dance.]
    ("You" implied)
6. He feels like a failure because he did not pass the midterm.
7. [Listening to Tamara's problems.] Jeff wondered if he really wanted to date her anymore.
8. The patient talked to the police detectives. [Who came to investigate his accident.]
9. Stacy went off her diet this afternoon/she ate fast food.
10. Her parents made her feel important and special in many ways. [For example, attending every one of her soccer games.]
11. Lend me two dollars, so I can get a cup of coffee,/then I'll be able to wake up. ("You" implied)
12. Marek sealed the envelope and put it in the mail,/then he realized that he had forgotten to enclose the check.
13. Dora and Robert bought souvenirs for all of their relatives.
14. A free lunch was served. [To those who attended the seminar.]
15. The scoreboard shows two outs/that must be a mistake.
16. Sergei told me the good news. [Which made me very happy.]

17. Fortunately, <u>Stan</u> <u>didn't have</u> the car ~~for the day~~.

18. <u>Cheyenne</u> <u>went</u> ~~to the circus with her son.~~[Since <u>she</u> <u>had</u> the day ~~off work.~~]

19. <u>Kari Kruise</u> <u>has</u> a morning show ~~on my favorite radio station,~~/<u>I</u> <u>listen</u> ~~to her~~ religiously.

20. [To be selected ~~for the scholarship.~~]<u>An applicant</u> <u>must be interviewed</u> ~~by the scholarship committee~~.

B. Correct the fragments and run-together sentences in Part A by rewriting each incorrect sentence. *Answers will vary.*

Unit Test II

A. Underline the subjects once and the verbs twice in the following paragraph. Cross out the prepositional phrases first. Then put the fragments in brackets ([ ]) and put a slash (/) between the run-together sentences.

    <u>I</u> <u>began</u> snow boarding when <u>I</u> <u>was</u> two years old,/<u>I</u> <u>have</u> always <u>loved</u> the cold <u>weather</u> and the thrill ~~of racing down the hill.~~[The <u>wind</u> <u>stinging</u> my cheeks.]<u>I</u> <u>began</u> racing ~~with a snow-boarding team.~~[When <u>I</u> <u>was</u> five years old.]<u>We</u> <u>traveled</u> ~~to different resorts on the weekends~~/<u>I</u> <u>did</u> dry-land training every day ~~during the week~~. <u>Being</u> ~~on the team~~ <u>was</u> fun because <u>most</u> ~~of my friends~~ <u>were</u> ~~on the team.~~[When <u>I</u> <u>got</u> ~~to high school.~~]<u>I</u> <u>was</u> able to teach snow boarding ~~at our local ski area~~. Now <u>I'm</u> ~~on my own,~~/<u>I</u> still <u>love</u> to be ~~in the cold.~~[And to snow board ~~with my family~~ when <u>I</u> <u>can</u>.]

B. Correct the fragments and run-together sentences in Part A by rewriting the paragraph. *Answers will vary.*

REGULAR AND IRREGULAR VERBS

✔ CHECKLIST for Using Regular and Irregular Verbs

> ✔ Are regular verbs in their correct forms?
> ✔ Are irregular verbs in their correct forms?

Test Yourself

Underline the complete verb in each of the following sentences. Then mark an X if the form of the verb is incorrect.

- _____ The pipe has bursted.
- _____ Sim reacted to the scene calmly.
- _____ I bought my car at an auction.
- _____ We had hid in the basement.
- _____ Sorry, I eated all the cookies.

(Answers are in Appendix 4.)

TEACHING REGULAR AND IRREGULAR VERBS

Have students create mnemonic devices for the irregular verbs that give them the most trouble. For instance, a silly poem based on the game of Battleship might help students remember *sink, sank, sunk:*

If you *sink* my battle-
   ship,
then you *sank* it.
But I must say,
"You've *sunk* my
   battleship!"

   Have students cre-
ate as many mnemonic
devices as they can to
help them remember
irregular verbs. Then
ask them to read their
devices to the class.

All verbs are either regular or irregular. *Regular verbs* form the past and past participle by adding *-d* or *-ed* to the present tense. If a verb does not form its past tense and past participle this way, it is called an *irregular verb.*

REGULAR VERBS

Here are the principal parts (present, past, and past participle forms) of some regular verbs. **Regular verbs** form the past tense and past participle by adding *-d* or *-ed.* The past participle is the verb form often used with helping verbs like *have, has,* or *had.*

Some Regular Verbs

PRESENT TENSE	PAST TENSE	PAST PARTICIPLE (USED WITH HELPING WORDS LIKE *HAVE, HAS, HAD*)
talk	talked	talked
sigh	sighed	sighed
drag	dragged	dragged
enter	entered	entered
consider	considered	considered

INSTRUCTOR'S RESOURCE MANUAL

For more exercises and for quizzes, see the *Instructor's Resource Manual*, Section II, Part V.

The different forms of a verb tell when something happened—in the *present* (I *talk*) or in the *past* (I *talked*, I *have talked*, I *had talked*).

REVIEWING REGULAR VERBS

What is a regular verb?

A regular verb forms its past tense and past participle by adding -d or -ed.

Identify three forms of a regular verb.

| _____ *present* _____ | _____ *past* _____ | _____ *past participle* _____ |

◆ **P r a c t i c e   1   Identifying** Put an X to the left of the incorrect verb forms in the following chart.

Present Tense	Past Tense	Past Participle
1. _____ clap	_____ clapped	_____ clapped
2. _____ help	_X_ helpt	_____ helped
3. _X_ watched	_____ watched	_____ watched
4. _____ gaze	_____ gazed	_X_ gazd
5. _X_ reclined	_____ reclined	_____ reclined

◆ *P r a c t i c e   2* **Completing** Write the correct forms of the following regular verbs.

	Present Tense	Past Tense	Past Participle
1. smoke	smoke	smoked	smoked
2. create	create	created	created
3. paste	paste	pasted	pasted
4. buzz	buzz	buzzed	buzzed
5. pick	pick	picked	picked

◆ *P r a c t i c e   3* **Writing Your Own** Write five sentences using at least five of the words from Practice 1. *Answers will vary.*

IRREGULAR VERBS

Irregular verbs do not form their past tense and past participle with *-d* or *-ed*. That is why they are irregular. Some follow certain patterns (*spring, sprang, sprung; ring, rang, rung; drink, drank, drunk; sink, sank, sunk*). But the only sure way to know the forms of an irregular verb is to spend time learning them. As you write, you can check a dictionary or the following list.

Irregular Verbs

PRESENT	PAST	PAST PARTICIPLE (USED WITH HELPING WORDS LIKE *HAVE, HAS, HAD*)
am	was	been
are	were	been
be	was	been
bear	bore	borne, born
beat	beat	beaten
begin	began	begun

bend	bent	bent
bid	bid	bid
bind	bound	bound
bite	bit	bitten
blow	blew	blown
break	broke	broken
bring	brought (not *brang*)	brought (not *brung*)
build	built	built
burst	burst (not *bursted*)	burst
buy	bought	bought
choose	chose	chosen
come	came	come
cost	cost (not *costed*)	cost
cut	cut	cut
deal	dealt	dealt
do	did (not *done*)	done
draw	drew	drawn
drink	drank	drunk
drive	drove	driven
eat	ate	eaten
fall	fell	fallen
feed	fed	fed
feel	felt	felt
fight	fought	fought
find	found	found
flee	fled	fled
fly	flew	flown
forget	forgot	forgotten
forgive	forgave	forgiven
freeze	froze	frozen
get	got	got, gotten
go	went	gone

grow	grew	grown
hang[1] (a picture)	hung	hung
has	had	had
have	had	had
hear	heard	heard
hide	hid	hidden
hurt	hurt (not *hurted*)	hurt
is	was	been
know	knew	known
lay	laid	laid
lead	led	led
leave	left	left
lend	lent	lent
lie[2]	lay	lain
lose	lost	lost
meet	met	met
pay	paid	paid
prove	proved	proved, proven
put	put	put
read [rēēd]	read [rĕd]	read [rĕd]
ride	rode	ridden
ring	rang	rung
rise	rose	risen
run	ran	run
say	said	said
see	saw (not *seen*)	seen
set	set	set
shake	shook	shaken
shine[3] (a light)	shone	shone
shrink	shrank	shrunk
sing	sang	sung
sink	sank	sunk
sit	sat	sat

sleep	slept	slept
speak	spoke	spoken
spend	spent	spent
spread	spread	spread
spring	sprang (not *sprung*)	sprung
stand	stood	stood
steal	stole	stolen
stick	stuck	stuck
stink	stank (not *stunk*)	stunk
strike	struck	struck, stricken
strive	strove	striven, strived
swear	swore	sworn
sweep	swept	swept
swell	swelled	swelled, swollen
swim	swam	swum
swing	swung	swung
take	took	taken
teach	taught	taught
tear	tore	torn
tell	told	told
think	thought	thought
throw	threw	thrown
understand	understood	understood
wake	woke	woken
wear	wore	worn
weave	wove	woven
win	won	won
wring	wrung	wrung
write	wrote	written

1. *Hang* meaning "execute by hanging" is regular: *hang, hanged, hanged.*
2. *Lie* meaning "tell a lie" is regular: *lie, lied, lied.*
3. *Shine* meaning "brighten by polishing" is regular: *shine, shined, shined.*

REVIEWING IRREGULAR VERBS

What is the difference between regular and irregular verbs?

Irregular verbs do not form their past tense and past participle with -d or -ed.

What is the best way to learn how irregular verbs form their past tense and past participle?

The best way to learn them is to become familiar with them.

◆ **P r a c t i c e   4   Identifying** Put an X to the left of the incorrect verb forms in the following chart.

Present Tense	Past Tense	Past Participle
1. _____ bear	_X_ beared	_____ borne
2. _____ shrink	_____ shrank	_X_ shrank
3. _____ swing	_____ swung	_X_ swang
4. _____ deal	_X_ dealed	_____ dealt
5. _X_ chose	_____ chose	_____ chosen

◆ **P r a c t i c e   5   Completing** Write the correct forms of the following irregular verbs.

	Present Tense	Past Tense	Past Participle
1. am	am	was	been
2. write	write	wrote	written
3. sweep	sweep	swept	swept
4. fall	fall	fell	fallen
5. swell	swell	swelled	swelled, swollen

◆ **P r a c t i c e   6   Writing Your Own** Write five sentences using at least five of the words from the chart in Practice 5. *Answers will vary.*

USING *LIE/LAY* AND *SIT/SET* CORRECTLY

Two pairs of verbs are often used incorrectly—*lie/lay* and *sit/set*.

Lie/Lay

	Present Tense	Past Tense	Past Participle
lie (recline or lie down)	lie	lay	(have, has, had) lain
lay (put or place down)	lay	laid	(have, has, had) laid

The verb *lay* always takes an object. You must lay something down:

> Lay down *what?*
> Lay down *your books*.

Sit/Set

	Present Tense	Past Tense	Past Participle
sit (get into a seated position)	sit	sat	(have, has, had) sat
set (put or place down)	set	set	(have, has, had) set

Like the verb *lay*, the verb *set* must always have an object. You must set something down:

> Set *what?*
> Set *the presents* over here.

REVIEWING *Lie/Lay* AND *Sit/Set*

What do lie and lay mean?

Lie means recline or lie down; lay means put or place down.

What are the principal parts of lie and lay?

Lie, lay, lain and lay, laid, laid

What do sit and set mean?

Sit means get into a seated position; set means put or place down.

> *What are the principal parts of sit and set?*
>
> Sit, sat, sat and set, set, set
> _____
>
> *Which of these verbs always take an object?*
>
> Lay and set
> _____

◆ **P r a c t i c e   7   Identifying** Choose the correct verb in the following sentences.

1. After I (sat, set) down, I felt much better.
2. All day I have (lain, laid) in my room watching TV.
3. He has (lay, laid) the blanket down for our picnic.
4. We had to (sat, set) our watches to exactly the same time.
5. (Lie, Lay) the pieces of the puzzle out on the table, please.

◆ **P r a c t i c e   8   Completing** Fill in each blank in the following sentences with the correct form of *lie/lay* or *sit/set*.

1. Suzy has ____lain____ in the bathtub for so long that her skin has wrinkled.
2. I could have ____lain/sat____ in the moonlight looking at the stars all night.
3. The cook ____laid/set____ out all the ingredients.
4. Please ____set____ those heavy boxes down before you strain your back.
5. I think I will go and ____lie/sit____ down for a while.

◆ **P r a c t i c e   9   Writing Your Own** Write five sentences using variations of *lie/lay* or *sit/set*. *Answers will vary.*

CHAPTER REVIEW

You might want to reread your answers to the questions in all the review boxes before you do the following exercises.

◆ *Review* **P r a c t i c e   1   Identifying** Write out the past tense and past participle of each verb listed here and then identify the verb as either regular or irregular.

	Present Tense	Past Tense	Past Participle	Type of Verb
1.	brush	brushed	brushed	regular
2.	fix	fixed	fixed	regular
3.	wear	wore	worn	irregular
4.	buy	bought	bought	irregular
5.	suffer	suffered	suffered	regular
6.	have	had	had	irregular
7.	type	typed	typed	regular
8.	feel	felt	felt	irregular
9.	touch	touched	touched	regular
10.	teach	taught	taught	irregular

♦ **Review P r a c t i c e 2 Completing** Fill in each blank in the following sentences with a regular or irregular verb that makes sense. *Answers may vary.*

1. Yesterday, I _____sat_____ at my computer and tried to write my essay.

2. Tilda _____came_____ over to my house last night.

3. I always smile and _____wave_____ my hand to the people on the Mardi Gras floats.

4. Geraldo has _____spilled_____ his drink all over the waitress.

5. Carlos and Tom have _____missed_____ class again.

6. You should never _____drop/shake_____ an infant; doing so can cause brain damage and death.

7. The groom smiled at his bride and _____placed_____ the ring on her third finger.

8. The plumbing in the house has _____sprung_____ a leak.

9. Mary Ann _____hung_____ the picture in her bedroom.

10. All cozy in my bed, I _____slept_____ right through the earthquake.

◆ ***Review   Practice   3*** **Writing   Your   Own** Write a paragraph explaining the most important parts of your daily routine. Be sure to explain why each activity is important. *Answers will vary.*

◆ ***Review   Practice   4*** **Editing Your Writing** Exchange paragraphs from Review Practice 3 with another student, and do the following: *Answers will vary.*

1. Circle any verb forms that are not correct.

2. Suggest a correction for these incorrect forms.

Then return the paper to its writer, and use the information in this chapter to correct the verb forms in your own paragraph. Record your errors on the Error Log in Appendix 6.

VERB TENSE

✔ CHECKLIST for Correcting Tense Problems

> ✔ Are present-tense verbs in the correct form?
> ✔ Are past-tense verbs in the correct form?
> ✔ Are *-ing* verbs used with the correct helping verbs?
> ✔ Are the forms of *be, do,* and *have* used correctly?

Test Yourself

Underline the complete verb in each sentence. Then mark an X if the form of the verb is incorrect.

- _____ Jean always laugh when I tell that joke.
- _____ Mark jumped over the hurdle and crossed the finish line.
- _____ I had spoke to the salesclerk about a discount.
- _____ Students ain't allowed to bring food and drink into the computer lab.
- _____ My two cats be playing in the sunshine.

(Answers are in Appendix 4.)

When we hear the word "verb," we often think of action. We also know that action occurs in time. We are naturally interested in whether something happened today or yesterday or if it will happen at some time in the future. The time of an action is indicated by the **tense** of a verb, specifically in the ending of a verb or in a helping word. This chapter discusses the most common errors in using verb tense.

change the sentence into its assigned tense moves one space forward on the grid. For instance, the following sentence might be given to the Past and Present teams: "We will search for the answer." If the Past team changes the sentence to "We searched for the answer," its horse and buggy moves forward one space; if the Present team changes it to "We search for the answer," its car moves forward; and so on.

The first vehicle to reach the end of the grid wins.

INSTRUCTOR'S
RESOURCE MANUAL
For more sample sentences, for more exercises, and for quizzes, see the *Instructor's Resource Manual,* Section II, Part V.

PRESENT TENSE

One of the most common errors in college writing is reversing the present-tense endings—adding an *-s* where none is needed and omitting the *-s* where it is required. This error causes problems in subject-verb agreement. Make sure you understand this mistake, and then proofread carefully to avoid it in your writing.

Present Tense

Singular		Plural	
INCORRECT	CORRECT	INCORRECT	CORRECT
NOT *I walks*	*I walk*	**NOT** *we walks*	*we walk*
NOT *you walks*	*you walk*	**NOT** *you walks*	*you walk*
NOT *he, she, it walk*	*he, she, it walks*	**NOT** *they walks*	*they walk*

You also need to be able to spot these same errors in sentences.

Incorrect	Correct
That car run me off the road.	**That car ran** me off the road.
My mother hate my boyfriend.	**My mother hates** my boyfriend.
You speaks too fast.	**You speak** too fast.
They trims the trees once a year.	**They trim** the trees once a year.

REVIEWING PRESENT-TENSE ERRORS
···

What is the most common error in using the present tense?

Reversing the present-tense endings—adding -s when not needed or

omitting it when it is required

How can you prevent this error?

By learning the correct forms and proofreading carefully

◢ **P r a c t i c e   1 A   Identifying** Underline the present-tense errors in each of the following sentences.

1. I <u>loves</u> to sit in a cool theater on a hot summer day. *(love)*
2. You <u>babbles</u> too much. *(babble)*
3. My baby sister <u>play</u> well with her cousin. *(plays)*
4. We <u>seems</u> to be lost. *(seem)*
5. Next week, they <u>plans</u> on going to the party after the show. *(plan)*

◢ **P r a c t i c e   1 B   Correcting** Correct the present-tense errors in Practice 1A by rewriting each sentence. *See Practice 1A.*

◢ **P r a c t i c e   2   Completing** Fill in each blank in the following paragraph with the correct present-tense verbs. *Answers may vary.*

My brother always (1) _____*asks*_____ me to help him with his paper route. Usually I don't mind because he (2) _____*gives*_____ me money and we (3) _____*get*_____ to work together. It's strange, too, because I actually (4) _____*enjoy*_____ rolling up the papers. But lately my brother has been sleeping late while I do all the work. So I told him I was going on strike until I got either more money or more help. Do you know what he did? He fired me! Can you (5) _____*believe*_____ that?

◢ **P r a c t i c e   3   Writing Your Own** Write a sentence of your own for each of the following present-tense verbs. *Answers will vary.*

1. relieve _____

2. feels _____

3. skates _____

4. asks _____

5. skip _____

PAST TENSE

Just as we know that a verb is in the present tense by its ending, we can tell that a verb is in the past tense by its ending. Regular verbs form the past tense by adding *-d* or *-ed*. But some writers forget the ending when they are writing the past tense. Understanding this problem and then proofreading carefully will help you catch this error.

Past Tense

Singular		Plural	
INCORRECT	CORRECT	INCORRECT	CORRECT
NOT *I walk*	*I walked*	**NOT** *we walk*	*we walked*
NOT *you walk*	*you walked*	**NOT** *you walk*	*you walked*
NOT *he, she, it walk*	*he, she, it walked*	**NOT** *they walk*	*they walked*

You also need to be able to spot these same errors in sentences.

Incorrect	Correct
She run fast.	**She ran** fast.
He see the game.	**He saw** the game.
The girl study hard.	**The girl studied** hard.
Yes, **we learn** a lot.	Yes, **we learned** a lot.

REVIEWING PAST-TENSE ERRORS

What is the most common sentence error made with the past tense?

Forgetting the past-tense ending (-d or -ed)

How can you prevent this error?

By learning the correct forms and proofreading carefully

◆ *P r a c t i c e 4 A* **Identifying** Underline the past-tense errors in the following sentences.

1. When we were in high school, we <u>talk</u> on the phone for hours. *(talked)*
2. The radio station <u>play</u> the song over and over again. *(played)*

3. Yesterday you <u>edit</u> your work. *(edited)*

4. She <u>close</u> all the windows when she left. *(closed)*

5. I just <u>realize</u> that I have already done these exercises. *(realized)*

P r a c t i c e   4 B   Correcting Correct the past-tense errors in Practice 4A by rewriting each sentence. *See Practice 4A.*

P r a c t i c e   5   Completing Fill in each blank in the following paragraph with the correct past-tense verb. *Answers will vary.*

Yesterday, it was so hot that several of my friends (1) _____ to go to the beach. They (2) _____ a lunch, put on their swimsuits, and (3) _____ into the car. Sadly, I had a cold, so I (4) _____ home. Boy, am I glad I did. My friends were stuck in traffic for two hours with no air conditioning. This is the one time I (5) _____ my lucky stars for a cold.

P r a c t i c e   6   Writing Your Own Write a sentence of your own for each of the following past-tense verbs. *Answers will vary.*

1. rained _____

2. fixed _____

3. sipped _____

4. lifted _____

5. visited _____

USING HELPING WORDS WITH PAST PARTICIPLES

Helping words are used with the past participle form, *not* with the past-tense form. It is incorrect to use a helping verb (such as *is, was, were, have, has,* or *had*) with the past tense. Make sure you understand how to use helping words with past participles, and then proofread your written work to avoid making these errors.

Incorrect	Correct
They **have went.**	They **have gone.**
She **has decide** to get married.	She **has decided** to get married.
I **have ate** breakfast already.	I **have eaten** breakfast already.
We **had took** the test early.	We **had taken** the test early.

REVIEWING ERRORS WITH HELPING
WORDS AND PAST PARTICIPLES

What is the most common sentence error made with past participles?

Using a helping word with the past tense instead of the past participle

How can you prevent this error?

By learning the correct forms and proofreading carefully

Practice 7A **Identifying** Underline the incorrect helping words and past participles in each of the following sentences.

1. I <u>have sang</u> that song in French. *(have sung)*
2. Kendra and Misty <u>have hid</u> all the Easter eggs. *(have hidden)*
3. The plane <u>has flew</u> over the ocean. *(has flown)*
4. We <u>have did</u> all the necessary repairs to the fence. *(have done)*
5. She <u>has forget</u> the phone number. *(has forgotten)*

Practice 7B **Correcting** Correct the helping verb and past participle errors in Practice 7A by rewriting each sentence. *See Practice 7A.*

Practice 8 **Completing** Fill in each blank in the following paragraph with helping verbs and past participles that make sense. *Answers will vary.*

It all started in elementary school. I was a new student and didn't know a single person. For two weeks, I (1) _____ my lunch alone. No one had even talked to me. Even though I didn't show it, my classmates' neglect (2) _____ my feelings. My little heart (3) _____. But one day, a wonderful boy named John happened to notice me. I (4) _____ my lunch, so he decided to share his with me. From that day forward, we (5) _____ the best of friends.

◆ *P r a c t i c e 9* **Writing Your Own** Write a sentence of your own for each of the following helping words and past participles. *Answers will vary.*

1. have drunk _____

2. has seen _____

3. had woven _____

4. has risen _____

5. have hidden _____

USING *-ing* VERBS CORRECTLY

Verbs ending in *-ing* describe action that is going on or that was going on for a while. To be a complete verb, an *-ing* verb is always used with a helping verb. Two common errors occur with *-ing* verbs:

1. Using *be* or *been* instead of the correct helping verb
2. Using no helping verb at all

Learn the correct forms, and proofread carefully to catch these errors.

Incorrect	Correct
The car **be going** too fast.	The car **is going** too fast.
	The car **was going** too fast.
The car **been going** too fast.	The car **has been going** too fast.
	The car **had been going** too fast.
We **watching** a movie.	We **are watching** a movie.
	We **have been watching** a movie.
	We **were watching** a movie.
	We **had been watching** a movie.

REVIEWING *-ing* VERB ERRORS

What two kinds of errors occur with -ing verbs?

Using be or been instead of the correct helping verb

Not using any helping verb at all

How can you prevent these errors?

By learning the correct forms and proofreading carefully

◆ *P r a c t i c e 1 0 A* **Identifying** Underline the incorrect helping verbs and *-ing* forms in each of the following sentences.

1. The cat <u>be chasing</u> the dog! *(is chasing)*
2. The patient <u>been waiting</u> for the doctor for over an hour. *(has been waiting)*
3. That building <u>be leaning</u> to the side for over 20 years. *(has been leaning)*
4. I <u>feeling</u> sick because I ate an entire pizza by myself. *(am feeling)*
5. We <u>be driving</u> down Sunset Boulevard. *(are driving)*

◆ *P r a c t i c e 1 0 B* **Correcting** Correct the verb form errors in Practice 10A by rewriting each sentence. *See Practice 10A.*

◆ *P r a c t i c e 1 1* **Completing** Fill in each blank in the following paragraph with the correct helping verb and *-ing* form. *Answers will vary.*

I (1) _____ one of the best days of my life. It started while I (2) _____ my clothes and found $20 in my pocket. Then on my way to work, I was pulled over by a police officer. While he (3) _____ out the ticket, I made him laugh so hard that he tore it up and let me go with a warning. But the best part of my day happened while I was at work. I (4) _____ to the radio when I heard my name announced. I had just won a trip to Hawaii! I (5) _____ up and down and screaming. My boss was so happy for me that he gave me the rest of the day off.

◆ *P r a c t i c e   1 2*   **Writing Your Own** Write a sentence of your own for each of the following verbs. *Answers will vary.*

1. is wishing ————————————————————

2. has been writing ————————————————

3. were laying ——————————————————

4. was driving ——————————————————

5. had been sailing —————————————————

PROBLEMS WITH *be*

The verb *be* can cause problems in both the present tense and the past tense. The following chart demonstrates these problems. Learn how to use these forms correctly, and then always proofread your written work carefully to avoid these errors.

The Verb *be*

Present Tense

Singular		Plural	
INCORRECT	CORRECT	INCORRECT	CORRECT
NOT *I be/ain't*	*I am/am not*	**NOT** *we be/ain't*	*we are/are not*
NOT *you be/ain't*	*you are/are not*	**NOT** *you be/ain't*	*you are/are not*
NOT *he, she, it be/ain't*	*he, she, it is/is not*	**NOT** *they be/ain't*	*they are/are not*

Past Tense

Singular		Plural	
INCORRECT	CORRECT	INCORRECT	CORRECT
NOT *I were*	*I was*	**NOT** *we was*	*we were*
NOT *you was*	*you were*	**NOT** *you was*	*you were*
NOT *he, she, it were*	*he, she, it was*	**NOT** *they was*	*they were*

REVIEWING PROBLEMS WITH *be*

What are two common errors made with be?

In the present tense, using be and ain't instead of the correct verb forms

In the past tense, confusing was and were

How can you prevent these errors?

By learning the correct forms and proofreading carefully

◆ **P r a c t i c e 1 3 A**   **Identifying** Underline the incorrect forms of *be* in each of the following sentences.

1. I <u>ain't</u> going to travel by plane. *(am not)*
2. You <u>is</u> going to have to study for this exam. *(are)*
3. He <u>be</u> the person you need to talk to about enrollment. *(is)*
4. You <u>was</u> supposed to take your clothes off before you ironed them. *(were)*
5. They <u>was</u> not having any fun. *(were)*

◆ **P r a c t i c e 1 3 B**   **Correcting** Correct the incorrect forms of *be* in Practice 13A by rewriting each sentence. *See Practice 13A.*

◆ **P r a c t i c e 1 4**   **Completing** Fill in each blank in the following paragraph with the correct form of *be*.

Crystal (1) ___*is*___ an adventurous person. She (2) ___*is*___ willing to try just about anything, and she usually talks me into going along with her. We have jumped out of a plane, off a bridge, and off a mountain—with a parachute or a bungee cord, of course. But when she decided we should have our belly buttons pierced, I panicked. Now, I (3) ___*am*___ not a coward, but I knew this little adventure (4) ___*was*___ going to hurt. Danger I like, but pain—well, that's a different story. This (5) ___*was*___ one adventure I had to say no to.

◆ *P r a c t i c e **1 5**   **Writing Your Own** Write a sentence of your own for each of the following verbs. *Answers will vary.*

1. am not _____

2. is _____

3. was _____

4. are _____

5. were _____

PROBLEMS WITH *do*

Another verb that causes sentence problems in the present and past tenses is *do*. The following chart shows these problems. Learn the correct forms, and proofread to avoid errors.

The Verb *do*

Present Tense

Singular		Plural	
INCORRECT	CORRECT	INCORRECT	CORRECT
NOT *I does*	*I do*	**NOT** *we does*	*we do*
NOT *you does*	*you do*	**NOT** *you does*	*you do*
NOT *he, she, it do*	*he, she, it does*	**NOT** *they does*	*they do*

Past Tense

Singular		Plural	
INCORRECT	CORRECT	INCORRECT	CORRECT
NOT *I done*	*I did*	**NOT** *we done*	*we did*
NOT *you done*	*you did*	**NOT** *you done*	*you did*
NOT *he, she, it done*	*he, she, it did*	**NOT** *they done*	*they did*

REVIEWING PROBLEMS WITH *do*

What are two common errors made with do?

In the present tense, confusing does and do

In the past tense, confusing done and did

How can you prevent these errors?

By learning the correct forms and proofreading carefully

Practice 16A **Identifying** Underline the incorrect forms of *do* in each of the following sentences.

1. We always <u>does</u> the prewriting exercises before organizing our essays. *(do)*
2. She <u>done</u> it again. *(did)*
3. You <u>does</u> a good job even when you don't have to. *(do)*
4. Yes, that computer certainly <u>do</u> need a new modem. *(does)*
5. Henry, you <u>done</u> let the cat out! *(remove done)*

Practice 16B **Correcting** Correct the incorrect forms of *do* in Practice 16A by rewriting each sentence. *See Practice 16A.*

Practice 17 **Completing** Fill in each blank in the following paragraph with the correct form of *do*.

I (1) _____*do*_____ believe it was love at first sight. She had the prettiest brown eyes and the silkiest blonde hair I had ever seen. My friends warned me that she wasn't right for me, but they (2) _____*did*_____n't understand—we were made for each other. Now, I admit that she (3) _____*did/does*_____ slobber a bit and her hair (4) _____*did/does*_____ shed in the summer, but she's always happy to see me and doesn't mind my stupid mistakes. Adopting Porsche, my golden retriever, was the best thing I ever (5) _____*did*_____.

◈ *P r a c t i c e   1 8*   **Writing Your Own** Write a sentence of your own for each of the following verbs. *Answers will vary.*

1. do _____

2. does _____

3. did _____

4. does _____

5. do _____

PROBLEMS WITH *have*

Along with *be* and *do*, the verb *have* causes sentence problems in the present and past tenses. The following chart demonstrates these problems. Learn the correct forms, and proofread to avoid errors with *have*.

The Verb *have*

Present Tense

Singular		Plural	
INCORRECT	CORRECT	INCORRECT	CORRECT
NOT *I has*	*I have*	**NOT** *we has*	*we have*
NOT *you has*	*you have*	**NOT** *you has*	*you have*
NOT *he, she, it have*	*he, she, it has*	**NOT** *they has*	*they have*

Past Tense

Singular		Plural	
INCORRECT	CORRECT	INCORRECT	CORRECT
NOT *I has*	*I had*	**NOT** *we has*	*we had*
NOT *you have*	*you had*	**NOT** *you has*	*you had*
NOT *he, she, it have*	*he, she, it had*	**NOT** *they has*	*they had*

REVIEWING PROBLEMS WITH *have*

What are two common errors made with have?

In the present tense, confusing has and have

In the past tense, confusing has or have and had

How can you prevent these errors?

By learning the correct forms and proofreading carefully

P r a c t i c e   1 9 A   Identifying Underline the incorrect forms of *have* in each of the following sentences.

1. We <u>has</u> already taken up too much space. *(have)*
2. Yesterday, I <u>has</u> money in my account; today I <u>has</u> none. *(had, have)*
3. If George is late, then he <u>have</u> to come in through the back entrance. *(has)*
4. You <u>has</u> a great deal of courage when dealing with angry customers. *(have)*
5. Sabine and Jackie <u>has</u> taken the rest of the afternoon off. *(have)*

P r a c t i c e   1 9 B   Correcting Correct the incorrect forms of *have* in Practice 19A by rewriting each sentence. *See Practice 19A.*

P r a c t i c e   2 0   Completing Fill in each blank in the following paragraph with the correct form of *have*.

"I (1) ____have____ a secret," said my little brother Bubba, "but you (2) ___have___ to promise not to tell." Now Bubba (3) ____has____ the most wonderful imagination, and I knew to expect the unexpected since we (4) ____have____ shared many secrets in the past. So I said, "OK, what is it?" He leaned closer, cupped his hand to my ear, and whispered, "Babies don't really come from the stork." "No!" I exclaimed, pretending to be shocked. "Where do they come from?" I asked. "Why, they come from eggs," he proudly said. I (5) ____had____ the hardest time keeping a straight face.

◆ *P r a c t i c e 2 1*   **Writing Your Own** Write a sentence of your own for each of the following verbs. *Answers will vary.*

1. have _____

2. has _____

3. had _____

4. has _____

5. have _____

CHAPTER REVIEW

You might want to reread your answers to the questions in all the review boxes before you do the following exercises.

◆ *Review P r a c t i c e 1*   **Identifying** Underline the incorrect verb forms in the following sentences. Check problem areas carefully: Is an -s needed, or is there an unnecessary -s ending? Do all past-tense regular verbs end in -d or -ed? Is the past participle used with helping words? Is the correct helping verb used with -ing verbs? Are the forms of *be, do,* and *have* correct?

1. Janet and Henry <u>likes</u> to go for long drives in the mountains. *(like)*
2. Our high school band <u>has strove</u> to be the best in the nation. *(has striven)*
3. I <u>be</u> sorry for your troubles. *(am)*
4. I <u>enjoys</u> a hot cup of coffee while I work. *(enjoy)*
5. You <u>done</u> a wise thing when you signed up for classes early. *(did)*
6. The birds <u>be flying</u> south for the winter. *(are flying)*
7. I <u>have wove</u> the tapestry threads back together. *(have woven)*
8. That fat cat <u>been sleeping</u> in the sun all day. *(has been sleeping)*
9. Those two girls think they <u>has</u> all the answers. *(have)*
10. Last Christmas, we <u>bake</u> most of our gifts. *(baked)*

◆ *Review P r a c t i c e 2*   **Correcting** Correct the errors in Review Practice 1 by rewriting each sentence. *See Review Practice 1.*

◆ ***Review Practice 3***   **Writing Your Own** Write a short paragraph describing your favorite pet. Be careful to use all verbs in the correct tense. Check in particular for errors with *be*, *do*, and *have*. *Answers will vary.*

◆ ***Review Practice 4***   **Editing Through Collaboration** Exchange paragraphs from Review Practice 3 with another student, and do the following: *Answers will vary.*

1. Underline any incorrect tenses.
2. Circle any incorrect verb forms.

Then return the paper to its writer, and use the information in this chapter to correct any verb errors in your own paragraph. Record your errors on the Error Log in Appendix 6.

SUBJECT-VERB AGREEMENT

CHECKLIST for Correcting Subject-Verb Agreement Problems

> ✔ Do all subjects agree with their verbs?

Test Yourself

Underline the subjects once and the complete verbs twice in the following sentences. Put an X by the sentence if its subject and verb do not agree.

- _____ Neither the shorts nor the shirt fit me.
- _____ Chips and dip is my favorite snack.
- _____ There were a large storm last night.
- _____ Some of the soil along with the fertilizer are for the orchard.
- _____ Cotton and silk is more comfortable than wool.

(Answers are in Appendix 4.)

Almost every day, we come across situations that require us to reach an agreement with someone. For example, you and a friend might have to agree on which movie to see, or you and your manager might have to agree on how many hours you'll work in the coming week. Whatever the issue, agreement is essential in most aspects of life—including writing. In this chapter, you will learn how to resolve conflicts in your sentences by making sure your subjects and verbs agree.

TEACHING SUBJECT-VERB AGREEMENT
Create several sentences that demonstrate subject-verb agreement errors. (You could use the examples from the chapter as models.) Put words and phrases from these sentences on index cards. Then put three or four long strips of Velcro horizontally across a piece of poster board, and place squares of the other side of the Velcro on the backs of the index cards.

Now attach index cards to the poster board so that you create a few simple sentences with no words separating the subjects and their verbs. Next, add phrase cards to the sentences, separating the subjects and verbs to show students that verbs do not change

even though informa-
tion may come between
a subject and its verb.
    Demonstrate some
common agreement
errors by placing
incorrect verbs with
subjects.
    Once students
understand how sub-
jects and verbs agree,
test your students by
putting sentences with
subject-verb agreement
errors on the board and
asking them to come to
the board to find and
correct the errors.

INSTRUCTOR'S
RESOURCE MANUAL
For more sample
sentences, for more
exercises, and for
quizzes, see the
*Instructor's Resource
Manual*, Section II,
Part V.

SUBJECT-VERB AGREEMENT

Subject-verb agreement simply means that singular subjects must be paired with singular verbs and plural subjects with plural verbs. Look at this example:

Singular: **She works** in Baltimore.

The subject *she* is singular because it refers to only one person. The verb *works* is singular and matches the singular subject. Here is the same sentence in plural form:

Plural: **They work** in Baltimore.

The subject *they* is plural, referring to more than one person, and the verb *work* is also plural.

REVIEWING SUBJECT-VERB AGREEMENT

What is the difference between singular and plural?

Singular refers to only one subject. Plural refers to more than one subject.

What kind of verb goes with a singular subject?

A singular verb goes with a singular subject.

What kind of verb goes with a plural subject?

A plural verb goes with a plural subject.

◆ *P r a c t i c e   1*   **Identifying** Underline the verb that agrees with its subject in each of the following sentences.

1. In her free time, Cassie (be, <u>is</u>) a volunteer nurse.
2. The girls usually (<u>store</u>, stores) their gear in the lockers.
3. Rocky, my 80-pound dog, (eat, <u>eats</u>) more food in a day than I do.
4. I (<u>do</u>, does) all of my reading for my classes at least one week ahead of time.
5. You (has, <u>have</u>) something green in your hair.

◆ *P r a c t i c e   2*   **Completing** Fill in each blank in the following sentences with a present-tense verb that agrees with its subject. *Answers will vary.*

1. Every evening, Michael _____ by the fire.

2. They _____ many questions.

3. Neil _____ everything chocolate.

4. We rarely _____ down that path, for it is always dark and eerie.

5. He _____ to only classical music.

◆ *P r a c t i c e   3*   **Writing Your Own** Write five sentences of your own, and underline the subjects and verbs. Make sure that your subjects and verbs agree. *Answers will vary.*

WORDS SEPARATING SUBJECTS AND VERBS

With sentences that are as simple and direct as *She works in Baltimore,* checking that the subject and verb agree is easy. But problems can arise when words come between the subject and the verb. Often the words between the subject and verb are prepositional phrases. If you follow the advice given in Chapter 34, you will be able to find the subject and verb: *Cross out all the prepositional phrases in a sentence. The subject and verb will be among the words that are left.* Here are some examples:

                                              s   v
Prepositional Phrases: The **notebook** ~~for history class~~ **is** ~~in my~~
                             ~~backpack~~.

When you cross out the prepositional phrases, you can tell that the singular subject, *notebook,* and the singular verb, *is,* agree.

                                              s   v
Prepositional Phrases: The **roses** ~~in my garden~~ **bloom** ~~in April~~.

When you cross out the prepositional phrases, you can tell that the plural subject, *roses,* and the plural verb, *bloom,* agree.

REVIEWING WORDS SEPARATING SUBJECTS AND VERBS

What words often come between subjects and verbs?

Prepositional phrases often come between subjects and verbs.

> ***What is an easy way to identify the subject and verb in a sentence?***
>
> *Cross out the prepositional phrases first.*

◆ **P r a c t i c e 4 Identifying** Underline the subject once and the verb twice in each of the following sentences. Cross out the prepositional phrases first. Put an X to the left of any sentence in which the subject and verb do not agree.

1. ___X___ Cindy, unlike many people today, do so much for others.

2. ___X___ That man in the red pants think a lot about his social life.

3. ___X___ Frog legs, in spite of what most people say, tastes like frog legs.

4. _____ The flowers in the garden smell nice.

5. ___X___ The economy in America seem to be getting stronger.

◆ **P r a c t i c e 5 Completing** Fill in each blank in the following sentences with a present-tense verb that agrees with its subject. *Answers will vary.*

1. My little brother, despite being told otherwise, still _____ in Santa Claus.

2. The train for San Francisco _____ in the station at 7:45 p.m.

3. MTV, unlike VH1, _____ to air more music videos.

4. The boxes in the hallway _____ in the moving van.

5. The wind during a thunderstorm always _____ me.

◆ **P r a c t i c e 6 Writing Your Own** Write five sentences of your own with at least one prepositional phrase in each, and underline the subjects and verbs. Make sure that your subjects and verbs agree. *Answers will vary.*

MORE THAN ONE SUBJECT

Sometimes a subject consists of more than one person, place, thing, or idea. These subjects are called **compound** (as discussed in Chapter 30). Follow these three rules when matching a verb to a compound subject:

1. When compound subjects are joined by *and,* use a plural verb.

    Plural: Thursday and Friday were hot days.

    The singular words *Thursday and Friday* together make a plural subject. Therefore, the plural verb *were* is needed.

2. When the subject appears to have more than one part but the parts refer to a single unit, use a singular verb.

    Singular: Macaroni and cheese is Eli's favorite food.

    Macaroni is one item and *cheese* is one item, but Eli does not eat one without the other, so they form a single unit. Because they are a single unit, they require a singular verb—*is.*

3. When compound subjects are joined by *or* or *nor,* make the verb agree with the subject closest to it.

    Singular: Neither hot dogs nor chicken was on the menu.

    The part of the compound subject closest to the verb is *chicken,* which is singular. Therefore, the verb must be singular—*was.*

    Plural: Neither chicken nor hot dogs were on the menu.

    This time, the part of the compound subject closest to the verb is *hot dogs,* which is plural. Therefore, the verb must be plural—*were.*

REVIEWING SUBJECT-VERB AGREEMENT
WITH MORE THAN ONE SUBJECT

Do you use a singular or plural verb with compound subjects joined by and?

A plural verb
_____

Why should you use a singular verb with a subject like macaroni and cheese?

Because it forms a single unit
_____

If one part of a compound subject joined by or *or* nor *is singular and the other is plural, how do you decide whether to use a singular or plural verb?*

Make the verb agree with the subject closest to it.
_____

◆ *P r a c t i c e* *7* **Identifying** Underline the verb that agrees with its subject in each of the following sentences. Cross out the prepositional phrases first.

1. You and I (was, <u>were</u>) going the wrong way ~~down a one-way street~~.
2. Chicken and dumplings (taste, <u>tastes</u>) better ~~with a little salt and pepper~~.
3. Either the mosquitoes or the wind (cause, <u>causes</u>) my skin problems.
4. Celery and peanut butter (<u>is</u>, are) my favorite snack.
5. Neither the professor nor the students (knows, <u>know</u>) the answer ~~to this question~~.

◆ *P r a c t i c e* *8* **Completing** Fill in each blank in the following sentences with a present-tense verb that agrees with its subject. Avoid *is*, *are*, *was*, and *were*. Cross out the prepositional phrases first. *Answers will vary.*

1. Either lilies or tulips _____ well ~~in the spring~~.
2. Pie and ice cream _____ the best dessert.
3. The ants and flies ~~in the house~~ _____ me.
4. The train and the passengers _____ sometime this evening.
5. Neither the entrees nor the dessert _____ appetizing tonight.

◆ *P r a c t i c e* *9* **Writing Your Own** Write a sentence of your own for each of the following compound subjects. Make sure that your subjects and verbs agree. *Answers will vary.*

1. either the handouts or the manuscript _____

2. brooms and brushes _____

3. neither the nurses nor the doctor _____

4. ham and cheese _____

5. the horse and her foal _____

VERBS BEFORE SUBJECTS

When the subject follows its verb, the subject may be hard to find, which makes the process of agreeing subjects and verbs difficult. Subjects come after verbs in two particular situations—when the sentence begins with *here* or *there* and when a question begins with *Who, What, Where, When, Why,* or *How.* Here are some examples:

Verb Before Subject: Here **are** the **decorations** for the party.

Verb Before Subject: There **is iced tea** in the refrigerator.

In sentences that begin with *here* or *there*, the verb always comes before the subject. Don't forget to cross out prepositional phrases to help you identify the subject. One of the words that's left will be the subject, and then you can check that the verb agrees with it.

$$\overset{v}{} \qquad \overset{s}{}$$

Verb Before Subject: Who **is** that attractive **man** in the blue suit?

$$\overset{v}{} \qquad \overset{s}{} \quad \overset{v}{}$$

Verb Before Subject: Where **are** the valuable **paintings kept?**

$$\overset{v}{} \; \overset{s}{} \; \overset{v}{}$$

Verb Before Subject: When **are you flying** to Rome?

In questions that begin with *Who, What, When, Where, Why,* and *How,* the verb comes before the subject or is split by the subject, as in the last two examples.

REVIEWING VERBS BEFORE SUBJECTS

Where will you find the verb in sentences that begin with here *or* there?

Before the subject
_____

Where will you find the verb in questions that begin with who, what, where, when, why, *and* how?

Before the subject
_____

◈ *P r a c t i c e 1 0* **Identifying** Underline the subject once and the verb twice in each of the following sentences. Cross out the prepositional phrases first.

1. Here <u>lies</u> the <u>cause</u> ~~of the problem despite the evidence~~.

2. Who <u>is</u> the <u>leader</u> ~~of your group~~?

3. How <u>do</u> <u>you</u> <u>feel</u> ~~after your recent operation~~?

4. Where ~~in the world~~ <u>are</u> my <u>keys</u>?

5. There ~~on the table~~ <u>are</u> your <u>books</u>.

◈ *P r a c t i c e 1 1* **Completing** Fill in each blank in the following sentences with a verb that agrees with its subject. Cross out the prepositional phrases first. *Answers will vary.*

1. Where _____ the rest ~~of the apricot pie~~?

2. ~~Over the hill~~, there _____ a great swimming hole.

3. Why _____ their dirty clothes ~~on the bathroom floor~~?

4. How many times _____ your sister asked you to fix that hair dryer?

5. What _____ this mess ~~in the front yard~~?

◈ *P r a c t i c e 1 2* **Writing Your Own** Write a sentence of your own for each of the following words and phrases. Make sure that your subjects and verbs agree. *Answers will vary.*

1. there may be _____

2. what has been _____

3. how did he _____

4. when is _____

5. here is _____

COLLECTIVE NOUNS

Collective nouns name a group of people or things. Examples include such nouns as *army, audience, band, class, committee, crew, crowd, family, flock, gang, jury, majority, minority, orchestra, senate, team,* and *troop.*

Collective nouns can be singular or plural. They are singular when they refer to a group as a single unit. They are plural when they refer to the individual actions or feelings of the group members.

$$\overset{s}{} \qquad \overset{v}{}$$

Singular: The string **quartet performs** three times a year.

Quartet refers to the entire unit or group. Therefore, it requires the singular verb *performs*.

$$\overset{s}{} \qquad \overset{v}{}$$

Plural: The string **quartet get** their new instruments on Monday.

Here *quartet* refers to the individual members, who will each get a new instrument, so the plural verb *get* is used.

REVIEWING COLLECTIVE NOUNS

When is a collective noun singular?

When it refers to a group as a single unit

When is a collective noun plural?

When it refers to the individual actions or feelings of the group members

---

◆ **P r a c t i c e   1 3   Identifying** Underline the correct verb in each of the following sentences. Cross out the prepositional phrases first.

1. The audience (listen, <u>listens</u>) intently ~~to the guest speaker~~.
2. The majority (<u>have</u>, has) voted ~~at different polling booths~~.
3. The orchestra (play, <u>plays</u>) different selections, depending ~~on the concert~~.
4. Our high school cheerleading squad (is, <u>are</u>) all going ~~to different colleges~~.
5. The litter ~~of puppies~~ (get, <u>gets</u>) a bath today.

◆ **P r a c t i c e   1 4   Completing** Fill in each blank in the following sentences with a present-tense verb that agrees with its subject. Cross out the prepositional phrases first. *Answers will vary.*

1. A flock ~~of geese~~ always _____ south ~~for the winter~~.
2. The crew _____ trouble making sure everyone has a good time.
3. The school orchestra _____ this competition every year.

4. The army _____ students who have degrees ~~as officers~~.

5. The senate _____ according ~~to individual beliefs~~.

◆ **P r a c t i c e   1 5**   **Writing Your Own** Write a sentence of your own using each of the following words as a plural subject. Make sure that your subjects and verbs agree. *Answers will vary.*

1. committee _____

2. gang _____

3. class _____

4. minority _____

5. group _____

INDEFINITE PRONOUNS

Indefinite pronouns do not refer to anyone or anything specific. Some indefinite pronouns are always singular, and some are always plural. A few can be either singular or plural, depending on the other words in the sentence. When an indefinite pronoun is the subject of a sentence, the verb must agree with the pronoun. Here is a list of indefinite pronouns.

Indefinite Pronouns

ALWAYS SINGULAR		ALWAYS PLURAL	EITHER SINGULAR OR PLURAL
another	*neither*	*both*	*all*
anybody	*nobody*	*few*	*any*
anyone	*none*	*many*	*more*
anything	*no one*	*others*	*most*
each	*nothing*	*several*	*some*
either	*one*		
everybody	*other*		
everyone	*somebody*		
everything	*someone*		
little	*something*		
much			

Singular: **No one** ever **changes** at work.

Everybody refuses to work harder.

Plural: **Many take** long lunches and **go** home early.

Others stay late but **are** tired and unmotivated.

The pronouns that can be either singular or plural are singular when they refer to singular words and plural when they refer to plural words.

Singular: **Some** of Abby's *day* **was** hectic.

Some is singular because it refers to *day*, which is singular. The singular verb *was* agrees with the singular subject *some*.

Plural: **Some** of Abby's co-*workers* **were** late.

Some is plural because it refers to *co-workers*, which is plural. The plural verb *were* agrees with the plural subject *some*.

REVIEWING INDEFINITE PRONOUNS

What is an indefinite pronoun?

A pronoun that doesn't refer to anyone or anything specific

When are all, any, more, most, *and* some *singular or plural?*

They are singular when they refer to singular words and plural when

they refer to plural words.

♦ **P r a c t i c e   1 6   Identifying** Underline the verb that agrees with its subject in each of the following sentences. Cross out the prepositional phrases first.

1. All ~~of my money~~ (<u>is</u>, are) gone.
2. Both ~~of the pools~~ (was, <u>were</u>) treated ~~with chlorine~~.

3. No one (do, <u>does</u>) more work than she.

4. Something (fly, <u>flies</u>) ~~into my window~~ every night and (buzz, <u>buzzes</u>) ~~around my head.~~

5. Most ~~of Omar's friends~~ (<u>seem</u>, seems) friendly.

◆ **Practice 17** **Completing** Fill in each blank in the following sentences with a present-tense verb that agrees with its subject. Cross out the prepositional phrases first. *Answers will vary.*

1. Most ~~of the people~~ _____ ~~to work in the mornings.~~

2. No one really _____ if he will accept the job.

3. Both _____ the consequences ~~of their actions.~~

4. None ~~of the fake contestants~~ _____ it was a joke.

5. Somebody _____ moving my things ~~off my desk.~~

◆ **Practice 18** **Writing Your Own** Write a sentence of your own using each of the following words as a subject, combined with one of the following verbs: *is, are, was, were.* Make sure that your subjects and verbs agree. *Answers will vary.*

1. anything _____

2. others _____

3. some _____

4. any _____

5. several _____

CHAPTER REVIEW

You might want to review your answers to the questions in all the review boxes before you do the following exercises.

◆ **Review Practice 1** **Identifying** Underline the subject once and the verb twice in each of the following sentences. Cross out the prepositional phrases first. Then put an X to the left of each sentence in which the subject and verb do not agree. Correct the subjects and verbs that don't agree by rewriting the incorrect sentences.

1. __X__ There sit the <u><u>man</u></u> who will be the next president of the United States. *(sits)*

2. __X__ The <u>moon</u> and the <u>stars</u> in the evening sky shines brightly. *(shine)*

3. __X__ The <u>team</u> usually <u>practice</u> off the track every Tuesday. *(practices)*

4. _____ Some of the fish in that tank <u>appear</u> to be sick.

5. _____ Doctor, how <u><u>is</u></u> the <u>patient</u> in room 204?

6. __X__ <u>Something</u> very sharp <u>keep</u> punching me in the back. *(keeps)*

7. __X__ <u>Sour cream and onion</u> <u><u>are</u></u> my favorite type of dip. *(is)*

8. __X__ Here <u>are</u> the <u>recipe</u> from my grandmother. *(is)*

9. __X__ Neither the <u>chairs</u> nor the <u>table</u> <u>match</u> the décor in this room. *(matches)*

10. _____ My <u>gang</u> of artistic friends <u>finds</u> the new trends exciting.

◆ *Review* **P r a c t i c e 2 Completing** Fill in each blank in the following sentences with a present-tense verb that agrees with its subject. *Answers will vary.*

1. My gang _____ late for the show.

2. Neither wind nor rain nor snow _____ us from going outside.

3. Here _____ where Eugene's great-grandmother built her first house.

4. Several of the guests _____ the secret code to the room back stage.

5. None of the water _____ safe for drinking.

6. Where _____ the tourists go for information about hotels?

7. Nothing _____ to be wrong with the car.

8. The track team _____ 5 miles every day, regardless of the weather.

9. Steven's mother and father _____ planning a vacation to Paris.

10. There in that apartment building _____ my former high school principal.

◈ *Review **P r a c t i c e** 3* **Writing Your Own** Write a paragraph explaining why you did or did not join a committee, team, or other group. Make sure that your subjects and verbs agree. *Answers will vary.*

◈ *Review **P r a c t i c e** 4* **Editing Through Collaboration** Exchange paragraphs from Review Practice 3 with another student, and do the following: *Answers will vary.*

1. Underline the subject once in each sentence.
2. Underline the verbs twice.
3. Put an X by any verbs that do not agree with their subjects.

Then return the paper to its writer, and use the information in this chapter to correct any subject-verb agreement errors in your own paragraph. Record your errors on the Error Log in Appendix 6.

MORE ON VERBS

☑ CHECKLIST for Correcting Tense and Voice Problems

> ✔ Are verb tenses consistent?
> ✔ Are sentences written in the active voice?

Test Yourself

Label each sentence I if the verb tenses are inconsistent or P if it uses the passive voice.

- _____ George raced across the field and the ball was caught.
- _____ The old record was broken by Justin.
- _____ That painting was done by a famous artist.
- _____ In the future, we may live on Mars, and we have produced our food in greenhouses.
- _____ First, the baker prepares the dough, and then she will cut out the cookies.

(Answers are in Appendix 4.)

Verbs communicate the action and time of each sentence. So it is important that you use verb tense consistently. Also, you should strive to write in the active, not the passive, voice. This chapter provides help with both of these sentence skills.

CONSISTENT VERB TENSE

Verb tense refers to the time an action takes place—in the present, the past, or the future. The verb tenses in a sentence should be consistent. That is,

TEACHING MORE ON VERBS

Create a short paragraph with inconsistent tenses. You might use words like "today" and "yesterday" to help create confusion. For example, "I am studying today for the hardest final I have ever taken. I had been studying for over two weeks, and I still will not feel like I'm prepared. The test was given tomorrow."

Have students rewrite the paragraph three times, once for each tense: past, present, and future. Make sure they adjust all words to indicate the correct time (for example, use "today" with the present and "yesterday" with the past).

INSTRUCTOR'S
RESOURCE MANUAL
For more sample
paragraphs, for more
exercises, and for
quizzes, see the
*Instructor's Resource
Manual*, Section II,
Part V.

if you start out using one tense, you should not switch tenses unless absolutely necessary. Switching tenses can be confusing. Here are some examples:

                                             Present   Present

Inconsistent: When the sun **sinks** into the bay and the moon **rises**

                                             Past

from behind the trees, the pelicans **flew** away to the south.

                                             Present   Present

Consistent: When the sun **sinks** into the bay and the moon **rises**

                                             Present

from behind the trees, the pelicans **fly** away to the south.

                                             Past   Present

Inconsistent: They **skidded** off the road yesterday when the rain **is** heavy.

                                             Past

Consistent: They **skidded** off the road yesterday when the rain

                                             Past

was heavy.

                                             Future

Inconsistent: My brother **will receive** his degree in June, and then

                                             Present

he **moves** to Boston.

                                             Future

Consistent: My brother **will receive** his degree in June, and then

                                             Future

he **will move** to Boston.

REVIEWING CONSISTENT VERB TENSES

Why should verb tenses be consistent?

Because time should be consistent within a sentence

> **What problem do inconsistent verb tenses create?**
>
> *Inconsistent verb tenses can be confusing for the reader.*

◆ **P r a c t i c e   1 A   Identifying** In the following sentences, write C if the verb tense is consistent or I if it is inconsistent.

1. ___I___ Scott walked to the store and buy some milk.

2. ___I___ Last evening, Charles waited at the park for his friends, but they never make it.

3. ___I___ According to the instructor, we will need to bring a change of clothes, and we have to get all of our medical records updated.

4. ___I___ They grilled fresh fish over the fire and sleep under the stars.

5. ___C___ The salesclerk was rude to me, yet I thanked her anyway.

◆ **P r a c t i c e   1 B   Correcting** Correct the verb tense errors in Practice 1A by rewriting the inconsistent sentences. *Answers will vary.*

◆ **P r a c t i c e   2   Completing** Fill in each blank in the following sentences with consistent verbs. *Answers will vary.*

1. During Kendra's vacation, she _____ along the beach and _____ souvenirs for her friends and family.

2. Out of the box _____ the cat, and then he _____ under the table.

3. Oh, no, I _____ to bring the decorations for the prom, and I _____ the invitations sitting on my kitchen counter.

4. Actors and singers generally _____ a lot of media coverage and _____ featured on many special television shows.

5. Madonna's music and videos _____ many people, but her loyal fans _____ her.

◆ **P r a c t i c e   3   Writing Your Own** Write five sentences of your own with at least two verbs in each. Make sure your tenses are consistent. *Answers will vary.*

USING THE ACTIVE VOICE

In the **active voice,** the subject performs the action. In the **passive voice,** the subject receives the action. Compare the following two examples:

Passive Voice: The mayor **was accused** of stealing **by the police.**

Active Voice: **The police accused** the mayor of stealing.

The active voice adds energy to your writing. Here is another example. Notice the difference between active and passive.

Passive Voice: **The cake was baked** for Tim's birthday **by my grandmother.**

Active Voice: **My grandmother baked the cake** for Tim's birthday.

REVIEWING ACTIVE AND PASSIVE VOICE

What is the difference between the active and passive voice?

In the active voice, the subject performs the action. In the passive voice,

the subject receives the action.

Why is the active voice usually better than the passive?

It adds energy to your writing.

◆ *Practice 4A*   **Identifying** Write A if the sentence is in the active voice and P if it is in the passive voice.

1. ___A___ The astronauts landed on the moon and planted a flag.

2. ___P___ Flowers are being sent to the funeral home.

3. ___A___ Jordan hit the ball over the fence into the neighbor's yard.

4. ___P___ The experimental medicines were shipped to the laboratory for further testing.

5. ___P___ People who heckle the politicians will be escorted from the building.

◆ *Practice 4B*   **Correcting** Rewrite the passive sentences in Practice 4A in the active voice. *Answers will vary.*

◆ **P r a c t i c e 5 Completing** Complete the following sentences in the active voice. *Answers will vary.*

1. Many boxes of clothes ————————————————.

2. A can of hairspray ————————————————.

3. A plate of food ————————————————.

4. The boy's ball ————————————————.

5. The trip ————————————————.

◆ **P r a c t i c e 6 Writing Your Own** Write five sentences in the passive voice. Then rewrite them in the active voice. *Answers will vary.*

CHAPTER REVIEW

You might want to reread your answers to the questions in all the review boxes before you do the following exercises.

◆ **Review P r a c t i c e 1 Identifying** Label each sentence I if the verb tenses are inconsistent, P if it is in the passive voice, or C if it is correct. Then correct the inconsistent and passive sentences by rewriting them. *Answers will vary.*

1. __C__ You should pick up the trash in the yard.

2. __I__ The yacht keeps listing to the left and will need to be fixed before anyone can board her.

3. __P__ The ornaments sitting above the fireplace were given to my grandmother by famous people and were some of her favorite belongings.

4. __I__ Tomorrow, you and I will go to the lake and fished for trout.

5. __I__ I drank the Sprite and eat all the cookies.

6. __I__ Ken wished he had remembered his girlfriend's birthday and prays that she will forgive him.

7. __P__ The wad of gum was placed under the desk by a naughty boy.

8. __P__ The piano is played by Jeannie, and the songs are sung by Mark.

9. __P__ Your purchases will be sent to you later this week.

10. __C__ Caring individuals think of others before themselves and perform unselfish acts.

◈ **Review P r a c t i c e 2**   **Completing** Fill in each blank with consistent, active verbs. *Answers will vary.*

1. Mike _____ the house on time but _____ stuck in traffic.

2. I _____ the hot coffee too quickly and _____ my tongue.

3. The pebble in my shoe _____ my foot, so I _____ down.

4. The bird _____ out the window and _____ south.

5. Clare still _____ in the Easter Bunny, but then she _____ only 3 years old.

◈ **Review P r a c t i c e 3**   **Writing Your Own** Write a paragraph about a recent, difficult decision you have made. Be sure to give the reasons for your decision. Keep your tenses consistent, and use the active voice. *Answers will vary.*

◈ **Review P r a c t i c e 4**   **Editing Through Collaboration** Exchange paragraphs from Review Practice 3 with another student, and do the following: *Answers will vary.*

1. Circle all verbs that are not consistent in tense.

2. Underline any verbs in the passive voice.

Then return the paper to its writer, and use the information in this chapter to correct any verb consistency or voice errors in your own paragraph. Record your errors on the Error Log in Appendix 6.

UNIT TESTS

Here are some exercises that test your understanding of all the material in this unit: Regular and Irregular Verbs, Verb Tense, Subject-Verb Agreement, and More on Verbs (Consistent/Inconsistent and Active/Passive).

Unit Test I

A. Underline all the verb errors in the following sentences.

1. Dennis has <u>set</u> in that chair for so long that his legs <u>has</u> gone numb. *(sat) (have)*
2. My grandparents in New England <u>likes</u> to sit on the front porch in the summer time. *(like)*
3. Parents with small children <u>finds</u> it hard to spend quiet time together. *(find)*
4. The car is broken; it <u>need</u> a new starter. *(needs)*
5. You have <u>sank</u> the golf ball. *(sunk)*
6. Mr. and Mrs. Titus have <u>spoke</u> to the person in charge. *(spoken)*
7. I <u>type</u> that report a couple of weeks ago and <u>hope</u> my employer liked it. *(typed) (hoped)*
8. Last year, we <u>watch</u> the Fourth of July fireworks from our house. *(watched)*
9. Neither the steak nor the hamburgers <u>needs</u> seasoning on the grill. *(need)*
10. She <u>grow</u> tulips every spring. *(grows)*
11. I love to <u>lay</u> in the sun while listening to music. *(lie)*
12. We <u>be</u> having so much fun that we <u>doesn't</u> want to go home. *(are) (don't)*
13. Since there are no vacancies at the hotel, we <u>has</u> nowhere to go. *(have)*
14. <u>The water was spilled on the floor by you.</u> *(You spilled water on the floor.)*
15. Mrs. Turner always <u>smile</u> whenever she sees me. *(smiles)*
16. Your tuition and parking fee <u>is</u> due at the beginning of school. *(are)*
17. There <u>go</u> my dog down the street again. *(goes)*
18. The police crew routinely <u>stop</u> drivers on the road to test for drunk driving. *(stops)*
19. Everything always <u>go</u> wrong on Friday the thirteenth. *(goes)*
20. When the surf breaks through the reef, it gushes into our backyard and <u>flooded</u> the deck. *(floods)*

B. Correct the verb errors in Part A by rewriting each incorrect sentence.

Unit Test II

A. Underline the verb errors in the following paragraph.

Every child *want* a hobby growing up. Not every child *be* inter-

[*wants*]

ested in playing sports or singing, but most children *likes* activities

[*is*]

[*like*]

that *interested* them. Children should not just *set* around after

[*interest*]

[*sit*]

school. Kids *are allowed* by hobbies to express themselves freely. This

[*Hobbies allow kids*]

help them develop social skills, and it *do* a lot for their self-

[*helps*]

[*does*]

confidence. Hobbies *kept* them occupied with productive activities.

[*keep*]

Hobbies have also *connect* many kids with caring adults, who then

[*connected*]

encourage them at their hobbies. Adults also *has* kids set fun goals for

[*have*]

themselves. Kids *are kept* occupied and out of trouble by hobbies.

[*Hobbies keep kids*]

B. Correct the verb errors in Part A by rewriting the paragraph.

PRONOUN PROBLEMS

CHAPTER 41

 CHECKLIST for Using Pronouns

> ✔ Are all subject pronouns used correctly?
> ✔ Are all object pronouns used correctly?
> ✔ Are all possessive pronouns used correctly?
> ✔ Are pronouns used in *than* or *as* comparisons in the correct form?
> ✔ Are the pronouns *this*, *that*, *these*, and *those* used correctly?

Test Yourself

Correct the pronoun errors in the following sentences.

- The ball was their's to begin with.
- Tom told Valerie and I the most exciting story.
- James can type a lot faster than me.
- Those there running shoes are Kim's.
- Me and Julio are going to the movies tonight.

(Answers are in Appendix 4.)

Pronouns are words that take the place of nouns. They help us avoid repeating nouns. In this chapter, we'll discuss five types of pronoun problems: (1) using the wrong pronoun as a subject, (2) using the wrong pronoun as an object, (3) using an apostrophe with a possessive pronoun, (4) misusing pronouns in comparisons, and (5) misusing demonstrative pronouns.

TEACHING PRONOUN PROBLEMS

Divide students into groups of three or four, and provide them with a paragraph that has several pronoun errors. Here is an example:

Mine brother can be so selfish. He has difficulty sharing. He believes that these here books are only to be read by he or that them there clothes are only for he to wear. He was always more selfish than me. I always loved to share my stuff with others. You would not even believe he had the same parents as me because him is so selfish. I hope someday someone teaches him about the art of sharing.

Ask students to correct all the pronoun errors in the paragraph.

The first group to correct all the pronoun errors wins.

INSTRUCTOR'S
RESOURCE MANUAL

For more sample
paragraphs, for more
exercises, and for
quizzes, see the
*Instructor's Resource
Manual,* Section II,
Part V.

PRONOUNS AS SUBJECTS

Single pronouns as subjects usually don't cause problems.

Subject Pronoun: **I** attended the opera with my aunt and uncle.

Subject Pronoun: **They** relocated to New York.

You wouldn't say "*Me* attended the game" or "*Them* went to Los Angeles." But an error often occurs when a sentence has a compound subject and one or more of the subjects is a pronoun.

NOT   **The boys and us** competed all the time.

Correct: **The boys and we** competed all the time.

NOT   **Her and me** decided to go to Paris.

Correct: **She and I** decided to go to Paris.

To test whether you have used the correct form of the pronoun in a compound subject, try each subject alone.

Subject Pronoun?   **The boys and us** competed for the trophy.

Test: **The boys** competed for the trophy. **YES**

Test: **Us** competed for the trophy. **NO**

Test: **We** competed for the trophy. **YES**

Correction: **The boys and we** competed for the trophy.

Here is a list of subject pronouns.

Subject Pronouns

Singular	Plural
I	*we*
you	*you*
he, she, it	*they*

REVIEWING PRONOUNS AS SUBJECTS

Name two subject pronouns.

Answers will include two of the following: I, you, he, she, it, we, or they.

> *How can you test whether you are using the correct pronoun as the subject of a sentence?*
>
> Try each subject separately in its sentence.

◆ **P r a c t i c e 1 Identifying** Underline the pronouns used as subjects in each of the following sentences.

1. Diane and <u>he</u> will be gone for at least a week.
2. <u>He</u> is going to have to work faster if <u>he</u> wants to meet the deadline.
3. "<u>I</u> really don't want to go," <u>he</u> said.
4. <u>We</u> cannot use the elevator because <u>it</u> is not working.
5. <u>She</u> and <u>I</u> have been best friends since <u>I</u> can remember.

◆ **P r a c t i c e 2 Completing** Fill in each blank in the following paragraph with a subject pronoun.

      At first, my friends had me convinced that (1) ___*I*___ should go on the annual deep-sea fishing trip. (2) ___*They*___ spoke on and on about how much fun the last trip was. But before long, Brian admitted that (3) ___*he*___ got sick once the boat was out at sea. Then Misty explained how the captain of the boat cut off the heads of the fish and gutted them. (4) ___*She*___ found the whole process exciting. (5) ___*You*___ can just imagine my reaction! I don't think I'll be joining my friends on their fishing trip.

◆ **P r a c t i c e 3 Writing Your Own** Write a sentence of your own for each of the following subject pronouns. *Answers will vary.*

1. they ——————————————————————————

2. you ——————————————————————————

3. he ——————————————————————————

4. it ——————————————————————————

5. I ——————————————————————————

PRONOUNS AS OBJECTS

One of the most frequent pronoun errors is using a subject pronoun when the sentence calls for an object pronoun. The sentence may require an object after a verb, showing that someone or something receives the action of the verb. Or it may be an object of a preposition that is required (see page 514 for a list of prepositions).

NOT   She gave **Kenisha and I** some money.
Correct: She gave **Kenisha and me** some money.

NOT   The secret is between **you and I.**
Correct: The secret is between **you and me.**

Like the subject pronoun error, the object pronoun error usually occurs with compound objects. Also like the subject pronoun error, you can test whether you are using the correct pronoun by using each object separately.

Object Pronoun?   She gave **Kenisha and I** some money.
Test: She gave **Kenisha** some money. **YES**
Test: She gave **I** some money. **NO**
Test: She gave **me** some money. **YES**
Correction: She gave **Kenisha and me** some money.

Here is a list of object pronouns:

Object Pronouns

Singular	Plural
me	*us*
you	*you*
him, her, it	*them*

REVIEWING PRONOUNS AS OBJECTS

In what two places are pronouns used as objects?

After a verb and after a preposition

How can you test whether you have used the correct pronoun as the object in a sentence?

Try each object separately in its sentence.

◆ **P r a c t i c e 4 Identifying** Underline the correct object pronoun in each of the following sentences.

1. Natalie's grandmother raised (her, she) since she was 5.
2. The wonderful neighbors welcomed (we, us) to the community with a cake.
3. Corrina accidentally sprayed my sister and (I, me) with the hose.
4. All are going on the trip except for you and (him, he).
5. For (her, she), I will sit through this awful movie.

◆ **P r a c t i c e 5 Completing** Fill in each blank in the following sentences with an object pronoun. *Answers will vary.*

1. Between the two of _____, we should be able to fix the problem.
2. He asked you and _____ to the same dance.
3. Unlike _____, I am going to take emergency gear on this hiking trip.
4. According to you and _____, the test will take one hour.
5. The priest took _____ on a tour of the temple.

◆ **P r a c t i c e 6 Writing Your Own** Write a sentence of your own for each of the following object pronouns. *Answers will vary.*

1. us _____

2. him _____

3. me _____

4. them _____

5. her _____

POSSESSIVE PRONOUNS

Possessive pronouns show ownership (*my house*, *her baseball*, *our family*). (See pages 508–509 for a list of pronouns.) An apostrophe is used with nouns to show ownership (*Jack's dog, the farmer's tractor, the people's opinions*). But an apostrophe is never used with possessive pronouns.

Possessive Pronouns

Singular	Plural
my, mine	our, ours
your, yours	you, yours
his, her, hers	their, theirs

NOT   That house is **their's.**
Correct: That house is **theirs.**

NOT   The book on the table is **your's.**
Correct: The book on the table is **yours.**

NOT   The dog chased **it's** tail.
Correct: The dog chased **its** tail.

REVIEWING POSSESSIVE PRONOUNS

When do you use an apostrophe with a noun?

An apostrophe is used to show ownership with a noun.

Do possessive pronouns take apostrophes?

No, possessive pronouns never take apostrophes.

◆ *P r a c t i c e 7* **Identifying** Underline the correct possessive pronoun in each of the following sentences.

1. The computer needs <u>its</u> monitor fixed.
2. Both of <u>my</u> aunts live in New Mexico.

3. That piece of cake on the counter is <u>hers</u>.

4. The children left <u>their</u> toys in the driveway.

5. Hey! That was <u>his</u>.

♦ **P r a c t i c e 8** **Completing** Fill in each blank in the following sentences with a possessive pronoun. *Answers will vary.*

1. These books aren't _____, so they must be _____.

2. _____ dogs bothered the neighbors so much that we had to move.

3. The filming crew left _____ equipment on the set.

4. Look at John's dog carrying _____ bowl in his mouth.

5. The copy machine won't work because _____ ink cartridge is empty.

♦ **P r a c t i c e 9** **Writing Your Own** Write a sentence of your own for each of the following possessive pronouns. *Answers will vary.*

1. mine _____

2. theirs _____

3. his _____

4. its _____

5. our _____

PRONOUNS IN COMPARISONS

Sometimes pronoun problems occur in comparisons with *than* or *as*. An object pronoun may be mistakenly used instead of a subject pronoun. To find out if you are using the right pronoun, you should finish the sentence as shown here.

NOT   She can analyze poems better than **me.**

Correct: She can analyze poems better than **I** [can analyze poems].

NOT   Lilly is not as good a piano player as **him.**

Correct: Lilly is not as good a piano player as **he** [is].

Hint: Sometimes an object pronoun is required in a *than* or *as* comparison. But errors rarely occur in this case because the subject pronoun sounds so unnatural.

NOT   Kay dislikes him more than she dislikes **I.**

Correct: Kay dislikes him more than she dislikes **me.**

REVIEWING PRONOUNS IN COMPARISONS

What causes pronoun problems in comparisons?

Problems can occur when an object pronoun is mistakenly used instead

of a subject pronoun.

How can you test whether to use a subject pronoun or an object pronoun in a than *or as* comparison?

Finish the sentence to test whether to use a subject pronoun or an

object pronoun.

P r a c t i c e 1 0 **Identifying** Underline the correct pronoun in each of the following comparisons.

1. Mark is much neater than (I, me).
2. Cindy, the head majorette at our high school, can twirl a baton as well as (we, us).
3. Simone is not as talented an artist as (him, he).
4. Those other puppies are much fatter than (they, them).
5. Carlos is just as happy as (she, her).

P r a c t i c e 1 1 **Completing** Fill in each blank in the following sentences with an appropriate pronoun for comparison. *Answers will vary.*

1. After he appeared in *Star Wars*, Harrison Ford became a bigger star than

   _____ .

2. Joey can throw a ball as far as _____.

3. My friends managed to stay longer in the haunted house than _____ did.

4. He makes you just as mad as he makes _____.

5. Julia, whose parents are well-known artists, is a more talented painter than _____.

◆ *P r a c t i c e 1 2* **Writing Your Own** Write a sentence of your own using each of the following pronouns in *than* or *as* comparisons. *Answers will vary.*

1. I _____

2. she _____

3. they _____

4. we _____

5. he _____

DEMONSTRATIVE PRONOUNS

There are four demonstrative pronouns: *this, that, these,* and *those.* **Demonstrative pronouns** point to specific people or objects. Use *this* and *these* to refer to items that are near and *that* and *those* to refer to items farther away. Look at the following examples.

Demonstrative (near):	**This** is my room.
Demonstrative (near):	**These** are yesterday's notes.
Demonstrative (farther):	**That** is the town hall.
Demonstrative (farther):	**Those** are the cheerleaders for the other team.

Sometimes demonstrative pronouns are not used correctly.

	Incorrect	**Correct**
NOT	this here, that there	this, that
NOT	these here, these ones	these
NOT	them, those there, those ones	those

NOT	**Them** are the clothes she bought.
Correct:	**Those** are the clothes she bought.

NOT	I'd like to have **these here** books.
Correct:	I'd like to have **these** books.

NOT	I found **those ones** in the attic.
Correct:	I found **those** in the attic.

NOT	**Those there** are the ones I like.
Correct:	**Those** are the ones I like.

When demonstrative pronouns are used with nouns, they become adjectives.

Pronoun:	**That** is mine.
Adjective:	**That computer** is hers.

Pronoun:	**Those** are actions you may regret.
Adjective:	You may regret **those actions.**

The problems that occur with demonstrative pronouns can also occur when these pronouns act as adjectives.

NOT	Please give me **that there** paper.
Correct:	Please give me **that** paper.

Reviewing Demonstrative Pronouns
....

Name the four demonstrative pronouns.

　　this　　　　　*that*　　　　　*these*　　　　*those*
_____ _____ _____ _____

Give two examples of errors with demonstrative pronouns.

Students should use two from this here, that there, them, these here,

these ones, those there, and those ones.

◆ **P r a c t i c e 1 3 A**   **Identifying** Underline the demonstrative pronoun errors in each of the following sentences.

1. The babies usually play with <u>those there</u> toys. *(those)*

2. <u>This here</u> test is just too difficult. *(This)*

3. I believe <u>that there</u> pair of shoes will do nicely for this outfit. *(that)*

4. <u>These ones</u> should be brought in out of the rain. *(These)*

5. I can carry <u>this here</u> if you'll take <u>that there</u>. *(this, that)*

◆ **P r a c t i c e 1 3 B**   **Correcting** Correct the demonstrative pronoun errors in Practice 13A by rewriting the incorrect sentences. *See Practice 13A.*

◆ **P r a c t i c e 1 4**   **Completing** Fill in each blank in the following sentences with a logical demonstrative pronoun. *Answers will vary.*

1. _____ are the skates he wanted.

2. Would you like _____ curtains for your house?

3. _____ Corvette belongs to my uncle.

4. She baked _____ cookies herself.

5. I want _____ for my bathroom.

◆ **P r a c t i c e 1 5**   **Writing Your Own** Write four sentences of your own, one using each demonstrative pronoun. Be sure you don't use these pronouns as adjectives in your sentences. *Answers will vary.*

CHAPTER REVIEW

You might want to reread your answers to the questions in all the review boxes before you do the following exercises.

◆ ***Review Practice 1*** **Identifying** Underline the pronoun errors in each of the following sentences.

1. The football team and <u>us</u> went out for pizza after the game. *(we)*
2. I think the fish is trying to tell you <u>its'</u> tank needs to be cleaned. *(its)*
3. That secret was supposed to remain between you and <u>I</u>. *(me)*
4. My brother at age 4 was as big as <u>him</u> at age 6. *(he)*
5. <u>These here</u> tarts are the best I've ever tasted. *(These)*
6. Due to the power outage, <u>him and me</u> had dinner by candlelight. *(he and I)*
7. I do believe you are stronger than <u>him</u>. *(he)*
8. <u>Hers'</u> money is already spent even though she started out with $100. *(Her)*
9. One of my high school teachers taught me and <u>she</u> how to fly a plane. *(her)*
10. I know that <u>those there</u> CDs belong to me. *(those)*

◆ ***Review Practice 2*** **Completing** Correct the pronoun errors in Review Practice 1 by rewriting the incorrect sentences. *See Review Practice 1.*

◆ ***Review Practice 3*** **Writing Your Own** Write a short paragraph about your most treasured object. Why is it one of your favorite possessions? *Answers will vary.*

◆ ***Review Practice 4*** **Editing Through Collaboration** Exchange paragraphs from Review Practice 3 with another student, and do the following: *Answers will vary.*

1. Circle all pronouns.
2. Check that all the subject and object pronouns are used correctly. Also check that possessive pronouns, pronouns used in comparisons, and demonstrative pronouns are used correctly. Put an X through any that are not in the correct form.

Then return the paper to its writer, and use the information in this chapter to correct the pronoun errors in your own paragraph. Record your errors on the Error Log in Appendix 6.

PRONOUN REFERENCE AND POINT OF VIEW

✔️ CHECKLIST for Correcting Problems with Pronoun Reference and Point of View

> ✔ Does every pronoun have a clear antecedent?
>
> ✔ Are pronouns as close as possible to the words they refer to?
>
> ✔ Do you maintain a single point of view?

Test Yourself

Underline the pronouns in these sentences. Then put an X over any pronouns that are confusing or unclear.

- It says to schedule your own appointments.
- Millie and Tanya were planning to go to Las Vegas, but her car broke.
- I created a backup plan because you should always be prepared for the unexpected.
- You know they are covering up evidence of alien beings.
- Jimmy forgot the answer to questions 1 and 10, but he remembered it the next day.

(Answers are in Appendix 4.)

Anytime you use a pronoun, it must clearly refer to a specific word in the sentence. The word it refers to is called its **antecedent.** Two kinds of problems occur with pronoun references: The antecedent may be unclear, or the antecedent may be missing altogether. You should also be careful to stick to the same point of view in your writing. If, for example, you start out talking about "I," you should not shift to "you" in the middle of the sentence.

TEACHING PRONOUN REFERENCE AND POINT OF VIEW
Provide students with a series of pictures that have a unique point of view. Ask them to study each picture to guess who they think might have taken the picture and from what point of view (for example, a young woman, trying to show the beauty of a father and child).

After the students have analyzed a few pictures, have them change their positions about who they think took the picture and what his or her point of view might be. Shifting their opinions will probably be difficult.

Point out to students that this kind of difficulty occurs when students shift point of view in their sentences or don't provide a reference for readers when using pronouns. Readers will experience the same

619

type of confusion when pronoun reference and point of view shift unnecessarily or are unclear.

INSTRUCTOR'S RESOURCE MANUAL

For more exercises and for quizzes, see the *Instructor's Resource Manual*, Section II, Part V.

PRONOUN REFERENCE

Sometimes a sentence is confusing because the reader can't tell what a pronoun is referring to. The confusion may occur because the pronoun's antecedent is unclear or is completely missing.

Unclear Antecedents

In the following examples, the word each pronoun is referring to is unclear.

Unclear:	A bucket and an oar lay in the boat. As Rachel reached for **it,** the boat moved. (Was Rachel reaching for *the bucket* or *the oar*? Only Rachel knows for sure.)
Clear:	A bucket and an oar lay in the boat. As Rachel reached for **the bucket,** the boat moved.
Clear:	A bucket and an oar lay in the boat. As Rachel reached for **the oar,** the boat moved.
Unclear:	Michael told Oliver that **he** should change jobs. (Does *he* refer to *Michael* or *Oliver*? Only the writer knows.)
Clear:	Michael told Oliver that **Oliver** should change jobs.
Clear:	Talking with Oliver, **Michael** said that **he** should change jobs.

How can you be sure that every pronoun you use has a clear antecedent? First, you can proofread carefully. Probably an even better test, though, is to ask a friend to read what you have written and tell you if your meaning is clear or not.

Missing Antecedents

Every pronoun should have a clear antecedent, the word it refers to. But what happens when there is no antecedent at all? The writer's message is not communicated. Two words in particular should alert you to the possibility of missing antecedents: *it* and *they.*

The following sentences have missing antecedents:

Missing Antecedent:	In a recent political poll, **it** shows that most people consider their votes unimportant. (What does *it* refer to? It has no antecedent.)

Clear:	A **recent political poll** shows that most people consider their votes unimportant.
Missing Antecedent:	**They** say that a fool and his money are soon parted. (Who is *they*?)
Clear:	**An old saying** states that a fool and his money are soon parted.

REVIEWING PRONOUN REFERENCE

What is an antecedent?

The word a pronoun refers to

How can you be sure every pronoun you use has a clear antecedent?

Proofread carefully, and ask a friend to read your writing and tell you

if your meaning is unclear.

What two words warn you that an antecedent may be missing?

it   they

◆ ***Practice   1A*** **Identifying** Underline the pronouns in each of the following sentences. Then put an X next to any sentences with missing or unclear antecedents.

1. ___X___ According to recent surveys, <u>it</u> says that more people are getting a college education.

2. ___X___ <u>My</u> red pen should be in <u>my</u> purse, but <u>I</u> can't find <u>it</u>.

3. _____ The sitting room must have <u>its</u> baseboards cleaned.

4. ___X___ Talking with Kesha and Mindy, <u>I</u> learned that <u>she</u> is moving to Texas!

5. ___X___ <u>They</u> say <u>you</u> can catch more flies with honey than with vinegar.

◆ ***Practice   1B*** **Correcting** Correct the sentences with pronoun errors in Practice 1A by rewriting them. *Answers will vary.*

P r a c t i c e 2 **Completing** Correct the unclear or missing pronoun references in the following sentences by rewriting them. Pronouns that should be corrected are underlined. *Answers will vary.*

1. <u>It</u> says that we are all required to be at the meeting.
2. <u>They</u> always told me to treat people the way I want to be treated.
3. According to Sue and Hanna, <u>she</u> has been accepted into Yale.
4. We have chocolate and vanilla ice cream, but <u>it</u> tastes better.
5. <u>It</u> indicates that we should have turned left at the first light.

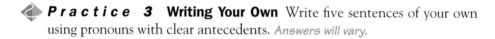 ***P r a c t i c e 3*** **Writing Your Own** Write five sentences of your own using pronouns with clear antecedents. *Answers will vary.*

SHIFTING POINT OF VIEW

Point of view refers to whether a statement is made in the first person, the second person, or the third person. Each person—or point of view—requires different pronouns. The following chart lists the pronouns for each point of view.

Point of View

First Person:	*I, we*
Second Person:	*you, you*
Third Person:	*he, she, it, they*

If you begin writing from one point of view, you should stay in that point of view. Do not shift to another point of view. For example, if you start out writing "I," you should continue with "I" and not shift to "you." Shifting point of view is a very common error in college writing.

Shift: If a **person** doesn't study, **you** will not do well in school.

Correct: If a **person** doesn't study, **he or she** will not do well in school.

Shift: I changed jobs because **you** have more opportunities here.

Correct: I changed jobs because **I** have more opportunities here.

> REVIEWING POINT OF VIEW
>
> *What is point of view?*
>
> *Point of view refers to whether a statement is made in the first,*
>
> *second, or third person.*
>
> *What does it mean to shift point of view?*
>
> *A shift occurs when a writer begins in one person and changes to another.*

◆ *P r a c t i c e **4 A**   **Identifying** Underline the pronouns that shift in point of view in the following sentences.

1. If you don't eat a good diet, <u>they</u> may find <u>their</u> health suffering. *(you, your)*
2. One can always find unique merchandise at the more exclusive stores, but <u>you</u> have to be willing to pay the price. *(one has)*
3. I hinted that I didn't want to take part in the play, but <u>you</u> never know if <u>you</u>'ve gotten the message across. *(I, I've)*
4. I see a couple of concerts a year because <u>everyone</u> needs a little culture in <u>his</u> or <u>her</u> life. *(I need, my)*
5. I've already started writing my research paper because <u>you</u> should never wait until the last minute. *(I)*

◆ *P r a c t i c e **4 B**   **Correcting** Correct the point-of-view errors in Practice 4A by rewriting the incorrect sentences. *See Practice 4A. Answers may vary.*

◆ *P r a c t i c e **5**   **Completing** Complete the following sentences with pronouns that stay in the same point of view.

1. I decided to pack lightly and carry my luggage on board the airplane, so _____*I*_____ know my luggage will arrive when I do.
2. I should taste these dishes since _____*I*_____ never know if I'm going to like them until I try them.
3. A person is expected to follow the rules of the road; otherwise, ___*he or she*___ may cause an accident.

4. I always wear a smile on my face since ___*I*___ never know who might be around.

5. One should pay attention; then ___*one*___ might not feel so confused.

◆ *P r a c t i c e 6* **Writing Your Own** Write a sentence of your own for each of the following pronouns. Be sure the pronouns have clear antecedents and do not shift point of view. *Answers will vary.*

1. they _____

2. you _____

3. I _____

4. it _____

5. we _____

CHAPTER REVIEW

You might want to reread your answers to the questions in all the review boxes before you do the following exercises.

◆ *Review P r a c t i c e 1* **Identifying** Label the following sentences U if the antecedent is unclear, M if the antecedent is missing, or S if the sentence shifts point of view. Then correct the pronoun errors by rewriting the incorrect sentences.

1. ___*S*___ If one forgets the answer, then you should look it up.

2. ___*M*___ They say you should never accept rides from strangers.

3. ___*U*___ Janie bought milk, bread, cheese, and lettuce at the grocery store, but she left it in the car.

4. ___*S*___ A person should always look both ways before crossing the street; otherwise, you might get hit by a car.

5. ___*U*___ Stacy and Myra have already left for the show, but she forgot her wallet.

6. ___*M*___ It explains that the majority of the citizens are in favor of the proposed freeway.

7. ___*S*___ I asked my friends about my decision because you always value your friends' advice.

8. ___M___ It pointed out that "every cloud has a silver lining."

9. ___U___ Steven told Jason that he was going to be late.

10. ___U___ I ordered two pairs of jeans, a pair of shorts, and a pair of shoes from a catalog. I received it one week later.

◆ **Review P r a c t i c e 2 Completing** Correct the pronoun errors in the following sentences by rewriting each incorrect sentence. *Answers will vary.*

1. I am going to purchase the most expensive champagne I can find, for you know that will impress the guests.

2. According to this announcement, it says we need to arrive no later than 2:00 p.m.

3. Jake and Dean will probably get into good colleges, even though he has a higher GPA.

4. A person should manage time wisely since you only have 24 hours in a day.

5. They are always carrying on about how bad the humidity is in the South.

6. Before Carla and Trisha left town, she bought a new swimsuit.

7. We were gossiping about Jarrett and Jeremy when he walked right by us.

8. One should study for the test if you want to pass it.

9. I had my hands full with a squirming puppy and a hissing cat until I decided to set him down.

10. You know what they say: "Never go to bed with a wet head."

◆ **Review P r a c t i c e 3 Writing Your Own** Write a paragraph about a new experience you have had. Include at least six different pronouns. *Answers will vary.*

◆ **Review P r a c t i c e 4 Editing Through Collaboration** Exchange paragraphs from Review Practice 3 with another student, and do the following: *Answers will vary.*

1. Underline all pronouns.

2. Draw arrows to the words they modify.

3. Put an X through any pronouns that do not refer to a clear antecedent or that shift point of view.

Then return the paper to its writer, and use the information in this chapter to correct any pronoun reference and point-of-view errors in your own paragraph. Record your errors on the Error Log in Appendix 6.

PRONOUN AGREEMENT

✅ CHECKLIST for Correcting Pronoun Agreement Problems

> ✔ Do all pronouns and their antecedents agree in number (singular or plural)?
>
> ✔ Do any pronouns that refer to indefinite pronouns agree in number?
>
> ✔ Are any pronouns used in a sexist way?

TEACHING PRONOUN AGREEMENT
Create two sets of index cards: one of musical performers (made from pictures cut out of magazines) and another of personal pronouns. The performer cards should have pictures of both single performers and groups. Divide the students into small groups, and divide the performer cards evenly among the groups.

Provide sentences on the board, and ask teams to identify pronoun antecedent errors in the sentences. When a team gets an answer correct, give it a random pronoun card. The team should then match the pronoun card with a performer card (for example, a "her" card could go with Faith Hill or Madonna, a "their" card with Aerosmith or 'N Sync).

Test Yourself

Underline the pronoun in each sentence, and draw an arrow to its antecedent. Put an X over any pronouns that do not agree with their antecedents.

- Somebody left his lights on in his car.
- A judge must put aside her bias.
- Each of the children needs their permission slip signed.
- None of the fans could keep their voices quiet.
- A motorcyclist must take care of her gear.

(Answers are in Appendix 4.)

As you learned in Chapter 35, subjects and verbs must agree for clear communication. If the subject is singular, the verb must be singular; if the subject is plural, the verb must be plural. The same holds true for pronouns and the words they refer to—their *antecedents*. They must agree in number—both singular or both plural. Usually, pronoun agreement is not a problem, as these sentences show:

Singular:	**Dr. Gomez** told **his** patient to stop smoking.
Plural:	**Carlos** and **Gina** took **their** children to Disney World.

INDEFINITE PRONOUNS

The first team to correctly match all their performer cards with pronoun cards wins.

Pronoun agreement may become a problem with indefinite pronouns. Indefinite pronouns that are always singular give writers the most trouble.

NOT	**One** of the students finished **their** test early. (How many students finished early? Only one, so use a singular pronoun.)
Correct:	**One** of the students finished **her** test early.
Correct:	**One** of the students finished **his** test early.

INSTRUCTOR'S RESOURCE MANUAL

For sample sentences, for more exercises and for quizzes, see the *Instructor's Resource Manual*, Section II, Part V.

NOT	**Somebody** just drove **their** new car into a ditch. (How many people just drove a car into a ditch? One person, so use a singular pronoun.)
Correct:	**Somebody** just drove **her** new car into a ditch.
Correct:	**Somebody** just drove **his** new car into a ditch.

Here is a list of indefinite pronouns that are always singular.

Singular Indefinite Pronouns

another	everybody	neither	one
anybody	everyone	nobody	other
anyone	everything	none	somebody
anything	little	no one	someone
each	much	nothing	something
either			

Hint: A few indefinite pronouns can be either singular or plural, depending on their meaning in the sentence. These pronouns are *any, all, more, most,* and *some.*

Singular:	**Some** of the money was left over, so we gave **it** to charity.
Plural:	**Some** of the donations were left over, so we gave **them** to charity.

In the first sentence, *money* is singular, so the singular pronoun *it* is used. In the second sentence, *donations* is plural, so the plural pronoun *them* is used.

REVIEWING INDEFINITE PRONOUNS

Why should a pronoun agree with the word it refers to?

To communicate clearly

Name five indefinite pronouns that are always singular. Answers will vary.

_____ _____ _____ _____ _____

◆ **P r a c t i c e 1 Identifying** Underline the correct pronoun from the choices in parentheses, and be prepared to explain your choices.

1. All of the infants had (his or her, <u>their</u>) footprints and handprints recorded at the hospital.
2. None of the cars needs (<u>its</u>, their) tires changed.
3. Anyone can get (<u>his or her</u>, their) high school diploma.
4. Before anybody can join the club, (<u>he or she</u>, they) must fill out an enrollment form.
5. The farmers and the farmworkers need (his or her, <u>their</u>) work hours shortened.

◆ **P r a c t i c e 2 Completing** Fill in each blank in the following sentences with a pronoun that agrees with its antecedent.

1. Fabiola and Fabian asked _____*their*_____ questions at the same time.
2. Everyone should listen more closely to ____*his or her*____ teacher.
3. Matt lost ____*his*____ backpack at the park.
4. Someone who could do a thing like that should have ____*his or her*____ head examined.
5. Something in the car leaked all ____*its*____ fluids onto the driveway.

◆ **P r a c t i c e 3 Writing Your Own** Write a sentence of your own for each of the following pronouns. Answers will vary.

1. none _____

2. other _____

3. no one _____

4. everything _____

5. someone _____

AVOIDING SEXISM

In the first section of this chapter, you learned that you should use singular pronouns to refer to singular indefinite pronouns. For example, the indefinite pronoun *someone* requires a singular pronoun, *his* or *her*, not the plural *their*. But what if you don't know whether the person referred to is male or female? Then you have a choice: (1) you can say "he or she" or "his or her"; (2) you can make the sentence plural; or (3) you can rewrite the sentence to avoid the problem altogether. What you should not do is ignore half the population by referring to all humans as males.

NOT   If **anyone** wants to go, **they** are welcome to do so.

NOT   If **anyone** wants to go, **he** is welcome to do so.

Correct: If **anyone** wants to go, **he or she** is welcome to do so.

Correct: **People** who want to go are welcome to do so.

NOT   **Everyone** remembered to bring **their** lunch.

NOT   **Everyone** remembered to bring **his** lunch.

Correct: **Everyone** remembered to bring **his or her** lunch.

Correct: **All** the students remembered to bring **their** lunch.

Sexism in writing can also occur in ways other than with indefinite pronouns. We often assume that doctors, lawyers, and bank presidents are men and that nurses, schoolteachers, and secretaries are women. But that is not very accurate.

NOT   Ask a **fireman** if **he** thinks the wiring is safe.
(Why automatically assume that the person fighting fires is a male instead of a female?)

Correct: Ask a **firefighter** if **he or she** thinks the wiring is safe.

NOT   The **mailman** delivered my neighbor's mail to my house by mistake.
(Since both men and women deliver mail, the more correct term is *mail carrier.*)

Correct: The **mail carrier** delivered my neighbor's mail to my house by mistake.

NOT An **assistant** cannot reveal **her** boss's confidential business.
(Why leave the men who are assistants out of this sentence?)

Correct: An **assistant** cannot reveal **his or her** boss's confidential business.

Correct: **Assistants** cannot reveal **their** boss's confidential business.

REVIEWING SEXISM IN WRITING

What is sexism in writing?

  Assuming that the people in a group are all male or all female

What are two ways to get around the problem of using male pronouns to refer to both women and men?

  Use he or she   *Make the sentence plural*

Give two other examples of sexism in writing. Examples will vary.

◆ *P r a c t i c e 4 A* **Identifying** Underline the sexist references in the following sentences.

1. The chairperson should keep <u>his</u> board informed of new developments. *(his or her)*
2. A nurse gives <u>her</u> time and patience freely. *(his or her)*
3. Each person is responsible for make–up work if <u>they</u> miss an assignment. *(he or she misses)*
4. Everybody must bring food if <u>they</u> plan to eat. *(he or she plans)*
5. A good sailor knows <u>his</u> knots. *(his or her)*

◆ *P r a c t i c e 4 B* **Correcting** Correct the sexist pronouns in Practice 4A by rewriting the incorrect sentences. *See Practice 4A.*

◆ *P r a c t i c e 5* **Completing** Fill in each blank in the following sentences with an appropriate pronoun.

1. A technician might become frustrated with ____*his or her*____ job.
2. A hairdresser who attracts celebrity customers can name ____*his or her*____ price.
3. An accountant needs help with ____*his or her*____ accounts.
4. Somebody wrote ____*his or her*____ phone number on the bathroom wall.
5. Another child has forgotten ____*his or her*____ lunch.

◆ **P r a c t i c e 6 Writing Your Own** Write a sentence of your own for each of the following antecedents. Include at least one pronoun in each sentence. *Answers will vary.*

1. doctor _____

2. politician _____

3. police officer _____

4. spokesperson _____

5. FBI agent _____

CHAPTER REVIEW

You might want to reread your answers to the questions in all the review boxes before you do the following exercises.

◆ *Review P r a c t i c e **1** **Identifying** Underline and correct the pronoun errors in the following sentences.

1. Anyone who wants <u>their</u> book signed should stand in this line. *(his or her)*
2. A good assistant keeps <u>her</u> dictionary within easy reach. *(his or her)*
3. A surfer can lose <u>his</u> wave. *(his or her)*
4. Only one of the contestants turned in <u>their</u> enrollment form on time. *(his or her)*
5. The politician who cares about <u>his</u> people will win the election. *(his or her)*
6. Each of the photographers has <u>their</u> own camera. *(his or her)*
7. Everyone needs <u>their</u> funny bone tickled every now and then. *(his or her)*
8. A tattoo artist should always clean <u>her</u> equipment before each new client. *(his or her)*

9. A teacher should always ask <u>her</u> students if they understand the assignment. *(his or her)*

10. Someone that messy should clean <u>their</u> room more often. *(his or her)*

◆ **Review Practice 2** **Completing** Fill in each blank in the following sentences with an appropriate pronoun.

1. Neither of the criminals wanted _____*his or her*_____ picture taken.

2. A racecar driver depends on _____*his or her*_____ car and skill to win the race.

3. A housecleaner brings _____*his or her*_____ own supplies.

4. Each of the boys can do _____*his*_____ own work.

5. None of the students wanted to disappoint _____*his or her*_____ teacher.

6. At the reunion, everyone talked to _____*his or her*_____ friends.

7. Another person left _____*his or her*_____ homework behind.

8. Somebody needs to water _____*his or her*_____ lawn.

9. Everyone should be nice to _____*his or her*_____ neighbors.

10. Nobody should park _____*his or her*_____ car in a no-parking zone.

◆ **Review Practice 3** **Writing Your Own** Write a paragraph describing your favorite type of music. Why is it your favorite? *Answers will vary.*

◆ **Review Practice 4** **Editing Through Collaboration** Exchange paragraphs from Review Practice 3 with another student, and do the following: *Answers will vary.*

1. Underline any pronouns.

2. Circle any pronouns that do not agree with the words they refer to.

Then return the paper to its writer, and use the information in this chapter to correct any pronoun agreement errors in your own paragraph. Record your errors on the Error Log in Appendix 6.

UNIT TESTS

Here are some exercises that test your understanding of all the material in this unit: Pronoun Problems, Pronoun Reference and Point of View, and Pronoun Agreement.

Unit Test I

A. Underline the pronoun errors in the following sentences.

1. Of all the science entries, we thought <u>ours'</u> was the best. *(ours)*

2. I do not talk as much as <u>him</u>. *(he)*

3. Each of the girls needs to have <u>their</u> hair cut. *(her)*

4. These clothes are too outrageous to be mine; they must be <u>yours'</u>. *(yours)*

5. A parent needs to pick up <u>her</u> child from school. *(his or her)*

6. No one should harm <u>their</u> body. *(his or her)*

7. During the earthquake, <u>those there</u> shelves shook loose. *(those)*

8. Brenda can sew better than <u>me</u>. *(I)*

9. Emma and Candace have gone to the beach for the weekend, but <u>she</u> is going to have to return home sooner than expected. *(Answers will vary.)*

10. With a bit more practice, you will be just as good at these video games as <u>them</u>. *(they)*

11. Between Olga and Valerie, <u>she</u> should be able to finish the work on time. *(Answers will vary.)*

12. <u>You</u> try to be nice to strangers because we never know when we might need help. *(We)*

13. A body can only take on so much before <u>you</u> suffer from stress. *(it suffers)*

14. You can always seek help from the counselors if <u>someone</u> has questions. *(you)*

15. Neither of the doctors could diagnose <u>their</u> patient's illness. *(his or her)*

16. I realize that she sings better than <u>him</u>. *(he)*

17. Most of the stories need <u>its</u> titles rewritten. *(their)*

18. <u>These here</u> mosquitoes are about to drive me crazy. *(These)*

19. Another person must have left <u>his</u> books in class. *(his or her)*

20. At least one nurse forgot <u>her</u> uniform. *(his or her)*

B. Correct the pronoun errors in Part A by rewriting each incorrect sentence.

Unit Test II

A. Underline the pronoun errors in the following paragraph.

Many scientists say that soft music helps calm people's nerves. Some school officials are beginning to play soft music for <u>his or her</u> *[their]* students at the beginning of the day and after lunch to calm them down. The scientists' studies show that if a person sits down and listens to soft, relaxing music for at least five minutes every day, <u>they</u> *[he or she]* can reduce <u>your</u> *[his or her]* heart rate and lower <u>your</u> *[his or her]* blood pressure. For a person who has heart problems, <u>this here</u> *[this]* is a good way to supplement <u>their</u> *[his or her]* medical care. Scientists have studied <u>it</u> *[this problem]* for a long time, so people should be as wise as <u>them</u> *[they]* and follow <u>his or her</u> *[their]* advice. <u>This</u> *[This idea]* will benefit <u>them</u> *[people]* greatly.

B. Correct the pronoun errors in Part A by rewriting the paragraph.

ADJECTIVES

✅ CHECKLIST for Using Adjectives Correctly

> ✔ Are all adjectives that show comparison used correctly?
> ✔ Are the forms of *good* and *bad* used correctly?

Test Yourself

Underline the adjectives in the following sentences. Then put an X over the adjectives that are used incorrectly.

- The kites were very colorful.
- She has the worstest hair color that I have ever seen.
- We were more busier this week than last week.
- He is the oldest of the two brothers.
- The Ford Mustang is more better than the Nissan Sentra.

(Answers are in Appendix 4.)

Adjectives are modifiers. They help us communicate more clearly (I have a *green* car; I want a *red* one) and vividly (the movie was *funny* and *romantic*). Without adjectives, our language would be drab and boring.

USING ADJECTIVES

Adjectives are words that modify—or describe—nouns or pronouns. Adjectives often tell how something or someone looks: *dark, light, tall, short, large, small.* Most adjectives come before the words they modify, but with linking verbs (such as *is, are, look, become,* and *feel*), adjectives follow the words they modify.

INSTRUCTOR'S
RESOURCE MANUAL
For more sample
sentences, for more
exercises, and for
quizzes, see the
*Instructor's Resources
Manual*, Section II,
Part V.

Adjectives Before a Noun: We felt the **cold, icy** snow.

Adjectives After a Linking Verb: The snow was **cold** and **icy**.

REVIEWING ADJECTIVES

What are adjectives?

Adjectives modify or describe nouns or pronouns.

Where can you find adjectives in a sentence?

Before a noun or pronoun or after a linking verb

◆ **P r a c t i c e 1   Identifying** In the following sentences, underline the adjectives, and circle the words they modify.

1. Michael left a shiny red apple on the wooden desk on Monday morning.
2. Mrs. Johnson gave the 2-year-old boy a piece of hard candy.
3. Our family doctor wants us to come in for our annual checkups.
4. I read a great book by John Grisham last week.
5. Grandma's beautiful garden is a quiet place for me to read, draw, or take a quick nap.

◆ **P r a c t i c e 2   Completing** Fill in each blank in the following sentences with logical adjectives. *Answers will vary.*

During my (1) _____ year of high school, I asked the head cheerleader to go to the prom with me. I was (2) _____ when she agreed to be my date, and I really wanted to impress her. I rented an expensive tuxedo, bought a (3) _____ corsage for her to wear on her wrist, and made sure to pick her up on time. The (4) _____ price was worth it because when we arrived at the dance, all of my buddies patted me on the back and said, "You two look (5) _____ together!"

◆ **P r a c t i c e 3   Writing Your Own** Write a sentence of your own for each of the following adjectives. *Answers will vary.*

1. curious _____

2. durable _____

3. thirteen _____

4. helpful _____

5. short-tempered _____

COMPARING WITH ADJECTIVES

Most adjectives have three forms: a **basic** form, a **comparative** form (used to compare two items or indicate a greater degree), and a **superlative** form (used to compare three or more items or indicate the greatest degree).

For positive comparisons, adjectives form the comparative and superlative in two different ways.

1. For one-syllable adjectives and some two-syllable adjectives, use *-er* to compare two items and *-est* to compare three or more items.

Basic	Comparative (used to compare two items)	Superlative (used to compare three or more items)
bold	bolder	boldest
warm	warmer	warmest
foggy	foggier	foggiest
cozy	cozier	coziest

2. For some two-syllable adjectives and all longer adjectives, use *more* to compare two items and *most* to compare three or more items.

Basic	Comparative (used to compare two items)	Superlative (used to compare three or more items)
friendly	more friendly	most friendly
peaceful	more peaceful	most peaceful
wonderful	more wonderful	most wonderful
appropriate	more appropriate	most appropriate

For negative comparisons, use *less* to compare two items and *least* to compare three or more items.

Basic	Comparative (used to compare two items)	Superlative (used to compare three or more items)
loud	less loud	least loud
funny	less funny	least funny
popular	less popular	least popular

Hint: Some adjectives are not usually compared. For example, one person cannot be "more dead" than another. Here are some more examples.

broken	*final*	*square*
empty	*impossible*	*supreme*
equal	*singular*	*unanimous*

REVIEWING ADJECTIVE FORMS

When do you use the comparative form of an adjective?

To compare two items

When do you use the superlative form of an adjective?

To compare three or more items

How do one-syllable and some two-syllable adjectives form the comparative and superlative in positive comparisons?

Add -er for the comparative and -est for the superlative.

How do some two-syllable adjectives and all longer adjectives form the comparative and superlative in positive comparisons?

With more and most

How do you form negative comparisons?

With less and least

◆ *P r a c t i c e* **4** **Identifying** Underline the adjectives, and note whether they are basic (B), comparative (C), or superlative (S).

1. ___S___ The most logical decision would be to appoint Sam to the position.

2. ___B___ Today the students showed how dedicated they can be.

3. ___C___ Mita was happier about the engagement than her father was.

4. ___S___ The strongest students always score the highest on the exam.

5. ___C___ The food Nora and Richard ate on vacation was less healthy than what they eat at home.

◆ *P r a c t i c e* **5** **Completing** Fill in each blank in the following paragraph with the correct comparative or superlative form of the adjective in parentheses.

One summer afternoon, I was hiking high in the mountains when the sky above me grew suddenly (1) ____darker____ (dark) than I have ever seen it. It looked like rain was going to fall soon, and I happened to be in an (2) ____unsheltered____ (unsheltered) place on the mountain. I looked around to find the (3) ____most suitable____ (suitable) tree to sit under, but there weren't any that would protect me. Even the (4) ____thickest____ (thick) tree was very puny and wouldn't keep the rain off of my head. Quickly, I realized I had no option but to run (5) ____faster____ (fast) than the rain to find shelter farther down the hill.

◆ *P r a c t i c e* **6** **Writing Your Own** Write a sentence of your own for each of the following adjectives.

1. a superlative form of *pretty* ____prettiest/least pretty____

2. the basic form of *sensible* ____sensible____

3. a comparative form of *talented* ____more/less talented____

4. a superlative form of *disgusting* ____most/least disgusting____

5. a comparative form of *tall* ____taller/less tall____

COMMON ADJECTIVE ERRORS

Two types of problems occur with adjectives used in comparisons.

1. Instead of using one method for forming the comparative or superlative, both are used. That is, both *-er* and *more* or *less* are used to compare two items or both *-est* and *most* or *least* are used to compare three or more items.

   NOT   My youngest son is **more taller** than his brothers.
   Correct: My youngest son is **taller** than his brothers.

   NOT   This is the **most happiest** day of my life.
   Correct: This is the **happiest** day of my life.

2. The second type of error occurs when the comparative or superlative is used with the wrong number of items. The comparative form should be used for two items and the superlative for three or more items.

   NOT   Marina is the **smartest** of the two sisters.
   Correct: Marina is the **smarter** of the two sisters.

   NOT   History is the **harder** of my three classes this semester.
   Correct: History is the **hardest** of my three classes this semester.

REVIEWING COMMON ADJECTIVE ERRORS

Can you ever use -er + more or -est + most?

No—you can't use both methods of comparison at the same time.

When do you use the comparative form of an adjective?

When comparing two items

When do you use the superlative form of an adjective?

When comparing three or more items

◆ **P r a c t i c e   7 A**   **Identifying** Underline the adjectives in the following sentences that are used incorrectly in comparisons. Mark sentences that are correct C.

1. _____ The *rudest* <u>most rudest</u> customers are usually the ones who are trying to get something for free.

2. _____ Bob and Chad are both good-looking, but Bob is *smarter* <u>smartest</u>.

3. __*C*__ This class would be <u>more fun</u> if we could meet outside sometimes.

4. _____ The *rainiest* <u>most rainiest</u> day of the year was April 15.

5. _____ The *biggest* <u>bigger</u> house in town is at 1859 Pine Street.

◆ **P r a c t i c e   7 B**   **Correcting** Correct the adjective errors in Practice 7A by rewriting the incorrect sentences. *See Practice 7A.*

◆ **P r a c t i c e   8**   **Completing** Choose the correct adjective forms in the following paragraph to complete the sentences.

Giving the dog a bath is the (1) ___*most difficult*___ (more difficult, most difficult) chore in our house, and somehow it always seems to be my job. My sister Stephanie and I share most of the chores, but I am definitely (2) ___*more responsible*___ (more responsible, most responsible) than she is. Usually, I do my chores without complaining, but bathing the dog is just unfair. We have an Australian sheepdog, and he is the (3) ___*clumsiest*___ (clumsiest, most clumsiest) thing alive. He seems to find every puddle of mud and sticky stuff to step in, and it quickly gets all over his fur. Unfortunately, though, he has a great dislike for baths, so the struggle to wash him is (4) ___*trickier*___ (trickiest, trickier) than it should be. And Stephanie is no help at all. While I'm fighting to hose him down, she just stands back and laughs at me, which makes me even (5) ___*madder*___ (madder, more madder).

◆ *P r a c t i c e   9*   **Writing Your Own** Write a sentence of your own for each of the following adjectives. *Answers will vary.*

1. strongest _____

2. more truthful _____

3. most gracious _____

4. larger _____

5. most frightening _____

USING *GOOD* AND *BAD* CORRECTLY

The adjectives *good* and *bad* are irregular. They do not form the comparative and superlative like most other adjectives. Here are the correct forms for these two irregular adjectives:

Basic	Comparative (used to compare two items)	Superlative (used to compare three or more items)
good	better	best
bad	worse	worst

Problems occur with *good* and *bad* when writers don't know how to form their comparative and superlative forms.

NOT   more better, more worse, worser, most best, most worst, bestest, worstest

Correct: better, worse, best, worst

These errors appear in sentences in the following ways:

NOT   That is the **worstest** food I've ever tasted.

Correct: That is the **worst** food I've ever tasted.

NOT   Air pollution is getting **more worse** every year.

Correct: Air pollution is getting **worse** every year.

REVIEWING *Good* AND *Bad*
....

What are the three forms of good?

_____*good*_____   _____*better*_____   _____*best*_____

What are the three forms of bad?

_____*bad*_____   _____*worse*_____   _____*worst*_____

◆ **P r a c t i c e   1 0 A**   **Identifying** In the following sentences, underline the forms of *good* and *bad* used correctly, and circle the forms of *good* and *bad* used incorrectly.

1. Both options are good, but getting a raise is (more better) *better* than getting time off from work.

2. Giving that presentation in my psychology class was the (worstest) *worst* experience of my college career.

3. Giving your time to a charity is (more good) *better* than just giving your money.

4. Sean wanted to go to Princeton, but his grades were worse than he thought.

5. Doing the laundry is (more worse) *worse* than getting a root canal.

◆ **P r a c t i c e   1 0 B**   **Correcting** Correct the errors with *good* and *bad* in Practice 10A by rewriting the incorrect sentences. *See Practice 10A.*

◆ **P r a c t i c e   1 1**   **Completing** Using the correct forms of *good* or *bad*, complete the following paragraph.

The (1) _____*worst*_____ day of my life was July 8, 2001. I remember it (2) _____*better*_____ than any other. I had just bought a brand new convertible and was taking it to the beach for a couple of days of fun in the sun. Fortunately, my (3) _____*best*_____ friend, Tara, was with me, because just 20 miles outside town, the engine of my dream car overheated! What was (4) _____*worse*_____ was neither of us had a cell phone, and the closest pay phone was more than a mile away. We finally found a phone and called another friend, and then we waited and waited for a tow truck. After spending more than $3,000 in repairs, I found that my dream car had become my (5) _____*worst*_____ nightmare.

◆ *P r a c t i c e* **1 2**   **Writing Your Own** Write a sentence of your own for each of the following forms of *good* and *bad*. *Answers will vary.*

1. best _____

2. bad _____

3. worse _____

4. better _____

5. worst _____

CHAPTER REVIEW

You might want to reread your answers to the questions in all the review boxes before you do the following exercises.

◆ *Review P r a c t i c e   1*   **Identifying** Label the following adjectives basic (B), comparative (C), superlative (S), or not able to be compared (X).

1. __*C*__ sillier

2. __*S*__ most ridiculous

3. __*X*__ dead

4. __*B*__ tempting

5. __*C*__ more stubborn

6. __*S*__ meatiest

7. __*S*__ most appealing

8. __*X*__ broken

9. __*B*__ tired

10. __*C*__ lovelier

◆ *Review Practice 2* **Completing** Supply the comparative and superlative forms for each of the following adjectives.

Basic	Comparative	Superlative
1. welcome	*more/less welcome*	*most/least welcome*
2. justifiable	*more/less justifiable*	*most/least justifiable*
3. scary	*scarier, less scary*	*scariest, least scary*
4. kind	*kinder, less kind*	*kindest, least kind*
5. mystical	*more/less mystical*	*most/least mystical*
6. strong	*stronger, less strong*	*strongest, least strong*
7. foolish	*more/less foolish*	*most/least foolish*
8. confusing	*more/less confusing*	*most/least confusing*
9. extraordinary	*more/less extraordinary*	*most/least extraordinary*
10. loving	*more/less loving*	*most/least loving*

◆ *Review Practice 3* **Writing Your Own** Write a paragraph describing the first pet you ever owned. What kind of animal was it? What did it look like? How did it act? What did you name it, and why did you choose that name? *Answers will vary.*

◆ *Review Practice 4* **Editing Through Collaboration** Exchange paragraphs from Review Practice 3 with another student, and do the following: *Answers will vary.*

1. Underline all the adjectives.
2. Circle those that are not in the correct form.

Then return the paper to its writer, and use the information in this chapter to correct any adjective errors in your own paragraph. Record your errors on the Error Log in Appendix 6.

ADVERBS

✔ CHECKLIST for Using Adverbs

> ✔ Are all adverbs that show comparison used correctly?
>
> ✔ Are *good/well* and *bad/badly* used correctly?

TEACHING ADVERBS
Choose a student, and give him or her oral directions, like "walk to the other side of the room." The student should follow the directions.
   Next, add an adverb to the sentence, and have the student again follow directions ("walk *slowly* to the other side of the room").
   Continue changing or adding more adverbs to the directions so that students can see how adverbs affect the meaning of a sentence. Don't forget to add negative as well as positive words to remind students of the full range of adverbs ("do *not* walk to the other side of the room").

Test Yourself

Underline the adverbs in the following sentences. Then put an X over the adverbs that are used incorrectly.

- The pants fit me too loose, so I returned them to the store.
- Tori wasn't never so happy as after she won the lottery.
- When Madeline returned from Paris, she said she had a real good time.
- We happily made more ice cream when our first supply ran out.
- I wanted so bad to win the race, but I couldn't catch up.

(Answers are in Appendix 4.)

Like adjectives, adverbs help us communicate more clearly (she talked *slowly*) and more vividly (he sang *beautifully*). They make their sentences more interesting.

USING ADVERBS

Adverbs modify verbs, adjectives, and other adverbs. They answer the questions *how? when? where? how often?* and *to what extent?* Look at the following examples.

How: My grandfather walked **slowly** up the stairs.

When: Classes **always** begin after Labor Day.

Where: Music lessons are held **here.**

How often: I shop at K-Mart **regularly.**

To what extent: The airport is **extremely** busy during the holidays.

INSTRUCTOR'S
RESOURCE MANUAL
For more sample
sentences, for more
exercises, and for
quizzes, see the
*Instructor's Resource
Manual,* Section II,
Part V.

Some words are always adverbs, including *here, there, not, never, now, again, almost, often,* and *well.*

Other adverbs are formed by adding *-ly* to an adjective:

Adjective	Adverb
dim	dimly
soft	softly
careless	carelessly

Hint: Not all words that end in *-ly* are adverbs. Some, such as *friendly, early, lonely, chilly,* and *lively,* are adjectives.

REVIEWING ADVERBS

What are adverbs?

Adverbs modify verbs, adjectives, and other adverbs.

What five questions do adverbs answer?

How?   When?   Where?   How often?   To what extent?

List four words that are always adverbs.

Answers will vary.

How do many adverbs end?

In –ly

◆ *P r a c t i c e 1*   **Identifying** In the following sentences, underline the adverbs, and circle the words they modify.

1. We drove quickly to Los Angeles so that we wouldn't miss the concert.
2. I never saw that girl again.
3. Dirk suddenly changed his mind and agreed to host the party.
4. Stephen successfully completed the nursing program.
5. When the children became impatient during the drive, we continuously told them, "We're almost there."

◆ **P r a c t i c e 2**   **Completing** Fill in each blank in the following sentences with an adverb that makes sense. *Answers will vary.*

Sam's mom (1) _____ drove him to the airport, where he caught a plane to Houston, Texas. He was going to visit his grandparents (2) _____. Sam was only 10 years old, but he had (3) _____ flown alone before. When the plane landed in Houston, Sam (4) _____ grabbed his carry-on luggage and (5) _____ ran to meet "Papa" and "Nonny."

◆ **P r a c t i c e 3**   **Writing Your Own** Write a sentence of your own for each of the following adverbs. *Answers will vary.*

1. now _____

2. briskly _____

3. innocently _____

4. lazily _____

5. often _____

COMPARING WITH ADVERBS

Like adjectives, most adverbs have three forms: a **basic** form, a **comparative** form (used to compare two items), and a **superlative** form (used to compare three or more items).

For positive comparisons, adverbs form the comparative and superlative forms in two different ways:

1. For one-syllable adverbs, use -*er* to compare two items and -*est* to compare three or more items.

Basic	Comparative (used to compare two items)	Superlative (used to compare three or more items)
soon	sooner	soonest
fast	faster	fastest

2. For adverbs of two or more syllables, use *more* to compare two items and *most* to compare three or more items.

Basic	Comparative (used to compare two items)	Superlative (used to compare three or more items)
strangely	more strangely	most strangely
carefully	more carefully	most carefully
happily	more happily	most happily

For negative comparisons, adverbs, like adjectives, use *less* to compare two items and *least* to compare three or more items.

Basic	Comparative (used to compare two items)	Superlative (used to compare three or more items)
close	less close	least close
quickly	less quickly	least quickly
creatively	less creatively	least creatively

Hint: Like adjectives, certain adverbs are not usually compared. Something cannot last "more eternally" or work "more invisibly." The following adverbs cannot logically be compared.

endlessly	*eternally*	*infinitely*
equally	*impossibly*	*invisibly*

REVIEWING ADVERB FORMS

When do you use the comparative form of an adverb?

To compare two items

When do you use the superlative form of an adverb?

To compare three or more items

How do one-syllable adverbs form the comparative and superlative in positive comparisons?

Add -er for the comparative and -est for the superlative.

How do adverbs of two or more syllables form the comparative and superlative in positive comparisons?

With more and most

How do you form negative comparisons with adverbs?

With less and least

◆ *P r a c t i c e* **4** **Identifying** Underline the adverbs, and note whether they are basic (B), comparative (C), or superlative (S).

1. __C__ When Jack joined the gym, he began to lose weight <u>more quickly</u>.

2. __C__ The sun shone <u>more brightly</u> after the rain stopped.

3. __S__ Valencia is the <u>most rapidly</u> growing city in southern California.

4. __C__ People enroll <u>less often</u> in the morning classes than the afternoon classes.

5. __B__ Priscilla <u>rudely</u> interrupted her mother and walked out of the room.

◆ *P r a c t i c e* **5** **Completing** Fill in each blank in the following paragraph with the correct comparative or superlative form of the adverb in parentheses.

At one time, *Highlights* was the (1) _____*most widely*_____ (widely) read children's magazine. It had (2) _____*more simply*_____ (simply) written stories for the younger readers and (3) _____*more intellectually*_____ (intellectually) challenging games for the older kids than any other magazine. Because of the wide variety of material in each issue, *Highlights* was the (4) _____*most highly*_____ (highly) acclaimed publication for American youth. Now, though, *Highlights* has lots of competition, and big publishers are creating magazines for young readers (5) _____*more often*_____ (often) than they used to.

◆ ***P r a c t i c e 6*** **Writing Your Own** Write a sentence of your own for each of the following adverbs. *Answers will vary.*

1. a superlative form of *readily* _____

2. a comparative form of *eagerly* _____

3. the basic form of *unhappily* _____

4. a superlative form of *angrily* _____

5. a comparative form of *honestly* _____

ADJECTIVE OR ADVERB?

One of the most common errors with modifiers is using an adjective when an adverb is called for. Keep in mind that adjectives modify nouns and pronouns, whereas adverbs modify verbs, adjectives, and other adverbs. Adverbs *do not* modify nouns or pronouns. Here are some examples.

NOT   She spoke too **slow.** [adjective]
Correct: She spoke too **slowly.** [adverb]

NOT   We were **real** sorry about the accident. [adjective]
Correct: We were **really** sorry about the accident. [adverb]

> ### REVIEWING THE DIFFERENCE BETWEEN ADJECTIVES AND ADVERBS
>
> **How do you know whether to use an adjective or an adverb in a sentence?**
>
> *Adjectives modify nouns and pronouns. Adverbs modify verbs,*
>
> *adjectives, and other adverbs.*
>
> **Give an example of an adverb in a sentence.**
>
> *Examples will vary.*
>
> **Give an example of an adjective in a sentence.**
>
> *Examples will vary.*

◆ **P r a c t i c e   7 A   Identifying** Underline the adverbs in the following sentences. Write C next to the sentences that are correct.

1. _____ Adam Sandler's character snored <u>loud</u> in *Little Nicky*. *(loudly)*

2. ___*C*___ I rocked the baby <u>gently</u> to put her to sleep. *(gently)*

3. _____ Mr. Simpson talked <u>too quick</u>, and I didn't understand the assignment. *(quickly)*

4. _____ Before we left the zoo, we checked the map <u>careful</u> to make sure we'd seen everything. *(carefully)*

5. _____ Cook the beans <u>slow</u> so they don't burn. *(slowly)*

◆ **P r a c t i c e   7 B   Correcting** Correct the adverb errors in Practice 7A by rewriting the incorrect sentences. *See Practice 7A.*

◆ **P r a c t i c e   8   Completing** Choose the correct adverb to complete the sentences in the following paragraph.

Zack and I went to Six Flags Magic Mountain last weekend and had a (1) ____*really*____ (real, really) good time. When we pulled into the parking lot, we could hear the roller coasters zooming

(2) ____*loudly*____ (loudly, loud) overhead, and we could smell the yummy junk food. After we got through the gates, we ran (3) ____*quickly*____ (quick, quickly) to the line for the ride Shockwave. The line moved along (4) ____*smoothly*____ (smoothly, smooth), and we were on the ride within 20 minutes. When Shockwave was over, we (5) ____*gladly*____ (glad, gladly) got in line to ride it again.

◆ *P r a c t i c e 9*   **Writing Your Own** Write a sentence of your own for each of the following adverbs.

1. specifically _____

2. tightly _____

3. greatly _____

4. sadly _____

5. coldly _____

DOUBLE NEGATIVES

Another problem that involves adverbs is the **double negative**—using two negative words in one clause. Examples of negative words include *no, not, never, none, nothing, neither, nowhere, nobody, barely,* and *hardly.* A double negative creates the opposite meaning of what is intended.

Double Negative: She **never** had **no** time to rest.

The actual meaning of these double negatives is "She did have time to rest."

Correction: She had **no** time to rest.

Double Negative: My brother does **not** give me **nothing.**

The actual meaning of these double negatives is "My brother does give me something."

Correction: My brother does **not** give me **anything.**

Double negatives often occur with contractions.

Double Negative: There **aren't hardly** any apples left.

The actual meaning of these double negatives is "There are plenty of apples left."

Correction: There are **hardly** any apples left.

Using two negatives is confusing and grammatically wrong. Be on the lookout for negative words, and use only one per clause.

REVIEWING DOUBLE NEGATIVES

What is a double negative?

Using two negative words where one will do

List five negative words.

Answers will vary.

Why should you avoid double negatives?

They convey the opposite meaning of what is intended.

◆ **P r a c t i c e   1 0 A**   **Identifying** Mark each of the following sentences either correct (C) or incorrect (X).

1. ___X___ He didn't never study, but he always passed the tests. (*didn't* never did study)

2. ___X___ Tabitha wasn't hardly 4 years old when her mother passed away. (*wasn't* hardly)

3. ___X___ Nobody showed up for none of the practices last week. (*none* any)

4. ___C___ Hawkins doesn't really know what he wants to do.

5. ___X___ I wouldn't go nowhere with him. (*nowhere* anywhere)

◆ **P r a c t i c e   1 0 B**   **Correcting** Correct the double negatives in Practice 10A by rewriting the incorrect sentences. *See Practice 10A.*

◆ **P r a c t i c e   1 1**   **Completing** Choose the correct negative modifiers to complete the following paragraph.

Last summer, I went to the beach and (1) ___was hardly___ (was hardly, wasn't hardly) prepared for the sunshiny weather. I didn't buy (2) ___any___ (any, no) sunscreen before I left because I had a decent tan already. To my surprise, I started to burn after only three hours on the beach, and there (3) ___wasn't anything___ (wasn't nothing, wasn't anything) I could do about it. I thought the burning feeling wouldn't (4) ___ever___ (ever, never) go away. And no matter what lotions and ointments I put on, I couldn't get (5) ___any___ (no, any) relief. Next time, I'll remember to bring an umbrella.

◆ **P r a c t i c e   1 2**   **Writing Your Own** Write a sentence of your own for each of the following negative adverbs. *Answers will vary.*

1. never _____

2. not _____

3. barely _____

4. nobody _____

5. nowhere _____

USING *GOOD/WELL* AND *BAD/BADLY* CORRECTLY

The pairs *good/well* and *bad/badly* are so frequently misused that they deserve special attention.

Good is an adjective; *well* is an adverb.

Use *good* with a noun (n) or after a linking verb (lv).

                                 n
Adjective: Juan is a **good** boy.

                        lv
Adjective: She looks **good.**

Use *well* for someone's health or after an action verb (av).

                   lv

Adverb: He is **well** again. [health]

                      av

Adverb: The baby sleeps **well** at night.

Bad is an adjective; *badly* is an adverb.
Use *bad* with a noun (n) or after a linking verb (lv). Always use *bad* after *feel* if you're talking about emotions.

                             n

Adjective: He seems like a **bad** person.

                     lv

Adjective: I feel **bad** that I got a ticket.

Use *badly* with an adjective (adj) or after an action verb (av).

                            adj

Adverb: The house was **badly** burned.

                     av

Adverb: He swims **badly.**

REVIEWING *Good/Well* AND *Bad/Badly*

When should you use the adjective good?

With a noun or after a linking verb

When should you use the adverb well?

For someone's health, after an action verb, or after feel for emotions

When should you use the adjective bad?

With a noun or after a linking verb

When should you use the adverb badly?

With an adjective or after an action verb

◆ **P r a c t i c e   1 3 A   Identifying** Label each of the following sentences either correct (C) or incorrect (X).

1. ___X___ I want to do good in this job so my boss will like me. (~~good~~ well)

2. ___X___ My favorite team is playing bad this week. (~~bad~~, badly)

3. ___C___ Vilma sings well and is pursuing a career in opera.

4. ___C___ Rachel said she felt bad about Mr. Brown's accident.

5. ___X___ I wanted so bad to go diving, but I couldn't. (~~bad~~, badly)

◆ **P r a c t i c e   1 3 B   Correcting** Correct the adverb errors in Practice 13A by rewriting the incorrect sentences. *See Practice 13A.*

◆ **P r a c t i c e   1 4   Completing** Choose the correct modifiers to complete the following paragraph.

When Scott was in high school, there was only one thing he could do really (1) _____well_____ (good, well). He struggled with academics, he played most sports very (2) _____badly_____ (bad, badly), and he was never popular with the girls. But his one strength was music. From the moment he picked up his first guitar, he was always (3) _____good_____ (good, well) at creating songs. Fortunately, his natural talent earned him several (4) _____good_____ (good, well) scholarship offers from big-name universities. Unfortunately, his (5) _____bad_____ (bad, badly) study habits in high school made college more difficult for him, but he survived.

◆ **P r a c t i c e   1 5   Writing Your Own** Write a sentence of your own for each of the following modifiers. *Answers will vary.*

1. well _____

2. badly _____

3. good _____

4. bad _____

5. well _____

CHAPTER REVIEW

You might want to reread your answers to the questions in all the review boxes before you do the following exercises.

◆ **Review Practice 1** **Identifying** Underline the correct word in each of the following sentences.

1. Tia and Sue Ann studied together for the midterm, but Tia took notes (<u>more</u>, most) thoroughly.
2. We don't have (no, <u>any</u>) money for rent this month.
3. His speech seemed to go on (<u>endlessly</u>, more endlessly, most endlessly).
4. Of all the teachers at this school, Mrs. Thompson speaks the (more clearly, <u>most clearly</u>).
5. Jose drives (more fast, <u>faster</u>) than I do.
6. During the baseball game, I struck out (<u>less</u>, least) often than Jack did.
7. She plays the flute very (good, <u>well</u>) and is in the orchestra.
8. My senior year in high school, I was voted (less, <u>least</u>) likely to drop out of college.
9. He hurt his knee so (bad, <u>badly</u>), it required medical attention.
10. The children were (real, <u>really</u>) tired after spending the day at the lake.

◆ **Review Practice 2** **Completing** Fill in each blank in the following paragraph with an adverb that makes sense. Try not to use any adverb more than once. *Answers will vary.*

Working as a food server can be very challenging. I take my job (1) _____ than the other servers, so I can (2) _____ count on coming home with better tips. But sometimes there are customers I just can't please, no matter how (3) _____ I want to. Also, there are the minor problems that happen (4) _____, like the kitchen running out of chicken or the bartender forgetting to make the drinks for my table. Because I'm determined to do my job (5) _____, though, my customers like me and keep coming back.

◆ *Review P r a c t i c e   3*   **Writing Your Own** If you could prepare any-thing you wanted for dinner tonight, what would you make? Write a para-graph about this meal. How would you prepare it? How would you serve it? How many courses would it consist of? *Answers will vary.*

◆ *Review P r a c t i c e   4*   **Editing Through Collaboration** Exchange paragraphs from Review Practice 3 with another student, and do the fol-lowing: *Answers will vary.*

1. Underline all the adverbs.

2. Circle those that are not in the correct form.

3. Put an X above any double negatives.

Then return the paper to its writer, and use the information in this chapter to correct any adverb errors in your own paragraph. Record your errors on the Error Log in Appendix 6.

CHAPTER **46**

MODIFIER ERRORS

✓ CHECKLIST for Identifying and Correcting Modifier Problems

TEACHING MODIFIER
ERRORS
Have students get out a
piece of paper and draw
pictures representing
the following sen-
tences: "Picking flow-
ers, my nose became
red and itchy," and "I
chased the dog wearing
my underwear." Collect
the pictures, and point
out to the students that
most of them drew the
pictures incorrectly
(most of them will—
especially for the first
example).
Explain that liter-
ally, the first sentence
says the nose was pick-
ing the flowers and the
second says the dog was
wearing the underwear.
Showing students
how misplaced modi-
fiers change the mean-
ing of sentences can
help them identify their
own modifier errors.

> ✔ Are modifiers as close as possible to the words they modify?
> ✔ Are any sentences confusing because the words that the modifiers refer to are missing?

Test Yourself

Underline the modifier problem in each sentence.

- After studying together, his grades really improved.
- Before doing the laundry, the car needed to be washed.
- To get a good job, the interview must go well.
- The professor told the class he was retiring before he dismissed them.
- I wrote a letter to the newspaper that complained about rising power bills.

(Answers are in Appendix 4.)

As you know, a modifier describes another word or group of words. Sometimes, however, a modifier is too far from the words it refers to (*misplaced modifier*), or the word it refers to is missing altogether (*dangling modifier*). As a result, the sentence is confusing.

MISPLACED MODIFIERS

A modifier should be placed as close as possible to the word or words it modifies, but this does not always happen. A **misplaced modifier** is too far from the word or words it refers to, making the meaning of the sentence unclear. Look at these examples.

INSTRUCTOR'S
RESOURCE MANUAL
For more sample
sentences, for more
exercises, and for
quizzes, see the
*Instructor's Resource
Manual*, Section II,
Part V.

Misplaced: The instructor explained why plagiarism is wrong **on Friday.**

(Is plagiarism wrong only on Friday? Probably not. So the modifier *on Friday* needs to be moved closer to the word it actually modifies.)

Correct: The instructor explained **on Friday** why plagiarism is wrong.

Misplaced: In most states, it is illegal to carry liquor in a car **that has been opened.**

(It is the liquor, not the car, that must not have been opened. So the modifier *that has been opened* needs to be moved closer to the word it modifies.)

Correct: In most states, it is illegal to carry liquor **that has been opened in a car.**

Certain modifiers that limit meaning are often misplaced, causing problems. Look at how meaning changes by moving the limiting word *only* in the following sentences:

Only Aunt Emily says that Lilly was a bad cook.
(Aunt Emily says this, but no one else does.)

Aunt Emily **only** says that Lilly was a bad cook.
(Aunt Emily says this, but she doesn't really mean it.)

Aunt Emily says **only** that Lilly was a bad cook.
(Aunt Emily says this but nothing more.)

Aunt Emily says that **only** Lilly was a bad cook.
(Lilly—and no one else—was a bad cook.)

Aunt Emily says that Lilly **only** was a bad cook.
(Aunt Emily says that there were some who were good cooks and Lilly was the only bad one.)

Aunt Emily says that Lilly was **only** a bad cook.
(Lilly was a bad cook, but she wasn't bad at other things.)

Aunt Emily says that Lilly was a bad cook **only.**
(Lilly was a bad cook, but she wasn't bad at other things.)

Here is a list of common limiting words.

almost	*hardly*	*merely*	*only*
even	*just*	*nearly*	*scarcely*

REVIEWING MISPLACED MODIFIERS

What is a misplaced modifier?

A modifier that is not as close as possible to the word it refers to

How can you correct a misplaced modifier?

Place it as close as possible to the word or words it refers to.

Practice 1A **Identifying** Underline the misplaced modifiers in the following sentences.

1. Tina told Tom that <u>to win the lottery</u> she had a great chance.
2. The car leaked all its oil by the time I called a mechanic <u>in the driveway</u>.
3. Brittany went to the mall with Jim <u>wearing her favorite hat</u>.
4. I sold Luigi my old watch after I bought an expensive new one <u>for $10</u>.
5. We made a pie in the kitchen <u>with lots of blueberries</u>.

Practice 1B **Correcting** Correct the misplaced modifiers in Practice 1A by rewriting the incorrect sentences. *Answers will vary.*

Practice 2 **Completing** Fill in each blank in the following paragraph with a modifier that makes sense. Include at least two phrases.
Answers will vary.

Several years ago, Rodger owned a (1) _____ farm in Kentucky where he grew corn and wheat. He also had (2) _____ orchards of apples that he (3) _____ harvested every September. His children had (4) _____ the farm. Shortly before Rodger died, he trained his children (5) _____ the family business.

◆ *P r a c t i c e* **3** **Writing Your Own** Write a sentence of your own for each of the following modifiers. *Answers will vary.*

1. before summer _____

2. since the company hired him _____

3. while driving to the store _____

4. after she bought the car _____

5. though no one was there _____

DANGLING MODIFIERS

Modifiers are "dangling" when they have nothing to refer to in a sentence. **Dangling modifiers** (starting with an *-ing* word or with *to*) often appear at the beginning of a sentence. Here is an example.

> Dangling: **Reaching the top of the hill,** the view was beautiful.

A modifier usually modifies the words closest to it. So the phrase *Reaching the top of the hill* modifies *view*. But it's not the view that reaches the top of the hill. In fact, there is no logical word in the sentence that the phrase modifies. It is left dangling. You can correct a dangling modifier in one of two ways—by inserting the missing word that is being referred to or by rewriting the sentence.

> Correct: **Reaching the top of the hill,** we saw a beautiful view.
>
> Correct: **When we reached the top of the hill,** the view we saw was beautiful.

> Dangling: **To get into the movie,** an ID must be presented.
>
> Correct: **To get into the movie,** you must present an ID.
>
> Correct: You must present an ID **to get into the movie.**

> Dangling: The garage was empty **after moving the tools.**
>
> Correct: **After moving the tools,** we had an empty garage.
>
> Correct: The garage was empty **after we moved the tools.**

REVIEWING DANGLING MODIFIERS
....

What is a dangling modifier?

A modifier that has nothing to refer to in its sentence

How do you correct a dangling modifier?

By inserting the missing word that is being referred to or by rewriting

the sentence

P r a c t i c e   4 A   **Identifying** Underline the dangling modifiers in the following sentences.

1. To get a good deal, time must be spent comparing prices.
2. Screaming for help, the chair fell over with the little boy in it.
3. As an only daughter with four brothers, there was never enough food in the house.
4. To get a driver's license, two tests must be passed.
5. Giving the dog a bath, the bathroom floor became flooded.

P r a c t i c e   4 B   **Correcting** Correct the dangling modifiers in Practice 4A by rewriting the incorrect sentences. *Answers will vary.*

P r a c t i c e   5   **Completing** Fill in each blank in the following paragraph with a modifier that makes sense. Include at least two phrases.
Answers will vary.

      (1) _____ professional baseball teams begin spring training. The coaches plan on (2) _____ weight lifting and lots of running. Hundreds of (3) _____ athletes begin training each season, but within days, many get cut from the major league teams. These men usually get placed on (4) _____ teams. These men hope to play well throughout the season and (5) _____ move up.

P r a c t i c e   6   **Writing Your Own** Write a sentence of your own for each of the following phrases. *Answers will vary.*

1. warm and bright _____

2. shaking my hand _____

3. to understand the opposite sex _____

4. getting a chance to see the ocean _____

5. to win an argument _____

CHAPTER REVIEW

You might want to reread your answers to the questions in all the review boxes before you do the following exercises.

◆ *Review Practice 1* **Identifying** Underline the modifier errors in the following sentences.

1. <u>Turning in my essay late</u>, my computer crashed.
2. I am flying to Atlanta on Friday and returning Monday <u>to attend a wedding</u>.
3. <u>To make a perfect chocolate dessert</u>, the oven temperature must be carefully watched.
4. I put away my clothes and then called some friends <u>in the closet</u>.
5. <u>Throwing the ball across the room</u>, the lamp fell over and broke.
6. Jennifer complained that she forgot to send out invitations <u>in an angry voice</u>.
7. I found a pressed flower in my Shakespeare textbook <u>from my wedding</u>.
8. <u>Driving to the movie theater</u>, teenagers kept stepping out into the street in front of us.
9. Maria has a picture of her cousins at the beach <u>in her locker</u>.
10. <u>To please your parents</u>, good grades should be earned on every report card.

◆ *Review Practice 2* **Completing** Rewrite the sentences in Review Practice 1 so that the phrases you underlined are as close as possible to the words they modify. *Answers will vary.*

◆ *Review Practice 3* **Writing Your Own** Write a paragraph about your greatest accomplishment. What did you do? How hard did you work for it? What was your reward? *Answers will vary.*

R e v i e w   P r a c t i c e   4   **Editing Through Collaboration** Exchange paragraphs from Review Practice 3 with another student, and do the following: *Answers will vary.*

1. Underline any misplaced modifiers.

2. Put brackets around any dangling modifiers.

Then return the paper to its writer, and use the information in this chapter to correct any modifier problems in your own paragraph. Record your errors on the Error Log in Appendix 6.

UNIT TESTS

Here are some exercises that test your understanding of all the material in this unit: Adjectives, Adverbs, and Modifier Errors.

Unit Test I

A. Underline the modifier errors in the following sentences.

1. During the test, Professor Gupta said we could talk <u>quiet</u> with our lab partners. *quietly*

2. <u>While weeding my flower beds</u>, the snails were all over. *While weeding my flower beds, I saw that*

3. He swam badly during the meet <u>after staying up too late the night before</u>. *After staying up too late the night before, he*

4. Tell your boss that you are <u>more better</u> at your job than he realizes. *better*

5. Pauly didn't get his mother <u>nothing</u> for her birthday. *anything*

6. Curtis got distracted, and his car drifted more <u>sudden</u> than he expected <u>to the center divider</u>. *drifted to the center divider; suddenly.*

7. The pilot flew the jet as if there wasn't <u>nothing</u> to fear. *anything*

8. Turn your paper in at the end of class <u>to your teacher</u>. *Turn your paper in to your teacher*

9. If you do <u>good</u> on the midterm, you don't have to take the final exam. *well*

10. Handle the antiques more <u>gentle</u> than you did this morning because they are fragile. *gently*

11. I heard the <u>most worst</u> pickup line on TV the other day. *worst*

12. Nadia walked <u>proud</u> across the stage at her graduation. *proudly*

13. Anabel tiptoed <u>quiet</u> through the bedroom so she wouldn't wake the baby. *quietly*

14. <u>To avoid writing bad checks</u>, your account balance should be checked often. *To avoid writing bad checks, I*

15. Zena went to Alicia's house to get a cookie recipe <u>next door</u>. *house next door*

16. Dr. Romano told the <u>most funniest</u> jokes while he was examining my broken arm. *funniest*

17. Grandpa <u>can't barely</u> hear anymore. *can barely*

18. Women wore girdles laced up <u>tight</u> <u>to look like they had very small waists</u>. *To look like they had very small waists, women; tightly*

19. When Beth changed the oil in her car, she put the oil cap on too <u>loose</u>, and it fell off. *loosely*

20. The <u>most prepared</u> of the two athletes was Kareem. *more prepared*

B. Correct the modifier errors in Part A by rewriting each incorrect sentence.

Unit Test II

A. Underline the modifier errors in the following paragraph.

    more expensive
Health care in America is getting <u>expensiver</u> every year. Compared to
                                          most
other employers, I think my employer is ~~more~~ realistic about coverage.
To save money
ᴧ<u>Some</u> companies are <u>~~not~~ hardly</u> taking care of their employees ~~to save

money~~; many no longer offer a complete benefits package to full- or part-
                        who work hard
time employees. Many people ᴧ<u>cannot</u> afford <u>~~no~~</u> individual insurance plan~~s~~
on top of their monthly bills ~~who work hard~~. Having to pay for insurance,
people are not purchasing   *quickly*
ᴧeye and dental exams ~~are often not purchased~~. People are <u>quick</u> running out
of options for affordable health care. If employers can't afford to offer their
employees insurance plans, maybe in the future companies can find a <u>~~more~~

better</u> way to accommodate those who work for them.

B. Correct the modifier errors in Part A by rewriting the paragraph.

END PUNCTUATION

✔ CHECKLIST for Using End Punctuation

✔ Does each sentence end with a period, a question mark, or an exclamation point?

✔ Are question marks used when asking questions?

✔ Do sentences that exclaim end with exclamation points?

TEACHING END PUNCTUATION

Distribute a lively, animated paragraph with the end punctuation taken out. Read the paragraph aloud to the class to show how dull the paragraph is without the punctuation.

Then hand out the paragraph with the punctuation inserted, and ask three or four students to read the paragraph with a lot of enthusiasm. This shows students how end punctuation defines parameters, but it also demonstrates the variety with which people express punctuation marks.

INSTRUCTOR'S RESOURCE MANUAL

For sample paragraphs, for more exercises, and for quizzes, see the *Instructor's Resource Manual*, Section II, Part V.

Test Yourself

Add the appropriate end punctuation to the following sentences.

• How are we going to get there

• That's amazing

• Get me a Pepsi, please

• This will never happen to me

• Can you make your own dinner tonight

(Answers are in Appendix 4.)

End punctuation signals the end of a sentence in three ways: The period ends a statement, the question mark signals a question, and the exclamation point marks an exclamation.

PERIOD

1. A period is used with statements, mild commands, and indirect questions.

    Statement: The boy rode to school on the bus.

    Command: Ride the bus to school today.

Indirect Question: I asked him why he rode the bus to school today.

2. A period is also used with abbreviations and numbers.

Abbreviations: Mr. Johnson lives at 9 Kings Rd., next door to Dr. Tina Lopez.

Numbers: $16.95   4.5 $876.98   .066

REVIEWING PERIODS

What are the three main uses of a period?

To mark the end of statements, mild comments, and indirect questions

What are two other uses of a period?

With abbreviations and numbers

◆ *P r a c t i c e 1* **Identifying** In the following sentences, circle the periods used incorrectly, and add those that are missing.

1. Walt is buying the house on the corner of Sonora Ave. and Eureka St.
2. I bought a new computer monitor for $210.0.0.
3. Mr. Bernard just married Ms. Walters.
4. Tara's dentist is named Dr. Jones, and his office is on 4th. St.
5. Bring your child to the library on the corner of Jackson Drive. and Lovejoy Pl.

◆ *P r a c t i c e 2* **Completing** Add periods to the following paragraph where they are needed.

    Jane Seymour is a very talented actress who stars in a TV series called *Dr. Quinn, Medicine Woman.* Ms. Seymour also has twin boys who are in grade school, and she wrote a book about her experience mothering twins. Her husband is very supportive of her acting and writing activities. He helps with the children and even offered quotes for her book. The book sells for about $20.50 and is published by St. Martin's Press.

◆ *P r a c t i c e 3* **Writing Your Own** Write a sentence of your own for each of the following descriptions. *Answers will vary.*

1. a statement about cooking
2. a statement including a dollar amount
3. a statement including an address with an abbreviated street name
4. an indirect question about a psychology midterm
5. a command to do a household chore

QUESTION MARK

The question mark is used after a direct question.

Question Mark: Do you have homework to do?

Question Mark: "Can you get your homework done on time?" her mother asked.

REVIEWING QUESTION MARKS

What is the main role of a question mark?

To indicate that a question is being asked

Give an example of a question.

Examples will vary.

 P r a c t i c e 4 Identifying In the following sentences, circle the question marks used incorrectly, and add those that are needed.

1. Did you buy that jacket only last week.*?*
2. I wonder when the party starts*?*
3. Stephanie said, "Are you wearing my watch?" *no changes*
4. Tina asked Whit how he was feeling*?*
5. This is my biggest concern: How are we going to protect the rain forests.*?*

P r a c t i c e 5 Completing Add question marks to the following paragraph where they are needed.

What are the three most important things to remember about writing.*?*First, choose topics that you are interested in. Why should you write about something that bores you. ?Second, remember that writing is a process. Should you ever turn in your first draft. ?No way. Writing gets better and better the more drafts you write. Third, give yourself plenty of time for editing and revision. Don't you think it's better that you catch the errors before your instructor does. ?Writing will be less of a chore if you remember these things and apply them to each assignment.

◆ *P r a c t i c e   6*   **Writing Your Own** Write a sentence of your own for each of the following descriptions. *Answers will vary.*

1. a direct question about driving _____

2. an indirect question about your favorite sport _____

3. a direct question about a family member _____

4. an indirect question about the next major holiday _____

5. a direct question about lunch _____

EXCLAMATION POINT

The exclamation point indicates strong feeling.

   If it is used too often, it is not as effective as it could be. You shouldn't use more than one exclamation point at a time.

Exclamation Point:	Never!
Exclamation Point:	You don't mean it!
Exclamation Point:	Take your hands off me or I'll scream!
Exclamation Point:	"You scared me to death!" she said.

REVIEWING EXCLAMATION POINTS

What is the main use of an exclamation point?

To show strong emotion _____

Give an example of an exclamation.

Examples will vary. _____

◆ *P r a c t i c e*   *7*   **Identifying** Circle the punctuation used incorrectly, and add those that are needed.

1. That's outrageous⊙!

2. I can't believe it⊙!

3. He said① "Great job, Julian!"

4. You can't mean that②!

5. "Don't hurt my baby⊙!" yelled the mother.

◆ *P r a c t i c e*   *8*   **Completing** Add exclamation points to the following paragraph where they are appropriate.

> Paintball is my favorite pastime, and I play every weekend. It's so much fun./Last Saturday, Steve and Jay were on one team, and Tim and I were on another. Within an hour, Tim and I cornered Jay and took him out. "Pop./Pop.'/ But suddenly, Steve came around a tree and pointed his paintball gun right at Tim.
> "Duck,/" I yelled.
> Tim quickly hit the ground, but it was too late. "Pop./Pop.'/
> "Yeah,/" Steve yelled as he hit Tim right in the chest with paintballs.
> But I was even quicker. "Pop.'/ One shot and Steve had red paint right in the middle of his stomach.
> "Last remaining survivor again,/" I screamed in delight.

◆ *P r a c t i c e*   *9*   **Writing Your Own** Write five sentences of your own using exclamation points correctly. *Answers will vary.*

CHAPTER REVIEW

You might want to reread your answers to the questions in all the review boxes before you do the following exercises.

◆ *Review P r a c t i c e*   *1*   **Identifying** For each sentence, add the correct end punctuation.

1. Do you have any tattoos?

2. Stop lying to me.

3. Are you sure you can help me?

4. No! Not yet!

5. Is there a problem with this software*?*

6. Sometimes I think I'll never graduate*.*

7. My cousin wants to know if we're going to leave soon*.*

8. Take the keys to my car*.*

9. That's impossible*!*

10. You should study tomorrow while you're off work*.*

◆ *Review Practice 2* **Completing** Turn sentences 1–5 into questions and sentences 6–10 into exclamations.

1. The plumber came today. *Did the plumber come today?*

2. The Jets are going to win the Super Bowl. *Are the Jets going to win the Super Bowl?*

3. Delores made the afghan. *Did Delores make the afghan?*

4. You are going to be my date. *Are you going to be my date?*

5. The baby hasn't been fed yet. *Has the baby been fed yet?*

6. Don't forget to do the dishes. *!*

7. We have ten minutes to get on the plane. *!*

8. Are you serious? *You're serious!*

9. I don't want to tell you. *!*

10. This is a great day. *!*

◆ *Review Practice 3* **Writing Your Own** Write a paragraph about an emotional experience or event in your life. Was it exciting, happy, sad, disappointing, frustrating, or challenging? What happened? Who was involved? Include all three types of end punctuation—period, question mark, and exclamation point. *Answers will vary.*

◆ *Review Practice 4* **Editing Through Collaboration** Exchange paragraphs from Review Practice 3 with another student, and do the following: *Answers will vary.*

1. Circle any errors in end punctuation.

2. Suggest the correct punctuation above your circle.

Then return the paragraph to its writer, and use the information in this chapter to correct any end punctuation errors in your own paragraph. Record your errors on the Error Log in Appendix 6.

COMMAS

✔ CHECKLIST for Using Commas

- ✔ Are commas used to separate items in a series?
- ✔ Are commas used to set off introductory material?
- ✔ Is there a comma before *and, but, for, nor, or, so,* and *yet* when they are followed by an independent clause?
- ✔ Are commas used to set off interrupting material in a sentence?
- ✔ Are commas used to set off direct quotations?
- ✔ Are commas used correctly in numbers, dates, addresses, and letters?

TEACHING COMMAS

Write 10 sentences that contain comma errors. Put each sentence on a small poster board so that you have 10 poster boards. Then create a duplicate set of poster boards. Divide the class into two teams. Place a set of 10 poster boards in front of each team with the sentences facing down.

Begin a tag team relay in which each team uses a marker to fix or supply the commas. When the first person finishes the first sentence, he or she hands the marker to the next person, who moves to the next sentence. The second person places commas in the second sentence and then hands the marker to the next person, and so on. Time the teams.

When the students have completed all the

Test Yourself

Add commas to the following sentences.

- We drove to the beach and we had a picnic.
- Before I eat breakfast I take a multivitamin.
- "This is my favorite restaurant" said Matt.
- E-mail though makes corresponding easy and fast.
- They were married on February 26 2004 in Las Vegas Nevada.

(Answers are in Appendix 4.)

The **comma** is the most frequently used punctuation mark, but it is also the most often misused. Commas make reading sentences easier because they separate the parts of sentences. Following the rules in this chapter will help you write clear sentences that are easy to read.

COMMAS WITH ITEMS IN A SERIES

Use commas to separate items in a series.
This means that you should put a comma between all items in a series.

Series: The house had three bedrooms, two baths, and a pool.

Series: She caught the fish, cleaned it, and then cooked it.

Series: William can have a new car if his grades improve, if he gets a job, and if he does his chores at home.

Sometimes this rule applies to a series of adjectives in front of a noun, but sometimes it does not. Look at these two examples.

Adjectives with Commas: The **foggy, cold** weather is finally over.

Adjectives Without Commas: The **loose bottom** knob fell off my TV.

Both of these examples are correct. So how do you know whether or not to use commas? You can use one of two tests. One test is to insert the word "and" between the adjectives. If the sentence makes sense, use a comma. Another test is to switch the order of the adjectives. If the sentence still reads clearly, use a comma between the two words.

Test 1:   The **foggy and cold** weather is finally over. **OK, so use a comma**

Test 2:   The **cold, foggy** weather is finally over. **OK, so use a comma**

Test 1:   The **loose and bottom** knob fell off my TV. **NO comma**

Test 2:   The **bottom loose** knob fell off my TV. **NO comma**

REVIEWING COMMAS WITH ITEMS IN A SERIES

Why use commas with items in a series?

To separate the items

Where do these commas go?

After all items in the series except the last

---

sentences, check to make sure that all the commas are correctly placed. Add five seconds to the team's time for each incorrect or missed comma. The team to finish with the lowest time wins.

INSTRUCTOR'S RESOURCE MANUAL

For sample sentences, for more exercises, and for quizzes, see the *Instructor's Resource Manual*, Section II, Part V.

◆ ***P r a c t i c e   1*   Identifying** In the following sentences, circle the commas that are used incorrectly, and add any commas that are missing.

1. In my free time, I like to read, sew, and make jelly.
2. My girlfriend is very good, at tennis, volleyball, and golf.
3. The best things, about gardening are the relaxation, the sense of accomplishment, and the feeling of being one with nature.
4. To play professional basketball, one must practice regularly, play competitively, and get a big break.
5. The sofa, the ottoman, and the computer desk are going to be donated to Goodwill.

◆ ***P r a c t i c e   2*   Completing** Add the missing commas to the following paragraph.

   We are flying to Dallas this weekend to attend a friend's wedding. Before we leave, I need to do the laundry, pay the bills, and arrange for a house sitter. My husband's childhood friend is the one getting married, so he also hopes to see some of his other friends there— especially Gene, Brad, and Dwayne. During the past two months, we bought airline tickets, arranged for a rental car, and reserved a hotel room. Now all we have to do is make it to the airport on time! I'm also trying to decide whether to wear navy, pink, or gray, and my husband is getting his best suit altered. Though it has required lots of time, energy, and money, we are really looking forward to this trip.

◆ ***P r a c t i c e   3*   Writing Your Own** Write a sentence of your own for each of the following sets of items. *Answers will vary.*

1. three things to do at the mall _____
2. three sports you like to play _____
3. three items on a to-do list _____
4. three popular magazines _____
5. three of your favorite snack foods _____

COMMAS WITH INTRODUCTORY WORDS

Use a comma to set off an introductory word, phrase, or clause from the rest of its sentence.

If you are unsure whether to add a comma, try reading the sentence with your reader in mind. If you want your reader to pause after the introductory word or phrase, you should insert a comma.

Introductory Word:	**No,** it didn't rain.
Introductory Word:	**Really,** the weather wasn't as bad as we thought it would be.
Introductory Phrase:	**On the whole,** this is a great town to live in.
Introductory Phrase:	**To prove this to my relatives,** I took them for a tour of the town.
Introductory Clause:	**As the doors opened,** the light poured in.
Introductory Clause:	**When the movie was over,** everyone was silent.

REVIEWING COMMAS WITH INTRODUCTORY WORDS

Why use commas with introductory words, phrases, and clauses?

To set them off from the rest of the sentence

How can you tell if a comma is needed?

Read the sentence to see if you want your reader to pause after the

introductory words.

◆ *P r a c t i c e* **4** **Identifying** In the following sentences, circle the commas that are used incorrectly, and add any commas that are missing.

1. Three years, ago, we lived in Boise.
2. As the fire continued, to burn, the firefighters feared it would get out of control.
3. Sure, I can take you to the store.
4. After spilling the water, the little boy began to cry.
5. The next time you go, to Macy's, can you pick up a gift certificate for me?

◆ *P r a c t i c e* **5** **Completing** Add the missing commas to the following paragraph.

When Terina was 7 years old, we took her to Disneyland. Since she was tall enough to ride all of the rides, she really enjoyed herself. First, we had to take pictures with Mickey and Minnie. Of course, we couldn't miss them! Next, we got in line for Space Mountain, which turned out to be her favorite ride. By the end of the day, we had ridden Space Mountain five times.

◆ *P r a c t i c e   6*   **Writing Your Own** Write a sentence of your own for each of the following introductory words, phrases, or clauses. *Answers will vary.*

1. well _____

2. when we thought it was almost over _____

3. yes _____

4. as the mail carrier arrived _____

5. wanting to win the lottery _____

COMMAS WITH INDEPENDENT CLAUSES

Use a comma before *and, but, for, nor, or, so,* and *yet* when they join two independent clauses. (Remember that an independent clause must have both a subject and a verb.)

Independent Clauses:	The boy flew to London, **and** he took a boat to France.
Independent Clauses:	He enjoyed the flight, **but** he liked the boat ride more.

Hint: Do not use a comma when a single subject has two verbs.

no
s   v   comma   v

The **boy flew** to London and **left** for France the next day.

Adding a comma when none is needed is one of the most common errors in college writing assignments. Only if the second verb has its own subject should you add a comma.

s   v   comma   s   v

The **boy flew** to London, and **he left** for France the next day.

REVIEWING COMMAS WITH COORDINATING CONJUNCTIONS

Name three coordinating conjunctions.

<u>Answers will vary.</u> _____ _____

When should you use a comma before a coordinating conjunction?

<u>When it joins two independent clauses</u>

Should you use a comma before a coordinating conjunction when a single subject has two verbs?

<u>No—only if the second verb has its own subject</u>

P r a c t i c e   7   Identifying In the following sentences, underline the subjects once and the coordinating conjunctions twice. Then circle any commas that are used incorrectly, and add any commas that are missing.

1. My <u>computer</u> crashed, <u><u>so</u></u> I lost my whole research paper.
2. The <u>car</u> looks great, <u><u>and</u></u> drives even better.
3. <u>Going</u> to the mountains was a good idea, <u><u>and</u></u> <u>we</u> had a very nice time.
4. The <u>cat</u> will curl up on the sofa, <u><u>or</u></u> the rug by the fireplace.
5. My <u>cousin</u> wants to get married, <u><u>but</u></u> <u>I</u> think she's too young.

P r a c t i c e   8   Completing Add the missing commas to the following paragraph.

   For my last birthday, my grandmother gave me $100, so I wanted to spend it on clothes. I went to the mall, and I found three outfits that were perfect. I couldn't decide on just one, but I didn't have enough money for them all. I needed the dressy outfit more, yet the casual outfit was a great bargain. Finally, I settled on one pantsuit, but I'm saving money to go back and get the others. I'll go back within a month, or maybe I'll just wait until after my next holiday gift.

P r a c t i c e   9   Writing Your Own Write a sentence of your own using each of the following coordinating conjunctions to separate two independent clauses. *Answers will vary.*

1. or _____

2. and _____

3. so _____

4. but _____

5. yet _____

COMMAS WITH INTERRUPTERS

Use a comma before and after a word or phrase that interrupts the flow of a sentence.

Most words that interrupt a sentence are not necessary for understanding the main point of a sentence. Setting them off makes it easier to recognize the main point.

Word:	My next-door neighbor, **Carlos,** is from Portugal.
Word:	I didn't hear the phone ring, **however,** because I was in the shower.
Phrase:	My textbook, ***Ancient Rome,*** is on the desk.
Phrase:	One of the most popular vacation spots, **according to recent surveys,** is Disneyland.
Phrase:	Mr. Colby, **president of the school board,** has been elected mayor.

A very common type of interrupter is a clause that begins with *who, whose, which, when,* or *where* and is not necessary for understanding the main point of the sentence:

Clause:	The new mall, **which is downtown,** has three restaurants.

Because the information "which is downtown" is not necessary for understanding the main idea of the sentence, it is set off with commas.

Clause:	Carol Roth, **who has a Ph.D. in history,** is my new neighbor.

The main point here is that Carol Roth is my new neighbor. Since the other information isn't necessary for understanding the sentence, it can be set off with commas.

Hint: Do not use commas with *who, whose, which, when,* or *where* if the information is necessary for understanding the main point of the sentence.

My friend **who is a circus clown** just arrived in town.

Because the information in the *who* clause is necessary to understand which friend just arrived in town, you should not set it off with commas.

Hint: Do not use commas to set off clauses beginning with *that:*

The mall **that is downtown** has three restaurants.

REVIEWING COMMAS WITH INTERRUPTERS

Why should you use commas to set off words and phrases in the middle of a sentence?

To make the main point easier to recognize

When should you use commas with who, whose, which, when, or where?

When the interrupting words are not necessary for understanding the

main point

When should you not use commas before these words?

When the information is necessary to the point of the sentence

---

◆ **P r a c t i c e 1 0 Identifying** Label each sentence C if commas are used correctly with the underlined words and phrases or X if they are not.

1. ___C___ Jacquelyn Smith, <u>who used to be a model</u>, has a line of clothing at Kmart.

2. ___X___ My girlfriend <u>Cheri</u>, is almost 23 years old.

3. ___C___ The AMC theater, <u>my favorite hangout</u>, is located on Main Street.

4. ___X___ Joe's leather jacket, <u>which he's had only four months</u> has a broken zipper.

5. ___X___ *Air Force One,* <u>the airplane</u>, used by the United States president, is the most secure aircraft in the world.

◆ *P r a c t i c e* **1 1** **Completing** Insert commas around the interrupting words and phrases in the following paragraph.

My favorite grandmother, Gram, turned 80 this year. My grandfather died last August, and we didn't want Gram living alone. She was able to take care of herself, however, and didn't want to go to a retirement home. Recently, we visited Rosewood, which is a very popular retirement community, and she was impressed with the facilities. There are group homes, of course, with "around the clock" care, but there are also condominiums where residents can live alone or with roommates. The entire neighborhood is monitored by security guards, which is reassuring, and the medical staff is always available. Gram's been there for three weeks now and said, when we asked, that she's never been happier.

◆ *P r a c t i c e* **1 2** **Writing Your Own** Write a sentence of your own for each of the following phrases. *Answers will vary.*

1. who is very brave _____

2. which costs over $100 _____

3. however _____

4. the mayor's wife _____

5. taking the keys _____

COMMAS WITH DIRECT QUOTATIONS

Use commas to mark direct quotations.

A direct quotation records a person's exact words. Commas set off the exact words from the rest of the sentence, making it easier to understand who said what.

Direct Quotation: My friends often say, **"You are so lucky."**

Direct Quotation: **"You are so lucky,"** my friends often say.

Direct Quotation: **"You are so lucky,"** says my grandmother, **"to have good friends."**

Hint: If a quotation ends with a question mark or an exclamation point, do not use a comma. Only one punctuation mark is needed.

NOT   "What did he want?," she asked.

Correct: "What did he want?" she asked.

REVIEWING COMMAS WITH DIRECT QUOTATIONS

Why should you use commas with a direct quotation?

To help the reader understand who said what

Should you use a comma if the quotation ends with a question mark or an exclamation point? Why or why not?

No—only one punctuation mark is needed.

◆ **P r a c t i c e   1 3   Identifying** In the following sentences, circle the commas that are used incorrectly, and add any commas that are missing.

1. Tonya noted, "I want the Kings to win tonight."
2. "If you go now," he said, "don't come back."
3. "Are you absolutely sure?," David asked.
4. "That cat," Christine said, "sets off my allergies."
5. Mr. Avery remarked, "The paper will not be accepted late."

◆ **P r a c t i c e   1 4   Completing** Add the missing commas to the following passage.

"Are you going to the game tonight?" Dirk asked Lonnie.
"Of course," she replied, "I wouldn't miss it."
"But the Mets will probably be slaughtered," Dirk said.
"What difference does that make?" she questioned.
Dirk answered, "I just don't want to pay money to watch them lose."
"Well, I'm a real loyal fan!" Lonnie emphasized as she walked away.

◆ **P r a c t i c e   1 5   Writing Your Own** Write five sentences of your own using commas to set off direct quotations. *Answers will vary.*

OTHER USES OF COMMAS

Use commas in the following ways.

> **Numbers:** What is **2,502,500** divided by **10,522?**
>
> **Dates:** My great grandfather was born in December 1888 in London and died on **July 23, 1972,** in Denver.

Notice that there is a comma both before and after the year.

> **Addresses:** Ashley moved from **Chicago, Illinois,** to **15305 Jefferson Ave., Boston, MA 09643.**

Notice that there is no comma between the state and zip code.

> **Letters:** **Dear Alisha,**
>
> **Yours truly,**

REVIEWING OTHER USES OF COMMAS

Give one example of commas in each of the following situations:
Examples will vary.

Numbers _____

Dates _____

Addresses _____

Letters _____

Why are these commas important?

They clarify information in everday writing.

◆ *P r a c t i c e **16*** **Identifying** In the following sentences, circle the commas that are used incorrectly, and add any commas that are missing.

1. The new Honda Accord costs more than $23,000.

2. Michael Finley plays basketball with the Mavericks and lives in Dallas, Texas.

3. My five-year anniversary is June 16,2005.

4. Jamie lives in Los Altos, California,with her two kids.

5. Yours truly,Deena

P r a c t i c e 17 **Completing** Add the missing commas to the following paragraph.

Norma graduated from Centenary College in Shreveport, Louisiana on June 5, 1999. There were more than 3,000 people in the audience, including Norma's friends and family. Her parents drove all the way from Tulsa, Oklahoma and they stayed in Louisiana all weekend. After the graduation ceremonies, Norma and her loved ones spent the weekend visiting the New Orleans area and other parts of Louisiana that Norma didn't get to see while attending school.

P r a c t i c e 18 **Writing Your Own** Write a sentence of your own for each of the following items. *Answers will vary.*

1. your date of birth

   _____

2. the city and state where you were born

   _____

3. your full address, including the ZIP code

   _____

4. the estimated number of people who attend your school

   _____

5. the amount of money you would like to make per year after college graduation

   _____

CHAPTER REVIEW

You might want to reread your answers to the questions in all the review boxes before you do the following exercises.

◆ ***Review Practice 1***   **Identifying**   Add the missing commas to the following sentences.

1. When I was 12 years old, my father took me to Honolulu, Hawaii.

2. Seth wanted more dessert, but he was on a diet.

3. Although James read that book before, he couldn't remember how it ended.

4. The Prelude is, of course, the best Honda vehicle.

5. I proudly cheered as Nick, my best friend, scored a touchdown.

6. "We will begin discussing genetics next Tuesday," said the professor.

7. Azaleas, carnations, and roses are my favorite flowers.

8. The beautiful, tall, brown-haired model walked down the catwalk.

9. There are 300,400 people in this county.

10. Craig and I started dating on August 7, 2001.

◆ ***Review Practice 2***   **Completing**   Add the missing commas to the following paragraph.

    My only cat, Mango, is Siamese. I still remember when she was born; it was February 14, 1997, Valentine's Day. There are more than 1,000 different breeds of cats, but the Siamese are the most strikingly beautiful. Mango is a friendly cat, however, unlike most Siamese. When I first brought her home, my friends said, "She'll be a spoiled brat," but I have come to love her.

◆ ***Review Practice 3***   **Writing Your Own**   Write a paragraph about the importance of computer knowledge. What are the benefits of computer technology? Why should we be familiar with it? *Answers will vary.*

◆ ***Review Practice 4***   **Editing Through Collaboration**   Exchange paragraphs from Review Practice 3 with another student, and do the following: *Answers will vary.*

1. Circle any misplaced commas.

2. Suggest corrections for the incorrect commas.

Then return the paper to its writer, and use the information in this chapter to correct any comma errors in your own paragraph. Record your errors on the Error Log in Appendix 6.

APOSTROPHES

CHECKLIST for Using Apostrophes

> ✔ Are apostrophes used correctly in contractions?
> ✔ Are apostrophes used correctly to show possession?

Test Yourself

Add an apostrophe or an apostrophe and *-s* to the following sentences.

- The flight crew was surprised by the pilots rudeness when he boarded the plane.
- Its important that the car has its engine checked every 3,000 miles.
- Whats going to happen after Dominic is gone?
- The mens bathroom is located on the third floor.
- James house is the third one on the left.

(Answers are in Appendix 4.)

The **apostrophe** looks like a single quotation mark. Its two main purposes are to indicate where letters have been left out and to show ownership.

MARKING CONTRACTIONS

Use an apostrophe to show that letters have been omitted to form a contraction.

TEACHING
APOSTROPHES
Create a game of
Jeopardy! with the
following categories:
"Understanding
Contractions,"
"Forming
Contractions,"
"Identifying Correct
and Incorrect
Possessives," and
"Forming Possessives."
Write questions like
the following to fit each
category.
*Understanding
Contractions:*
  Answer: The word
    that *can't* stands
    for
  Question: What is
    cannot?
Forming Contractions:
  Answer: The con-
    traction made
    from the words
    should have
  Question: What is
    should've?

Identifying Correct and Incorrect Possessives:
   Answer: Of *hers, his,* and *it's,* the word that is an incorrect posses-sive pronoun
   Question: What is *it's?*
Forming Possessives
   Answer: Another way to write "the house of the fam-ily named Jones"
   Question: What is "the Joneses' house"?
   Divide the class into teams to play the game. The team to get the most correct answers wins.

INSTRUCTOR'S RESOURCE MANUAL
For directions on how to play the game and a complete set of ques-tions and answers, for more exercises, and for quizzes, see the *Instructor's Resource Manual,* Section II, Part V.

A **contraction** is the shortening of one or more words. Our everyday speech is filled with contractions.

I have	=	I've (*h* and *a* have been omitted)
you are	=	you're (*a* has been omitted)
let us	=	let's (*u* has been omitted)

Here is a list of commonly used contractions.

Some Common Contractions

I am	=	*I'm*	*we have*	=	*we've*
I would	=	*I'd*	*we will*	=	*we'll*
I will	=	*I'll*	*they are*	=	*they're*
you have	=	*you've*	*they have*	=	*they've*
you will	=	*you'll*	*do not*	=	*don't*
he is	=	*he's*	*did not*	=	*didn't*
she will	=	*she'll*	*have not*	=	*haven't*
it is	=	*it's*	*could not*	=	*couldn't*

Hint: Two words that are frequently misused are *it's* and *its.*

it's = contraction: it is (*or it has*)	**It's** too late to go to the movie.
its = pronoun: belonging to it	**Its** eyes are really large.

To see if you are using the correct word, say the sentence with the words *it is.* If that is what you want to say, add an apostrophe to the word.

?   I think **its** burning.

Test: I think it is burning.   **YES, add an apostrophe**

This sentence makes sense with *it is,* so you should write *it's.*

Correct: I think **it's** burning.

?   The dog wagged **its** tail.

Test: The dog wagged it is tail.   **NO, so no apostrophe**

This sentence does not make sense with *it is,* so you should not use the apostrophe in *its.*

Correct: The dog wagged **its** tail.

REVIEWING CONTRACTIONS

What is the purpose of an apostrophe in a contraction?

To show that letters have been omitted

Write five contractions, and tell which letters have been omitted.

Answers will vary.

What is the difference between it's and its?

It's stands for it is or it has, and its is a possessive pronoun.

◆ *P r a c t i c e* **1** **Identifying** In the following sentences, circle the apostrophes that are used incorrectly, and add any apostrophes that are missing.

1. I've got to find a better job.
2. The attorney said she's working overtime on this case.
3. They'll be glad to see you at the party.
4. It's a good thing they did'nt bring their baby to the wedding.
5. Cameron doesnt get paid until Friday.

◆ *P r a c t i c e* **2** **Completing** Write contractions for the following words.

1. she + would = _she'd_

2. did + not = _didn't_

3. will + not = _won't_

4. they + will = *they'll* _____

5. should + have = *should've* _____

◆ **P r a c t i c e   3**   **Writing Your Own** Write a sentence of your own for each of the contractions you wrote in Practice 2. *Answers will vary.*

SHOWING POSSESSION

Use an apostrophe to show possession.

1. For a singular word, use *'s* to indicate possession or ownership. You can always replace a possessive with *of* plus the noun or pronoun.

the soldier's rifle	=	the rifle **of the soldier**
someone's house	=	the house **of someone**
doctor's office	=	the office **of the doctor**
yesterday's paper	=	the paper **of yesterday**

2. For plural nouns ending in *-s*, use only an apostrophe.

the soldiers' rifles	=	the rifles **of the soldiers**
the doctors' office	=	the office **of the doctors**
the painters' studio	=	the studio **of the painters**
the students' grades	=	the grades **of the students**
the brothers' boat	=	the boat **of the brothers**

3. For plural nouns that do not end in *-s*, add *'s*.

the men's pants	=	the pants **of the men**
the deer's antlers	=	the antlers **of the deer**
the criteria's importance	=	the importance **of the criteria**

REVIEWING POSSESSIVES
....

How do you mark possession or ownership for a singular word?

Add 's to the word.

How do you mark possession or ownership for a plural word that ends in -s?

Add an apostrophe after the -s ending.

How do you mark possession or ownership for a plural word that doesn't end in -s?

Add 's to the word

◆ **P r a c t i c e   4   Identifying** In the following sentences, circle the apostrophes that are used incorrectly, and add any apostrophes that are missing.

1. The boy's bicycle had a flat tire.
2. The disaster was Jennifer's fault.
3. Our two cat's water bowl was empty.
4. We knew the airline's food would be tasty.
5. Todays temperature reached 83 degrees.

◆ **P r a c t i c e   5   Completing** Write a possessive for each of the following phrases.

1. the feet of Charles ___Charles's feet___

2. the guests of Dr. Blakeney ___Dr. Blakeney's guests___

3. the tide of the ocean ___the ocean's tide___

4. the shirts of the men ___the men's shirts___

5. the assignment of the students ___the students' assignment___

◆ **P r a c t i c e   6   Writing Your Own** Write a sentence of your own for each of the possessives you wrote in Practice 5. *Answers will vary.*

COMMON APOSTROPHE ERRORS

Two common errors occur with apostrophes. The following guidelines will help you avoid these errors.

No Apostrophe with Possessive Pronouns

Do not use an apostrophe with a possessive pronoun.

Possessive pronouns already show ownership, so they do not need an apostrophe.

Error	Correct
his'	his
her's or hers'	hers
it's or its'	its
your's or yours'	yours
our's or ours'	ours
their's or theirs'	theirs

No Apostrophe to Form the Plural

Do not use an apostrophe to form a plural word.

This error occurs most often with plural words ending in *-s*. An apostrophe indicates possession or contraction; it does *not* indicate the plural. Therefore, a plural word never takes an apostrophe unless it is possessive.

NOT   The **clothes'** are in the dryer.

Correct: The **clothes** are in the dryer.

NOT   She bought a case of **soda's** last week.

Correct: She bought a case of **sodas** last week.

NOT   Get your coffee and **donut's** here.

Correct: Get your coffee and **donuts** here.

REVIEWING APOSTROPHE ERRORS

List three possessive pronouns.

Answers will vary. _____ _____

Why don't possessive pronouns take apostrophes?

They are possessive without apostrophes.

> *What is wrong with the apostrophe in each of the following sentences?*
> *The last float in the parade is* ours'.
>
> The pronoun ours is possessive without an apostrophe.
>
> *There must be 100* floats' *in the parade.*
>
> Floats is plural only, not possessive.

◆ **P r a c t i c e 7 Identifying** In the following sentences, circle the apostrophes that are used incorrectly, and add any apostrophes that are missing.

1. I've been to that store five time's, and I've never seen shoes like yours'.
2. My brother's are working for my father's company.
3. Sam left his' cars window's down, and it is starting to rain.
4. The soccer player's are meeting at noon.
5. The big story in the newspaper's is yesterday's flood.

◆ **P r a c t i c e 8 Completing** Write a possessive for each of the following phrases.

1. the house belonging to them ___their house___

2. the pants she owns ___her pants___

3. the soda you are holding ___your soda___

4. the price of it ___its price___

5. the feet of him ___his feet___

◆ **P r a c t i c e 9 Writing Your Own** Write a sentence of your own for each of the possessives you wrote in Practice 8. *Answers will vary.*

CHAPTER REVIEW

You might want to reread your answers to the questions in all the review boxes before you do the following exercises.

◆ **Review Practice 1** **Identifying** In the following sentences, circle the apostrophes that are used incorrectly, and add any apostrophes that are missing.

1. Mr. Thompson's diner serves many pasta entrée's.
2. Two plumber's came to fix the leaks.
3. I thought I picked up my purse, but it was really her's.
4. Naomi was'nt pleased with the restaurant's service.
5. The rose's in my front yard haven't bloomed yet.
6. It's amazing that Tricia cut her hair as short as yours.
7. His' new house is in Highland Park.
8. You've got to see Ming's new jet ski's.
9. Our high school's head cheerleader is getting a full athletic scholarship to college.
10. Mary's parent's ordered four pizza's for her party.

◆ **Review Practice 2** **Completing** Add the missing apostrophes to the following sentences.

1. The truck's brakes went out while it was coming over the hill.
2. We haven't heard from Ben since he left his father's ranch and headed for ours.
3. My next-door neighbor's uncle is a big Hollywood actor.
4. Sarah's diet consisted of hot dogs and sodas.
5. The freeways are crowded because yesterday's fire still hasn't been contained.
6. I think it's time for us to go to our house and for you to go to yours.
7. Devon's kids were playing dominoes.
8. Maurice can't ever beat me at backgammon.
9. Stella's going to the game with us.
10. Both cars' gas tanks are empty.

◆ **Review Practice 3** **Writing Your Own** Write a paragraph about your favorite teacher. What was his or her name? What was special about this person? *Answers will vary.*

◆ *Review Practice 4* **Editing Through Collaboration** Exchange
paragraphs from Review Practice 3 with another student, and do the
following: *Answers will vary.*

1. Circle any misplaced or missing apostrophes.
2. Indicate whether they mark possession (P) or contraction (C).

Then return the paper to its writer, and use the information in this chapter
to correct any apostrophe errors in your own paragraph. Record your errors
on the Error Log in Appendix 6.

QUOTATION MARKS

✔ CHECKLIST for Using Quotation Marks

TEACHING
QUOTATION MARKS
Present the class with
an excerpt from a play
(one with numerous
stage directions and
comments) written as
one long paragraph
with no quotation
marks to distinguish
the spoken language
from the stage direc-
tions. Have a student
read the excerpt from
the play. Students
will see how difficult
distinguishing the
stage remarks from
the words is and will
then understand the
value of marking direct
quotations.
Then have students
work in groups of three
or four to punctuate
the paragraph correctly
by adding quotation
marks and proper
spacing.

- ✔ Are quotation marks used to indicate someone's exact words?
- ✔ Are all periods and commas inside quotation marks?
- ✔ Are words capitalized correctly in quotations?
- ✔ Are quotation marks used to indicate the title of a short work, such as a short story or a poem?

Test Yourself

Add quotation marks where needed in the following sentences.

- Can we go out to dinner tonight? she asked.
- Jeri screamed, Don't go in there!
- If you can't find my house, Tom said, call me on your cell phone.
- My favorite poem is The Red Wheelbarrow by William Carlos Williams.
- David said, I'll fix your car this weekend.

(Answers are in Appendix 4.)

Quotation marks are punctuation marks that work together in pairs. Their most common use is to indicate someone's exact words. They are also used to mark the title of a short piece of writing, such as a short story or a poem.

DIRECT QUOTATIONS

Use quotation marks to indicate a **direct quotation**—someone's exact words.

Here are some examples that show the three basic forms of a direct quotation.

Direct Quotation: "I will not lend you the money," said the banker.

Here the quoted words come first.

Direct Quotation: The banker said, "I will not lend you the money."

Here the quoted words come after the speaker is named.

Direct Quotation: "I will not," the banker said, "lend you the money."

In this example, the quoted words are interrupted, and the speaker is named in the middle. This form emphasizes the first few words.

INDIRECT QUOTATIONS

If you just talk about someone's words, you do not need quotation marks. Indirect quotations usually include the word *that*, as in *said that*. In questions, the wording is often *asked if*. Look at these examples of **indirect quotations.**

Direct Quotation: "I lost my job at the supermarket," said Bob.

These are Bob's exact words, so you must use quotation marks.

Indirect Quotation: Bob **said that** he lost his job at the supermarket.

This sentence explains what Bob said but does not use Bob's exact words. So quotation marks should not be used.

Direct Quotation: "The train trip took eight hours," said Kira.
Indirect Quotation: Kira **said that** the train trip took eight hours.

Direct Quotation: "Did you get the car fixed?" Mom asked.
Indirect Quotation: Mom **asked if** I had gotten the car fixed.

INSTRUCTOR'S RESOURCE MANUAL

For sample paragraphs, for more exercises and for quizzes, see the *Instructor's Resource Manual*, Section II, Part V.

REVIEWING QUOTATION MARKS WITH QUOTATIONS

How do you show that you are repeating someone's exact words?

Put the words in quotation marks

What is an indirect quotation?

An explanation of someone's words but not the exact words

P r a c t i c e 1 Identifying In the following sentences, circle the quotation marks used incorrectly, and add any quotation marks that are missing.

1. "Help me!"yelled the drowning woman."

2. "If you can't take the heat," my mom used to say,"stay out of the kitchen."

3. Martina asked, "Have you found my jacket?" *Correct*

4. Steffan said,"My goal is to"get into the Olympics."

5. Chonda said that "she enjoyed the movie last night."

P r a c t i c e 2 Completing Add the missing quotation marks to the following paragraph.

When I went into the salon, my hairdresser asked,"How do you want your hair cut today?"I don't really know,"I replied,"but I brought in a couple of pictures of haircuts I like.""Those are cute"she said."Do you think my hair would look good like that?"I asked. "Absolutely!"she exclaimed. Then she set to work with the scissors. When she was finished, I looked in the mirror in horror."That's not what I had in mind,"I told her."But it looks just like the pictures,"she said."How can you say that?"I exclaimed."The haircuts I showed you are shoulder-length, and mine is now above my ears!""Well,"she said,"it will always grow back."

P r a c t i c e 3 Writing Your Own Write a sentence of your own for each of the following expressions. *Answers will vary.*

1. a question asked by Claudia _____

2. a statement spoken by the manager _____

3. an exclamation spoken by Becky _____

4. an indirect question that Jared asked _____

5. a statement spoken by the electrician _____

CAPITALIZING AND USING OTHER PUNCTUATION MARKS WITH QUOTATION MARKS

When you are quoting someone's complete sentences, begin with a capital letter and use appropriate end punctuation—a period, a question mark, or an exclamation point. You do not need to capitalize the first word of a quotation if it is only part of a sentence. Here are some examples.

Capitalize the first letter of the words being quoted, and put a period at the end of the sentence if it is a statement. Separate the spoken words from the rest of the sentence with a comma.

"**He** doesn't seem very nice," she said.
He said, "**T**urn off the music."

If the quotation ends with a question mark or an exclamation point, use that punctuation instead of a comma or a period.

"**Why** do you want to know?" she asked.
He yelled, "**T**urn off that music!"

In a quotation that is interrupted, capitalize the first word being quoted, but do not capitalize words in the middle of the sentence. Use a comma both before and after the interruption. End with a period if it is a statement.

"**Yes,**" said the bus driver, "this bus goes downtown."

You do not need to capitalize the first word of a quotation that is only part of a sentence.

I don't think that he will ever "**f**ind himself."

Hint: Look at the examples again. Notice that periods and commas always go inside the quotation marks.

    NOT   "Yes", he said, "we're ready to leave".
    Correct: "Yes," he said, "we're ready to leave."

REVIEWING CAPITALIZATION AND PUNCTUATION
WITH QUOTATION MARKS

When you quote someone's exact words, why should you begin with a capital letter?

Because the word begins a sentence

Where do commas go in relation to quotation marks? Where do periods go?

Both commas and periods go inside quotation marks.

P r a c t i c e   4   Identifying In the following sentences, circle the quotation marks, capital letters, and other punctuation marks that are used incorrectly, and add any missing quotation marks and punctuation.

1. "Is there a doctor in the house"?"the man screamed.
2. "I can't believe", she said, "That you've never seen the ocean."
3. Margarita asked, "Are you ever going to meet me for coffee"??"
4. "This is the last time", he promised, "that I come home late."
5. Garrett said, "I want to take the trolley to the restaurant on the corner."

P r a c t i c e   5   Completing Add the missing quotation marks and punctuation to the following paragraph.

I was having car problems, so I drove to the auto shop on the corner. "What do you think is wrong with my car?"I asked the mechanic."I can't tell you,"he said,"until I take a look at it myself."I replied,"I'll leave it with you this afternoon, and you can tell me later today what you find out.""That would be great,"he said. Finally, around 4:00 p.m., he called me on the phone."Your car needs a new clutch,"he said. "No way!"I exclaimed. "Sorry, mister,"he calmly replied,"but that's all I found to be wrong with it."I explained,"But I just replaced the clutch four months ago.""Well,"he said"I hope you saved your receipt and warranty paperwork."

P r a c t i c e   6   Writing Your Own Write a sentence of your own for each of the following direct quotations, punctuated correctly. *Answers will vary.*

1. "No, I won't" _____

2. "How are we going to do that" _____

3. "This is the most important priority" _____

4. "Yes" "you can come to the party" _____

5. "Don't worry" "you didn't miss anything" _____

QUOTATION MARKS AROUND TITLES

Put quotation marks around the titles of short works that are parts of larger works. The titles of longer works are put in italics (or underlined).

Quotation Marks	Italics/Underlining
"The Yellow Wallpaper" (short story)	*American Short Stories* (book)
"Song of Myself" (poem)	*Leaves of Grass* (book)
"My Girl" (song)	*The Temptations' Greatest Hits* (CD)
"Explore New Orleans" (magazine article)	*New Orleans Monthly* (magazine)
"Convicts Escape" (newspaper article)	*New York Times* (newspaper)
"The Wedding" (episode on TV series)	*Friends* (TV series)

REVIEWING QUOTATION MARKS WITH TITLES

When do you put quotation marks around a title?

When it is a short work that is part of a larger work

When do you italicize (or underline) a title?

When it is a longer work

◆ *P r a c t i c e 7*   **Identifying**   Put an X in front of each sentence with errors in quotation marks or italics/underlining. Add any missing quotation marks and italics or underlining.

1. ___X___ My favorite song by the Beatles is *Yellow Submarine*. *("Yellow Submarine")*

2. ___X___ When Juliet was in high school, she read Shirley Jackson's famous short story The Lottery. *("The Lottery")*

3. _____ Getting through *Moby Dick* by Herman Melville took me three weeks.

4. ___X___ My first boyfriend recited William Blake's poem The Garden of Love to me on my front porch. *("The Garden of Love")*

5. ___X___ The "New York Times" ran a long article called *Japan's Princess Gives Birth* about Crown Princess Masako. *(New York Times, "Japan's Princess Gives Birth")*

◆ **P r a c t i c e 8   Completing** Place quotation marks around the titles of short works, and underline the titles of long works in the following paragraph.

   Mark got a great job with the <u>Chicago</u> <u>Tribune</u> last summer. He is now working as the editor of the entertainment section, and he writes a column called "Making a Mark." In his column, he reviews celebrity events and activities, such as concerts, hit movies, and best-selling books. For one article, he interviewed several people from <u>Survivor</u>, the popular reality TV show. He also attended a Dixie Chicks concert and quoted lines from the song "There's Your Trouble" on their album <u>Wide</u> <u>Open</u> <u>Spaces</u>. Another article featured Nikki Giovanni, who read her poem "Dream" during their interview. Mark has become friends with some very interesting and well-known people, and he is now looking forward to speaking with Steven Spielberg on the set of the latest sequel to <u>Jurassic</u> <u>Park</u>.

◆ **P r a c t i c e 9   Writing Your Own** Write a sentence of your own for each of the following items. Make up a title if you can't think of one.
Answers will vary.

1. a short story _____

2. a song _____

3. a TV show _____

4. a CD _____

5. a magazine article _____

CHAPTER REVIEW

You might want to reread your answers to the questions in all the review boxes before you do the following exercises.

◀ *Review P r a c t i c e **1** **Identifying*** Add the missing quotation marks and punctuation to the following sentences.

1. Patty sang Whitney Houston's "You Give Good Love" at the karaoke party.

2. Our next writing assignment is a critical review of Robert Browning's poem "My Last Duchess."

3. "You don't have to go to work today," I told Gerard.

4. Marjorie won the short story contest with a tale she wrote about her grandmother called "It's a Happy Day."

5. Devonne asked, "Where does Jack live?"

6. When Princess Diana died, the <u>Boston</u> <u>Globe</u> ran an article called "Too Soon."

7. The scores came in, and our coach yelled, "Great job, team!"

8. "I can't make it to the meeting," she said, "but I'll call you tonight to find out what I missed."

9. "What do you want to eat for breakfast?" Charise asked.

10. I submitted an article to <u>Golf</u> <u>Magazine</u> called "How to Swing like Tiger Woods."

◀ *Review P r a c t i c e **2** **Completing*** Add the missing quotation marks, commas, and underlining for italics to the following dialogue.

"Hurry up," I said, "or we're going to be late for the Beastie Boys Concert."
"I'm coming," John replied. "Just hold your horses!"
"The write-up in <u>USA</u> <u>Today</u> said this was going to be their biggest concert ever," I told him. I asked John if he too had read that article, but he said that he hadn't.
"I didn't have time to read today," he explained, "because I was busy buying a CD of their greatest hits. Now," John said, "I'm really excited about the concert tonight!"

◀ *Review P r a c t i c e **3** **Writing Your Own*** In paragraph form, record a conversation you had this week. Who were you talking to? What did you talk about? What were your exact words? *Answers will vary.*

◆ *Review P r a c t i c e 4* **Editing Through Collaboration** Exchange paragraphs from Review Practice 3 with another student, and do the following: *Answers will vary.*

1. Circle any incorrect or missing quotation marks.

2. Underline any faulty punctuation.

3. Put an X over any incorrect use of italics/underlining.

Then return the paper to its writer, and use the information in this chapter to correct any errors with quotation marks and italics/underlining in your own paragraph. Record your errors on the Error Log in Appendix 6.

OTHER PUNCTUATION MARKS

✔ CHECKLIST for Using Semicolons, Colons, Dashes, and Parentheses

> ✔ Are semicolons used to join two closely related complete sentences?
> ✔ Are long items in a series that already contain commas separated by semicolons?
> ✔ Are colons used correctly to introduce a list?
> ✔ Are dashes used to emphasize or further explain a point?
> ✔ Are parentheses used to include additional, but not necessary, information?

Test Yourself

Add semicolons, colons, dashes, or parentheses to the following sentences.

- Kris left for the dance Sean decided to stay home.
- We wanted to win therefore we practiced every day.
- The computer's advertised price didn't include several important things a monitor, a printer, and speakers.
- Ramon asked the best question during the interview "Why should we vote for you?"
- Bring the jelly to a "rolling boil" a boil that cannot be stirred down.

(Answers are in Appendix 4.)

This chapter explains the uses of the **semicolon, colon, dash,** and **parentheses.** We'll look at these punctuation marks one by one.

TEACHING OTHER PUNCTUATION MARKS
Before class, put a series of sentence parts and punctuation marks on small pieces of cardboard. The sentence parts should include clauses, phrases, and single parts of speech.
 Assign several pieces of cardboard to each student, and have the students begin by wearing one card. Then have students who are sentence parts stand in front of the class to form a sentence. For example, seven students might make the following sentence:
 I went grocery shopping (clause)
 after school (prepositional phrase)
 because (subordinating conjunction)
 I needed food (clause)
 fruit/milk/bread (3 words)

SEMICOLONS

Semicolons are used to separate equal parts of a sentence. They are also used to avoid confusion when listing items in a series.

1. Use a semicolon to separate two closely related independent clauses.

    An independent clause is a group of words with a subject and a verb that can stand alone as a sentence. You might use a semicolon instead of a coordinating conjunction (*and, but, for, nor, or, so, yet*) or a period. Any one of the three options would be correct.

	Independent	Independent
Semicolon:	Sam never drove to school; **he** always rode his bike.	
Conjunction:	Sam never drove to school, **for** he always rode his bike.	
Period:	Sam never drove to school. **He** always rode his bike.	

2. Use a semicolon to join two independent clauses that are connected by such words as *however, therefore, furthermore, moreover, for example,* or *consequently.* Put a comma after the connecting word.

	Independent	Independent
Semicolon:	Traveling can be expensive; **nevertheless,** it's always enjoyable.	
Semicolon:	Brad is very smart; **furthermore,** he was offered seven scholarships.	
Semicolon:	He has trouble in math; **therefore,** he hired a tutor.	

3. Use a semicolon to separate items in a series when any of the items contain commas.

NOT	On the flight to New York, Mei Lin read a popular new thriller with a surprise ending, took a long, relaxing nap, and watched an incredibly dull movie about a rock star.
Correct:	On the flight to New York, Mei Lin read a popular new thriller with a surprise ending; took a long, relaxing nap; and watched an incredibly dull movie about a rock star.

REVIEWING SEMICOLONS

How are semicolons used between two independent clauses?

To separate the clauses

How are semicolons used with items in a series?

To separate the items when commas are included

◆ *P r a c t i c e 1* **Identifying** In the following sentences, circle the semicolons that are used incorrectly, and add any commas and semicolons that are missing.

1. The car needed new front tires; the old ones were quite bald.
2. Lisa's 10-month-old son didn't take a nap today; however, he was very pleasant.
3. I must have lost my keys; I can't find them anywhere.
4. Our team is the strongest, and we are prepared to win.
5. Mr. Banderas teaches Spanish; writes novels, books, and short stories; and reviews movies in his spare time.

◆ *P r a c t i c e 2* **Completing** Add semicolons to the following paragraph.

When I was in junior high, my school had a big dance; I dreaded it from the day it was announced. I didn't have a boyfriend; I didn't have the right clothes, shoes, or hairstyle; and I didn't have any money saved up for things like that. Even worse, I knew my parents felt I was too young to go; nonetheless, I knew my friends would keep asking me if I was going. Finally, I thought of a good excuse: I told my friends my grandmother was having major surgery. My friends probably knew I was lying; however, nobody said anything more to me about it.

◆ *P r a c t i c e 3* **Writing Your Own** Write five sentences of your own using semicolons correctly. *Answers will vary.*

COLONS

1. The main use of the colon is to introduce a list or thought. Here are some examples:

   Colon: Buy the following items for the trip**:** toothpaste, tooth-brush, razor, soap, and makeup.

   Colon: The fair had some new attractions**:** a double ferris wheel, a roller coaster, and an antique merry-go-round.

   Colon: The choice was simple**:** return the merchandise.

   The most common error with colons is using one where it isn't needed.

2. Do not use a colon after the words *such as* or *including*. A complete sentence must come before a colon.

   NOT   Cook only fresh vegetables, **such as:** green beans, broccoli, and spinach.

   Correct: Cook only fresh vegetables, **such as** green beans, broccoli, and spinach.

   NOT   We went to many countries in Europe, **including:** Spain and Portugal.

   Correct: We went to many countries in Europe, **including** Spain and Portugal.

3. In addition, you should not use a colon after a verb or after a preposition. Remember that a complete sentence must come before a colon.

   NOT   The movies to be reviewed **are:** *American Beauty* and *Wonder Boys.*

   Correct: The movies to be reviewed **are** *American Beauty* and *Wonder Boys.*

   NOT   The box was full **of:** books, old dolls, and scrapbooks.

   Correct: The box was full **of** books, old dolls, and scrapbooks.

REVIEWING COLONS

What is the main use of a colon?

To introduce a list

> *Why should you not use a colon after such words as is or of?*
>
> A colon must come after a complete sentence.

◆ *P r a c t i c e   4*   **Identifying** In the following sentences, circle the colons that are used incorrectly, and add any colons that are missing.

1. The best things about summer are: swimming, biking, and picnics.

2. The man asked me for the following items: my driver's license, my Social Security number, and my credit cards.

3. We accidentally left many things at home, such as: my toothbrush, our hair dryer, and the baby's bottle.

4. I was most impressed by: the atmosphere, the prices, and the service.

5. The most expensive parts to repair were: the carburetor, the ignition system, and the fuel injector.

◆ *P r a c t i c e   5*   **Completing** Add colons to the following paragraph.

Reading is an excellent way to spend free time. A good book can do many things: take you to a faraway place, introduce you to different people, and expose you to extraordinary experiences. I especially like two kinds of books: science fiction and romance novels. These genres are totally opposite, I know, but they have just what I like: action, strange characters, and suspension of disbelief. When I am reading, I am in a world of my own. I escape all of my everyday problems: my difficult job, my nagging mother, and sometimes even my homework.

◆ *P r a c t i c e   6*   **Writing Your Own** Write five sentences of your own using colons correctly. *Answers will vary.*

DASHES AND PARENTHESES
Dashes

1. Use dashes to emphasize or draw attention to a point.

   Dash: I know what I want to be—a doctor.

   In this example, the beginning of the sentence introduces an idea, and the dash then sets off the answer.

   Dash: Money and time—these are what I need.

In this example, the key words are set off at the beginning, and the explanation follows. Beginning this way adds some suspense to the sentence.

Dashes: I know what I want in a husband—a sense of humor—and I plan to get it.

The dashes divide this sentence into three distinct parts, which makes the reader pause and think about each part.

Parentheses

Whereas dashes set off material that the writer wants to emphasize, parentheses do just the opposite. They are always used in pairs.

2. Use parentheses to set off information that is interesting or helpful but not necessary for understanding the sentence.

Parentheses: When in Rome **(as the saying goes)**, do as the Romans do.

Parentheses: The senator's position on the proposal **(Senate Bill 193)** has changed several times.

3. Parentheses are also used to mark a person's life span and to number items in a sentence.

Parentheses: Herman Melville **(1819–1891)** wrote the classic *Moby Dick*.

Parentheses: My boss gave me three things to do today: **(1)** answer the mail, **(2)** file receipts, and **(3)** send out bills.

REVIEWING DASHES AND PARENTHESES

What is the difference between dashes and parentheses?

Dashes emphasize information, and parentheses set off unnecessary

but helpful information.

When do you use dashes?

To emphasize or draw attention to a point

When do you use parentheses?

To set off information that isn't necessary to the main point of a sentence

◈ *P r a c t i c e* **7** **Identifying** Use dashes or parentheses with the underlined words in the following sentences.

1. One powerful tool for student research is becoming more popular than the library—the Internet.
2. My brother—the police chief—keeps his phone number unlisted.
3. Nick (head of the math department) hires the new teachers. *(or dashes)*
4. I signaled the oncoming car (by flashing my lights) but it still didn't turn its headlights on.
5. Cheryl got her passport so she can (1) visit other countries, (2) go diving in all of the seven seas, and (3) photograph royalty.

◈ *P r a c t i c e* **8** **Completing** Add dashes and parentheses to the following paragraph.

> In high school, I volunteered to work on the yearbook. Mrs. Brady was our instructor—a round lady with bright red cheeks and a strange laugh. She immediately set us to work on several things (mostly after school) as we accumulated photos and news about the school's major events. I remember one lesson I learned in that class—never procrastinate. If I failed to finish an assignment (something that rarely happened) someone else would do it instead, and that person's work would be published instead of mine. I'll never forget my year with Mrs. Brady.

◈ *P r a c t i c e* **9** **Writing Your Own** Write three sentences of your own using dashes and two using parentheses. *Answers will vary.*

CHAPTER REVIEW

You might want to reread your answers to the questions in all the review boxes before you do the following exercises.

◈ *Review P r a c t i c e* **1** **Identifying** Add semicolons, colons, dashes, and parentheses to the following sentences.

1. We are going to the grocery store; we have nothing in the pantry.

2. There are only three people I trust: Krista, Tanya, and Lucy.

3. He is always home; however, he doesn't ever help out around the house.

4. I bought the car in my favorite color—neon yellow. *(or colon)*

5. Put the flowers on the table outside (the one by the wall) and the presents can go there too. *(or dashes)*

6. My favorite book was made into a movie—*Beloved*.

7. There are many things to do today: pick up the dry cleaning, vacuum the carpets, and wash the dishes.

8. The chicken coop needs to be cleaned out; it is full of leaves and tree branches.

9. We will pick up Derek, Jenny, and Carmen; go to the beach; and lie out all day.

10. I got your favorite ice cream for your birthday—fudge ripple. *(or colon)*

◆ *Review* **P r a c t i c e   2** **Completing** Add semicolons, colons, dashes, and parentheses to the following paragraph.

Today was an extremely windy day, so we decided to fly kites. We drove to Kite Hill (a place where I went as a kid) and we climbed to the very top. We took out the kites and other necessary things: masking tape, string, and ribbons. This way we were prepared to repair our kites, if necessary. The wind was perfect; we couldn't have asked for better weather. There was only one thing we forgot—the picnic lunch! Fortunately, Lamar remembered to pack the cooler with sodas—mostly Diet Coke—for something to drink when we got thirsty. After about four hours of flying kites (it felt like 14), the group decided to head back home.

◆ *Review* **P r a c t i c e   3** **Writing Your Own** Write a paragraph explaining some of your five-year goals. What do you plan to be doing in five years? What do you want to have accomplished? *Answers will vary.*

Review P r a c t i c e 4 **Editing Through Collaboration** Exchange paragraphs from Review Practice 3 with another student, and do the following: *Answers will vary.*

1. Circle any incorrect or missing semicolons.
2. Circle any incorrect or missing colons.
3. Circle any incorrect or missing dashes.
4. Circle any incorrect or missing parentheses.

Then return the paper to its writer, and use the information in this chapter to correct any punctuation errors in your own paragraph. Record your errors on the Error Log in Appendix 6.

UNIT TESTS

Here are some exercises that test your understanding of all the material in this unit: End Punctuation, Commas, Apostrophes, Quotation Marks, Semicolons, Colons, Dashes, and Parentheses.

Unit Test I

Correct the punctuation errors in the following sentences.

1. The normal human body temperature is 986°.
2. We are having grilled chicken, asparagus, and French bread for dinner tonight.
3. The car looks great, and drives even better.
4. Is your mother paying your tuition?
5. We were late to school, as usual, because we had to stop for gas.
6. You make me so angry!
7. Emily's car is newer than ours.
8. My mother still lives at 4901 El Sendero Ave., San Antonio, TX 78233.
9. "Without question," Cameron said, "that is the best option we have."
10. People shouldn't start smoking because it's a hard habit to break.
11. My favorite animals at the zoo were the monkeys, the hippos, and the zebras.
12. Wanting to get better grades, Mary studied all weekend.
13. My computer crashed, so I lost my whole research paper.

14. The conference will cover three important issues: race relations, the economy, and global warming.

15. My sister joined the Army last June; she committed to four years.

16. My favorite movies are romances, dramas, and horror films.

17. "Don't even think about it!" Janelle exclaimed.

18. His two uncles' briefcases are both leather.

19. Martina asked if I had found her jacket.

20. Brad Pitt's worst movie ever, Fight Club, was still better than the best Mike Myers movie, *Austin Powers*. *(Fight Club)*

Unit Test II

Correct the punctuation errors in the following paragraph.

Waiting on tables is a lot harder than most people think! It's a job that involves people skills, organization, and quick thinking. While servers are responsible for four tables in most restaurants, some smaller restaurants give their servers' up to ten tables. A restaurant's staff (made up of hosts, hostesses, cooks, and servers) must remember two very important points about service: promptness, and pleasantness., It is not always easy to be prompt and pleasant,. Many customers wonder how servers carry large heavy tray's?. Waiting tables can be hard;, but it can be rewarding—a good way to earn some money on a fairly flexible schedule.

CAPITALIZATION

✔ CHECKLIST for Editing Capitalization

> ✔ Are all proper nouns capitalized?
> ✔ Are all words in titles capitalized correctly?
> ✔ Have you followed the other rules for capitalizing correctly?

Test Yourself

Correct the capitalization errors in the following sentences.

- According to uncle Bob, mother makes the best texas sheet cake.
- Antonio is a native american.
- "the shortest path," he said, "Is down baker street."
- Issa loves to go to walt disney world.
- Last year, I saw the red hot chili peppers in concert.

(Answers are in Appendix 4.)

Because every sentence begins with a capital letter, **capitalization** is the best place to start discussing the mechanics of good writing. Capital letters signal where sentences begin. They also call attention to certain kinds of words, making sentences easier to read and understand.

Correct capitalization coupled with correct punctuation adds up to good, clear writing. Here are some guidelines to help you capitalize correctly.

1. Capitalize the first word of every sentence, including the first word of a quotation that forms a sentence.

> **M**y favorite city is Rome.
> "**R**ome is my favorite city," he said.
> He said, "**M**y favorite city is Rome."

TEACHING CAPITALIZATION

Show students copies of real e-mails that contain no capitalization whatsoever. At the same time, show students copies of chat room conversations where people who type in all caps are told to "stop yelling."

Have students rewrite the e-mails with correct capitalization.

After the exercise, talk to students about how capitalization marks sentence boundaries.

INSTRUCTOR'S RESOURCE MANUAL

For sample sentences, for more exercises, and for quizzes, see the *Instructor's Resource Manual*, Section II, Part V.

Do not capitalize the second part of a quotation that is split.

"**M**y favorite city," he said, "is Rome."

2. Capitalize all proper nouns. Do not capitalize common nouns.

Common Nouns	Proper Nouns
person	Eleanor Roosevelt
state	Minnesota
building	Empire State Building
river	Mississippi River
airplane	*Air Force One*

Here are some examples of proper nouns.

People:	Sarah, Julia Roberts, Tiger Woods
Groups:	Australians, Apaches, Europeans, British, Latino
Languages:	Russian, Italian, French
Religions, Religious Books, Holy Days:	Catholicism, Buddhism, Koran, Bible, Yom Kippur, Kwanzaa, Easter
Organizations:	Boston Red Sox, Democratic Party, American Civil Liberties Union, Kiwanis Club, Alpha Gamma Delta
Places:	Smoky Mountains National Park, Antarctica, Louisville, Jefferson County, Madison Avenue, Highway 101, Golden Gate Bridge, John F. Kennedy International Airport
Institutions, Agencies, Businesses:	Washington High School, Baltimore Public Library, United Way, Grady Memorial Hospital, Time Warner
Brand Names, Ships, Aircraft:	Mustang, Wisk, Pepsi, **U.S.S.** *Alabama*, *Challenger*

3. Capitalize titles used with people's names or in place of their names.

Mr. Ralph W. Gerber, **M**s. Rachel Lorca, **D**r. Leticia Johnson Aunt Jane, Grandpa Bob, Cousin Maria, Sis, Nana

Do not capitalize words that identify family relationships.

NOT	I saw my **G**randfather yesterday.
Correct:	I saw my grandfather yesterday.
Correct:	I saw **G**randfather yesterday.

4. Capitalize the titles of creative works.

Books:	*The **C**atcher in the **R**ye*
Short Stories:	"**S**onny's **B**lues"
Plays:	*The **G**lass **M**enagerie*
Poems:	"**M**y **L**ast **D**uchess"
Articles:	"**T**wo **N**ew **I**nns **N**ow **O**pen for **B**usiness"
Magazines:	*Newsweek*
Songs:	"**C**heeseburger in **P**aradise"
Albums or CDs:	*Jimmy **B**uffet's **G**reatest **H**its*
Films:	*Lady and the **T**ramp*
TV Series:	*The **W**est **W**ing*
Works of Art:	*The **B**edroom at **A**rles*
Computer Programs:	**A**pple **W**orks

Do not capitalize *a, an, the,* or short prepositions unless they are the first or last word in a title.

5. Capitalize days of the week, months, holidays, and special events.

Monday, July, Presidents' Day, Thanksgiving, Cinco de Mayo, Mardi Gras

Do not capitalize the names of seasons: *summer, fall, winter, spring.*

6. Capitalize the names of historical events, periods, and documents:

the French Revolution, the Jurassic Period, World War II, the Sixties, the Battle of Bunker Hill, the Magna Carta

7. Capitalize specific course titles and the names of language courses.

Economics 201, Philosophy 101, Spanish 200, Civilizations of the Ancient World

Do not capitalize a course or subject you are referring to in a general way unless the course is a language.

my economics course, my philosophy course, my Spanish course, my history course

8. Capitalize references to regions of the country but not words that merely indicate direction.

> If you travel **n**orth from Houston, you will end up in the **M**idwest, probably in Kansas or Nebraska.

9. Capitalize the opening of a letter and the first word of the closing.

> **D**ear **D**r. Hamlin, **D**ear **S**ir,
>
> **B**est wishes, **S**incerely,

Notice that a comma comes after the opening and closing.

REVIEWING CAPITALIZATION

Why is capitalization important in your writing?

It signals the beginning of a sentence and calls attention to certain

kinds of words so that sentences are easier to read and understand.

What is the difference between a proper noun and a common noun?

Common nouns are everyday words; proper nouns name specific people

and things.

◆ **P r a c t i c e 1** **Identifying** Correct the capitalization errors in the following sentences.

1. The <u>irs</u> is auditing <u>aunt</u> Joan. *(IRS, Aunt)*

2. Debbie and Sue bought their mother a bottle of <u>chanel's</u> <u>coco</u> perfume for <u>mother's</u> Day. *(Chanel's, Coco, Mother's)*

3. In our History class, we are studying the <u>great wall</u> of <u>china</u>. *(history, Great Wall, China)*

4. This <u>Winter</u>, <u>emilio</u> will visit <u>uncle</u> Luis, who lives somewhere in the <u>south</u>. *(winter, Emilio, Uncle, South)*

5. David Bowie's song "<u>changes</u>" is a classic from the <u>seventies</u>. *(Changes, Seventies)*

◆ **P r a c t i c e 2** **Completing** Fill in each blank with words that complete the sentence. Be sure to capitalize words correctly. (You can make up titles if necessary.) *Answers will vary.*

1. In my _____ class, we had to read _____.

2. Blanca bought a new truck, a _____.

3. _____ should be in charge of the charity drive.

4. I wish I could get tickets to see _____ in concert.

5. We are going to _____ for our vacation.

♦ **P r a c t i c e   3   Writing Your Own** Write five sentences of your own that cover at least five of the capitalization rules. *Answers will vary.*

CHAPTER REVIEW

You might want to reread your answers to the questions in all the review boxes before you do the following exercises.

♦ **Review P r a c t i c e   1   Identifying** Correct the capitalization errors in the following sentences.

1. In April's edition of *people* magazine, LeAnn <u>rimes</u> talks about her love of <u>Country</u> music. *(People, Rimes, country)*

2. We decided to get married even though he's a member of the <u>democratic party</u> and I am a member of the <u>republican party</u>. *(Democratic Party, Republican Party)*

3. Raphael was born on October 31, 1972—he was a <u>halloween</u> baby. *(Halloween)*

4. Many <u>Fathers</u>, <u>Sons</u>, and <u>Brothers</u> fought against each other in the <u>american civil war</u>. *(fathers, sons, brothers, American Civil War)*

5. Ernesto's uncle has a beautiful statue of the <u>buddha</u> in his garden. *(Buddha)*

6. I watch *late night with David Letterman* for entertainment. *(Late Night with)*

7. Christy can speak both <u>english</u> and <u>spanish</u>. *(English, Spanish)*

8. We celebrate both <u>christmas</u> and <u>kwanzaa</u>. *(Christmas, Kwanzaa)*

9. My <u>Father</u> used to drive me around town in his 1968 convertible <u>ford mustang</u>. *(father, Ford Mustang)*

10. The spider said to the fly, "<u>welcome</u> to my home." *(Welcome)*

♦ **Review P r a c t i c e   2   Completing** Fill in each blank with words that complete the sentence. Be sure to capitalize words correctly. *Answers will vary.*

1. Over the weekend, I watched my favorite movie, _____.

2. In history, we are studying the _____.

3. I was born on _____.

4. Ashley wears nothing but _____ clothes.

5. Fred and _____ both plan to major in _____.

6. He has an unusual accent because he's from _____.

7. If you travel _____ on Highway 101, you will eventually reach Santa Cruz.

8. My favorite relative, _____, will visit soon.

9. Every summer, we go to _____ to fish.

10. Even though she's a _____ and I'm a _____, we are still the best of friends.

◆ *Review Practice 3* **Writing Your Own** Write a paragraph about the most unusual person you've met or the most unusual place you've visited. What made this person or place unique? *Answers will vary.*

◆ *Review Practice 4* **Editing Through Collaboration** Exchange paragraphs from Review Practice 3 with another student, and do the following tasks: *Answers will vary.*

1. Circle any capital letters that don't follow the capitalization rules.

2. Write the rule number next to the error for the writer to refer to.

Then return the paper to its writer, and use the information in this chapter to correct any capitalization errors in your own paragraph. Record your errors on the Error Log in Appendix 6.

ABBREVIATIONS
AND NUMBERS

CHAPTER

53

✅ CHECKLIST for Using Abbreviations and Numbers

> ✔ Are titles before and after proper names abbreviated correctly?
>
> ✔ Are government agencies and other organizations abbreviated correctly?
>
> ✔ Are numbers *zero* through *nine* spelled out?
>
> ✔ Are numbers 10 and over written as figures (10, 25, 1–20, 324)?

Test Yourself

Correct the abbreviation and number errors in these sentences.

- He earned two million three hundred thousand dollars last year.
- My cat had 5 kittens.
- Sherril moved from England to the U.S.
- Mister Johnson always drinks hot chocolate in the mornings.
- I work for the Internal Revenue Service.

(Answers are in Appendix 4.)

Like capitalization, **abbreviations** and **numbers** are also mechanical features of writing that help us communicate what we want to say. Following the rules that govern their use will make your writing as precise as possible.

TEACHING
ABBREVIATIONS
AND NUMBERS
Have students work in groups of three or four to write a paragraph that is filled with abbreviation and number errors. Have them be as inventive as possible yet still make the paragraph coherent.

Have the groups exchange paragraphs and try to decipher the paragraphs they now have. Point out how distracting abbreviations and numbers can be when they are not used correctly.

INSTRUCTOR'S
RESOURCE MANUAL
For a sample paragraph, for more exercises, and for quizzes, see the *Instructor's Resource Manual*, Section II, Part V.

ABBREVIATIONS

1. Abbreviate titles before proper names.

    Mr. Michael Charles, **Mrs.** Marschel, **Ms.** Susan Deffaa, **Dr.** Frank Hilbig, **Rev.** Billy Graham, **Sen.** Diane Feinstein, **Sgt.** Arturo Lopez

    Abbreviate religious, governmental, and military titles when used with an entire name. Do not abbreviate them when used only with a last name.

    NOT   We thought that **Gov.** Peterson would be reelected.
    Correct: We thought that **Governor** Peterson would be reelected.
    Correct: We thought **Gov.** Richard Peterson would be reelected.

    Professor is not usually abbreviated: **Professor** Mya Belle is teaching this class.

2. Abbreviate academic degrees.

    B.S. (Bachelor of Science)
    R.N. (Registered Nurse)

3. Use the following abbreviations with numbers.

    a.m. or **A.M.**   **p.m.** or **P.M.**   **B.C.** and **A.D.**

4. Abbreviate *United States* only when it is used as an adjective.

    NOT   The **U.S.** is in North America.
    Correct: The **United States** is in North America.
    Correct: The **U.S.** Senate will consider this bill today.

5. Abbreviate only the names of well-known government agencies, businesses, and educational institutions by using their initials without periods.

    FBI (Federal Bureau of Investigation)
    NBC (National Broadcasting Corporation)
    USC (University of Southern California)
    ACLU (American Civil Liberties Union)

6. Abbreviate state names when addressing mail or writing out the postal address. Otherwise, spell out the names of states.

    Maria's new address is 7124 Funston Street, San Francisco, **CA** 90555.
    Maria has moved to San Francisco, **California.**

R EVIEWING A BBREVIATIONS

When you write, are you free to abbreviate any words you want?

No, relatively few abbreviations are acceptable in writing.

◆ **P r a c t i c e 1 Identifying** Correct the underlined words in each of the following sentences.

1. <u>Prof.</u> Smith said that I was a wonderful writer. *(Professor)*

2. The <u>United States</u> economy has many markets. *(U.S.)*

3. When I can't sleep, I watch <u>Music Television</u>. *(MTV)*

4. Last night, <u>sergeant</u> David Montgomery devised the winning strategy. *(Sgt.)*

5. Candice moved to 237 Bella Avenue, Houma, <u>Louisiana</u> 79337. *(LA)*

◆ **P r a c t i c e 2 Completing** In each sentence, write either an abbreviation or the complete word, whichever is correct.

1. We were caught speeding at 10 _____*p.m.*_____ (p.m., post meridian).

2. Alisha will be attending _*California State University*_ (CSU, California State University) and will get her _____*B.A.*_____ (B.A., bachelor of arts) degree in English.

3. Darryl and Pat are visiting relatives in Orlando, _____*Florida*_____ (FL, Florida).

4. We moved to the _*United States*_ (U.S., United States) when I was four years old.

5. (Sen., Senator) _____*Senator*_____ Matthews always has a kind word.

◆ **P r a c t i c e 3 Writing Your Own** Write a sentence of your own for each of the following abbreviations. *Answers will vary.*

1. Mr. _____

2. a.m. _____

3. ABC _____

4. A.A. _____

5. U.S. _____

NUMBERS

Most writers ask the same question about using numbers: When should a number be spelled out, and when is it all right to use numerals? The following simple rules will help you make this decision.

1. Spell out numbers from *zero* to *nine*. Use figures for numbers 10 and higher.

> I have **three** dogs.
>
> My mother-in-law has **19** grandchildren and **11** great-grandchildren.

Do not mix spelled-out numbers and figures in a sentence if they refer to the same types of items. Use numerals for all numbers in that case.

NOT   I have **three** dogs, **18** goldfish, and **two** canaries.

Correct: I have **3** dogs, **18** goldfish, and **2** canaries.

2. For very large numbers, use a combination of figures and words.

> The state's new budget is approximately **$32 million.**
>
> Computer sales for the company reached **2.1 million** units.

3. Always spell out a number that begins a sentence. If this becomes awkward, reword the sentence.

> **Thirty-five** people died in the crash.
>
> Approximately **260,000** people live in Mobile, Alabama.

4. Use figures for dates, addresses, zip codes, telephone numbers, identification numbers, and time.

> On August **1, 1965,** my parents moved to **215** Circle Drive, Santa Fe, NM **71730.**
>
> My new telephone number is **(555) 877-1420.**
>
> My Social Security number is **123-45-6789.**
>
> My alarm went off at **5:00** a.m.

5. Use figures for fractions, decimals, and percentages.

> To make the dessert, you need **1/2** cup of butter and **16** ounces of chocolate.

His blood-alcohol level was **.09.**

Over **5 percent** of Californians are of Hispanic background.

Notice that *percent* is written out and is all one word.

6. Use figures for exact measurements, including amounts of money. Use a dollar sign for amounts over $1.

The room measures **9** feet by **12** feet.

She bought gas for **$2.79** a gallon today—**25** cents more than yesterday.

7. Use figures for the parts of a book.

Chapter **10**   page **120**   Exercise **8**   questions **1** and **7**

Notice that *Chapter* and *Exercise* are capitalized.

REVIEWING NUMBERS

What is the general rule for spelling out numbers as opposed to using numerals?

Spell out numbers zero through nine, and use figures for 10 and higher.

◆ **P r a c t i c e   4   Identifying** Correct any errors with numbers in each of the following sentences.

1. On August <u>third</u>, 2001, <u>sixteen</u> dogs escaped from the pound. *(3, 16)*
2. The park, which measures approximately <u>two thousand</u> square feet, will cost <u>five thousand dollars</u> to landscape. *(2,000, $5,000)*
3. Mr. Thompson's old telephone number was <u>three, nine, nine, four, two, zero, nine</u> *(399-4209)*
4. Almost <u>twenty-five</u> percent of my income comes from sales. *(25)*
5. The earthquake that hit at <u>six forty-five</u> last night measured 6.0 on the Richter scale. *(6:45)*

◆ **P r a c t i c e   5   Completing** Fill in each blank in the following sentences with numbers in the proper form. *Answers will vary.*

1. Please read Chapter _____ and answer questions _____ through _____.

2. I have _____ pencils, _____ bluebooks, and _____ note cards; I am ready for this test.

3. _____ percent of my time is spent doing homework.

4. Christmas is on _____ every year.

5. He made $ _____ million last year.

◆ **P r a c t i c e   6   Write Your Own** Write a sentence demonstrating each of the following rules for numbers. *Answers will vary.*

1. Spell out numbers *zero* through *nine*. Use figures for numbers 10 and higher.
2. For very large numbers, use a combination of figures and words.
3. Always spell out a number that begins a sentence.
4. Use figures for dates, addresses, zip codes, telephone numbers, identification numbers, and time.
5. Use figures for fractions, decimals, and percentages.

CHAPTER REVIEW

You might want to reread your answers to the questions in all the review boxes before you do the following exercises.

◆ ***Review Practice 1*** **Identifying** Circle the abbreviation errors and underline the number errors in each of the following sentences. Some sentences contain more than one error.

1. According to Prof. Gleason, there is a process to writing. *(Professor)*
2. At exactly 7:00 post meridiem, everyone will jump out of his or her hiding place and yell, "Surprise!" *(p.m. or P.M.)*
3. The crew will need explosives to blast the twenty-nine-ton boulder. *(29-ton)*
4. Gen. Brevington's retirement banquet will be held on January twenty-nine, 2004. *(General, 29)*
5. Only 2 of the 8 children remembered their permission slips. *(two, eight)*
6. Of all the people polled, only ten percent were in favor of the new law. *(10)*
7. 9 days from now, Columbia Broadcasting System is airing a special on former United States President Bill Clinton. *(Nine, CBS, U.S.)*

8. You can receive an (associate of arts) degree from your local community college. *(A.A.)*

9. The answers to questions <u>four</u> and <u>five</u> are in Chapter 21. *(4, 5)*

10. After winning the lottery for <u>two million five hundred thousand dollars</u>, Janene moved to Beverly Hills, (CA). *($2.5 million, California)*

◆ ***Review   Practice   2   Completing*** Correct the errors in Review Practice 1 by rewriting the sentences. *See Review Practice 1.*

◆ ***Review   Practice   3   Writing Your Own*** Write a paragraph explaining the quickest route from your house to your school. Use numbers and abbreviations in your paragraph. *Answers will vary.*

◆ ***Review   Practice   4   Editing Through Collaboration*** Exchange paragraphs from Review Practice 3 with another student, and do the following: *Answers will vary.*

1. Underline all abbreviations, numbers, and figures.

2. Circle any abbreviations, numbers, or figures that are not in their correct form.

Then return the paper to its writer, and use the information in this chapter to correct any abbreviation and number errors in your own paragraph. Record your errors on the Error Log in Appendix 6.

UNIT TESTS

Here are some exercises that test your understanding of all the material in this unit: Capitalization, Abbreviations, and Numbers.

Unit Test I

A. Underline the errors in capitalization, abbreviations, and numbers in the following sentences.

1. My brother plans to earn his <u>bachelor of science</u> in physics. *(B.S.)*

2. She invested <u>one thousand four hundred dollars</u> last year. *($1,400)*

3. In a pinch, you can substitute <u>one-half</u> cup of shortening for <u>one-half</u> cup of butter. *(1/2, 1/2)*

4. After lunch at the <u>hard rock café</u>, let's shop on Rodeo <u>drive</u>. *(Hard Rock Café, Drive)*

5. The owners of the company expect profits of <u>six million five hundred thousand dollars</u> this year. *($6.5 million)*

6. My dog had <u>4</u> puppies. *(four)*

7. Of all the countries my aunt has visited, the <u>U.S.</u> is her favorite. *(United States)*

8. "That looks great," said the hairdresser, "<u>But</u> we need to take a little more off the top." *(but)*

9. The police officer clocked me driving too fast in front of the <u>Columbia Broadcasting System</u> building. *(CBS)*

10. Marcus visited Australia and then returned to the <u>U.S.</u> *(United States)*

11. The fence will cost <u>five hundred dollars</u> to fix. *($500)*

12. This semester, I plan on taking <u>psychology</u> 101 and <u>sociology</u> 200. *(Psychology, Sociology)*

13. <u>Bro.</u> Thomas visited me in the hospital. *(Brother)*

14. <u>Mister</u> Matthews takes a walk every night before he goes to bed. *(Mr.)*

15. Before taking the exam, review questions 5 through <u>twenty</u> in Exercise <u>twenty-nine</u>. *(20, 29)*

16. Charlton Heston is a vocal member of the <u>national rifle association</u> (NRA). *(National Rifle Association)*

17. I wake up at exactly 5:30 <u>ante meridiem</u> every morning. *(a.m.)*

18. I work for the <u>fbi</u>, not the <u>cia</u>. *(FBI, CIA)*

19. Monique purchased <u>three</u> bags of balloons, 10 rolls of streamers, <u>two</u> banners, and <u>one</u> piñata for the party. *(3, 2, 1)*

20. The letter opened with these words: "<u>my dearest Ralph</u>." *(My Dearest Ralph)*

B. Correct the errors in capitalization, abbreviations, and numbers in Part A by rewriting each incorrect sentence.

Unit Test II

A. Underline the errors in capitalization, abbreviations, and numbers in the following paragraph.

    Last <u>Spring</u>, *[spring]* my family and I went to Alaska on vacation. We went for <u>eleven</u> *[11]* days; we stayed from <u>monday</u>, *[Monday]* June <u>third</u> *[3]* through <u>thursday</u>, *[Thursday]* June <u>fourteenth</u>. *[14]* Some of my extended family, including <u>grandpa</u> *[Grandpa]* Joe and <u>auntie</u> *[Auntie]* Jane, came with us. While we were there, we ate at Fish and <u>chips</u>, *[Chips]* which is a small diner on the coast. I found so many cute souvenirs for my <u>Friends</u>; *[friends]* I even found a postcard to mail to my elderly friend, <u>Misses</u> *[Mrs.]* Calen. However, I couldn't remember if her address was 6260 Minden <u>Dr</u>, *[Drive]* Carlsbad, <u>New Mexico</u> *[NM]* 88220 or 6220 Minden <u>Ave</u>, *[Avenue]* Carlsbad, <u>New Mexico</u> *[NM]* 88260, so I had to give the postcard to her when I got home. Even with all of the souvenirs I bought, the trip cost me only <u>nine-hundred dollars</u>, *[$900]* which is only <u>thirty</u> *[30]* percent of what our last family trip cost me.

B. Correct the errors in capitalization, abbreviations, and numbers in Part A by rewriting the paragraph.

CHAPTER 54

VARYING SENTENCE STRUCTURE

✅ CHECKLIST for Varying Sentence Patterns

✔ Do you add introductory material to vary your sentence patterns?

✔ Do you occasionally reverse the order of some subjects and verbs?

✔ Do you move sentence parts to add variety to your sentences?

✔ Do you sometimes use questions and exclamations to vary your sentence structure?

TEACHING VARYING SENTENCE STRUCTURE

Put students into groups of three or four, and provide them with a paragraph made up of simple sentences. All groups should receive the same paragraph.

Have each group make its paragraph more lively by using the guidelines in this chapter to vary sentence structure.

Then have the groups read their paragraphs to the rest of the class, and let the students decide which paragraph is most exciting. Why did they choose the paragraph they did?

INSTRUCTOR'S RESOURCE MANUAL

For sample paragraphs, for more exercises, and for quizzes, see the *Instructor's Resource Manual*, Section II, Part V.

Test Yourself

Turn each of the following pairs of sentences into one sentence that is more interesting.

- I work too much. I am tired.
- My cat is very lazy. She sleeps more than 14 hours a day.
- He enjoys reading. He likes mysteries.
- I live in an old house. My family has lived here for generations.
- My brother loves to eat. He will eat anything.

(Answers are in Appendix 4.)

Reading the same sentence pattern sentence after sentence can become very monotonous for your readers. This chapter will help you solve this problem in your writing. Look at the following example.

I have always loved animals. I am about to get my own dog for the first time. I am ready to be responsible enough to take care of it. I am excited about this new phase in my life. I got a part-time job. I can't wait to get my own dog.

This paragraph has some terrific ideas, but they are expressed in such a monotonous way that the readers might doze off. What this paragraph needs is variety in its sentence structure. Here are some ideas for keeping your readers awake and ready to hear your good thoughts.

ADD INTRODUCTORY WORDS

Add some introductory words to your sentences so that they don't all start the same way.

> **For as long as I can remember,** I have always loved animals. **Now** I am about to get my own dog for the first time. I am ready to be responsible enough to take care of it. I am excited about this new phase in my life. **To pay for my new friend,** I got a part-time job. I can't wait to get my own dog.

◆ *P r a c t i c e 1* **Identifying** Underline the sentence in each pair that could be turned into an introductory word, phrase, or clause.

1. Misty had a terrible stomachache. <u>It was late last night</u>. *(Late last night,)*
2. <u>We went to the river.</u> We skipped over the rocks. *(When we went to the river,)*
3. <u>We went to McDonald's for breakfast.</u> We saw our friends. *(When we went to McDonald's for breakfast,)*
4. The sunsets are beautiful. <u>It was spring.</u> *(In the spring,)*
5. He is afraid of dogs. <u>He was bitten by a dog once.</u> *(Because he was bitten by a dog once,)*

◆ *P r a c t i c e 2* **Completing** Rewrite the sentences in Practice 1 by turning each sentence you underlined into an introductory word, phrase, or clause. *See Practice 1.*

◆ *P r a c t i c e 3* **Writing Your Own** Write five sentences of your own with introductory elements. *Answers will vary.*

REVERSE WORDS

Reverse the order of some subjects and verbs. For example, instead of *I am so excited,* try *Am I ever excited.* You can also add or drop words and change punctuation to make the sentence read smoothly.

> For as long as I can remember, I have always loved animals. Now I am about to get my own dog for the first time. I am ready to be

responsible enough to take care of it. **Am I ever excited** about this new phase in my life. To pay for my new friend, I got a part-time job. I can't wait to get my own dog.

◆ *P r a c t i c e   4*   **Identifying** Underline the words or phrases you could reverse in each of the following sentences.

1. I am happy to know you. *(Am I happy to know you!)*
2. All the ingredients went into the pot. *(Into the pot went all the ingredients.)*
3. The cat jumped out of the hat. *(Out of the hat jumped the cat.)*
4. The children were happy. *(Were the children happy!)*
5. The strange creature appeared out of nowhere. *(Out of nowhere appeared the strange creature.)*

◆ *P r a c t i c e   5*   **Completing** Rewrite the sentences in Practice 4 by reversing the words you underlined. *See Practice 4.*

◆ *P r a c t i c e   6*   **Writing Your Own** Write five sentences of your own with subjects and verbs reversed. *Answers will vary.*

MOVE SENTENCE PARTS

Move some parts of the sentence around. Experiment to see which order works best.

For as long as I can remember, I have always loved animals. Now I am about to get my own dog for the first time. I am ready to be responsible enough to take care of it. Am I ever excited about this new phase in my life. **My part-time job can help me pay for my new friend.** I can't wait to get my own dog.

◆ *P r a c t i c e   7*   **Identifying** Underline any parts of the following sentences that can be moved around.

1. To bake these cookies, you will need 2 cups of flour. *(Move to beginning of sentence.)*
2. Finally, I knew the truth. *(Move to end.)*
3. I was very full after lunch. *(Move to beginning.)*
4. You will find your shoes underneath your bed. *(Move to beginning.)*
5. If you enjoyed the film, you will probably like the book. *(Move to end.)*

◆ *P r a c t i c e* **8** **Completing** Rewrite the sentences in Practice 7, moving the words you underlined. *See Practice 7.*

◆ *P r a c t i c e* **9** **Writing Your Own** Write two sentences of your own. Then rewrite each sentence two different ways. *Answers will vary.*

VARY SENTENCE TYPE

Use a question, a command, or an exclamation occasionally.

> For as long as I can remember, I have always loved animals. **Have you?** Now I am about to get my own dog for the first time. I am ready to be responsible enough to take care of it. **Am I ever excited about this new phase in my life!** My part-time job can help me pay for my new friend. I can't wait to get my own dog.

◆ *P r a c t i c e* **10** **Identifying** Identify each of the following sentences as a statement (S), a question (Q), a command (C), or an exclamation (E).

1. __Q__ When is the meal being served

2. __Q__ Did you see that object flying in the sky

3. __C__ Bring me a glass of iced tea and a bowl of grapes

4. __C__ First do the prewriting exercises

5. __S, E__ I just hate it when that happens

◆ *P r a c t i c e* **11** **Completing** Complete the following sentences, making them into questions, commands, or exclamations. Then supply the correct punctuation. *Answers will vary.*

1. Wow, I can't believe ⎯⎯⎯⎯⎯⎯⎯⎯⎯⎯⎯⎯⎯

2. At the first intersection ⎯⎯⎯⎯⎯⎯⎯⎯⎯⎯⎯⎯

3. Why is ⎯⎯⎯⎯⎯⎯⎯⎯⎯⎯⎯⎯⎯⎯⎯⎯⎯⎯⎯

4. Hand me ⎯⎯⎯⎯⎯⎯⎯⎯⎯⎯⎯⎯⎯⎯⎯⎯⎯⎯

5. Did you hear ⎯⎯⎯⎯⎯⎯⎯⎯⎯⎯⎯⎯⎯⎯⎯⎯

◆ **P r a c t i c e 1 2** **Writing Your Own** Write two statements, two questions, two commands, and two exclamations of your own. *Answers will vary.*

REVIEWING WAYS TO VARY SENTENCE PATTERNS

Why is varying sentence patterns important in your writing?

Sentence variety keeps the readers interested.

Name four ways to vary your sentence patterns.

Add introductory words and phrases.

Reverse the order of some subjects and verbs.

Move some parts of your sentences around.

Use a question, a command, or an exclamation occasionally.

What other kinds of sentences besides statements can you use for variety?

questions   commands   exclamations

CHAPTER REVIEW

You might want to reread your answers to the questions in the review box before you do the following exercises.

◆ **Review P r a c t i c e 1** **Identifying** Underline the words or groups of words that have been added or moved in each revised sentence. Then use the following key to tell which rule was applied to the sentence:

1. Add introductory words.
2. Reverse the order of subject and verb.
3. Move parts of the sentence around.
4. Use a question, a command, or an exclamation occasionally.

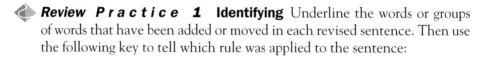

    1. Eat your peas. You aren't finished with dinner yet.

         _1_ If you eat your peas, you'll be finished with dinner.

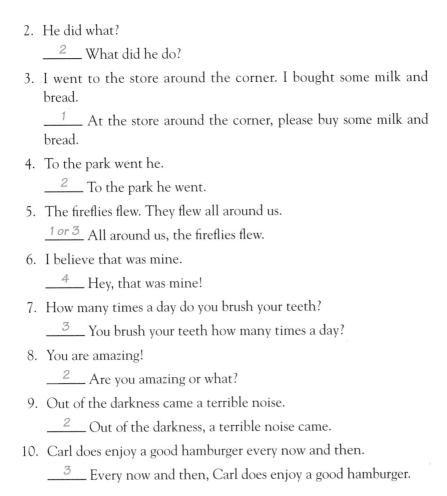

2. He did what?

    ___2___ What did he do?

3. I went to the store around the corner. I bought some milk and bread.

    ___1___ At the store around the corner, please buy some milk and bread.

4. To the park went he.

    ___2___ To the park he went.

5. The fireflies flew. They flew all around us.

    ___1 or 3___ All around us, the fireflies flew.

6. I believe that was mine.

    ___4___ Hey, that was mine!

7. How many times a day do you brush your teeth?

    ___3___ You brush your teeth how many times a day?

8. You are amazing!

    ___2___ Are you amazing or what?

9. Out of the darkness came a terrible noise.

    ___2___ Out of the darkness, a terrible noise came.

10. Carl does enjoy a good hamburger every now and then.

    ___3___ Every now and then, Carl does enjoy a good hamburger.

◆ **Review P r a c t i c e 2 Completing** Vary the structure of the following sentences with at least three of the four ideas you just learned. *Answers will vary.*

A good teacher should be encouraging toward students. He or she should understand when a student is having problems and spend some one-on-one time together. The teacher should then help the student identify problems and give helpful instruction to solve the problem. A good teacher never makes fun of a student.

◆ **Review P r a c t i c e 3 Writing Your Own** Write a paragraph about a good deed you have performed. What made you decide to do what you did? Try to use each of the four ways you have learned to make sentences interesting. *Answers will vary.*

Review Practice 4 **Editing Through Collaboration** Exchange paragraphs from Review Practice 3 with another student, and do the following: *Answers will vary.*

1. Put brackets around any sentences that sound monotonous.
2. Suggest a way to vary each of these sentences.

Then return the paper to its writer, and use the information in this chapter to vary the sentence structure in your own paragraph. Record your errors on the Error Log in Appendix 6.

PARALLELISM

 CHECKLIST for Using Parallelism

> ✔ Can you use parallelism to add coherence to your sentences and paragraphs?
> ✔ Are all items in a series grammatically balanced?

Test Yourself

Underline the parts in each of the following sentences that seem awkward or unbalanced.

- Tony enjoys hockey, football, and runs.
- My mom and dad give money to help the homeless and for building new homes.
- I finished high school, started college, and I am beginning a new job.
- I love the mountains because they're cool, clean, and feel refreshing.
- Listening to music, watching television, or to read a book are good ways to relax.

(Answers are in Appendix 4.)

When sentences are **parallel,** they are balanced. That is, words, phrases, or clauses in a series start with the same grammatical form. Parallel structures make your sentences interesting and clear.

Following is a paragraph that could be greatly improved with parallel structures.

TEACHING PARALLELISM

Draw a picture of two sets of train tracks that run parallel to each other. Draw a second picture of two sets of train tracks that eventually cross each other. Ask students the following question: If both tracks have trains heading toward each other and you were on one of the trains, which set of tracks would you prefer your train to be on? Of course students will choose the parallel tracks. Ask them to discuss their choice.

Now explain to students that when sentences are not parallel, they are often like two trains heading for each other and about to collide. Then discuss how faulty parallelism can "wreck" an idea just as trains not on parallel tracks can collide.

Show them how parallelism is important to move ideas along

smoothly. Use the
examples in the text to
prove your point.

INSTRUCTOR'S
RESOURCE MANUAL
For more exercises and
for quizzes, see the
*Instructor's Resource
Manual,* Section II,
Part V.

My brother Ricardo was not excited when he was called in to work at the hospital today. He had been looking forward to this day off—his first in three weeks. He was planning to work out in the morning, swimming in the afternoon, and going to a movie in the evening. Instead he will be helping the patients, assisting the nurses, and will aid the doctors.

Words and phrases in a series should be parallel, which means they should start with the same type of word. Parallelism makes your sentence structure smoother and more interesting. Look at this sentence, for example.

NOT   He had planned to **work out** in the morning,

swimming in the afternoon, and

going to a movie in the evening.

Parallel: He had planned to **work out** in the morning,

swim in the afternoon, and

go to the movies in the evening.

Parallel: He had planned on **working out** in the morning,

swimming in the afternoon, and

going to the movies in the evening.

Here is another sentence that would read better if the parts were parallel:

NOT   Instead he will be **helping** the patients,

assisting the nurses, and

will aid the doctors.

Parallel: Instead he will be **helping** the patients,

assisting the nurses, and

aiding the doctors.

Parallel: Instead he will be helping **the patients,**

the nurses, and

the doctors.

Now read the paragraph with these two sentences made parallel or balanced.

My brother Ricardo was not excited when he was called in to work at the hospital today. He had been looking forward to this day off—his first in three weeks. He had planned to work out in the morning, swim in the afternoon, and go to a movie in the evening. Instead he will be helping the patients, the nurses, and the doctors.

REVIEWING PARALLELISM

What is parallelism?

Starting words, phrases, and clauses in a series with the same

grammatical form

Why should you use parallelism in your writing?

To make your writing interesting and clear

◆ *P r a c t i c e 1*   **Identifying** Underline the parallel structures in each of the following sentences.

1. Scott plans to <u>hide in his cabin</u>, <u>do some fishing</u>, and <u>work on his novel</u>.
2. The car needs new <u>windows</u>, <u>tires</u>, and <u>paint</u>.
3. Georgia believes <u>that she is the most wonderful person in the world</u> and <u>that she deserves everyone's love and attention</u>.
4. They <u>camped under the stars</u>, <u>swam in the cool lakes</u>, and <u>enjoyed the fresh air</u>.
5. Because of the <u>pouring rain</u>, <u>extreme cold</u>, and <u>bitter wind</u>, we decided to stay inside.

◆ *P r a c t i c e 2*   **Completing** Make the underlined elements parallel in each of the following sentences. *Answers will vary.*

1. He will wear only clothes <u>that have designer labels</u> and <u>they are expensive</u>.

   _____

2. <u>Regular exercise</u>, <u>drinking plenty of water</u>, and <u>eating lots of good food</u> will help keep you healthy.

   _____

3. Dierdra went to the mall <u>to get a bite to eat</u>, <u>to do some shopping</u>, and <u>will visit friends</u>.

   _____

4. Please do not <u>tap pens</u>, <u>talk to others</u>, or <u>eating food during the exam</u>.

_____

5. On his trip, he <u>took pictures of mountains</u>, <u>fed animals</u>, and <u>some enjoy-able people</u>.

_____

◆ *P r a c t i c e   3* **Writing Your Own** Write five sentences of your own using parallel structures in each. *Answers will vary.*

CHAPTER REVIEW

You might want to reread your answers to the questions in the review box before you do the following exercises.

◆ *Review P r a c t i c e   1*   **Identifying** Underline the parallel structures in each of the following sentences.

1. <u>Football</u>, <u>basketball</u>, and <u>hockey</u> are all competitive sports.
2. Because of <u>the terrible weather</u>, <u>the horrible traffic</u>, and <u>the missed bus</u>, we didn't make our flight.
3. When I'm in love, <u>the sun always shines</u>, <u>the stars always sparkle</u>, and <u>the moon always glows</u>.
4. Marilyn went to the city's annual air show <u>because she wanted to see the jet planes</u> and <u>because she wanted to try the interesting foods</u>.
5. The <u>biting mosquitoes</u>, <u>barking dogs</u>, and <u>burning sun</u> made me miserable.
6. Please <u>feed</u>, <u>bathe</u>, and <u>change</u> the baby before I get home.
7. If Harvey <u>cleans the house</u>, <u>does his homework</u>, and <u>begs for forgiveness</u>, he may get out of his punishment.
8. I believe <u>that people should be treated fairly</u> and <u>that everyone should get a second chance</u>.
9. He was suspended because he <u>fought</u>, <u>cheated</u>, and <u>disrespected</u> others.
10. Today Mother <u>paid the bills</u>, <u>balanced the checkbook</u>, and <u>washed the car</u>.

◆ *Review P r a c t i c e   2* **Completing** Complete each of the following sentences with parallel structures. *Answers will vary.*

1. I enjoy _____, _____, and _____ in the summer.

2. Because of _____ and because of _____, Miriam didn't go to the movies.

3. You can be successful in college if you _____, _____, and _____.

4. Even though Jeremy _____, _____, and _____, he still can't find the problem.

5. _____, _____, and _____ are essential items when hiking.

6. She cooks foods that _____ and _____.

7. My favorite foods are _____, _____, and _____.

8. If I have to hear her _____, _____, and _____ one more time, I'm going to scream.

9. The instructor has already explained _____, _____, and _____.

10. If you _____, _____, and _____, you just might survive boot camp.

◆ *Review P r a c t i c e 3* **Writing Your Own** Write a paragraph about the best holiday you've ever had. What was the holiday? Why was it the best? Use two examples of parallelism in your paragraph. *Answers will vary.*

◆ *Review P r a c t i c e 4* **Editing Through Collaboration** Exchange paragraphs from Review Practice 3 with another student, and do the following: *Answers will vary.*

1. Underline any items in a series.

2. Put brackets around any of these items that are not grammatically parallel.

Then return the paper to its writer, and use the information in this chapter to correct any parallelism errors in your own paragraph. Record your errors on the Error Log in Appendix 6.

COMBINING SENTENCES

✓ CHECKLIST for Combining Sentences

> ✔ Do you combine sentences to avoid too many short, choppy sentences in a row?
>
> ✔ Do you use different types of sentences?

TEACHING
COMBINING
SENTENCES
Have each student
write a list of 10 simple
sentences on a common
subject (such as educa-
tion, war, politics,
ecology, animal rights,
or final exams). Then
have students work
in pairs to create the
following sentence
patterns from the
simple sentences:
   Three compound
      sentences
   Three complex
      sentences
   Three compound-
      complex
      sentences
Have the class discuss
the different effects of
these sentence types.

INSTRUCTOR'S
RESOURCE MANUAL
For more exercises
and for quizzes, see the
*Instructor's Resource
Manual,* Section II,
Part V.

Test Yourself

Combine each set of sentences into one sentence.

- My brother is taking tennis lessons. He takes his lessons from a professional player.
- The baby is crying. She's hungry.
- It's too hot outside. Let's go for a swim.
- We moved overseas when I was 11 years old. I learned much about different cultures.
- I like to travel. Africa has many interesting animals and plants. I want to go to Africa.

(Answers are in Appendix 4.)

Still another way to add variety to your writing is to combine short, choppy sentences into longer sentences. You can combine simple sentences to make compound or complex sentences. You can also combine compound and complex sentences.

SIMPLE SENTENCES

A **simple sentence** consists of one independent clause. Remember that a clause has a subject and a main verb.

In the following examples, notice that a simple sentence can have more than one subject and more than one verb. (For more on compound subjects and compound verbs, see Chapter 30.)

S V
I have several very good friends.

S V   V
I have good friends and enjoy being with them.

S   S   V
Martin and Louis are good friends.

S   S   V   V
Martin and I do interesting things and go to interesting places.

REVIEWING SIMPLE SENTENCES

What does a simple sentence consist of?

One independent clause

Write a simple sentence.

Answers will vary.

◆ **P r a c t i c e   1   Identifying** Underline the subjects once and the verbs twice in each of the following sentences. Then label the simple sentences SS.

1. _____ Most cats don't like the water, but most dogs do.

2. _SS_ Tommy and I like listening to the same types of music and watching the same types of shows.

3. _____ I feel that our luck is about to change.

4. _SS_ We left quickly because of the smell.

5. _SS_ We have pictures of the family throughout the house.

◆ **P r a c t i c e   2   Completing** Make simple sentences out of the sentences in Practice 1 that are not simple. *Answers will vary.*

◈ *P r a c t i c e 3* **Writing Your Own** Write a simple sentence of your own for each of the following subjects and verbs. *Answers will vary.*

1. Jessy and Miguel _____

2. we're eating and drinking _____

3. the playful kittens _____

4. looking and listening _____

5. the hot pan _____

COMPOUND SENTENCES

A **compound sentence** consists of two or more independent clauses joined by a coordinating conjunction (*and, but, for, nor, or, so,* or *yet*). In other words, you can create a compound sentence from two (or more) simple sentences.

Simple:	I can swim fast.
Simple:	I am a good long-distance swimmer.
	s v s v
Compound:	I can swim fast, **and** I am a good long-distance swimmer.

Simple:	She has a very stressful job.
Simple:	She works out at the gym three times a week.
	s v s v
Compound:	She has a very stressful job, **so** she works out at the gym three times a week.

Simple:	My parents are leaving for Hawaii on Tuesday.
Simple:	They won't be here for my birthday party.
	s v
Compound:	My parents are leaving for Hawaii on Tuesday, **so**
	s v
	they won't be here for my birthday party.

Hint: As the examples show, a comma comes before the coordinating conjunction in a compound sentence.

REVIEWING COMPOUND SENTENCES

What does a compound sentence consist of?

Two or more independent clauses

Write a compound sentence.

Answers will vary.

◆ *P r a c t i c e   4*   **Identifying** Underline the independent clauses in the following sentences, and circle the coordinating conjunctions.

1. I am not sick, and I feel fine.
2. You cannot bring food or drink in this building, but you can eat in the cafeteria.
3. We try not to gossip, for we know the damage loose lips can cause.
4. I do not like raspberries, yet I do like raspberry pie.
5. Christy likes fast cars, so she is going to buy a sports car.

◆ *P r a c t i c e   5*   **Completing** Combine each pair of simple sentences into a compound sentence. *Answers will vary.*

1. I am leaving. I am late for an appointment.
2. Quickly, move out of the way. The angry elephant is going to charge us.
3. We usually take a month-long vacation. We are always happy to return home.
4. This food has been sitting out all day in the hot sun. It smells awful.
5. I have a lot of cousins. I haven't met them all.

◆ *P r a c t i c e   6*   **Writing Your Own** Write five compound sentences of your own. *Answers will vary.*

COMPLEX SENTENCES

A **complex sentence** is composed of one independent clause and at least one dependent clause. A **dependent clause** begins with either a subordinating conjunction or a relative pronoun.

Subordinating Conjunctions

after	*because*	*since*	*until*
although	*before*	*so*	*when*
as	*even if*	*so that*	*whenever*
as if	*even though*	*than*	*where*
as long as	*how*	*that*	*wherever*
as soon as	*if*	*though*	*whether*
as though	*in order that*	*unless*	*while*

Relative Pronouns

who	*whom*	*whose*	*which*	*that*

You can use subordinating conjunctions and relative pronouns to make a simple sentence (an independent clause) into a dependent clause. Then you can add the new dependent clause to an independent clause to produce a complex sentence that adds interest and variety to your writing.

How do you know which simple sentence should be independent and which should be dependent? The idea that you think is more important should be the independent clause. The less important idea will then be the dependent clause.

Following are some examples of how to combine simple sentences to make a complex sentence.

Simple: Myra has a large collection of movie videos.

Simple: Myra watches the same few films over and over.

Dep

Complex: **Even though** Myra has a large collection of movie

Ind

videos, she watches the same few films over and over.

This complex sentence stresses that Myra watches the same films over and over. The size of her collection is of secondary importance.

Ind

Complex: She has a big collection of movie videos, **though** she

Dep

watches the same few films over and over.

In the previous complex sentence, the size of the collection is most important, so it is the independent clause.

Simple: The winner of the lottery was Laura.

Simple: Laura is my cousin.

$$\overset{\text{Ind}}{} \qquad\qquad\qquad\qquad \overset{\text{Dep}}{}$$

Complex: The winner of the lottery was Laura, **who** is my cousin.

This complex sentence answers the question "Who won the lottery?" The information about Laura being the cousin is of secondary importance.

$$\overset{\text{Ind}}{} \qquad\qquad\qquad \overset{\text{Dep}}{}$$

Complex: My cousin is Laura, **who** won the lottery.

This complex sentence answers the question "Who is your cousin?" The information that she won the lottery is secondary.

REVIEWING COMPLEX SENTENCES

What does a complex sentence consist of?

An independent clause and at least one dependent clause

Write a complex sentence.

Answers will vary.

◆ **P r a c t i c e 7 Identifying** Label the underlined part of each sentence as either an independent (Ind) or a dependent (Dep) clause.

1. _Dep_ <u>Although I was tired</u>, I still went to school.

2. _Dep_ Here is the furniture <u>that you ordered</u>.

3. _Ind_ <u>Trish moved to the coast</u> because she likes the beach.

4. _Dep_ My doctor is Janet Woo, <u>who is also my mom</u>.

5. _Ind_ If we cannot study at your house, <u>then let's study at the library</u>.

◆ **P r a c t i c e 8 Completing** Finish each sentence, and label the new clause either dependent (Dep) or independent (Ind). *Answers will vary.*

1. __*Ind*__ Whenever John's face turns red, _____.
2. __*Ind*__ _____ because he forgot to call home.
3. __*Dep*__ Maya's mother, who _____, is a great cook.
4. __*Dep*__ I like the blue one, _____.
5. __*Dep*__ He climbed the mountain _____.

◆ **P r a c t i c e   9   Writing Your Own** Write five complex sentences, making sure you have one independent clause and at least one dependent clause in each. *Answers will vary.*

COMPOUND-COMPLEX SENTENCES

If you combine a compound sentence with a complex sentence, you produce a **compound-complex sentence.** That means your sentence has at least two independent clauses (to make it compound) and at least one dependent clause (to make it complex). Here are some examples.

Simple: My cousin likes scuba diving.

Simple: He is planning a trip to Hawaii.

Simple: He is excited about diving in Hawaii.

                                           Ind   Ind

Compound-Complex: My cousin likes scuba diving, **so** he is

                                                 Dep

        planning a trip to Hawaii, **which** he is very excited about.

Simple: She bought a new house.

Simple: It has a pool and a spa.

Simple: The house was very expensive.

                                         Ind   Dep

Compound-Complex: She bought a new house, **which** has a

                                               Ind

        pool and a spa, **but** it was very expensive.

Simple: Today's weather is very bad.

Simple: The rain could make it difficult to drive.

Simple: This could delay your departure for home.

	Ind Ind
Compound-Complex:	Today's weather is very bad, **and** the rain

                                                          Dep
                    could make it difficult to drive, **which** could
                    delay your arrival home.

Hint: Notice that we occasionally have to change words in combined sentences so that the sentences make sense.

REVIEWING COMPOUND-COMPLEX SENTENCES

What does a compound-complex sentence consist of?

  At least two independent clauses and one dependent clause

Write a compound-complex sentence.

  Answers will vary.

◆ **P r a c t i c e   1 0   Identifying** Underline the clauses in each of the following compound-complex sentences. Then identify each clause as either independent (Ind) or dependent (Dep).

        Dep   Ind   Ind
1. Whenever I travel, I set an alarm clock, and I arrange for a wake-up call.

        Ind   Dep   Ind
2. Sandy likes Anthony because he is nice, but she also likes Mark.

        Dep   Ind   Ind
3. After they fought, they decided to make up, and now they are inseparable.

      Ind   Dep   Ind
4. The traffic, which is usually bad around noon, is very heavy today, so

        Ind
   you'd better leave soon.

            Ind   Dep   Ind
5. We went to the Virgin Islands because we love the sun, yet it rained the

   whole time.

◆ **P r a c t i c e 1 1   Completing** Expand each sentence into a compound-complex sentence. *Answers will vary.*

1. The boy likes oranges and pears.

   _____

2. The box was very heavy, but he lifted it anyway.

_____

3. Jill says that she will never fly in a plane.

_____

4. John will be 21 soon.

_____

5. I am watching MTV and getting some rest.

_____

◆ **P r a c t i c e   1 2**   **Writing Your Own** Write five compound-complex sentences of your own. *Answers will vary.*

CHAPTER REVIEW

You might want to reread your answers to the questions in all the review boxes before you do the following exercises.

◆ **Review   P r a c t i c e   1**   **Identifying** Underline the independent clauses in each sentence. Then label the sentence simple (SS), compound (C), complex (CX), or compound-complex (CCX). The following definitions might help you.

Simple (SS)	= one independent clause
Compound (C)	= two or more independent clauses joined by *and, but, for, nor, or, so,* or *yet*
Complex (CX)	= one independent clause and at least one dependent clause
Compound-complex (CCX)	= at least two independent clauses and one or more dependent clauses

1. __SS__ Casey and Floyd have left the building.

2. __CX__ Even though he is quiet, he is very friendly.

3. ___C___ Marcy and David are boyfriend and girlfriend, and <u>they are going to the prom together</u>.

4. ___SS___ <u>The dog and cat ate my dinner last night</u>.

5. ___C___ Mrs. Glancy is my close friend, and <u>she visits me often</u>.

6. ___CCX___ Marc is happy because Sheila is here, and <u>he wants to ask her on a date</u>.

7. ___SS___ <u>The folders are in the desk drawer</u>.

8. ___C___ The dog needs to be fed, and <u>he needs a bath</u>.

9. ___CCX___ The gifts, which you bought yesterday, <u>have been wrapped</u>, and <u>they are ready to be delivered</u>.

10. ___CX___ Because her alarm didn't go off, <u>she was late for work</u>.

◆ **Review P r a c t i c e 2 Completing** Combine each set of sentences to make the sentence pattern indicated in parentheses. You may need to change some wording in the sentences so they make sense. The list of sentence types in Review Practice 1 may help you with this exercise. *Answers will vary.*

1. Antoine bikes in the morning. He wants to stay in shape. He goes to the gym every weekend. (compound-complex)

2. I like to play in the mud. I always get dirty. (compound)

3. You should leave now. You should be at your appointment 15 minutes early to fill out paperwork. (complex)

4. Penny brought a stray dog home. Penny loves animals. Her mother wouldn't let her keep it. (compound-complex)

5. I slammed the car door on my thumb. I broke it. (complex)

6. I love to chew gum and pop bubbles. I can't chew gum in class. (complex)

7. The little girl lost her doll. She has looked everywhere for it. She is crying. (compound-complex)

8. The sun is shining. The birds are singing. (compound)

9. The reports are missing. I need them now. (compound)

10. It is October. The leaves are turning brown and falling from the tree. (complex)

◆ **Review P r a c t i c e 3 Writing Your Own** Write a paragraph about your fondest wish. What is it, and why do you wish for it? *Answers will vary.*

◆ ***Review P r a c t i c e 4***   **Editing Through Collaboration** Exchange paragraphs from Review Practice 3 with another student, and do the following: *Answers will vary.*

1. Put brackets around any sentences that you think should be combined.

2. Underline sentences that are incorrectly combined (for example, ones that have a weak connecting word or no connecting word).

Then return the paper to its writer, and use the information in this chapter to combine sentences in your own paragraph. Record your errors on the Error Log in Appendix 6.

UNIT TESTS

Here are some exercises that test your understanding of all the material in this unit: varying sentence structure, parallelism, and combining sentences.

Unit Test I

A. Underline and label the errors in each of the following sentences in variety, parallelism, and sentence combining.

1. We went on a trip to Canada. We visited many relatives. We had never even met these relatives before. *(variety, sentence combining)*

2. Myra should not eat before swimming. She will get sick. *(variety, sentence combining)*

3. She's been in trouble before. She usually gets out of it. She knows how. *(variety, sentence combining)*

4. I worked late last night. I had a deadline to meet. The deadline was on my project. *(variety, sentence combining)*

5. I like the water. I don't know how to swim. *(variety, sentence combining)*

6. We decided we would do nothing but relax, read, and <u>swimming this weekend</u>. *(parallelism)*

7. Salsa dancing is hard. You can do it if you practice. Practice takes time. *(variety, sentence combining)*

8. Hanna loves working with small children. She's a babysitter. *(variety, sentence combining)*

9. The two boys dared each other. They jumped into the cold pool. It was 3 a.m. *(variety, sentence combining)*

10. The neighbors are complaining. The neighbors didn't like the loud noises. *(variety, sentence combining)*

11. Becky likes math. Math is her major. *(variety, sentence combining)*

12. You will have to buy lunch. You can bring your own. *(variety, sentence combining)*

13. Take this letter to the post office for me. It is important. It will need postage. *(variety, sentence combining)*

14. He was racing across the field, was jumping over the hedges, and <u>fell into the pond</u>. *(parallelism)*

15. You are smart. You will understand this problem. This problem is complex. *(variety, sentence combining)*

16. The monkeys are jumping from tree to tree. They are lively. *(variety, sentence combining)*

17. Leo shouldn't watch so much television. He should not stay up so late at night. *(variety, sentence combining)*

18. My nieces are sleeping in my bed, wearing my clothes, and <u>will drive me crazy</u>. *(parallelism)*

19. He isn't going to work today because he feels ill. He has plenty of sick leave left. *(sentence combining)*

20. Our car broke down. Juanita and I decided to fly to Las Vegas. *(variety, sentence combining)*

B. Correct the errors you identified in Part A by rewriting each incorrect sentence. *Answers will vary.*

Unit Test II

A. Underline and label the errors in the following paragraph in variety, parallelism, and sentence combining.

(1)
Learning to write is like learning to ride a bike. (2) Learning to write is fun once people learn how. (3) Learning to write involves learning several of the components of writing. (4) Some of the components of writing are grammar, audience, and to organize. (5) People are sometimes nervous about writing. (6) They don't know how to approach an assignment. (7) Once people master each component of writing, they usually enjoy journals, writing creative fiction, and even to write research papers. (8) Writing can become easy and fun. (9) People need to give writing a chance. (10) People just need to practice. (11) They would see their writing improve.

(1-3) sentence variety, sentence combining
(4) parallelism
(5-6) sentence combining
(7) parallelism
(8-9) sentence combining
(10-11) sentence combining

B. Correct the errors you identified in Part A by rewriting the paragraph. *Answers will vary.*

STANDARD AND NONSTANDARD ENGLISH

✔ CHECKLIST for Choosing the Right Word

> ✔ Do you consistently use standard English in your paper?
>
> ✔ Is your paper free of nonstandard, ungrammatical words?
>
> ✔ Have you changed any slang to standard English?

Test Yourself

Label the following sentences as correct, incorrect, or slang.

- You shoulda seen Claudia's new hairstyle. _____
- Where are my friends at? _____
- Your new bike is really hot. _____
- Randy was enthused about his date. _____
- Fatboy Slim's new video rocks. _____

(Answers are in Appendix 4.)

Choosing the right words for what you want to say is an important part of effective communication. This chapter will help you find the right words and phrases for the audience you are trying to reach.

Look, for example, at the following sentences. They all have a similar message, expressed in different words.

I want to do good in college, being as I can get a good job.

I be studying hard in college, so I can get a good job.

I'm going to hit the books so I can rake in the bucks.

I want to do well in college so I can get a good job.

TEACHING STANDARD AND NONSTANDARD ENGLISH

Give students a short scene (such as a portion of the balcony scene in *Romeo and Juliet*), and have them rewrite it using modern-day slang.

After students have finished this exercise, talk to them about the importance of knowing audience and purpose as a writer.

INSTRUCTOR'S RESOURCE MANUAL

For more exercises and for quizzes, see the *Instructor's Resource Manual*, Section II, Part V.

Which of these sentences would you probably say to a friend or to someone in your family? Which would you most likely say in a job interview? Which would be good for a college paper?

The first three sentences are nonstandard English. They might be said or written to a friend or family member, but they would not be appropriate in an academic setting or in a job situation. Only the fourth sentence would be appropriate in an academic paper or in a job interview.

STANDARD AND NONSTANDARD ENGLISH

Most of the English language falls into one of two categories—either *standard* or *nonstandard*. **Standard English** is the language of college, business, and the media. It is used by reporters on television, by newspapers, in most magazines, and on Web sites created by schools, government, business, and organizations. Standard English is always grammatically correct and free of slang.

Nonstandard English does not follow all the rules of grammar and often includes slang. Nonstandard English is not necessarily wrong, but it is more appropriate in some settings (with friends and family) than others. It is not appropriate in college or business writing. To understand the difference between standard and nonstandard English, compare the following paragraphs.

Nonstandard English

I was stoked to find out I would be getting a $300 refund on my taxes. My first thought was to blow it on a trip, maybe somewheres like Las Vegas. But none of my friends was enthused by that. Then I thought being as I watch television alot, I would buy a new TV with a built-in VCR. My brother got hisself one last year. Then it hit me, hey, I'm gonna need some money to buy new duds for my job. Alright, I decided, I gotta buy clothes with the dough, irregardless of what I'd like to do with it.

Standard English

I was thrilled when I found out I would be getting a $300 refund on my taxes. My first thought was to spend it on a trip, maybe somewhere like Las Vegas. But none of my friends was enthusiastic about that. Then I thought that since I watch television a lot, I would buy a new TV with a built-in VCR. My brother got himself one last year. Then I realized that I am going to need some money to buy new clothes for my job. All right, I decided, I have to buy clothes with the money, regardless of what I'd like to do with it.

In the rest of this chapter, you will learn how to recognize and correct ungrammatical English and how to avoid slang in your writing.

REVIEWING STANDARD AND NONSTANDARD ENGLISH

Where do you hear standard English in your daily life?

On TV, in the media, in schools, in newspapers

What is nonstandard English?

English that does not follow the rules of grammar and usage

Give two examples of nonstandard English.

Examples will vary.

NONSTANDARD ENGLISH

Nonstandard English is ungrammatical. It does not follow the rules of standard English that are required in college writing. The academic and business worlds expect you to be able to recognize and avoid nonstandard English. This is not always easy because some nonstandard terms are used so often in speech that many people think they are acceptable in writing. The following list might help you choose the correct words in your own writing

ain't

> **NOT**   My economics professor **ain't** giving us the test today.
> **CORRECT** My economics professor **isn't** giving us the test today.

anywheres

> **NOT**   Lashawn buys her clothes **anywheres** she can find them.
> **CORRECT** Lashawn buys her clothes **anywhere** she can find them.

be

> **NOT**   I **be** so happy.
> **CORRECT** I **am** so happy.

(For additional help with *be*, see Chapter 38, "Verb Tense.")

being as, being that

NOT Emilio will not get to go home over the weekend, **being as** he has to work.

CORRECT Emilio will not get to go home over the weekend **because** he has to work.

coulda/could of, shoulda/should of

NOT He **could of** earned a better grade on the test if he'd studied.

CORRECT He **could have** (or **could've**) earned a better grade on the test if he'd studied.

different than

NOT She is **different than** us.

CORRECT She is **different from** us.

drug

NOT She **drug** the mattress across the room.

CORRECT She **dragged** the mattress across the room.

enthused

NOT Mary was **enthused** about the wedding.

CORRECT Mary was **enthusiastic** about the wedding.

everywheres

NOT My dog follows me **everywheres** I go.

CORRECT My dog follows me **everywhere** I go.

goes

NOT Then Lorie **goes,** "I'm leaving without you."

CORRECT Then Lorie **said,** "I'm leaving without you."

CORRECT Then Lorie **said** that she was leaving without me.

hisself

NOT Jackson made **hisself** a cheeseburger.

CORRECT Jackson made **himself** a cheeseburger.

in regards to

NOT We received a letter **in regards to** your complaint.

CORRECT We received a letter **in regard to** your complaint.

irregardless

NOT	**Irregardless** of how long you study French, you'll never speak it like a native.
CORRECT	**Regardless** of how long you study French, you'll never speak it like a native.

kinda/kind of, sorta/sort of

NOT	The rooms smells **kinda** sweet, **sorta** like vanilla.
CORRECT	The room smells **rather** sweet, **much like** vanilla.

most

NOT	**Most** everyone accepted the invitation.
CORRECT	**Almost** everyone accepted the invitation.

must of

NOT	I **must of** lost my purse at the party.
CORRECT	I **must have** lost my purse at the party.

off of

NOT	Billy jumped **off of** the back of the truck.
CORRECT	Billy jumped **off** the back of the truck.

oughta

NOT	Sometimes I think I **oughta** watch less television.
CORRECT	Sometimes I think I **ought to** watch less television.

real

NOT	My boyfriend was **real** mad when I went out with another boy.
CORRECT	My boyfriend was **really** mad when I went out with another boy.

somewheres

NOT	Your jeans are **somewheres** in that pile of clothes.
CORRECT	Your jeans are **somewhere** in that pile of clothes.

suppose to

NOT	You were **suppose to** turn that paper in yesterday.
CORRECT	You were **supposed to** turn that paper in yesterday.

theirselves

> **NOT**   They helped **theirselves** to the food in the buffet line.
>
> **CORRECT** They helped **themselves** to the food in the buffet line.

use to

> **NOT**   I **use to** have a truck.
>
> **CORRECT** I **used to** have a truck.

ways

> **NOT**   Curt's car broke down a long **ways** from home.
>
> **CORRECT** Curt's car broke down a long **way** from home.

where . . . at

> **NOT**   **Where** is the nearest bakery **at?**
>
> **CORRECT** **Where** is the nearest bakery?

REVIEWING NONSTANDARD ENGLISH

What is one reason using nonstandard English in written work is easy to do?

We hear it so often, we think it is standard.

Give four examples of nonstandard English; then correct them.
Examples will vary.

_____   _____

_____   _____

_____   _____

_____   _____

◆ **P r a c t i c e 1 A**   **Identifying** Underline the ungrammatical words or phrases in each of the following sentences.

1. Do you know <u>where</u> the children are <u>at</u>? *(drop "at")*

2. Then John <u>goes</u>, "There is no way I'm going to touch that." *(says)*

3. Our production of *Romeo and Juliet* is <u>kinda</u> like the original, but <u>sorta</u> modern. *(much, rather)*

4. I <u>coulda</u> stayed at home instead of sitting here listening to this boring lecture. *(could have or could've)*

5. Justin was <u>suppose to</u> mail the invitations. *(supposed to)*

♦ **Practice 1B** **Correcting** Correct the ungrammatical words and expressions in Practice 1A by rewriting the incorrect sentences. *See Practice 1A.*

♦ **Practice 2** **Completing** Underline the ungrammatical word or words in each phrase, and change them to standard English.

1. <u>Anywheres</u> I go   *Anywhere*

2. She <u>drug</u> it   *dragged*

3. We are a long <u>ways</u>   *way*

4. He made <u>hisself</u>   *himself*

5. <u>Being that</u> Susan   *Because*

♦ **Practice 3** **Writing Your Own** Write five sentences of your own using the grammatical words and phrases you chose in Practice 2. *Answers will vary.*

SLANG

Another example of nonstandard English is **slang,** popular words and expressions that come and go, much like the latest fashions. For example, in the 1950s, someone might call his or her special someone *dreamy.* In the 1960s, you might hear a boyfriend or girlfriend described as *groovy,* and in the 1990s, *sweet* was the popular slang term. Today your significant other might be *hot* or *dope.*

These expressions are slang because they are part of the spoken language that changes from generation to generation and from place to place. As you might suspect, slang communicates to a limited audience who share common interests and experiences. Some slang words, such as *cool* and *neat,* have become part of our language, but most slang is temporary. What's in today may be out tomorrow, so the best advice is to avoid slang in your writing.

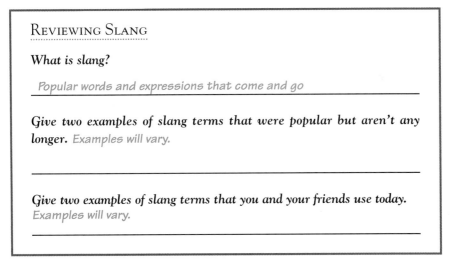

REVIEWING SLANG

What is slang?

Popular words and expressions that come and go

Give two examples of slang terms that were popular but aren't any longer. Examples will vary.

Give two examples of slang terms that you and your friends use today. Examples will vary.

P r a c t i c e 4   Identifying Underline the slang words and expressions in each of the following sentences.

1. *Return of the Mummy* <u>rocks</u>!
2. "<u>Wassup</u>?" I yelled to my <u>homies</u>.
3. This party is <u>da bomb</u>.
4. My mom <u>tripped out</u> when I got my tattoo.
5. Stewart is <u>zoning</u> on the video game.

P r a c t i c e 5   Completing Translate the following slang expressions into standard English.

1. Talk to the hand *Don't talk to me; I'm not listening to you.*

2. hella good *really good*

3. flyboy *popular guy; friend*

4. right back atcha *I could say the same thing to you.*

5. a wanna-be *someone who wants to be someone or something he or she is not*

P r a c t i c e 6   Writing Your Own List five slang words or expressions, and use them in sentences of your own. Then rewrite each sentence using standard English to replace the slang expressions. *Answers will vary.*

CHAPTER REVIEW

You might want to reread your answers to the questions in all the review boxes before you do the following exercises.

◆ *Review Practice 1* **Identifying** Underline the ungrammatical or slang words in the following sentences.

1. You really need to <u>chill out</u>.
2. He <u>ain't</u> going to know what's going on.
3. I was so <u>enthused</u> when I won the contest.
4. He's really <u>jammin'</u> to the music.
5. Hey, stop <u>buggin'</u> me.
6. Oops, I fell <u>off of</u> the ski lift.
7. He's no <u>different than</u> you or me.
8. She's thinks she's <u>all that</u>.
9. You <u>oughta</u> take art lessons.
10. Sandra is really <u>phat</u>.

◆ *Review Practice 2* **Completing** Correct any nonstandard English in each of the following sentences by rewriting the sentences. *Answers may vary.*

1. I <u>be</u> wide awake and can't sleep. *(am)*
2. <u>Irregardless</u> of them, Rufus is talking to <u>hisself</u>. *(Regardless, himself)*
3. Tony's making <u>big money</u> at his new job. *(a good salary)*
4. Those singers are <u>bad</u>. *(really good)*
5. My girlfriend was <u>real</u> mad when I forgot Valentine's Day. *(really)*
6. <u>In regards to</u> your question, I don't have an answer. *(In regard to)*
7. <u>Watcha doin'</u>? *(What are you doing?)*
8. Who's the <u>real slim shady</u>? *(person who is genuine)*
9. Jane <u>could of</u> found extra blankets if you were cold. *(could've)*
10. You are <u>solid</u>, man. *(honest)*

◆ *Review Practice 3* **Writing Your Own** Write a paragraph on how you spend your free time. Do you spend it with your friends or alone? What do you do and why? *Answers will vary.*

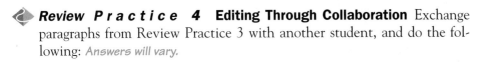

◆ *Review Practice 4* **Editing Through Collaboration** Exchange paragraphs from Review Practice 3 with another student, and do the following: *Answers will vary.*

1. Underline any ungrammatical language.

2. Circle any slang.

Then return the paper to its writer, and use the information in this chapter to correct any nonstandard or slang expressions in your own paragraph. Record your errors on the Error Log in Appendix 6.

CHAPTER **58** EASILY CONFUSED WORDS

✔ CHECKLIST for Easily Confused Words

> ✔ Is the correct word chosen from the easily confused words?
> ✔ Are the following words used correctly: *its/it's, their/there/they're, to/too/two, who's/whose, your/you're?*

TEACHING EASILY
CONFUSED WORDS
Provide students with
the following poem
(author unknown), and
ask them to rewrite it
correctly.

*Ode to the Spell-
Checker*
Eye halve a spelling
   chequer,
It came with my pea
   sea.
It plainly marques
   for my revue
Miss steaks eye kin
   knot sea.

Eye strike a key and
   type a word
And weight four it
   two say
Weather eye am
   wrong oar write
It shows me straight
   a weigh.

As soon as a mist
   ache is maid
It nose bee fore two
   long,
And eye can put the
   error rite
Its rare lea ever
   wrong.

Test Yourself

Choose the correct word in parentheses.

- Miranda couldn't (choose, chose) a college.
- (It's, Its) time to leave for the show.
- I can't (hear, here) with all this noise.
- (Weather, Whether) you go or not, I'm still going to attend.
- (Who's, Whose) responsible for this mess?

(Answers are in Appendix 4.)

Some words are easily confused. They may look alike, sound alike, or have similar meanings, but they all play different roles in the English language. This chapter will help you choose the right words for your sentences.

EASILY CONFUSED WORDS, PART I

a/an: Use *a* before words that begin with a consonant. Use *an* before words that begin with a vowel (*a, e, i, o, u*).

> **a** bill, **a** cat, **a** zebra
> **an** artichoke, **an** Indian, **an** occasion

accept/except: *Accept* means "receive." *Except* means "other than."

> Mary will not **accept** the gift.
>
> Everyone went **except** Harry.

advice/advise: *Advice* means "helpful information." *Advise* means "give advice or help."

> My mother usually gives me very good **advice.**
>
> My parents **advise** me when I'm trying to make an important decision.

affect/effect: *Affect* (verb) means "influence." *Effect* means "bring about" (verb) or "a result" (noun).

> She hopes having children won't **affect** her chance at promotion.
>
> I believe that changes in the law will **effect** positive changes in society.
>
> The weather had a bad **effect** on his health.

already/all ready: *Already* means "in the past." *All ready* means "completely prepared."

> I have **already** taken that class.
>
> We had packed the car and were **all ready** to go when the accident happened.

among/between: Use *among* when referring to three or more people or things. Use *between* when referring to only two people or things.

> The students discussed the issues **among** themselves.
>
> I can't decide **between** the two dresses.

bad/badly: *Bad* means "not good." *Badly* means "not well."

> That meat is **bad,** so don't eat it.
>
> He felt **bad** about the accident.
>
> He was hurt **badly** in the accident.

beside/besides: *Beside* means "next to." *Besides* means "in addition (to)."

> She sat **beside** him at lunch.
>
> **Besides** sleeping, I can think of nothing else I want to do.

Eye have run this
  poem threw it;
I am shore your
  pleased two no.
Its letter perfect awl
  the weigh;
My chequer told me
  sew!

INSTRUCTOR'S
RESOURCE MANUAL

For more exercises and
for quizzes, see the
*Instructor's Resource
Manual,* Section II,
Part V.

brake/break: *Brake* means "stop" or "the parts that stop a moving vehicle." *Break* means "shatter, come apart" or "a rest between work periods."

She didn't **brake** soon enough to avoid the other car.

I watched the limb **break** off the tree.

Can we take a **break?**

breath/breathe: *Breath* means "air." *Breathe* means "taking in air."

Take a long, slow **breath.**

The air we have to **breathe** is unhealthy.

choose/chose: *Choose* means "select." *Chose* is the past tense of choose.

Please **choose** an answer.

He **chose** the wrong answer.

REVIEWING WORDS THAT ARE EASILY CONFUSED, PART I

Do you understand the differences in the sets of words in Part I of the list? Answers will vary.

_____

Have you ever confused any of these words? If so, which ones? Answers will vary.

_____

 Practice 1 **Identifying** Underline the correct word in each of the following sentences.

1. I can (advice, <u>advise</u>) you on what courses to take.
2. The little boy behaved (bad, <u>badly</u>) when his father left.
3. We were (already, <u>all ready</u>) to leave the house when she realized she didn't have her purse.
4. (<u>Among</u>, Between) the three of us, we should have enough money to buy lunch.
5. The cold water took my (<u>breath</u>, breathe) away.

◆ *P r a c t i c e 2*   **Completing** Complete the following sentences with a correct word from Part I of this list.

1. I _____*chose*_____ you to be on my team last year.

2. _____*Except*_____ for the humidity, we had a wonderful trip.

3. We have to keep the secret _____*between*_____ you and me.

4. Corkey was a _____*bad*_____ dog; he chewed up my shoes.

5. Take my _____*advice*_____ and bring a jacket.

◆ *P r a c t i c e 3*   **Writing Your Own** Use each pair of words correctly in a sentence of your own. *Answers will vary.*

1. a/an _____

2. breath/breathe _____

3. affect/effect _____

4. already/all ready _____

5. beside/besides _____

EASILY CONFUSED WORDS, PART II

coarse/course: *Coarse* refers to something that is rough. *Course* refers to a class, a process, or a part of a meal.

> This pavement is **coarse.**
> My **course** in math is very interesting.
> I will prepare a four–**course** meal.

desert/dessert: *Desert* refers to dry, sandy land or means "abandon." *Dessert* refers to the last course of a meal.

> It is difficult to live in the **desert.**
> He **deserted** his family.
> We had strawberry shortcake for **dessert.**

Hint: You can remember that **dessert** has two s's if you think of *strawberry shortcake*.

does/dose: *Does* means "performs." *Dose* refers to a specific portion of medicine.

> My sister **does** whatever she wants.
>
> Children should have only a small **dose** of the medicine.

fewer/less: *Fewer* refers to things that can be counted. *Less* refers to things that cannot be counted.

> There are **fewer** cotton fields than there used to be.
>
> She has much **less** time now that she has a new job.

good/well: *Good* modifies nouns. *Well* modifies verbs, adjectives, and adverbs. *Well* also refers to a state of health.

> Bill looks **good** in his new suit.
>
> I'm afraid I didn't do **well** on the test.
>
> Kate isn't feeling **well** today.

hear/here: *Hear* refers to the act of listening. *Here* means "in this place."

> My father can't **hear** as well as he used to.
>
> **Here** is the book you asked for.

it's/its: *It's* is the contraction for *it is* or *it has*. *Its* is a possessive pronoun.

> The teacher said **it's** important to answer all the questions.
>
> The dog chased **its** tail.

knew/new: *Knew* is the past tense of *know*. *New* means "recent."

> I thought everyone **knew** I had a **new** boyfriend.

know/no: *Know* means "understand." *No* means "not any" or is the opposite of *yes*.

> We all **know** that we have **no** hope of defeating the other team.

lay/lie: *Lay* means "set down." (Its principal parts are *lay, laid, laid*.) *Lie* means "recline." (Its principal parts are *lie, lay, lain*.)

> He **lays** brick for a living.
>
> He **laid** down the heavy sack.
>
> She **lies** down at 2 p.m. every day for a nap.
>
> I **lay** in the grass.

(For additional help with *lie* and *lay*, see Chapter 37, "Regular and Irregular Verbs.")

loose/lose: *Loose* means "free" or "unattached." *Lose* means "misplace" or "not win."

> Hal's pants are too **loose.**

> If I **lose** another $10, I'm going to quit gambling.

passed/past: *Passed* is the past tense of pass. *Past* refers to an earlier time or means "beyond."

> John **passed** by his old house on the way to school.

> It is interesting to study the **past.**

> The dog ran **past** me and into the street.

REVIEWING WORDS THAT ARE EASILY CONFUSED, PART II

Do you understand the differences in the sets of words in Part II of the list? Answers will vary.

_____

Have you ever confused any of these words? If so, which ones? Answers will vary.

_____

P r a c t i c e 4 Identifying Underline the correct word in each of the following sentences.

1. We (passed, past) Edward on the freeway.
2. I think you have made a (good, well) choice.
3. With her second job, Marsha has (fewer, less) time to spend with her friends.
4. (It's, Its) going to be a beautiful day.
5. I cannot (loose, lose) this ring; it was given to me by my grandmother.

P r a c t i c e 5 Completing Complete the following sentences with a correct word from Part II of this list.

1. The restaurant served peach cobbler for _____*dessert*_____.
2. How do you like my _____*new*_____ car?

3. Mike _____*does*_____ not want to go to the concert with us.

4. This business _____*course*_____ will benefit me on the job.

5. I am not feeling _____*well*_____ today.

◆ **P r a c t i c e   6**   **Writing Your Own** Use each pair of words correctly in a sentence of your own. *Answers will vary.*

1. fewer/less _____

2. knew/new _____

3. hear/here _____

4. it's/its _____

5. lay/lie _____

EASILY CONFUSED WORDS, PART III

principal/principle: *Principal* means "main, most important," "a school official," or "a sum of money." A *principle* is a rule. (Think of *principle* and *rule*—both end in *-le.*)

My **principal** reason for moving is to be closer to my family.
Mr. Kobler is the **principal** at Westside Elementary School.
He lives by one main **principle**—honesty.

quiet/quite: *Quiet* means "without noise." *Quite* means "very."

The house was **quiet.**
I am **quite** happy with my new car.

raise/rise: *Raise* means "increase" or "lift up." *Rise* means "get up from a sitting or reclining position."

The state is going to **raise** the tax on cigarettes.
Jane can **rise** slowly from her wheelchair.

set/sit: *Set* means "put down." *Sit* means "take a seated position."

Set the vase on the table.
I don't like to **sit** at a desk for long period of time.

(For additional help with *sit* and *set*, see Chapter 37, "Regular and Irregular Verbs.")

than/then: *Than* is used in making comparisons. *Then* means "next."

My mother is younger **than** my father.
I took piano lessons; **then** I took guitar lessons.

their/there/they're: *Their* is possessive. *There* indicates location. *They're* is the contraction of *they are*.

Their house burned down last year.
Too many people are living **there.**
They're all going to London.

threw/through: *Threw*, the past tense of throw, means "tossed." *Through* means "finished" or "passing from one point to another."

The pitcher **threw** the ball.
I am **through** with dinner.
My brother and I rode **through** the forest on our bikes.

to/too/two: *To* means "toward" or is used with a verb. *Too* means "also" or "very." *Two* is a number.

I went to the store **to** buy some bread.
I bought some artichokes **too,** even though they were **too** expensive for my budget.
My mother has **two** sisters.

wear/were/where: *Wear* means "have on one's body." *Were* is the past tense of *be*. *Where* refers to a place.

Can you **wear** shorts to school?
Where were you yesterday?

weather/whether: *Weather* refers to outdoor conditions. *Whether* expresses possibility.

No one knows **whether** the **weather** will get better or worse.

who's/whose: *Who's* is a contraction of *who is* or *who has*. *Whose* is a possessive pronoun.

Who's going to decide **whose** car to take?

your/you're: *Your* means "belonging to you." *You're* is the contraction of *you are*.

Your attention to details proves **you're** a good worker.

REVIEWING WORDS THAT ARE EASILY CONFUSED, PART III

Do you understand the differences in the sets of words in Part III of this list? Answers will vary.

_____

Have you ever confused any of these words? If so, which ones? Answers will vary.

_____

◆ **P r a c t i c e   7   Identifying** Underline the correct word in each of the following sentences.

1. Janene was (quiet, <u>quite</u>) pleased with your work.
2. (Your, <u>You're</u>) the best choice for this task.
3. Please (set, <u>sit</u>) here and wait for the doctor.
4. (<u>Who's</u>, Whose) planning on going to tonight's game?
5. Our (<u>principal</u>, principle) is retiring at the end of the year.

◆ **P r a c t i c e   8   Completing** Complete the following sentences with a correct word from Part III of this list.

1. After the performance, the audience _____*threw*_____ flowers at the performer's feet.
2. Beatrice's _____*principal*_____ reason for quitting her job was the pay.
3. Finish your homework, and _____*then*_____ you can watch television.
4. _____*Where*_____ are you going dressed like that?
5. Why did you _____*wear*_____ shorts in the winter?

◆ **P r a c t i c e   9   Writing Your Own** Use each set of words correctly in a sentence of your own. Answers will vary.

1. raise/rise _____

2. their/there/they're _____

3. your/you're _____

4. set/sit _____

5. who's/whose _____

CHAPTER REVIEW

You might want to reread your answers to the questions in all the review boxes before you do the following exercises.

◆ *Review Practice 1* **Identifying** Underline the correct word in each of the following sentences.

1. Your influence is having a positive (affect, <u>effect</u>) on people's lives.
2. (<u>Who's</u>, Whose) that girl with Paul?
3. Jade needs to stand (hear, <u>here</u>) when her name is announced.
4. (Your, <u>You're</u>) the one for me.
5. There are many different plants that grow in the (<u>desert</u>, dessert).
6. Sydney (choose, <u>chose</u>) the smallest puppy of the litter.
7. The picture has come (<u>loose</u>, lose) from its frame.
8. Please sit (<u>beside</u>, besides) me during the ceremony.
9. Your counselor gave you good (<u>advice</u>, advise), and you should take it.
10. Over (their, <u>there</u>, they're) is the house where I grew up.

◆ *Review Practice 2* **Completing** Complete the following sentences with a correct word from all three parts of the list. *Answers may vary.*

1. We _____*knew*_____ each other when we were children.
2. Contestants should send in __*new, their, two, loose*__ photographs of themselves.
3. The _____*weather*_____ outside was so nice that we decided to walk.
4. If you leave now, you will _____*break*_____ up our happy home.

5. The crowd was so _____*quiet*_____ that you could hear people breathing.

6. Quantitative analysis is the most challenging _____*course*_____ I have ever taken.

7. Jeffrey did not _____*hear*_____ the phone ringing.

8. I laughed so hard that I couldn't catch my _____*breath*_____.

9. Because of our uninvited houseguests, we have _____*less, no*_____ food in the house.

10. Faith has _____*already*_____ donated to the cause.

♦ **Review Practice 3   Writing Your Own** Write a paragraph explaining the qualities of a good friend. What are the qualities, and why do you think they are important? Try to use some of the easily confused words from this chapter. *Answers will vary.*

♦ **Review Practice 4   Editing Through Collaboration** Exchange paragraphs from Review Practice 3 with another student, and do the following:

1. Circle any words used incorrectly.

2. Write the correct form of the word above the error.

Then return the paper to its writer, and use the information in this chapter to correct any confused words in your own paragraph. Record your errors on the Error Log in Appendix 6.

SPELLING

✔ CHECKLIST for Identifying Misspelled Words

✔ Do you follow the basic spelling rules?

✔ Are all words spelled correctly?

Test Yourself

Correct the misspelled words in the following sentences.

- What is your new addres?
- Turn left on the third avenu.
- I was using the wrong calender when I made out the schedule.
- The dealer delt me a good hand.
- Please get all the items on the grocry list.

(Answers are in Appendix 4.)

If you think back over your education, you will realize that teachers believe spelling is important. There is a good reason they feel this way: Spelling errors send negative messages. Misspellings seem to leap out at readers, creating serious doubts about the writer's abilities in general. Because you will not always have access to spell-checkers—and because spell-checkers do not catch all spelling errors—improving your spelling skills is important.

SPELLING HINTS

The spelling rules in this chapter will help you become a better speller. But first, here are some practical hints that will also help you improve your spelling.

TEACHING SPELLING
Create a word search game (single letters in columns and rows of approximately 20 letters each), and provide students with a list of misspelled words. Tell students that the correctly spelled words are the words they are searching for inside the word search game. The first student to uncover all the correctly spelled words wins.

INSTRUCTOR'S RESOURCE MANUAL
For sample word search games, for more exercises, and for quizzes, see the *Instructor's Resource Manual*, Section II, Part V.

1. Start a personal spelling list of your own. Use the list of commonly misspelled words on pages 780–784 as your starting point.

2. Study the lists of easily confused words in Chapter 58.

3. Avoid all nonstandard expressions (see Chapter 57).

4. Use a dictionary when you run across words you don't know.

5. Run the spell-check program if you are writing on a computer. Keep in mind, however, that spell-check cannot tell if you have incorrectly used one word in place of another (such as *to, too,* or *two*).

REVIEWING HINTS FOR BECOMING A BETTER SPELLER

Name two things you can do immediately to become a better speller.

Answers will vary.

Why can't you depend on a spell-check program to find every misspelled word?

Because it won't find confused words that are spelled correctly.

Practice 1A   Identifying Underline the misspelled words in each of the following sentences. Refer to the list of easily confused words in Chapter 58 and to the spelling list in this chapter as necessary.

1. "We want to go <u>to</u>," cried the children. *(too)*
2. The <u>baloon</u> floated away in the breeze. *(balloon)*
3. With John's promotion came a better <u>salry</u>. *(salary)*
4. This vacation has had a relaxing <u>affect</u> on my attitude. *(effect)*
5. It was an <u>akward</u> situation when the bride wouldn't say, "I do." *(awkward)*

Practice 1B   Correcting Correct the spelling errors in Practice 1A by rewriting the incorrect sentences. *See Practice 1A.*

Practice 2   Completing Fill in each blank in the following sentences with hints that help with spelling.

1. Use a ___*dictionary*___ to look up words you don't know.
2. You can always use the ___*spell-check program*___ on your computer, but you should remember that it cannot catch confused words, only misspelled words.

3. Start a ___*spelling list*___ to help you remember words you commonly misspell.

4. Study the list of ___*confused words*___ in Chapter ___*58*___.

5. Try to avoid all ___*nonstandard*___ English.

◆ *P r a c t i c e 3* **Writing Your Own** Choose the correctly spelled word in each pair, and write a sentence using it. Refer to the spelling list on pages 780–784 if necessary. *Sentences will vary.*

1. concieve/<u>conceive</u> _____

2. <u>absence</u>/absense _____

3. vaccum/<u>vacuum</u> _____

4. <u>library</u>/libary _____

5. delt/<u>dealt</u> _____

SPELLING RULES

Four basic spelling rules can help you avoid many misspellings. It pays to spend a little time learning them now.

1. **Words that end in -e:** When adding a suffix beginning with a vowel (*a, e, i, o, u*), drop the final *-e*.

   achieve + -ing   =   achieving
   include + -ed   =   included
   value + -able   =   valuable

   When adding a suffix beginning with a consonant, keep the final *-e*.

   aware + -ness   =   awareness
   improve + -ment   =   improvement
   leisure + -ly   =   leisurely

2. **Words with *ie* and *ei*:** Put *i* before *e* except after *c* or when sounded like *ay* as in *neighbor* and *weigh*.

c + ei	(no c) + ie
receive	grieve
conceive	niece

deceive	friend
neighbor	relief

3. **Words that end in -y:** When adding a suffix to a word that ends in a consonant plus -y, change the y to *i*.

happy + -er	=	happier
dry + -ed	=	dried
easy + -est	=	easiest

4. **Words that double the final consonant:** When adding a suffix starting with a vowel to a one-syllable word, double the final consonant.

big + -est	=	biggest
quit + -er	=	quitter
bet + -ing	=	betting

With words of more than one syllable, double the final consonant if (1) the final syllable is stressed and (2) the word ends in a single vowel plus a single consonant.

begin + -ing	=	beginning
transmit + -ing	=	transmitting
excel + -ed	=	excelled

The word *travel* has more than one syllable. Should you double the final consonant? No, you should not, because the stress is on the *first* syllable (*tra´ vel*). The word ends in a vowel and a consonant, but that is not enough. Both parts of the rule must be met.

REVIEWING FOUR BASIC SPELLING RULES

What is the rule for adding a suffix to words ending in -e (such as date + -ing)?

Drop the final -e when adding a suffix that begins with a vowel, and keep

the -e when adding a suffix that begins with a consonant.

What is the rule for spelling ie and ei words (such as receive, neighbor, *and* friend)?

Put i before e except after c or when sounded like "ay" as in neighbor

and weigh.

When do you change y to i before a suffix (such as sunny + -est*)?*

When the word ends in a consonant plus -y

When do you double the final consonant of a word before adding a suffix (such as cut, begin, *or* travel + -ing*)?*

When a one-syllable word ends in a consonant or when words of more

than one syllable have the stress on the final syllable and end in a vowel

plus a consonant

P r a c t i c e 4 A **Identifying** Underline the spelling errors in each of the following sentences.

1. It's not like we're commiting a crime. *(committing)*
2. The boundarys have been clearly marked. *(boundaries)*
3. You are so wierd. *(weird)*
4. Our bagage was lost somewhere in New York. *(baggage)*
5. The facilitys are near one another. *(facilities)*

P r a c t i c e 4 B **Correcting** Correct the spelling errors in Practice 4A by rewriting the incorrect sentences. *See Practice 4A.*

P r a c t i c e 5 **Completing** Complete the following spelling rules.

1. When adding a suffix beginning with a vowel to a word that ends in -e,
   drop the final -e .
2. With words of more than one syllable, _____double_____ the final consonant if (1) the final syllable is _____stressed_____ and (2) the word ends in a single _____vowel_____ plus a single _____consonant_____.
3. Put *i* before *e* except after _____c_____ or when sounded like _____"ay"_____ as in neighbor and weigh .
4. When adding a suffix starting with a _____vowel_____ to a one-syllable word, _____double_____ the final consonant.

5. When adding a suffix to a word the ends in a consonant plus -y, change the _____y_____ to _____i_____.

◆ *P r a c t i c e* **6** **Writing Your Own** Make a list of words you commonly misspell. Then choose five of the words, and use each correctly in a sentence. *Answers will vary.*

MOST COMMONLY MISSPELLED WORDS

Use the following list of commonly misspelled words to check your spelling when you write.

abbreviate	amateur	banana
absence	ambulance	bankrupt
accelerate	ancient	banquet
accessible	anonymous	beautiful
accidentally	anxiety	beggar
accommodate	anxious	beginning
accompany	appreciate	behavior
accomplish	appropriate	benefited
accumulate	approximate	bicycle
accurate	architect	biscuit
ache	arithmetic	bought
achievement	artificial	boundary
acknowledgment	assassin	brilliant
acre	athletic	brought
actual	attach	buoyant
address	audience	bureau
adequate	authority	burglar
advertisement	autumn	business
afraid	auxiliary	cabbage
aggravate	avenue	cafeteria
aisle	awkward	calendar
although	baggage	campaign
aluminum	balloon	canoe

canyon	condemn	dictionary
captain	conference	difficulty
career	congratulate	diploma
carriage	conscience	disappear
cashier	consensus	disastrous
catastrophe	continuous	discipline
caterpillar	convenience	disease
ceiling	cooperate	dissatisfied
cemetery	corporation	divisional
census	correspond	dormitory
certain	cough	economy
certificate	counterfeit	efficiency
challenge	courageous	eighth
champion	courteous	elaborate
character	cozy	electricity
chief	criticize	eligible
children	curiosity	embarrass
chimney	curious	emphasize
coffee	curriculum	employee
collar	cylinder	encourage
college	dairy	enormous
column	dangerous	enough
commit	dealt	enthusiastic
committee	deceive	envelope
communicate	decision	environment
community	definition	equipment
comparison	delicious	equivalent
competent	descend	especially
competition	describe	essential
complexion	description	establish
conceive	deteriorate	exaggerate
concession	determine	excellent
concrete	development	exceptionally

excessive	gruesome	intelligence
exhaust	guarantee	interfere
exhilarating	guess	interrupt
existence	guidance	invitation
explanation	handkerchief	irrelevant
extinct	handsome	irrigate
extraordinary	haphazard	issue
familiar	happiness	jealous
famous	harass	jewelry
fascinate	height	journalism
fashion	hesitate	judgment
fatigue	hoping	kindergarten
faucet	humorous	knife
February	hygiene	knowledge
fiery	hymn	knuckles
financial	icicle	laboratory
foreign	illustrate	laborious
forfeit	imaginary	language
fortunate	immediately	laugh
forty	immortal	laundry
freight	impossible	league
friend	incidentally	legible
fundamental	incredible	legislature
gauge	independence	leisure
genius	indispensable	length
genuine	individual	library
geography	inferior	license
gnaw	infinite	lieutenant
government	influential	lightning
graduation	initial	likable
grammar	initiation	liquid
grief	innocence	listen
grocery	installation	literature

machinery	obstacle	prejudice
magazine	occasion	previous
magnificent	occurred	privilege
majority	official	procedure
manufacture	omission	proceed
marriage	omitted	pronounce
material	opportunity	psychology
mathematics	opponent	publicly
maximum	opposite	questionnaire
mayor	original	quotient
meant	outrageous	realize
medicine	pamphlet	receipt
message	paragraph	recipe
mileage	parallel	recommend
miniature	parentheses	reign
minimum	partial	religious
minute	particular	representative
mirror	pastime	reservoir
miscellaneous	patience	responsibility
mischievous	peculiar	restaurant
miserable	permanent	rhyme
misspell	persistent	rhythm
monotonous	personnel	salary
mortgage	persuade	satisfactory
mysterious	physician	scarcity
necessary	pitcher	scenery
neighborhood	pneumonia	schedule
niece	politician	science
nineteen	possess	scissors
ninety	prairie	secretary
noticeable	precede	seize
nuisance	precious	separate
obedience	preferred	significant

similar	terrible	vehicle
skiing	theater	vicinity
soldier	thief	villain
souvenir	thorough	visible
sovereign	tobacco	volunteer
spaghetti	tomorrow	weather
squirrel	tongue	Wednesday
statue	tournament	weigh
stomach	tragedy	weird
strength	truly	whose
subtle	unanimous	width
succeed	undoubtedly	worst
success	unique	wreckage
sufficient	university	writing
surprise	usable	yacht
syllable	usually	yearn
symptom	vacuum	yield
technique	valuable	zealous
temperature	various	zoology
temporary	vegetable	

REVIEWING COMMONLY MISSPELLED WORDS

Why is spelling important in your writing? *It is important because*

poor spelling sends a negative message to your reader.

Start a personal spelling log of your most commonly misspelled words.

_____ _____ _____ _____

_____ _____ _____ _____

_____ _____ _____ _____

◆ *P r a c t i c e   **7 A***   **Identifying** Underline any words that are misspelled in the following sentences.

1. This steak and lobster dinner is <u>incredable</u>. *(incredible)*
2. You shouldn't <u>condem</u> others for doing what you do. *(condemn)*
3. Valentine's Day is in <u>Febuary</u>. *(February)*
4. How long have you been <u>writting</u> that novel? *(writing)*
5. I know you will <u>suceed</u> in college. *(succeed)*

◆ *P r a c t i c e   **7 B***   **Correcting** Correct any spelling errors that you identified in Practice 7A by rewriting the incorrect sentences. *See Practice 7A.*

◆ *P r a c t i c e   **8***   **Completing** Correct the spelling errors in the following paragraph.

>   I was eating a plate of <u>spagetti</u> *(spaghetti)* when the phone rang. It was my <u>nieghbor</u> *(neighbor)*. He said, "The big fight is <u>begining</u> *(beginning)* in 15 minutes, and my television screen just went out." He then <u>beged</u> *(begged)* me to let him come over and watch it at my house. So I told him that was fine. He neglected to tell me, however, that he wouldn't be alone. He and seven of his rowdy <u>freinds</u> *(friends)* invaded my house, ate my <u>spagetti</u> *(spaghetti)* and drank my soda, and left a <u>catastrophy</u> *(catastrophe)* behind. I think the next time I have a party, I'll have it at his house.

◆ *P r a c t i c e   **9***   **Writing Your Own** Write a complete sentence for each word listed here. *Answers will vary.*

1. appreciate _____

2. laundry _____

3. marriage _____

4. excellent _____

5. opposite _____

CHAPTER REVIEW

You might want to reread your answers to the questions in all the review boxes before you do the following exercises.

> *Review Practice 1* **Identifying** Underline the misspelled words in each of the following sentences.

1. I'm trying to catch the <u>rythm</u> of this music. *(rhythm)*
2. You ate my <u>desert</u>. *(dessert)*
3. This essay shows <u>improvment</u>. *(improvement)*
4. Ramona is a <u>genuis</u> with figures. *(genius)*
5. The <u>firy</u>-hot peppers made my eyes water. *(fiery)*
6. Most teenagers want their <u>independance</u>. *(independence)*
7. If we stick to the <u>scedule</u>, we should make it home before <u>tomorow</u>. *(schedule, tomorrow)*
8. <u>Breath</u> deeply, and put your head between your legs. *(Breathe)*
9. My family lives in <u>seperate</u> states. *(separate)*
10. Dr. Murphy rides his <u>bycicle</u> to work every day. *(bicycle)*

> *Review Practice 2* **Completing** Correct the spelling errors in Review Practice 1 by rewriting the incorrect sentences. *See Review Practice 1.*

> *Review Practice 3* **Writing Your Own** Write a paragraph explaining how to become a better speller. Are there any hints that may help? *Answers will vary.*

> *Review Practice 4* **Editing Through Collaboration** Exchange paragraphs from Review Practice 3 with another student, and do the following:

1. Underline any words that are used incorrectly.
2. Circle any misspelled words.

Then return the paper to its writer, and use the information in this chapter to correct any spelling errors in your own paragraph. Record your errors on the Spelling Log in Appendix 7.

UNIT TESTS

Here are some exercises that test your understanding of all the material in this unit: Standard and Nonstandard English, Easily Confused Words, and Spelling.

Unit Test I

A. Underline the word choice and spelling errors in the following sentences.

1. I <u>use to</u> walk to work, but now I have a car. *(used to)*

2. I plan to <u>lay</u> in my bed all day reading a good book. *(lie)*

3. When she realized her zipper was open, she was very <u>embarassed</u>. *(embarrassed)*

4. I cannot <u>decieve</u> you; I ate the last cookie. *(deceive)*

5. Jefferson lost his surfboard <u>to</u>. *(too)*

6. If the students work hard, they can <u>rise</u> enough money for their trip. *(raise)*

7. If our star player doesn't get here soon, we will have to <u>forfiet</u> the game. *(forfeit)*

8. Please be <u>quite</u> while in the <u>libary</u>. *(quiet, library)*

9. My best friend <u>got busted</u> for staying out <u>to</u> late. *(got caught, too)*

10. <u>Beside</u> giving me a mother's unconditional love, my mom is also my best friend. *(Besides)*

11. <u>Their</u> already on the plane. *(They're)*

12. Speak louder—I can't <u>here</u> you. *(hear)*

13. Cassie is better with computers <u>then</u> he is. *(than)*

14. The <u>theif</u> stole Rhonda's stereo. *(thief)*

15. Leanne <u>choose</u> to volunteer at the homeless shelter. *(chose)*

16. Sam <u>must of</u> forgotten that we were <u>suppose</u> to have lunch today. *(must've (must have), supposed)*

17. Please <u>except</u> my congratulations on your promotion. *(accept)*

18. He's definitely <u>weirded out</u>. *(lost control)*

19. The <u>affect</u> was devastating on my ego. *(effect)*

20. The <u>course</u> material scratched the baby's skin. *(coarse)*

B. Correct the errors in Part A by rewriting each incorrect sentence.

Unit Test II

A. Underline the word choice and spelling errors in the following paragraph.

        Protecting the *environment*
<u>enviurnment</u> is important <u>everywheres</u>. People <u>use to</u>
everywhere *used to*

think less about the <u>enviurnment</u> <u>then</u> they do today. They couldn't
environment *than*

<u>concieve</u> of the fact that a problem was being created by car fumes and
conceive

other toxins. Now <u>their</u> are organizations dedicated to protecting the
there

<u>enviurnment</u>. These organizations help the <u>goverment</u> make laws that pro-
environment *government*

tect the <u>enviurnment</u>. <u>Than</u>, stricter laws help the <u>goverment</u> keep track of
environment *Then* *government*

<u>whose</u> causing pollution problems in the United States. People must begin
who's

to take <u>responsability</u> for doing <u>there</u> part to help protect <u>are</u> air, land, and
responsibility *their* *our*

water; this is the only way <u>are</u> children will have a clean place to live in the
our

future.

B. Correct the word choice and spelling errors in Part A by rewriting the
paragraph.

APPENDIX 1 Critical Thinking Log

Circle the critical thinking questions that you missed after each essay you read. Have your instructor explain the pattern of errors.

Reading	Content			Purpose and Audience			Paragraphs				Number Correct
Describing											
Mario Suarez	1	2	3	4	5	6	7	8	9	10	
Linda Hogan	1	2	3	4	5	6	7	8	9	10	
Narrating											
Lynda Barry	1	2	3	4	5	6	7	8	9	10	
Stan Higgins	1	2	3	4	5	6	7	8	9	10	
Illustrating											
Mike Rose	1	2	3	4	5	6	7	8	9	10	
Chana Shoenberger	1	2	3	4	5	6	7	8	9	10	
Analyzing a Process											
Roger Flax	1	2	3	4	5	6	7	8	9	10	
David Levy	1	2	3	4	5	6	7	8	9	10	
Comparing/Contrasting											
Stephanie Coontz	1	2	3	4	5	6	7	8	9	10	
Tony Cohan	1	2	3	4	5	6	7	8	9	10	
Dividing/Classifying											
Bernice Reagon	1	2	3	4	5	6	7	8	9	10	
Marion Winik	1	2	3	4	5	6	7	8	9	10	
Defining											
Wang Ping	1	2	3	4	5	6	7	8	9	10	
Michael Norlen	1	2	3	4	5	6	7	8	9	10	
Analyzing Causes/Effects											
Michael Alvear	1	2	3	4	5	6	7	8	9	10	
Stacey Colino	1	2	3	4	5	6	7	8	9	10	
Arguing											
Dave Grossman	1	2	3	4	5	6	7	8	9	10	
Willard and Cole	1	2	3	4	5	6	7	8	9	10	

The legend on the reverse side will help you identify your strengths and weaknesses in critical thinking.

Legend for Critical Thinking Log

Questions	Skill
1–2	Literal and interpretive understanding
3–6	Critical thinking and analysis
7–9	Analyzing sentences
10	Writing paragraphs

APPENDIX 2A

Revising
Describing
Peer Evaluation Form

Use the following questions to evaluate your partner's essay. Direct your comments to your partner.

Writer: _____ **Peer:** _____

Describing

1. Is the dominant impression clearly communicated? Explain your answer.

2. Does the essay use objective and subjective descriptions when needed? Explain your answer.

3. Does the essay draw on all five senses? Explain your answer.

4. Does the essay show rather than tell? Explain your answer.

Thesis Statement

5. Does the thesis statement contain the essay's controlling idea and an opinion about that idea?

6. Does the thesis appear as the last sentence of the introduction? Explain your answer.

Basic Elements

7. Does the essay have all the basic elements? Is each one effective? Explain your answer.

Development

8. Does each paragraph support the thesis statement? Does each paragraph contain enough specific details to develop its topic sentence? Explain your answer.

Unity

9. Do all the essay's topic sentences relate directly to the thesis statement? Do the details in each paragraph support its topic sentence? Explain your answer.

Organization

10. Is the essay organized logically? Is each body paragraph organized logically? Explain your answer.

Coherence

11. Are transitions used effectively so that paragraphs move smoothly and logically from one to the next? Do the sentences move smoothly and logically from one to the next? Explain your answer.

APPENDIX 2A Editing
Describing
Peer Evaluation Form

Use the following questions to help you find editing errors in your partner's essay. Mark the errors directly on your partner's paper using the editing symbols on the inside back cover.

Writer: _____   **Peer:** _____

Sentences

1. Does each sentence have a subject and verb?

    Mark any fragments you find with **frag.**

    Put a slash (/) between any fused sentences and comma splices.

2. Do all subjects and verbs agree?

    Mark any subject-verb agreement errors you find with **sv.**

3. Do all pronouns agree with their nouns?

    Mark any pronoun errors you find with **pro agr.**

4. Are all modifiers as close as possible to the words they modify?

    Mark any modifier errors you find with **ad** (adjective or adverb problem), **mm** (misplaced modifier), or **dm** (dangling modifier).

Punctuation and Mechanics

5. Are sentences punctuated correctly?

    Mark any punctuation errors you find with the appropriate symbol under Unit 5 of the editing symbols (inside back cover).

6. Are words capitalized properly?

    Mark any capitalization errors you find with **lc** (lowercase) or **cap** (capital).

Word Choice and Spelling

7. Are words used correctly?

    Mark any words that are used incorrectly with **wc** (word choice) or **ww** (wrong word).

8. Are words spelled correctly?

    Mark any misspelled words you find with **sp.**

APPENDIX 2B Revising Narrating Peer Evaluation Form

Use the following questions to evaluate your partner's essay. Direct your comments to your partner.

Writer: _____ **Peer:** _____

Narrating

1. What is the essay's main point? If you're not sure, show the writer how he or she can make the main point clearer.

2. Does the writer use the five W's and one H to construct the essay? Where does the essay need more information?

3. Does the writer develop the essay with vivid details? Where can more details be added?

4. Does the writer build excitement with careful pacing? Explain your answer.

Thesis Statement

5. Does the thesis statement contain the essay's controlling idea and an opinion about that idea?

6. Does the thesis appear as the last sentence of the introduction? Explain your answer.

Basic Elements

7. Does the essay have all the basic elements. Is each one effective? Explain your answer.

Development

8. Does each paragraph support the thesis statement? Does each paragraph contain enough specific details to develop its topic sentence? Explain your answer.

Unity

9. Do all the essay's topic sentences relate directly to the thesis statement? Do the details in each paragraph support its topic sentence? Explain your answer.

Organization

10. Is the essay organized logically? Is each body paragraph organized logically? Explain your answer.

Coherence

11. Are transitions used effectively so that paragraphs move smoothly and logically from one to the next? Do the sentences move smoothly and logically from one to the next? Explain your answer.

APPENDIX 2B
Editing
Narrating
Peer Evaluation Form

Use the following questions to help your partner find editing errors in his or her essay. Mark the errors directly on your partner's paper using the editing symbols on the inside back cover.

Writer: _____ **Peer:** _____

Sentences

1. Does each sentence have a subject and verb?

   Mark any fragments you find with **frag.**

   Put a slash (/) between any fused sentences and comma splices.

2. Do all subjects and verbs agree?

   Mark any subject-verb agreement errors you find with **sv.**

3. Do all pronouns agree with their nouns?

   Mark any pronoun errors you find with **pro agr.**

4. Are all modifiers as close as possible to the words they modify?

   Mark any modifier errors you find with **ad** (adjective or adverb problem), **mm** (misplaced modifier), or **dm** (dangling modifier).

Punctuation and Mechanics

5. Are sentences punctuated correctly?

   Mark any punctuation errors you find with the appropriate symbol under Unit 5 of the editing symbols (inside back cover).

6. Are words capitalized properly?

   Mark any capitalization errors you find with **lc** (lowercase) or **cap** (capital).

Word Choice and Spelling

7. Are words used correctly?

   Mark any words that are used incorrectly with **wc** (word choice) or **ww** (wrong word).

8. Are words spelled correctly?

   Mark any misspelled words you find with **sp.**

APPENDIX 2C

Revising Illustrating Peer Evaluation Form

Use the following questions to evaluate your partner's essay. Direct your comments to your partner.

Writer: _____ **Peer:** _____

Illustrating

1. What is the essay's main point? If you're not sure, show the writer how he or she can make the main point clearer.

2. Did the writer choose examples that are relevant to the main point? If not, which examples need to be changed?

3. Does the writer choose examples that the reader can identify with? If not, which examples need to be changed?

4. Does the writer use a sufficient number of examples to make his or her point? Where can more examples be added?

Thesis Statement

5. Does the thesis statement contain the essay's controlling idea and an opinion about that idea?

6. Does the thesis appear as the last sentence of the introduction? Explain your answer.

Basic Elements

7. Does the essay have all the basic elements. Is each one effective? Explain your answer.

Development

8. Does each paragraph support the thesis statement? Does each paragraph contain enough specific details to develop its topic sentence? Explain your answer.

Unity

9. Do all the essay's topic sentences relate directly to the thesis statement? Do the details in each paragraph support its topic sentence? Explain your answer.

Organization

10. Is the essay organized logically? Is each body paragraph organized logically? Explain your answer.

Coherence

11. Are transitions used effectively so that paragraphs move smoothly and logically from one to the next? Do the sentences move smoothly and logically from one to the next? Explain your answer.

APPENDIX 2C

Editing
Illustrating
Peer Evaluation Form

Use the following questions to help you find editing errors in your partner's essay. Mark the errors directly on your partner's paper using the editing symbols on the inside back cover.

Writer: _____ **Peer:** _____

Sentences

1. Does each sentence have a subject and verb?

   Mark any fragments you find with **frag.**

   Put a slash (/) between any fused sentences and comma splices.

2. Do all subjects and verbs agree?

   Mark any subject-verb agreement errors you find with **sv.**

3. Do all pronouns agree with their nouns?

   Mark any pronoun errors you find with **pro agr.**

4. Are all modifiers as close as possible to the words they modify?

   Mark any modifier errors you find with **ad** (adjective or adverb problem), **mm** (misplaced modifier), or **dm** (dangling modifier).

Punctuation and Mechanics

5. Are sentences punctuated correctly?

   Mark any punctuation errors you find with the appropriate symbol under Unit 5 of the editing symbols (inside back cover).

6. Are words capitalized properly?

   Mark any capitalization errors you find with **lc** (lowercase) or **cap** (capital).

Word Choice and Spelling

7. Are words used correctly?

   Mark any words that are used incorrectly with **wc** (word choice) or **ww** (wrong word).

8. Are words spelled correctly?

   Mark any misspelled words you find with **sp.**

APPENDIX 2D Revising
Analyzing a Process
Peer Evaluation Form

Use the following questions to evaluate your partner's essay. Direct your comments to your partner.

Writer: _____ **Peer:** _____

Analyzing a Process

1. Does the writer state in the thesis statement what the reader should be able to do or understand by the end of the essay? If not, what information does the thesis statement need to be clearer?

2. Does the writer know his or her audience? Explain your answer.

3. Does the remainder of the essay explain the rest of the process? If not, what seems to be missing?

4. Does the writer end the process essay by considering the process as a whole? Explain your answer.

Thesis Statement

5. Does the thesis statement contain the essay's controlling idea and an opinion about that idea?

6. Does the thesis appear as the last sentence of the introduction? Explain your answer.

Basic Elements

7. Does the essay have all the basic elements. Is each one effective? Explain your answer.

Development

8. Does each paragraph support the thesis statement? Does each paragraph contain enough specific details to develop its topic sentence? Explain your answer.

Unity

9. Do all the essay's topic sentences relate directly to the thesis statement? Do the details in each paragraph support its topic sentence? Explain your answer.

Organization

10. Is the essay organized logically? Is each body paragraph organized logically? Explain your answer.

Coherence

11. Are transitions used effectively so that paragraphs move smoothly and logically from one to the next? Do the sentences move smoothly and logically from one to the next? Explain your answer.

APPENDIX 2D

Editing
Analyzing a Process
Peer Evaluation Form

Use the following questions to help you find editing errors in your partner's essay. Mark the errors directly on your partner's paper using the editing symbols on the inside back cover.

Writer: _____ **Peer:** _____

Sentences

1. Does each sentence have a subject and verb?

   Mark any fragments you find with **frag.**

   Put a slash (/) between any fused sentences and comma splices.

2. Do all subjects and verbs agree?

   Mark any subject-verb agreement errors you find with **sv.**

3. Do all pronouns agree with their nouns?

   Mark any pronoun errors you find with **pro agr.**

4. Are all modifiers as close as possible to the words they modify?

   Mark any modifier errors you find with **ad** (adjective or adverb problem), **mm** (misplaced modifier), or **dm** (dangling modifier).

Punctuation and Mechanics

5. Are sentences punctuated correctly?

   Mark any punctuation errors you find with the appropriate symbol under Unit 5 of the editing symbols (inside back cover).

6. Are words capitalized properly?

   Mark any capitalization errors you find with **lc** (lowercase) or **cap** (capital).

Word Choice and Spelling

7. Are words used correctly?

   Mark any words that are used incorrectly with **wc** (word choice) or **ww** (wrong word).

8. Are words spelled correctly?

   Mark any misspelled words you find with **sp.**

APPENDIX 2E

Revising
Comparing and Contrasting
Peer Evaluation Form

Use the following questions to evaluate your partner's essay. Direct your comments to your partner.

Writer: _____   **Peer:** _____

Comparing and Contrasting

1. Does the writer state the point he or she is trying to make with a comparison in the thesis statement? If not, what part of the comparison does the writer need to focus on?

2. Does the writer choose items to compare and contrast that will make his or her point most effectively? What details need to be added to make the comparison more effective?

3. Does the writer use as many specific details and examples as possible to expand the comparison? Explain your answer.

4. Is the comparison developed in a balanced way? Explain your answer.

Thesis Statement

5. Does the thesis statement contain the essay's controlling idea and an opinion about that idea?

6. Does the thesis appear as the last sentence of the introduction? Explain your answer.

Basic Elements

7. Does the essay have all the basic elements. Is each one effective? Explain your answer.

Development

8. Does each paragraph support the thesis statement? Does each paragraph contain enough specific details to develop its topic sentence? Explain your answer.

Unity

9. Do all the essay's topic sentences relate directly to the thesis statement? Do the details in each paragraph support its topic sentence? Explain your answer.

Organization

10. Is the essay organized logically? Is each body paragraph organized logically? Explain your answer.

Coherence

11. Are transitions used effectively so that paragraphs move smoothly and logically from one to the next? Do the sentences move smoothly and logically from one to the next? Explain your answer.

APPENDIX 2E
Editing Comparing and Contrasting Peer Evaluation Form

Use the following questions to help you find editing errors in your partner's essay. Mark the errors directly on your partner's paper using the editing symbols on the inside back cover.

Writer: _____ **Peer:** _____

Sentences

1. Does each sentence have a subject and verb?

   Mark any fragments you find with **frag.**

   Put a slash (/) between any fused sentences and comma splices.

2. Do all subjects and verbs agree?

   Mark any subject-verb agreement errors you find with **sv.**

3. Do all pronouns agree with their nouns?

   Mark any pronoun errors you find with **pro agr.**

4. Are all modifiers as close as possible to the words they modify?

   Mark any modifier errors you find with **ad** (adjective or adverb problem), **mm** (misplaced modifier), or **dm** (dangling modifier).

Punctuation and Mechanics

5. Are sentences punctuated correctly?

   Mark any punctuation errors you find with the appropriate symbol under Unit 5 of the editing symbols (inside back cover).

6. Are words capitalized properly?

   Mark any capitalization errors you find with **lc** (lowercase) or **cap** (capital).

Word Choice and Spelling

7. Are words used correctly?

   Mark any words that are used incorrectly with **wc** (word choice) or **ww** (wrong word).

8. Are words spelled correctly?

   Mark any misspelled words you find with **sp.**

APPENDIX 2F

Revising
Dividing and Classifying
Peer Evaluation Form

Use the following questions to evaluate your partner's essay. Direct your comments to your partner.

Writer: _____   **Peer:** _____

Dividing and Classifying

1. What is the overall purpose for the essay, and is it stated in the thesis statement? If not, where does the essay need clarification?

2. Did the writer divide the topic into categories that don't overlap? Explain your answer.

3. Did the writer clearly explain each category? Explain your answer.

Thesis Statement

4. Does the thesis statement contain the essay's controlling idea and an opinion about that idea?

5. Does the thesis appear as the last sentence of the introduction? Explain your answer.

Basic Elements

6. Does the essay have all the basic elements. Is each one effective? Explain your answer.

Development

7. Does each paragraph support the thesis statement? Does each paragraph contain enough specific details to develop its topic sentence? Explain your answer.

Unity

8. Do all the essay's topic sentences relate directly to the thesis statement? Do the details in each paragraph support its topic sentence? Explain your answer.

Organization

9. Is the essay organized logically? Is each body paragraph organized logically? Explain your answer.

Coherence

10. Are transitions used effectively so that paragraphs move smoothly and logically from one to the next? Do the sentences move smoothly and logically from one to the next? Explain your answer.

APPENDIX 2F

Editing
Dividing and Classifying
Peer Evaluation Form

Use the following questions to help you find editing errors in your partner's essay. Mark the errors directly on your partner's paper using the editing symbols on the inside back cover.

Writer: _____ **Peer:** _____

Sentences

1. Does each sentence have a subject and verb?

   Mark any fragments you find with **frag.**

   Put a slash (/) between any fused sentences and comma splices.

2. Do all subjects and verbs agree?

   Mark any subject-verb agreement errors you find with **sv.**

3. Do all pronouns agree with their nouns?

   Mark any pronoun errors you find with **pro agr.**

4. Are all modifiers as close as possible to the words they modify?

   Mark any modifier errors you find with **ad** (adjective or adverb problem), **mm** (misplaced modifier), or **dm** (dangling modifier).

Punctuation and Mechanics

5. Are sentences punctuated correctly?

   Mark any punctuation errors you find with the appropriate symbol under Unit 5 of the editing symbols (inside back cover).

6. Are words capitalized properly?

   Mark any capitalization errors you find with **lc** (lowercase) or **cap** (capital).

Word Choice and Spelling

7. Are words used correctly?

   Mark any words that are used incorrectly with **wc** (word choice) or **ww** (wrong word).

8. Are words spelled correctly?

   Mark any misspelled words you find with **sp.**

APPENDIX 2G Revising Defining Peer Evaluation Form

Use the following questions to evaluate your partner's paragraph. Direct your comments to your partner.

Writer: _____ **Peer:** _____

Defining

1. Did the writer choose a word or idea carefully and give readers a working definition of it in the thesis statement? Explain your answer.

2. Does the writer define his or her term or idea by synonym, category, or negation? Is this approach effective? Why or why not?

3. Does the writer use examples to expand on his or her definition of the term or idea? Where does the definition need more information?

4. Does the writer use other rhetorical strategies, such as description, comparison, or process analysis, to support the definition? Explain your answer.

Thesis Statement

5. Does the thesis statement contain the essay's controlling idea and an opinion about that idea?

6. Does the thesis appear as the last sentence of the introduction? Explain your answer.

Basic Elements

7. Does the essay have all the basic elements. Is each one effective? Explain your answer.

Development

8. Does each paragraph support the thesis statement? Does each paragraph contain enough specific details to develop its topic sentence? Explain your answer.

Unity

9. Do all the essay's topic sentences relate directly to the thesis statement? Do the details in each paragraph support its topic sentence? Explain your answer.

Organization

10. Is the essay organized logically? Is each body paragraph organized logically? Explain your answer.

Coherence

11. Are transitions used effectively so that paragraphs move smoothly and logically from one to the next? Do the sentences move smoothly and logically from one to the next? Explain your answer.

APPENDIX 2G   Editing Defining Peer Evaluation Form

Use the following questions to help you find editing errors in your partner's essay. Mark the errors directly on your partner's paper using the editing symbols on the inside back cover.

Writer: _____   **Peer:** _____

Sentences

1. Does each sentence have a subject and verb?

   Mark any fragments you find with **frag.**

   Put a slash (/) between any fused sentences and comma splices.

2. Do all subjects and verbs agree?

   Mark any subject-verb agreement errors you find with **sv.**

3. Do all pronouns agree with their nouns?

   Mark any pronoun errors you find with **pro agr.**

4. Are all modifiers as close as possible to the words they modify?

   Mark any modifier errors you find with **ad** (adjective or adverb problem), **mm** (misplaced modifier), or **dm** (dangling modifier).

Punctuation and Mechanics

5. Are sentences punctuated correctly?

   Mark any punctuation errors you find with the appropriate symbol under Unit 5 of the editing symbols (inside back cover).

6. Are words capitalized properly?

   Mark any capitalization errors you find with **lc** (lowercase) or **cap** (capital).

Word Choice and Spelling

7. Are words used correctly?

   Mark any words that are used incorrectly with **wc** (word choice) or **ww** (wrong word).

8. Are words spelled correctly?

   Mark any misspelled words you find with **sp.**

APPENDIX 2H

Revising
Analyzing Causes and Effects
Peer Evaluation Form

Use the following questions to evaluate your partner's essay. Direct your comments to your partner.

Writer: _____ **Peer:** _____

Analyzing Causes and Effects

1. Does the thesis statement make a clear statement about what is being analyzed? If not, what information does it need to be clearer?

2. Did the writer choose facts and details to support the topic sentence? What details need to be added?

3. Does the writer confuse coincidence with causes or effects? Explain your answer.

4. Does the writer include the real causes and effects for his or her topic? What details are unnecessary?

Thesis Statement

5. Does the thesis statement contain the essay's controlling idea and an opinion about that idea?

6. Does the thesis appear as the last sentence of the introduction? Explain your answer.

Basic Elements

7. Does the essay have all the basic elements. Is each one effective? Explain your answer.

Development

8. Does each paragraph support the thesis statement? Does each paragraph contain enough specific details to develop its topic sentence? Explain your answer.

Unity

9. Do all the essay's topic sentences relate directly to the thesis statement? Do the details in each paragraph support its topic sentence? Explain your answer.

Organization

10. Is the essay organized logically? Is each body paragraph organized logically? Explain your answer.

Coherence

11. Are transitions used effectively so that paragraphs move smoothly and logically from one to the next? Do the sentences move smoothly and logically from one to the next? Explain your answer.

APPENDIX 2H
Editing
Analyzing Causes and Effects
Peer Evaluation Form

Use the following questions to help you find editing errors in your partner's essay. Mark the errors directly on your partner's paper using the editing symbols on the inside back cover.

Writer: _____ **Peer:** _____

Sentences

1. Does each sentence have a subject and verb?

   Mark any fragments you find with **frag.**

   Put a slash (/) between any fused sentences and comma splices.

2. Do all subjects and verbs agree?

   Mark any subject-verb agreement errors you find with **sv.**

3. Do all pronouns agree with their nouns?

   Mark any pronoun errors you find with **pro agr.**

4. Are all modifiers as close as possible to the words they modify?

   Mark any modifier errors you find with **ad** (adjective or adverb problem), **mm** (misplaced modifier), or **dm** (dangling modifier).

Punctuation and Mechanics

5. Are sentences punctuated correctly?

   Mark any punctuation errors you find with the appropriate symbol under Unit 5 of the editing symbols (inside back cover).

6. Are words capitalized properly?

   Mark any capitalization errors you find with **lc** (lowercase) or **cap** (capital).

Word Choice and Spelling

7. Are words used correctly?

   Mark any words that are used incorrectly with **wc** (word choice) or **ww** (wrong word).

8. Are words spelled correctly?

   Mark any misspelled words you find with **sp.**

APPENDIX 21 Revising Arguing Peer Evaluation Form

Use the following questions to evaluate your partner's essay. Direct your comments to your partner.

Writer: _____ **Peer:** _____

Arguing

1. Does the writer state his or her opinion on the subject matter in the thesis statement? What information is missing?

2. Who is the intended audience for this essay? Does the writer adequately persuade this audience? Why or why not?

3. Does the writer choose appropriate evidence to support the thesis statement? What evidence is needed? What evidence is unnecessary?

4. Does the writer anticipate the opposing points of view? Explain your answer.

5. Does the writer find some common ground? Explain your answer.

6. Does the writer maintain a reasonable tone? Explain your answer.

Thesis Statement

7. Does the thesis statement contain the essay's controlling idea and an opinion about that idea?

8. Does the thesis appear as the last sentence of the introduction? Explain your answer.

Basic Elements

9. Does the essay have all the basic elements. Is each one effective? Explain your answer.

Development

10. Does each paragraph support the thesis statement? Does each paragraph contain enough specific details to develop its topic sentence? Explain your answer.

Unity

11. Do all the essay's topic sentences relate directly to the thesis statement? Do the details in each paragraph support its topic sentence? Explain your answer.

Organization

12. Is the essay organized logically? Is each body paragraph organized logically? Explain your answer.

Coherence

13. Are transitions used effectively so that paragraphs move smoothly and logically from one to the next? Do the sentences move smoothly and logically from one to the next? Explain your answer.

APPENDIX 21 Editing
Arguing
Peer Evaluation Form

Use the following questions to help you find editing errors in your partner's essay. Mark the errors directly on your partner's paper using the editing symbols on the inside back cover.

Writer: _____ **Peer:** _____

Sentences

1. Does each sentence have a subject and verb?

    Mark any fragments you find with **frag.**

    Put a slash (/) between any fused sentences and comma splices.

2. Do all subjects and verbs agree?

    Mark any subject-verb agreement errors you find with **sv.**

3. Do all pronouns agree with their nouns?

    Mark any pronoun errors you find with **pro agr.**

4. Are all modifiers as close as possible to the words they modify?

    Mark any modifier errors you find with **ad** (adjective or adverb problem), **mm** (misplaced modifier), or **dm** (dangling modifier).

Punctuation and Mechanics

5. Are sentences punctuated correctly?

    Mark any punctuation errors you find with the appropriate symbol under Unit 5 of the editing symbols (inside back cover).

6. Are words capitalized properly?

    Mark any capitalization errors you find with **lc** (lowercase) or **cap** (capital).

Word Choice and Spelling

7. Are words used correctly?

    Mark any words that are used incorrectly with **wc** (word choice) or **ww** (wrong word).

8. Are words spelled correctly?

    Mark any misspelled words you find with **sp.**

APPENDIX 3A

Revising
Writing an Essay with Sources
Peer Evaluation Form

Use the following questions to evaluate your partner's paper. Direct your comments to your partner.

Writer: _____ **Peer:** _____

Writing an Essay with Sources

1. Did the writer choose a subject that is neither too broad nor too narrow? Explain your answer.

2. Did the writer find sources that are relevant, reliable, and recent to support the thesis? Explain your answer.

3. Do you see any problems with plagiarism in the writer's paper? Explain your answer.

4. Does the writer incorporate sources and document properly? Check the writer's sources and documentation format—in the paper and at the end. Explain your answer.

Thesis Statement

7. Does the thesis statement contain the essay's controlling idea and an opinion about that idea?

8. Does the thesis appear as the last sentence of the introduction? Explain your answer.

Basic Elements

9. Does the essay have all the basic elements. Is each one effective? Explain your answer.

Development

10. Does each paragraph support the thesis statement? Does each paragraph contain enough specific details to develop its topic sentence? Explain your answer.

Unity

11. Do all the essay's topic sentences relate directly to the thesis statement? Do the details in each paragraph support its topic sentence? Explain your answer.

Organization

12. Is the essay organized logically? Is each body paragraph organized logically? Explain your answer.

Coherence

13. Are transitions used effectively so that paragraphs move smoothly and logically from one to the next? Do the sentences move smoothly and logically from one to the next? Explain your answer.

APPENDIX 3B
Editing
Writing an Essay with Sources
Peer Evaluation Form

Use the following questions to help you find editing errors in your partner's essay. Mark the errors directly on your partner's paper using the editing symbols on the inside back cover.

Writer: _____ **Peer:** _____

Sentences

1. Does each sentence have a subject and verb?

    Mark any fragments you find with **frag.**

    Put a slash (/) between any fused sentences and comma splices.

2. Do all subjects and verbs agree?

    Mark any subject-verb agreement errors you find with **sv.**

3. Do all pronouns agree with their nouns?

    Mark any pronoun errors you find with **pro agr.**

4. Are all modifiers as close as possible to the words they modify?

    Mark any modifier errors you find with **ad** (adjective or adverb problem), **mm** (misplaced modifier), or **dm** (dangling modifier).

Punctuation and Mechanics

5. Are sentences punctuated correctly?

    Mark any punctuation errors you find with the appropriate symbol under Unit 5 of the editing symbols (inside back cover).

6. Are words capitalized properly?

    Mark any capitalization errors you find with **lc** (lowercase) or **cap** (capital).

Word Choice and Spelling

7. Are words used correctly?

    Mark any words that are used incorrectly with **wc** (word choice) or **ww** (wrong word).

8. Are words spelled correctly?

    Mark any misspelled words you find with **sp.**

Here are the answers to the Test Yourself questions from the beginning of each chapter in the Handbook (Part V): Where are your strengths? Where are your weaknesses?

Introduction: Parts of Speech (p. 503)

     adj   *n* *v* *adv* *adj* *n* *adj* *adj*   *n*   *adj*   *n*
Professional basketball is definitely this nation's best spectator sport. The talented players

  v prep conj prep   *n adv adv pro*   *n* *adv v* *n prep v* *adj*
move up and down the court so quickly that the audience never has a chance to become bored.

int pro/v adv *v* *adj* *adj*   *n* *adj*   *n* *conj pro* *adj*   *n* *v pro prep v*
Boy, I'll never forget that Saturday night last February when my favorite uncle took me to see

   adj *n* *prep*   *n*   *pro v*   *adj* *adj* *n prep*   *n conj*
the Spurs game against the Trailblazers. It was an important home game for San Antonio, so

   n *v* *adj*   *n* *v* *adv*   *prep*   *pro prep* *n conj pro* *v*
the arena was packed. The Spurs were behind throughout most of the game, but they pulled

  prep conj v prep   *adj* *n prep* *adj adj*   *n*   *int pro v*   *adv* *v adv adj*
through and won with a three-pointer in the last few seconds. Wow! I have never seen so many

  n prep pro n conj   *v* *prep* *n prep pro* *n*
people on their feet and screaming at the top of their lungs.

Introduction: Phrases (p. 520)

Using the computer, of the research, for my report

To be totally confident, for spelling and grammar errors

in the gray house, at the end, of Maple Avenue, behind the bank

is going, to be a professional dancer

do want, to join us, for dinner, this evening

Introduction: Clauses (p. 522)

Magdalena will be a great attorney

because she argues so well

You don't understand the math concept

so I will keep going over it with you

If Shane is going to drive

he should have car insurance

We finished the big test

and then we all went out for pizza

I enjoyed the vacation

even though I had one really bad seafood dinner

Chapter 34: Subjects and Verbs (p. 527)

<u>You</u> <u><u>are</u></u> my best friend.

<u><u>Hang</u></u> up your clothes. (<u>You</u>)

<u>They</u> really <u><u>wanted</u></u> to be here tonight.

<u>He</u> <u><u>made</u></u> a sandwich and <u><u>put</u></u> it in a brown paper bag.

<u>Susie</u> and <u>Tom</u> <u><u>went</u></u> to the dance.

The insurance <u>agent</u> never <u><u>called</u></u> me today.

Chapter 35: Fragments (p. 535)

_____   I wanted to go to the gym yesterday.

__X___   Whose tie doesn't match his suit.

__X___   Giving up his seat for an elderly woman.

_____   Paul asked for the most popular menu item.

__X___   While the captain was away from the cockpit.

Chapter 36: Fused Sentences and Comma Splices (p. 548)

The rainstorm washed out my garden, / I had just planted spring bulbs.

When we cleaned the house, we found the TV remote control / it was between the sofa cushions.

People in authority are often criticized and seldom thanked.

The kids didn't find all of the Easter eggs during the hunt, / when we finally found them, they were rotten.

You should ask Aubri to cut your hair / she's been cutting mine for four years.

Chapter 37: Regular and Irregular Verbs (p. 558)

__X__	The pipe has bursted.
_____	Sim reacted to the scene calmly.
_____	I bought my car at an auction.
__X__	We had hid in the basement.
__X__	Sorry, I eated all the cookies.

Chapter 38: Verb Tense (p. 569)

__X__	Jea always laugh when I tell that joke.
_____	Mark jumped over the hurdle and crossed the finish line.
__X__	I had spoke to the sales clerk about a discount.
__X__	Students ain't allowed to bring food and drink into the computer lab.
__X__	My two cats be playing in the sunshine.

Chapter 39: Subject-Verb Agreement (p. 585)

__X__	Neither the shorts nor the shirt fit me.
_____	Chips and dip is my favorite snack.
__X__	There were a large storm last night.
__X__	Some of the soil along with the fertilizer are for the orchard.
__X__	Cotton and silk are more comfortable than wool.

Chapter 40: More on Verbs (p. 599)

_____   George raced across the field and caught the ball.

___P___   The old record was broken by Justin.

___P___   That painting was done by a famous artist.

___I___   In the future, we may live on Mars, and we produce our foods in greenhouses.

___I___   First, the baker prepares the dough, and then she will cut out the cookies.

Chapter 41: Pronoun Problems (p. 607)

The ball was ~~their's~~ **theirs** to begin with.

Tom told Valerie and ~~I~~ **me** the most exciting story.

James can type a lot faster than ~~me~~ **I**.

Those ~~there~~ running shoes are Kim's.

~~Me and~~ Julio and **I** are going to the movies tonight.

Chapter 42: Pronoun Reference and Point of View (p. 619)

It says to schedule **your** own appointments.
(X above It)

Millie and Tanya were going to go to Las Vegas, but **her** car broke.
(X above her)

I created a backup plan, because **you** should always be prepared for the unexpected.
(X above you)

You know **they** are covering up evidence of alien beings.
(X above You)

Jimmy forgot the answer to questions 1 and 10, but **he** remembered **it** the next day.
(X above it)

Chapter 43: Pronoun Agreement (p. 626)

Somebody left **his** lights on in **his** car.
(X above both his)

A judge must put aside **her** bias.
(X above her)

Each of the children needs **their** permission slip signed. [X above "their"]

None of the fans could keep **their** voices quiet. [X above "their"]

A motorcyclist must take care of **her** gear. [X above "her"]

Chapter 44: Adjectives (p. 635)

The kites were very **colorful**.

She has the **worstest hair** color. [X above "worstest"]

We were **more busier this** week than **last** week. [X above "busier"]

He is the **oldest** of the **two** brothers. [X above "oldest"]

The **Ford** Mustang is **more better** than the **Nissan** Sentra. [X above "better"]

Chapter 45: Adverbs (p. 646)

The pants fit me **too loose**, so I returned them to the store. [X above "loose"]

Tori was**n't never so** happy as after she won the lottery. [X above "n't"]

When Madeline returned from Paris, she said she had a **real** good time. [X above "real"]

We **happily** made more ice cream when our first supply ran out.

I wanted **so bad** to win the race, but I could**n't** catch up. [X above "bad"]

Chapter 46: Modifier Errors (p. 660)

After studying together, his grades really improved.

Before doing the laundry, the car needed to be washed.

To get a good job, the interview must go well.

The professor told the class he was retiring **before he dismissed them**.

I wrote a letter to the newspaper **that complained about rising power bills**.

Chapter 47: End Punctuation (p. 668)

How are we going to get there?

That's amazing!

Get me a Pepsi, please.

This will never happen to me!

Can you make your own dinner tonight?

Chapter 48: Commas (p. 674)

We drove to the beach, and we had a picnic.

Before I eat breakfast, I take a multivitamin.

"This is my favorite restaurant," said Matt.

E-mail, though, makes corresponding easy and fast.

They were married on September 21, 2004, in Las Vegas, Nevada.

Chapter 49: Apostrophes (p. 687)

The flight crew was surprised by the pilot's rudeness when he boarded the plane.

It's important that the car has its engine checked every 3,000 miles.

What's going to happen after Dominic is gone?

The men's bathroom is located on the third floor.

James's house is the third one on the left.

Chapter 50: Quotation Marks (p. 696)

"Can we go out to dinner tonight?" she asked.

Jeri screamed, "Don't go in there!"

"If you can't find my house," Tom said, "call me on your cell phone."

My favorite poem is "The Red Wheelbarrow" by William Carlos Williams.

David said, "I'll fix your car this weekend."

Chapter 51: Other Punctuation Marks (p. 705)

Kris left for the dance; Sean decided to stay home.

We wanted to win; therefore, we practiced every day.

The computer's advertised price didn't include several things: a monitor, a printer, and speakers.

Ramon asked the best question during the interview—"Why should we vote for you?" (or :)

Bring the jelly to a "rolling boil" (a boil that cannot be stirred down).

Chapter 52: Capitalization (p. 715)

According to **U**ncle **B**ob, **M**other makes the best **T**exas sheet cake.

Antonio is a **N**ative **A**merican.

"**T**he shortest path," he said, "is down **B**aker **S**treet."

Issa loves to go to **W**alt **D**isney **W**orld.

Last year, I saw the **R**ed **H**ot **C**hili **P**eppers in concert.

Chapter 53: Abbreviations and Numbers (p. 721)

He earned **$2,300,000** last year.

My cat had **five** kittens.

Sherril moved from England to the **United States**.

Mr. Johnson always drinks hot chocolate in the mornings.

I work for the **IRS**.

Chapter 54: Varying Sentence Structure (p. 730)

Answers will vary.

Chapter 55: Parallelism (p. 737)

Tony enjoys <u>hockey</u>, <u>football</u>, and <u>runs</u>.

My mom and dad give money <u>to help the homeless</u> and <u>for building new homes</u>.

I <u>finished high school</u>, <u>started college</u>, and <u>I am beginning a new job</u>.

I love the mountains because they're <u>cool</u>, <u>clean</u>, and <u>feel refreshing</u>.

<u>Listening to music</u>, <u>watching television</u>, or <u>to read a book</u> are good ways to relax.

Chapter 56: Combining Sentences (p. 742)

Answers will vary.

Chapter 57: Standard and Nonstandard English (p. 754)

You <u>shoulda</u> seen Claudia's new hairstyle. (**Incorrect**)

<u>Where</u> are my friends <u>at</u>? (**Incorrect**)

Your new bike is really <u>hot</u>. (**Slang**)

Randy was <u>enthused</u> about his date. (**Slang**)

Fatboy Slim's new video <u>rocks</u>. (**Slang**)

Chapter 58: Easily Confused Words (p. 764)

Sally couldn't (<u>choose</u>, chose) a college.

(<u>It's</u>, Its) time to leave for the show.

I can't (<u>hear</u>, here) with all this noise.

(Weather, <u>Whether</u>) you go or not, I'm still going to attend.

(<u>Who's</u>, Whose) responsible for this mess?

Chapter 59: Spelling (p. 775)

What is your new ~~addres~~ address?

Turn left on the third ~~avenu~~ avenue.

I was using the wrong ~~calender~~ calendar when I made out the schedule.

The dealer ~~delt~~ dealt me a good hand.

Please get all the items on the ~~groery~~ grocery list.

Put an X in the square that corresponds to each question that you missed. Then record your errors in the categories below to find out where you might need help.

	a	b	c	d	e	f	g
1							
2							
3							
4							
5							
6							
7							
8							
9							
10							

Fragments
1b _____ 1c _____ 2b _____ 2e _____ 4d _____

4e _____ 5d _____ 6d _____ 10c _____

Fused sentences and comma splices
1a _____ 1d _____ 2d _____ 3d _____ 5c _____ 8b _____

8e _____ 9a _____ 10b _____ 10f _____

Subject-verb agreement
6e _____

Verb forms
3a _____ 3c _____ 9e _____

Pronoun errors
7b _____

Pronoun agreement
3b _____ 4a _____ 10a _____

Modifiers
5b _____ 10e _____

End punctuation
6g _____

Commas	4f _____	4g _____	5a _____	7e _____	7f _____	9b _____
	9c _____					
Apostrophes	10d _____					
Capitalization	2a _____	2c _____	7c _____	7d _____		
Confused words	4b _____	4c _____	6c _____	7g _____	8a _____	9d _____
Spelling	6a _____	6b _____	6f _____	7a _____	8c _____	8d _____
	9f _____					

APPENDIX 6 Error Log

List any grammar, punctuation, and mechanics errors you make in your writing on the following chart. Then, to the right of this label, record (1) the actual error from your writing, (2) the rule for correcting this error, and (3) your correction.

Error	
Comma	**Example** I went to the new seafood restaurant and I ordered the lobster.
	Rule Use a comma before and, but, for, nor, or, so, and yet when they join two independent clauses.
	Correction I went to the new seafood restaurant, and I ordered the lobster.
Error	**Example**
	Rule
	Correction
Error	**Example**
	Rule
	Correction
Error	**Example**
	Rule
	Correction
Error	**Example**
	Rule
	Correction
Error	**Example**
	Rule
	Correction
Error	**Example**
	Rule
	Correction
Error	**Example**
	Rule
	Correction

Error	Example		
	Rule		
	Correction		
Error	Example		
	Rule		
	Correction		
Error	Example		
	Rule		
	Correction		
Error	Example		
	Rule		
	Correction		
Error	Example		
	Rule		
	Correction		
Error	Example		
	Rule		
	Correction		
Error	Example		
	Rule		
	Correction		
Error	Example		
	Rule		
	Correction		
Error	Example		
	Rule		
	Correction		
Error	Example		
	Rule		
	Correction		

APPENDIX 7 Spelling Log

On this chart, record any words you misspell, and write the correct spelling in the space next to the misspelled word. In the right column, write a note to yourself to help you remember the correct spelling. (See the first line for an example.) Refer to this chart as often as necessary to avoid misspelling the same words again.

Misspelled Word	Correct Spelling	Definition/Notes
there	their	there = place; their = pronoun; they're = "they are"

CREDITS ❖

CHAPTER **32**

"A Family Dilemma: To Scout or Not to Scout," by Michael Alvear, *Newsweek*, November 6, 2000, © 2000.

"Happiness is Catching: Why Emotions are Contagious," by Stacey Colino, *Family Circle*, March 12, 1996.

CHAPTER **33**

"We are Training Our Kids to Kill," by Dave Grossman, *Saturday Evening Post*, July, 1999. Reprinted by permission of the author.

"Anti-Loitering Laws Can Reduce Gang Violence," by Richard K. Willard, *Supreme Court Debates*, February 1999, © 1999 Congressional Digest Corp. Reprinted by permission of The Congressional Digest Corp.

"Anti-Loitering Laws are Ineffective and Biased," by David Cole, *The Nation*, January 4 1999. Reprinted with permission from the January 4, 1999 issue of *The Nation*.

INDEX ❖